THE SUPERMAN CHRONICLES

VOLUME NINE

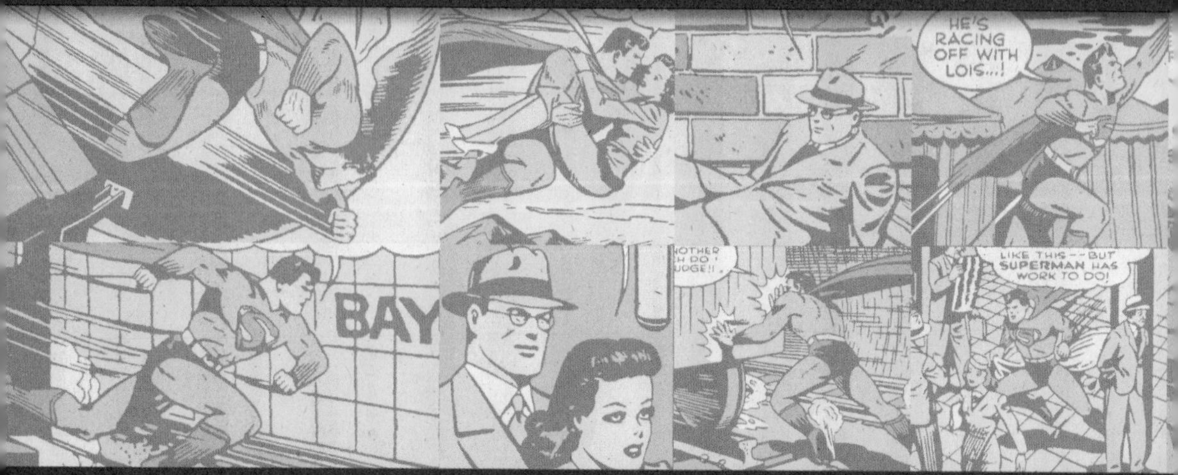
HE'S RACING OFF WITH LOIS...!
BAY
LIKE THIS--BUT SUPERMAN HAS WORK TO DO!

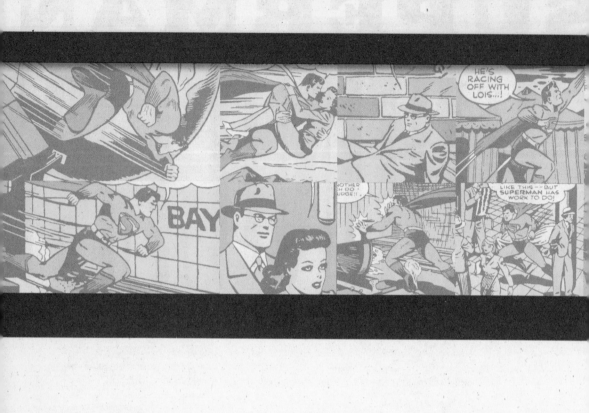

THE SUPERMAN CHRONICLES

VOLUME NINE

SUPERMAN CREATED BY JERRY SIEGEL & JOE SHUSTER
All stories written by Jerry Siegel and illustrated by John Sikela, and all covers illustrated by Fred Ray, unless otherwise noted.

ACTION COMICS NO. 48
-MAY 1942-
Cover 5

THE MERCHANT OF MURDER 6

SUPERMAN NO. 16
-MAY-JUNE 1942-
Cover 19

THE WORLD'S MEANEST MAN 20

TERROR FROM THE STARS* 33

THE CASE OF THE RUNAWAY SKYSCRAPERS 45

RACKET ON DELIVERY 58

ACTION COMICS NO. 49
-JUNE 1942-
Cover 71

THE WIZARD OF CHANCE 72
Penciller: John Sikela
Inker: Ed Dobrotka

WORLD'S FINEST COMICS NO. 6
-SUMMER 1942-
Cover 85

MAN OF STEEL VERSUS MAN OF METAL 86

ACTION COMICS NO. 50
-JULY 1942-
Cover 99

PLAY BALL!* 100
Penciller: Leo Nowak
Inker: Ed Dobrotka

SUPERMAN NO. 17
-JULY-AUGUST 1942-
Cover 113

MAN OR SUPERMAN? 114
Penciller: Joe Shuster
Inker: John Sikela

THE HUMAN BOMB 127
Artist: Leo Nowak

MUSCLES FOR SALE 139

WHEN TITANS CLASH 152

ACTION COMICS NO. 51
-AUGUST 1942-
Cover 165

THE CASE OF THE CRIMELESS CRIMES 166

ACTION COMICS NO. 52
-SEPTEMBER 1942-
Cover 179

THE EMPEROR OF AMERICA 180

*These stories were originally untitled and are titled here for reader convenience.

Whitney Ellsworth EDITOR – ORIGINAL SERIES ☆ Scott Nybakken EDITOR
Ian Sattler DIRECTOR EDITORIAL, SPECIAL PROJECTS AND ARCHIVAL EDITIONS EDITOR
Robbin Brosterman DESIGN DIRECTOR – BOOKS

DC COMICS

Diane Nelson PRESIDENT ☆ Dan DiDio and Jim Lee CO-PUBLISHERS ☆ Geoff Johns CHIEF CREATIVE OFFICER ☆ John Rood EXECUTIVE VP – SALES, MARKETI
AND BUSINESS DEVELOPMENT ☆ Amy Genkins SENIOR VP – BUSINESS AND LEGAL AFFAIRS ☆ Nairi Gardiner Senior VP – FINANCE ☆ Jeff Boison VP – PUBLISHI
OPERATIONS ☆ Mark Chiarello VP – ART DIRECTION AND DESIGN ☆ John Cunningham VP – MARKETING ☆ Terri Cunningham VP – TALENT RELATIONS AND
SERVICES ☆ Alison Gill SENIOR VP – MANUFACTURING AND OPERATIONS ☆ David Hyde VP – PUBLICITY ☆ Hank Kanalz SENIOR VP – DIGITAL
Jay Kogan VP – BUSINESS AND LEGAL AFFAIRS, PUBLISHING ☆ Jack Mahan VP – BUSINESS AFFAIRS, TALENT
Nick Napolitano VP – MANUFACTURING ADMINISTRATION ☆ Ron Perazza VP – ONLINE
Sue Pohja VP – BOOK SALES ☆ Courtney Simmons SENIOR VP – PUBLICITY
Bob Wayne SENIOR VP – SALES

DC Comics, 1700 Broadway, New York, NY 10019
A Warner Bros. Entertainment Company
Printed by Quad/Graphics, Dubuque, IA, USA 5/6/11.
First Printing.
ISBN: 978-1-4012-3122-4

Cover art by Fred Ray.

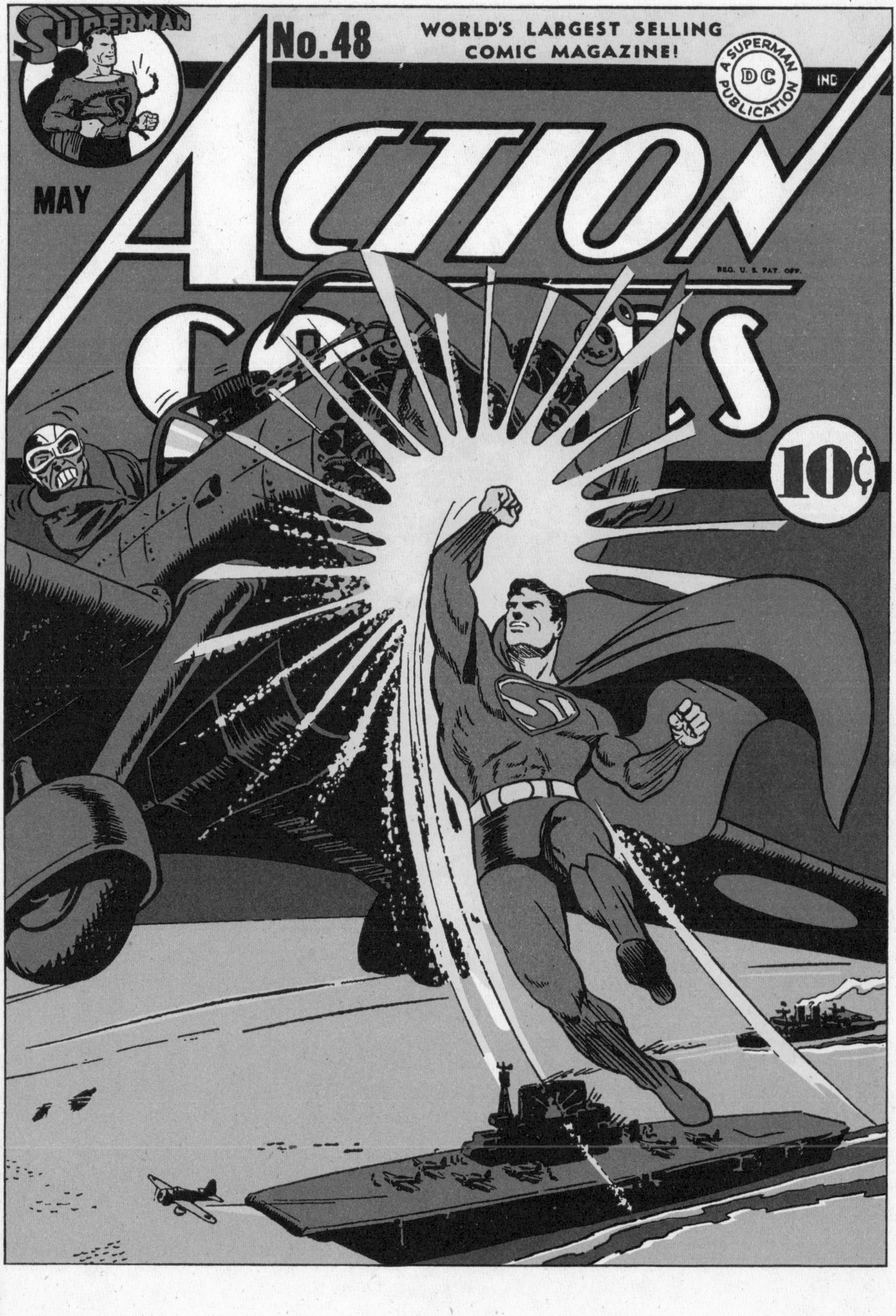
SUPERMAN
No. 48
WORLD'S LARGEST SELLING
COMIC MAGAZINE!
A SUPERMAN
DC
PUBLICATION
INC
MAY
ACTION
REG. U. S. PAT. OFF.
COMICS
10¢

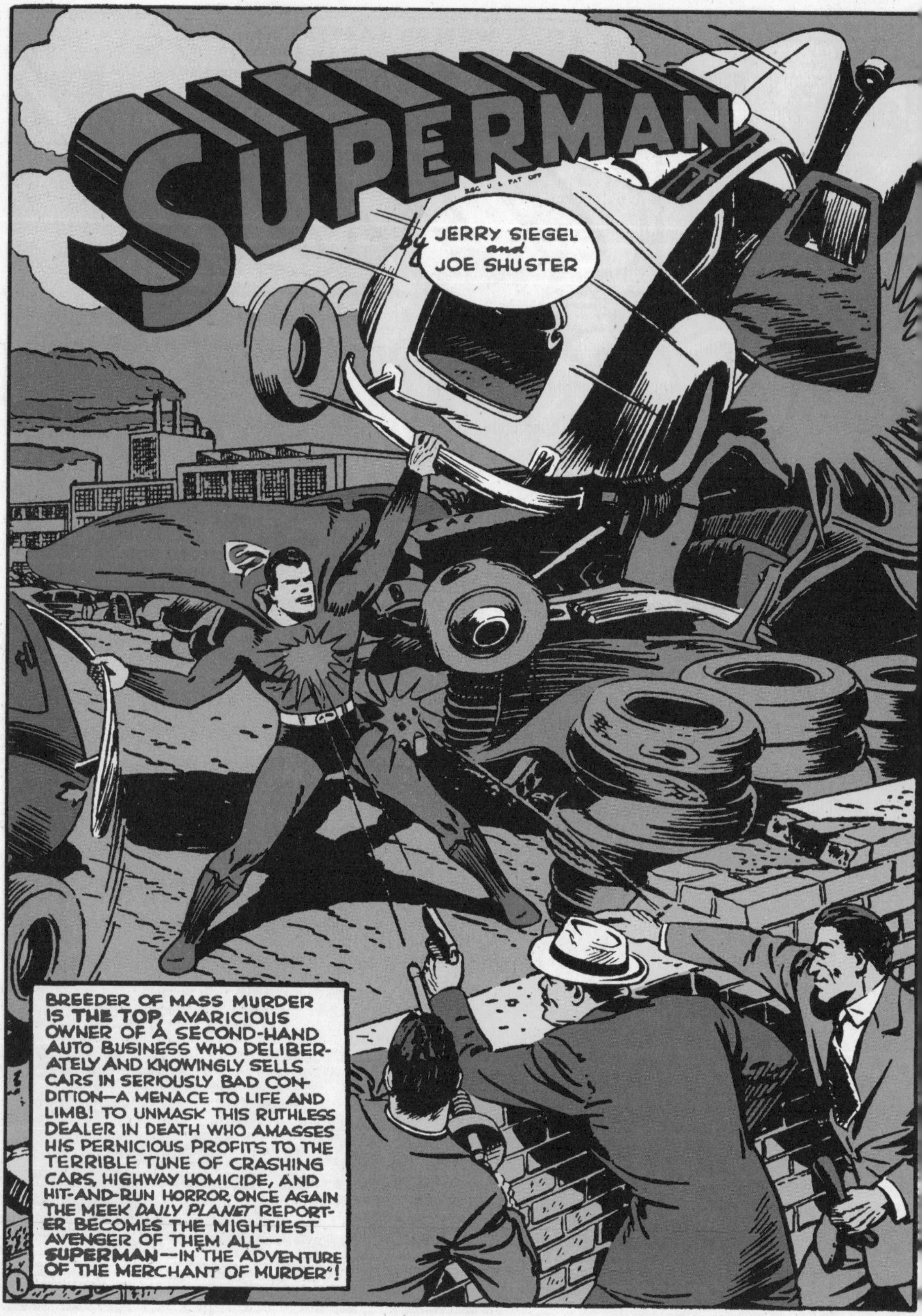
SUPERMAN
REG. U.S. PAT. OFF.
by JERRY SIEGEL and JOE SHUSTER
BREEDER OF MASS MURDER IS THE TOP, AVARICIOUS OWNER OF A SECOND-HAND AUTO BUSINESS WHO DELIBERATELY AND KNOWINGLY SELLS CARS IN SERIOUSLY BAD CONDITION—A MENACE TO LIFE AND LIMB! TO UNMASK THIS RUTHLESS DEALER IN DEATH WHO AMASSES HIS PERNICIOUS PROFITS TO THE TERRIBLE TUNE OF CRASHING CARS, HIGHWAY HOMICIDE, AND HIT-AND-RUN HORROR, ONCE AGAIN THE MEEK DAILY PLANET REPORTER BECOMES THE MIGHTIEST AVENGER OF THEM ALL—SUPERMAN—IN "THE ADVENTURE OF THE MERCHANT OF MURDER"!
1.

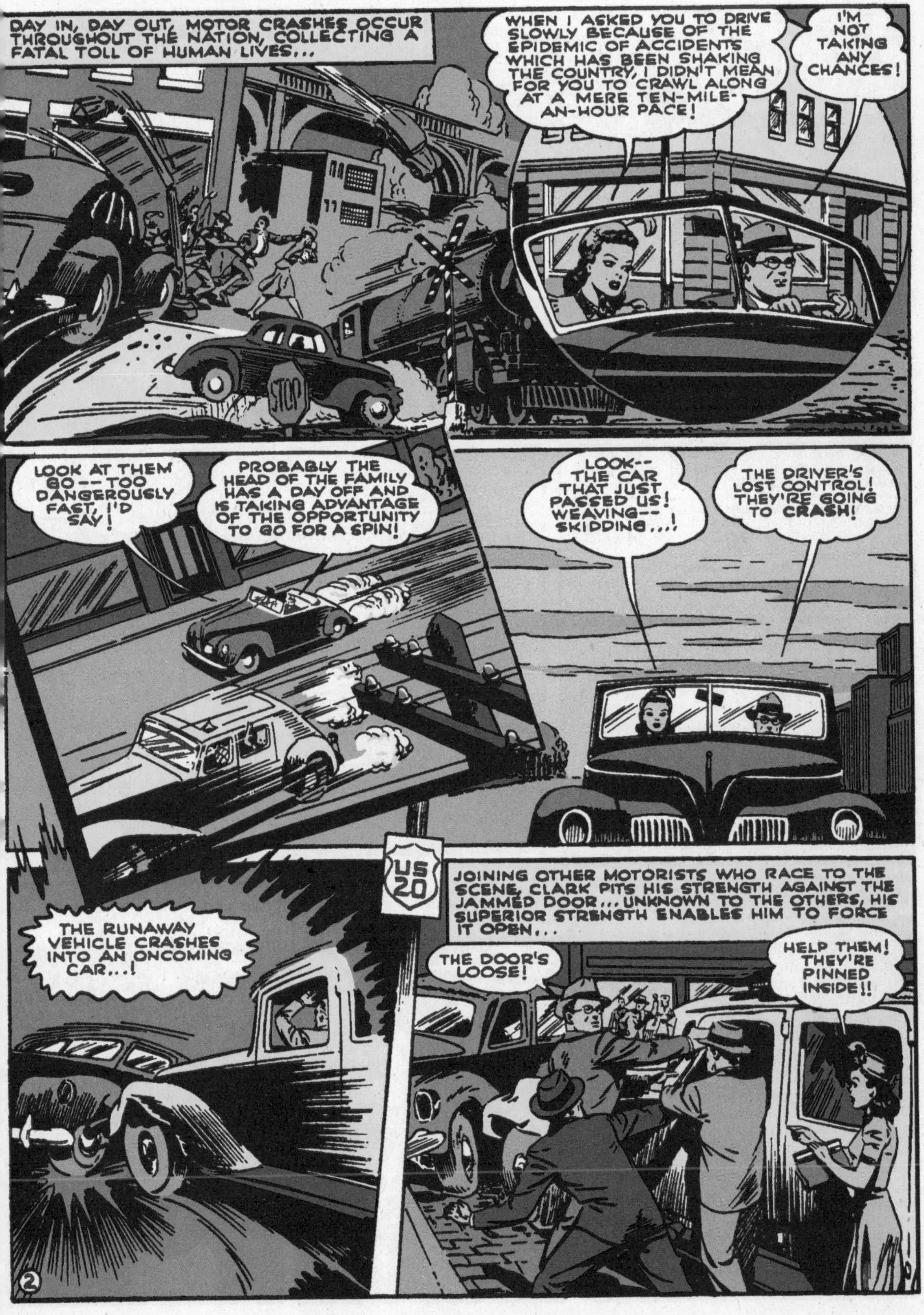
DAY IN, DAY OUT, MOTOR CRASHES OCCUR THROUGHOUT THE NATION, COLLECTING A FATAL TOLL OF HUMAN LIVES...
STOP
WHEN I ASKED YOU TO DRIVE SLOWLY BECAUSE OF THE EPIDEMIC OF ACCIDENTS WHICH HAS BEEN SHAKING THE COUNTRY, I DIDN'T MEAN FOR YOU TO CRAWL ALONG AT A MERE TEN-MILE-AN-HOUR PACE!
I'M NOT TAKING ANY CHANCES!
LOOK AT THEM GO--TOO DANGEROUSLY FAST, I'D SAY!
PROBABLY THE HEAD OF THE FAMILY HAS A DAY OFF AND IS TAKING ADVANTAGE OF THE OPPORTUNITY TO GO FOR A SPIN!
LOOK-- THE CAR THAT JUST PASSED US! WEAVING-- SKIDDING...!
THE DRIVER'S LOST CONTROL! THEY'RE GOING TO CRASH!
US 20
THE RUNAWAY VEHICLE CRASHES INTO AN ONCOMING CAR...!
JOINING OTHER MOTORISTS WHO RACE TO THE SCENE, CLARK PITS HIS STRENGTH AGAINST THE JAMMED DOOR... UNKNOWN TO THE OTHERS, HIS SUPERIOR STRENGTH ENABLES HIM TO FORCE IT OPEN...
THE DOOR'S LOOSE!
HELP THEM! THEY'RE PINNED INSIDE!!
2

DYING--JOHN'S DYING...AND TO THINK WE JUST BOUGHT THE CAR A FEW HOURS AGO... INVESTED ALL OUR SAVINGS IN IT....

WHY DOESN'T THE AMBULANCE HURRY?

HERE IT COMES!

AS THE POLICE AMBULANCE DRIVES OFF WITH THE CRASH VICTIMS, CLARK'S UNCANNY X-RAY VISION DISCLOSES TO HIM...

("--NO WONDER HE LOST CONTROL OF THE CAR... THE BRAKE-LINING IS WORN OUT...BUT THAT WOMAN SAID THEY JUST BOUGHT THE CAR!--")

WHEN THE POLICE PHOTOGRAPHER ARRIVES ON THE SCENE, CLARK MAKES A REQUEST...

PLEASE LET ME HAVE A SHOT OF THE WRECKAGE FROM THIS ANGLE...SEND IT UP TO THE NEWSPAPER OFFICE QUICKLY.

OKAY, KENT.

WHAT ARE YOU UP TO, CLARK?

SPEED 3531

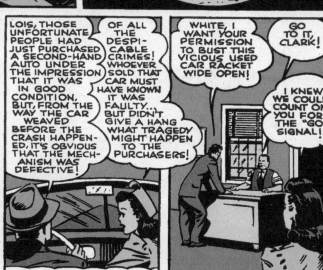

LOIS, THOSE UNFORTUNATE PEOPLE HAD JUST PURCHASED A SECOND-HAND AUTO UNDER THE IMPRESSION THAT IT WAS IN GOOD CONDITION, BUT, FROM THE WAY THE CAR WEAVED BEFORE THE CRASH HAPPENED, IT'S OBVIOUS THAT THE MECHANISM WAS DEFECTIVE!

OF ALL THE DESPICABLE CRIMES! WHOEVER SOLD THAT CAR MUST HAVE KNOWN IT WAS FAULTY...BUT DIDN'T GIVE A HANG WHAT TRAGEDY MIGHT HAPPEN TO THE PURCHASERS!

WHITE, I WANT YOUR PERMISSION TO BUST THIS VICIOUS USED CAR RACKET WIDE OPEN!

GO TO IT, CLARK!

I KNEW WE COULD COUNT ON YOU FOR THE "GO" SIGNAL!

AT THE OFFICE OF SID SPEED, PROPRIETOR OF SPEED MOTORS...

BUT "TOP"--I CAN'T HELP IT IF THIS DUMB CLUCK OF A REPORTER IS CAMPAIGNING FOR CITY SUPERVISION OF USED CAR SALES--

KENT DELIBERATELY PRINTED THAT PICTURE OF THE WRECKED CAR WHICH PLAINLY SHOWED THE NAME SPEED MOTORS ABOVE THE LICENSE PLATE...HE'S DANGEROUS... SILENCE HIM...!

I WANT TO TALK TO YOU RIGHT AWAY, KENT! CAN I EXPECT YOU?

I'LL BE RIGHT OVER! I'VE BEEN WANTING TO SEE YOU, MR. SPEED!

SO LONG, LOIS! SEE YOU LATER!

GOODBYE, CLARK! ("--YOU BET YOU WILL! IF YOU'RE GOING TO SPEED MOTORS I DON'T WANT TO MISS THE FIRE-WORKS!--")

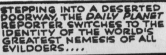

STEPPING INTO A DESERTED DOORWAY, THE *DAILY PLANET* REPORTER SWITCHES TO THE IDENTITY OF THE WORLD'S GREATEST NEMESIS OF ALL EVILDOERS....

MY CONVERSATION WITH MR. SPEED OUGHT TO BE INTERESTING--BUT NOT AS INTERESTING AS THE INFORMATION I MAY PICK UP WHILE RECONNOITERING AS SUPERMAN!

A MOMENT LATER--A HUMAN LIGHTNING BOLT STREAKS UP--UP INTO THE SKY....

I LIKE THE AIR UP HERE!

MOMENTS LATER, AS SUPERMAN DRIFTS LEISURELY OVER THE *SPEED MOTORS* BUILDING, USING HIS WIDE-SPREAD CAPE LIKE A SAIL.

SO THAT'S WHAT GOES ON...!

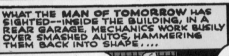

WHAT THE MAN OF TOMORROW HAS SIGHTED: INSIDE THE BUILDING, IN A REAR GARAGE, MECHANICS WORK BUSILY OVER SMASHED AUTOS, HAMMERING THEM BACK INTO SHAPE....

WHAT A JOB! IT WOULD BE EASIER TO BUILD NEW AUTOS THAN KNOCK THESE OLD WRECKS TOGETHER SO THEY LOOK HALF DECENT.

WHAT A RACKET! NO ONE WOULD EVER RECOGNIZE THESE SPIFFY-LOOKING HEAPS AS THE WRECKED CARS THAT WE TOWED IN HERE A FEW WEEKS AGO!

WHAT'RE YOU KICKIN' ABOUT? THE CUSTOMERS DON'T KNOW ENOUGH TO...AN' YOU'RE WELL PAID FOR YOUR WORK!

WHAT DOES SPEED CARE IF UNDER THE SHINY SURFACES THESE CARS ARE STILL OLD WRECKS AND SURE MEAT FOR MORE ACCIDENTS? ALL HE WANTS IS QUICK PROFITS--AND THE DEVIL TAKE THE CUSTOMER!

DOWN PLUMMETS THE MAN OF STEEL!

I WANT TO HEAR MORE!

("-PS-ST! LOOK!!-")

("-A SNOOPER! RUSH HIM!-")

BUT AS SPEED'S STRONGARM MEN RUSH HIM, THE MAN OF TOMORROW WHIRLS BEHIND THEM WITH SUPER-SPEED...

HUH? WH-WHERE IS HE?

BUT HE WAS HERE A SECOND AGO!

EVER THINK OF LOOKING BEHIND YOU?

OWW-WWW!!

④

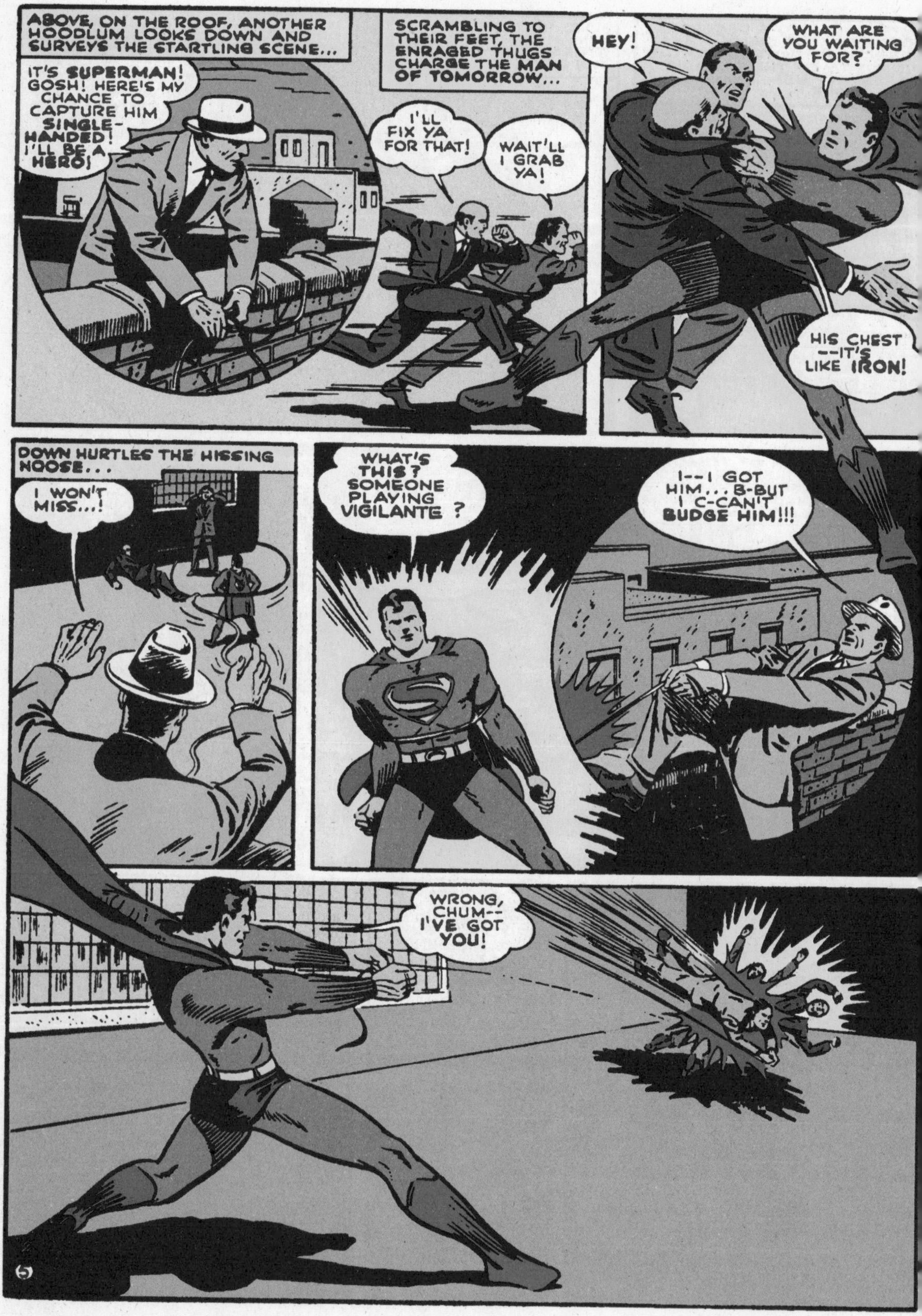
ABOVE, ON THE ROOF, ANOTHER HOODLUM LOOKS DOWN AND SURVEYS THE STARTLING SCENE...
IT'S SUPERMAN! GOSH! HERE'S MY CHANCE TO CAPTURE HIM SINGLE-HANDED! I'LL BE A HERO!
SCRAMBLING TO THEIR FEET, THE ENRAGED THUGS CHARGE THE MAN OF TOMORROW...
I'LL FIX YA FOR THAT!
WAIT'LL I GRAB YA!
HEY!
WHAT ARE YOU WAITING FOR?
HIS CHEST --IT'S LIKE IRON!
DOWN HURTLES THE HISSING NOOSE...
I WON'T MISS...!
WHAT'S THIS? SOMEONE PLAYING VIGILANTE ?
I--I GOT HIM... B-BUT I C-CAN'T BUDGE HIM!!!
WRONG, CHUM-- I'VE GOT YOU!

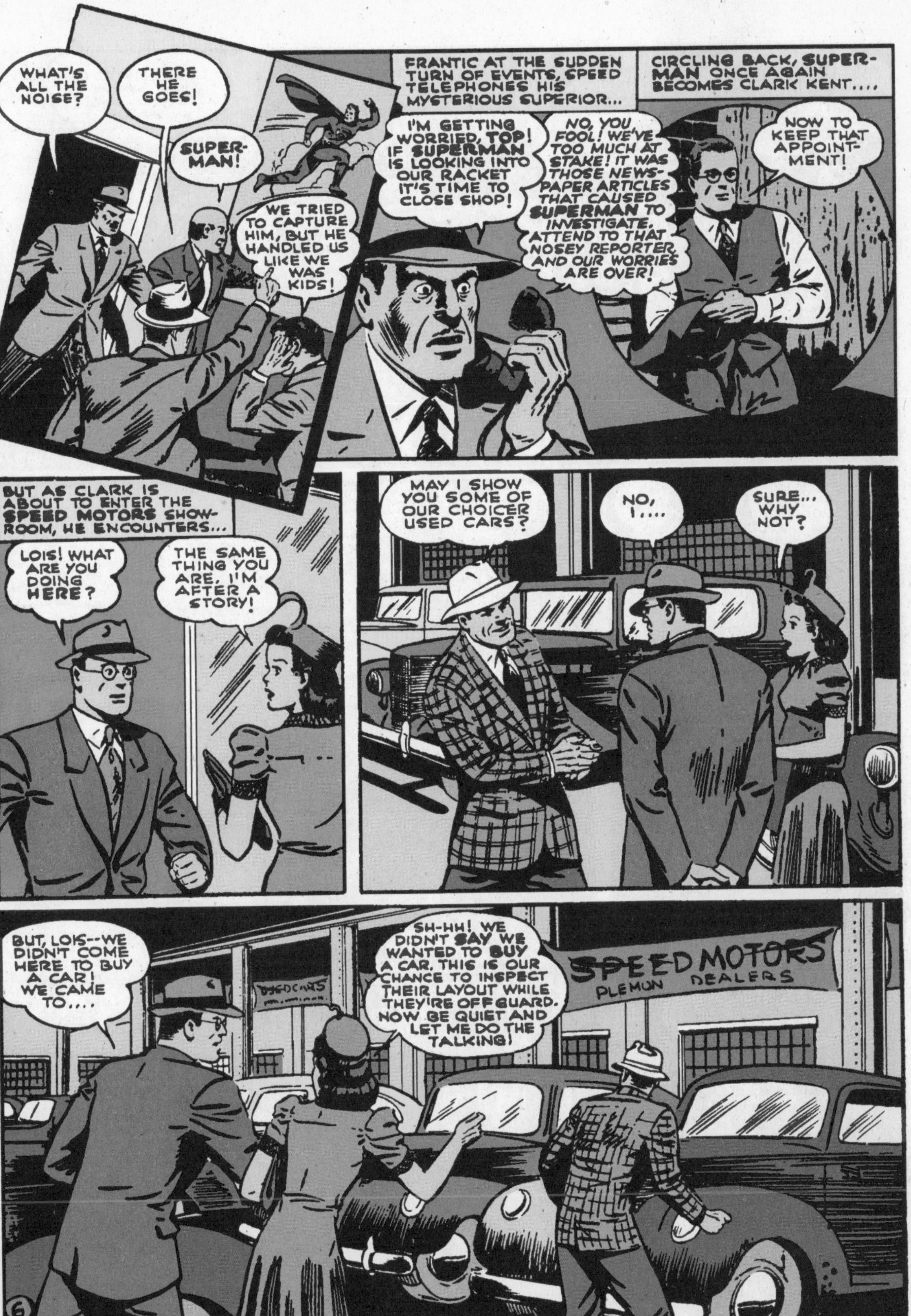
WHAT'S ALL THE NOISE?
THERE HE GOES!
SUPER-MAN!
WE TRIED TO CAPTURE HIM, BUT HE HANDLED US LIKE WE WAS KIDS!
FRANTIC AT THE SUDDEN TURN OF EVENTS, SPEED TELEPHONES HIS MYSTERIOUS SUPERIOR...
I'M GETTING WORRIED, TOP! IF SUPERMAN IS LOOKING INTO OUR RACKET IT'S TIME TO CLOSE SHOP!
NO, YOU FOOL! WE'VE TOO MUCH AT STAKE! IT WAS THOSE NEWS-PAPER ARTICLES THAT CAUSED SUPERMAN TO INVESTIGATE. ATTEND TO THAT NOSEY REPORTER AND OUR WORRIES ARE OVER!
CIRCLING BACK, SUPER-MAN ONCE AGAIN BECOMES CLARK KENT....
NOW TO KEEP THAT APPOINT-MENT!
BUT AS CLARK IS ABOUT TO ENTER THE SPEED MOTORS SHOW-ROOM, HE ENCOUNTERS...
LOIS! WHAT ARE YOU DOING HERE?
THE SAME THING YOU ARE. I'M AFTER A STORY!
MAY I SHOW YOU SOME OF OUR CHOICER USED CARS?
NO, I....
SURE... WHY NOT?
BUT, LOIS--WE DIDN'T COME HERE TO BUY A CAR! WE CAME TO....
SH-HH! WE DIDN'T SAY WE WANTED TO BUY A CAR. THIS IS OUR CHANCE TO INSPECT THEIR LAYOUT WHILE THEY'RE OFF GUARD. NOW BE QUIET AND LET ME DO THE TALKING!
SPEED MOTORS
PLEMUN DEALERS
6

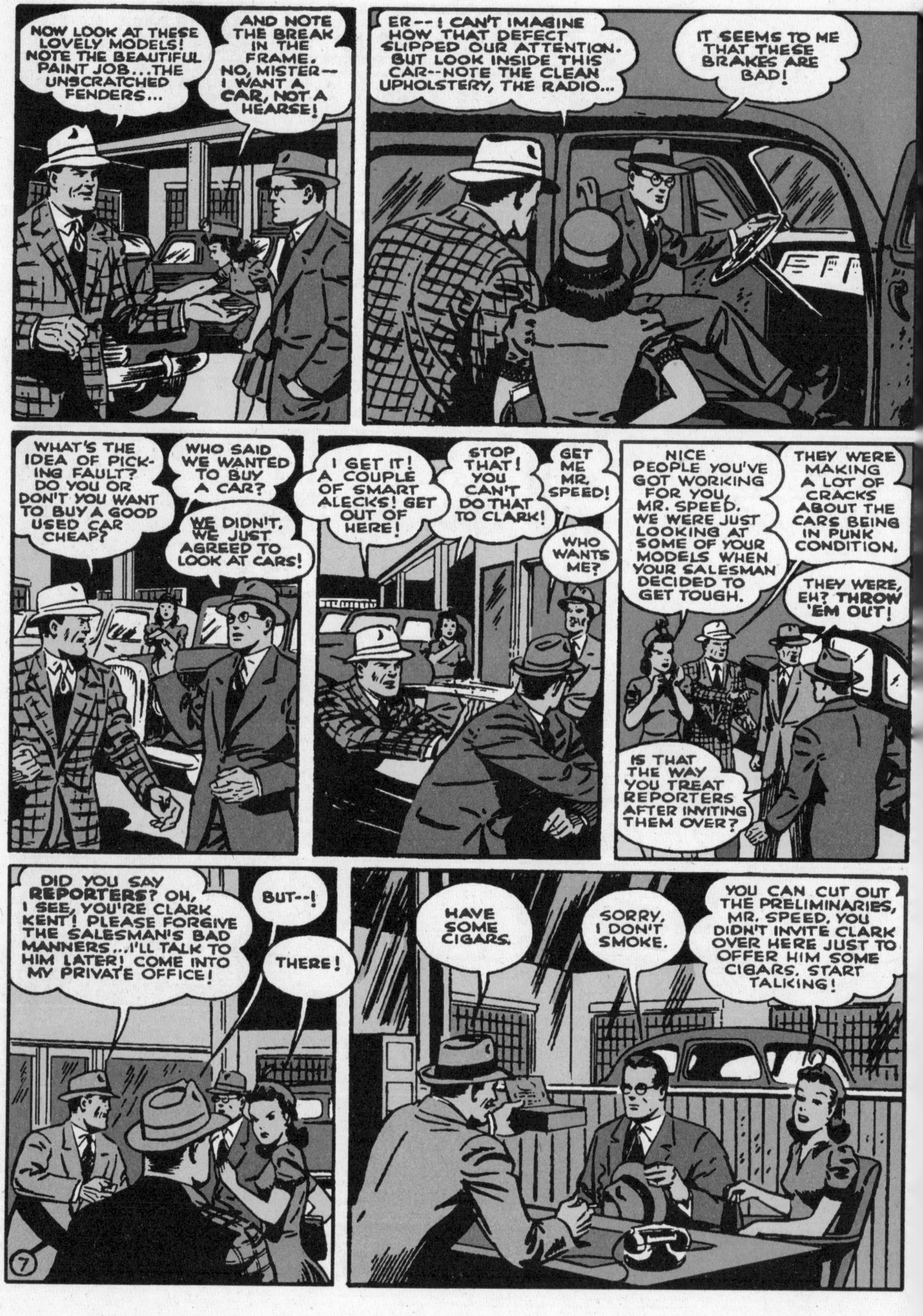
NOW LOOK AT THESE LOVELY MODELS! NOTE THE BEAUTIFUL PAINT JOB...THE UNSCRATCHED FENDERS...
AND NOTE THE BREAK IN THE FRAME. NO, MISTER-- I WANT A CAR, NOT A HEARSE!
ER--I CAN'T IMAGINE HOW THAT DEFECT SLIPPED OUR ATTENTION. BUT LOOK INSIDE THIS CAR--NOTE THE CLEAN UPHOLSTERY, THE RADIO...
IT SEEMS TO ME THAT THESE BRAKES ARE BAD!
WHAT'S THE IDEA OF PICKING FAULT? DO YOU OR DON'T YOU WANT TO BUY A GOOD USED CAR CHEAP?
WHO SAID WE WANTED TO BUY A CAR?
WE DIDN'T. WE JUST AGREED TO LOOK AT CARS!
I GET IT! A COUPLE OF SMART ALECKS! GET OUT OF HERE!
STOP THAT! YOU CAN'T DO THAT TO CLARK!
GET ME MR. SPEED!
WHO WANTS ME?
NICE PEOPLE YOU'VE GOT WORKING FOR YOU, MR. SPEED. WE WERE JUST LOOKING AT SOME OF YOUR MODELS WHEN YOUR SALESMAN DECIDED TO GET TOUGH.
THEY WERE MAKING A LOT OF CRACKS ABOUT THE CARS BEING IN PUNK CONDITION.
THEY WERE, EH? THROW 'EM OUT!
IS THAT THE WAY YOU TREAT REPORTERS AFTER INVITING THEM OVER?
DID YOU SAY REPORTERS? OH, I SEE, YOU'RE CLARK KENT! PLEASE FORGIVE THE SALESMAN'S BAD MANNERS...I'LL TALK TO HIM LATER! COME INTO MY PRIVATE OFFICE!
BUT--!
THERE!
7
HAVE SOME CIGARS.
SORRY, I DON'T SMOKE.
YOU CAN CUT OUT THE PRELIMINARIES, MR. SPEED. YOU DIDN'T INVITE CLARK OVER HERE JUST TO OFFER HIM SOME CIGARS. START TALKING!

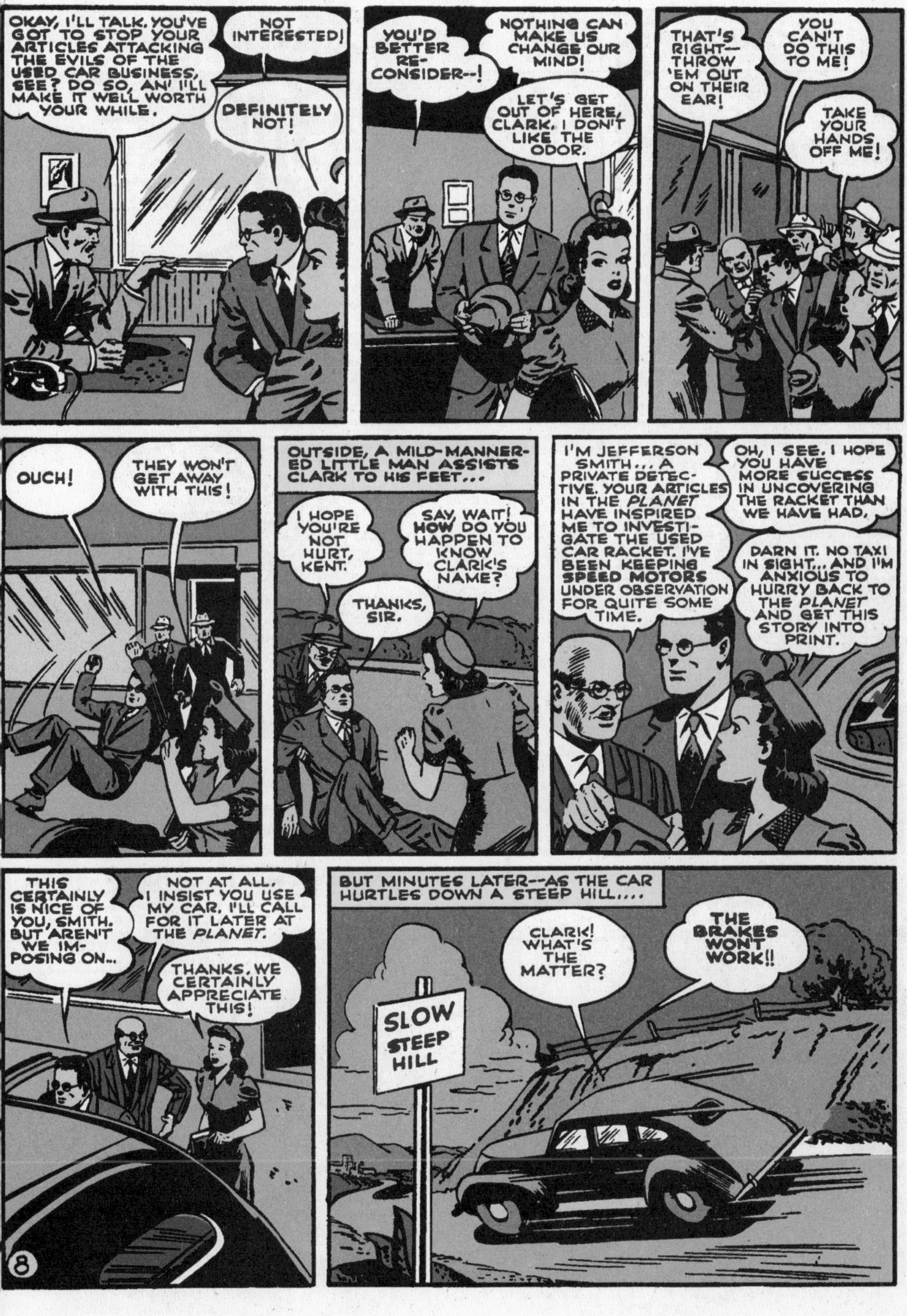

OKAY, I'LL TALK. YOU'VE GOT TO STOP YOUR ARTICLES ATTACKING THE EVILS OF THE USED CAR BUSINESS, SEE? DO SO, AN' I'LL MAKE IT WELL WORTH YOUR WHILE.
NOT INTERESTED!
DEFINITELY NOT!
YOU'D BETTER RE-CONSIDER--!
NOTHING CAN MAKE US CHANGE OUR MIND!
LET'S GET OUT OF HERE, CLARK. I DON'T LIKE THE ODOR.
THAT'S RIGHT--THROW 'EM OUT ON THEIR EAR!
YOU CAN'T DO THIS TO ME!
TAKE YOUR HANDS OFF ME!
OUCH!
THEY WON'T GET AWAY WITH THIS!
OUTSIDE, A MILD-MANNERED LITTLE MAN ASSISTS CLARK TO HIS FEET...
I HOPE YOU'RE NOT HURT, KENT.
SAY, WAIT! HOW DO YOU HAPPEN TO KNOW CLARK'S NAME?
THANKS, SIR.
I'M JEFFERSON SMITH... A PRIVATE DETECTIVE. YOUR ARTICLES IN THE PLANET HAVE INSPIRED ME TO INVESTIGATE THE USED CAR RACKET. I'VE BEEN KEEPING SPEED MOTORS UNDER OBSERVATION FOR QUITE SOME TIME.
OH, I SEE. I HOPE YOU HAVE MORE SUCCESS IN UNCOVERING THE RACKET THAN WE HAVE HAD.
DARN IT. NO TAXI IN SIGHT... AND I'M ANXIOUS TO HURRY BACK TO THE PLANET AND GET THIS STORY INTO PRINT.
THIS CERTAINLY IS NICE OF YOU, SMITH. BUT AREN'T WE IMPOSING ON...
NOT AT ALL. I INSIST YOU USE MY CAR. I'LL CALL FOR IT LATER AT THE PLANET.
THANKS. WE CERTAINLY APPRECIATE THIS!
8
BUT MINUTES LATER--AS THE CAR HURTLES DOWN A STEEP HILL....
SLOW STEEP HILL
CLARK! WHAT'S THE MATTER?
THE BRAKES WON'T WORK!!

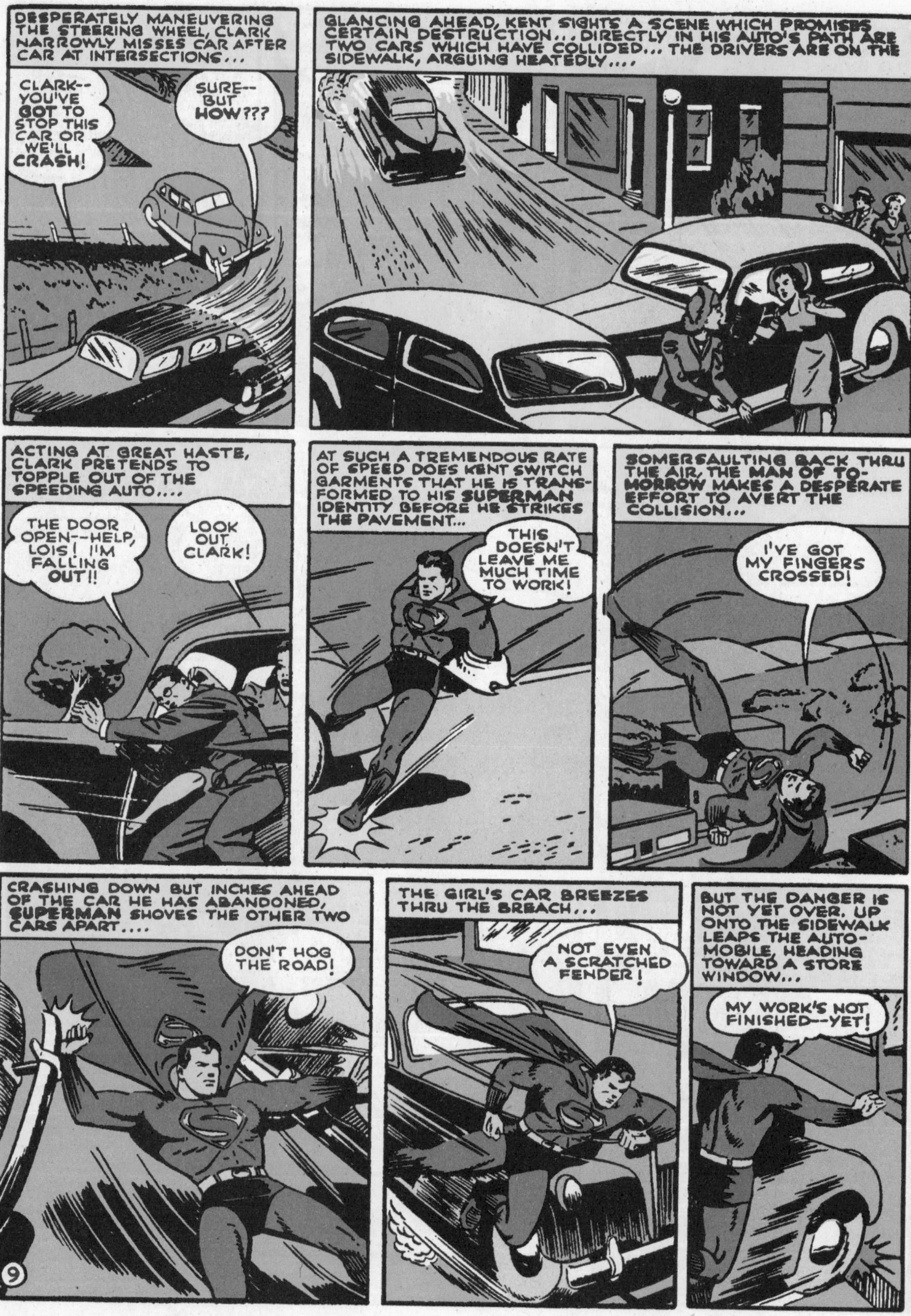
DESPERATELY MANEUVERING THE STEERING WHEEL, CLARK NARROWLY MISSES CAR AFTER CAR AT INTERSECTIONS...
CLARK--YOU'VE GOT TO STOP THIS CAR OR WE'LL CRASH!
SURE--BUT HOW???
GLANCING AHEAD, KENT SIGHTS A SCENE WHICH PROMISES CERTAIN DESTRUCTION... DIRECTLY IN HIS AUTO'S PATH ARE TWO CARS WHICH HAVE COLLIDED... THE DRIVERS ARE ON THE SIDEWALK, ARGUING HEATEDLY....
ACTING AT GREAT HASTE, CLARK PRETENDS TO TOPPLE OUT OF THE SPEEDING AUTO....
THE DOOR OPEN--HELP, LOIS! I'M FALLING OUT!!
LOOK OUT, CLARK!
AT SUCH A TREMENDOUS RATE OF SPEED DOES KENT SWITCH GARMENTS THAT HE IS TRANSFORMED TO HIS SUPERMAN IDENTITY BEFORE HE STRIKES THE PAVEMENT...
THIS DOESN'T LEAVE ME MUCH TIME TO WORK!
SOMERSAULTING BACK THRU THE AIR, THE MAN OF TOMORROW MAKES A DESPERATE EFFORT TO AVERT THE COLLISION...
I'VE GOT MY FINGERS CROSSED!
CRASHING DOWN BUT INCHES AHEAD OF THE CAR HE HAS ABANDONED, SUPERMAN SHOVES THE OTHER TWO CARS APART....
DON'T HOG THE ROAD!
9
THE GIRL'S CAR BREEZES THRU THE BREACH...
NOT EVEN A SCRATCHED FENDER!
BUT THE DANGER IS NOT YET OVER. UP ONTO THE SIDEWALK LEAPS THE AUTOMOBILE, HEADING TOWARD A STORE WINDOW...
MY WORK'S NOT FINISHED--YET!

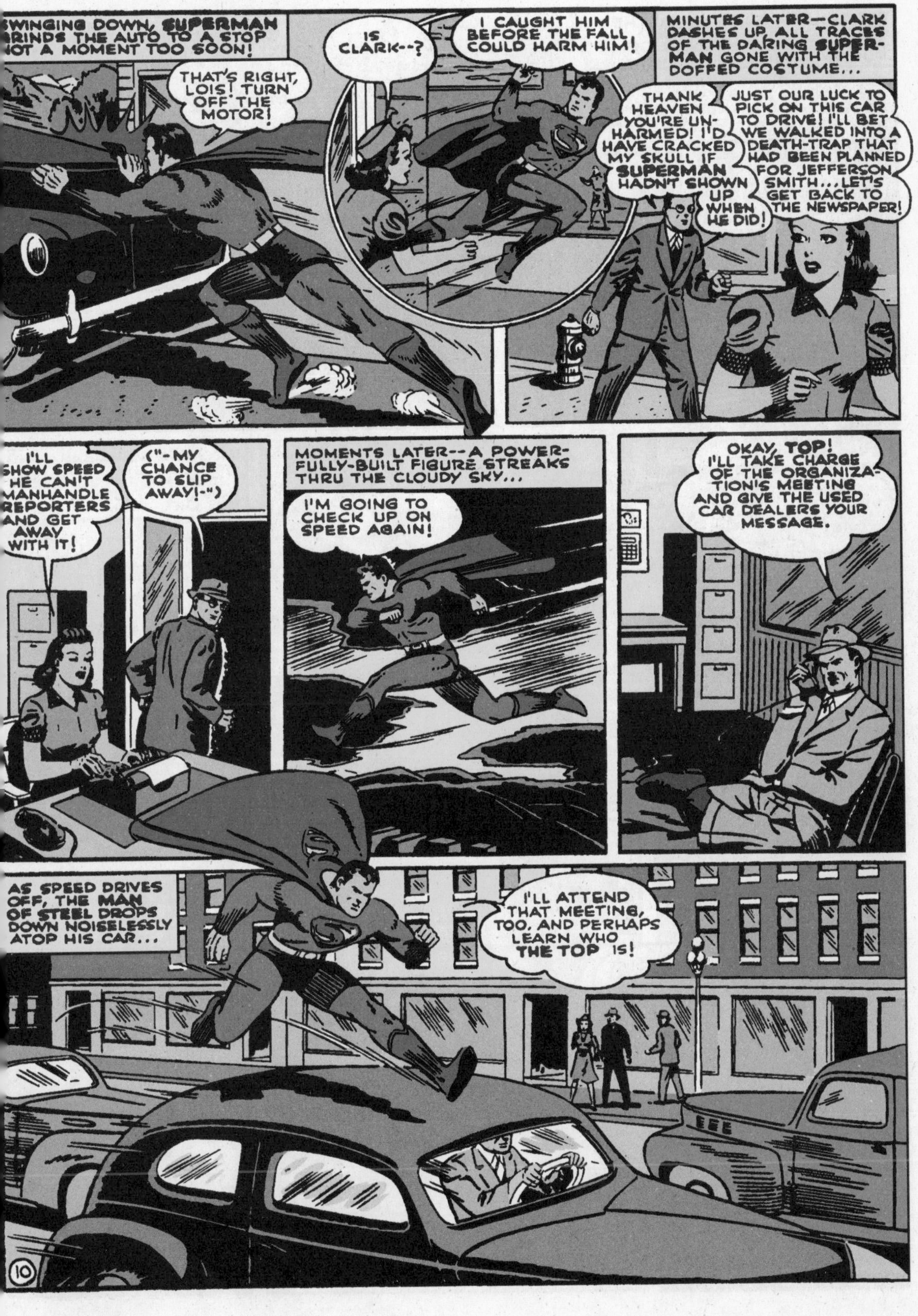
SWINGING DOWN, SUPERMAN BRINGS THE AUTO TO A STOP NOT A MOMENT TOO SOON!
THAT'S RIGHT, LOIS! TURN OFF THE MOTOR!
IS CLARK--?
I CAUGHT HIM BEFORE THE FALL COULD HARM HIM!
MINUTES LATER—CLARK DASHES UP, ALL TRACES OF THE DARING SUPERMAN GONE WITH THE DOFFED COSTUME...
THANK HEAVEN YOU'RE UNHARMED! I'D HAVE CRACKED MY SKULL IF SUPERMAN HADN'T SHOWN UP WHEN HE DID!
JUST OUR LUCK TO PICK ON THIS CAR TO DRIVE! I'LL BET WE WALKED INTO A DEATH-TRAP THAT HAD BEEN PLANNED FOR JEFFERSON SMITH... LET'S GET BACK TO THE NEWSPAPER!
I'LL SHOW SPEED HE CAN'T MANHANDLE REPORTERS AND GET AWAY WITH IT!
("-MY CHANCE TO SLIP AWAY!-")
MOMENTS LATER--A POWERFULLY-BUILT FIGURE STREAKS THRU THE CLOUDY SKY...
I'M GOING TO CHECK UP ON SPEED AGAIN!
OKAY, TOP! I'LL TAKE CHARGE OF THE ORGANIZATION'S MEETING AND GIVE THE USED CAR DEALERS YOUR MESSAGE.
AS SPEED DRIVES OFF, THE MAN OF STEEL DROPS DOWN NOISELESSLY ATOP HIS CAR...
I'LL ATTEND THAT MEETING, TOO, AND PERHAPS LEARN WHO THE TOP IS!
10

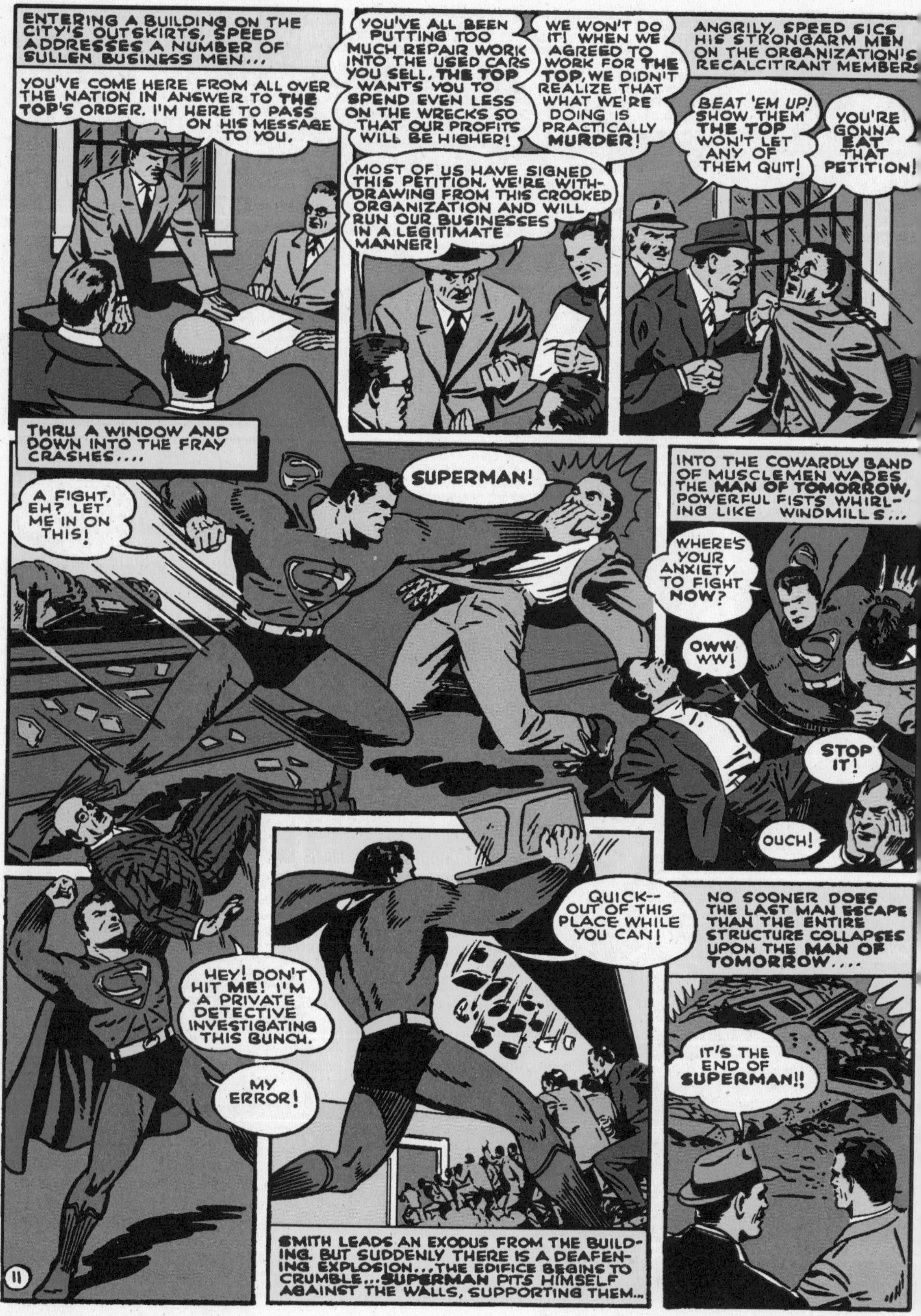
ENTERING A BUILDING ON THE CITY'S OUTSKIRTS, SPEED ADDRESSES A NUMBER OF SULLEN BUSINESS MEN...
YOU'VE COME HERE FROM ALL OVER THE NATION IN ANSWER TO THE TOP'S ORDER. I'M HERE TO PASS ON HIS MESSAGE TO YOU.
YOU'VE ALL BEEN PUTTING TOO MUCH REPAIR WORK INTO THE USED CARS YOU SELL. THE TOP WANTS YOU TO SPEND EVEN LESS ON THE WRECKS SO THAT OUR PROFITS WILL BE HIGHER!
WE WON'T DO IT! WHEN WE AGREED TO WORK FOR THE TOP, WE DIDN'T REALIZE THAT WHAT WE'RE DOING IS PRACTICALLY MURDER!
MOST OF US HAVE SIGNED THIS PETITION. WE'RE WITHDRAWING FROM THIS CROOKED ORGANIZATION AND WILL RUN OUR BUSINESSES IN A LEGITIMATE MANNER!
ANGRILY, SPEED SICS HIS STRONGARM MEN ON THE ORGANIZATION'S RECALCITRANT MEMBERS
BEAT 'EM UP! SHOW THEM THE TOP WON'T LET ANY OF THEM QUIT!
YOU'RE GONNA EAT THAT PETITION!
THRU A WINDOW AND DOWN INTO THE FRAY CRASHES....
A FIGHT, EH? LET ME IN ON THIS!
SUPERMAN!
INTO THE COWARDLY BAND OF MUSCLEMEN WADES THE MAN OF TOMORROW, POWERFUL FISTS WHIRLING LIKE WINDMILLS...
WHERE'S YOUR ANXIETY TO FIGHT NOW?
OWWWW!
STOP IT!
OUCH!
HEY! DON'T HIT ME! I'M A PRIVATE DETECTIVE INVESTIGATING THIS BUNCH.
MY ERROR!
11
QUICK-- OUT OF THIS PLACE WHILE YOU CAN!
SMITH LEADS AN EXODUS FROM THE BUILDING. BUT SUDDENLY THERE IS A DEAFENING EXPLOSION... THE EDIFICE BEGINS TO CRUMBLE... SUPERMAN PITS HIMSELF AGAINST THE WALLS, SUPPORTING THEM...
NO SOONER DOES THE LAST MAN ESCAPE THAN THE ENTIRE STRUCTURE COLLAPSES UPON THE MAN OF TOMORROW....
IT'S THE END OF SUPERMAN!!

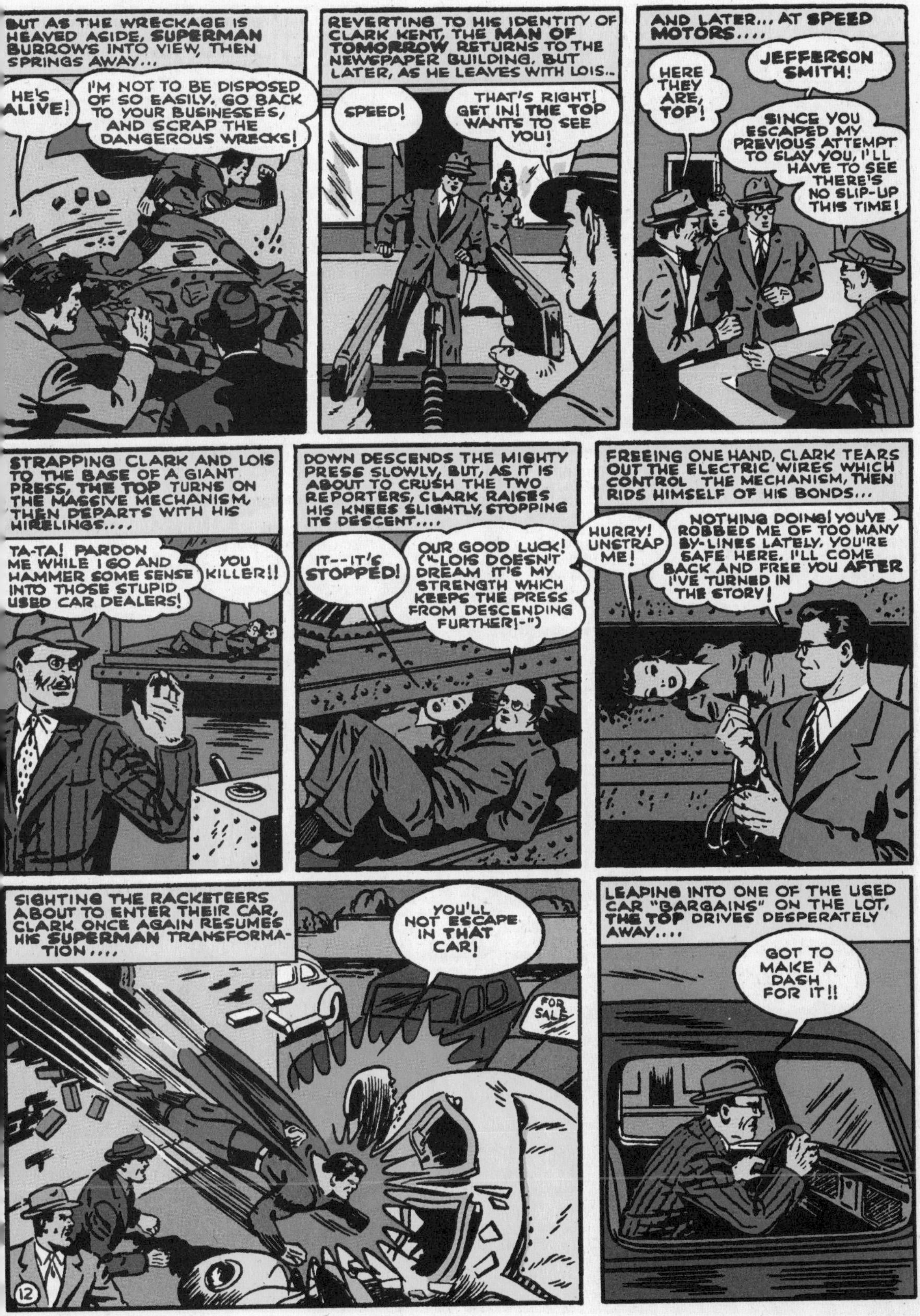
BUT AS THE WRECKAGE IS HEAVED ASIDE, SUPERMAN BURROWS INTO VIEW, THEN SPRINGS AWAY...
HE'S ALIVE!
I'M NOT TO BE DISPOSED OF SO EASILY. GO BACK TO YOUR BUSINESSES, AND SCRAP THE DANGEROUS WRECKS!
REVERTING TO HIS IDENTITY OF CLARK KENT, THE MAN OF TOMORROW RETURNS TO THE NEWSPAPER BUILDING. BUT LATER, AS HE LEAVES WITH LOIS..
SPEED!
THAT'S RIGHT! GET IN! THE TOP WANTS TO SEE YOU!
AND LATER... AT SPEED MOTORS....
HERE THEY ARE, TOP!
JEFFERSON SMITH!
SINCE YOU ESCAPED MY PREVIOUS ATTEMPT TO SLAY YOU, I'LL HAVE TO SEE THERE'S NO SLIP-UP THIS TIME!
STRAPPING CLARK AND LOIS TO THE BASE OF A GIANT PRESS, THE TOP TURNS ON THE MASSIVE MECHANISM, THEN DEPARTS WITH HIS HIRELINGS....
TA-TA! PARDON ME WHILE I GO AND HAMMER SOME SENSE INTO THOSE STUPID USED CAR DEALERS!
YOU KILLER!!
DOWN DESCENDS THE MIGHTY PRESS SLOWLY, BUT, AS IT IS ABOUT TO CRUSH THE TWO REPORTERS, CLARK RAISES HIS KNEES SLIGHTLY, STOPPING ITS DESCENT....
IT--IT'S STOPPED!
OUR GOOD LUCK! ("--LOIS DOESN'T DREAM IT'S MY STRENGTH WHICH KEEPS THE PRESS FROM DESCENDING FURTHER!-")
FREEING ONE HAND, CLARK TEARS OUT THE ELECTRIC WIRES WHICH CONTROL THE MECHANISM, THEN RIDS HIMSELF OF HIS BONDS...
HURRY! UNSTRAP ME!
NOTHING DOING! YOU'VE ROBBED ME OF TOO MANY BY-LINES LATELY. YOU'RE SAFE HERE. I'LL COME BACK AND FREE YOU AFTER I'VE TURNED IN THE STORY!
SIGHTING THE RACKETEERS ABOUT TO ENTER THEIR CAR, CLARK ONCE AGAIN RESUMES HIS SUPERMAN TRANSFORMATION....
YOU'LL NOT ESCAPE IN THAT CAR!
FOR SALE
12
LEAPING INTO ONE OF THE USED CAR "BARGAINS" ON THE LOT, THE TOP DRIVES DESPERATELY AWAY....
GOT TO MAKE A DASH FOR IT!!

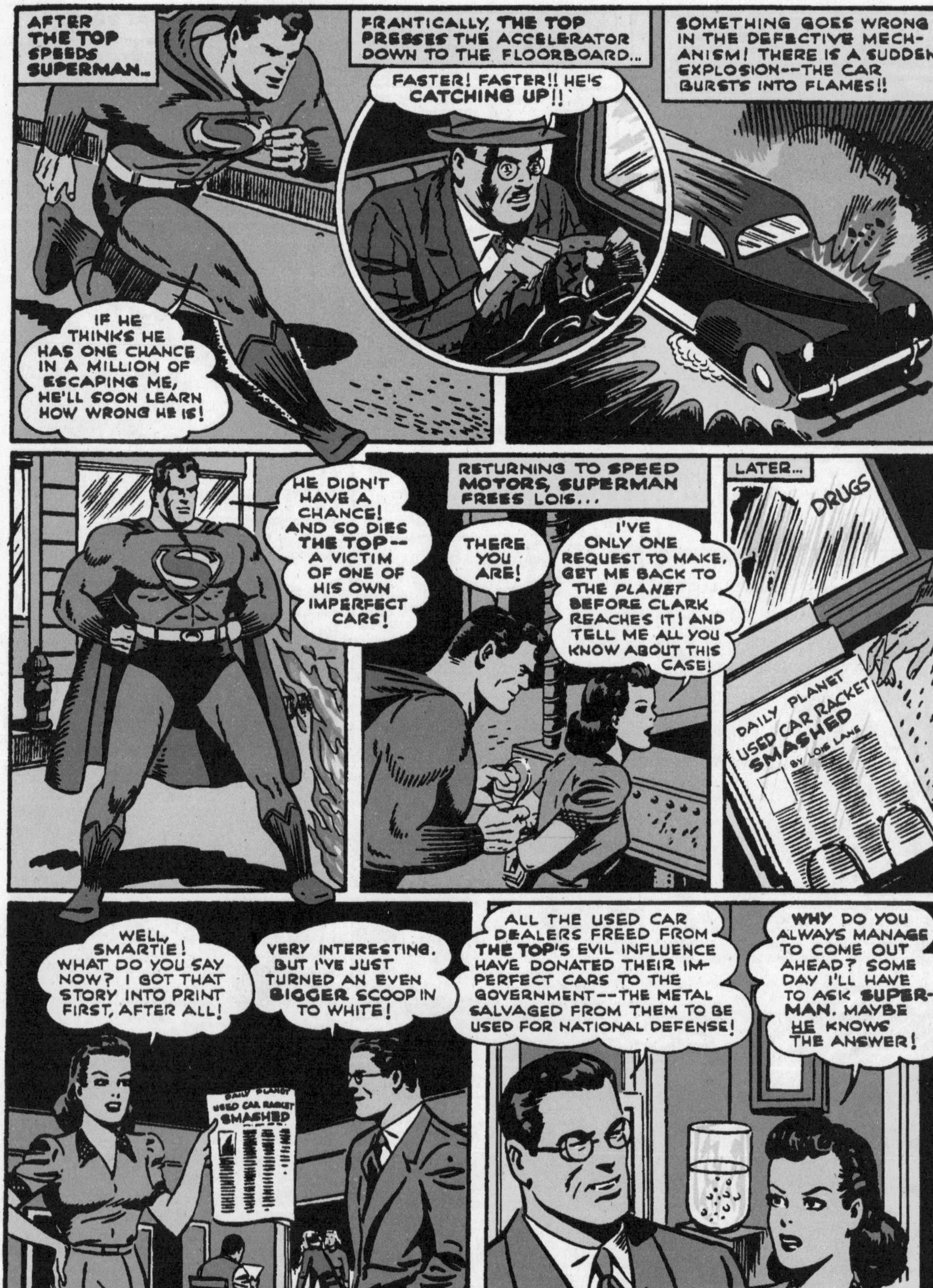
AFTER THE TOP SPEEDS SUPERMAN...
IF HE THINKS HE HAS ONE CHANCE IN A MILLION OF ESCAPING ME, HE'LL SOON LEARN HOW WRONG HE IS!
FRANTICALLY, THE TOP PRESSES THE ACCELERATOR DOWN TO THE FLOORBOARD...
FASTER! FASTER!! HE'S CATCHING UP!!
SOMETHING GOES WRONG IN THE DEFECTIVE MECHANISM! THERE IS A SUDDEN EXPLOSION--THE CAR BURSTS INTO FLAMES!!
HE DIDN'T HAVE A CHANCE! AND SO DIES THE TOP-- A VICTIM OF ONE OF HIS OWN IMPERFECT CARS!
RETURNING TO SPEED MOTORS, SUPERMAN FREES LOIS...
THERE YOU ARE!
I'VE ONLY ONE REQUEST TO MAKE. GET ME BACK TO THE PLANET BEFORE CLARK REACHES IT! AND TELL ME ALL YOU KNOW ABOUT THIS CASE!
LATER...
DRUGS
DAILY PLANET
USED CAR RACKET SMASHED
BY LOIS LANE
WELL, SMARTIE! WHAT DO YOU SAY NOW? I GOT THAT STORY INTO PRINT FIRST, AFTER ALL!
VERY INTERESTING. BUT I'VE JUST TURNED AN EVEN BIGGER SCOOP IN TO WHITE!
DAILY PLANET
USED CAR RACKET SMASHED
13
ALL THE USED CAR DEALERS FREED FROM THE TOP'S EVIL INFLUENCE HAVE DONATED THEIR IMPERFECT CARS TO THE GOVERNMENT--THE METAL SALVAGED FROM THEM TO BE USED FOR NATIONAL DEFENSE!
WHY DO YOU ALWAYS MANAGE TO COME OUT AHEAD? SOME DAY I'LL HAVE TO ASK SUPERMAN. MAYBE HE KNOWS THE ANSWER!
THE END

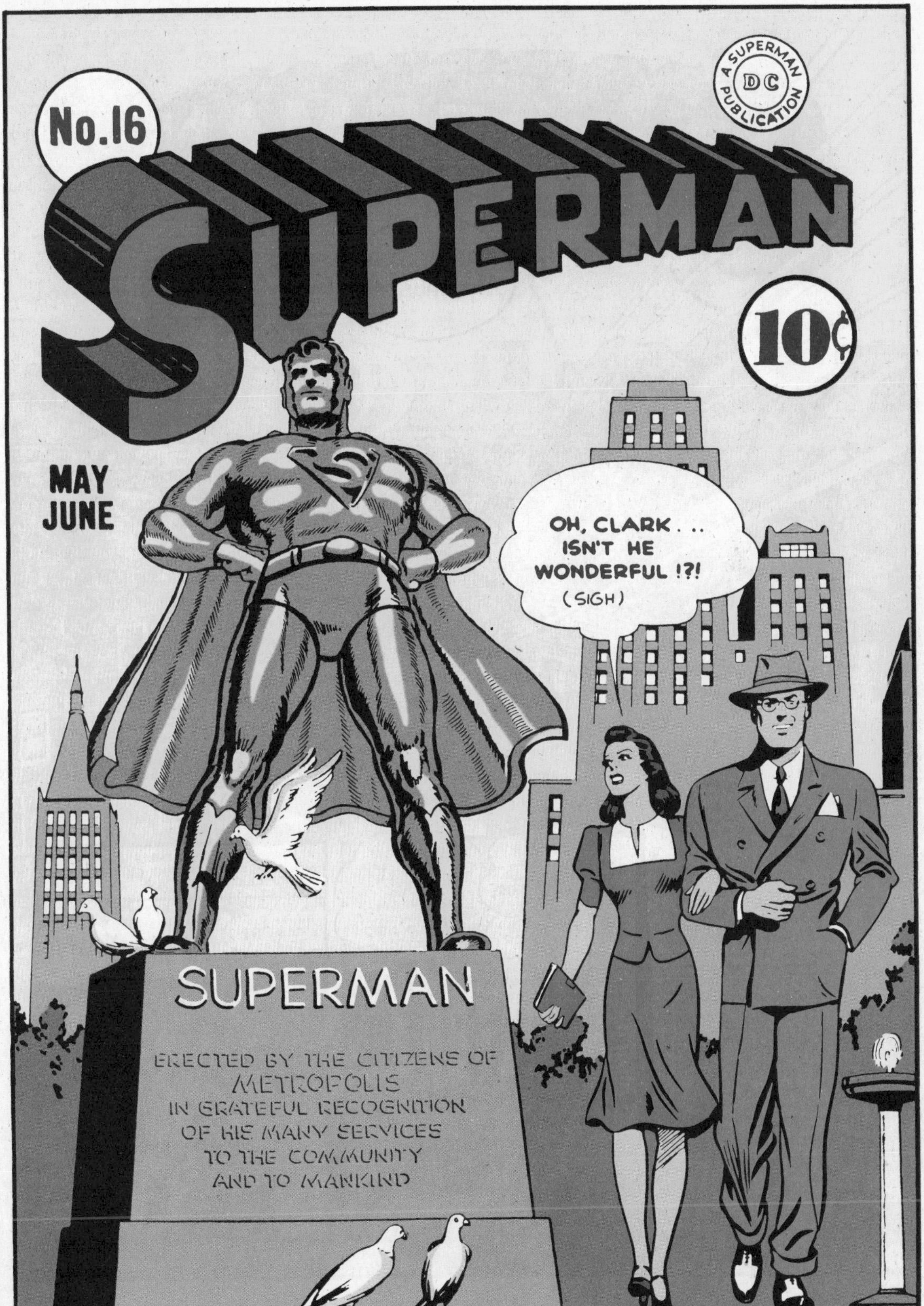
No. 16
A SUPERMAN DC PUBLICATION
SUPERMAN
10¢
MAY
JUNE
OH, CLARK . . .
ISN'T HE
WONDERFUL !?!
(SIGH)
SUPERMAN
ERECTED BY THE CITIZENS OF
METROPOLIS
IN GRATEFUL RECOGNITION
OF HIS MANY SERVICES
TO THE COMMUNITY
AND TO MANKIND

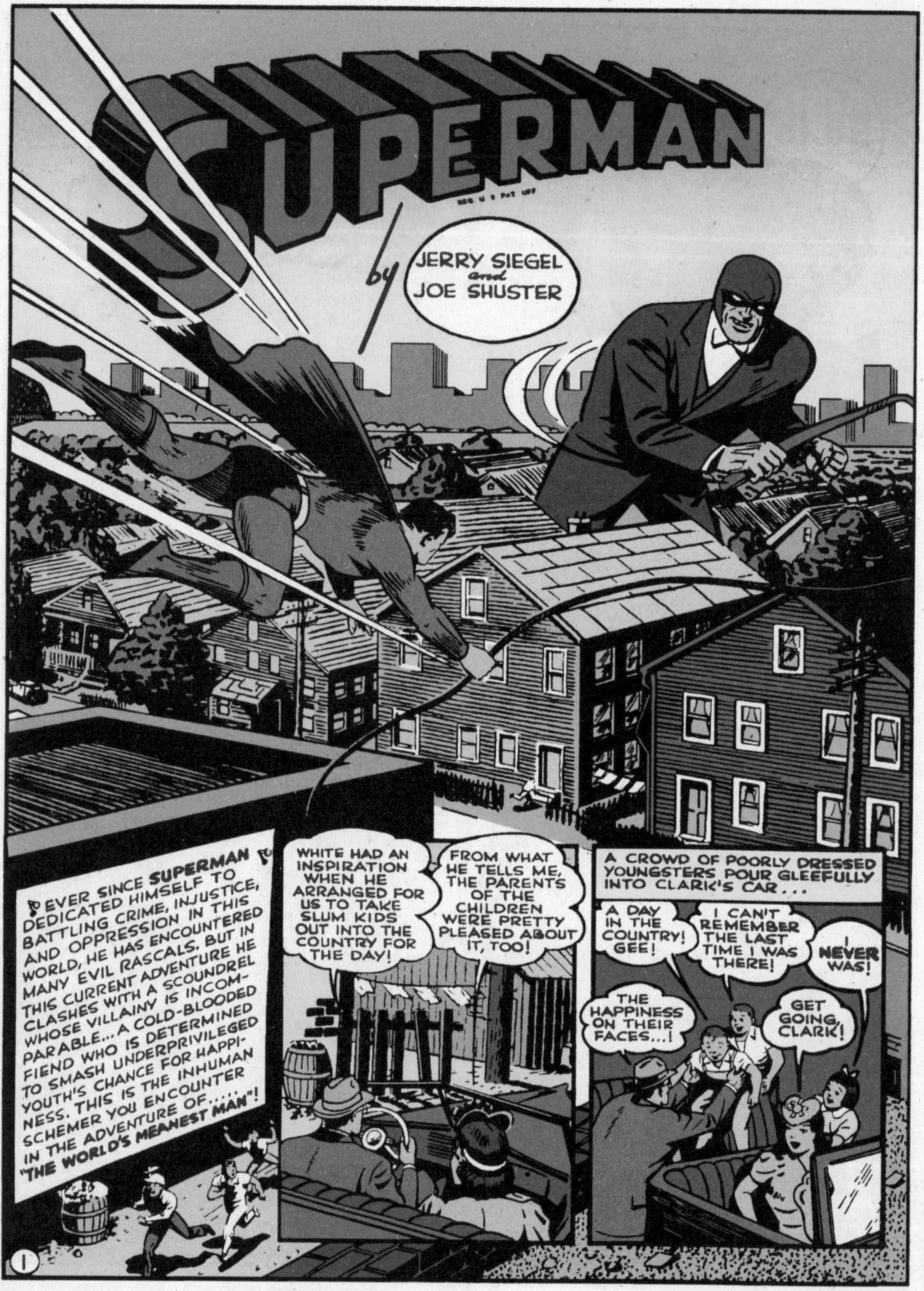
SUPERMAN
REG. U.S. PAT. OFF.
by JERRY SIEGEL and JOE SHUSTER
EVER SINCE SUPERMAN DEDICATED HIMSELF TO BATTLING CRIME, INJUSTICE, AND OPPRESSION IN THIS WORLD, HE HAS ENCOUNTERED MANY EVIL RASCALS. BUT IN THIS CURRENT ADVENTURE HE CLASHES WITH A SCOUNDREL WHOSE VILLAINY IS INCOMPARABLE... A COLD-BLOODED FIEND WHO IS DETERMINED TO SMASH UNDERPRIVILEGED YOUTH'S CHANCE FOR HAPPINESS. THIS IS THE INHUMAN SCHEMER YOU ENCOUNTER IN THE ADVENTURE OF..... "THE WORLD'S MEANEST MAN"!
1
WHITE HAD AN INSPIRATION WHEN HE ARRANGED FOR US TO TAKE SLUM KIDS OUT INTO THE COUNTRY FOR THE DAY!
FROM WHAT HE TELLS ME, THE PARENTS OF THE CHILDREN WERE PRETTY PLEASED ABOUT IT, TOO!
A CROWD OF POORLY DRESSED YOUNGSTERS POUR GLEEFULLY INTO CLARK'S CAR...
A DAY IN THE COUNTRY! GEE!
I CAN'T REMEMBER THE LAST TIME I WAS THERE!
I NEVER WAS!
THE HAPPINESS ON THEIR FACES...!
GET GOING, CLARK!

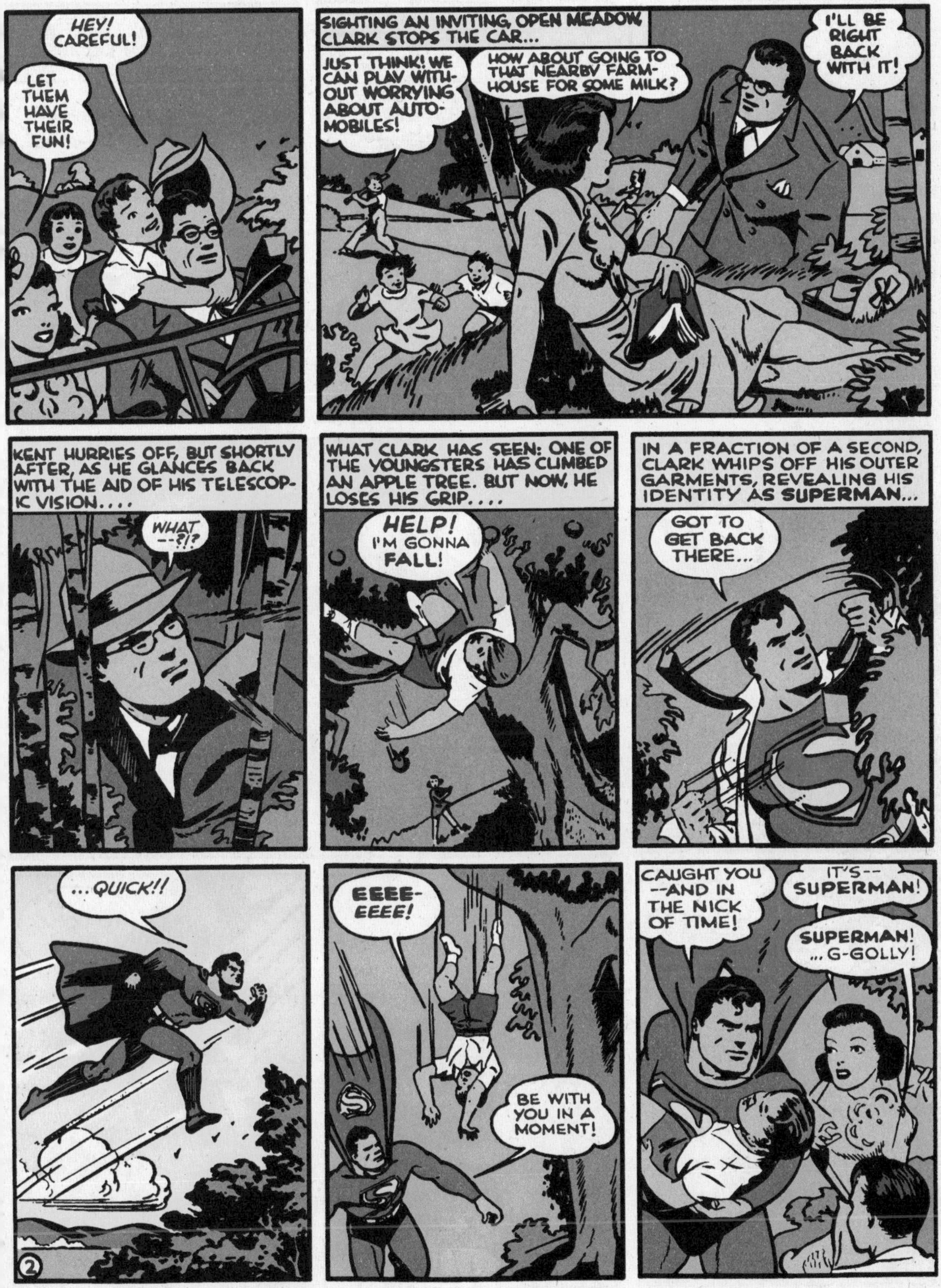
HEY! CAREFUL!
LET THEM HAVE THEIR FUN!
SIGHTING AN INVITING, OPEN MEADOW, CLARK STOPS THE CAR...
JUST THINK! WE CAN PLAY WITH-OUT WORRYING ABOUT AUTO-MOBILES!
HOW ABOUT GOING TO THAT NEARBY FARM-HOUSE FOR SOME MILK?
I'LL BE RIGHT BACK WITH IT!
KENT HURRIES OFF, BUT SHORTLY AFTER, AS HE GLANCES BACK WITH THE AID OF HIS TELESCOP-IC VISION....
WHAT --?!?
WHAT CLARK HAS SEEN: ONE OF THE YOUNGSTERS HAS CLIMBED AN APPLE TREE. BUT NOW, HE LOSES HIS GRIP....
HELP! I'M GONNA FALL!
IN A FRACTION OF A SECOND, CLARK WHIPS OFF HIS OUTER GARMENTS, REVEALING HIS IDENTITY AS SUPERMAN...
GOT TO GET BACK THERE...
...QUICK!!
2
EEEE-EEEE!
BE WITH YOU IN A MOMENT!
CAUGHT YOU --AND IN THE NICK OF TIME!
IT'S-- SUPERMAN!
SUPERMAN! ...G-GOLLY!

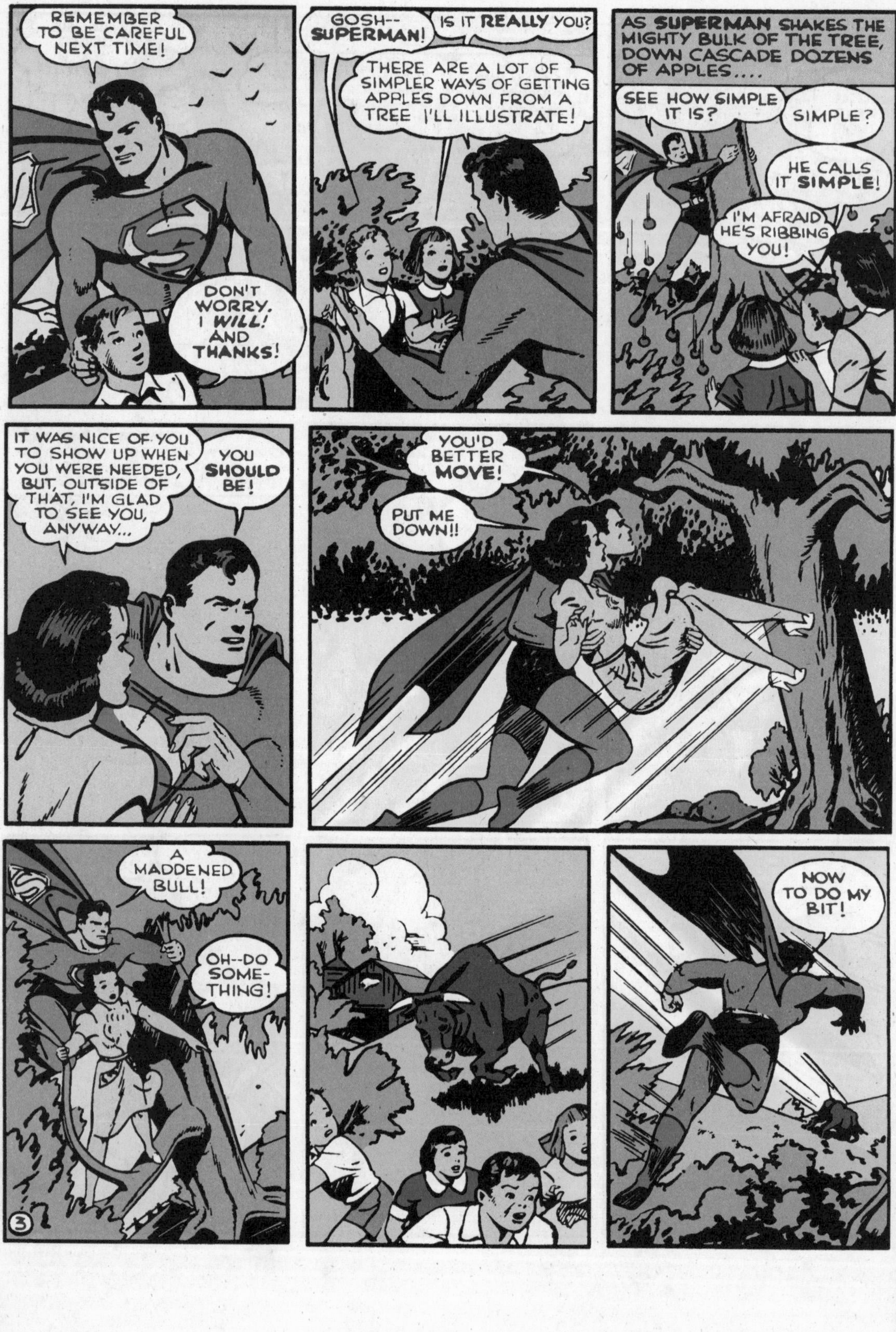
REMEMBER TO BE CAREFUL NEXT TIME!
DON'T WORRY. I **WILL!** AND **THANKS!**
GOSH-- **SUPERMAN!**
IS IT **REALLY** YOU?
THERE ARE A LOT OF SIMPLER WAYS OF GETTING APPLES DOWN FROM A TREE I'LL ILLUSTRATE!
AS **SUPERMAN** SHAKES THE MIGHTY BULK OF THE TREE, DOWN CASCADE DOZENS OF APPLES....
SEE HOW SIMPLE IT IS?
SIMPLE?
HE CALLS IT **SIMPLE!**
I'M AFRAID HE'S RIBBING YOU!
IT WAS NICE OF YOU TO SHOW UP WHEN YOU WERE NEEDED, BUT, OUTSIDE OF THAT, I'M GLAD TO SEE YOU, ANYWAY...
YOU **SHOULD** BE!
YOU'D BETTER **MOVE!**
PUT ME DOWN!!
A MADDENED BULL!
OH--DO SOME-THING!
NOW TO DO MY BIT!

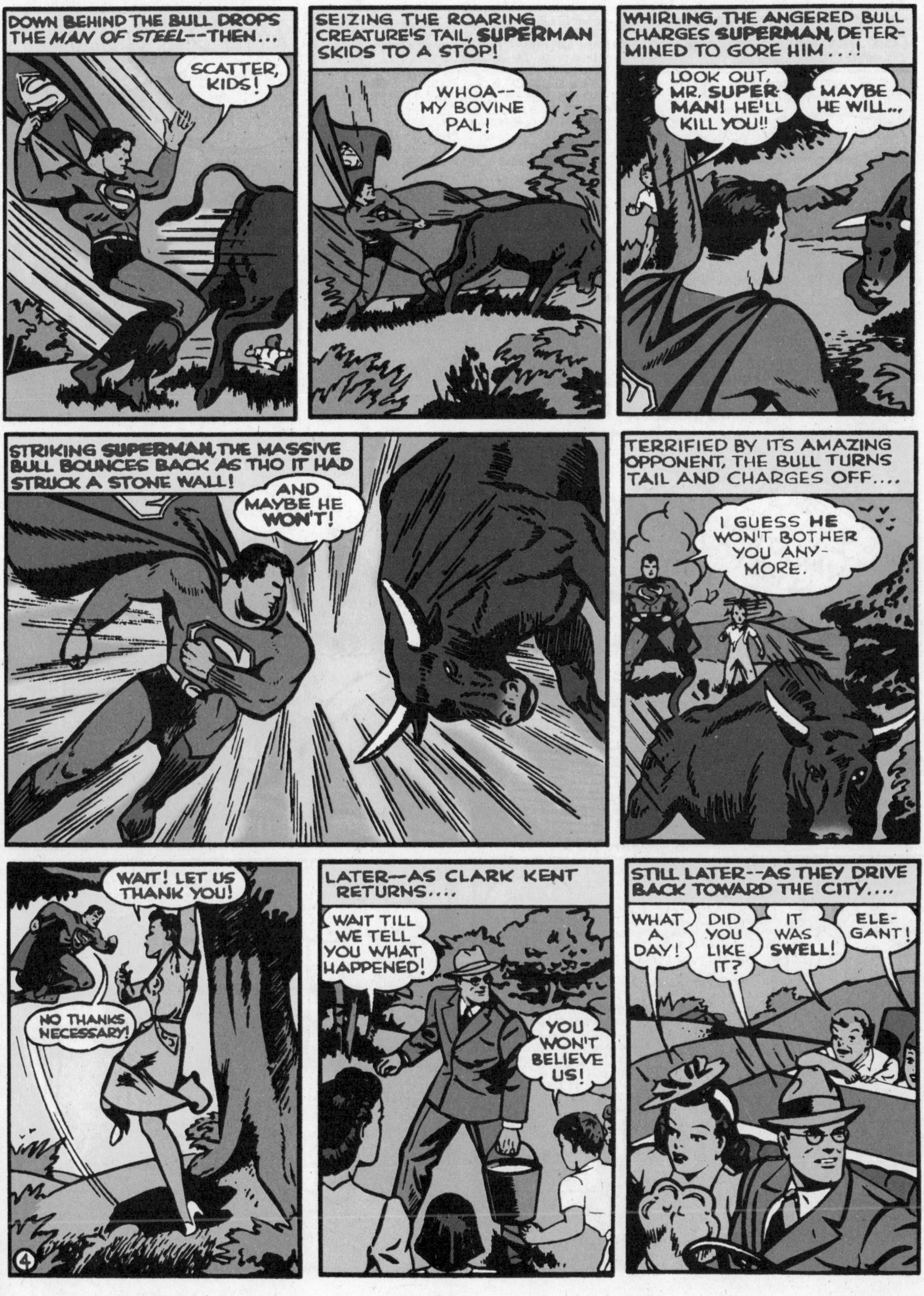

DOWN BEHIND THE BULL DROPS THE *MAN OF STEEL*--THEN...
SCATTER, KIDS!
SEIZING THE ROARING CREATURE'S TAIL, **SUPERMAN** SKIDS TO A STOP!
WHOA-- MY BOVINE PAL!
WHIRLING, THE ANGERED BULL CHARGES **SUPERMAN**, DETERMINED TO GORE HIM...!
LOOK OUT, MR. **SUPERMAN!** HE'LL KILL YOU!!
MAYBE HE WILL...
STRIKING **SUPERMAN**, THE MASSIVE BULL BOUNCES BACK AS THO IT HAD STRUCK A STONE WALL!
AND MAYBE HE **WON'T!**
TERRIFIED BY ITS AMAZING OPPONENT, THE BULL TURNS TAIL AND CHARGES OFF....
I GUESS **HE** WON'T BOTHER YOU ANYMORE.
WAIT! LET US THANK YOU!
NO THANKS NECESSARY!
4
LATER--AS CLARK KENT RETURNS....
WAIT TILL WE TELL YOU WHAT HAPPENED!
YOU WON'T BELIEVE US!
STILL LATER--AS THEY DRIVE BACK TOWARD THE CITY....
WHAT A DAY!
DID YOU LIKE IT?
IT WAS **SWELL!**
ELEGANT!

AFTER TAKING THE CHILDREN TO THEIR HOMES, CLARK AND LOIS RETURN TO THE *DAILY PLANET* OFFICE....

WELL, HOW'D IT GO?

SIMPLY GRAND!

GETTING OUT INTO THE COUNTRY MEANT SO MUCH TO THOSE UNDER-PRIVILEGED CHILDREN!

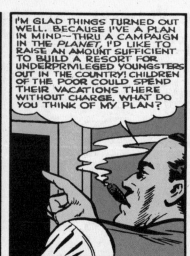

I'M GLAD THINGS TURNED OUT WELL. BECAUSE I'VE A PLAN IN MIND—THRU A CAMPAIGN IN THE *PLANET*, I'D LIKE TO RAISE AN AMOUNT SUFFICIENT TO BUILD A RESORT FOR UNDERPRIVILEGED YOUNGSTERS OUT IN THE COUNTRY! CHILDREN OF THE POOR COULD SPEND THEIR VACATIONS THERE WITHOUT CHARGE. WHAT DO YOU THINK OF MY PLAN?

IT'S--IT'S SWELL! WHITE, I NEVER QUITE REALIZED WHAT A BIG HEART YOU HAVE!

FOR A HARD-BOILED EDITOR, YOU'VE SURE GOT A SENTIMENTAL STREAK!

CUT OUT THE PALAVER AND GET BUSY, YOU TWO--POUND OUT SOME ARTICLES ANNOUNCING THE *PLANET'S* PLAN!

DAILY PLANET

FREE VACATION FARM ADVOCATED FOR UNDER-PRIVILEGED CHILDREN

DAILY PLANET

CAMPAIGN BEGINS; CONTRIBUTIONS URGED

A WEEK LATER...

WE MADE IT!

SWELL!

THE PEOPLE OF METROPOLIS ARE ALWAYS READY TO CONTRIBUTE TO A WORTHY CAUSE.

CHARLIE GRAYSON! WHEN DID YOU GET OUT OF JAIL?

YESTERDAY. I WANT TO CONTRIBUTE THIS CHECK TOWARD THE VACATION FARM CAMPAIGN. IF I COULD HAVE GONE TO A PLACE LIKE THAT WHEN I WAS A KID, MAYBE I WOULDN'T HAVE TURNED OUT TO BE A RACKETEER.

THAT'S MIGHTY BIG OF YOU, GRAYSON-- ESPECIALLY SINCE IT WAS THE *PLANET* WHICH EXPOSED YOUR ILLEGAL ACTIVITIES.

⑤

SO THEY'VE RAISED THE MONEY, EH? HM-MMM! WELL...THAT FREE VACATION RESORT ISN'T A SUCCESS YET..AND IF I CAN HELP IT, IT NEVER WILL BE!!

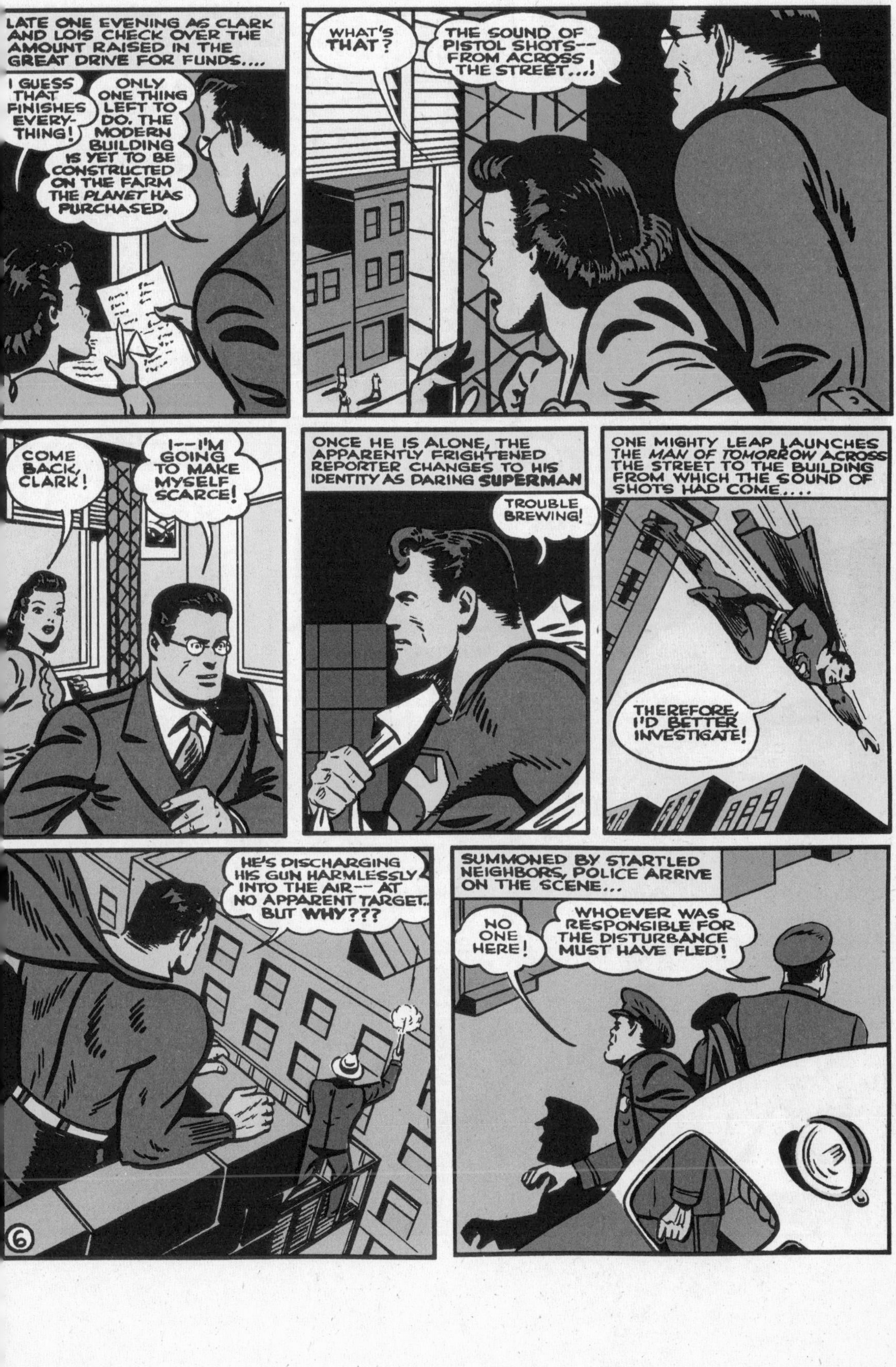
LATE ONE EVENING AS CLARK AND LOIS CHECK OVER THE AMOUNT RAISED IN THE GREAT DRIVE FOR FUNDS....
I GUESS THAT FINISHES EVERY-THING!
ONLY ONE THING LEFT TO DO. THE MODERN BUILDING IS YET TO BE CONSTRUCTED ON THE FARM THE PLANET HAS PURCHASED.
WHAT'S THAT?
THE SOUND OF PISTOL SHOTS-- FROM ACROSS THE STREET...!
COME BACK, CLARK!
I--I'M GOING TO MAKE MYSELF SCARCE!
ONCE HE IS ALONE, THE APPARENTLY FRIGHTENED REPORTER CHANGES TO HIS IDENTITY AS DARING SUPERMAN
TROUBLE BREWING!
ONE MIGHTY LEAP LAUNCHES THE MAN OF TOMORROW ACROSS THE STREET TO THE BUILDING FROM WHICH THE SOUND OF SHOTS HAD COME....
THEREFORE, I'D BETTER INVESTIGATE!
6
HE'S DISCHARGING HIS GUN HARMLESSLY INTO THE AIR-- AT NO APPARENT TARGET.. BUT WHY???
SUMMONED BY STARTLED NEIGHBORS, POLICE ARRIVE ON THE SCENE...
NO ONE HERE!
WHOEVER WAS RESPONSIBLE FOR THE DISTURBANCE MUST HAVE FLED!

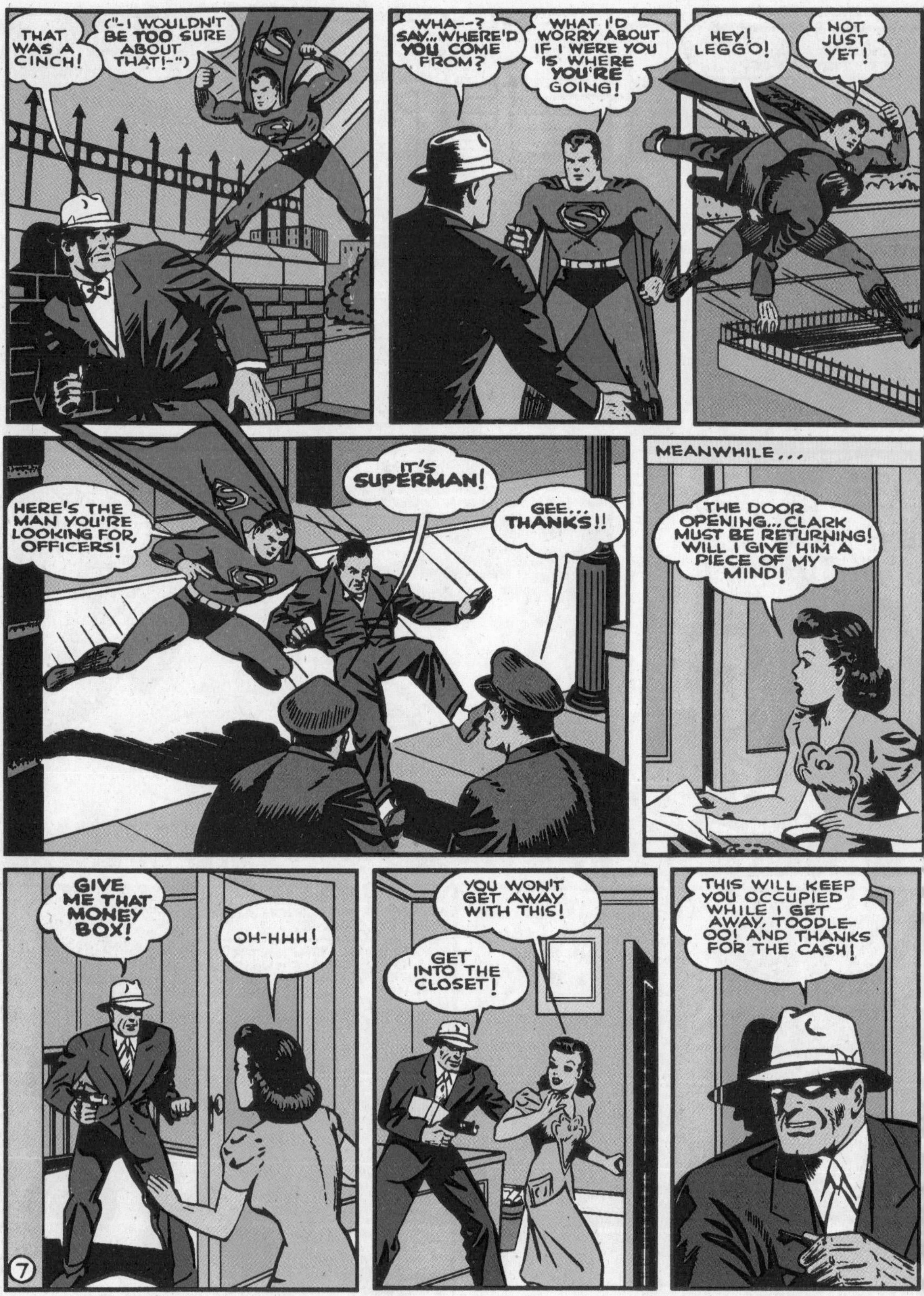
THAT WAS A CINCH!
("-I WOULDN'T BE TOO SURE ABOUT THAT!-")
WHA--? SAY... WHERE'D YOU COME FROM?
WHAT I'D WORRY ABOUT IF I WERE YOU IS WHERE YOU'RE GOING!
HEY! LEGGO!
NOT JUST YET!
HERE'S THE MAN YOU'RE LOOKING FOR, OFFICERS!
IT'S SUPERMAN!
GEE... THANKS!!
MEANWHILE...
THE DOOR OPENING... CLARK MUST BE RETURNING! WILL I GIVE HIM A PIECE OF MY MIND!
GIVE ME THAT MONEY BOX!
OH-HHH!
7
YOU WON'T GET AWAY WITH THIS!
GET INTO THE CLOSET!
THIS WILL KEEP YOU OCCUPIED WHILE I GET AWAY. TOODLE-OO! AND THANKS FOR THE CASH!

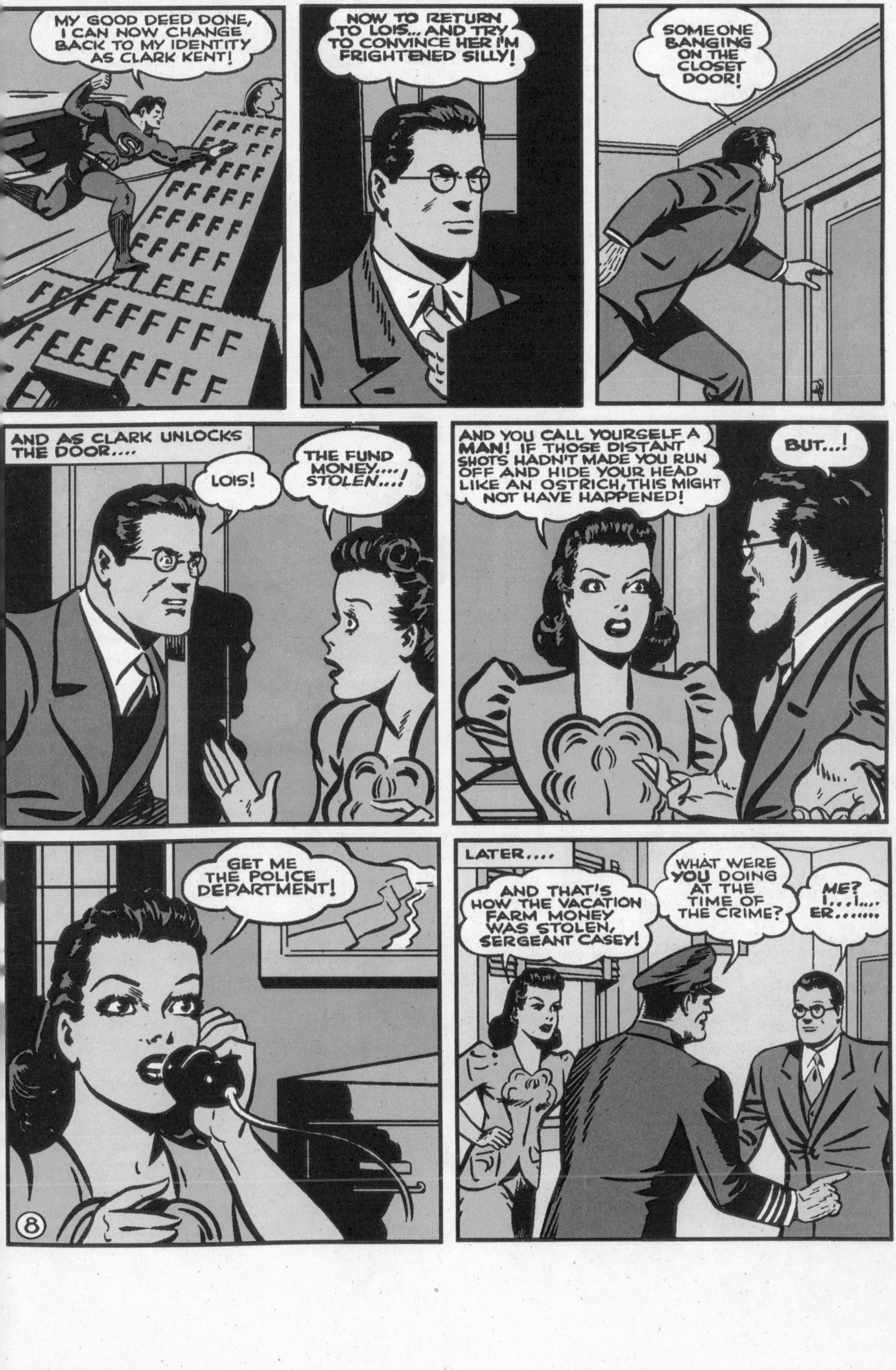
MY GOOD DEED DONE, I CAN NOW CHANGE BACK TO MY IDENTITY AS CLARK KENT!
NOW TO RETURN TO LOIS... AND TRY TO CONVINCE HER I'M FRIGHTENED SILLY!
SOMEONE BANGING ON THE CLOSET DOOR!
AND AS CLARK UNLOCKS THE DOOR....
LOIS!
THE FUND MONEY.... STOLEN...!
AND YOU CALL YOURSELF A MAN! IF THOSE DISTANT SHOTS HADN'T MADE YOU RUN OFF AND HIDE YOUR HEAD LIKE AN OSTRICH, THIS MIGHT NOT HAVE HAPPENED!
BUT...!
GET ME THE POLICE DEPARTMENT!
8
LATER....
AND THAT'S HOW THE VACATION FARM MONEY WAS STOLEN, SERGEANT CASEY!
WHAT WERE YOU DOING AT THE TIME OF THE CRIME?
ME? I...I.... ER.......

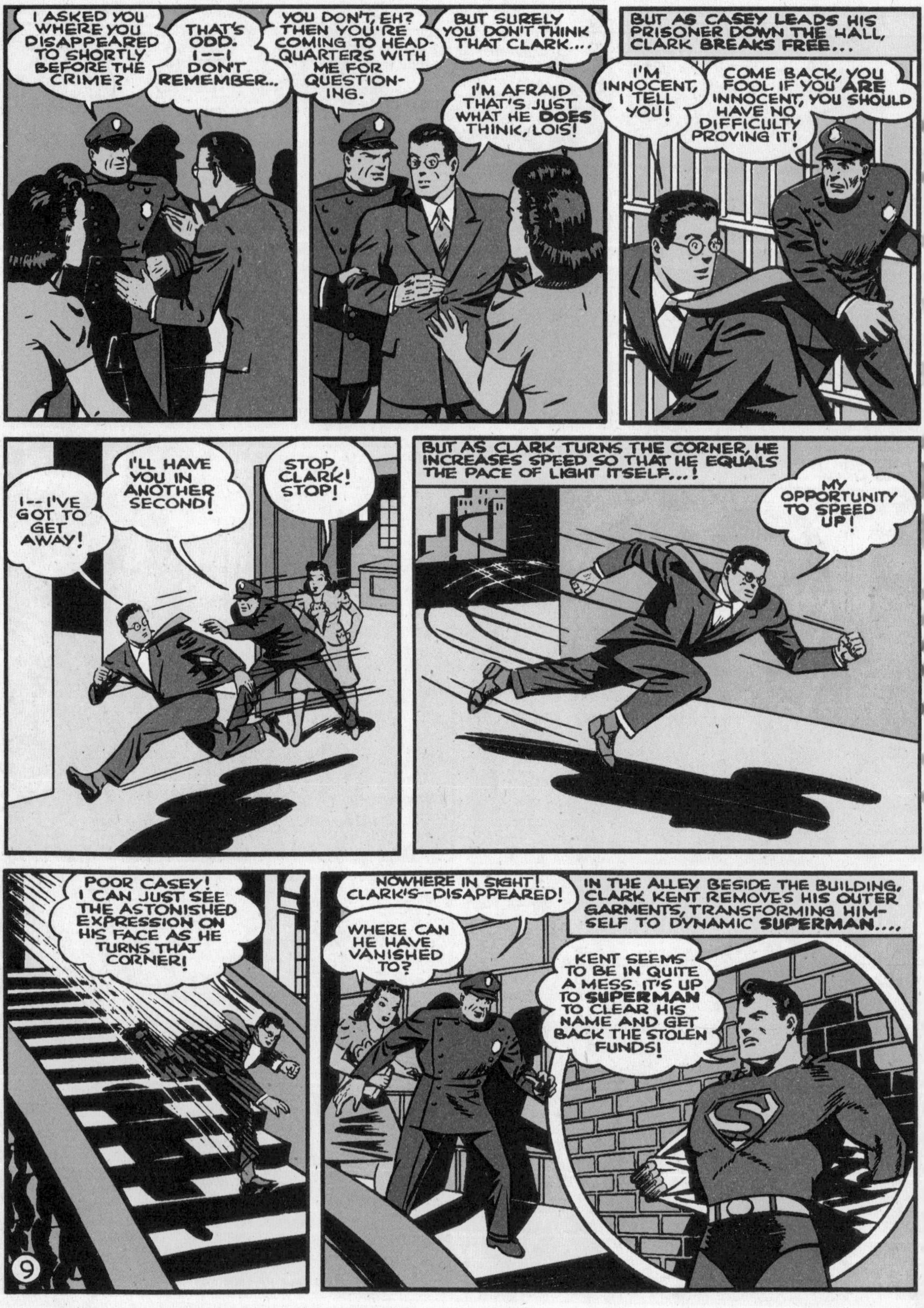
I ASKED YOU WHERE YOU DISAPPEARED TO SHORTLY BEFORE THE CRIME?
THAT'S ODD. I--I DON'T REMEMBER..
YOU DON'T, EH? THEN YOU'RE COMING TO HEAD-QUARTERS WITH ME FOR QUESTION-ING.
BUT SURELY YOU DON'T THINK THAT CLARK....
I'M AFRAID THAT'S JUST WHAT HE DOES THINK, LOIS!
BUT AS CASEY LEADS HIS PRISONER DOWN THE HALL, CLARK BREAKS FREE...
I'M INNOCENT, I TELL YOU!
COME BACK, YOU FOOL. IF YOU ARE INNOCENT, YOU SHOULD HAVE NO DIFFICULTY PROVING IT!
I--I'VE GOT TO GET AWAY!
I'LL HAVE YOU IN ANOTHER SECOND!
STOP, CLARK! STOP!
BUT AS CLARK TURNS THE CORNER, HE INCREASES SPEED SO THAT HE EQUALS THE PACE OF LIGHT ITSELF...!
MY OPPORTUNITY TO SPEED UP!
POOR CASEY! I CAN JUST SEE THE ASTONISHED EXPRESSION ON HIS FACE AS HE TURNS THAT CORNER!
9
NOWHERE IN SIGHT! CLARK'S--DISAPPEARED!
WHERE CAN HE HAVE VANISHED TO?
IN THE ALLEY BESIDE THE BUILDING, CLARK KENT REMOVES HIS OUTER GARMENTS, TRANSFORMING HIM-SELF TO DYNAMIC SUPERMAN....
KENT SEEMS TO BE IN QUITE A MESS. IT'S UP TO SUPERMAN TO CLEAR HIS NAME AND GET BACK THE STOLEN FUNDS!

AS THE MAN OF *STEEL* STREAKS TOWARD THE CITY JAIL.....

IT SEEMS MORE THAN MERE CO-INCIDENCE THAT THAT MAN WAS RAISING A DISTURBANCE ACROSS THE STREET JUST AT THE TIME THE *PLANET* WAS ROBBED!

AND AT THE JAIL...

I - I WAS JUST CELEBRAT-ING!

WELL, NEXT TIME YOU CELEBRATE BY SHOOTING OFF A GUN IN THE MIDDLE OF THE NIGHT, YOU'LL GET AN EVEN STIFFER FINE!

THE MAN DEPARTS, UNAWARE THAT A FIGURE TRAILS HIM FROM A VANTAGE POINT HIGH IN THE SKY...

THAT WAS *EASY!* NOW TO COLLECT!

LATER... AS SUPERMAN OBSERVES THE FELLOW ENTER A BUILDING...

HE MAY COLLECT MORE THAN HE EXPECTS!

INSIDE THE BUILDING, THE MAN RECEIVES HIS PAYMENT THRU A SMALL SLOT IN A STEEL DOOR...

YOU DID YOUR JOB WELL. WHILE YOU CREATED THAT DISTURBANCE, I WAS ABLE TO ROB THE *DAILY PLANET* WITHOUT INTERFERENCE.

THIS IS WHAT I CALL *EASY* MONEY!

STILL THINK IT'S EASY?

SUPERMAN!

ROB HELP-LESS YOUTH OF ITS CHANCE FOR HAPPINESS, WILL YOU?

NO! DON'T HURT ME! IT'S THE GUY WHO HIRED ME WHO'S TO BLAME! HE...!

BEFORE *SUPERMAN'S* CAPTIVE CAN REVEAL MORE, A BARRAGE OF BULLETS CUTS HIM SHORT...

YEEE-EEAHHH!

BANG! BANG!

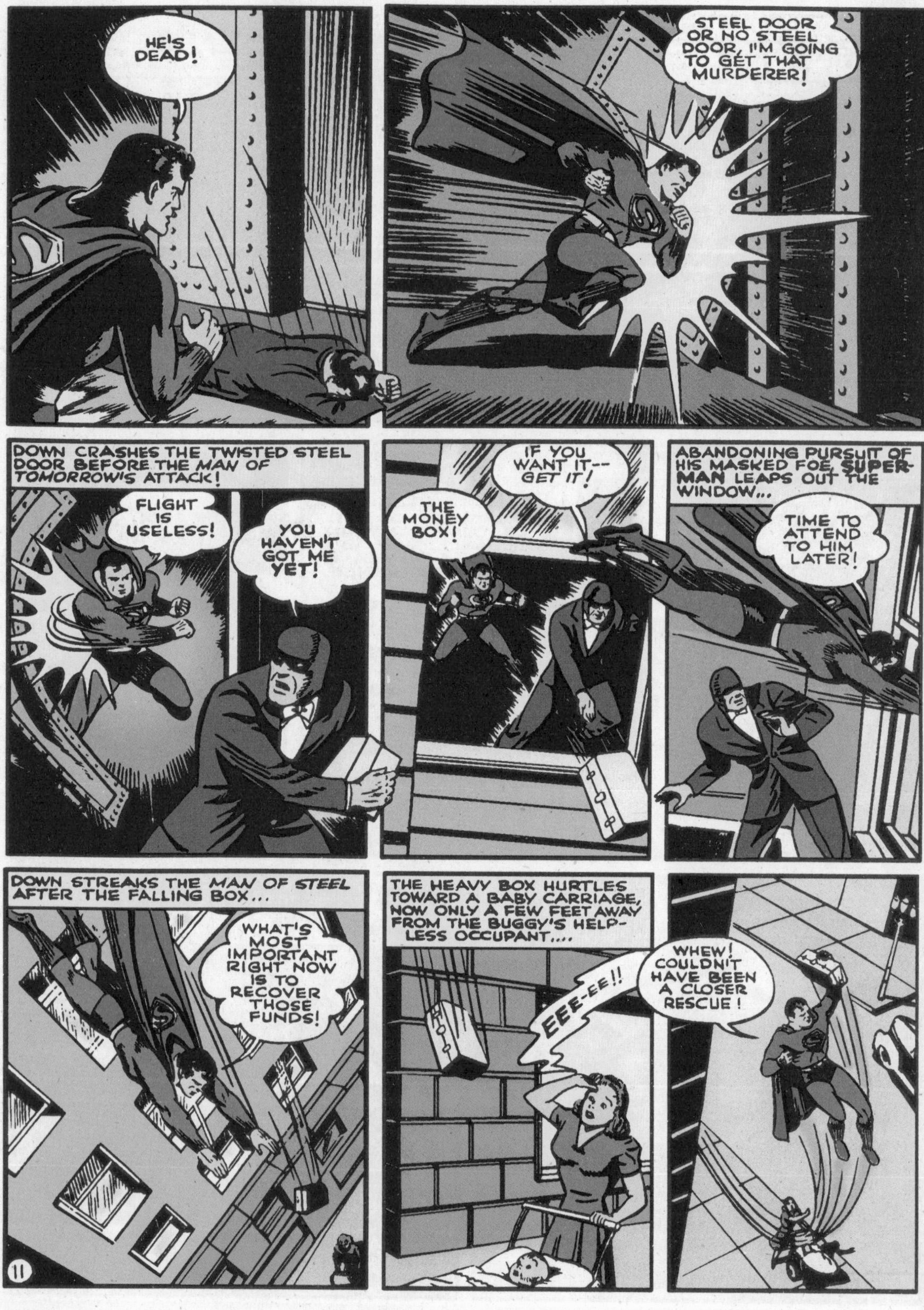
HE'S DEAD!
STEEL DOOR OR NO STEEL DOOR, I'M GOING TO GET THAT MURDERER!
DOWN CRASHES THE TWISTED STEEL DOOR BEFORE THE MAN OF TOMORROW'S ATTACK!
FLIGHT IS USELESS!
YOU HAVEN'T GOT ME YET!
IF YOU WANT IT-- GET IT!
THE MONEY BOX!
ABANDONING PURSUIT OF HIS MASKED FOE, SUPERMAN LEAPS OUT THE WINDOW...
TIME TO ATTEND TO HIM LATER!
DOWN STREAKS THE MAN OF STEEL AFTER THE FALLING BOX...
WHAT'S MOST IMPORTANT RIGHT NOW IS TO RECOVER THOSE FUNDS!
11
THE HEAVY BOX HURTLES TOWARD A BABY CARRIAGE, NOW ONLY A FEW FEET AWAY FROM THE BUGGY'S HELPLESS OCCUPANT....
EEE-EE!!
WHEW! COULDN'T HAVE BEEN A CLOSER RESCUE!

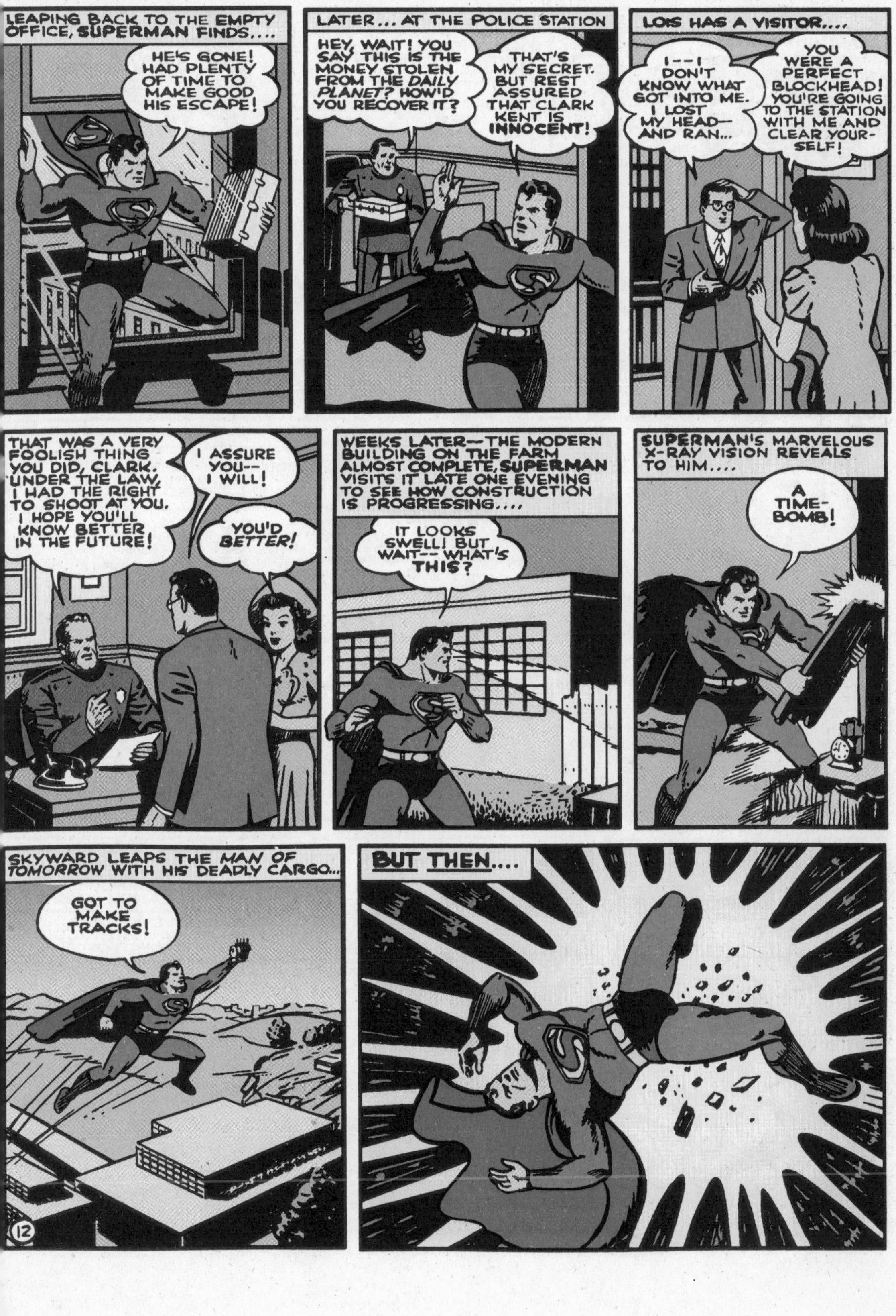
LEAPING BACK TO THE EMPTY OFFICE, SUPERMAN FINDS....
HE'S GONE! HAD PLENTY OF TIME TO MAKE GOOD HIS ESCAPE!
LATER... AT THE POLICE STATION
HEY, WAIT! YOU SAY THIS IS THE MONEY STOLEN FROM THE DAILY PLANET? HOW'D YOU RECOVER IT?
THAT'S MY SECRET. BUT REST ASSURED THAT CLARK KENT IS INNOCENT!
LOIS HAS A VISITOR....
I--I DON'T KNOW WHAT GOT INTO ME. I LOST MY HEAD-- AND RAN...
YOU WERE A PERFECT BLOCKHEAD! YOU'RE GOING TO THE STATION WITH ME AND CLEAR YOURSELF!
THAT WAS A VERY FOOLISH THING YOU DID, CLARK. UNDER THE LAW, I HAD THE RIGHT TO SHOOT AT YOU. I HOPE YOU'LL KNOW BETTER IN THE FUTURE!
I ASSURE YOU-- I WILL!
YOU'D BETTER!
WEEKS LATER--THE MODERN BUILDING ON THE FARM ALMOST COMPLETE, SUPERMAN VISITS IT LATE ONE EVENING TO SEE HOW CONSTRUCTION IS PROGRESSING....
IT LOOKS SWELL! BUT WAIT-- WHAT'S THIS?
SUPERMAN'S MARVELOUS X-RAY VISION REVEALS TO HIM....
A TIME-BOMB!
SKYWARD LEAPS THE MAN OF TOMORROW WITH HIS DEADLY CARGO...
GOT TO MAKE TRACKS!
12
BUT THEN....

DUE TO HIS IMPENETRABLE SKIN, THE *MAN OF STEEL* ESCAPES THE BLAST UNHARMED...

THE MASKED MAN AGAIN-- FLEEING... HE MUST BE THE ONE WHO PLANTED THAT BOMB!

SIGHTING *SUPERMAN* PLUMMETING DOWN BEFORE HIM, THE RUNNING MAN FIRES FRANTICALLY UP AT HIM...

NO! NO! KEEP AWAY!

YOU'RE WASTING YOUR BULLETS!

OO-OOOFF!

END OF THE LINE FOR YOU!

AS SUPERMAN REMOVES HIS FOE'S MASK...

YOU'RE CHARLIE GRAYSON, RACKETEER, WHOSE ACTIVITIES WERE EXPOSED BY THE *DAILY PLANET*!

THAT'S WHY I WANTED TO WRECK THE *PLANET'S* PET PHILANTHROPY... FOR REVENGE! AND I'D HAVE SUCCEEDED, IF IT HADN'T BEEN FOR *YOU!*

SUPERMAN STUNTS DIZZILY...

AND WILL YOU CONFESS TO SERGEANT CASEY?

YES! I'LL CONFESS EVERYTHING-- EVERYTHING!

LATER-- SUPERMAN LEAPS AWAY FROM THE POLICE STATION AS GRAYSON CONFESSES....

WHAT WOULD THE POLICE FORCE DO WITHOUT YOU?

NO DOUBT GET ALONG VERY NICELY!

WEEKS LATER... AS CLARK KENT AND LOIS LANE OBSERVE UNDERPRIVILEGED CHILDREN ENJOYING THE BENEFITS OF THE FREE VACATION FARM...

DOESN'T IT MAKE YOU FEEL PROUD TO KNOW YOU HAD SOMETHING TO DO WITH THE ESTABLISHMENT OF THIS FREE VACATION SPOT FOR KIDS?

IT CERTAINLY DOES, BUT, WE MUSTN'T FORGET THAT IF *SUPERMAN* HADN'T RECOVERED THE STOLEN FUNDS, ALL OUR PLANS WOULD HAVE BEEN BLASTED!

⑬

THE END

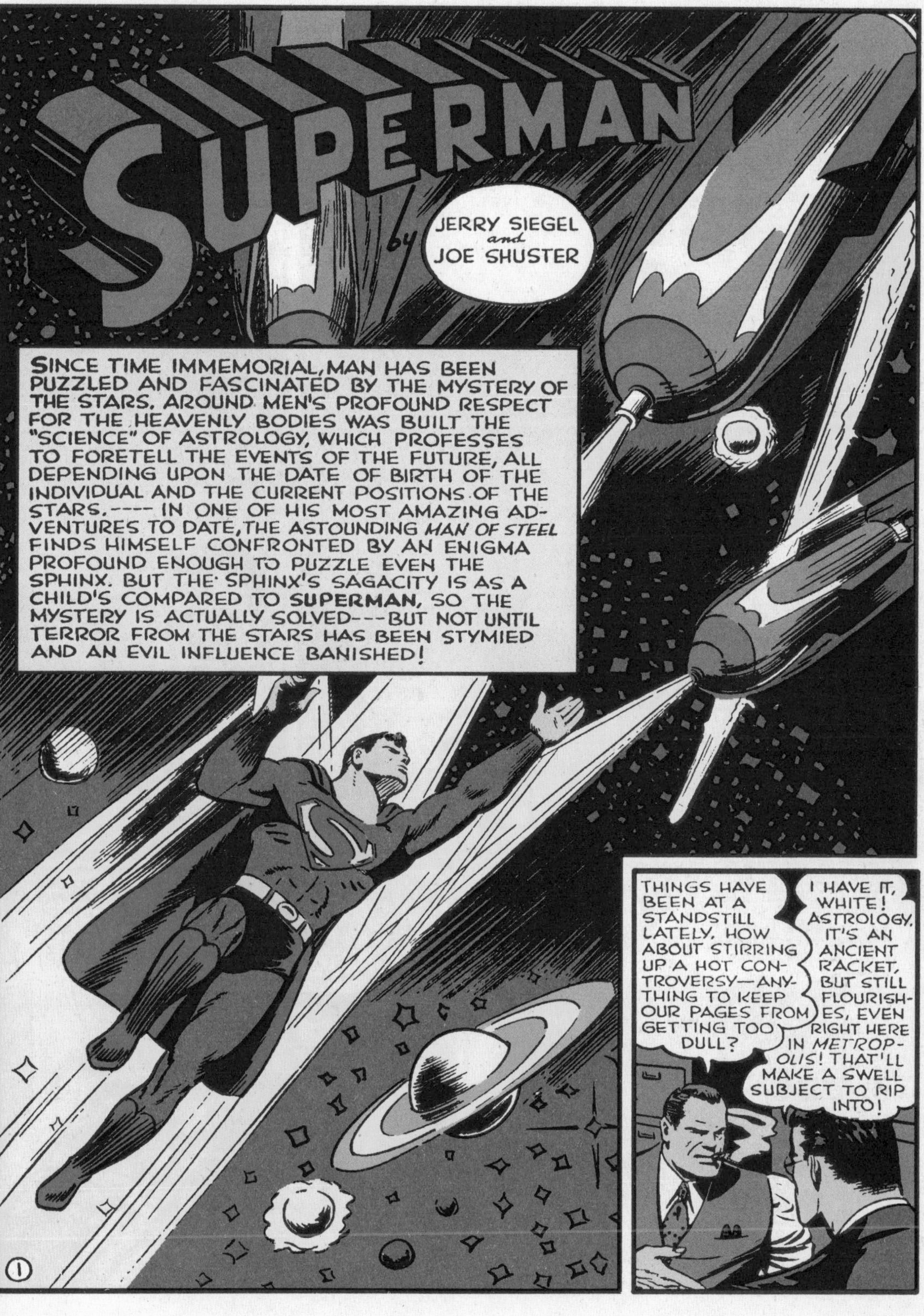
SUPERMAN
by JERRY SIEGEL and JOE SHUSTER
SINCE TIME IMMEMORIAL, MAN HAS BEEN PUZZLED AND FASCINATED BY THE MYSTERY OF THE STARS. AROUND MEN'S PROFOUND RESPECT FOR THE HEAVENLY BODIES WAS BUILT THE "SCIENCE" OF ASTROLOGY, WHICH PROFESSES TO FORETELL THE EVENTS OF THE FUTURE, ALL DEPENDING UPON THE DATE OF BIRTH OF THE INDIVIDUAL AND THE CURRENT POSITIONS OF THE STARS.---- IN ONE OF HIS MOST AMAZING ADVENTURES TO DATE, THE ASTOUNDING *MAN OF STEEL* FINDS HIMSELF CONFRONTED BY AN ENIGMA PROFOUND ENOUGH TO PUZZLE EVEN THE SPHINX. BUT THE SPHINX'S SAGACITY IS AS A CHILD'S COMPARED TO **SUPERMAN**, SO THE MYSTERY IS ACTUALLY SOLVED---BUT NOT UNTIL TERROR FROM THE STARS HAS BEEN STYMIED AND AN EVIL INFLUENCE BANISHED!
1
THINGS HAVE BEEN AT A STANDSTILL LATELY. HOW ABOUT STIRRING UP A HOT CONTROVERSY—ANYTHING TO KEEP OUR PAGES FROM GETTING TOO DULL?
I HAVE IT, WHITE! ASTROLOGY. IT'S AN ANCIENT RACKET, BUT STILL FLOURISHES, EVEN RIGHT HERE IN *METROPOLIS*! THAT'LL MAKE A SWELL SUBJECT TO RIP INTO!

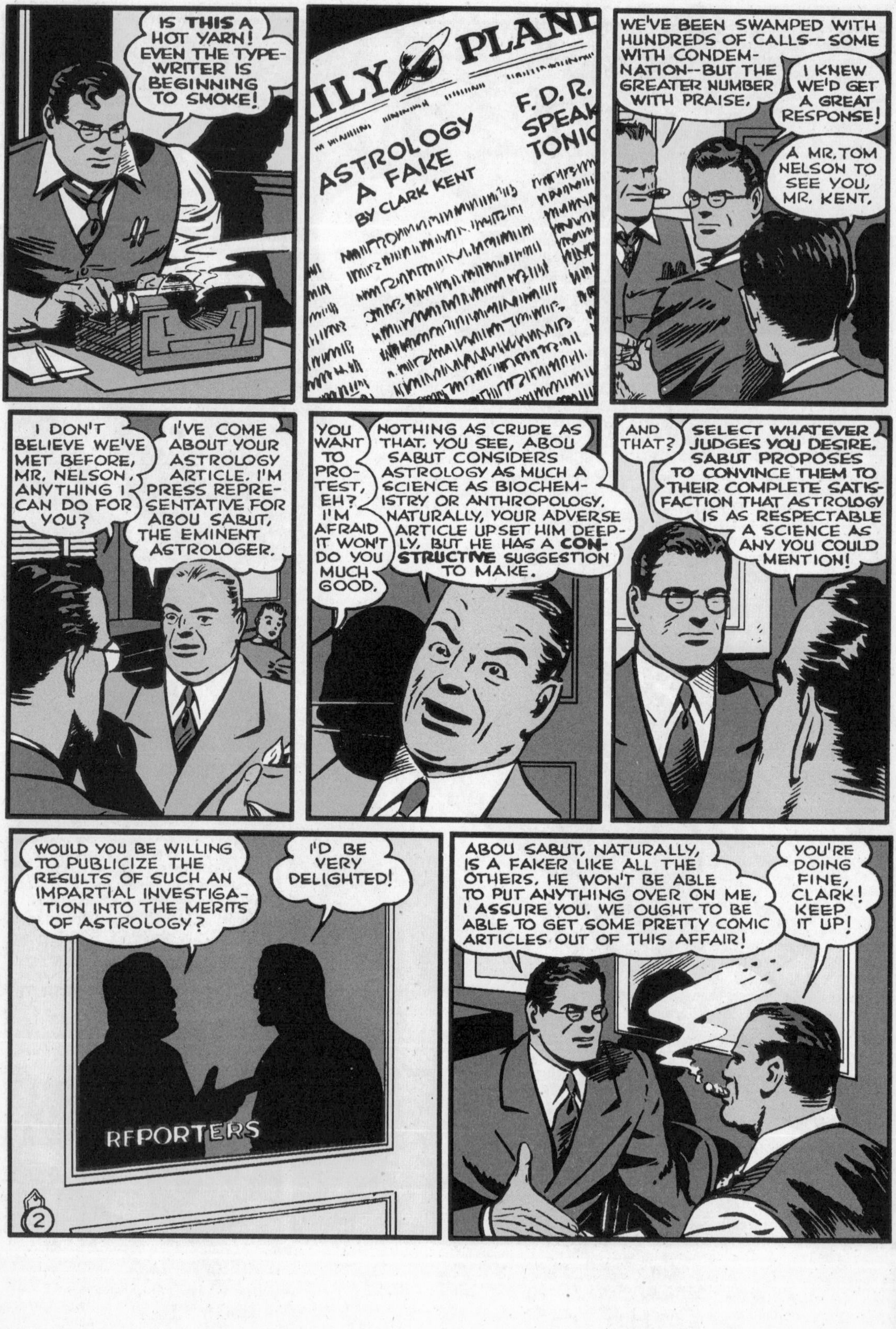
IS THIS A HOT YARN! EVEN THE TYPE-WRITER IS BEGINNING TO SMOKE!
DAILY PLANET
ASTROLOGY A FAKE
BY CLARK KENT
F. D. R. SPEAK TONIC
WE'VE BEEN SWAMPED WITH HUNDREDS OF CALLS--SOME WITH CONDEMNATION--BUT THE GREATER NUMBER WITH PRAISE.
I KNEW WE'D GET A GREAT RESPONSE!
A MR. TOM NELSON TO SEE YOU, MR. KENT.
I DON'T BELIEVE WE'VE MET BEFORE, MR. NELSON. ANYTHING I CAN DO FOR YOU?
I'VE COME ABOUT YOUR ASTROLOGY ARTICLE. I'M PRESS REPRESENTATIVE FOR ABOU SABUT, THE EMINENT ASTROLOGER.
YOU WANT TO PROTEST, EH? I'M AFRAID IT WON'T DO YOU MUCH GOOD.
NOTHING AS CRUDE AS THAT. YOU SEE, ABOU SABUT CONSIDERS ASTROLOGY AS MUCH A SCIENCE AS BIOCHEMISTRY OR ANTHROPOLOGY. NATURALLY, YOUR ADVERSE ARTICLE UPSET HIM DEEPLY. BUT HE HAS A CONSTRUCTIVE SUGGESTION TO MAKE.
AND THAT?
SELECT WHATEVER JUDGES YOU DESIRE. SABUT PROPOSES TO CONVINCE THEM TO THEIR COMPLETE SATISFACTION THAT ASTROLOGY IS AS RESPECTABLE A SCIENCE AS ANY YOU COULD MENTION!
WOULD YOU BE WILLING TO PUBLICIZE THE RESULTS OF SUCH AN IMPARTIAL INVESTIGATION INTO THE MERITS OF ASTROLOGY?
I'D BE VERY DELIGHTED!
REPORTERS
2
ABOU SABUT, NATURALLY, IS A FAKER LIKE ALL THE OTHERS. HE WON'T BE ABLE TO PUT ANYTHING OVER ON ME, I ASSURE YOU. WE OUGHT TO BE ABLE TO GET SOME PRETTY COMIC ARTICLES OUT OF THIS AFFAIR!
YOU'RE DOING FINE, CLARK! KEEP IT UP!

LATER THAT AFTERNOON...

MEET ABOU SABUT!

SO YOU DOUBT ASTROLOGY'S AUTHENTICITY?

I'M NOT THE ONLY ONE. THESE GENTLEMEN WITH ME SHARE MY DOUBTS.

ASTROLOGY IS A FRAUD-- BUT NO MORE A FAKE THAN YOU ARE!

YOU LEARNED ASTRONOMERS SICKEN ME, PROFESSOR DERMA. WE SHALL SEE WHO IS AND WHO IS NOT THE CHARLATAN. TELL ME YOUR BIRTHDATE.

I REFUSE!

TELL HIM, PROFESSOR! IF HIS FORECAST FAILS, IT WILL ONLY LEAD TO HIS OWN DOWNFALL!

HM-MM. VERY INTERESTING. ACCORDING TO MY CALCULATIONS, PROFESSOR, YOU HAVEN'T MORE THAN FIVE MINUTES TO LIVE!

I WON'T STAND FOR ANY MORE OF THIS NONSENSE! I'M GETTING OUT OF HERE!

WAIT! DON'T YOU WANT TO SEE HIM PROVED WRONG?

DISREGARDING CLARK'S PLEAS, THE PROFESSOR HURRIES OUT OF THE DAILY PLANET BUILDING INTO THE STREET'S HEAVY TRAFFIC...

NONSENSE... ABSOLUTELY NONSENSE...!

SUDDENLY, A TRUCK LOOMS OVER THE PROFESSOR... DESPERATELY, HE SEEKS TO ESCAPE IT-- THERE IS A SICKENING CRASH....!

3

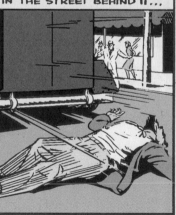

OFF SPEEDS THE TRUCK WITHOUT PAUSING, LEAVING A STILL, CRUMPLED FIGURE IN THE STREET BEHIND IT...

BUT CLARK KENT HAS WITNESSED THE STARTLING SIGHT! NOW HE WHIPS OFF HIS OUTER GARMENTS, REVEALING HIMSELF IN THE IDENTITY OF SUPERMAN...

A HIT-AND-RUN DRIVER! HE WON'T GET FAR!

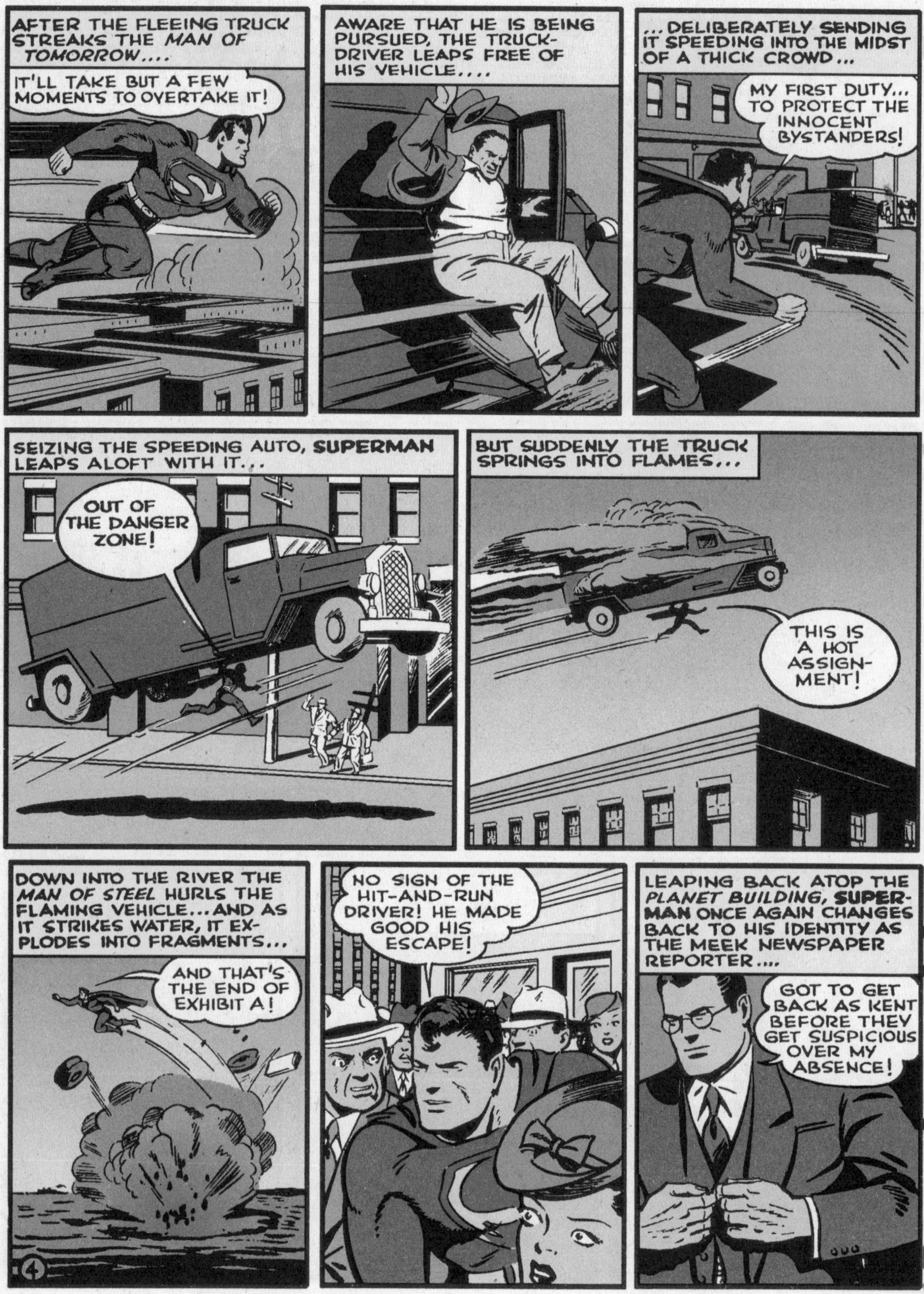
AFTER THE FLEEING TRUCK STREAKS THE MAN OF TOMORROW....
IT'LL TAKE BUT A FEW MOMENTS TO OVERTAKE IT!
AWARE THAT HE IS BEING PURSUED, THE TRUCK-DRIVER LEAPS FREE OF HIS VEHICLE....
...DELIBERATELY SENDING IT SPEEDING INTO THE MIDST OF A THICK CROWD...
MY FIRST DUTY... TO PROTECT THE INNOCENT BYSTANDERS!
SEIZING THE SPEEDING AUTO, SUPERMAN LEAPS ALOFT WITH IT...
OUT OF THE DANGER ZONE!
BUT SUDDENLY THE TRUCK SPRINGS INTO FLAMES...
THIS IS A HOT ASSIGN-MENT!
DOWN INTO THE RIVER THE MAN OF STEEL HURLS THE FLAMING VEHICLE...AND AS IT STRIKES WATER, IT EX-PLODES INTO FRAGMENTS...
AND THAT'S THE END OF EXHIBIT A!
4
NO SIGN OF THE HIT-AND-RUN DRIVER! HE MADE GOOD HIS ESCAPE!
LEAPING BACK ATOP THE PLANET BUILDING, SUPER-MAN ONCE AGAIN CHANGES BACK TO HIS IDENTITY AS THE MEEK NEWSPAPER REPORTER....
GOT TO GET BACK AS KENT BEFORE THEY GET SUSPICIOUS OVER MY ABSENCE!

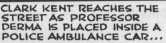

CLARK KENT REACHES THE STREET AS PROFESSOR DERMA IS PLACED INSIDE A POLICE AMBULANCE CAR...

IS HE --??

HE'S-- DEAD!

AND WITHIN FIVE MINUTES... JUST AS I PREDICTED!

COINCIDENCE... MERE COINCIDENCE!!

THAT'S ABSOLUTE NONSENSE!

SO FAR THE ASTROLOGIST HASN'T FAILED!

JUST COINCIDENCE? I'VE ALREADY MADE YOUR ASTROLOGICAL FORECAST, WARREN...ONLY TO DISCOVER YOUR JEWELRY STORE IS TO BE PILLAGED...AND AT ABOUT THIS MOMENT!

GOING SO SOON, MR. WARREN?

("--MY SUPER-SENSITIVE HEARING... DETECTING AN INTERESTING POLICE CALL!--")

I--I JUST REMEMBERED AN IMPORTANT APPOINTMENT. ("--THIS ASTROLOGER IS UNDOUBTEDLY TALKING THRU HIS HAT... BUT...I CAN'T AFFORD TO TAKE CHANCES!--")

PROCEED TO WARREN JEWELRY COMPANY... BURGLAR ALARM FLASH...!

A FEW MOMENTS EARLIER, ARMED THUGS MADE THEIR APPEARANCE AT WARREN'S JEWELRY STORE...

UP WITH YOUR HANDS!

AND NOT ONE FALSE MOVE OUTTA YOU!

I KN-KNOW BETTER!

BUT, DELIBERATELY, THE CASHIER STEPS ON AN ALARM BUTTON....

PLEASE EXCUSE ME WHILE I LOOK AT SOME RESEARCH MATERIAL.

ONLY TOO GLAD TO OBLIGE, MR. KENT.

⑤

CHANGING TO HIS SUPERMAN COSTUME, KENT SPEEDS OFF ALONG THE CITY'S STREETS..

IF THESE INCIDENTS KEEP UP, EVEN I MAY BEGIN TO BELIEVE THERE'S SOMETHING TO ASTROLOGY!

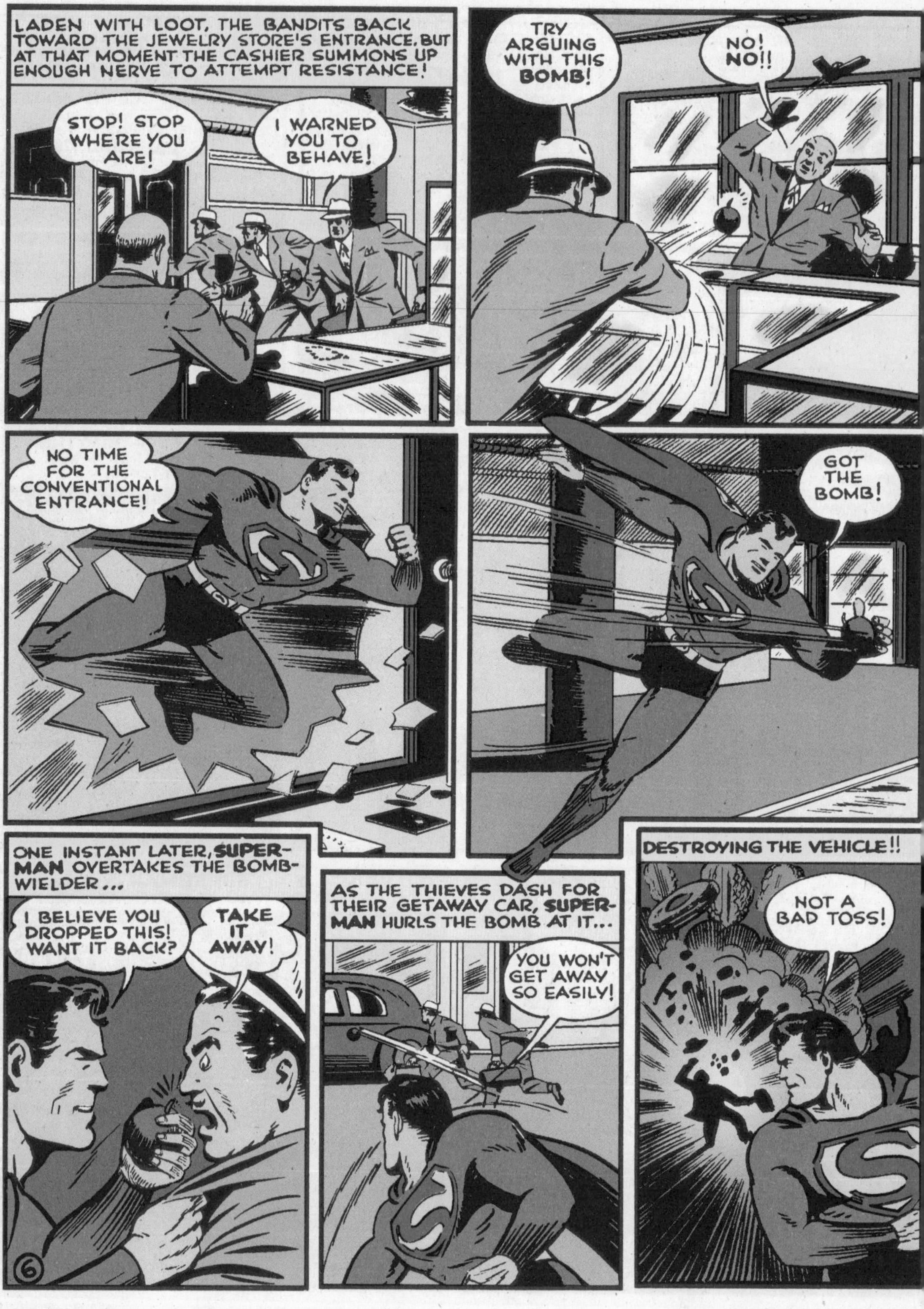
LADEN WITH LOOT, THE BANDITS BACK TOWARD THE JEWELRY STORE'S ENTRANCE, BUT AT THAT MOMENT THE CASHIER SUMMONS UP ENOUGH NERVE TO ATTEMPT RESISTANCE!
STOP! STOP WHERE YOU ARE!
I WARNED YOU TO BEHAVE!
TRY ARGUING WITH THIS BOMB!
NO! NO!!
NO TIME FOR THE CONVENTIONAL ENTRANCE!
GOT THE BOMB!
ONE INSTANT LATER, SUPERMAN OVERTAKES THE BOMB-WIELDER...
I BELIEVE YOU DROPPED THIS! WANT IT BACK?
TAKE IT AWAY!
6
AS THE THIEVES DASH FOR THEIR GETAWAY CAR, SUPERMAN HURLS THE BOMB AT IT...
YOU WON'T GET AWAY SO EASILY!
DESTROYING THE VEHICLE!!
NOT A BAD TOSS!

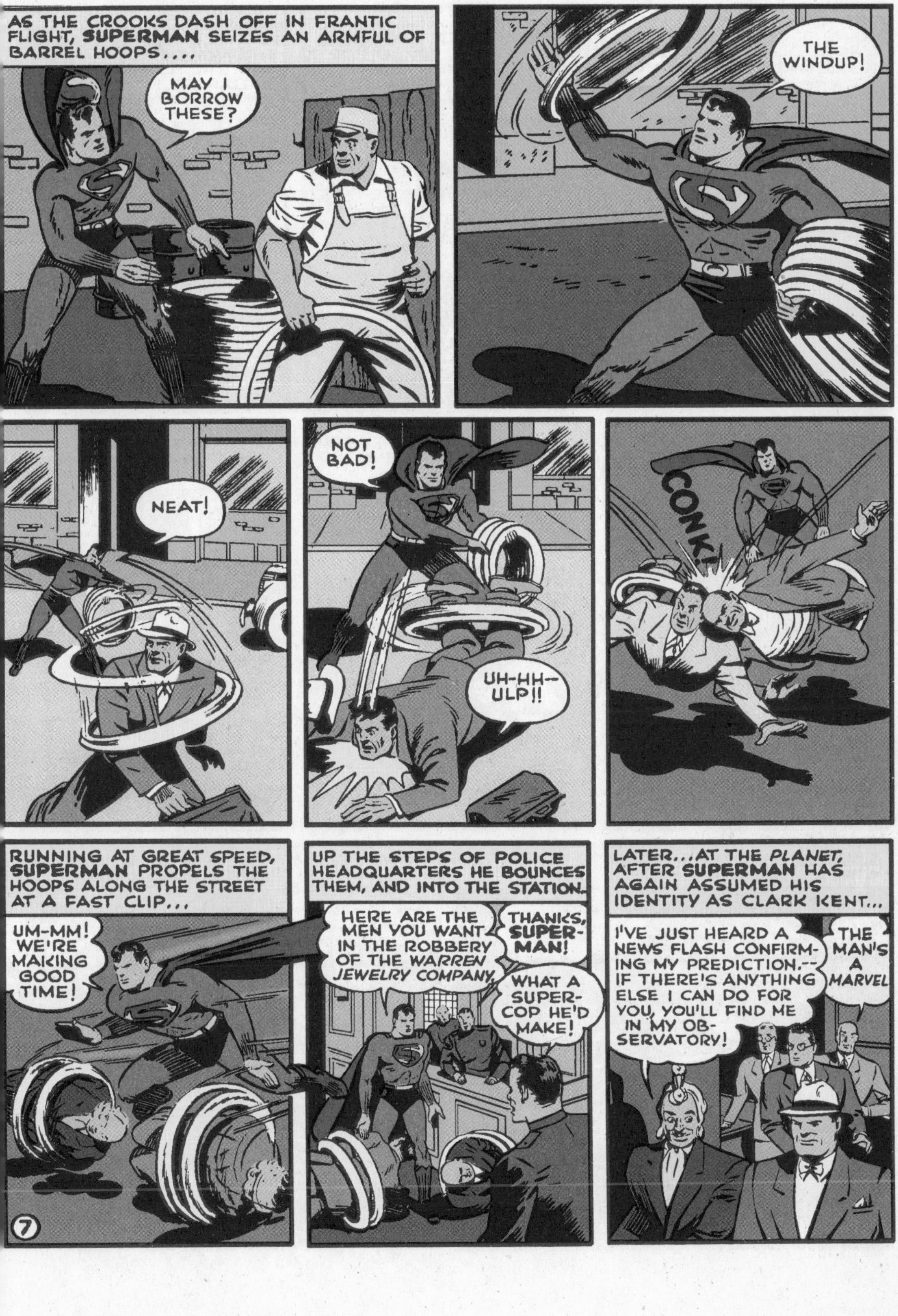
AS THE CROOKS DASH OFF IN FRANTIC FLIGHT, SUPERMAN SEIZES AN ARMFUL OF BARREL HOOPS....
MAY I BORROW THESE?
THE WINDUP!
NEAT!
NOT BAD!
UH-HH--ULP!!
CONK!
RUNNING AT GREAT SPEED, SUPERMAN PROPELS THE HOOPS ALONG THE STREET AT A FAST CLIP...
UM-MM! WE'RE MAKING GOOD TIME!
UP THE STEPS OF POLICE HEADQUARTERS HE BOUNCES THEM, AND INTO THE STATION.
HERE ARE THE MEN YOU WANT IN THE ROBBERY OF THE WARREN JEWELRY COMPANY.
THANKS, SUPERMAN!
WHAT A SUPER-COP HE'D MAKE!
LATER... AT THE PLANET, AFTER SUPERMAN HAS AGAIN ASSUMED HIS IDENTITY AS CLARK KENT...
I'VE JUST HEARD A NEWS FLASH CONFIRMING MY PREDICTION.-- IF THERE'S ANYTHING ELSE I CAN DO FOR YOU, YOU'LL FIND ME IN MY OBSERVATORY!
THE MAN'S A MARVEL
7

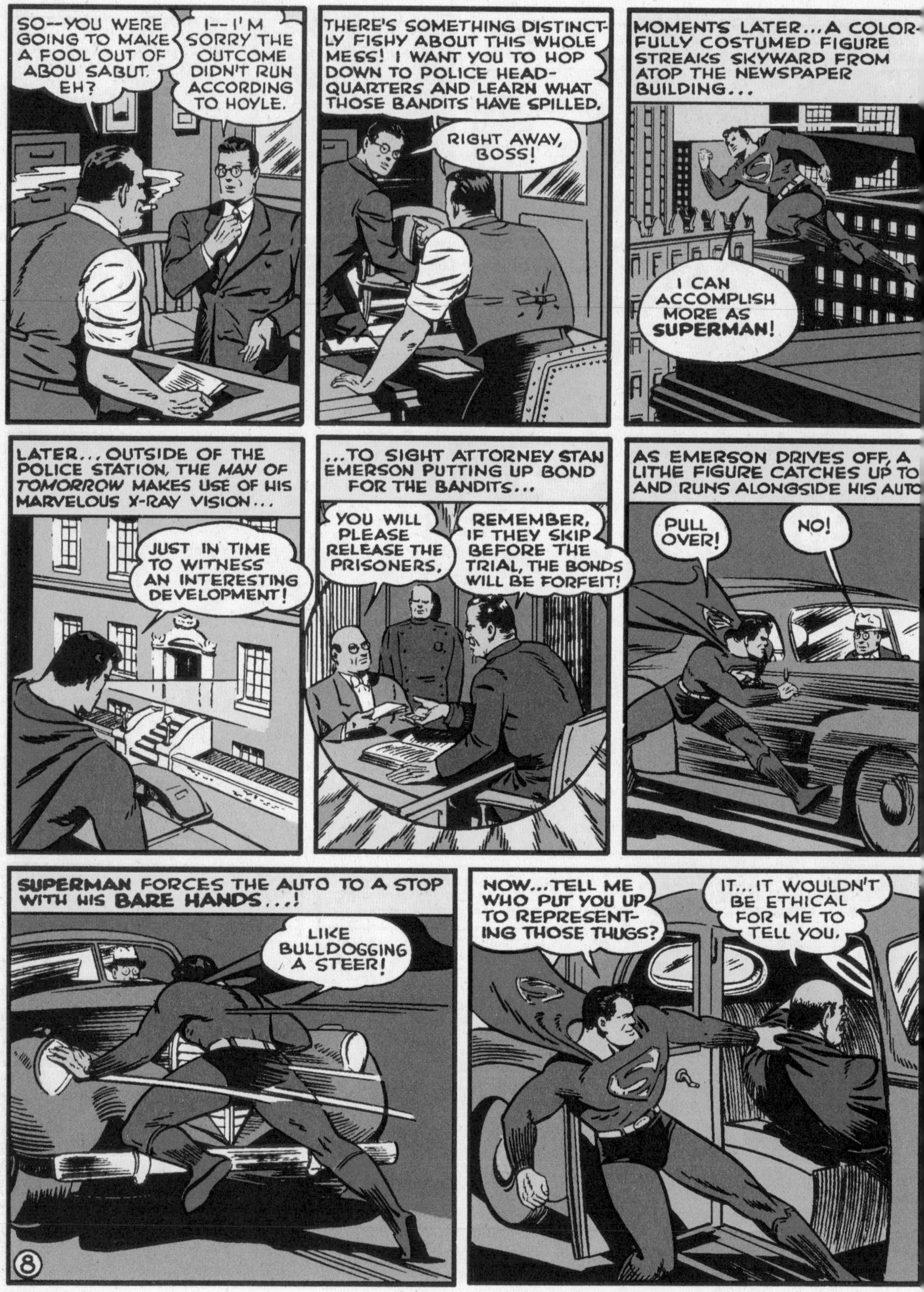
SO--YOU WERE GOING TO MAKE A FOOL OUT OF ABOU SABUT. EH?
I--I'M SORRY THE OUTCOME DIDN'T RUN ACCORDING TO HOYLE.
THERE'S SOMETHING DISTINCTLY FISHY ABOUT THIS WHOLE MESS! I WANT YOU TO HOP DOWN TO POLICE HEADQUARTERS AND LEARN WHAT THOSE BANDITS HAVE SPILLED.
RIGHT AWAY, BOSS!
MOMENTS LATER... A COLORFULLY COSTUMED FIGURE STREAKS SKYWARD FROM ATOP THE NEWSPAPER BUILDING...
I CAN ACCOMPLISH MORE AS SUPERMAN!
LATER... OUTSIDE OF THE POLICE STATION, THE MAN OF TOMORROW MAKES USE OF HIS MARVELOUS X-RAY VISION...
JUST IN TIME TO WITNESS AN INTERESTING DEVELOPMENT!
...TO SIGHT ATTORNEY STAN EMERSON PUTTING UP BOND FOR THE BANDITS...
YOU WILL PLEASE RELEASE THE PRISONERS.
REMEMBER, IF THEY SKIP BEFORE THE TRIAL, THE BONDS WILL BE FORFEIT!
AS EMERSON DRIVES OFF, A LITHE FIGURE CATCHES UP TO AND RUNS ALONGSIDE HIS AUTO
PULL OVER!
NO!
SUPERMAN FORCES THE AUTO TO A STOP WITH HIS BARE HANDS...!
LIKE BULLDOGGING A STEER!
8
NOW...TELL ME WHO PUT YOU UP TO REPRESENTING THOSE THUGS?
IT...IT WOULDN'T BE ETHICAL FOR ME TO TELL YOU.

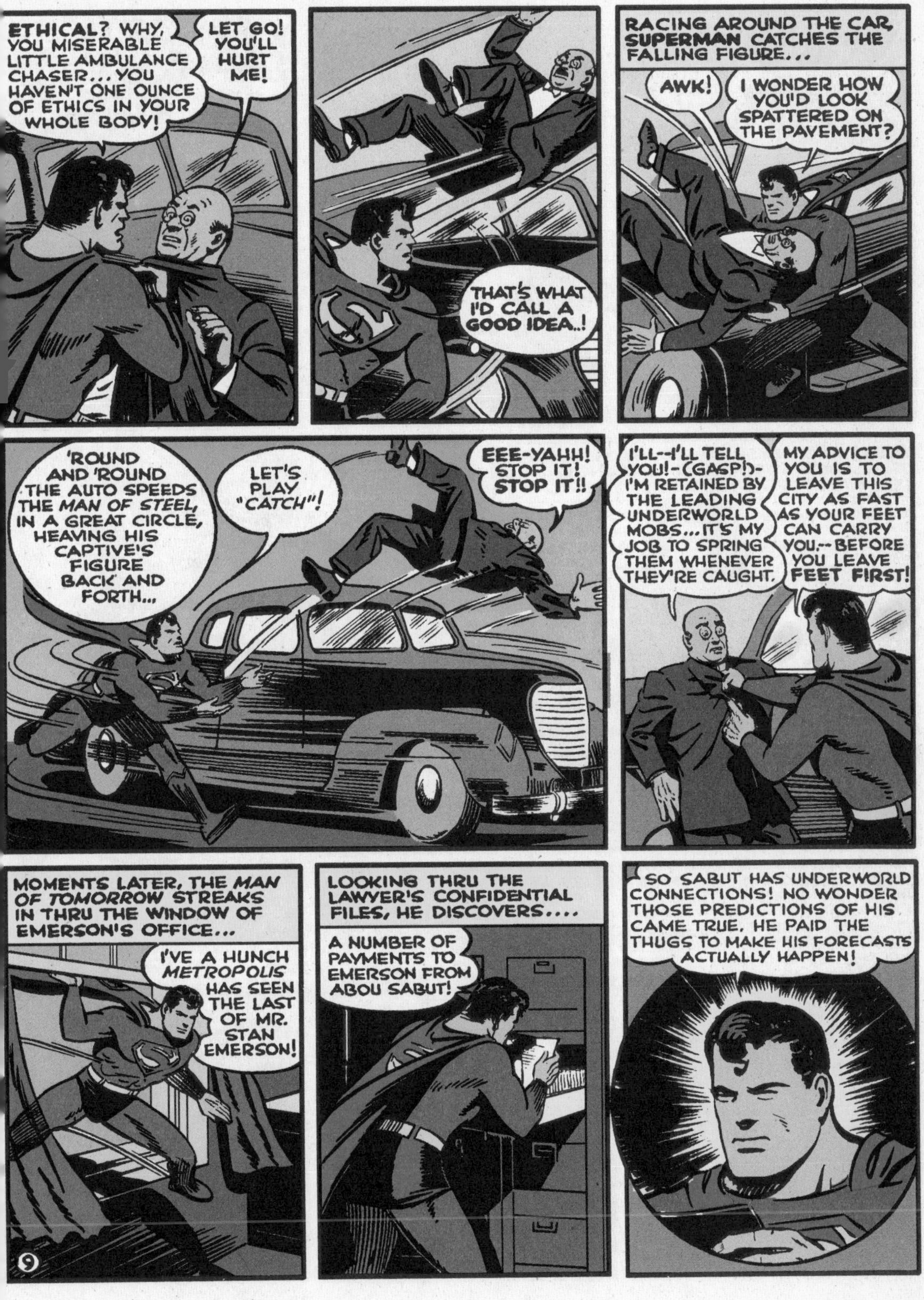
ETHICAL? WHY, YOU MISERABLE LITTLE AMBULANCE CHASER... YOU HAVEN'T ONE OUNCE OF ETHICS IN YOUR WHOLE BODY!
LET GO! YOU'LL HURT ME!
THAT'S WHAT I'D CALL A GOOD IDEA..!
RACING AROUND THE CAR, SUPERMAN CATCHES THE FALLING FIGURE...
AWK!
I WONDER HOW YOU'D LOOK SPATTERED ON THE PAVEMENT?
'ROUND AND 'ROUND THE AUTO SPEEDS THE MAN OF STEEL, IN A GREAT CIRCLE, HEAVING HIS CAPTIVE'S FIGURE BACK AND FORTH...
LET'S PLAY "CATCH"!
EEE-YAHH! STOP IT! STOP IT!!
I'LL--I'LL TELL YOU!-(GASP!)- I'M RETAINED BY THE LEADING UNDERWORLD MOBS...IT'S MY JOB TO SPRING THEM WHENEVER THEY'RE CAUGHT.
MY ADVICE TO YOU IS TO LEAVE THIS CITY AS FAST AS YOUR FEET CAN CARRY YOU,-- BEFORE YOU LEAVE FEET FIRST!
MOMENTS LATER, THE MAN OF TOMORROW STREAKS IN THRU THE WINDOW OF EMERSON'S OFFICE...
I'VE A HUNCH METROPOLIS HAS SEEN THE LAST OF MR. STAN EMERSON!
9
LOOKING THRU THE LAWYER'S CONFIDENTIAL FILES, HE DISCOVERS....
A NUMBER OF PAYMENTS TO EMERSON FROM ABOU SABUT!
SO SABUT HAS UNDERWORLD CONNECTIONS! NO WONDER THOSE PREDICTIONS OF HIS CAME TRUE. HE PAID THE THUGS TO MAKE HIS FORECASTS ACTUALLY HAPPEN!

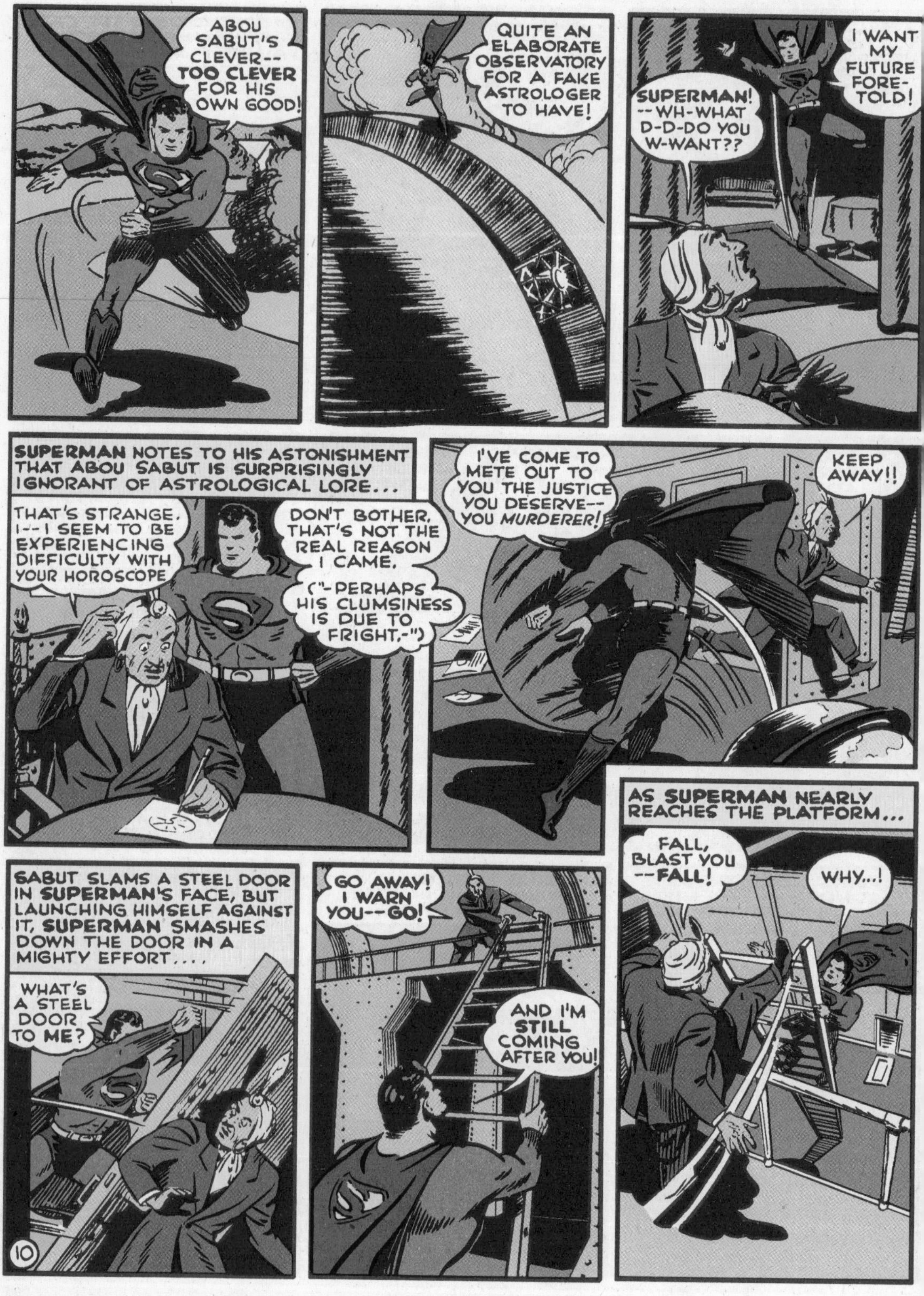
ABOU SABUT'S CLEVER-- TOO CLEVER FOR HIS OWN GOOD!
QUITE AN ELABORATE OBSERVATORY FOR A FAKE ASTROLOGER TO HAVE!
SUPERMAN! --WH-WHAT D-D-DO YOU W-WANT??
I WANT MY FUTURE FORE-TOLD!
SUPERMAN NOTES TO HIS ASTONISHMENT THAT ABOU SABUT IS SURPRISINGLY IGNORANT OF ASTROLOGICAL LORE...
THAT'S STRANGE. I--I SEEM TO BE EXPERIENCING DIFFICULTY WITH YOUR HOROSCOPE
DON'T BOTHER. THAT'S NOT THE REAL REASON I CAME.
("-PERHAPS HIS CLUMSINESS IS DUE TO FRIGHT.-")
I'VE COME TO METE OUT TO YOU THE JUSTICE YOU DESERVE-- YOU MURDERER!
KEEP AWAY!!
SABUT SLAMS A STEEL DOOR IN SUPERMAN'S FACE, BUT LAUNCHING HIMSELF AGAINST IT, SUPERMAN SMASHES DOWN THE DOOR IN A MIGHTY EFFORT....
WHAT'S A STEEL DOOR TO ME?
10
GO AWAY! I WARN YOU--GO!
AND I'M STILL COMING AFTER YOU!
AS SUPERMAN NEARLY REACHES THE PLATFORM...
FALL, BLAST YOU --FALL!
WHY...!

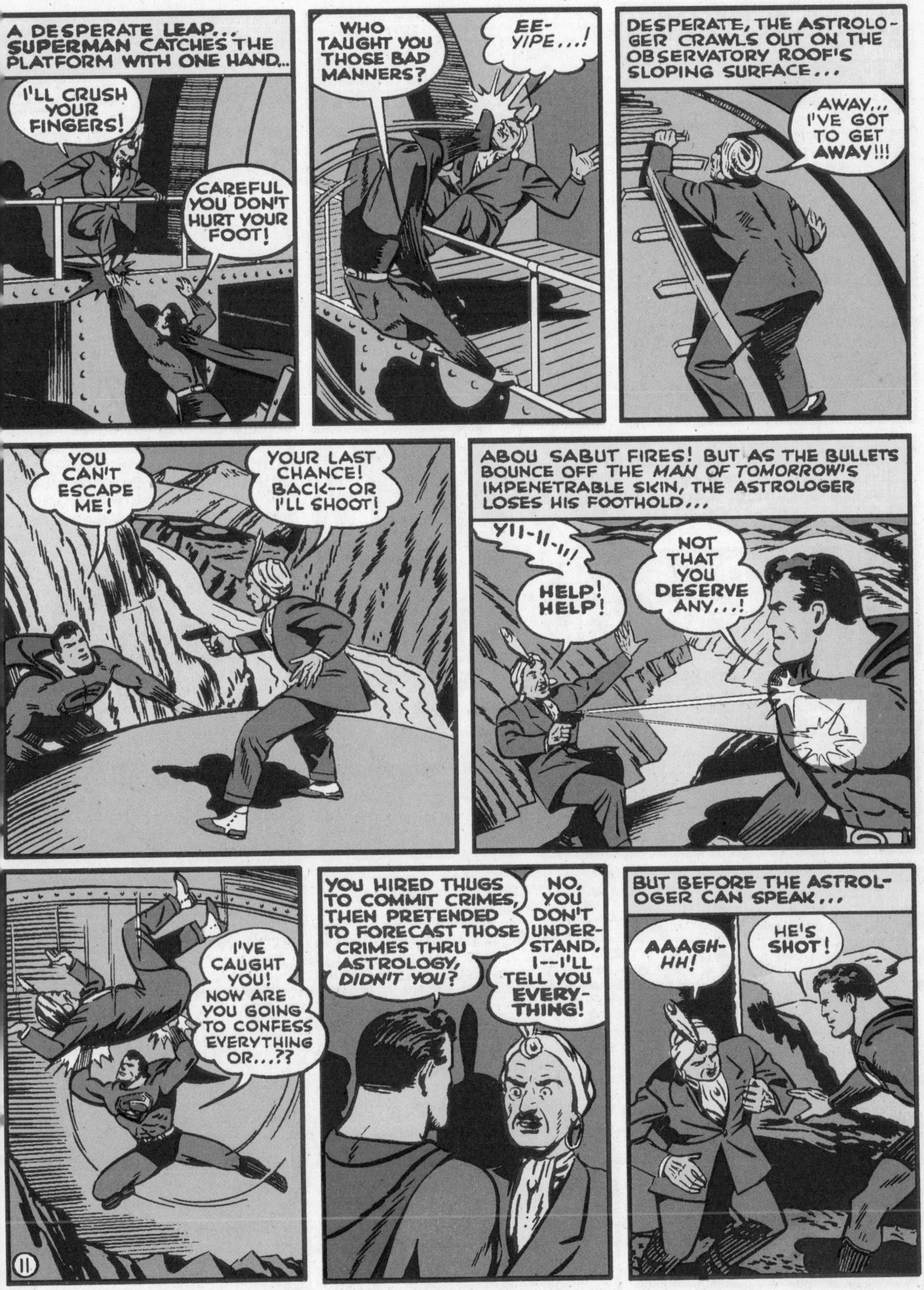

A DESPERATE LEAP... SUPERMAN CATCHES THE PLATFORM WITH ONE HAND...
I'LL CRUSH YOUR FINGERS!
CAREFUL YOU DON'T HURT YOUR FOOT!
WHO TAUGHT YOU THOSE BAD MANNERS?
EE-YIPE...!
DESPERATE, THE ASTROLOGER CRAWLS OUT ON THE OBSERVATORY ROOF'S SLOPING SURFACE...
AWAY... I'VE GOT TO GET AWAY!!!
YOU CAN'T ESCAPE ME!
YOUR LAST CHANCE! BACK--OR I'LL SHOOT!
ABOU SABUT FIRES! BUT AS THE BULLETS BOUNCE OFF THE *MAN OF TOMORROW'S* IMPENETRABLE SKIN, THE ASTROLOGER LOSES HIS FOOTHOLD...
YII-II-II!
HELP! HELP!
NOT THAT YOU DESERVE ANY...!
11
I'VE CAUGHT YOU! NOW ARE YOU GOING TO CONFESS EVERYTHING OR...??
YOU HIRED THUGS TO COMMIT CRIMES, THEN PRETENDED TO FORECAST THOSE CRIMES THRU ASTROLOGY, *DIDN'T YOU?*
NO, YOU DON'T UNDERSTAND, I--I'LL TELL YOU EVERYTHING!
BUT BEFORE THE ASTROLOGER CAN SPEAK...
AAAGH-HH!
HE'S SHOT!

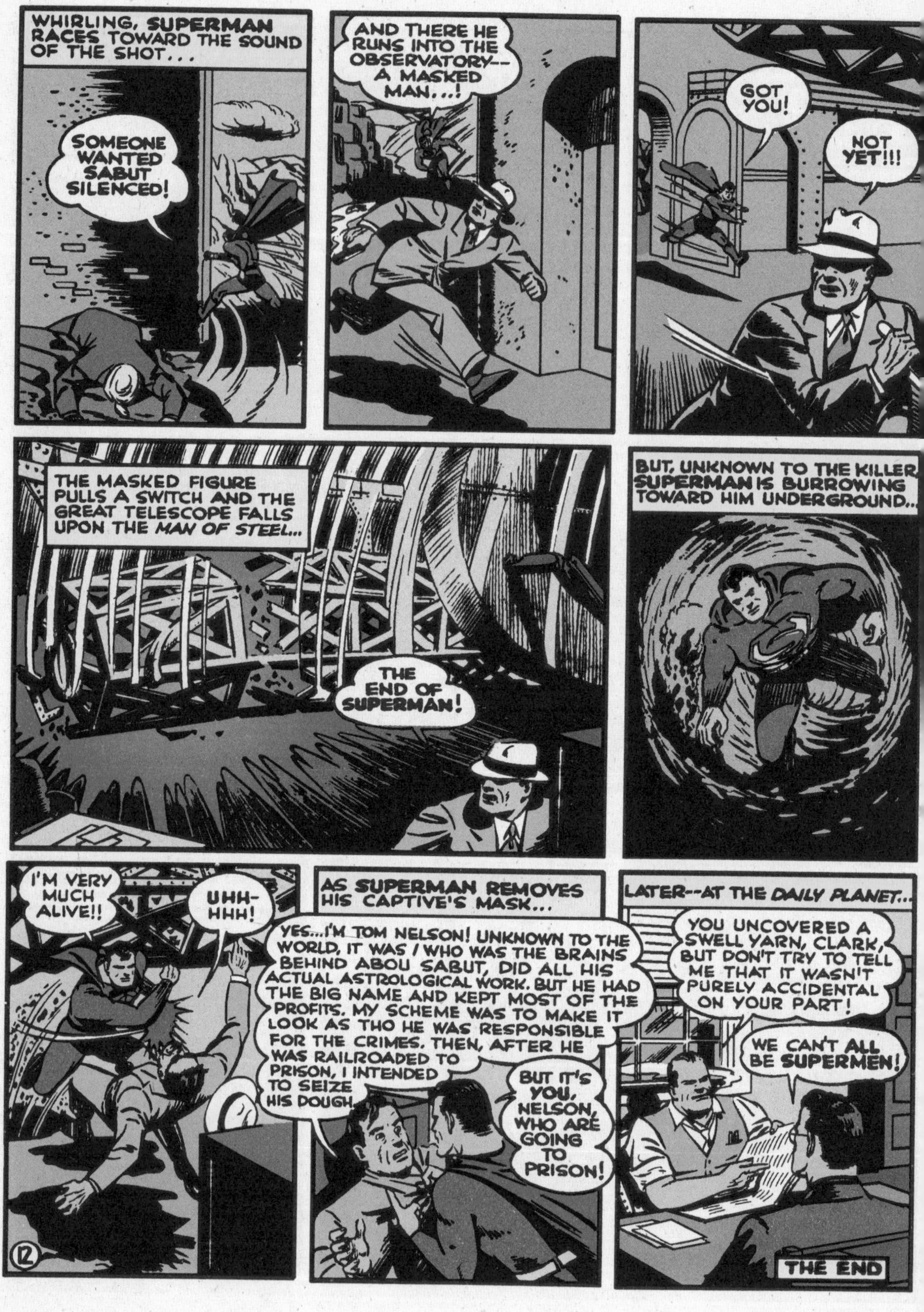
WHIRLING, SUPERMAN RACES TOWARD THE SOUND OF THE SHOT...
SOMEONE WANTED SABUT SILENCED!
AND THERE HE RUNS INTO THE OBSERVATORY-- A MASKED MAN...!
GOT YOU!
NOT YET!!!
THE MASKED FIGURE PULLS A SWITCH AND THE GREAT TELESCOPE FALLS UPON THE MAN OF STEEL...
THE END OF SUPERMAN!
BUT, UNKNOWN TO THE KILLER SUPERMAN IS BURROWING TOWARD HIM UNDERGROUND...
I'M VERY MUCH ALIVE!!
UHH-HHH!
12
AS SUPERMAN REMOVES HIS CAPTIVE'S MASK...
YES...I'M TOM NELSON! UNKNOWN TO THE WORLD, IT WAS I WHO WAS THE BRAINS BEHIND ABOU SABUT, DID ALL HIS ACTUAL ASTROLOGICAL WORK. BUT HE HAD THE BIG NAME AND KEPT MOST OF THE PROFITS. MY SCHEME WAS TO MAKE IT LOOK AS THO HE WAS RESPONSIBLE FOR THE CRIMES. THEN, AFTER HE WAS RAILROADED TO PRISON, I INTENDED TO SEIZE HIS DOUGH.
BUT IT'S YOU, NELSON, WHO ARE GOING TO PRISON!
LATER--AT THE DAILY PLANET...
YOU UNCOVERED A SWELL YARN, CLARK, BUT DON'T TRY TO TELL ME THAT IT WASN'T PURELY ACCIDENTAL ON YOUR PART!
WE CAN'T ALL BE SUPERMEN!
THE END

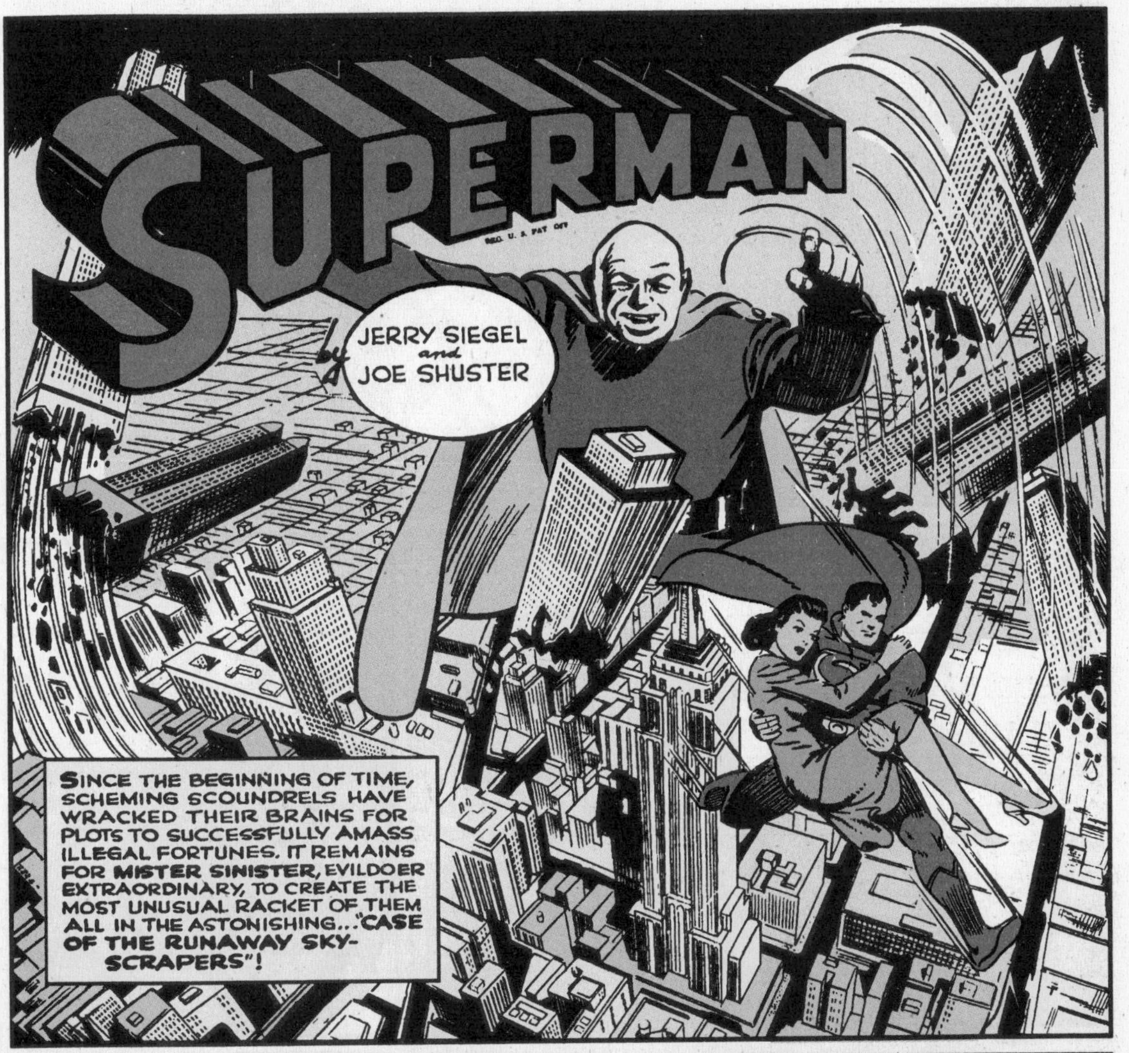
SUPERMAN
REG. U.S. PAT OFF
by JERRY SIEGEL and JOE SHUSTER
SINCE THE BEGINNING OF TIME, SCHEMING SCOUNDRELS HAVE WRACKED THEIR BRAINS FOR PLOTS TO SUCCESSFULLY AMASS ILLEGAL FORTUNES. IT REMAINS FOR MISTER SINISTER, EVILDOER EXTRAORDINARY, TO CREATE THE MOST UNUSUAL RACKET OF THEM ALL IN THE ASTONISHING..."CASE OF THE RUNAWAY SKY-SCRAPERS"!

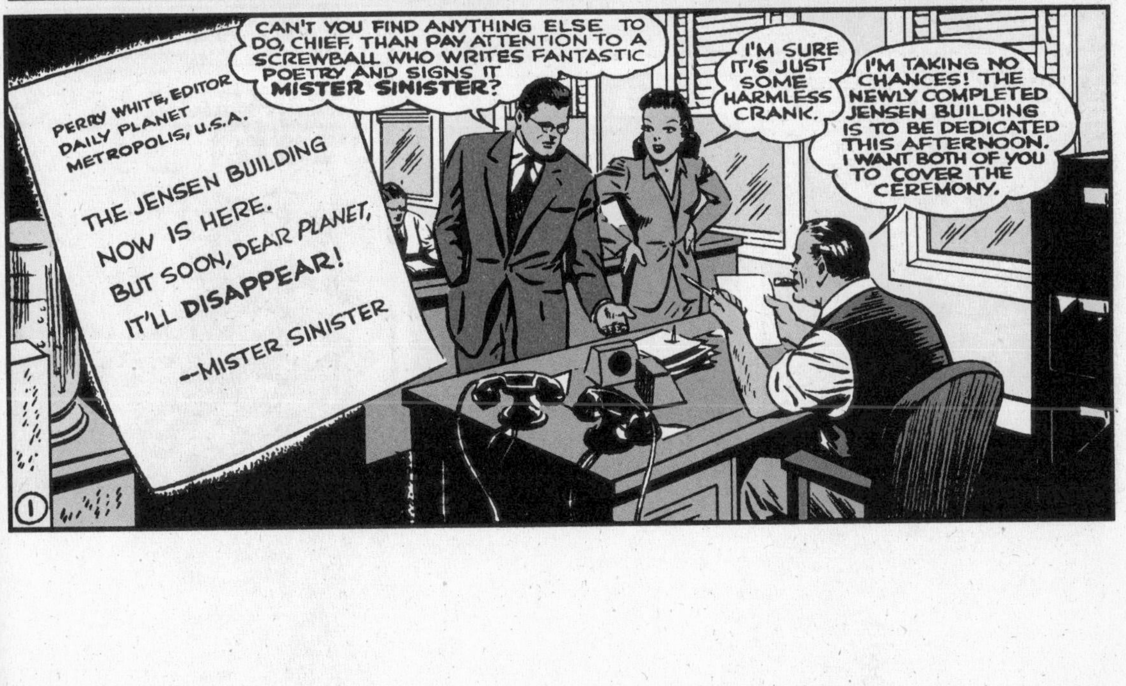
PERRY WHITE, EDITOR DAILY PLANET METROPOLIS, U.S.A.
THE JENSEN BUILDING NOW IS HERE. BUT SOON, DEAR PLANET, IT'LL DISAPPEAR! --MISTER SINISTER
CAN'T YOU FIND ANYTHING ELSE TO DO, CHIEF, THAN PAY ATTENTION TO A SCREWBALL WHO WRITES FANTASTIC POETRY AND SIGNS IT MISTER SINISTER?
I'M SURE IT'S JUST SOME HARMLESS CRANK.
I'M TAKING NO CHANCES! THE NEWLY COMPLETED JENSEN BUILDING IS TO BE DEDICATED THIS AFTERNOON. I WANT BOTH OF YOU TO COVER THE CEREMONY.
1

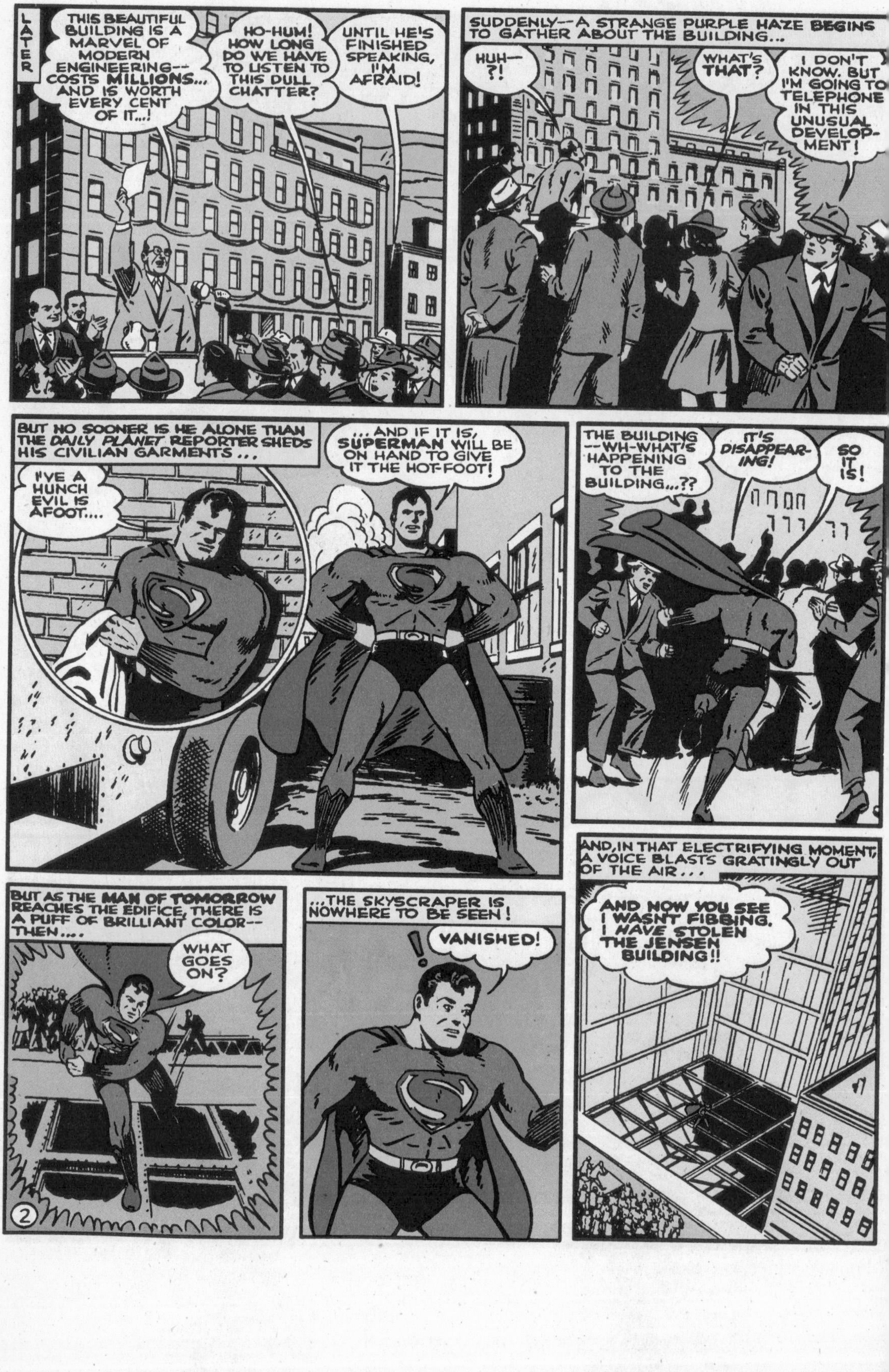
LATER
THIS BEAUTIFUL BUILDING IS A MARVEL OF MODERN ENGINEERING--COSTS MILLIONS... AND IS WORTH EVERY CENT OF IT...!
HO-HUM! HOW LONG DO WE HAVE TO LISTEN TO THIS DULL CHATTER?
UNTIL HE'S FINISHED SPEAKING, I'M AFRAID!
SUDDENLY--A STRANGE PURPLE HAZE BEGINS TO GATHER ABOUT THE BUILDING...
HUH--?!
WHAT'S THAT?
I DON'T KNOW. BUT I'M GOING TO TELEPHONE IN THIS UNUSUAL DEVELOPMENT!
BUT NO SOONER IS HE ALONE THAN THE DAILY PLANET REPORTER SHEDS HIS CIVILIAN GARMENTS...
I'VE A HUNCH EVIL IS AFOOT....
...AND IF IT IS, SUPERMAN WILL BE ON HAND TO GIVE IT THE HOT-FOOT!
THE BUILDING --WH-WHAT'S HAPPENING TO THE BUILDING...??
IT'S DISAPPEARING!
SO IT IS!
BUT AS THE MAN OF TOMORROW REACHES THE EDIFICE, THERE IS A PUFF OF BRILLIANT COLOR--THEN....
WHAT GOES ON?
2
...THE SKYSCRAPER IS NOWHERE TO BE SEEN!
VANISHED!
AND, IN THAT ELECTRIFYING MOMENT, A VOICE BLASTS GRATINGLY OUT OF THE AIR...
AND NOW YOU SEE I WASN'T FIBBING. I HAVE STOLEN THE JENSEN BUILDING!!

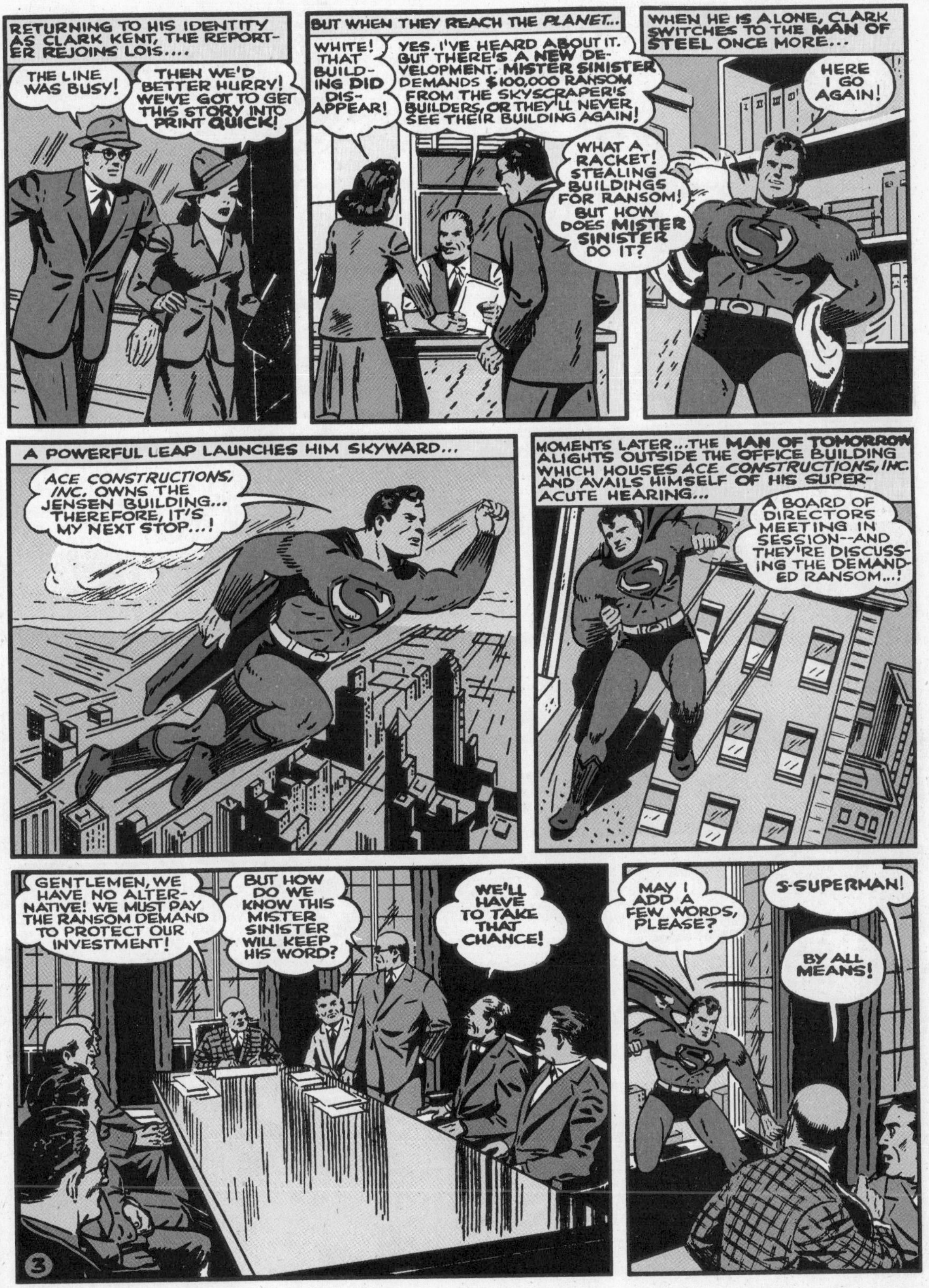

RETURNING TO HIS IDENTITY AS CLARK KENT, THE REPORTER REJOINS LOIS....
THE LINE WAS BUSY!
THEN WE'D BETTER HURRY! WE'VE GOT TO GET THIS STORY INTO PRINT QUICK!
BUT WHEN THEY REACH THE PLANET...
WHITE! THAT BUILDING DID DISAPPEAR!
YES. I'VE HEARD ABOUT IT. BUT THERE'S A NEW DEVELOPMENT. MISTER SINISTER DEMANDS $100,000 RANSOM FROM THE SKYSCRAPER'S BUILDERS, OR THEY'LL NEVER SEE THEIR BUILDING AGAIN!
WHAT A RACKET! STEALING BUILDINGS FOR RANSOM! BUT HOW DOES MISTER SINISTER DO IT?
WHEN HE IS ALONE, CLARK SWITCHES TO THE MAN OF STEEL ONCE MORE...
HERE I GO AGAIN!
A POWERFUL LEAP LAUNCHES HIM SKYWARD...
ACE CONSTRUCTIONS, INC. OWNS THE JENSEN BUILDING... THEREFORE, IT'S MY NEXT STOP...!
MOMENTS LATER...THE MAN OF TOMORROW ALIGHTS OUTSIDE THE OFFICE BUILDING WHICH HOUSES ACE CONSTRUCTIONS, INC. AND AVAILS HIMSELF OF HIS SUPER-ACUTE HEARING...
A BOARD OF DIRECTORS MEETING IN SESSION--AND THEY'RE DISCUSSING THE DEMANDED RANSOM...!
GENTLEMEN, WE HAVE NO ALTERNATIVE! WE MUST PAY THE RANSOM DEMAND TO PROTECT OUR INVESTMENT!
BUT HOW DO WE KNOW THIS MISTER SINISTER WILL KEEP HIS WORD?
WE'LL HAVE TO TAKE THAT CHANCE!
3
MAY I ADD A FEW WORDS, PLEASE?
S-SUPERMAN!
BY ALL MEANS!

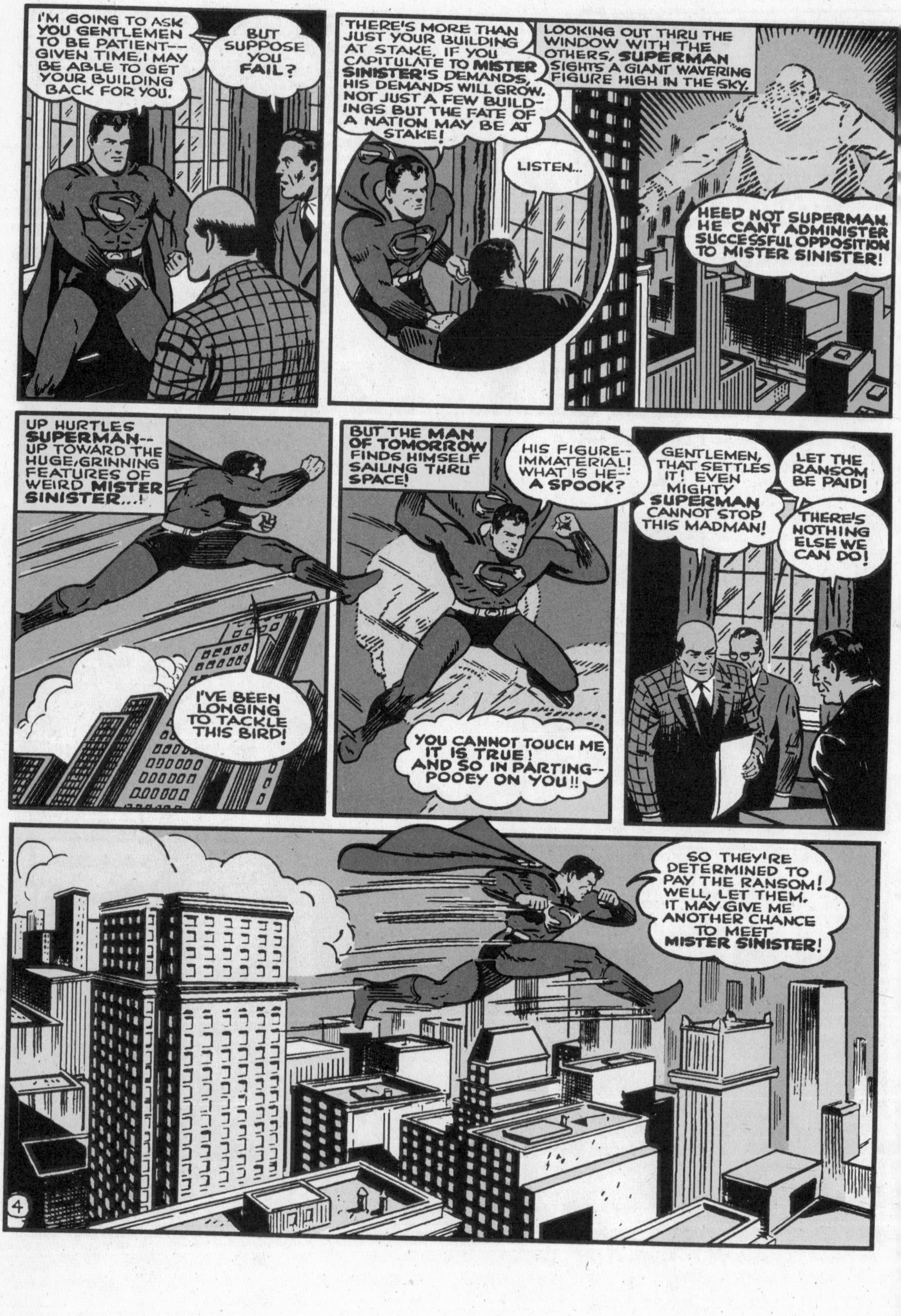
I'M GOING TO ASK YOU GENTLEMEN TO BE PATIENT-- GIVEN TIME, I MAY BE ABLE TO GET YOUR BUILDING BACK FOR YOU.
BUT SUPPOSE YOU FAIL?
THERE'S MORE THAN JUST YOUR BUILDING AT STAKE. IF YOU CAPITULATE TO MISTER SINISTER'S DEMANDS, HIS DEMANDS WILL GROW. NOT JUST A FEW BUILDINGS BUT THE FATE OF A NATION MAY BE AT STAKE!
LISTEN...
LOOKING OUT THRU THE WINDOW WITH THE OTHERS, SUPERMAN SIGHTS A GIANT WAVERING FIGURE HIGH IN THE SKY.
HEED NOT SUPERMAN. HE CANT ADMINISTER SUCCESSFUL OPPOSITION TO MISTER SINISTER!
UP HURTLES SUPERMAN-- UP TOWARD THE HUGE, GRINNING FEATURES OF WEIRD MISTER SINISTER...!
I'VE BEEN LONGING TO TACKLE THIS BIRD!
BUT THE MAN OF TOMORROW FINDS HIMSELF SAILING THRU SPACE!
HIS FIGURE-- IMMATERIAL! WHAT IS HE-- A SPOOK?
YOU CANNOT TOUCH ME, IT IS TRUE! AND SO IN PARTING-- POOEY ON YOU!!
GENTLEMEN, THAT SETTLES IT! EVEN MIGHTY SUPERMAN CANNOT STOP THIS MADMAN!
LET THE RANSOM BE PAID!
THERE'S NOTHING ELSE WE CAN DO!
SO THEY'RE DETERMINED TO PAY THE RANSOM! WELL, LET THEM. IT MAY GIVE ME ANOTHER CHANCE TO MEET MISTER SINISTER!
4

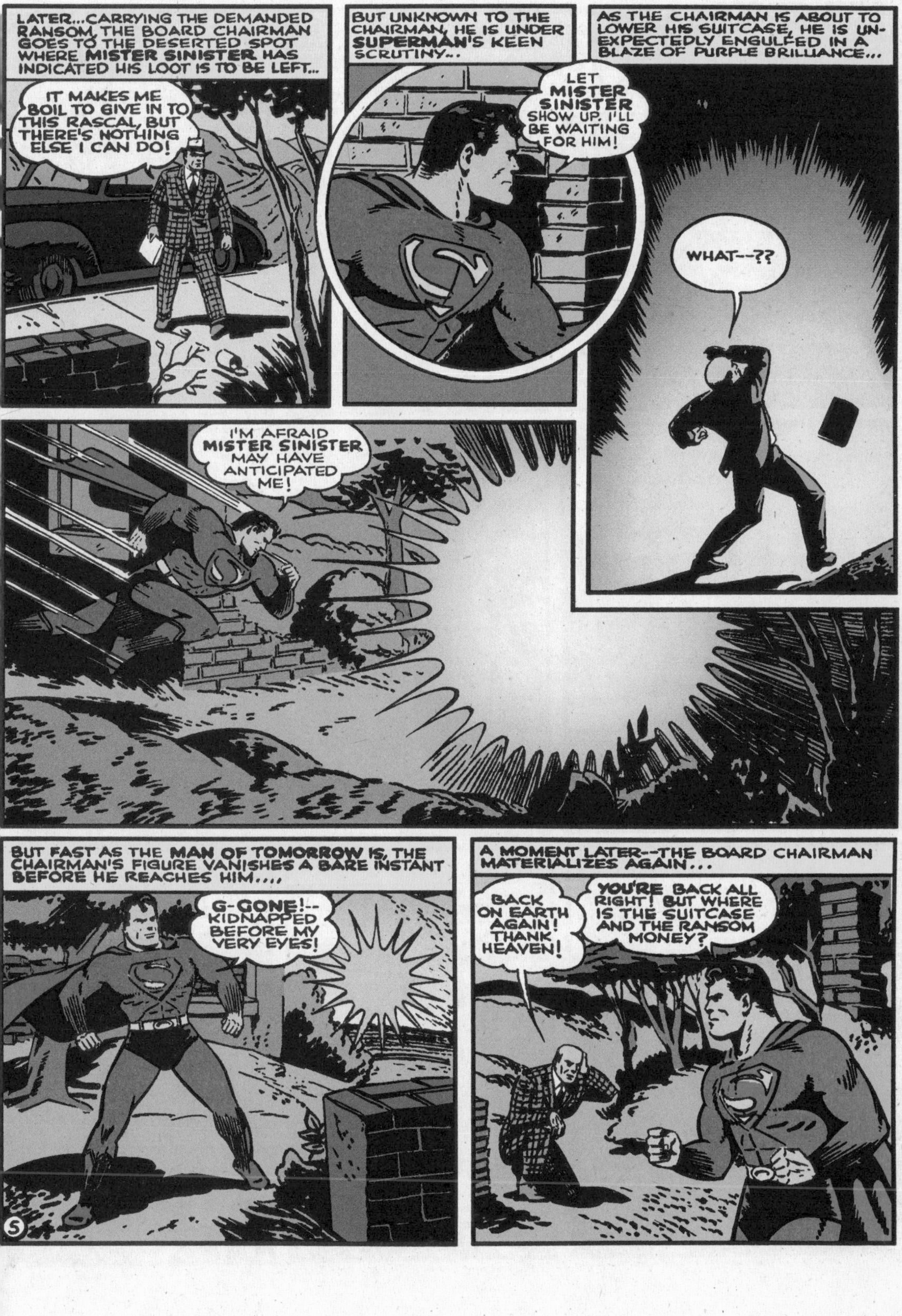
LATER...CARRYING THE DEMANDED RANSOM, THE BOARD CHAIRMAN GOES TO THE DESERTED SPOT WHERE MISTER SINISTER HAS INDICATED HIS LOOT IS TO BE LEFT...
IT MAKES ME BOIL TO GIVE IN TO THIS RASCAL, BUT THERE'S NOTHING ELSE I CAN DO!
BUT UNKNOWN TO THE CHAIRMAN, HE IS UNDER SUPERMAN'S KEEN SCRUTINY...
LET MISTER SINISTER SHOW UP. I'LL BE WAITING FOR HIM!
AS THE CHAIRMAN IS ABOUT TO LOWER HIS SUITCASE, HE IS UNEXPECTEDLY ENGULFED IN A BLAZE OF PURPLE BRILLIANCE...
WHAT--??
I'M AFRAID MISTER SINISTER MAY HAVE ANTICIPATED ME!
BUT FAST AS THE MAN OF TOMORROW IS, THE CHAIRMAN'S FIGURE VANISHES A BARE INSTANT BEFORE HE REACHES HIM....
G-GONE!-- KIDNAPPED BEFORE MY VERY EYES!
5
A MOMENT LATER--THE BOARD CHAIRMAN MATERIALIZES AGAIN...
BACK ON EARTH AGAIN! THANK HEAVEN!
YOU'RE BACK ALL RIGHT! BUT WHERE IS THE SUITCASE AND THE RANSOM MONEY?

I'VE GONE THRU A TERRIBLE EXPERIENCE--I SEEMED TO FIND MYSELF IN A WEIRD PURPLE-HUED WORLD...THUGS SNATCHED THE SUITCASE FROM ME... THEN **MISTER SINISTER** HIMSELF INFORMED ME THAT THE JENSEN BUILD-ING WOULD BE RETURNED AS HE HAD PROMISED.

THERE'S ONE SURE WAY WE CAN CHECK THAT STORY!

C-C-C-CAREFUL!!

DON'T WORRY, IF YOU FALL, YOU'LL NEVER KNOW WHAT HIT YOU!

THERE IT IS--THE JENSEN BUILDING...!!!

SO MISTER SINISTER KEPT HIS WORD!

OUR BUILDING--SAFE!

BUT, IF YOU'LL LOOK NEXT DOOR, YOU'LL NOTE THAT THE CARSON NATIONAL BANK HAS DISAPPEARED!

SO IT HAS!

AND YOU CAN THANK YOUR WEAK-KNEED BOARD OF DIRECTORS FOR IT! YOUR CRAVEN ATTITUDE HAS ENCOURAGED **MISTER SINISTER** TO TAKE DRASTIC STEPS!

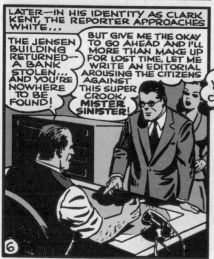

LATER--IN HIS IDENTITY AS CLARK KENT, THE REPORTER APPROACHES WHITE...

THE JENSEN BUILDING RETURNED-- A BANK STOLEN... AND YOU'RE NOWHERE TO BE FOUND!

BUT GIVE ME THE OKAY TO GO AHEAD AND I'LL MORE THAN MAKE UP FOR LOST TIME, LET ME WRITE AN EDITORIAL AROUSING THE CITIZENS AGAINST THIS SUPER CROOK, MISTER SINISTER!

RAPIDLY, CLARK DICTATES TO LOIS...

...AND THIS FIENDISH MONSTER MUST BE STOPPED IN HIS TRACKS BEFORE HE SMASHES LAW AND CIVILIZA-TION...--GOT THAT, LOIS?

I'M WITH YOU, CLARK!

I'VE GOT IT--KEEP GOING!

THE STORY IS GOOD, I MUST ADMIT. BUT I'LL CRUSH THE **PLANET** IF YOU DARE PRINT IT!!

MISTER SINISTER!

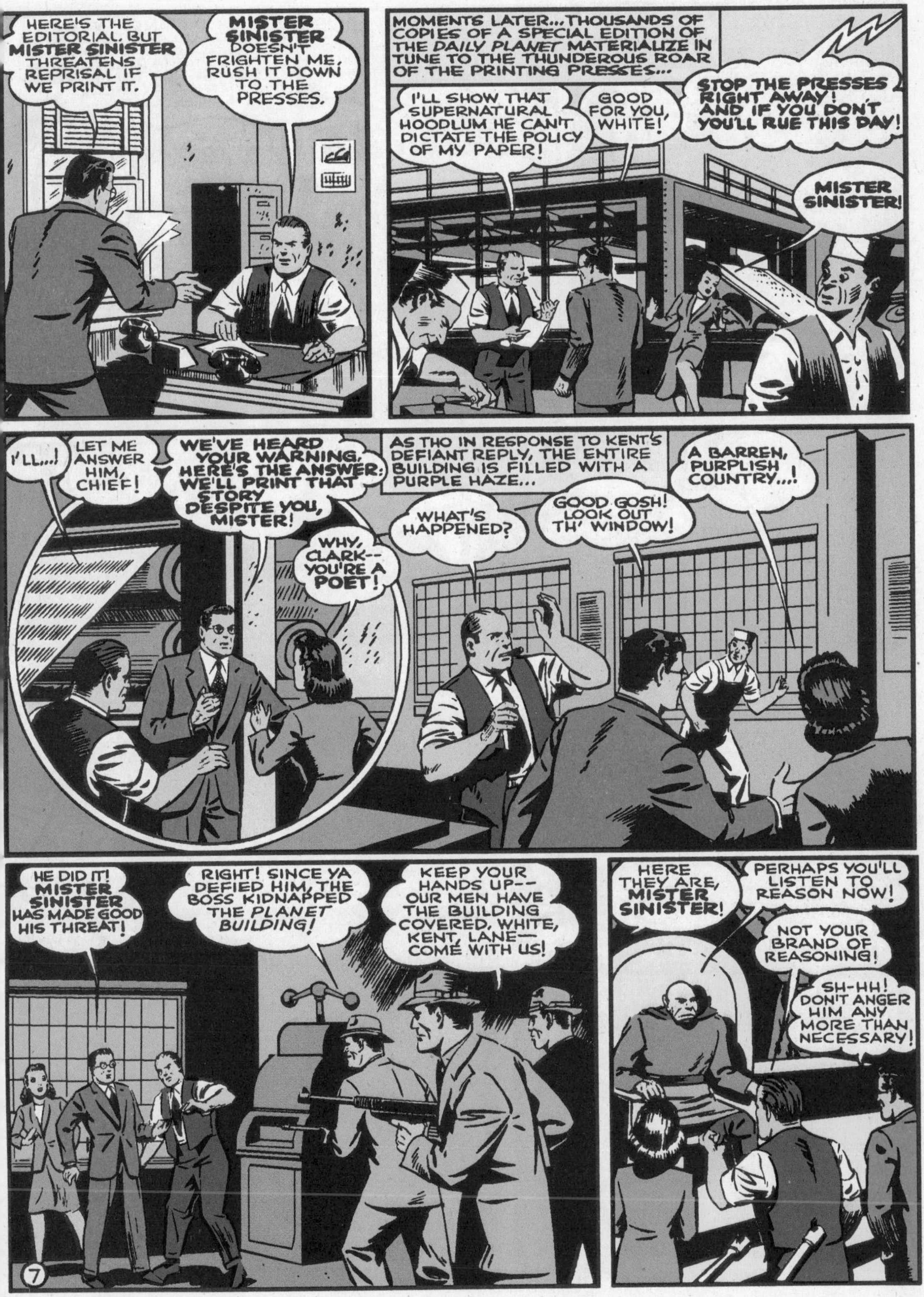
HERE'S THE EDITORIAL, BUT MISTER SINISTER THREATENS REPRISAL IF WE PRINT IT.
MISTER SINISTER DOESN'T FRIGHTEN ME. RUSH IT DOWN TO THE PRESSES.
MOMENTS LATER...THOUSANDS OF COPIES OF A SPECIAL EDITION OF THE DAILY PLANET MATERIALIZE IN TUNE TO THE THUNDEROUS ROAR OF THE PRINTING PRESSES...
I'LL SHOW THAT SUPERNATURAL HOODLUM HE CAN'T DICTATE THE POLICY OF MY PAPER!
GOOD FOR YOU, WHITE!
STOP THE PRESSES RIGHT AWAY! AND IF YOU DON'T YOU'LL RUE THIS DAY!
MISTER SINISTER!
I'LL...!
LET ME ANSWER HIM, CHIEF!
WE'VE HEARD YOUR WARNING. HERE'S THE ANSWER: WE'LL PRINT THAT STORY DESPITE YOU, MISTER!
WHY, CLARK-- YOU'RE A POET!
AS THO IN RESPONSE TO KENT'S DEFIANT REPLY, THE ENTIRE BUILDING IS FILLED WITH A PURPLE HAZE...
WHAT'S HAPPENED?
GOOD GOSH! LOOK OUT TH' WINDOW!
A BARREN, PURPLISH COUNTRY...!
HE DID IT! MISTER SINISTER HAS MADE GOOD HIS THREAT!
RIGHT! SINCE YA DEFIED HIM, THE BOSS KIDNAPPED THE PLANET BUILDING!
KEEP YOUR HANDS UP-- OUR MEN HAVE THE BUILDING COVERED, WHITE, KENT, LANE— COME WITH US!
7
HERE THEY ARE, MISTER SINISTER!
PERHAPS YOU'LL LISTEN TO REASON NOW!
NOT YOUR BRAND OF REASONING!
SH-HH! DON'T ANGER HIM ANY MORE THAN NECESSARY!

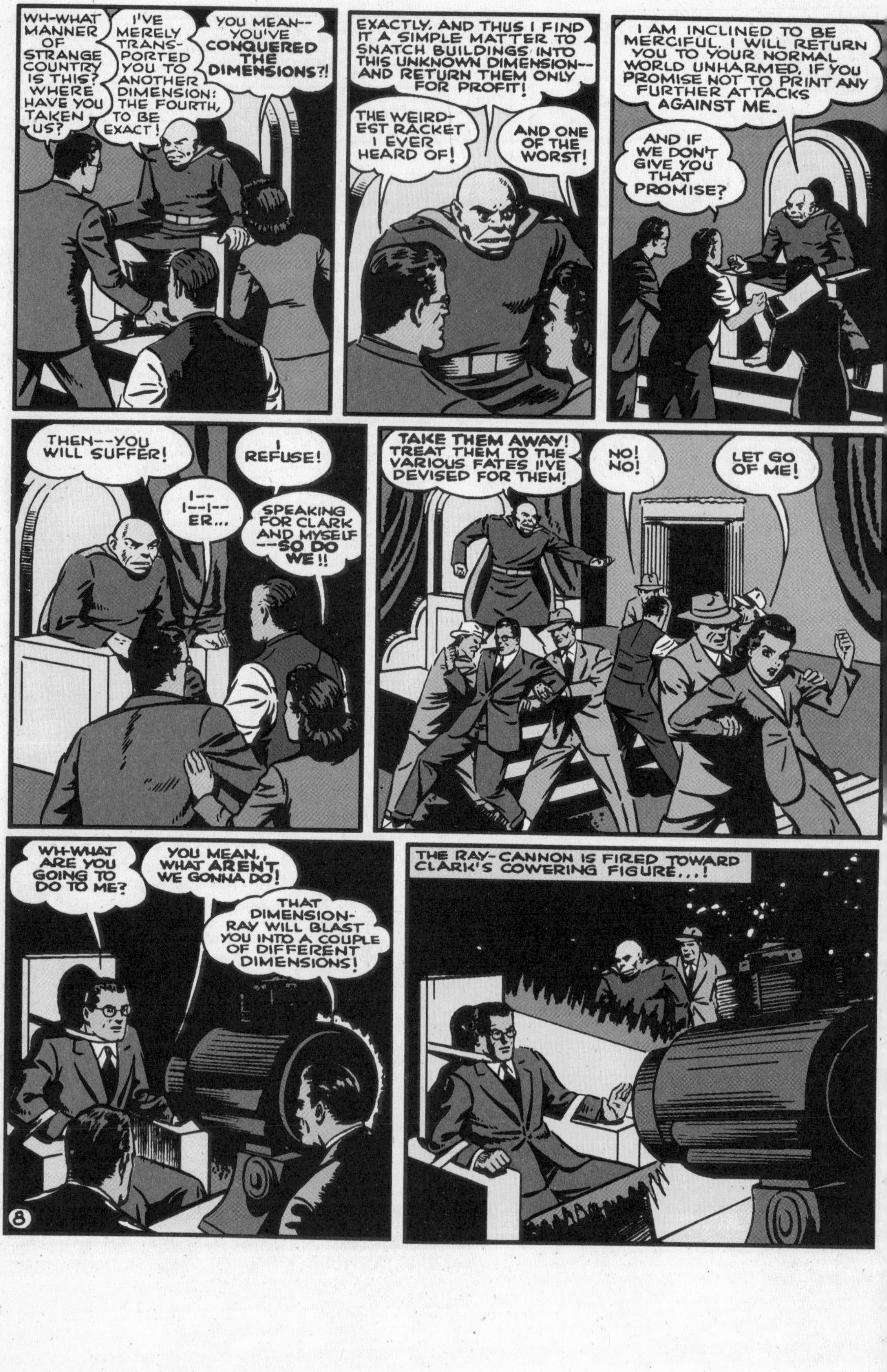
WH-WHAT MANNER OF STRANGE COUNTRY IS THIS? WHERE HAVE YOU TAKEN US?
I'VE MERELY TRANS-PORTED YOU TO ANOTHER DIMENSION: THE FOURTH, TO BE EXACT!
YOU MEAN--YOU'VE CONQUERED THE DIMENSIONS?!
EXACTLY, AND THUS I FIND IT A SIMPLE MATTER TO SNATCH BUILDINGS INTO THIS UNKNOWN DIMENSION--AND RETURN THEM ONLY FOR PROFIT!
THE WEIRD-EST RACKET I EVER HEARD OF!
AND ONE OF THE WORST!
I AM INCLINED TO BE MERCIFUL. I WILL RETURN YOU TO YOUR NORMAL WORLD UNHARMED, IF YOU PROMISE NOT TO PRINT ANY FURTHER ATTACKS AGAINST ME.
AND IF WE DON'T GIVE YOU THAT PROMISE?
THEN--YOU WILL SUFFER!
I REFUSE!
I--I--I--ER...
SPEAKING FOR CLARK AND MYSELF--SO DO WE!!
TAKE THEM AWAY! TREAT THEM TO THE VARIOUS FATES I'VE DEVISED FOR THEM!
NO! NO!
LET GO OF ME!
WH-WHAT ARE YOU GOING TO DO TO ME?
YOU MEAN, WHAT AREN'T WE GONNA DO!
THAT DIMENSION-RAY WILL BLAST YOU INTO A COUPLE OF DIFFERENT DIMENSIONS!
8
THE RAY-CANNON IS FIRED TOWARD CLARK'S COWERING FIGURE...!

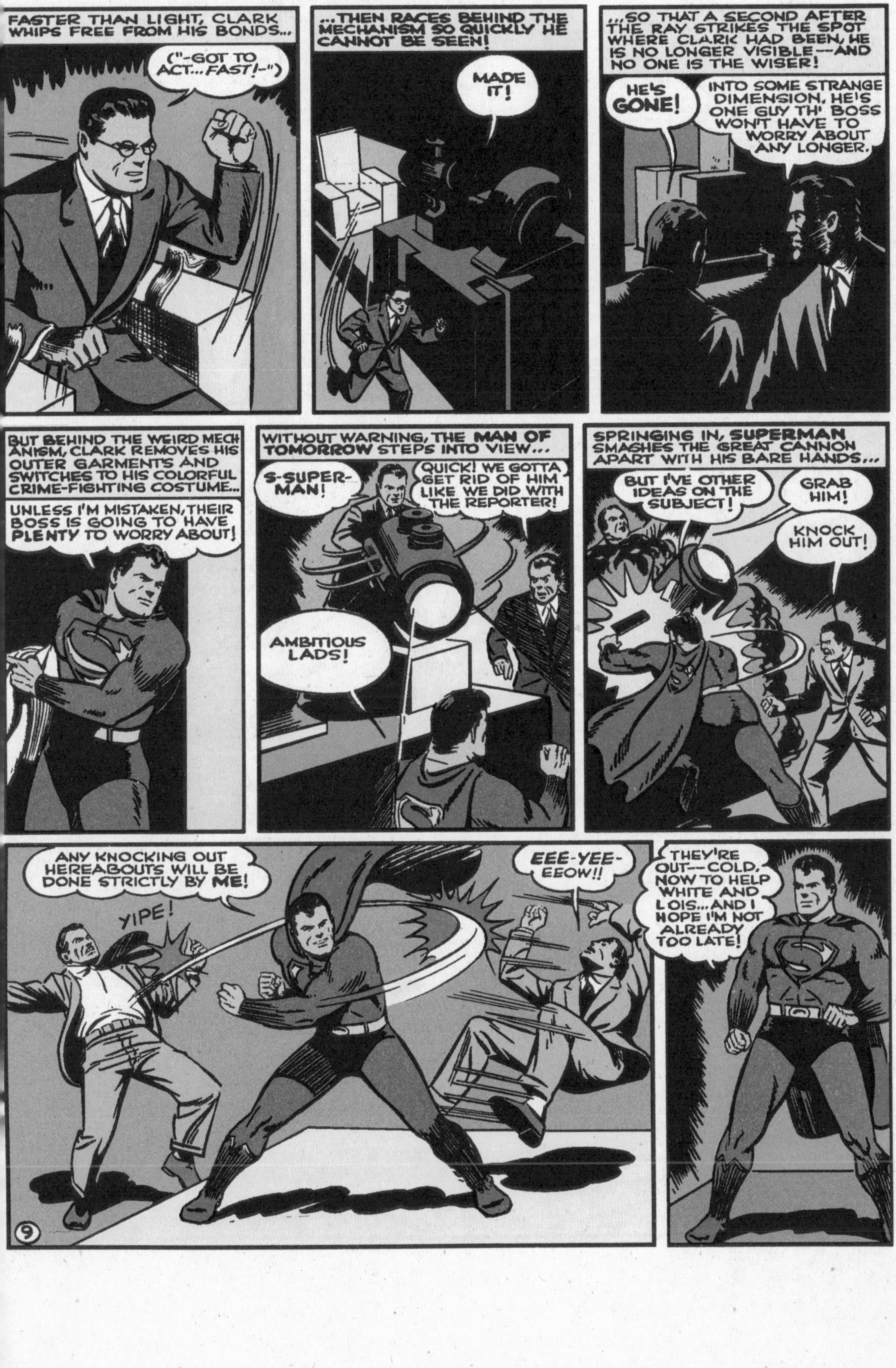
FASTER THAN LIGHT, CLARK WHIPS FREE FROM HIS BONDS...
("-GOT TO ACT...FAST!-")
...THEN RACES BEHIND THE MECHANISM SO QUICKLY HE CANNOT BE SEEN!
MADE IT!
...SO THAT A SECOND AFTER THE RAY STRIKES THE SPOT WHERE CLARK HAD BEEN, HE IS NO LONGER VISIBLE--AND NO ONE IS THE WISER!
HE'S GONE!
INTO SOME STRANGE DIMENSION, HE'S ONE GUY TH' BOSS WON'T HAVE TO WORRY ABOUT ANY LONGER.
BUT BEHIND THE WEIRD MECHANISM, CLARK REMOVES HIS OUTER GARMENTS AND SWITCHES TO HIS COLORFUL CRIME-FIGHTING COSTUME...
UNLESS I'M MISTAKEN, THEIR BOSS IS GOING TO HAVE PLENTY TO WORRY ABOUT!
WITHOUT WARNING, THE MAN OF TOMORROW STEPS INTO VIEW...
S-SUPER-MAN!
QUICK! WE GOTTA GET RID OF HIM LIKE WE DID WITH THE REPORTER!
AMBITIOUS LADS!
SPRINGING IN, SUPERMAN SMASHES THE GREAT CANNON APART WITH HIS BARE HANDS...
BUT I'VE OTHER IDEAS ON THE SUBJECT!
GRAB HIM!
KNOCK HIM OUT!
ANY KNOCKING OUT HEREABOUTS WILL BE DONE STRICTLY BY ME!
YIPE!
EEE-YEE-EEOW!!
THEY'RE OUT--COLD. NOW TO HELP WHITE AND LOIS...AND I HOPE I'M NOT ALREADY TOO LATE!
9

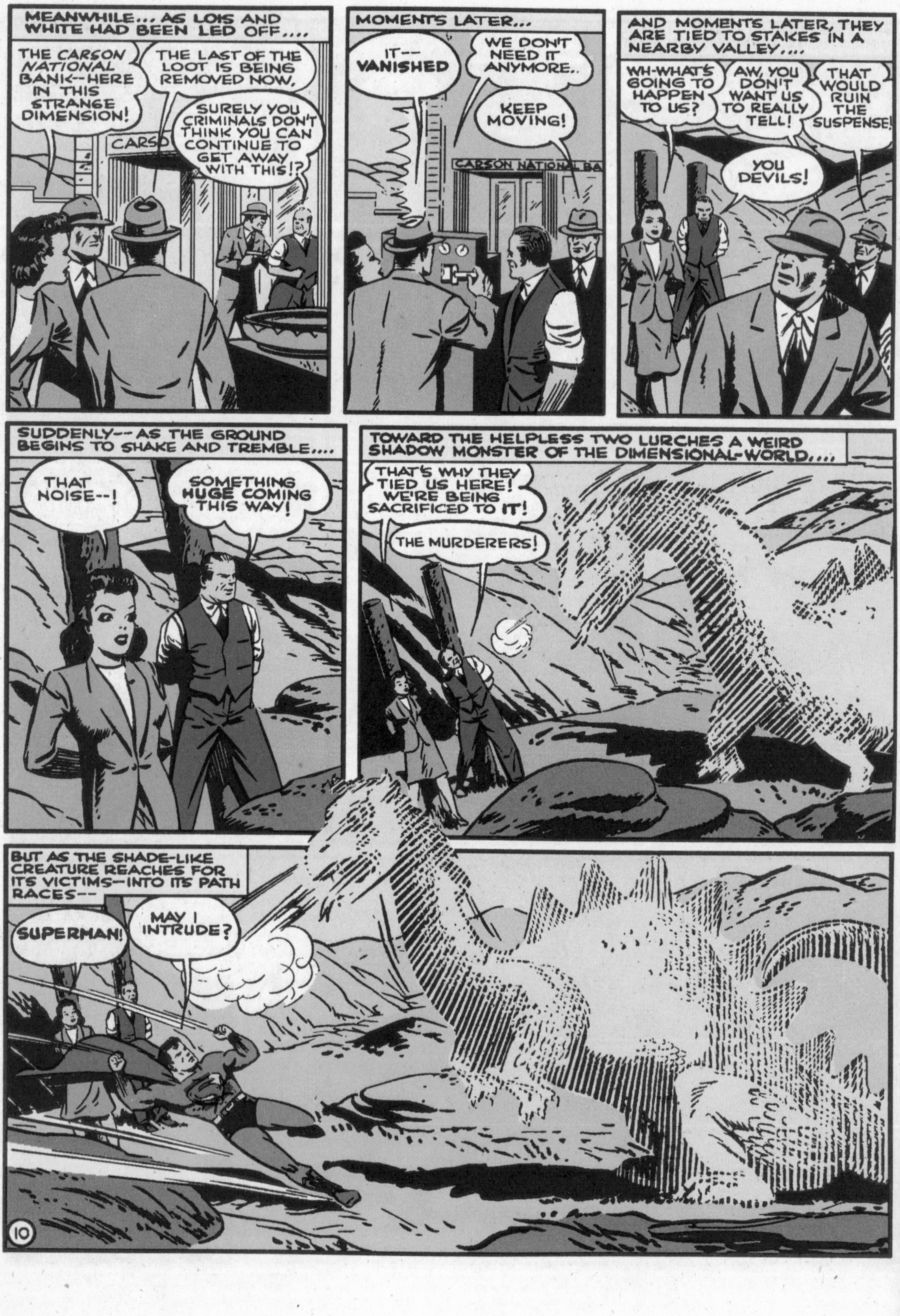
MEANWHILE... AS LOIS AND WHITE HAD BEEN LED OFF....
THE *CARSON NATIONAL* BANK--HERE IN THIS STRANGE DIMENSION!
THE LAST OF THE LOOT IS BEING REMOVED NOW,
SURELY YOU CRIMINALS DON'T THINK YOU CAN CONTINUE TO GET AWAY WITH THIS!?
CARSO
MOMENTS LATER...
IT-- **VANISHED**
WE DON'T NEED IT ANYMORE..
KEEP MOVING!
CARSON NATIONAL BA
AND MOMENTS LATER, THEY ARE TIED TO STAKES IN A NEARBY VALLEY....
WH-WHAT'S GOING TO HAPPEN TO US?
AW, YOU DON'T WANT US TO REALLY TELL!
THAT WOULD RUIN THE SUSPENSE!
YOU DEVILS!
SUDDENLY--AS THE GROUND BEGINS TO SHAKE AND TREMBLE....
THAT NOISE--!
SOMETHING **HUGE** COMING THIS WAY!
TOWARD THE HELPLESS TWO LURCHES A WEIRD SHADOW MONSTER OF THE DIMENSIONAL-WORLD....
THAT'S WHY THEY TIED US HERE! WE'RE BEING SACRIFICED TO **IT**!
THE MURDERERS!
BUT AS THE SHADE-LIKE CREATURE REACHES FOR ITS VICTIMS--INTO ITS PATH RACES--
SUPERMAN!
MAY I INTRUDE?
10

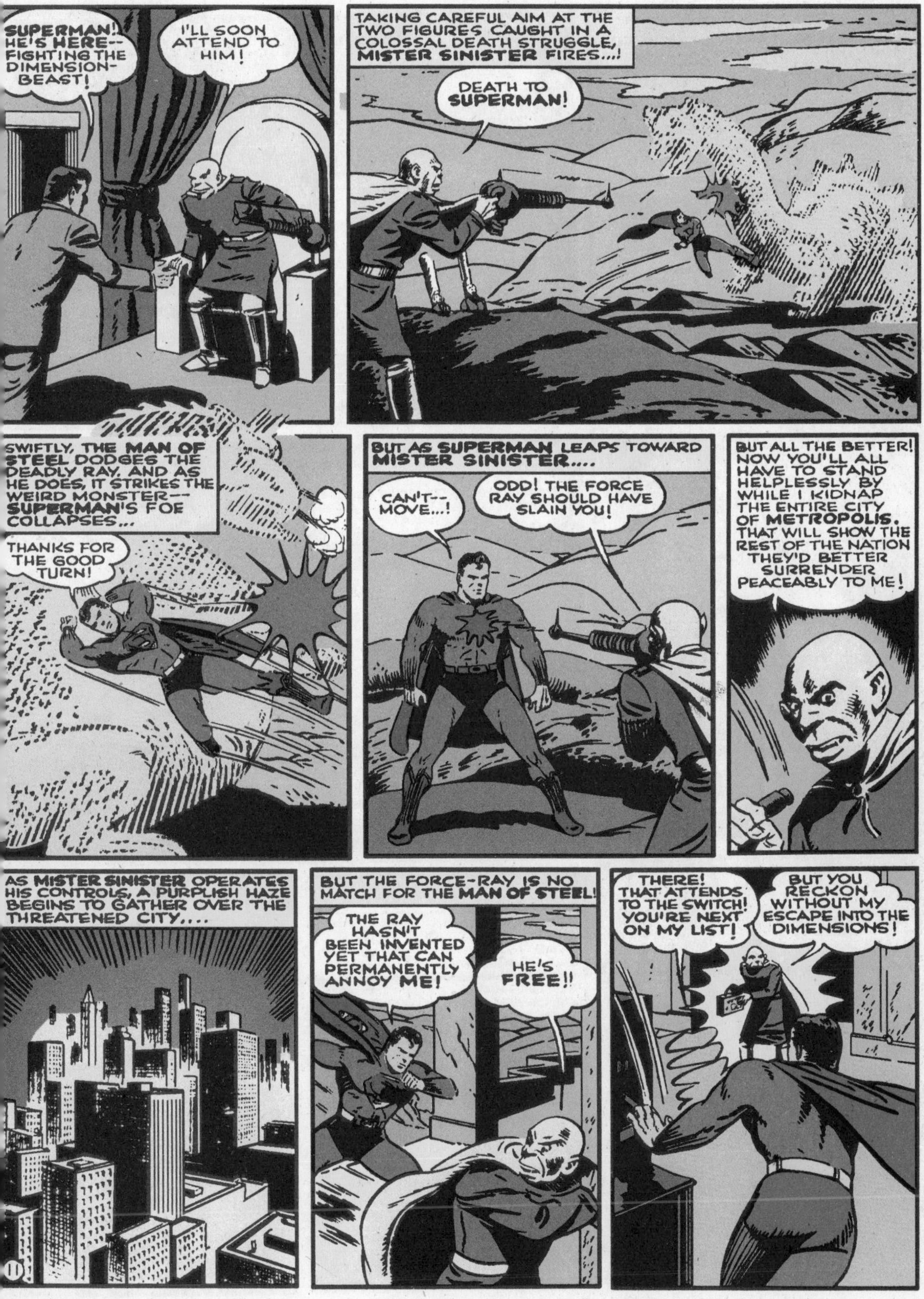
SUPERMAN! HE'S HERE-- FIGHTING THE DIMENSION-BEAST!
I'LL SOON ATTEND TO HIM!
TAKING CAREFUL AIM AT THE TWO FIGURES CAUGHT IN A COLOSSAL DEATH STRUGGLE, MISTER SINISTER FIRES...!
DEATH TO SUPERMAN!
SWIFTLY, THE MAN OF STEEL DODGES THE DEADLY RAY, AND AS HE DOES, IT STRIKES THE WEIRD MONSTER-- SUPERMAN'S FOE COLLAPSES...
THANKS FOR THE GOOD TURN!
BUT AS SUPERMAN LEAPS TOWARD MISTER SINISTER....
CAN'T-- MOVE...!
ODD! THE FORCE RAY SHOULD HAVE SLAIN YOU!
BUT ALL THE BETTER! NOW YOU'LL ALL HAVE TO STAND HELPLESSLY BY WHILE I KIDNAP THE ENTIRE CITY OF METROPOLIS. THAT WILL SHOW THE REST OF THE NATION THEY'D BETTER SURRENDER PEACEABLY TO ME!
AS MISTER SINISTER OPERATES HIS CONTROLS, A PURPLISH HAZE BEGINS TO GATHER OVER THE THREATENED CITY....
11
BUT THE FORCE-RAY IS NO MATCH FOR THE MAN OF STEEL!
THE RAY HASN'T BEEN INVENTED YET THAT CAN PERMANENTLY ANNOY ME!
HE'S FREE!!
THERE! THAT ATTENDS TO THE SWITCH! YOU'RE NEXT ON MY LIST!
BUT YOU RECKON WITHOUT MY ESCAPE INTO THE DIMENSIONS!

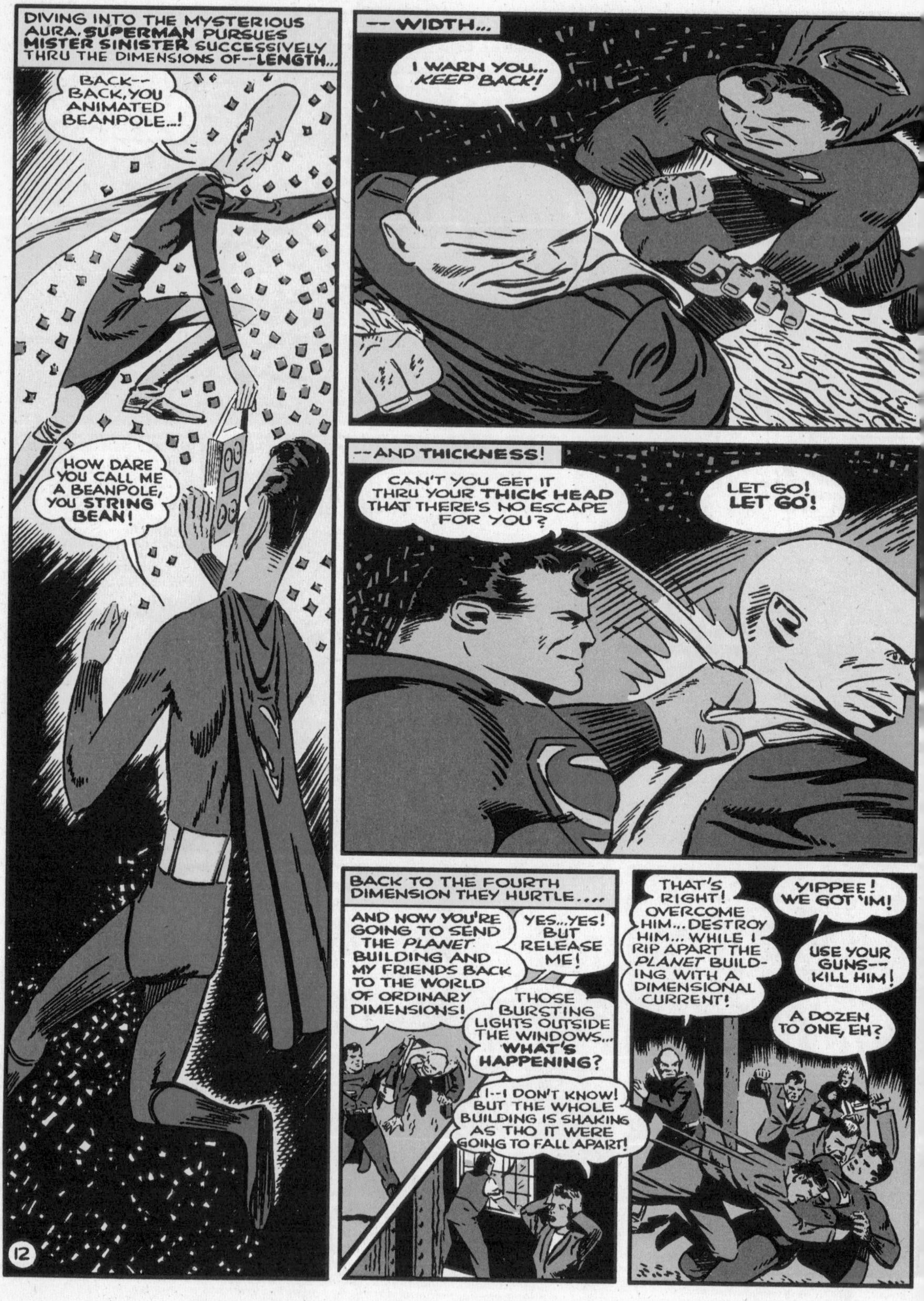
DIVING INTO THE MYSTERIOUS AURA, SUPERMAN PURSUES MISTER SINISTER SUCCESSIVELY THRU THE DIMENSIONS OF--LENGTH...
BACK--BACK, YOU ANIMATED BEANPOLE...!
HOW DARE YOU CALL ME A BEANPOLE, YOU STRING BEAN!
12
-- WIDTH...
I WARN YOU... KEEP BACK!
--AND THICKNESS!
CAN'T YOU GET IT THRU YOUR THICK HEAD THAT THERE'S NO ESCAPE FOR YOU?
LET GO! LET GO!
BACK TO THE FOURTH DIMENSION THEY HURTLE....
AND NOW YOU'RE GOING TO SEND THE PLANET BUILDING AND MY FRIENDS BACK TO THE WORLD OF ORDINARY DIMENSIONS!
YES...YES! BUT RELEASE ME!
THOSE BURSTING LIGHTS OUTSIDE THE WINDOWS... WHAT'S HAPPENING?
I--I DON'T KNOW! BUT THE WHOLE BUILDING IS SHAKING AS THO IT WERE GOING TO FALL APART!
THAT'S RIGHT! OVERCOME HIM... DESTROY HIM... WHILE I RIP APART THE PLANET BUILDING WITH A DIMENSIONAL CURRENT!
YIPPEE! WE GOT 'IM!
USE YOUR GUNS--KILL HIM!
A DOZEN TO ONE, EH?

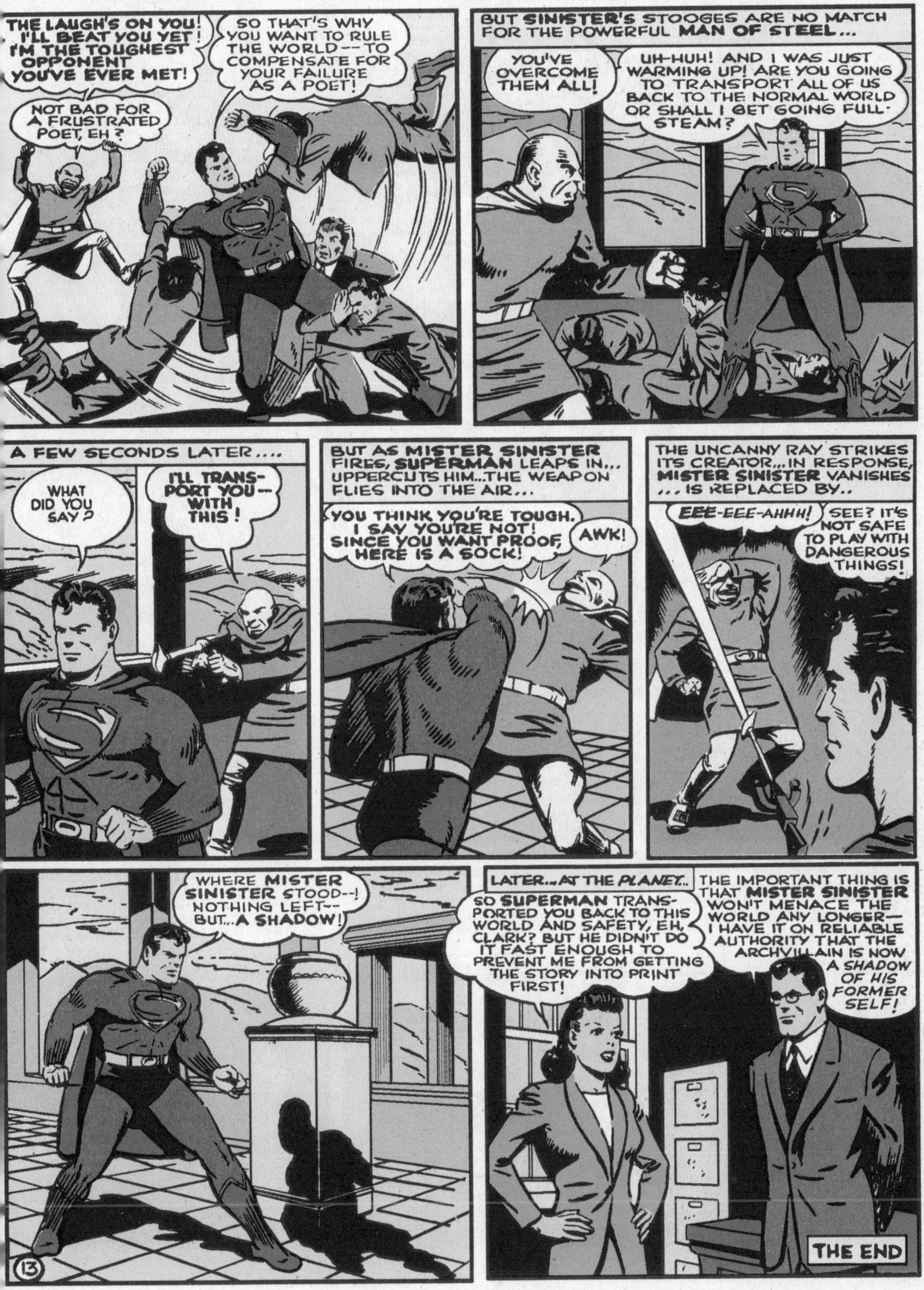
THE LAUGH'S ON YOU! I'LL BEAT YOU YET! I'M THE TOUGHEST OPPONENT YOU'VE EVER MET!
SO THAT'S WHY YOU WANT TO RULE THE WORLD--TO COMPENSATE FOR YOUR FAILURE AS A POET!
NOT BAD FOR A FRUSTRATED POET, EH?
BUT SINISTER'S STOOGES ARE NO MATCH FOR THE POWERFUL MAN OF STEEL...
YOU'VE OVERCOME THEM ALL!
UH-HUH! AND I WAS JUST WARMING UP! ARE YOU GOING TO TRANSPORT ALL OF US BACK TO THE NORMAL WORLD OR SHALL I GET GOING FULL-STEAM?
A FEW SECONDS LATER....
WHAT DID YOU SAY?
I'LL TRANSPORT YOU--WITH THIS!
BUT AS MISTER SINISTER FIRES, SUPERMAN LEAPS IN... UPPERCUTS HIM...THE WEAPON FLIES INTO THE AIR...
YOU THINK YOU'RE TOUGH. I SAY YOU'RE NOT! SINCE YOU WANT PROOF, HERE IS A SOCK!
AWK!
THE UNCANNY RAY STRIKES ITS CREATOR...IN RESPONSE, MISTER SINISTER VANISHES ...IS REPLACED BY..
EEE-EEE-AHHH!
SEE? IT'S NOT SAFE TO PLAY WITH DANGEROUS THINGS!
WHERE MISTER SINISTER STOOD--! NOTHING LEFT--BUT...A SHADOW!
13
LATER...AT THE PLANET...
SO SUPERMAN TRANSPORTED YOU BACK TO THIS WORLD AND SAFETY, EH, CLARK? BUT HE DIDN'T DO IT FAST ENOUGH TO PREVENT ME FROM GETTING THE STORY INTO PRINT FIRST!
THE IMPORTANT THING IS THAT MISTER SINISTER WON'T MENACE THE WORLD ANY LONGER--I HAVE IT ON RELIABLE AUTHORITY THAT THE ARCHVILLAIN IS NOW A SHADOW OF HIS FORMER SELF!
THE END

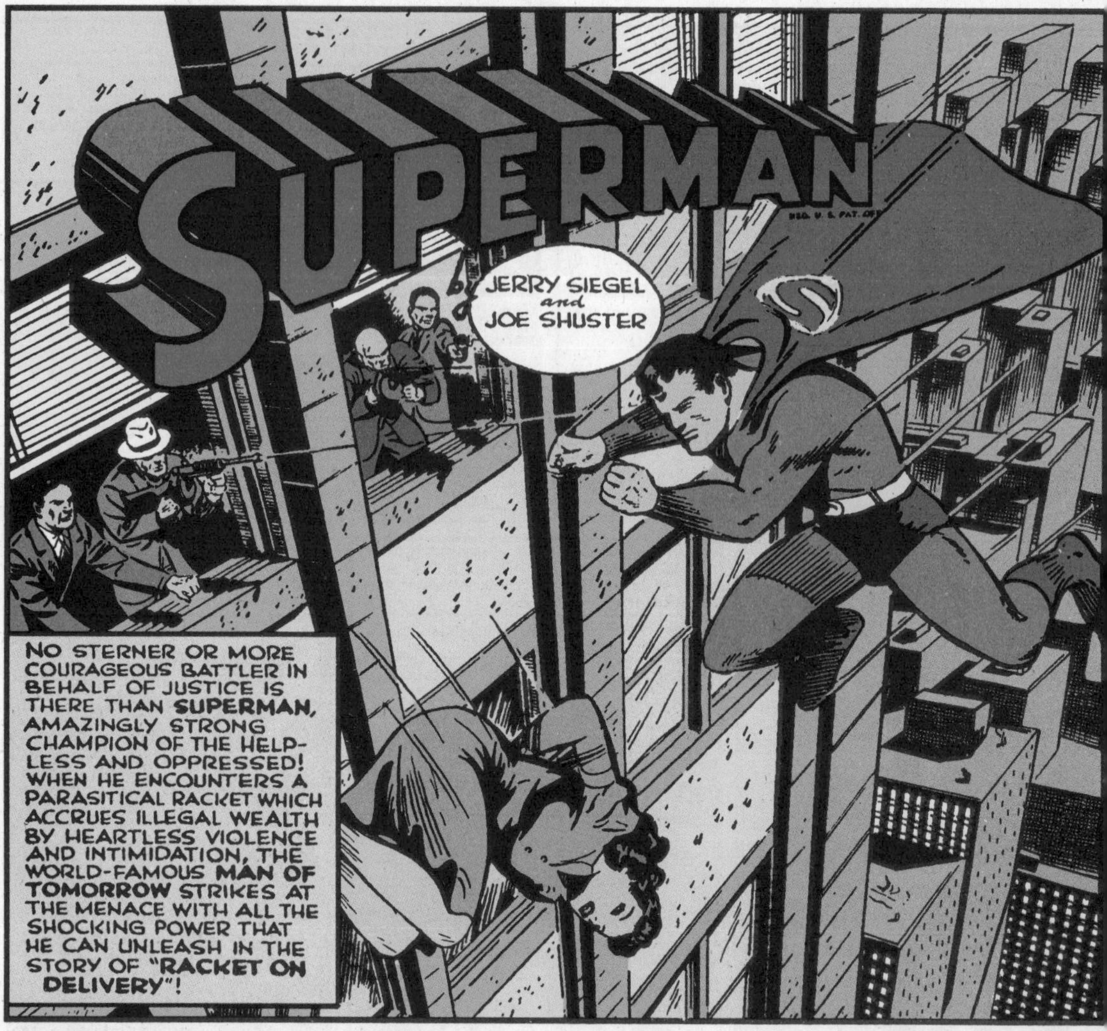
SUPERMAN
by JERRY SIEGEL and JOE SHUSTER
NO STERNER OR MORE COURAGEOUS BATTLER IN BEHALF OF JUSTICE IS THERE THAN **SUPERMAN**, AMAZINGLY STRONG CHAMPION OF THE HELPLESS AND OPPRESSED! WHEN HE ENCOUNTERS A PARASITICAL RACKET WHICH ACCRUES ILLEGAL WEALTH BY HEARTLESS VIOLENCE AND INTIMIDATION, THE WORLD-FAMOUS **MAN OF TOMORROW** STRIKES AT THE MENACE WITH ALL THE SHOCKING POWER THAT HE CAN UNLEASH IN THE STORY OF "**RACKET ON DELIVERY**"!

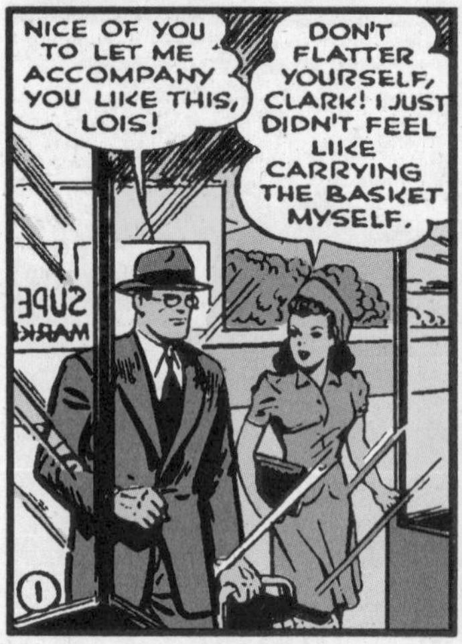
NICE OF YOU TO LET ME ACCOMPANY YOU LIKE THIS, LOIS!
DON'T FLATTER YOURSELF, CLARK! I JUST DIDN'T FEEL LIKE CARRYING THE BASKET MYSELF.
1

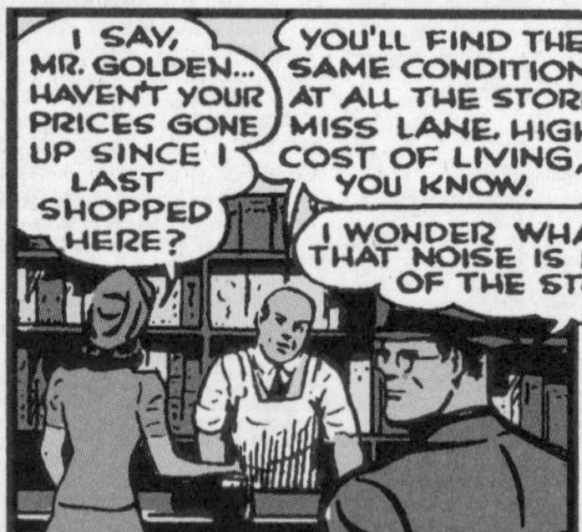
I SAY, MR. GOLDEN... HAVEN'T YOUR PRICES GONE UP SINCE I LAST SHOPPED HERE?
YOU'LL FIND THE SAME CONDITION AT ALL THE STORES, MISS LANE. HIGHER COST OF LIVING, YOU KNOW.
I WONDER WHAT ALL THAT NOISE IS IN BACK OF THE STORE?

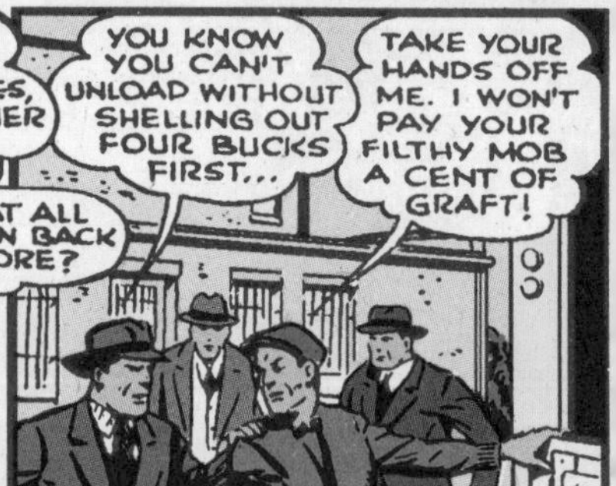
YOU KNOW YOU CAN'T UNLOAD WITHOUT SHELLING OUT FOUR BUCKS FIRST...
TAKE YOUR HANDS OFF ME. I WON'T PAY YOUR FILTHY MOB A CENT OF GRAFT!

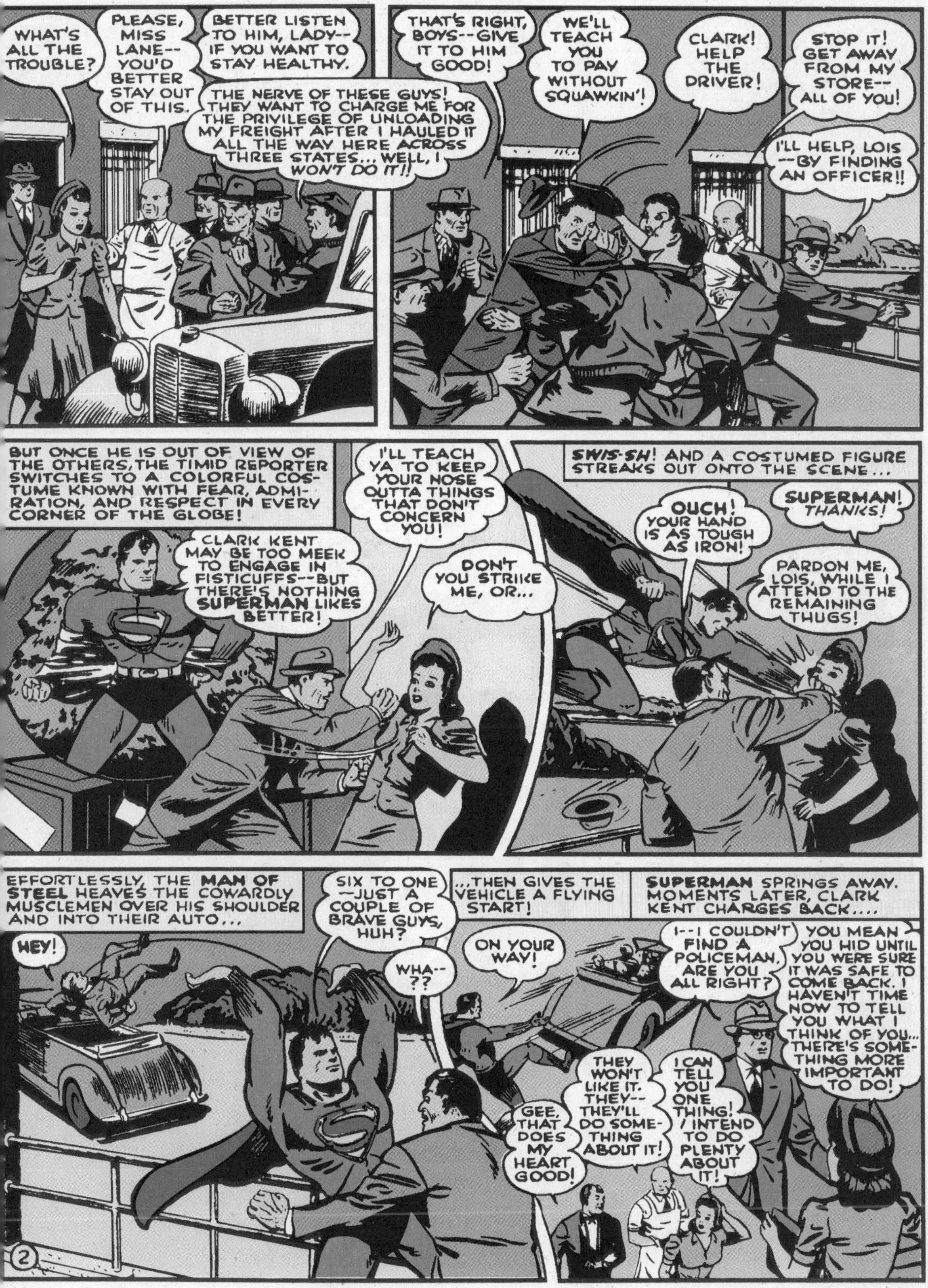
WHAT'S ALL THE TROUBLE?
PLEASE, MISS LANE-- YOU'D BETTER STAY OUT OF THIS.
BETTER LISTEN TO HIM, LADY-- IF YOU WANT TO STAY HEALTHY.
THE NERVE OF THESE GUYS! THEY WANT TO CHARGE ME FOR THE PRIVILEGE OF UNLOADING MY FREIGHT AFTER I HAULED IT ALL THE WAY HERE ACROSS THREE STATES... WELL, I *WON'T DO IT!!*
THAT'S RIGHT, BOYS--GIVE IT TO HIM GOOD!
WE'LL TEACH YOU TO PAY WITHOUT SQUAWKIN'!
CLARK! HELP THE DRIVER!
STOP IT! GET AWAY FROM MY STORE-- ALL OF YOU!
I'LL HELP, LOIS --BY FINDING AN OFFICER!!
BUT ONCE HE IS OUT OF VIEW OF THE OTHERS, THE TIMID REPORTER SWITCHES TO A COLORFUL COSTUME KNOWN WITH FEAR, ADMIRATION, AND RESPECT IN EVERY CORNER OF THE GLOBE!
CLARK KENT MAY BE TOO MEEK TO ENGAGE IN FISTICUFFS--BUT THERE'S NOTHING **SUPERMAN** LIKES BETTER!
I'LL TEACH YA TO KEEP YOUR NOSE OUTTA THINGS THAT DON'T CONCERN YOU!
DON'T YOU STRIKE ME, OR...
SWIS-SH! AND A COSTUMED FIGURE STREAKS OUT ONTO THE SCENE...
OUCH! YOUR HAND IS AS TOUGH AS IRON!
SUPERMAN! *THANKS!*
PARDON ME, LOIS, WHILE I ATTEND TO THE REMAINING THUGS!
EFFORTLESSLY, THE **MAN OF STEEL** HEAVES THE COWARDLY MUSCLEMEN OVER HIS SHOULDER AND INTO THEIR AUTO...
HEY!
SIX TO ONE --JUST A COUPLE OF BRAVE GUYS, HUH?
WHA-- ??
...THEN GIVES THE VEHICLE A FLYING START!
ON YOUR WAY!
SUPERMAN SPRINGS AWAY. MOMENTS LATER, CLARK KENT CHARGES BACK....
I--I COULDN'T **FIND A** POLICEMAN. ARE YOU ALL RIGHT?
YOU MEAN YOU HID UNTIL YOU WERE SURE IT WAS SAFE TO COME BACK. I HAVEN'T TIME NOW TO TELL YOU WHAT I THINK OF YOU... THERE'S SOMETHING MORE IMPORTANT TO DO!
GEE, THAT DOES MY HEART GOOD!
THEY WON'T LIKE IT. THEY-- THEY'LL DO SOMETHING ABOUT IT!
I CAN TELL YOU ONE THING! *I* INTEND TO DO PLENTY ABOUT IT!
2

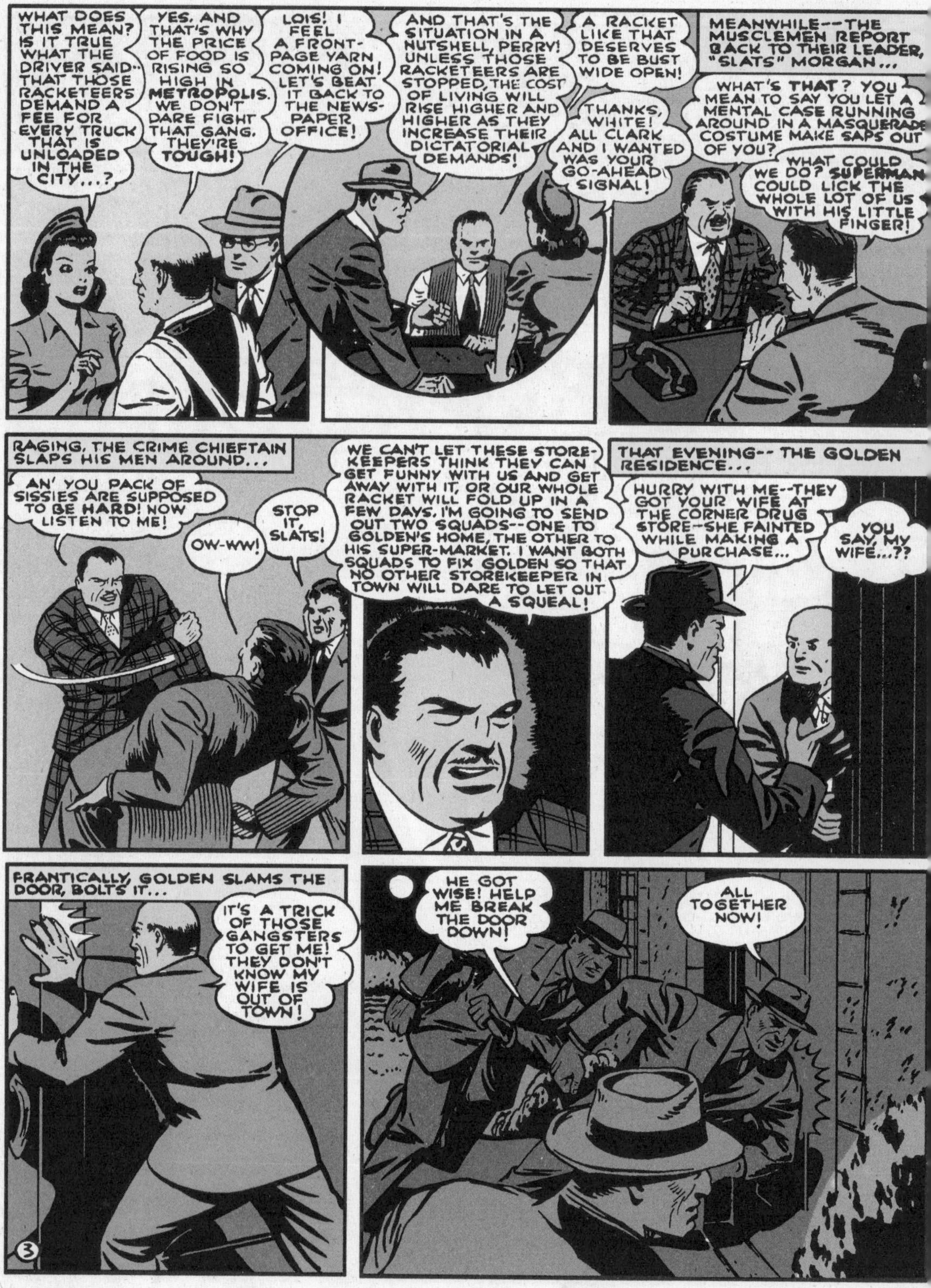
WHAT DOES THIS MEAN? IS IT TRUE WHAT THE DRIVER SAID--THAT THOSE RACKETEERS DEMAND A FEE FOR EVERY TRUCK THAT IS UNLOADED IN THE CITY...?
YES. AND THAT'S WHY THE PRICE OF FOOD IS RISING SO HIGH IN METROPOLIS. WE DON'T DARE FIGHT THAT GANG. THEY'RE TOUGH!
LOIS! I FEEL A FRONT-PAGE YARN COMING ON! LET'S BEAT IT BACK TO THE NEWS-PAPER OFFICE!
AND THAT'S THE SITUATION IN A NUTSHELL, PERRY! UNLESS THOSE RACKETEERS ARE STOPPED, THE COST OF LIVING WILL RISE HIGHER AND HIGHER AS THEY INCREASE THEIR DICTATORIAL DEMANDS!
A RACKET LIKE THAT DESERVES TO BE BUST WIDE OPEN!
THANKS, WHITE! ALL CLARK AND I WANTED WAS YOUR GO-AHEAD SIGNAL!
MEANWHILE--THE MUSCLEMEN REPORT BACK TO THEIR LEADER, "SLATS" MORGAN...
WHAT'S THAT? YOU MEAN TO SAY YOU LET A MENTAL CASE RUNNING AROUND IN A MASQUERADE COSTUME MAKE SAPS OUT OF YOU?
WHAT COULD WE DO? SUPERMAN COULD LICK THE WHOLE LOT OF US WITH HIS LITTLE FINGER!
RAGING, THE CRIME CHIEFTAIN SLAPS HIS MEN AROUND...
AN' YOU PACK OF SISSIES ARE SUPPOSED TO BE HARD! NOW LISTEN TO ME!
OW-WW!
STOP IT, SLATS!
WE CAN'T LET THESE STORE-KEEPERS THINK THEY CAN GET FUNNY WITH US AND GET AWAY WITH IT, OR OUR WHOLE RACKET WILL FOLD UP IN A FEW DAYS. I'M GOING TO SEND OUT TWO SQUADS--ONE TO GOLDEN'S HOME, THE OTHER TO HIS SUPER-MARKET. I WANT BOTH SQUADS TO FIX GOLDEN SO THAT NO OTHER STOREKEEPER IN TOWN WILL DARE TO LET OUT A SQUEAL!
THAT EVENING-- THE GOLDEN RESIDENCE...
HURRY WITH ME--THEY GOT YOUR WIFE AT THE CORNER DRUG STORE--SHE FAINTED WHILE MAKING A PURCHASE...
YOU SAY, MY WIFE...??
FRANTICALLY, GOLDEN SLAMS THE DOOR, BOLTS IT...
IT'S A TRICK OF THOSE GANGSTERS TO GET ME! THEY DON'T KNOW MY WIFE IS OUT OF TOWN!
3
HE GOT WISE! HELP ME BREAK THE DOOR DOWN!
ALL TOGETHER NOW!

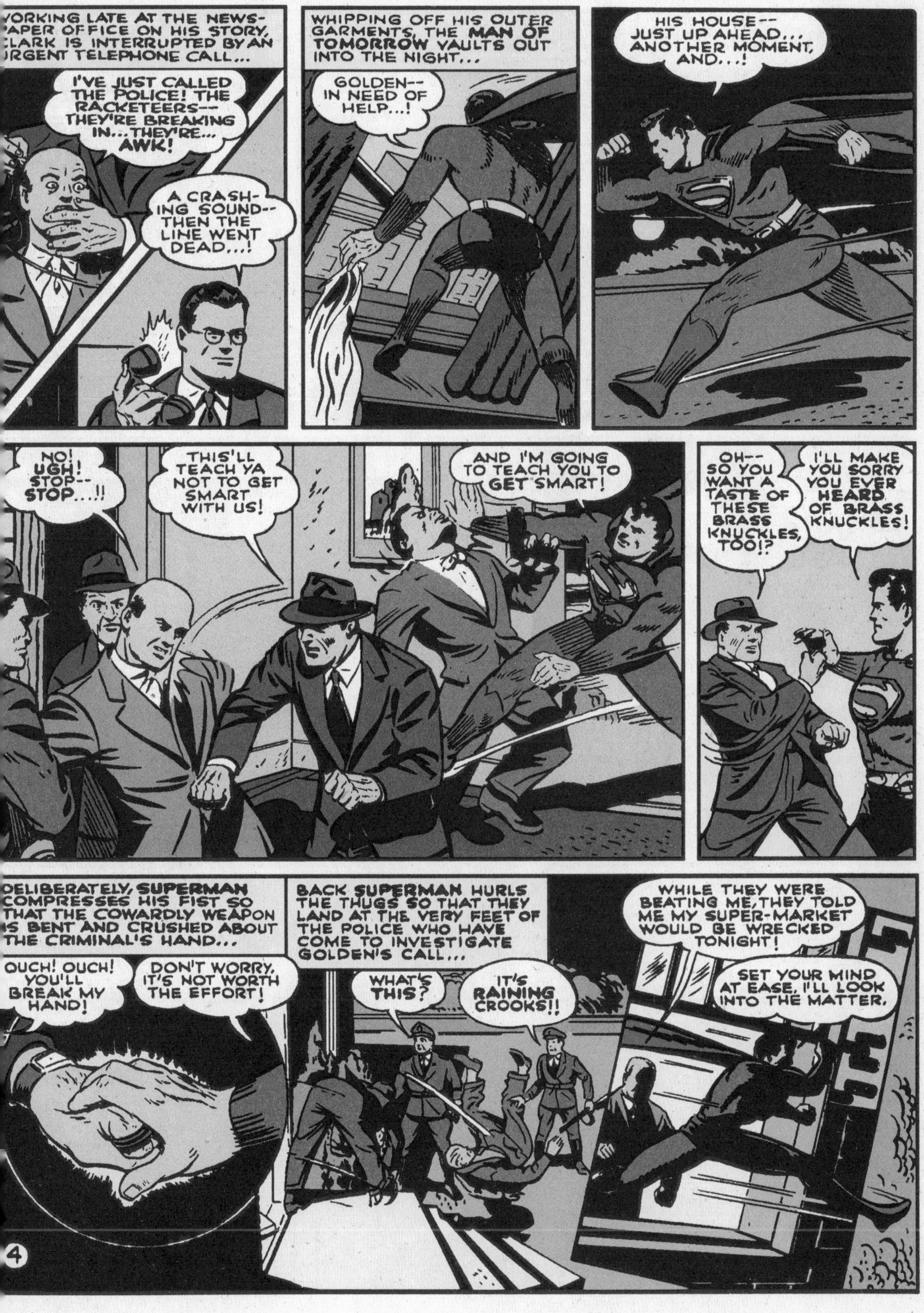
WORKING LATE AT THE NEWSPAPER OFFICE ON HIS STORY, CLARK IS INTERRUPTED BY AN URGENT TELEPHONE CALL...
I'VE JUST CALLED THE POLICE! THE RACKETEERS-- THEY'RE BREAKING IN... THEY'RE... AWK!
A CRASHING SOUND-- THEN THE LINE WENT DEAD...!
WHIPPING OFF HIS OUTER GARMENTS, THE MAN OF TOMORROW VAULTS OUT INTO THE NIGHT...
GOLDEN-- IN NEED OF HELP...!
HIS HOUSE-- JUST UP AHEAD... ANOTHER MOMENT, AND...!
NO! UGH! STOP-- STOP...!!
THIS'LL TEACH YA NOT TO GET SMART WITH US!
AND I'M GOING TO TEACH YOU TO GET SMART!
OH-- SO YOU WANT A TASTE OF THESE BRASS KNUCKLES, TOO!?
I'LL MAKE YOU SORRY YOU EVER HEARD OF BRASS KNUCKLES!
DELIBERATELY, SUPERMAN COMPRESSES HIS FIST SO THAT THE COWARDLY WEAPON IS BENT AND CRUSHED ABOUT THE CRIMINAL'S HAND...
OUCH! OUCH! YOU'LL BREAK MY HAND!
DON'T WORRY. IT'S NOT WORTH THE EFFORT!
4
BACK SUPERMAN HURLS THE THUGS SO THAT THEY LAND AT THE VERY FEET OF THE POLICE WHO HAVE COME TO INVESTIGATE GOLDEN'S CALL...
WHAT'S THIS?
IT'S RAINING CROOKS!!
WHILE THEY WERE BEATING ME, THEY TOLD ME MY SUPER-MARKET WOULD BE WRECKED TONIGHT!
SET YOUR MIND AT EASE. I'LL LOOK INTO THE MATTER.

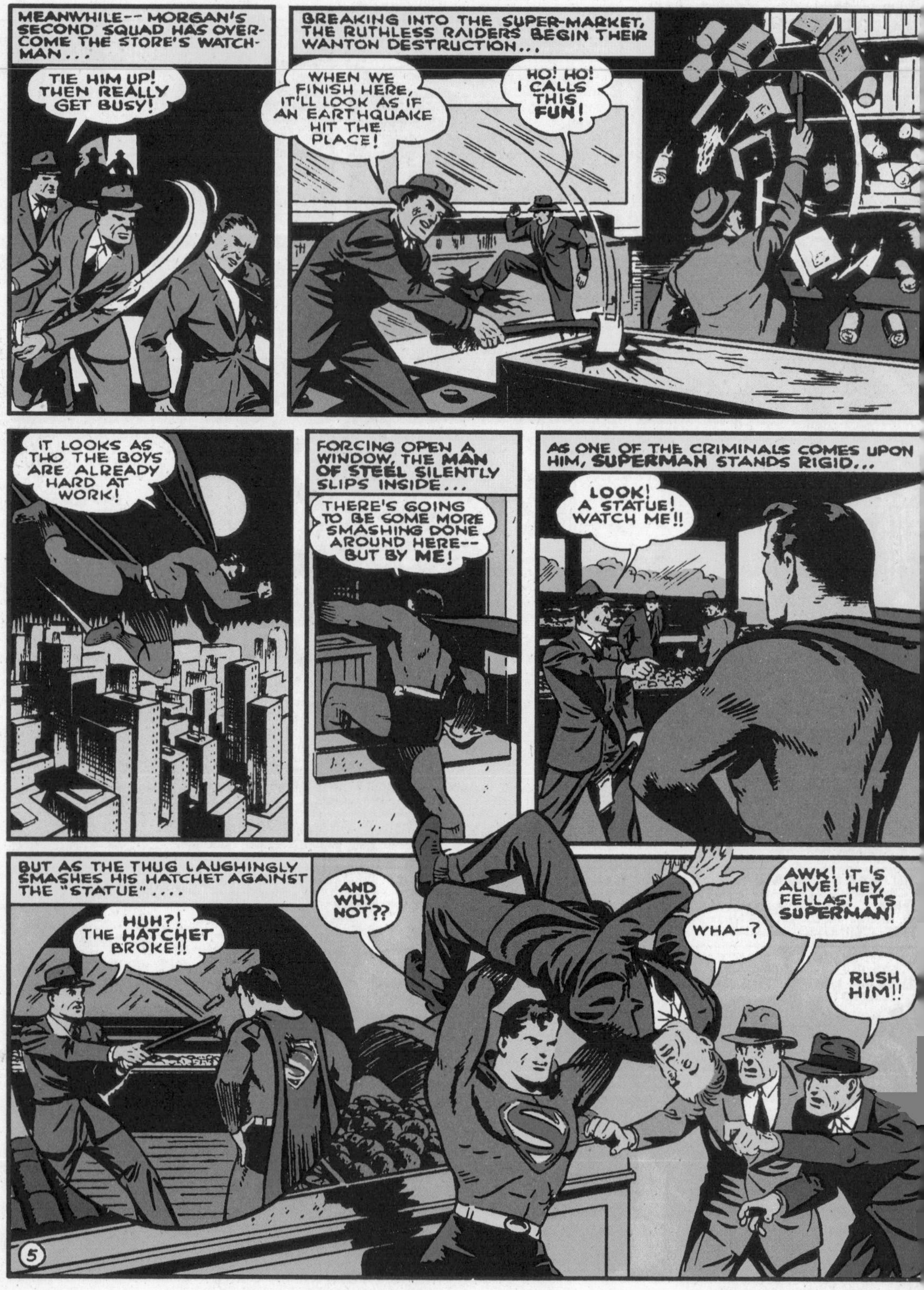
MEANWHILE-- MORGAN'S SECOND SQUAD HAS OVERCOME THE STORE'S WATCHMAN...
TIE HIM UP! THEN REALLY GET BUSY!
BREAKING INTO THE SUPER-MARKET, THE RUTHLESS RAIDERS BEGIN THEIR WANTON DESTRUCTION...
WHEN WE FINISH HERE, IT'LL LOOK AS IF AN EARTHQUAKE HIT THE PLACE!
HO! HO! I CALLS THIS FUN!
IT LOOKS AS THO THE BOYS ARE ALREADY HARD AT WORK!
FORCING OPEN A WINDOW, THE MAN OF STEEL SILENTLY SLIPS INSIDE...
THERE'S GOING TO BE SOME MORE SMASHING DONE AROUND HERE-- BUT BY ME!
AS ONE OF THE CRIMINALS COMES UPON HIM, SUPERMAN STANDS RIGID...
LOOK! A STATUE! WATCH ME!!
BUT AS THE THUG LAUGHINGLY SMASHES HIS HATCHET AGAINST THE "STATUE"....
HUH?! THE HATCHET BROKE!!
AND WHY NOT??
WHA--?
AWK! IT'S ALIVE! HEY, FELLAS! IT'S SUPERMAN!
RUSH HIM!!
5

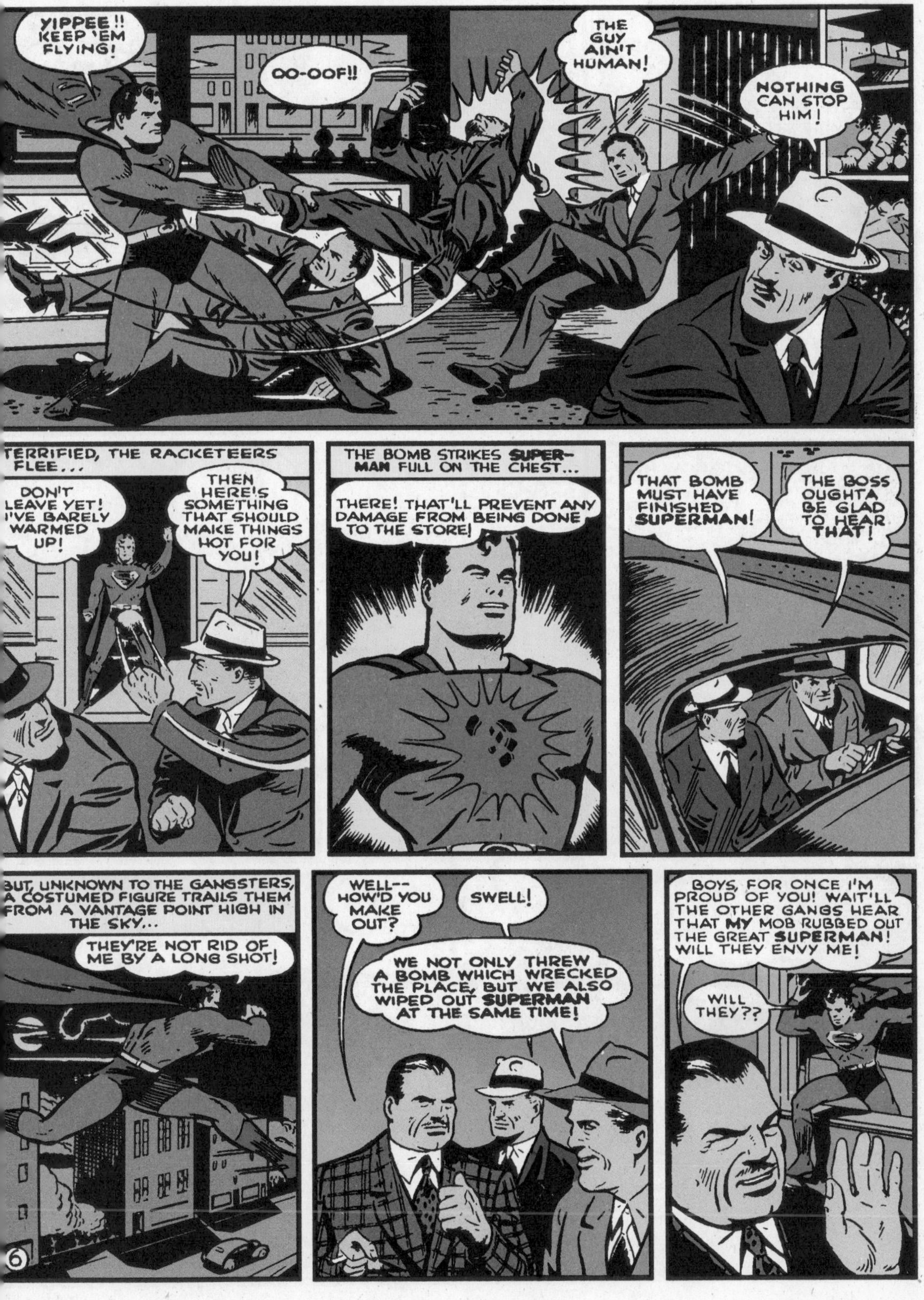
YIPPEE!! KEEP 'EM FLYING!
OO-OOF!!
THE GUY AIN'T HUMAN!
NOTHING CAN STOP HIM!
TERRIFIED, THE RACKETEERS FLEE...
DON'T LEAVE YET! I'VE BARELY WARMED UP!
THEN HERE'S SOMETHING THAT SHOULD MAKE THINGS HOT FOR YOU!
THE BOMB STRIKES SUPERMAN FULL ON THE CHEST...
THERE! THAT'LL PREVENT ANY DAMAGE FROM BEING DONE TO THE STORE!
THAT BOMB MUST HAVE FINISHED SUPERMAN!
THE BOSS OUGHTA BE GLAD TO HEAR THAT!
BUT, UNKNOWN TO THE GANGSTERS, A COSTUMED FIGURE TRAILS THEM FROM A VANTAGE POINT HIGH IN THE SKY...
THEY'RE NOT RID OF ME BY A LONG SHOT!
WELL-- HOW'D YOU MAKE OUT?
SWELL!
WE NOT ONLY THREW A BOMB WHICH WRECKED THE PLACE, BUT WE ALSO WIPED OUT SUPERMAN AT THE SAME TIME!
BOYS, FOR ONCE I'M PROUD OF YOU! WAIT'LL THE OTHER GANGS HEAR THAT MY MOB RUBBED OUT THE GREAT SUPERMAN! WILL THEY ENVY ME!
WILL THEY??

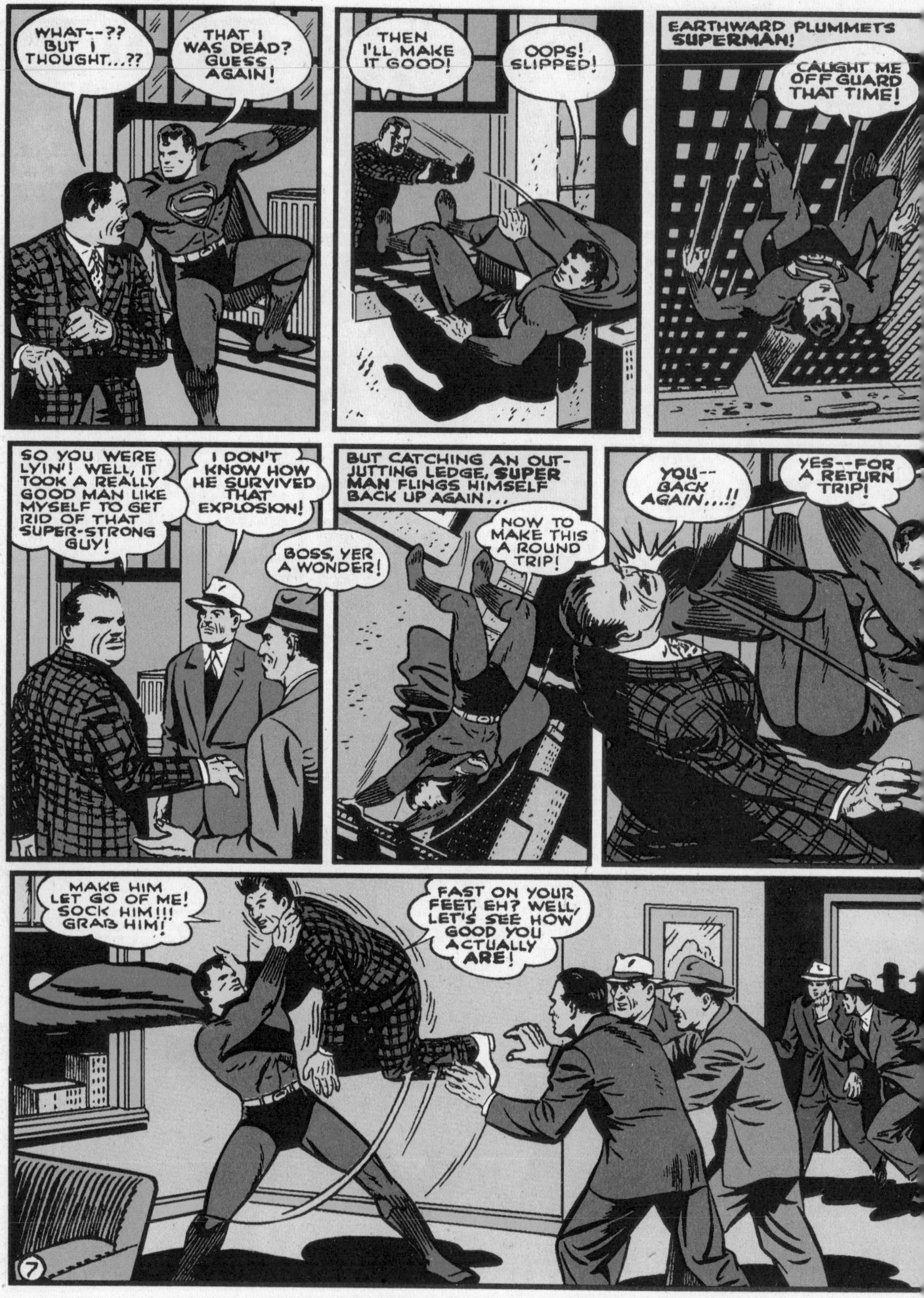
WHAT--?? BUT I THOUGHT...??
THAT I WAS DEAD? GUESS AGAIN!
THEN I'LL MAKE IT GOOD!
OOPS! SLIPPED!
EARTHWARD PLUMMETS SUPERMAN!
CAUGHT ME OFF GUARD THAT TIME!
SO YOU WERE LYIN'! WELL, IT TOOK A REALLY GOOD MAN LIKE MYSELF TO GET RID OF THAT SUPER-STRONG GUY!
I DON'T KNOW HOW HE SURVIVED THAT EXPLOSION!
BOSS, YER A WONDER!
BUT CATCHING AN OUT-JUTTING LEDGE, SUPER MAN FLINGS HIMSELF BACK UP AGAIN...
NOW TO MAKE THIS A ROUND TRIP!
YOU--BACK AGAIN...!!
YES--FOR A RETURN TRIP!
MAKE HIM LET GO OF ME! SOCK HIM!!! GRAB HIM!
FAST ON YOUR FEET, EH? WELL, LET'S SEE HOW GOOD YOU ACTUALLY ARE!
7

SUPERMAN SWINGS THE GANGLEADER'S BODY IN A LOW CIRCLE SO THAT THE THUGS ARE REPEATEDLY FORCED TO LEAP OVER THEIR CHIEF'S BODY...

THAT'S RIGHT! JUMP! JUMP!

MAKE HIM STOP!!

YOU DON'T THINK WE'RE ENJOYING THIS!

THIS IS YOUR LAST WARNING! IF YOU DON'T CUT OUT YOUR RACKETEERING, MY NEXT ENCOUNTER WITH YOU WILL BE THE LAST!

P-P-PUT M-ME D-D-DOWN!!!

IF MY FRIENDLY LITTLE WARNING DOESN'T WORK, I'LL HAVE TO RESORT TO STRONGER TACTICS!

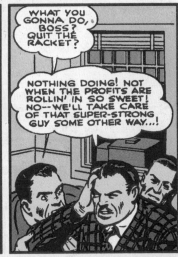

WHAT YOU GONNA DO, BOSS? QUIT THE RACKET?

NOTHING DOING! NOT WHEN THE PROFITS ARE ROLLIN' IN SO SWEET! NO-- WE'LL TAKE CARE OF THAT SUPER-STRONG GUY SOME OTHER WAY...!

NEXT DAY... AS THE MORNING EDITION ROLLS OFF THE THUNDERING PRESSES...

THINK THAT ARTICLE OUGHT TO DO IT, LOIS?

IT CERTAINLY SHOULD! I'M GLAD YOU REMEMBERED TO SIGN IT WITH BOTH OUR NAMES.

AND WHEN IT HITS THE STREETS...

WOW! WHAT A RACKET!

SO THAT'S WHY THE FOOD BUDGET'S BEEN STRAINED!

I'M GLAD THOSE CROOKS ARE BEING EXPOSED! I HOPE THEY GET THE JAIL TERMS THEY DESERVE!

OH-OH! THIS IS GOING TO RAISE THE ROOF AT HEAD-QUARTERS!

CLARK HAS A VISIT FROM VERNON HALE, ONE OF THE CITY'S MOST AGGRESSIVE COUNCILMEN...

THIS ARTICLE OF YOURS IS TERRIFIC, KENT! IF YOU'LL AC-COMPANY ME IN MY CAR TO THE POLICE COMMISSIONER'S OFFICE, I'LL BACK UP YOUR CHARGES AND DEMAND QUICK ACTION!

I'LL BE GLAD TO GO WITH YOU!

WAIT FOR ME! I'M GOING, TOO!!

8

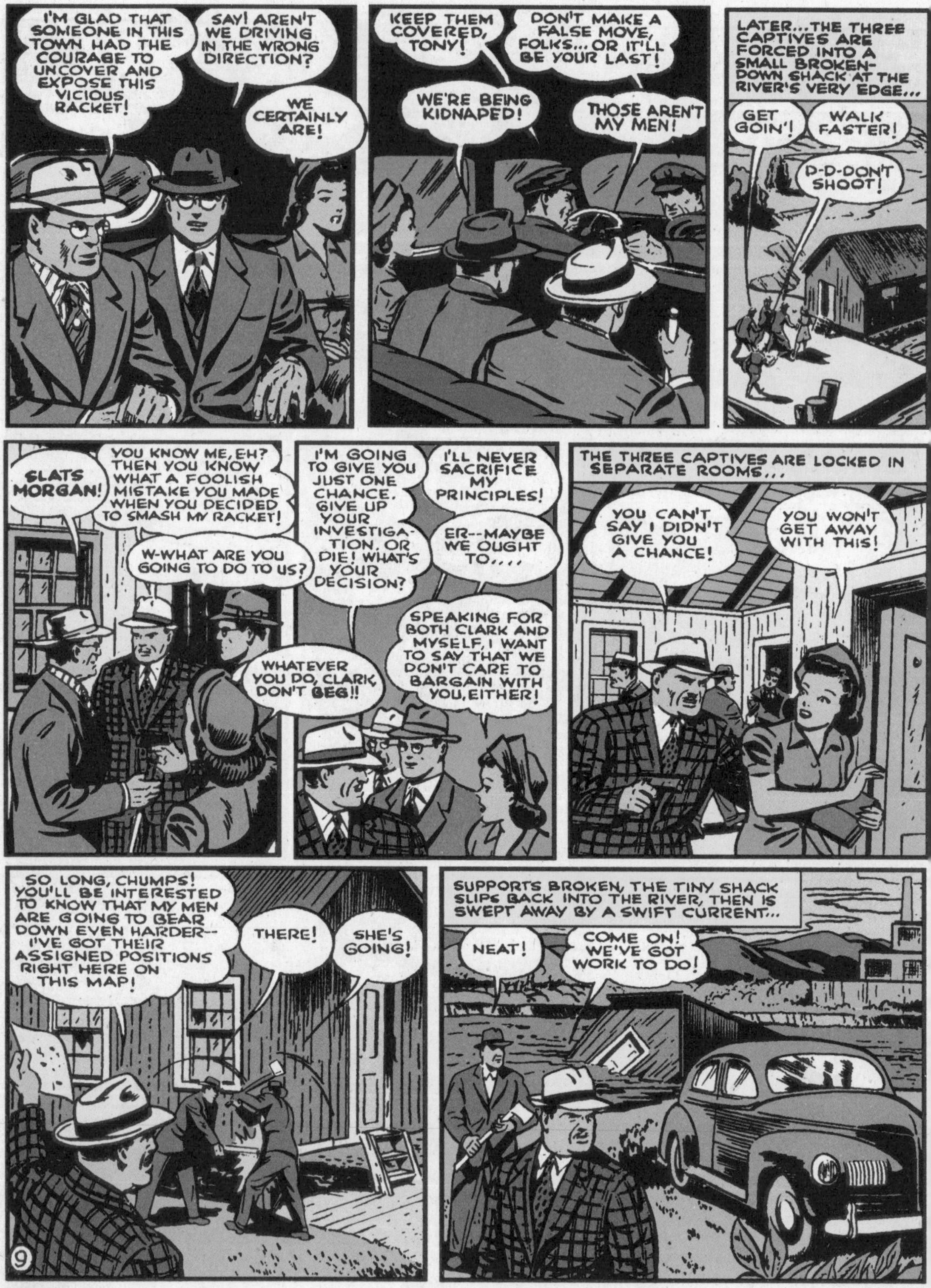
I'M GLAD THAT SOMEONE IN THIS TOWN HAD THE COURAGE TO UNCOVER AND EXPOSE THIS VICIOUS RACKET!
SAY! AREN'T WE DRIVING IN THE WRONG DIRECTION?
WE CERTAINLY ARE!
KEEP THEM COVERED, TONY!
DON'T MAKE A FALSE MOVE, FOLKS... OR IT'LL BE YOUR LAST!
WE'RE BEING KIDNAPED!
THOSE AREN'T MY MEN!
LATER... THE THREE CAPTIVES ARE FORCED INTO A SMALL BROKEN-DOWN SHACK AT THE RIVER'S VERY EDGE...
GET GOIN'!
WALK FASTER!
D-D-DON'T SHOOT!
SLATS MORGAN!
YOU KNOW ME, EH? THEN YOU KNOW WHAT A FOOLISH MISTAKE YOU MADE WHEN YOU DECIDED TO SMASH MY RACKET!
W-WHAT ARE YOU GOING TO DO TO US?
WHATEVER YOU DO, CLARK, DON'T BEG!!
I'M GOING TO GIVE YOU JUST ONE CHANCE. GIVE UP YOUR INVESTIGATION, OR DIE! WHAT'S YOUR DECISION?
I'LL NEVER SACRIFICE MY PRINCIPLES!
ER--MAYBE WE OUGHT TO....
SPEAKING FOR BOTH CLARK AND MYSELF, I WANT TO SAY THAT WE DON'T CARE TO BARGAIN WITH YOU, EITHER!
THE THREE CAPTIVES ARE LOCKED IN SEPARATE ROOMS...
YOU CAN'T SAY I DIDN'T GIVE YOU A CHANCE!
YOU WON'T GET AWAY WITH THIS!
SO LONG, CHUMPS! YOU'LL BE INTERESTED TO KNOW THAT MY MEN ARE GOING TO BEAR DOWN EVEN HARDER-- I'VE GOT THEIR ASSIGNED POSITIONS RIGHT HERE ON THIS MAP!
THERE!
SHE'S GOING!
9
SUPPORTS BROKEN, THE TINY SHACK SLIPS BACK INTO THE RIVER, THEN IS SWEPT AWAY BY A SWIFT CURRENT...
NEAT!
COME ON! WE'VE GOT WORK TO DO!

AS THE SHACK FLOATS DOWN THE RIVER, BUFFETED BY THE ANGRY CURRENT, KENT SWITCHES TO HIS IDENTITY AS SUPERMAN....

LOIS-- UNCONSCIOUS...

GOT HER! BUT I'VE GOT TO FIND HALE!

CAN'T LOCATE HIM--BETTER GET LOIS TO LAND...

YOU SAVED ME FROM THE RIVER! WAIT!

NO! THERE'S WORK TO BE DONE!

SWIFTLY, SUPERMAN OVER- TAKES MORGAN'S CAR... RIPS OFF THE HOOD...

HEY! STOP THAT!!

I KNOW YOU WON'T LISTEN TO MY REQUEST TO SLOW DOWN! SO...

--OUT WITH THE MOTOR!!

REMEMBER WHAT I TOLD YOU WHEN I LAST SAW YOU?

NO-- DON'T KILL ME! NO!!!

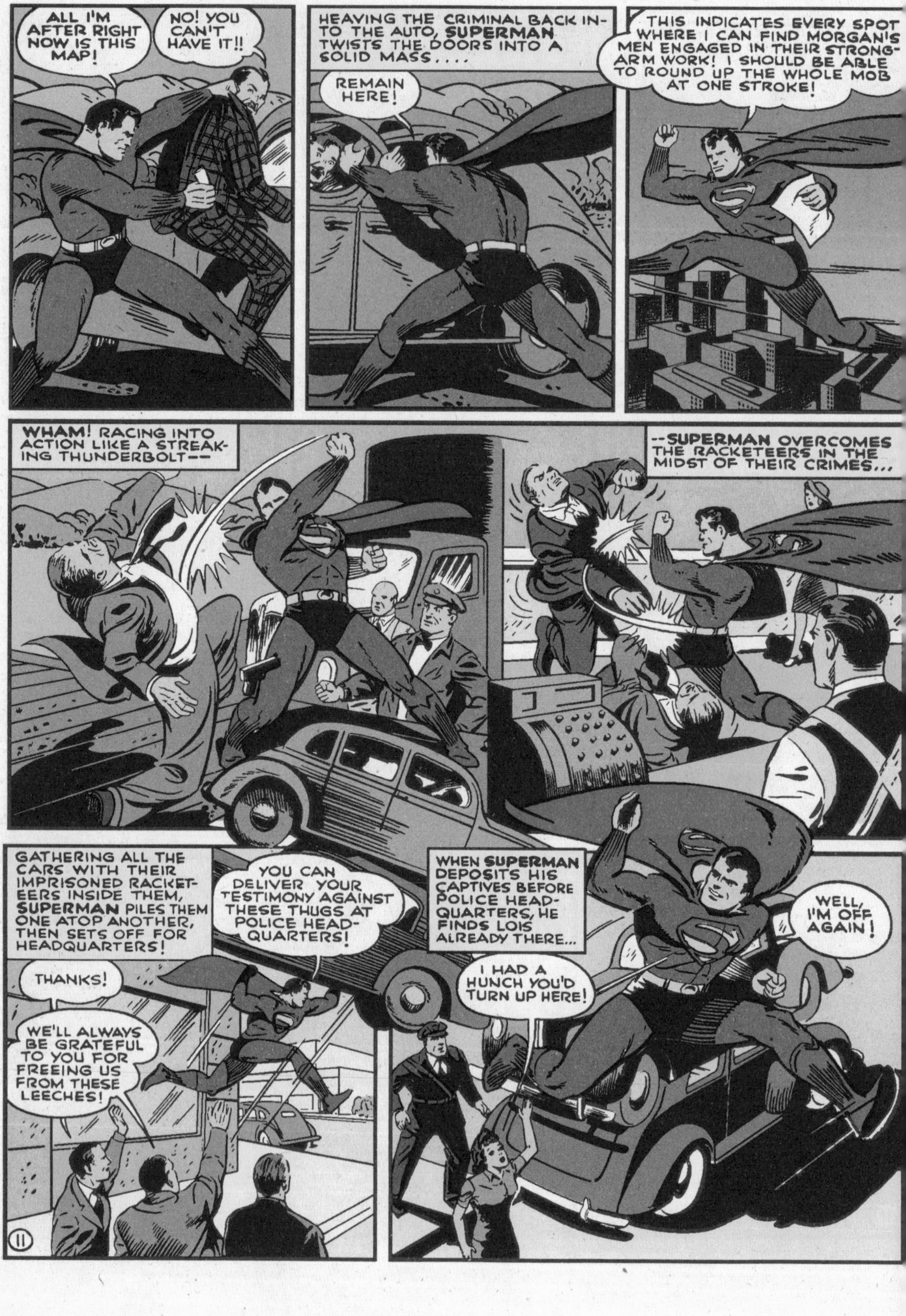
ALL I'M AFTER RIGHT NOW IS THIS MAP!
NO! YOU CAN'T HAVE IT!!
HEAVING THE CRIMINAL BACK IN-TO THE AUTO, SUPERMAN TWISTS THE DOORS INTO A SOLID MASS....
REMAIN HERE!
THIS INDICATES EVERY SPOT WHERE I CAN FIND MORGAN'S MEN ENGAGED IN THEIR STRONG-ARM WORK! I SHOULD BE ABLE TO ROUND UP THE WHOLE MOB AT ONE STROKE!
WHAM! RACING INTO ACTION LIKE A STREAK-ING THUNDERBOLT--
--SUPERMAN OVERCOMES THE RACKETEERS IN THE MIDST OF THEIR CRIMES...
GATHERING ALL THE CARS WITH THEIR IMPRISONED RACKET-EERS INSIDE THEM, SUPERMAN PILES THEM ONE ATOP ANOTHER, THEN SETS OFF FOR HEADQUARTERS!
YOU CAN DELIVER YOUR TESTIMONY AGAINST THESE THUGS AT POLICE HEAD-QUARTERS!
THANKS!
WE'LL ALWAYS BE GRATEFUL TO YOU FOR FREEING US FROM THESE LEECHES!
11
WHEN SUPERMAN DEPOSITS HIS CAPTIVES BEFORE POLICE HEAD-QUARTERS, HE FINDS LOIS ALREADY THERE...
I HAD A HUNCH YOU'D TURN UP HERE!
WELL, I'M OFF AGAIN!

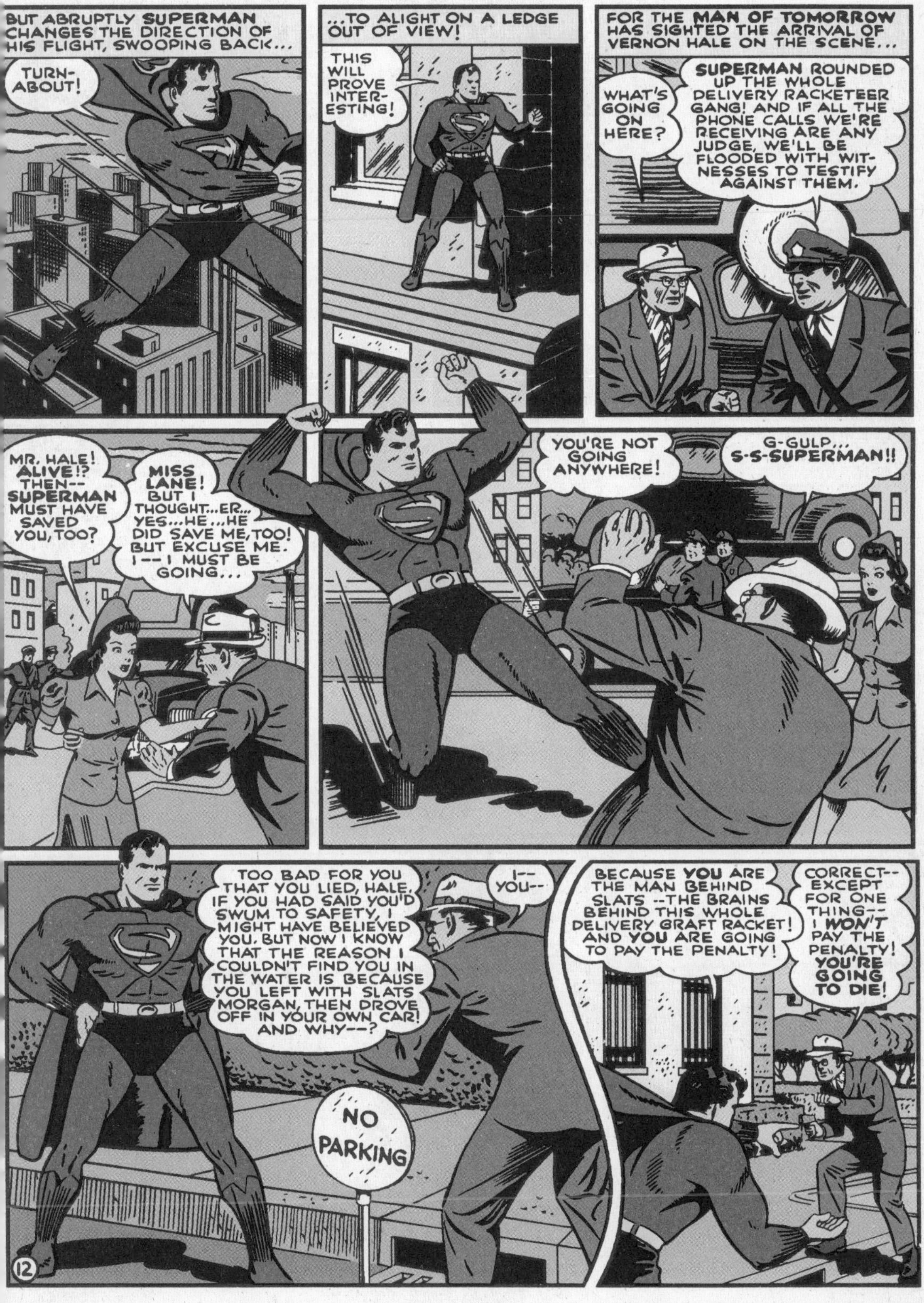
BUT ABRUPTLY SUPERMAN CHANGES THE DIRECTION OF HIS FLIGHT, SWOOPING BACK...
TURN-ABOUT!
...TO ALIGHT ON A LEDGE OUT OF VIEW!
THIS WILL PROVE INTER-ESTING!
FOR THE MAN OF TOMORROW HAS SIGHTED THE ARRIVAL OF VERNON HALE ON THE SCENE...
WHAT'S GOING ON HERE?
SUPERMAN ROUNDED UP THE WHOLE DELIVERY RACKETEER GANG! AND IF ALL THE PHONE CALLS WE'RE RECEIVING ARE ANY JUDGE, WE'LL BE FLOODED WITH WIT-NESSES TO TESTIFY AGAINST THEM.
MR. HALE! ALIVE!? THEN--SUPERMAN MUST HAVE SAVED YOU, TOO?
MISS LANE! BUT I THOUGHT...ER... YES...HE...HE DID SAVE ME, TOO! BUT EXCUSE ME. I--I MUST BE GOING...
YOU'RE NOT GOING ANYWHERE!
G-GULP... S-S-SUPERMAN!!
TOO BAD FOR YOU THAT YOU LIED, HALE. IF YOU HAD SAID YOU'D SWUM TO SAFETY, I MIGHT HAVE BELIEVED YOU. BUT NOW I KNOW THAT THE REASON I COULDN'T FIND YOU IN THE WATER IS BECAUSE YOU LEFT WITH SLATS MORGAN, THEN DROVE OFF IN YOUR OWN CAR! AND WHY--?
I--YOU--
NO PARKING
12
BECAUSE YOU ARE THE MAN BEHIND SLATS --THE BRAINS BEHIND THIS WHOLE DELIVERY GRAFT RACKET! AND YOU ARE GOING TO PAY THE PENALTY!
CORRECT--EXCEPT FOR ONE THING--I WON'T PAY THE PENALTY! YOU'RE GOING TO DIE!

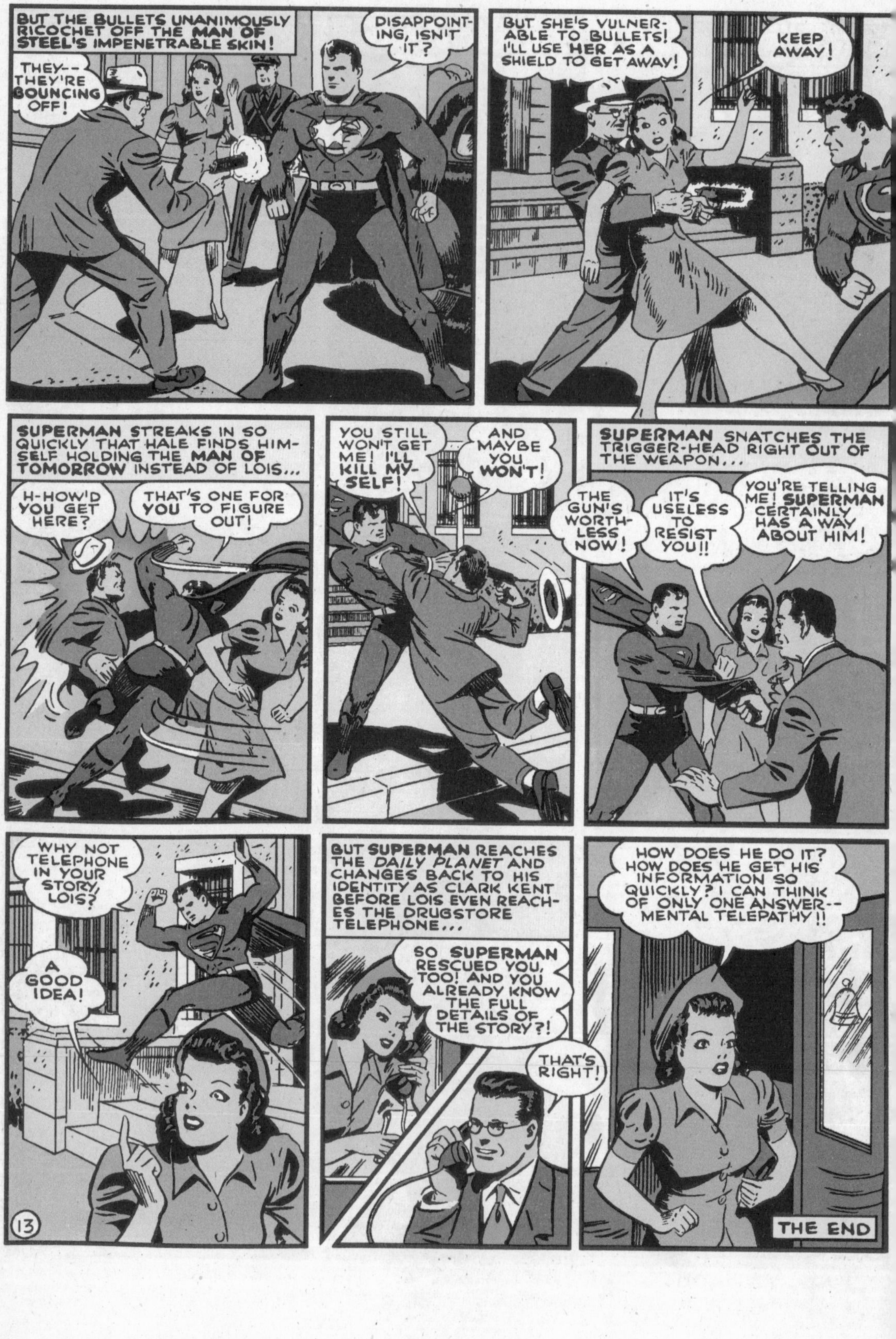
BUT THE BULLETS UNANIMOUSLY RICOCHET OFF THE MAN OF STEEL'S IMPENETRABLE SKIN!
THEY-- THEY'RE BOUNCING OFF!
DISAPPOINTING, ISN'T IT?
BUT SHE'S VULNERABLE TO BULLETS! I'LL USE HER AS A SHIELD TO GET AWAY!
KEEP AWAY!
SUPERMAN STREAKS IN SO QUICKLY THAT HALE FINDS HIMSELF HOLDING THE MAN OF TOMORROW INSTEAD OF LOIS...
H-HOW'D YOU GET HERE?
THAT'S ONE FOR YOU TO FIGURE OUT!
YOU STILL WON'T GET ME! I'LL KILL MYSELF!
AND MAYBE YOU WON'T!
SUPERMAN SNATCHES THE TRIGGER-HEAD RIGHT OUT OF THE WEAPON...
THE GUN'S WORTHLESS NOW!
IT'S USELESS TO RESIST YOU!!
YOU'RE TELLING ME! SUPERMAN CERTAINLY HAS A WAY ABOUT HIM!
WHY NOT TELEPHONE IN YOUR STORY, LOIS?
A GOOD IDEA!
13
BUT SUPERMAN REACHES THE DAILY PLANET AND CHANGES BACK TO HIS IDENTITY AS CLARK KENT BEFORE LOIS EVEN REACHES THE DRUGSTORE TELEPHONE...
SO SUPERMAN RESCUED YOU, TOO! AND YOU ALREADY KNOW THE FULL DETAILS OF THE STORY?!
THAT'S RIGHT!
HOW DOES HE DO IT? HOW DOES HE GET HIS INFORMATION SO QUICKLY? I CAN THINK OF ONLY ONE ANSWER-- MENTAL TELEPATHY!!
THE END

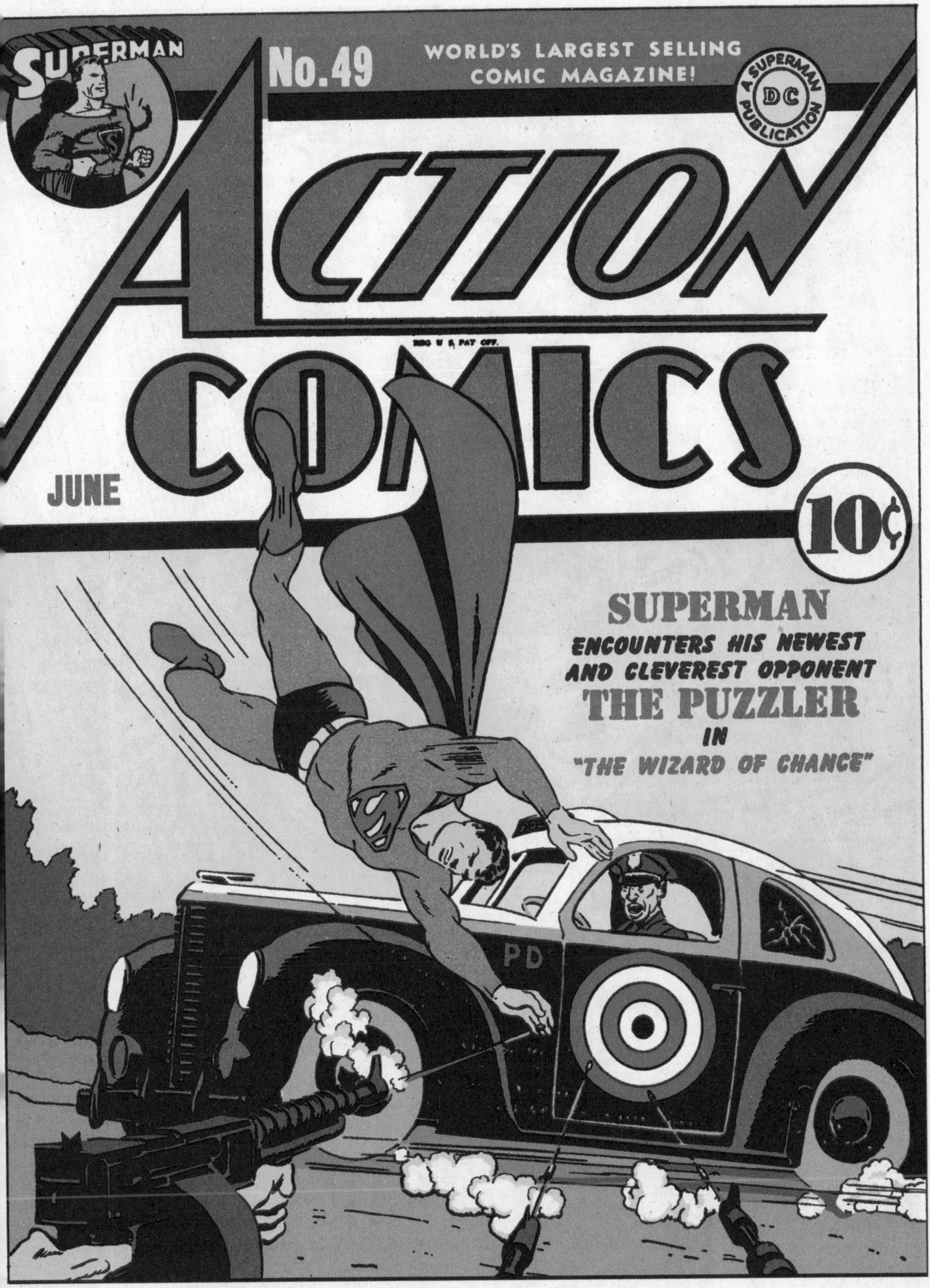
SUPERMAN
No.49
WORLD'S LARGEST SELLING COMIC MAGAZINE!
A SUPERMAN DC PUBLICATION
ACTION COMICS
REG. U. S. PAT. OFF.
JUNE
10¢
SUPERMAN
ENCOUNTERS HIS NEWEST AND CLEVEREST OPPONENT
THE PUZZLER
IN
"THE WIZARD OF CHANCE"
PD

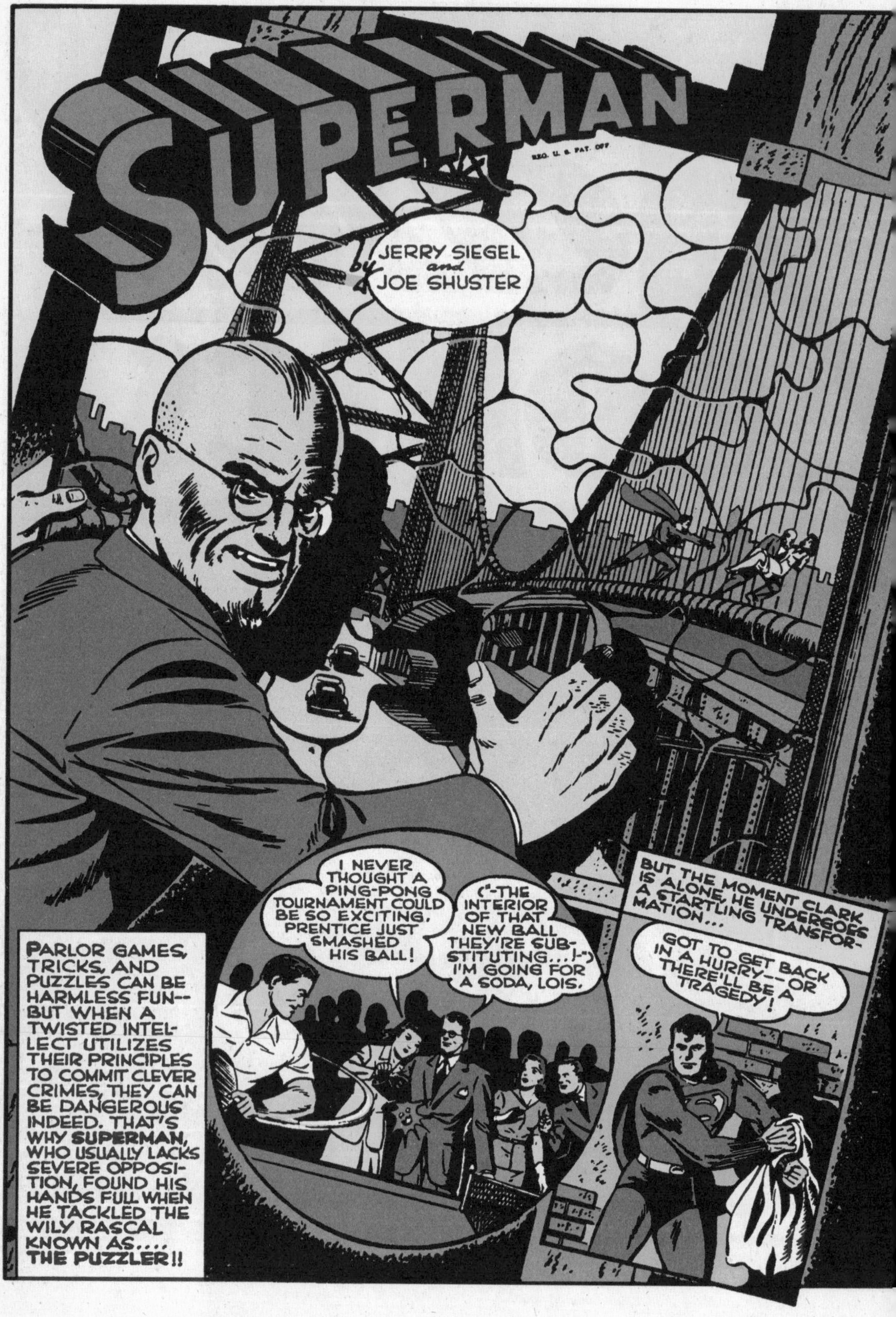
SUPERMAN
REG. U. S. PAT. OFF.
by JERRY SIEGEL and JOE SHUSTER
PARLOR GAMES, TRICKS, AND PUZZLES CAN BE HARMLESS FUN-- BUT WHEN A TWISTED INTELLECT UTILIZES THEIR PRINCIPLES TO COMMIT CLEVER CRIMES, THEY CAN BE DANGEROUS INDEED. THAT'S WHY SUPERMAN, WHO USUALLY LACKS SEVERE OPPOSITION, FOUND HIS HANDS FULL WHEN HE TACKLED THE WILY RASCAL KNOWN AS.... THE PUZZLER!!
I NEVER THOUGHT A PING-PONG TOURNAMENT COULD BE SO EXCITING. PRENTICE JUST SMASHED HIS BALL!
("-THE INTERIOR OF THAT NEW BALL THEY'RE SUBSTITUTING...!-") I'M GOING FOR A SODA, LOIS.
BUT THE MOMENT CLARK IS ALONE, HE UNDERGOES A STARTLING TRANSFORMATION...
GOT TO GET BACK IN A HURRY--OR THERE'LL BE A TRAGEDY!

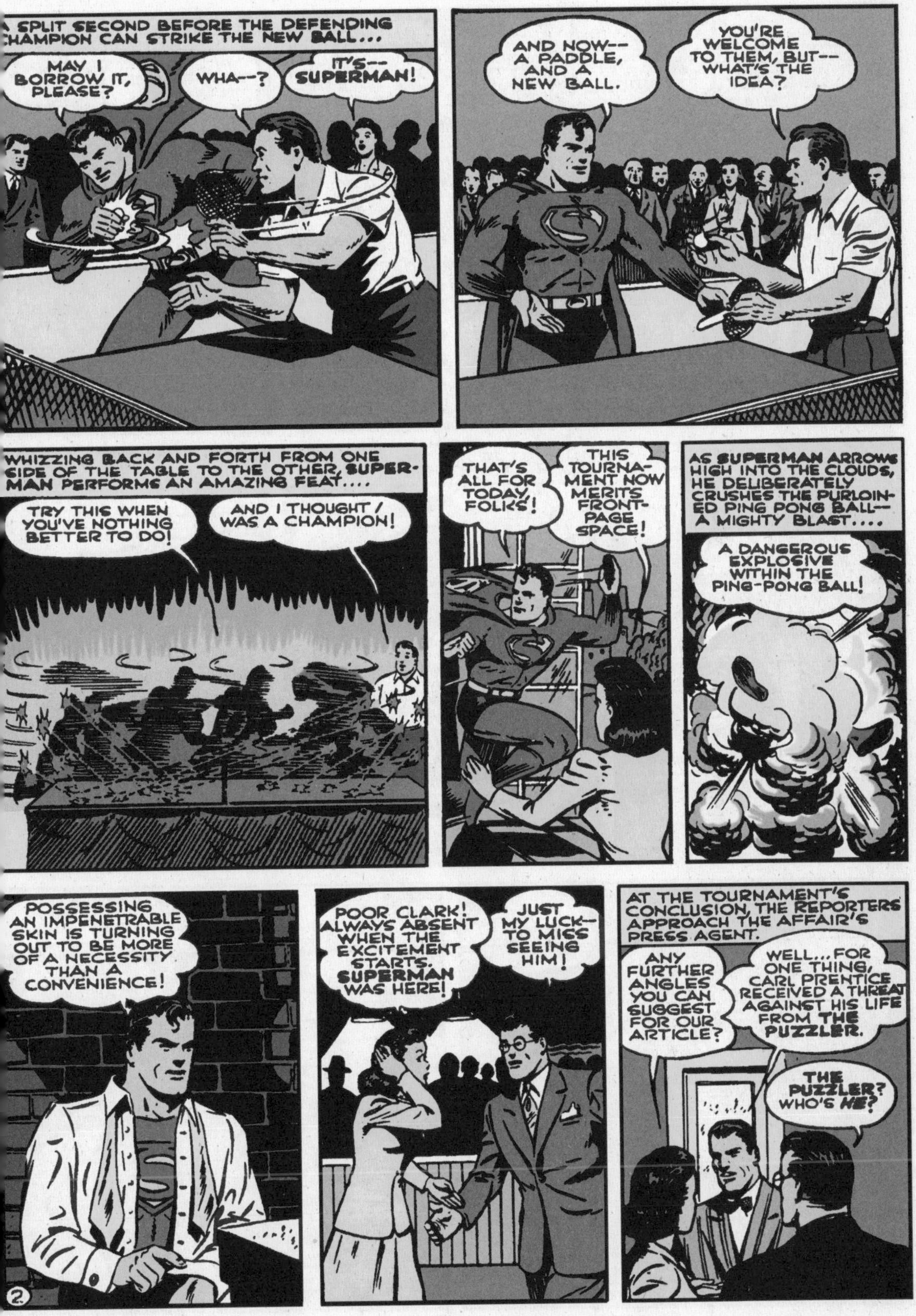

A SPLIT SECOND BEFORE THE DEFENDING CHAMPION CAN STRIKE THE NEW BALL...
MAY I BORROW IT, PLEASE?
WHA--?
IT'S-- SUPERMAN!
AND NOW-- A PADDLE, AND A NEW BALL.
YOU'RE WELCOME TO THEM, BUT-- WHAT'S THE IDEA?
WHIZZING BACK AND FORTH FROM ONE SIDE OF THE TABLE TO THE OTHER, SUPERMAN PERFORMS AN AMAZING FEAT....
TRY THIS WHEN YOU'VE NOTHING BETTER TO DO!
AND I THOUGHT I WAS A CHAMPION!
THAT'S ALL FOR TODAY, FOLKS!
THIS TOURNAMENT NOW MERITS FRONT-PAGE SPACE!
AS SUPERMAN ARROWS HIGH INTO THE CLOUDS, HE DELIBERATELY CRUSHES THE PURLOINED PING PONG BALL-- A MIGHTY BLAST....
A DANGEROUS EXPLOSIVE WITHIN THE PING-PONG BALL!
POSSESSING AN IMPENETRABLE SKIN IS TURNING OUT TO BE MORE OF A NECESSITY THAN A CONVENIENCE!
2
POOR CLARK! ALWAYS ABSENT WHEN THE EXCITEMENT STARTS. SUPERMAN WAS HERE!
JUST MY LUCK-- TO MISS SEEING HIM!
AT THE TOURNAMENT'S CONCLUSION, THE REPORTERS APPROACH THE AFFAIR'S PRESS AGENT.
ANY FURTHER ANGLES YOU CAN SUGGEST FOR OUR ARTICLE?
WELL... FOR ONE THING, CARL PRENTICE RECEIVED A THREAT AGAINST HIS LIFE FROM THE PUZZLER.
THE PUZZLER? WHO'S HE?

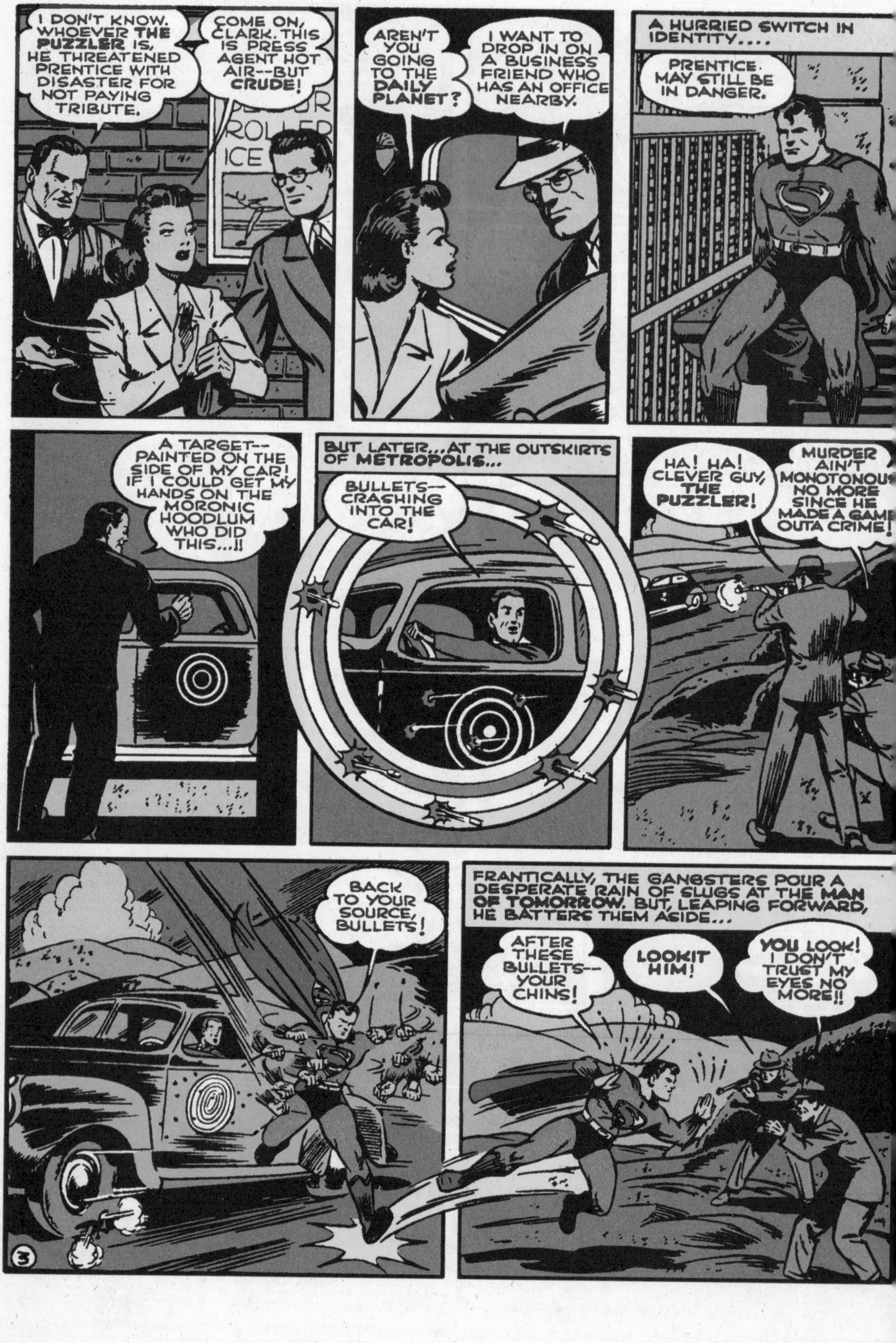

I DON'T KNOW. WHOEVER THE PUZZLER IS, HE THREATENED PRENTICE WITH DISASTER FOR NOT PAYING TRIBUTE.
COME ON, CLARK. THIS IS PRESS AGENT HOT AIR--BUT CRUDE!
ROLLER
ICE
AREN'T YOU GOING TO THE DAILY PLANET?
I WANT TO DROP IN ON A BUSINESS FRIEND WHO HAS AN OFFICE NEARBY.
A HURRIED SWITCH IN IDENTITY....
PRENTICE MAY STILL BE IN DANGER.
A TARGET--PAINTED ON THE SIDE OF MY CAR! IF I COULD GET MY HANDS ON THE MORONIC HOODLUM WHO DID THIS...!!
BUT LATER...AT THE OUTSKIRTS OF METROPOLIS...
BULLETS--CRASHING INTO THE CAR!
HA! HA! CLEVER GUY, THE PUZZLER!
MURDER AIN'T MONOTONOUS NO MORE SINCE HE MADE A GAME OUTA CRIME!
BACK TO YOUR SOURCE, BULLETS!
3
FRANTICALLY, THE GANGSTERS POUR A DESPERATE RAIN OF SLUGS AT THE MAN OF TOMORROW. BUT, LEAPING FORWARD, HE BATTERS THEM ASIDE...
AFTER THESE BULLETS--YOUR CHINS!
LOOKIT HIM!
YOU LOOK! I DON'T TRUST MY EYES NO MORE!!

SORRY I'VE NO HANDCUFFS --BUT THESE OUGHT TO DO!

HEY!

YOU CAN'T DO THIS TO US! AT LEAST, I HOPE YOU CAN'T!

SWIFTLY, SUPERMAN SEARCHES THEM, AND UPON EACH THUG FINDS...

HALF OF A NAIL-PUZZLE! I SUPPOSE THAT'S THE PUZZLER'S TRADEMARK!

TRY AND FIGURE IT OUT!

I'M SAYING NOTHING!

IN WITH YOU!

C-CAREFUL!

YIPE!

TRANSPORTING THE AUTO TO A POLICE STATION, SUPERMAN SPRINGS OFF....

THANKS FOR SAVING MY LIFE!

("-NOW TO RUSH THIS YARN INTO PRINT!-")

THAT EVENING...

THIS VIOLENCE IS ENTIRELY UNNECESSARY.

THROW A BRICK THRU THE POLICE STATION WINDOW WILL YOU!

A CELL IS JUST THE THING FOR YOU!

INSIDE THIS CANE--SMALL ELECTRIC BATTERIES. SHOCKING, EH?

SWIFTLY, THE PSEUDO-VAGABOND REMOVES HIS MAKE-UP...ANNEXES KEYS FROM ONE OF THE UNCONSCIOUS JAILERS...

GEE-- THE CHIEF!

IT'S-- THE PUZZLER!

ENGROSSING GAME, EH? I CALL IT-- "COPS AND ROBBERS"!!

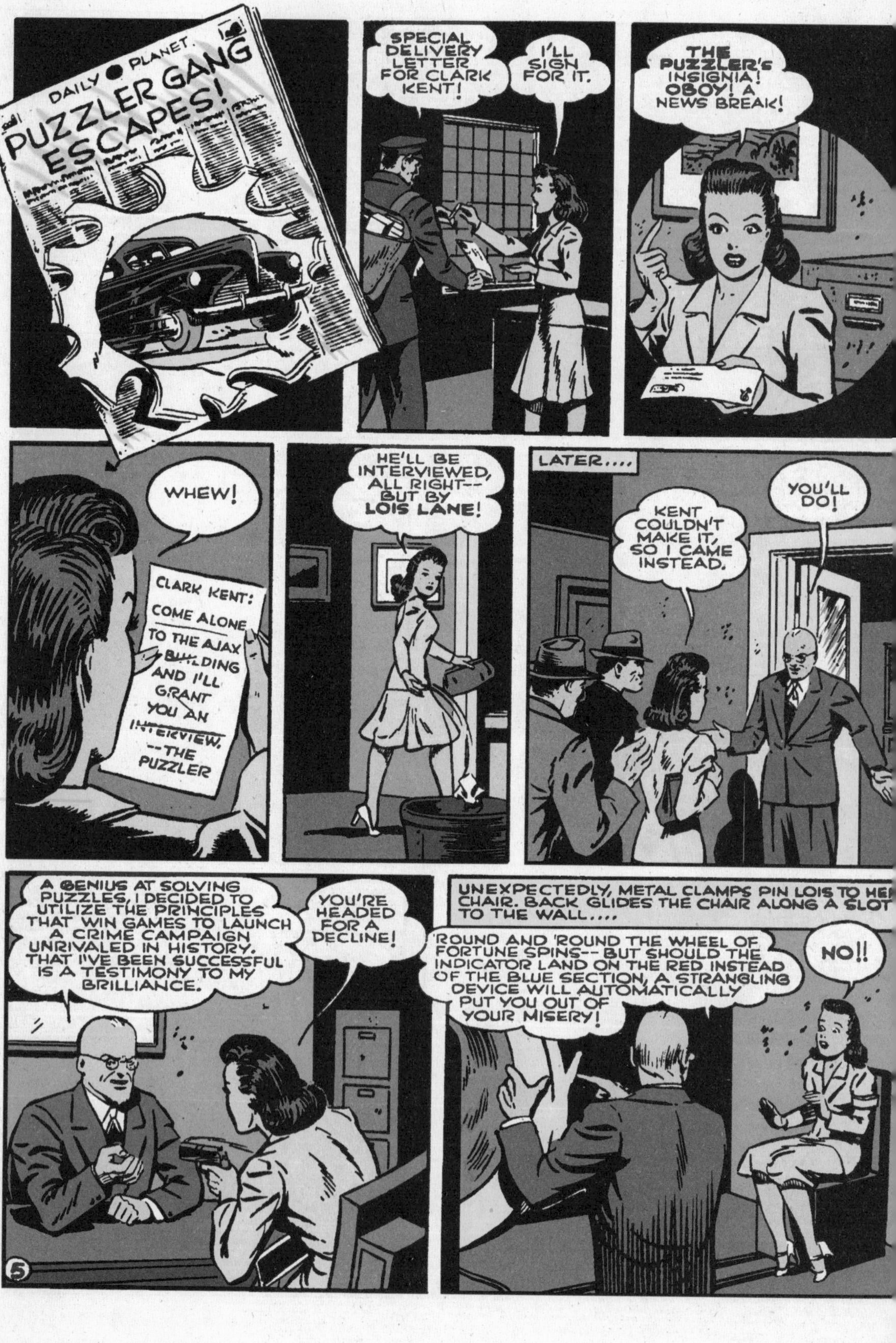
DAILY PLANET
PUZZLER GANG ESCAPES!
SPECIAL DELIVERY LETTER FOR CLARK KENT!
I'LL SIGN FOR IT.
THE PUZZLER's INSIGNIA! OBOY! A NEWS BREAK!
WHEW!
CLARK KENT: COME ALONE TO THE AJAX BUILDING AND I'LL GRANT YOU AN INTERVIEW. --THE PUZZLER
HE'LL BE INTERVIEWED, ALL RIGHT-- BUT BY LOIS LANE!
LATER....
KENT COULDN'T MAKE IT, SO I CAME INSTEAD.
YOU'LL DO!
A GENIUS AT SOLVING PUZZLES, I DECIDED TO UTILIZE THE PRINCIPLES THAT WIN GAMES TO LAUNCH A CRIME CAMPAIGN UNRIVALED IN HISTORY. THAT I'VE BEEN SUCCESSFUL IS A TESTIMONY TO MY BRILLIANCE.
YOU'RE HEADED FOR A DECLINE!
5
UNEXPECTEDLY, METAL CLAMPS PIN LOIS TO HER CHAIR. BACK GLIDES THE CHAIR ALONG A SLOT TO THE WALL....
'ROUND AND 'ROUND THE WHEEL OF FORTUNE SPINS-- BUT SHOULD THE INDICATOR LAND ON THE RED INSTEAD OF THE BLUE SECTION, A STRANGLING DEVICE WILL AUTOMATICALLY PUT YOU OUT OF YOUR MISERY!
NO!!

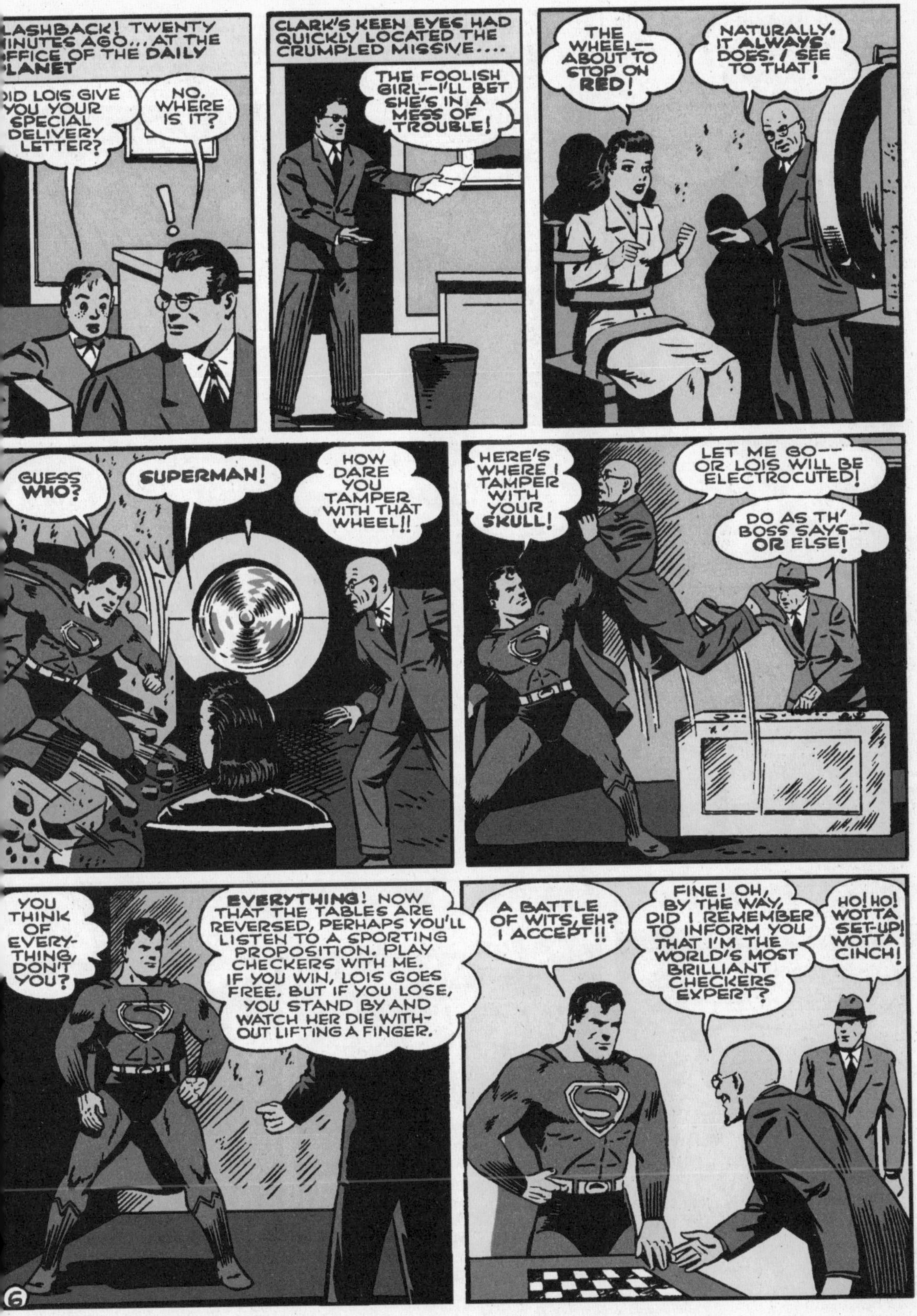

LASHBACK! TWENTY MINUTES AGO... AT THE OFFICE OF THE DAILY PLANET
DID LOIS GIVE YOU YOUR SPECIAL DELIVERY LETTER?
NO. WHERE IS IT?
!
CLARK'S KEEN EYES HAD QUICKLY LOCATED THE CRUMPLED MISSIVE....
THE FOOLISH GIRL--I'LL BET SHE'S IN A MESS OF TROUBLE!
THE WHEEL--ABOUT TO STOP ON RED!
NATURALLY. IT ALWAYS DOES. I SEE TO THAT!
GUESS WHO?
SUPERMAN!
HOW DARE YOU TAMPER WITH THAT WHEEL!!
HERE'S WHERE I TAMPER WITH YOUR SKULL!
LET ME GO--OR LOIS WILL BE ELECTROCUTED!
DO AS TH' BOSS SAYS--OR ELSE!
YOU THINK OF EVERY-THING, DON'T YOU?
EVERYTHING! NOW THAT THE TABLES ARE REVERSED, PERHAPS YOU'LL LISTEN TO A SPORTING PROPOSITION. PLAY CHECKERS WITH ME. IF YOU WIN, LOIS GOES FREE. BUT IF YOU LOSE, YOU STAND BY AND WATCH HER DIE WITH-OUT LIFTING A FINGER.
6
A BATTLE OF WITS, EH? I ACCEPT!!
FINE! OH, BY THE WAY, DID I REMEMBER TO INFORM YOU THAT I'M THE WORLD'S MOST BRILLIANT CHECKERS EXPERT?
HO! HO! WOTTA SET-UP! WOTTA CINCH!

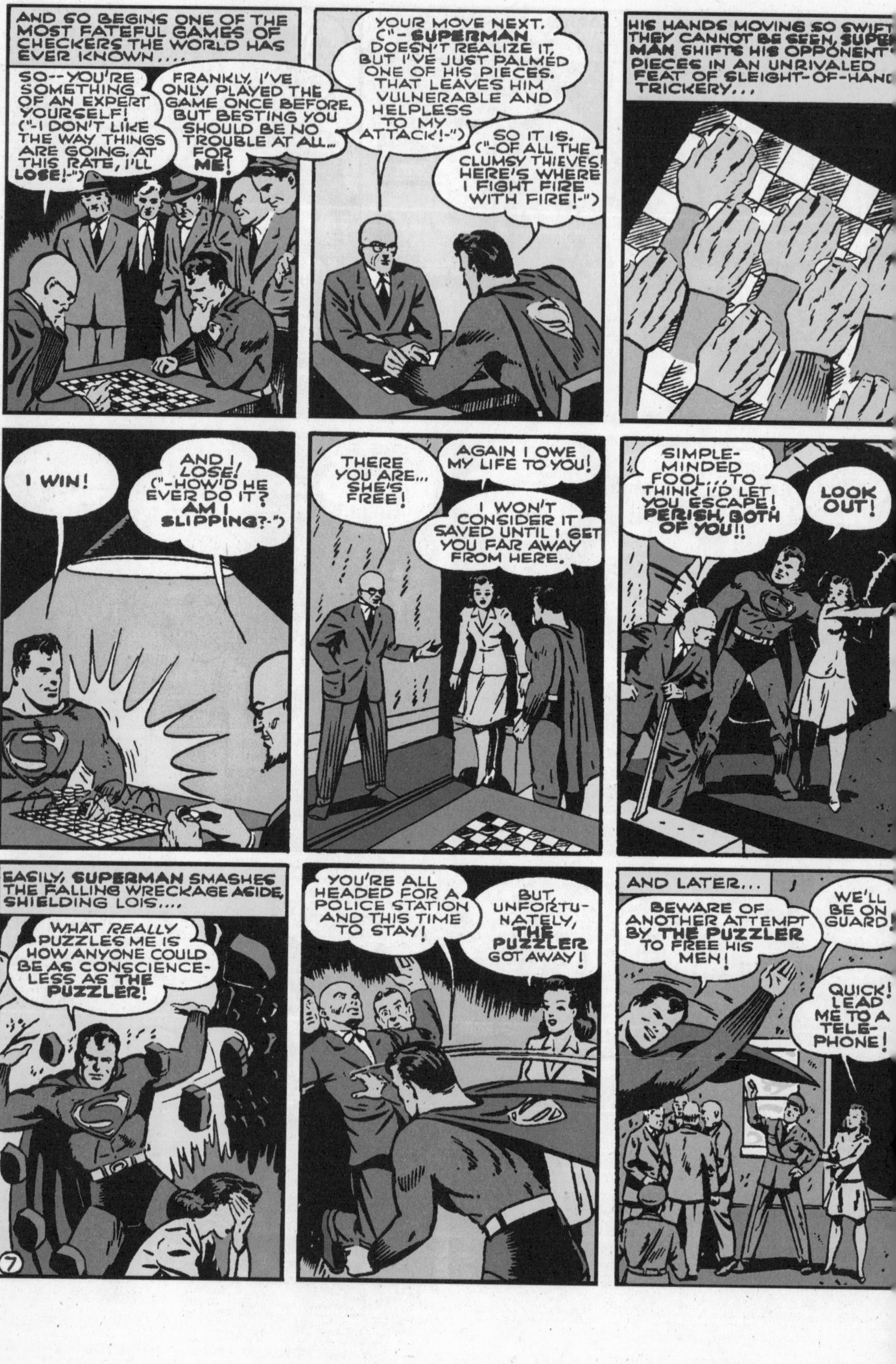

AND SO BEGINS ONE OF THE MOST FATEFUL GAMES OF CHECKERS THE WORLD HAS EVER KNOWN....
SO--YOU'RE SOMETHING OF AN EXPERT YOURSELF! ("-I DON'T LIKE THE WAY THINGS ARE GOING. AT THIS RATE, I'LL LOSE!-")
FRANKLY, I'VE ONLY PLAYED THE GAME ONCE BEFORE. BUT BESTING YOU SHOULD BE NO TROUBLE AT ALL... FOR ME!
YOUR MOVE NEXT. ("-SUPERMAN DOESN'T REALIZE IT, BUT I'VE JUST PALMED ONE OF HIS PIECES. THAT LEAVES HIM VULNERABLE AND HELPLESS TO MY ATTACK!-")
SO IT IS. ("-OF ALL THE CLUMSY THIEVES! HERE'S WHERE I FIGHT FIRE WITH FIRE!-")
HIS HANDS MOVING SO SWIFT THEY CANNOT BE SEEN, SUPE MAN SHIFTS HIS OPPONENT' PIECES IN AN UNRIVALED FEAT OF SLEIGHT-OF-HAN TRICKERY...
I WIN!
AND I LOSE! ("-HOW'D HE EVER DO IT? AM I SLIPPING?-")
THERE YOU ARE... SHE'S FREE!
AGAIN I OWE MY LIFE TO YOU!
I WON'T CONSIDER IT SAVED UNTIL I GET YOU FAR AWAY FROM HERE.
SIMPLE-MINDED FOOL... TO THINK I'D LET YOU ESCAPE! PERISH, BOTH OF YOU!!
LOOK OUT!
EASILY, SUPERMAN SMASHES THE FALLING WRECKAGE ASIDE, SHIELDING LOIS....
WHAT REALLY PUZZLES ME IS HOW ANYONE COULD BE AS CONSCIENCE-LESS AS THE PUZZLER!
7
YOU'RE ALL HEADED FOR A POLICE STATION AND THIS TIME TO STAY!
BUT, UNFORTU-NATELY, THE PUZZLER GOT AWAY!
AND LATER...
BEWARE OF ANOTHER ATTEMPT BY THE PUZZLER TO FREE HIS MEN!
WE'LL BE ON GUARD!
QUICK! LEAD ME TO A TELE-PHONE!

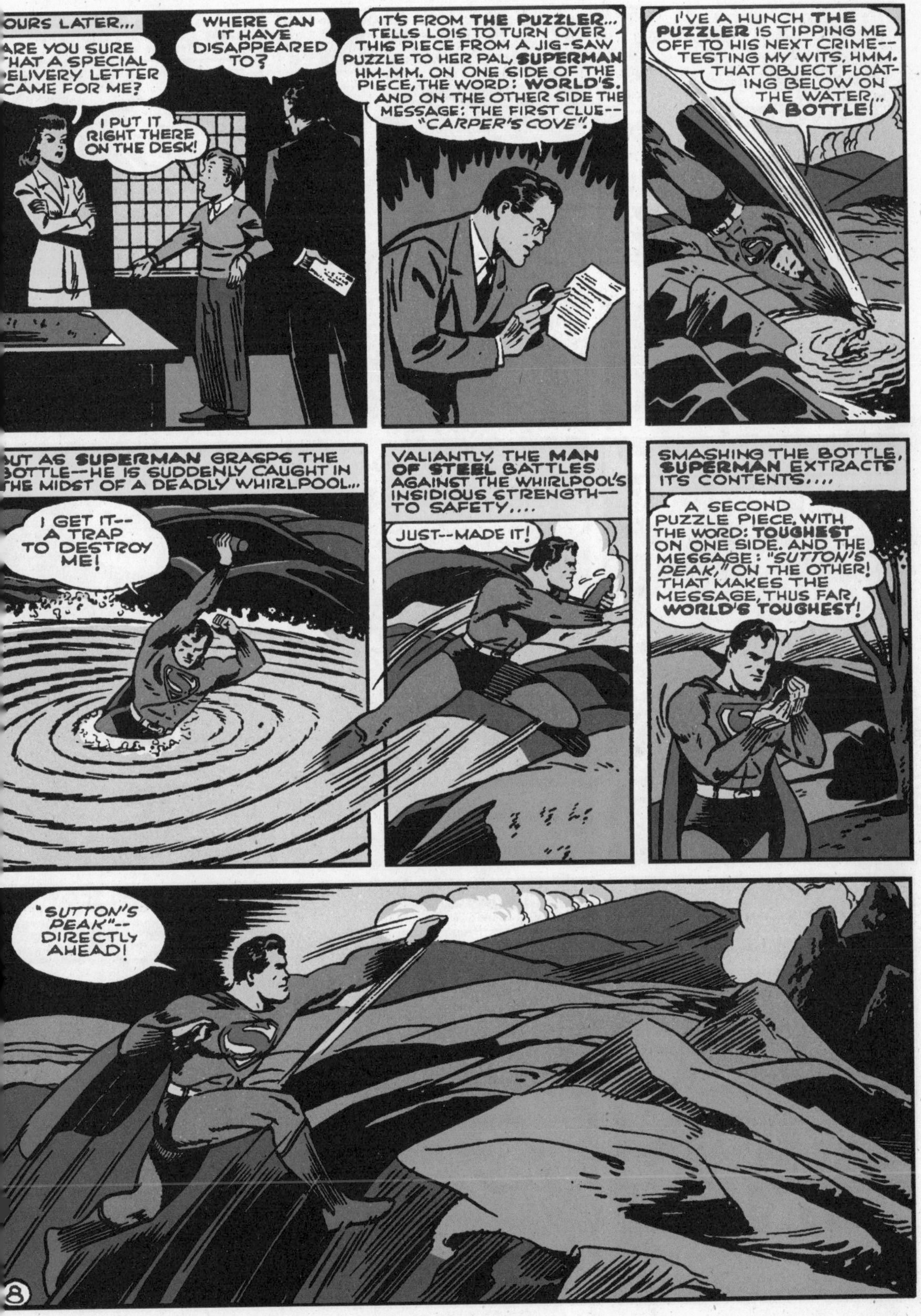

OURS LATER...
ARE YOU SURE THAT A SPECIAL DELIVERY LETTER CAME FOR ME?
I PUT IT RIGHT THERE ON THE DESK!
WHERE CAN IT HAVE DISAPPEARED TO?
IT'S FROM THE PUZZLER... TELLS LOIS TO TURN OVER THIS PIECE FROM A JIG-SAW PUZZLE TO HER PAL, SUPERMAN. HM-MM. ON ONE SIDE OF THE PIECE, THE WORD: WORLD'S. AND ON THE OTHER SIDE THE MESSAGE: THE FIRST CLUE--"CARPER'S COVE".
I'VE A HUNCH THE PUZZLER IS TIPPING ME OFF TO HIS NEXT CRIME--TESTING MY WITS. HMM. THAT OBJECT FLOATING BELOW ON THE WATER... A BOTTLE!
UT AS SUPERMAN GRASPS THE BOTTLE--HE IS SUDDENLY CAUGHT IN THE MIDST OF A DEADLY WHIRLPOOL...
I GET IT--A TRAP TO DESTROY ME!
VALIANTLY, THE MAN OF STEEL BATTLES AGAINST THE WHIRLPOOL'S INSIDIOUS STRENGTH--TO SAFETY....
JUST--MADE IT!
SMASHING THE BOTTLE, SUPERMAN EXTRACTS ITS CONTENTS....
A SECOND PUZZLE PIECE, WITH THE WORD: TOUGHEST ON ONE SIDE. AND THE MESSAGE: "SUTTON'S PEAK," ON THE OTHER! THAT MAKES THE MESSAGE, THUS FAR, WORLD'S TOUGHEST!
"SUTTON'S PEAK"--DIRECTLY AHEAD!
8

THERE'S NOTHING ABOUT. BUT WAIT! HIGH UP IN THE SKY-- A FLOATING BALLOON-- WITH A PUZZLE PIECE ATTACHED!!

SKYWARD HURTLES **SUPERMAN** BUT AS HE TOUCHES THE PUZZLE PIECE--THE BALLOON EXPLODES AND A DARK VAPOR ENGULFS HIM....

POISON GAS!

EARTHWARD PLUMMETS TH MAN OF TOMORROW, DAZED BY THE GAS...

FALLING-- FALLING-- A HOUSE BELOW-- GOT TO-- PULL OUT-- OF THIS...

THE SWIFT DESCENT CLEARS HIS MIND!

MISSED IT--BY INCHES!

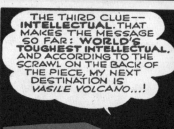

THE THIRD CLUE-- INTELLECTUAL. THAT MAKES THE MESSAGE SO FAR: WORLD'S TOUGHEST INTELLECTUAL AND ACCORDING TO THE SCRAWL ON THE BACK OF THE PIECE, MY NEXT DESTINATION IS VASILE VOLCANO...!

INTO THE CRATER OF THE DANGEROUS VOLCANO HURTLES **SUPERMAN**..

A CYLINDER ON A LEDGE BELOW...

THE MOMENT HE TOUCHES THE CYLINDER, A TRICK ARRANGE- MENT CAUSES AN EXPLOSION THAT SENDS HOT LAVA STREAM- ING TOWARD THE **MAN OF TOMORROW**....

⑨

THE FORCE OF THE EXPLOSION FLINGS **SUPERMAN** SKYWARD --UNHARMED...!

THE WORD: **GAME**-- "WORLD'S TOUGHEST INTELLECTUAL GAME!"

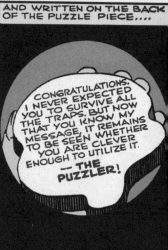

AND WRITTEN ON THE BACK OF THE PUZZLE PIECE....

CONGRATULATIONS. I NEVER EXPECTED YOU TO SURVIVE ALL THE TRAPS. BUT NOW THAT YOU KNOW MY MESSAGE, IT REMAINS TO BE SEEN WHETHER YOU ARE CLEVER ENOUGH TO UTILIZE IT. -- THE PUZZLER!

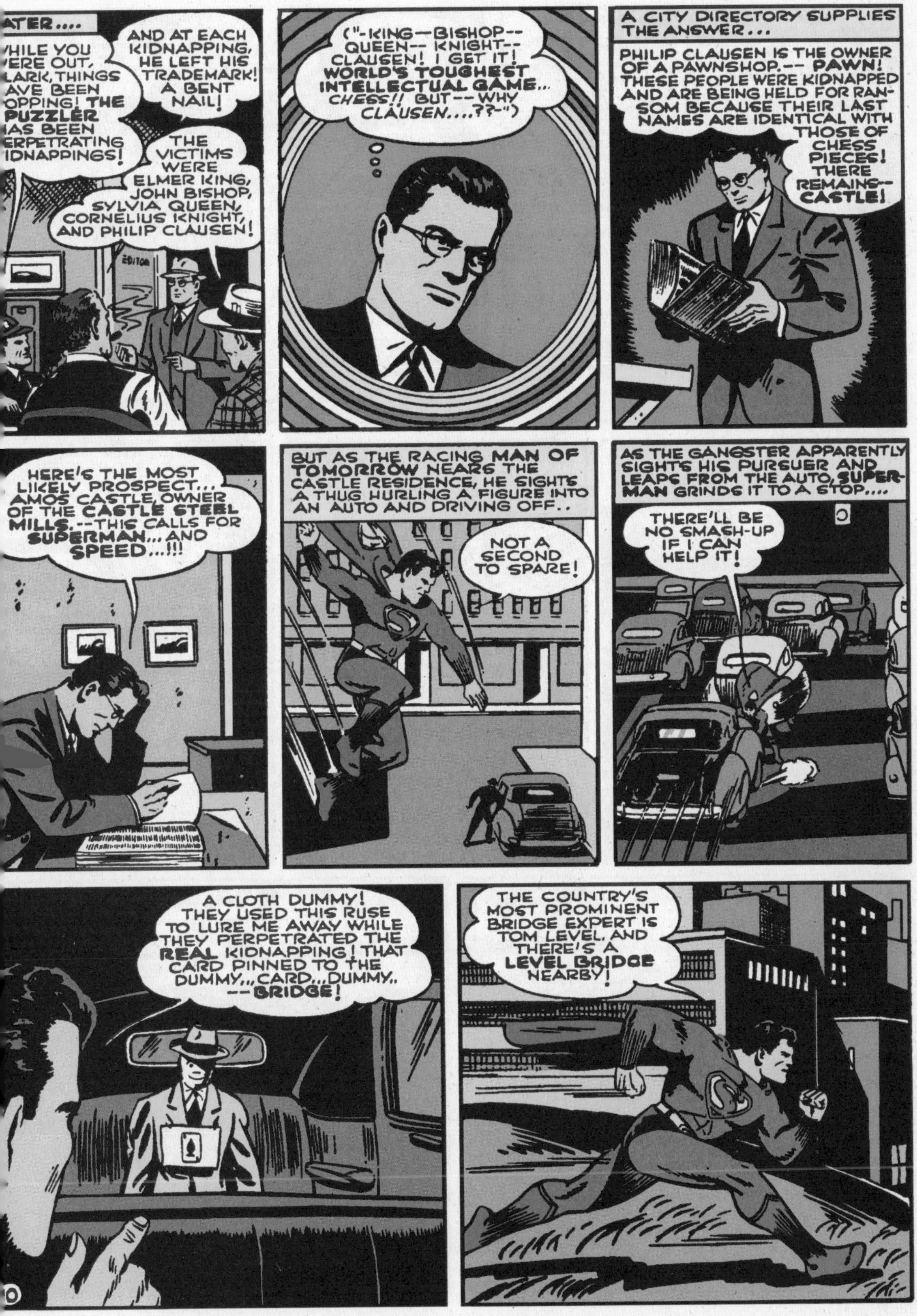
ATER....
HILE YOU ERE OUT, LARK, THINGS AVE BEEN OPPING! THE PUZZLER HAS BEEN ERPETRATING IDNAPPINGS!
AND AT EACH KIDNAPPING, HE LEFT HIS TRADEMARK! A BENT NAIL!
THE VICTIMS WERE ELMER KING, JOHN BISHOP, SYLVIA QUEEN, CORNELIUS KNIGHT, AND PHILIP CLAUSEN!
EDITOR
("-KING—BISHOP-- QUEEN-- KNIGHT-- CLAUSEN! I GET IT! WORLD'S TOUGHEST INTELLECTUAL GAME... CHESS!! BUT--WHY CLAUSEN....??-")
A CITY DIRECTORY SUPPLIES THE ANSWER...
PHILIP CLAUSEN IS THE OWNER OF A PAWNSHOP.-- PAWN! THESE PEOPLE WERE KIDNAPPED AND ARE BEING HELD FOR RANSOM BECAUSE THEIR LAST NAMES ARE IDENTICAL WITH THOSE OF CHESS PIECES! THERE REMAINS-- CASTLE!
HERE'S THE MOST LIKELY PROSPECT... AMOS CASTLE, OWNER OF THE CASTLE STEEL MILLS.--THIS CALLS FOR SUPERMAN... AND SPEED...!!!
BUT AS THE RACING MAN OF TOMORROW NEARS THE CASTLE RESIDENCE, HE SIGHTS A THUG HURLING A FIGURE INTO AN AUTO AND DRIVING OFF..
NOT A SECOND TO SPARE!
AS THE GANGSTER APPARENTLY SIGHTS HIS PURSUER AND LEAPS FROM THE AUTO, SUPERMAN GRINDS IT TO A STOP....
THERE'LL BE NO SMASH-UP IF I CAN HELP IT!
A CLOTH DUMMY! THEY USED THIS RUSE TO LURE ME AWAY WHILE THEY PERPETRATED THE REAL KIDNAPPING! THAT CARD PINNED TO THE DUMMY... CARD... DUMMY.. --BRIDGE!
THE COUNTRY'S MOST PROMINENT BRIDGE EXPERT IS TOM LEVEL, AND THERE'S A LEVEL BRIDGE NEARBY!

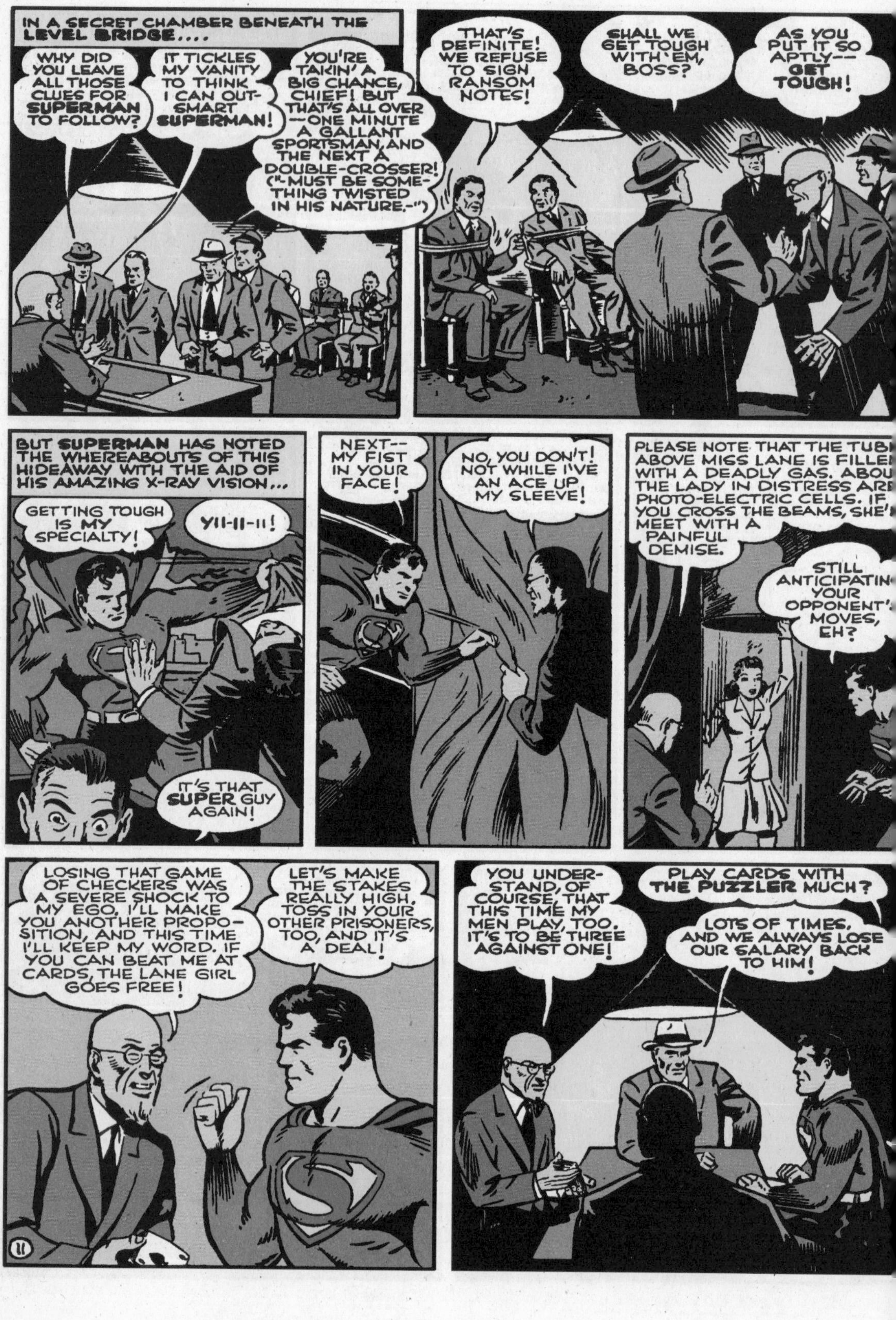
IN A SECRET CHAMBER BENEATH THE LEVEL BRIDGE....
WHY DID YOU LEAVE ALL THOSE CLUES FOR SUPERMAN TO FOLLOW?
IT TICKLES MY VANITY TO THINK I CAN OUT-SMART SUPERMAN!
YOU'RE TAKIN' A BIG CHANCE, CHIEF! BUT THAT'S ALL OVER --ONE MINUTE A GALLANT SPORTSMAN, AND THE NEXT A DOUBLE-CROSSER! ("-MUST BE SOMETHING TWISTED IN HIS NATURE.-")
THAT'S DEFINITE! WE REFUSE TO SIGN RANSOM NOTES!
SHALL WE GET TOUGH WITH 'EM, BOSS?
AS YOU PUT IT SO APTLY-- GET TOUGH!
BUT SUPERMAN HAS NOTED THE WHEREABOUTS OF THIS HIDEAWAY WITH THE AID OF HIS AMAZING X-RAY VISION...
GETTING TOUGH IS MY SPECIALTY!
YII-II-II!
IT'S THAT SUPER GUY AGAIN!
NEXT-- MY FIST IN YOUR FACE!
NO, YOU DON'T! NOT WHILE I'VE AN ACE UP MY SLEEVE!
PLEASE NOTE THAT THE TUB ABOVE MISS LANE IS FILLE WITH A DEADLY GAS. ABOU THE LADY IN DISTRESS AR PHOTO-ELECTRIC CELLS. IF YOU CROSS THE BEAMS, SHE' MEET WITH A PAINFUL DEMISE.
STILL ANTICIPATIN YOUR OPPONENT' MOVES, EH?
LOSING THAT GAME OF CHECKERS WAS A SEVERE SHOCK TO MY EGO, I'LL MAKE YOU ANOTHER PROPOSITION, AND THIS TIME I'LL KEEP MY WORD. IF YOU CAN BEAT ME AT CARDS, THE LANE GIRL GOES FREE!
LET'S MAKE THE STAKES REALLY HIGH. TOSS IN YOUR OTHER PRISONERS, TOO, AND IT'S A DEAL!
YOU UNDERSTAND, OF COURSE, THAT THIS TIME MY MEN PLAY, TOO. IT'S TO BE THREE AGAINST ONE!
PLAY CARDS WITH THE PUZZLER MUCH?
LOTS OF TIMES. AND WE ALWAYS LOSE OUR SALARY BACK TO HIM!

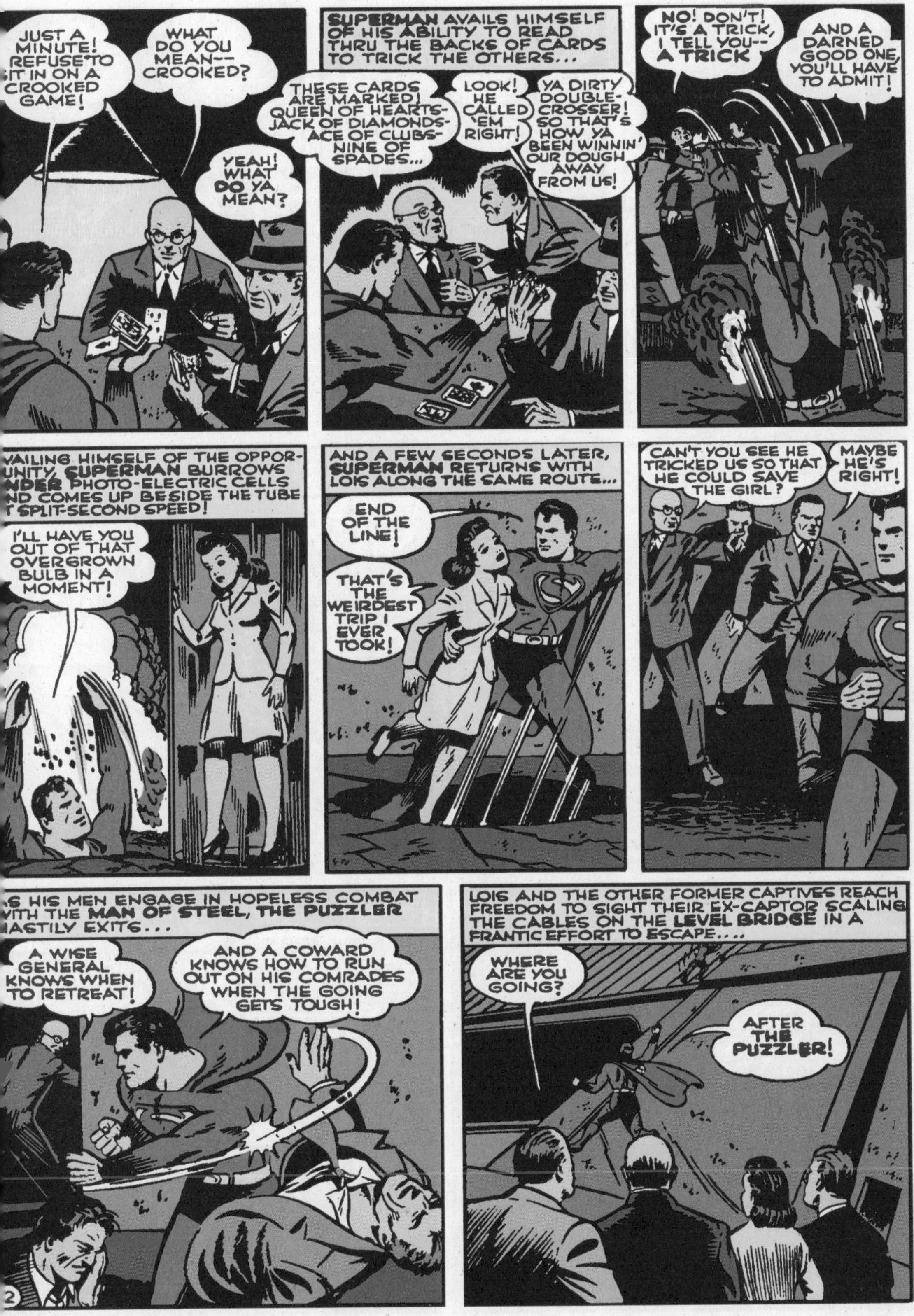
JUST A MINUTE! REFUSE TO IT IN ON A CROOKED GAME!
WHAT DO YOU MEAN-- CROOKED?
YEAH! WHAT DO YA MEAN?
SUPERMAN AVAILS HIMSELF OF HIS ABILITY TO READ THRU THE BACKS OF CARDS TO TRICK THE OTHERS...
THESE CARDS ARE MARKED! QUEEN OF HEARTS- JACK OF DIAMONDS- ACE OF CLUBS- NINE OF SPADES...
LOOK! HE CALLED 'EM RIGHT!
YA DIRTY DOUBLE-CROSSER! SO THAT'S HOW YA BEEN WINNIN' OUR DOUGH AWAY FROM US!
NO! DON'T! IT'S A TRICK, I TELL YOU-- A TRICK
AND A DARNED GOOD ONE, YOU'LL HAVE TO ADMIT!
VAILING HIMSELF OF THE OPPOR- UNITY, SUPERMAN BURROWS NDER PHOTO-ELECTRIC CELLS ND COMES UP BESIDE THE TUBE T SPLIT-SECOND SPEED!
I'LL HAVE YOU OUT OF THAT OVERGROWN BULB IN A MOMENT!
AND A FEW SECONDS LATER, SUPERMAN RETURNS WITH LOIS ALONG THE SAME ROUTE...
END OF THE LINE!
THAT'S THE WEIRDEST TRIP I EVER TOOK!
CAN'T YOU SEE HE TRICKED US SO THAT HE COULD SAVE THE GIRL?
MAYBE HE'S RIGHT!
S HIS MEN ENGAGE IN HOPELESS COMBAT ITH THE MAN OF STEEL, THE PUZZLER IASTILY EXITS...
A WISE GENERAL KNOWS WHEN TO RETREAT!
AND A COWARD KNOWS HOW TO RUN OUT ON HIS COMRADES WHEN THE GOING GETS TOUGH!
LOIS AND THE OTHER FORMER CAPTIVES REACH FREEDOM TO SIGHT THEIR EX-CAPTOR SCALING THE CABLES ON THE LEVEL BRIDGE IN A FRANTIC EFFORT TO ESCAPE....
WHERE ARE YOU GOING?
AFTER THE PUZZLER!

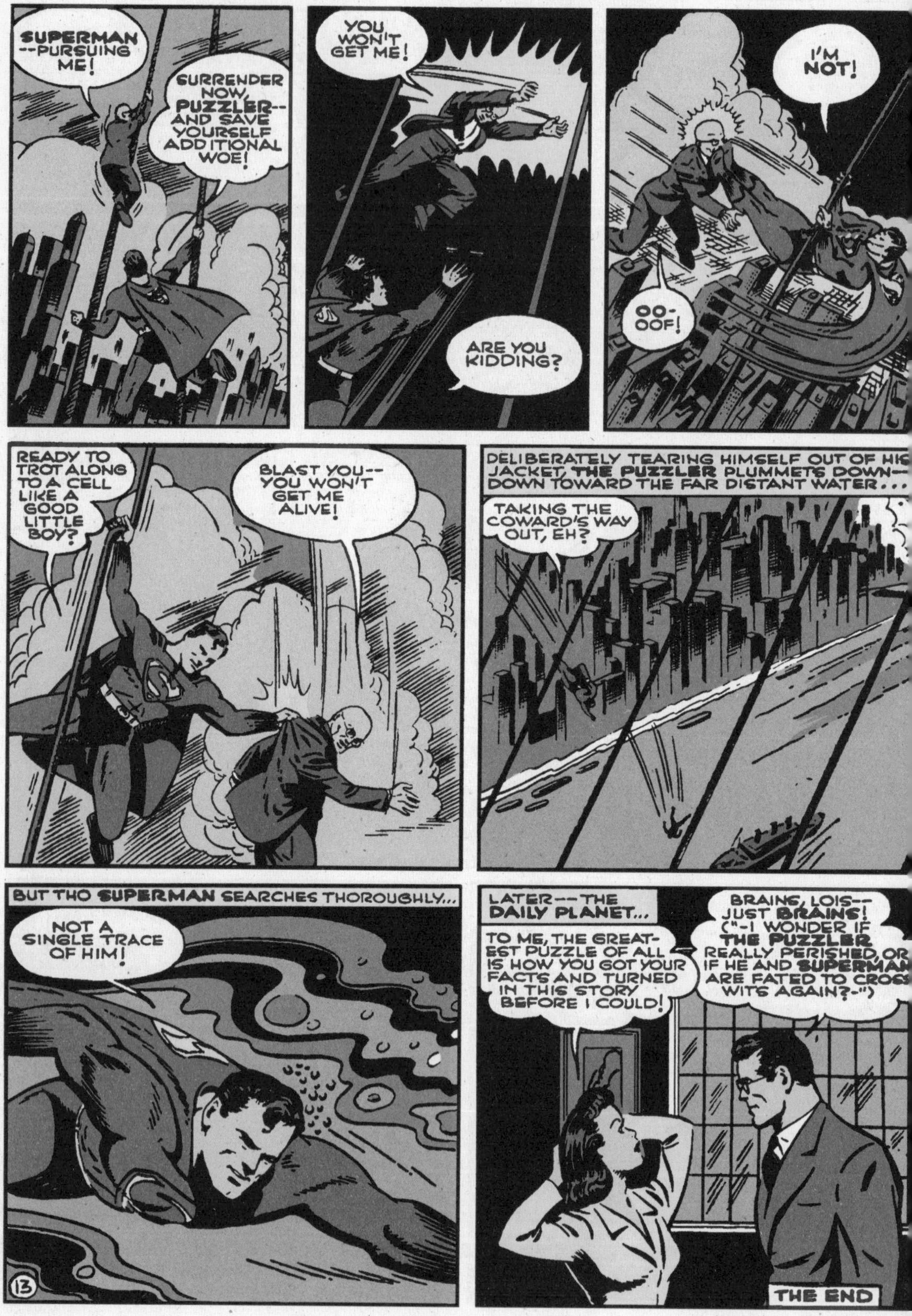

SUPERMAN --PURSUING ME!
SURRENDER NOW, PUZZLER-- AND SAVE YOURSELF ADDITIONAL WOE!
YOU WON'T GET ME!
ARE YOU KIDDING?
I'M NOT!
OO-OOF!
READY TO TROT ALONG TO A CELL LIKE A GOOD LITTLE BOY?
BLAST YOU-- YOU WON'T GET ME ALIVE!
DELIBERATELY TEARING HIMSELF OUT OF HI JACKET, THE PUZZLER PLUMMETS DOWN-- DOWN TOWARD THE FAR DISTANT WATER...
TAKING THE COWARD'S WAY OUT, EH?
BUT THO SUPERMAN SEARCHES THOROUGHLY...
NOT A SINGLE TRACE OF HIM!
13
LATER--THE DAILY PLANET...
TO ME, THE GREATEST PUZZLE OF ALL IS HOW YOU GOT YOUR FACTS AND TURNED IN THIS STORY BEFORE I COULD!
BRAINS, LOIS-- JUST BRAINS! ("-I WONDER IF THE PUZZLER REALLY PERISHED, OR IF HE AND SUPERMA ARE FATED TO CROS WITS AGAIN?-")
THE END

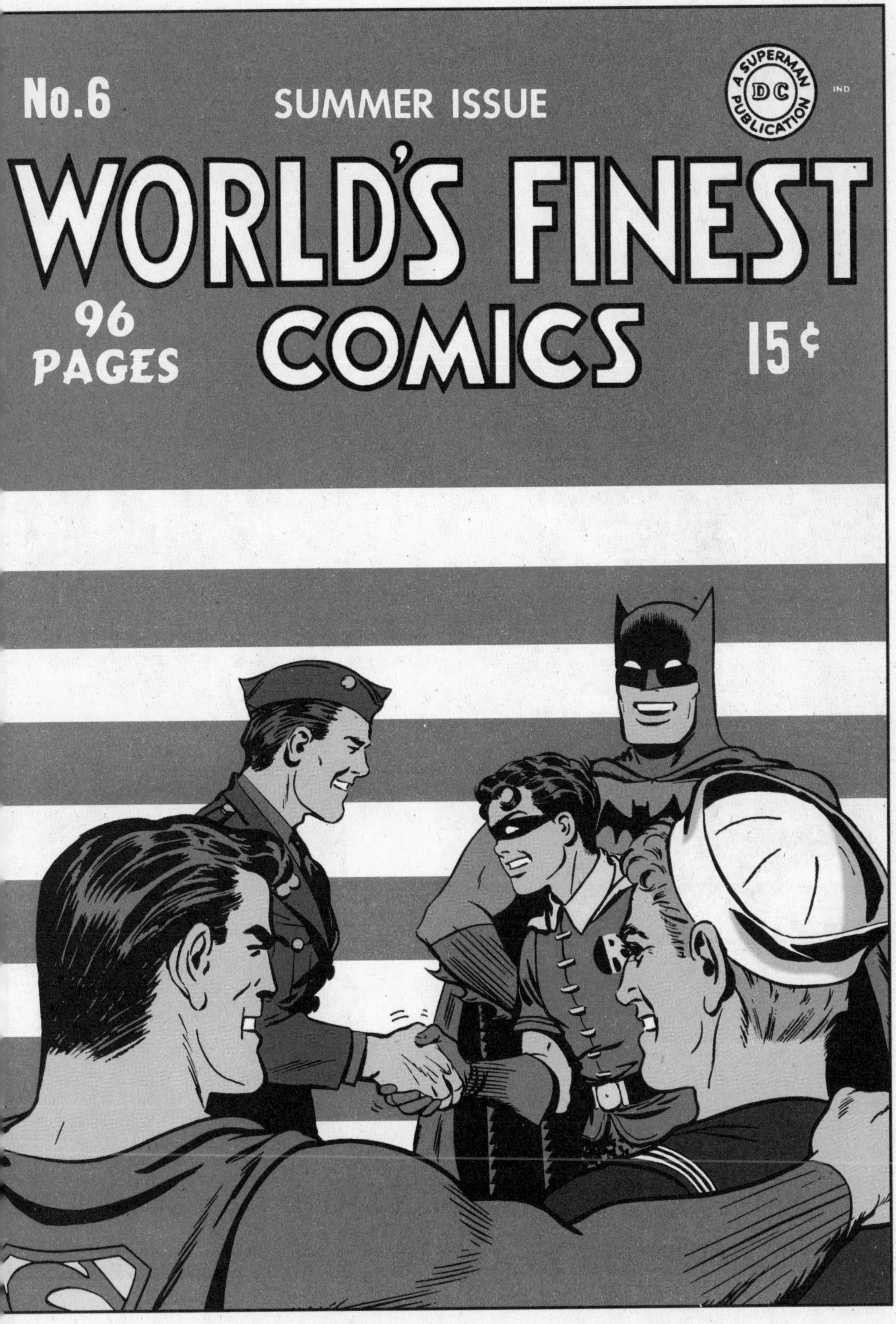
No.6
SUMMER ISSUE
A SUPERMAN DC PUBLICATION
IND
WORLD'S FINEST
96 PAGES
COMICS
15¢

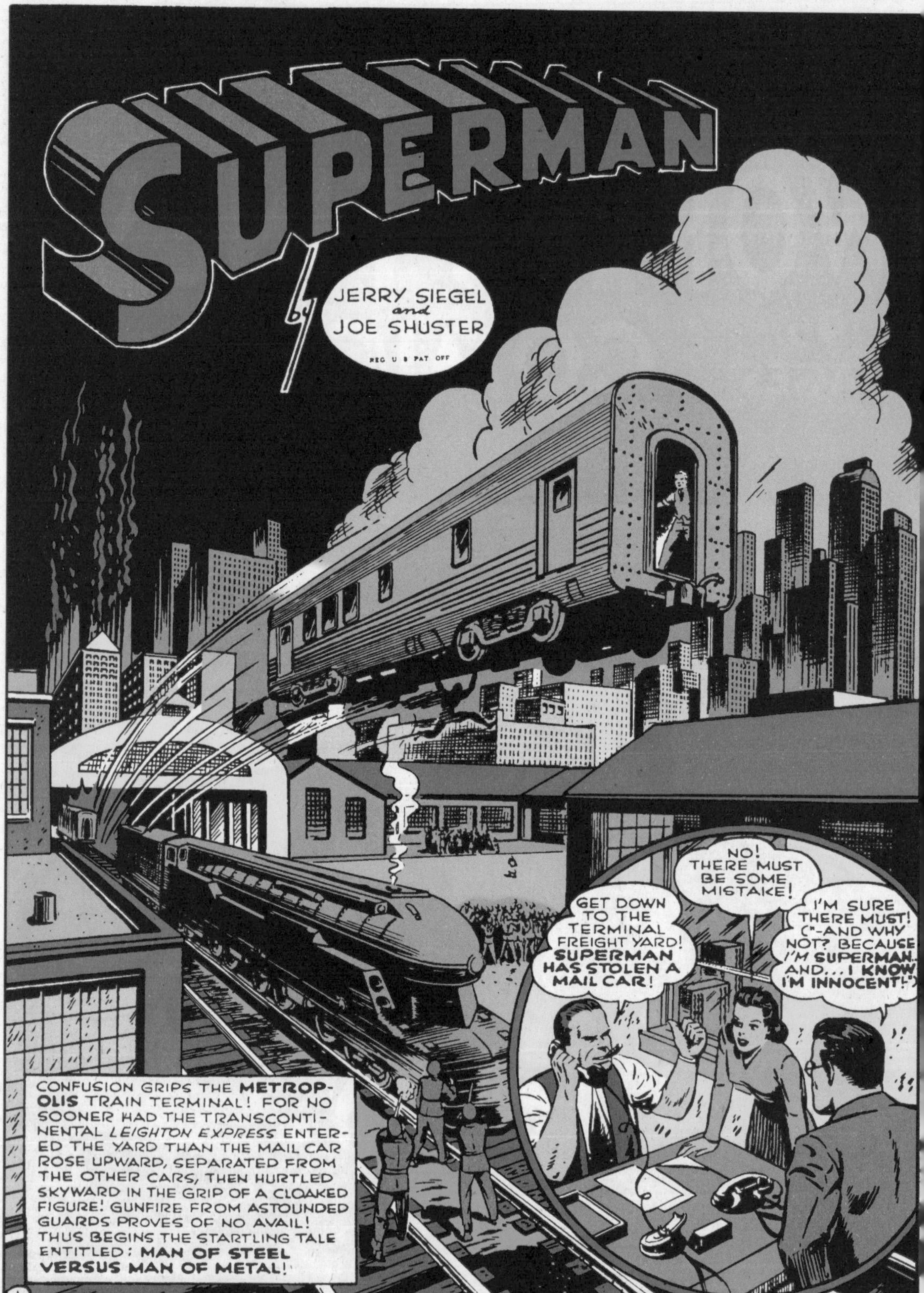
SUPERMAN
by JERRY SIEGEL and JOE SHUSTER
REG U S PAT OFF
CONFUSION GRIPS THE **METROPOLIS** TRAIN TERMINAL! FOR NO SOONER HAD THE TRANSCONTINENTAL *LEIGHTON EXPRESS* ENTERED THE YARD THAN THE MAIL CAR ROSE UPWARD, SEPARATED FROM THE OTHER CARS, THEN HURTLED SKYWARD IN THE GRIP OF A CLOAKED FIGURE! GUNFIRE FROM ASTOUNDED GUARDS PROVES OF NO AVAIL! THUS BEGINS THE STARTLING TALE ENTITLED: **MAN OF STEEL VERSUS MAN OF METAL**!
GET DOWN TO THE TERMINAL FREIGHT YARD! **SUPERMAN HAS STOLEN A MAIL CAR!**
NO! THERE MUST BE SOME MISTAKE!
I'M SURE THERE MUST! ("-AND WHY NOT? BECAUSE *I'M* **SUPERMAN**. AND... **I KNOW I'M INNOCENT!**")
1

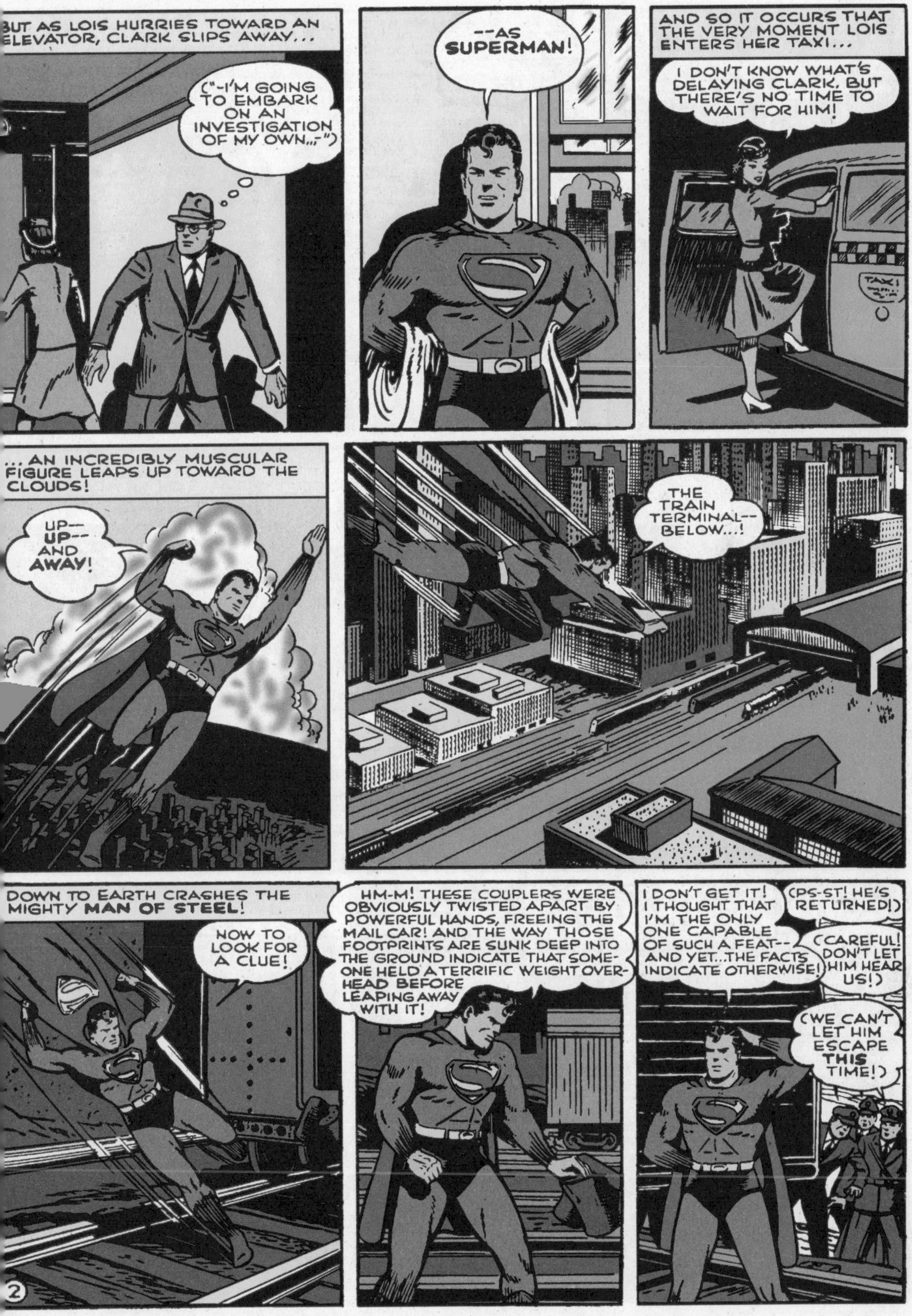
BUT AS LOIS HURRIES TOWARD AN ELEVATOR, CLARK SLIPS AWAY...
("-I'M GOING TO EMBARK ON AN INVESTIGATION OF MY OWN...-")
--AS SUPERMAN!
AND SO IT OCCURS THAT THE VERY MOMENT LOIS ENTERS HER TAXI...
I DON'T KNOW WHAT'S DELAYING CLARK, BUT THERE'S NO TIME TO WAIT FOR HIM!
TAXI
...AN INCREDIBLY MUSCULAR FIGURE LEAPS UP TOWARD THE CLOUDS!
UP-- UP-- AND AWAY!
THE TRAIN TERMINAL-- BELOW...!
DOWN TO EARTH CRASHES THE MIGHTY MAN OF STEEL!
NOW TO LOOK FOR A CLUE!
2
HM-M! THESE COUPLERS WERE OBVIOUSLY TWISTED APART BY POWERFUL HANDS, FREEING THE MAIL CAR! AND THE WAY THOSE FOOTPRINTS ARE SUNK DEEP INTO THE GROUND INDICATE THAT SOMEONE HELD A TERRIFIC WEIGHT OVERHEAD BEFORE LEAPING AWAY WITH IT!
I DON'T GET IT! I THOUGHT THAT I'M THE ONLY ONE CAPABLE OF SUCH A FEAT-- AND YET...THE FACTS INDICATE OTHERWISE!
(PS-ST! HE'S RETURNED!)
(CAREFUL! DON'T LET HIM HEAR US!)
(WE CAN'T LET HIM ESCAPE THIS TIME!)

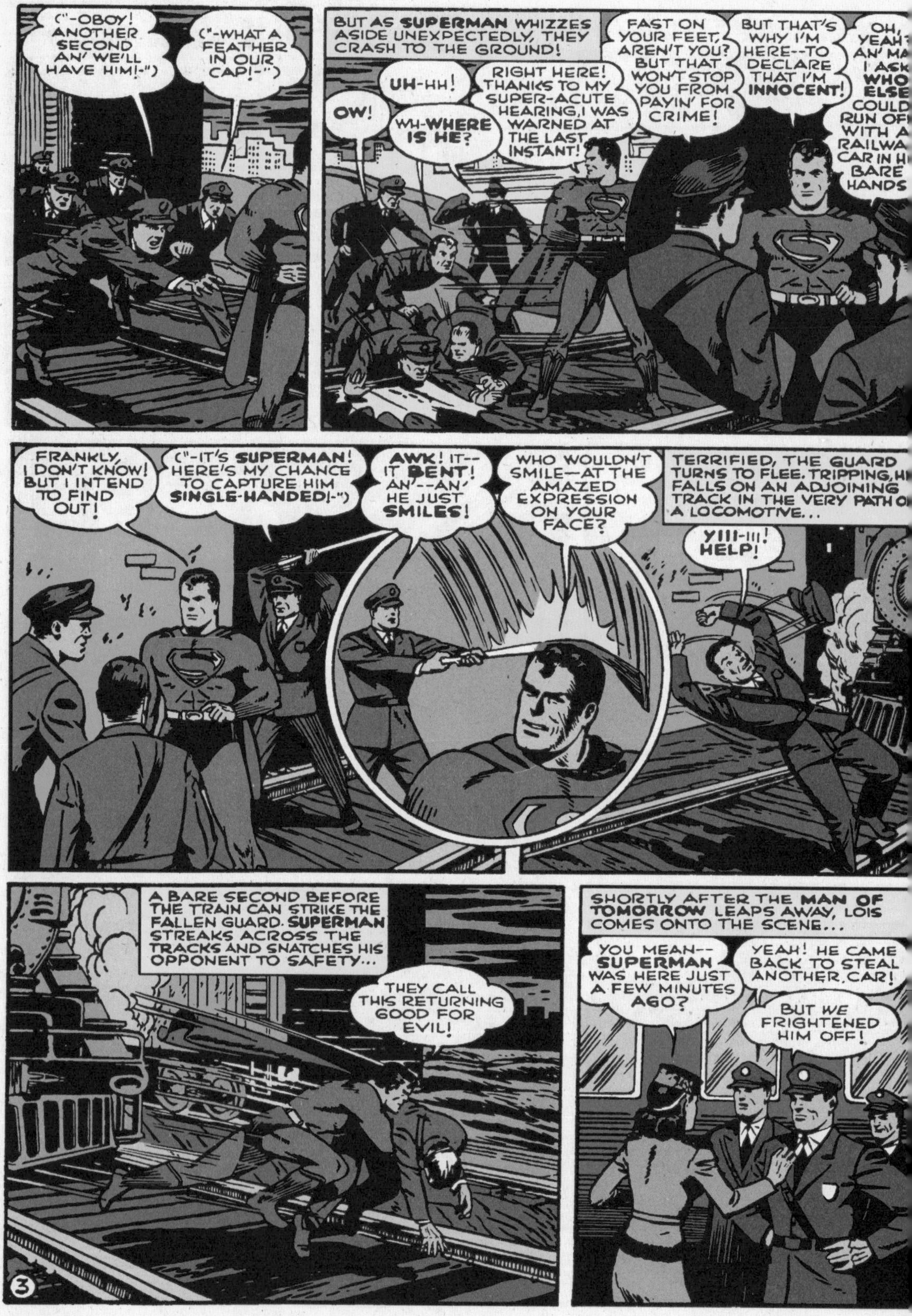
("-OBOY! ANOTHER SECOND AN' WE'LL HAVE HIM!-")
("-WHAT A FEATHER IN OUR CAP!-")
BUT AS **SUPERMAN** WHIZZES ASIDE UNEXPECTEDLY, THEY CRASH TO THE GROUND!
UH-HH!
OW!
WH-**WHERE IS HE?**
RIGHT HERE! THANKS TO MY SUPER-ACUTE HEARING, I WAS WARNED AT THE LAST INSTANT!
FAST ON YOUR FEET, AREN'T YOU? BUT THAT WON'T STOP YOU FROM PAYIN' FOR CRIME!
BUT THAT'S WHY I'M HERE--TO DECLARE THAT I'M **INNOCENT!**
OH, YEAH AN' MA I ASK WHO ELSE COULD RUN OF WITH A RAILWA CAR IN H BARE HANDS
FRANKLY, I DON'T KNOW! BUT I INTEND TO FIND OUT!
("-IT'S **SUPERMAN!** HERE'S MY CHANCE TO CAPTURE HIM **SINGLE-HANDED!**-")
AWK! IT--IT **BENT!** AN'--AN' HE JUST **SMILES!**
WHO WOULDN'T SMILE—AT THE AMAZED EXPRESSION ON YOUR FACE?
TERRIFIED, THE GUARD TURNS TO FLEE. TRIPPING, H FALLS ON AN ADJOINING TRACK IN THE VERY PATH O A LOCOMOTIVE...
YIII-III! HELP!
A BARE SECOND BEFORE THE TRAIN CAN STRIKE THE FALLEN GUARD, **SUPERMAN** STREAKS ACROSS THE TRACKS AND SNATCHES HIS OPPONENT TO SAFETY...
THEY CALL THIS RETURNING GOOD FOR EVIL!
3
SHORTLY AFTER THE **MAN OF TOMORROW** LEAPS AWAY, LOIS COMES ONTO THE SCENE...
YOU MEAN--**SUPERMAN** WAS HERE JUST A FEW MINUTES **AGO?**
YEAH! HE CAME BACK TO STEAL ANOTHER CAR!
BUT *WE* FRIGHTENED HIM OFF!

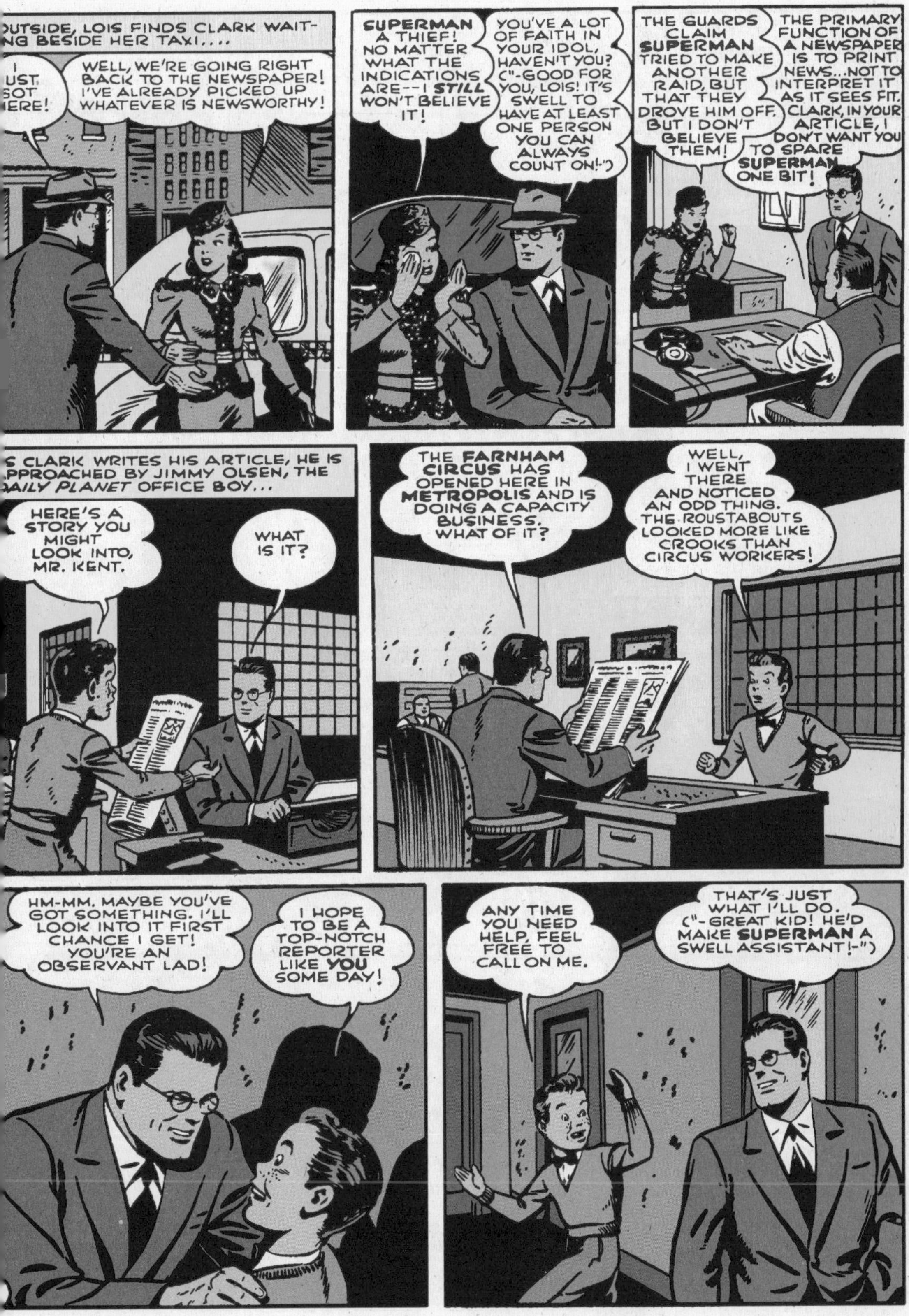

OUTSIDE, LOIS FINDS CLARK WAITING BESIDE HER TAXI....
I JUST GOT HERE!
WELL, WE'RE GOING RIGHT BACK TO THE NEWSPAPER! I'VE ALREADY PICKED UP WHATEVER IS NEWSWORTHY!
SUPERMAN A THIEF! NO MATTER WHAT THE INDICATIONS ARE--I STILL WON'T BELIEVE IT!
YOU'VE A LOT OF FAITH IN YOUR IDOL, HAVEN'T YOU? ("-GOOD FOR YOU, LOIS! IT'S SWELL TO HAVE AT LEAST ONE PERSON YOU CAN ALWAYS COUNT ON!-")
THE GUARDS CLAIM SUPERMAN TRIED TO MAKE ANOTHER RAID, BUT THAT THEY DROVE HIM OFF. BUT I DON'T BELIEVE THEM!
THE PRIMARY FUNCTION OF A NEWSPAPER IS TO PRINT NEWS...NOT TO INTERPRET IT AS IT SEES FIT. CLARK, IN YOUR ARTICLE, I DON'T WANT YOU TO SPARE SUPERMAN ONE BIT!
AS CLARK WRITES HIS ARTICLE, HE IS APPROACHED BY JIMMY OLSEN, THE DAILY PLANET OFFICE BOY...
HERE'S A STORY YOU MIGHT LOOK INTO, MR. KENT.
WHAT IS IT?
THE FARNHAM CIRCUS HAS OPENED HERE IN METROPOLIS AND IS DOING A CAPACITY BUSINESS. WHAT OF IT?
WELL, I WENT THERE AND NOTICED AN ODD THING. THE ROUSTABOUTS LOOKED MORE LIKE CROOKS THAN CIRCUS WORKERS!
HM-MM. MAYBE YOU'VE GOT SOMETHING. I'LL LOOK INTO IT FIRST CHANCE I GET! YOU'RE AN OBSERVANT LAD!
I HOPE TO BE A TOP-NOTCH REPORTER LIKE YOU SOME DAY!
ANY TIME YOU NEED HELP, FEEL FREE TO CALL ON ME.
THAT'S JUST WHAT I'LL DO. ("-GREAT KID! HE'D MAKE SUPERMAN A SWELL ASSISTANT!-")

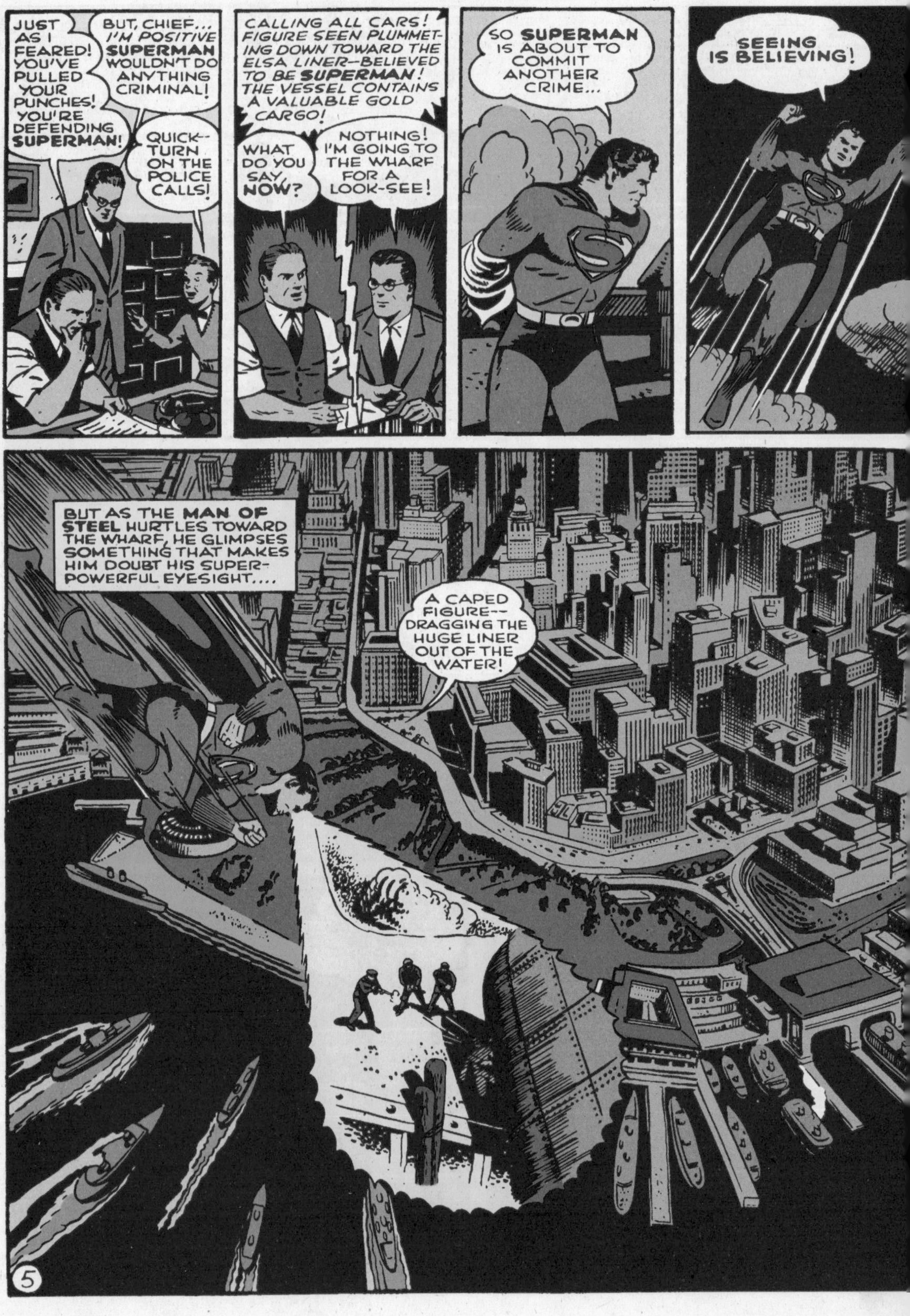
JUST AS I FEARED! YOU'VE PULLED YOUR PUNCHES! YOU'RE DEFENDING SUPERMAN!
BUT, CHIEF... I'M POSITIVE SUPERMAN WOULDN'T DO ANYTHING CRIMINAL!
QUICK-- TURN ON THE POLICE CALLS!
CALLING ALL CARS! FIGURE SEEN PLUMMETING DOWN TOWARD THE ELSA LINER--BELIEVED TO BE SUPERMAN! THE VESSEL CONTAINS A VALUABLE GOLD CARGO!
WHAT DO YOU SAY, NOW?
NOTHING! I'M GOING TO THE WHARF FOR A LOOK-SEE!
SO SUPERMAN IS ABOUT TO COMMIT ANOTHER CRIME...
SEEING IS BELIEVING!
BUT AS THE MAN OF STEEL HURTLES TOWARD THE WHARF, HE GLIMPSES SOMETHING THAT MAKES HIM DOUBT HIS SUPER-POWERFUL EYESIGHT....
A CAPED FIGURE-- DRAGGING THE HUGE LINER OUT OF THE WATER!
5

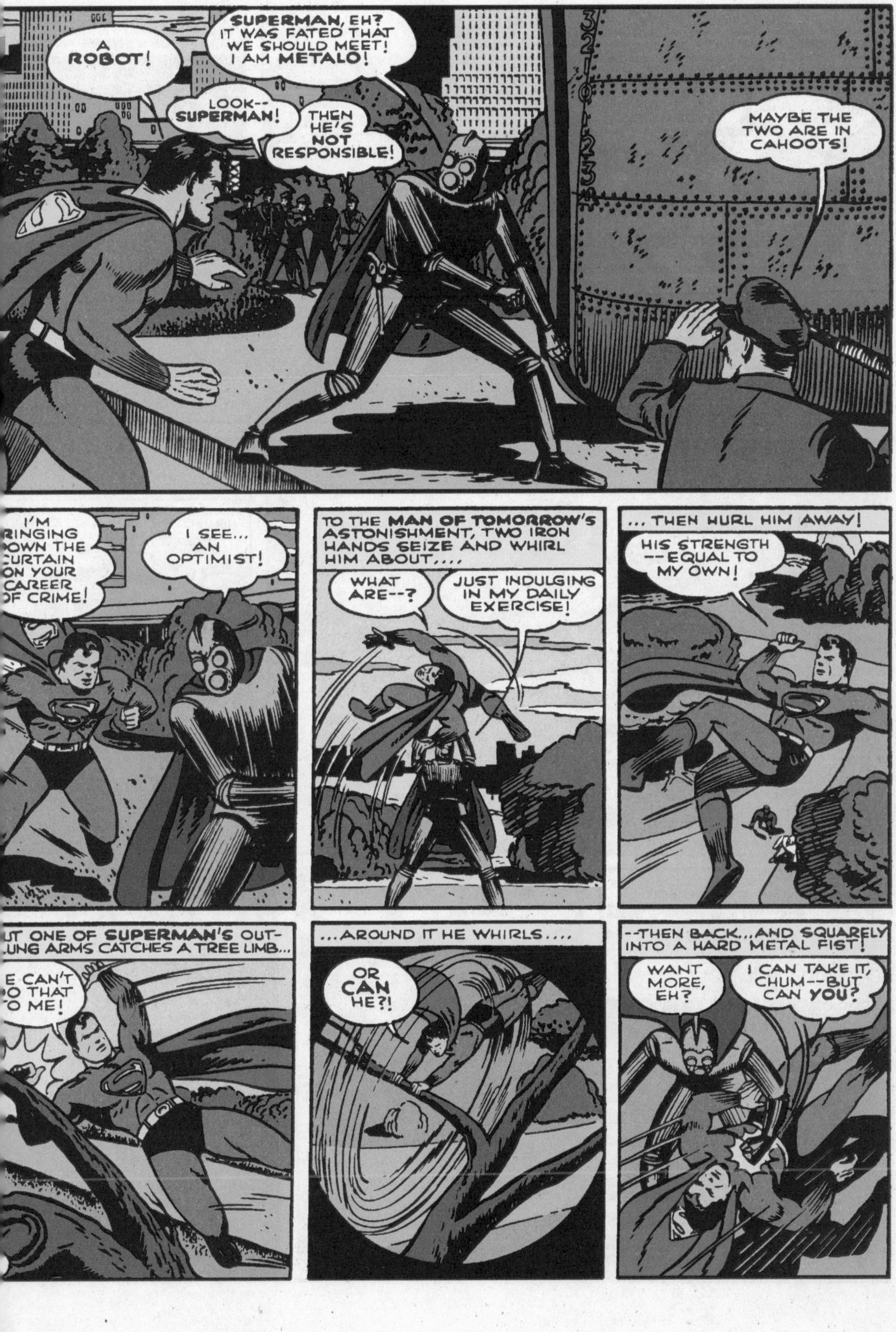
A ROBOT!
SUPERMAN, EH? IT WAS FATED THAT WE SHOULD MEET! I AM METALO!
LOOK-- SUPERMAN!
THEN HE'S NOT RESPONSIBLE!
MAYBE THE TWO ARE IN CAHOOTS!
I'M
RINGING
OWN THE
CURTAIN
ON YOUR
CAREER
OF CRIME!
I SEE... AN OPTIMIST!
TO THE MAN OF TOMORROW'S ASTONISHMENT, TWO IRON HANDS SEIZE AND WHIRL HIM ABOUT,...
WHAT ARE--?
JUST INDULGING IN MY DAILY EXERCISE!
... THEN HURL HIM AWAY!
HIS STRENGTH --EQUAL TO MY OWN!
UT ONE OF SUPERMAN'S OUT-
UNG ARMS CATCHES A TREE LIMB...
E CAN'T
O THAT
O ME!
...AROUND IT HE WHIRLS....
OR CAN HE?!
--THEN BACK...AND SQUARELY INTO A HARD METAL FIST!
WANT MORE, EH?
I CAN TAKE IT, CHUM--BUT CAN YOU?

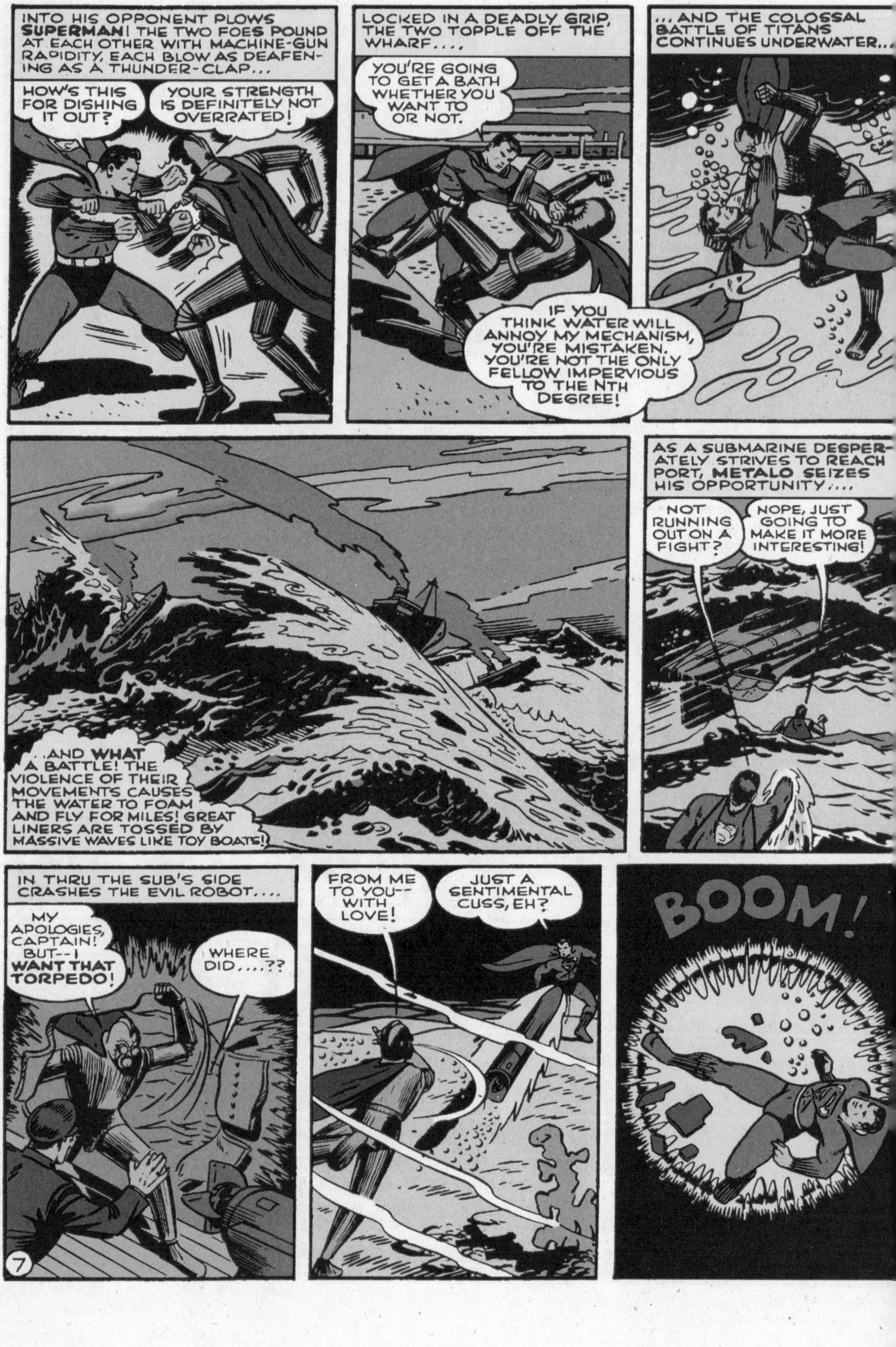
INTO HIS OPPONENT PLOWS SUPERMAN! THE TWO FOES POUND AT EACH OTHER WITH MACHINE-GUN RAPIDITY, EACH BLOW AS DEAFENING AS A THUNDER-CLAP...
HOW'S THIS FOR DISHING IT OUT?
YOUR STRENGTH IS DEFINITELY NOT OVERRATED!
LOCKED IN A DEADLY GRIP, THE TWO TOPPLE OFF THE WHARF....
YOU'RE GOING TO GET A BATH WHETHER YOU WANT TO OR NOT.
IF YOU THINK WATER WILL ANNOY MY MECHANISM, YOU'RE MISTAKEN. YOU'RE NOT THE ONLY FELLOW IMPERVIOUS TO THE Nth DEGREE!
...AND THE COLOSSAL BATTLE OF TITANS CONTINUES UNDERWATER...
...AND WHAT A BATTLE! THE VIOLENCE OF THEIR MOVEMENTS CAUSES THE WATER TO FOAM AND FLY FOR MILES! GREAT LINERS ARE TOSSED BY MASSIVE WAVES LIKE TOY BOATS!
AS A SUBMARINE DESPERATELY STRIVES TO REACH PORT, METALO SEIZES HIS OPPORTUNITY....
NOT RUNNING OUT ON A FIGHT?
NOPE, JUST GOING TO MAKE IT MORE INTERESTING!
IN THRU THE SUB'S SIDE CRASHES THE EVIL ROBOT....
MY APOLOGIES, CAPTAIN! BUT--I WANT THAT TORPEDO!
WHERE DID....??
7
FROM ME TO YOU-- WITH LOVE!
JUST A SENTIMENTAL CUSS, EH?
BOOM!

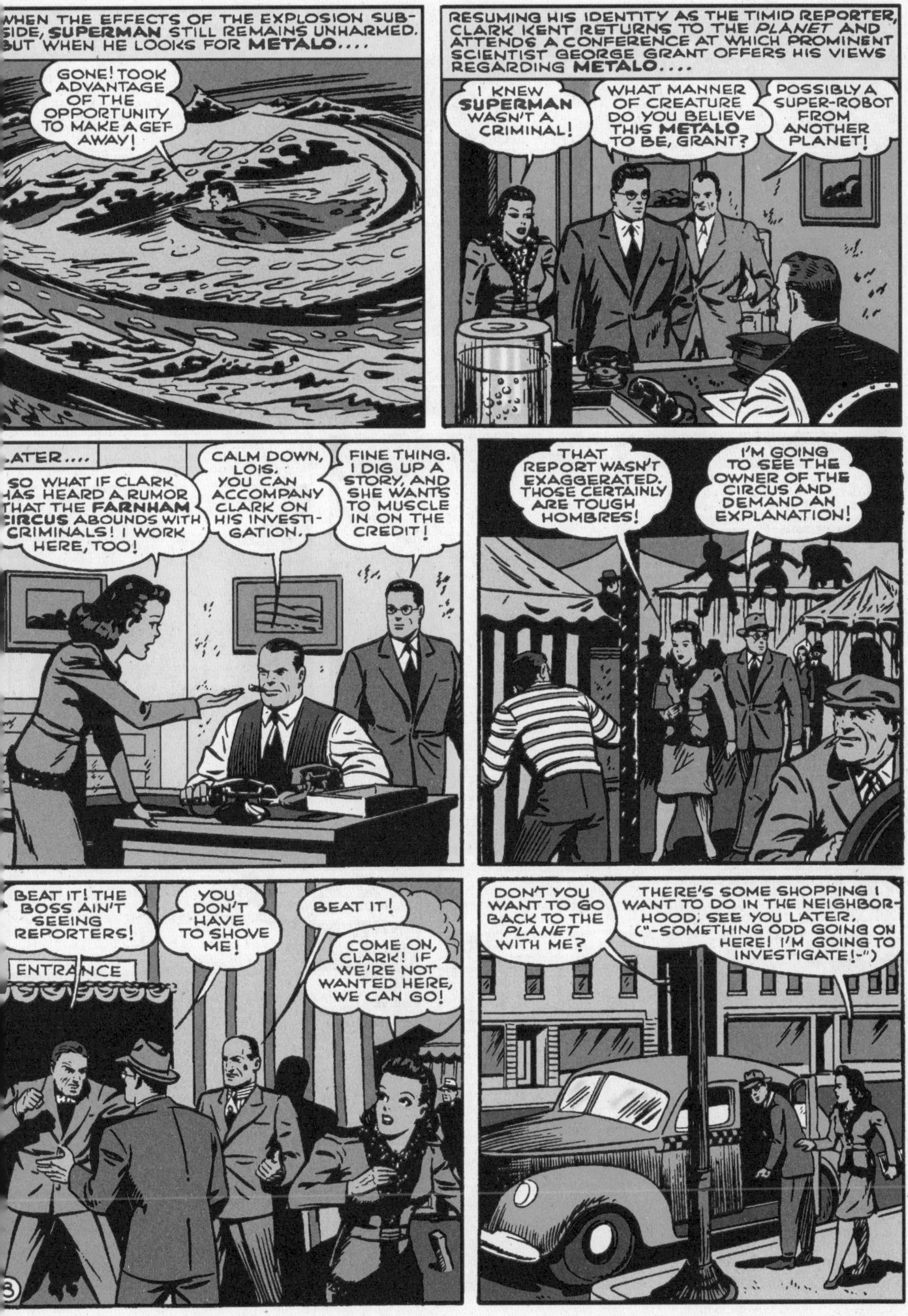
WHEN THE EFFECTS OF THE EXPLOSION SUBSIDE, SUPERMAN STILL REMAINS UNHARMED. BUT WHEN HE LOOKS FOR METALO....
GONE! TOOK ADVANTAGE OF THE OPPORTUNITY TO MAKE A GET-AWAY!
RESUMING HIS IDENTITY AS THE TIMID REPORTER, CLARK KENT RETURNS TO THE PLANET AND ATTENDS A CONFERENCE AT WHICH PROMINENT SCIENTIST GEORGE GRANT OFFERS HIS VIEWS REGARDING METALO....
I KNEW SUPERMAN WASN'T A CRIMINAL!
WHAT MANNER OF CREATURE DO YOU BELIEVE THIS METALO TO BE, GRANT?
POSSIBLY A SUPER-ROBOT FROM ANOTHER PLANET!
LATER....
SO WHAT IF CLARK HAS HEARD A RUMOR THAT THE FARNHAM CIRCUS ABOUNDS WITH CRIMINALS! I WORK HERE, TOO!
CALM DOWN, LOIS. YOU CAN ACCOMPANY CLARK ON HIS INVESTIGATION.
FINE THING. I DIG UP A STORY, AND SHE WANTS TO MUSCLE IN ON THE CREDIT!
THAT REPORT WASN'T EXAGGERATED. THOSE CERTAINLY ARE TOUGH HOMBRES!
I'M GOING TO SEE THE OWNER OF THE CIRCUS AND DEMAND AN EXPLANATION!
BEAT IT! THE BOSS AIN'T SEEING REPORTERS!
YOU DON'T HAVE TO SHOVE ME!
BEAT IT!
COME ON, CLARK! IF WE'RE NOT WANTED HERE, WE CAN GO!
ENTRANCE
8
DON'T YOU WANT TO GO BACK TO THE PLANET WITH ME?
THERE'S SOME SHOPPING I WANT TO DO IN THE NEIGHBORHOOD. SEE YOU LATER. ("-SOMETHING ODD GOING ON HERE! I'M GOING TO INVESTIGATE!-")

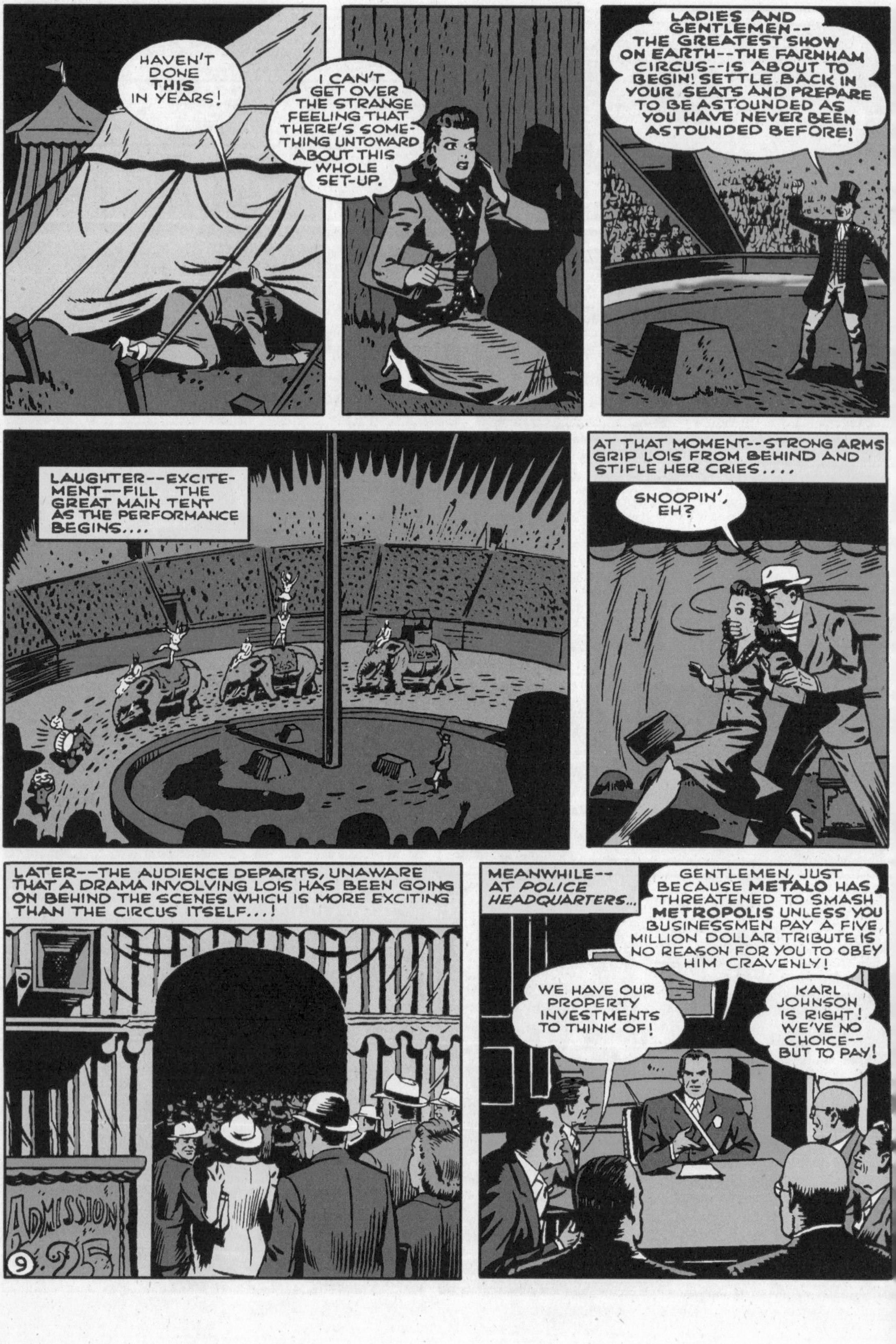
HAVEN'T DONE THIS IN YEARS!
I CAN'T GET OVER THE STRANGE FEELING THAT THERE'S SOMETHING UNTOWARD ABOUT THIS WHOLE SET-UP.
LADIES AND GENTLEMEN-- THE GREATEST SHOW ON EARTH--THE FARNHAM CIRCUS--IS ABOUT TO BEGIN! SETTLE BACK IN YOUR SEATS AND PREPARE TO BE ASTOUNDED AS YOU HAVE NEVER BEEN ASTOUNDED BEFORE!
LAUGHTER--EXCITEMENT--FILL THE GREAT MAIN TENT AS THE PERFORMANCE BEGINS....
AT THAT MOMENT--STRONG ARMS GRIP LOIS FROM BEHIND AND STIFLE HER CRIES....
SNOOPIN', EH?
LATER--THE AUDIENCE DEPARTS, UNAWARE THAT A DRAMA INVOLVING LOIS HAS BEEN GOING ON BEHIND THE SCENES WHICH IS MORE EXCITING THAN THE CIRCUS ITSELF...!
ADMISSION .25
9
MEANWHILE-- AT POLICE HEADQUARTERS...
GENTLEMEN, JUST BECAUSE METALO HAS THREATENED TO SMASH METROPOLIS UNLESS YOU BUSINESSMEN PAY A FIVE MILLION DOLLAR TRIBUTE IS NO REASON FOR YOU TO OBEY HIM CRAVENLY!
WE HAVE OUR PROPERTY INVESTMENTS TO THINK OF!
KARL JOHNSON IS RIGHT! WE'VE NO CHOICE-- BUT TO PAY!

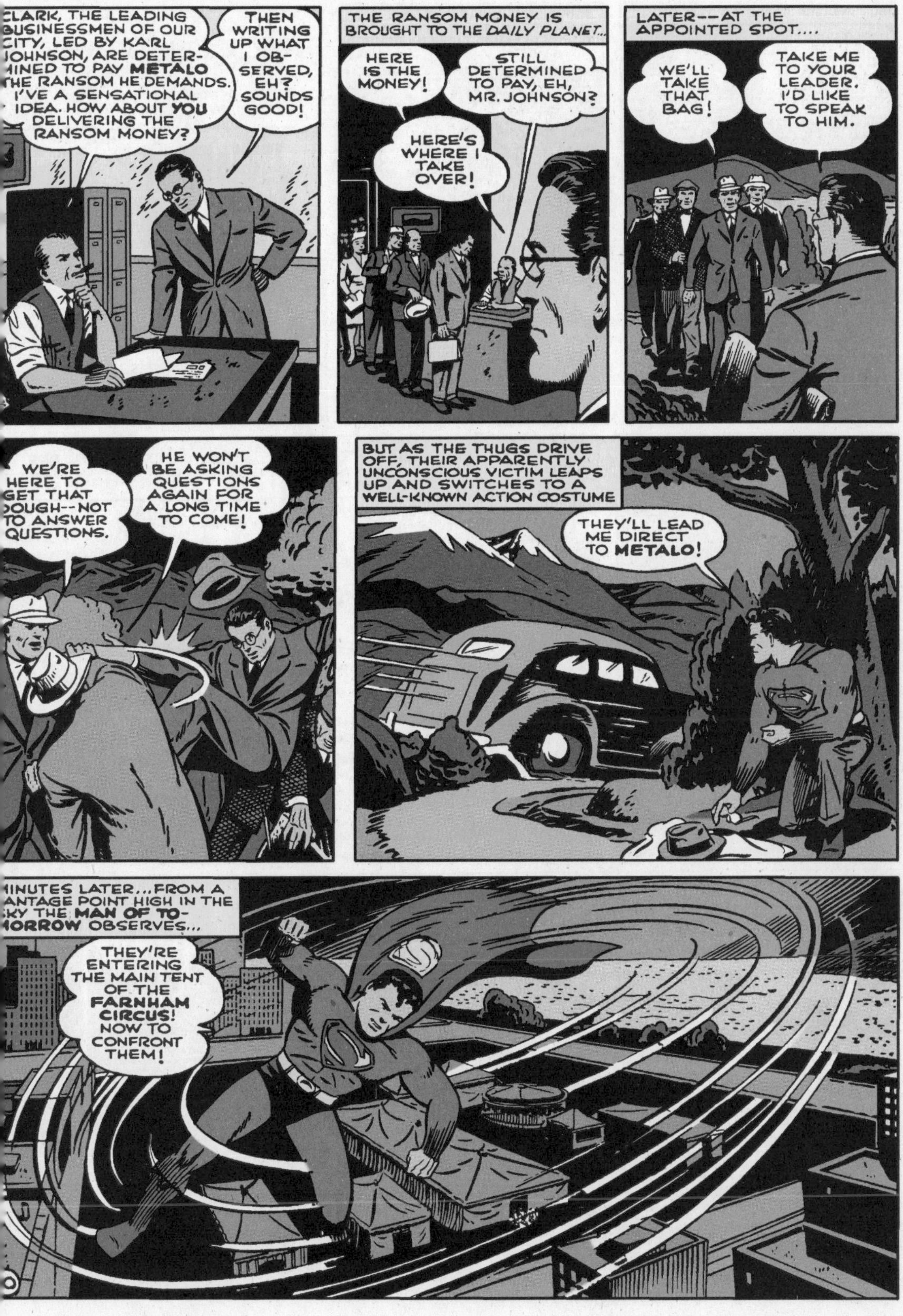
CLARK, THE LEADING BUSINESSMEN OF OUR CITY, LED BY KARL JOHNSON, ARE DETERMINED TO PAY **METALO** THE RANSOM HE DEMANDS. I'VE A SENSATIONAL IDEA. HOW ABOUT **YOU** DELIVERING THE RANSOM MONEY?
THEN WRITING UP WHAT I OBSERVED, EH? SOUNDS GOOD!
THE RANSOM MONEY IS BROUGHT TO THE *DAILY PLANET*...
HERE IS THE MONEY!
STILL DETERMINED TO PAY, EH, MR. JOHNSON?
HERE'S WHERE I TAKE OVER!
LATER--AT THE APPOINTED SPOT....
WE'LL TAKE THAT BAG!
TAKE ME TO YOUR LEADER. I'D LIKE TO SPEAK TO HIM.
WE'RE HERE TO GET THAT DOUGH--NOT TO ANSWER QUESTIONS.
HE WON'T BE ASKING QUESTIONS AGAIN FOR A LONG TIME TO COME!
BUT AS THE THUGS DRIVE OFF, THEIR APPARENTLY UNCONSCIOUS VICTIM LEAPS UP AND SWITCHES TO A WELL-KNOWN ACTION COSTUME
THEY'LL LEAD ME DIRECT TO **METALO**!
MINUTES LATER...FROM A VANTAGE POINT HIGH IN THE SKY THE **MAN OF TOMORROW** OBSERVES...
THEY'RE ENTERING THE MAIN TENT OF THE **FARNHAM CIRCUS**! NOW TO CONFRONT THEM!

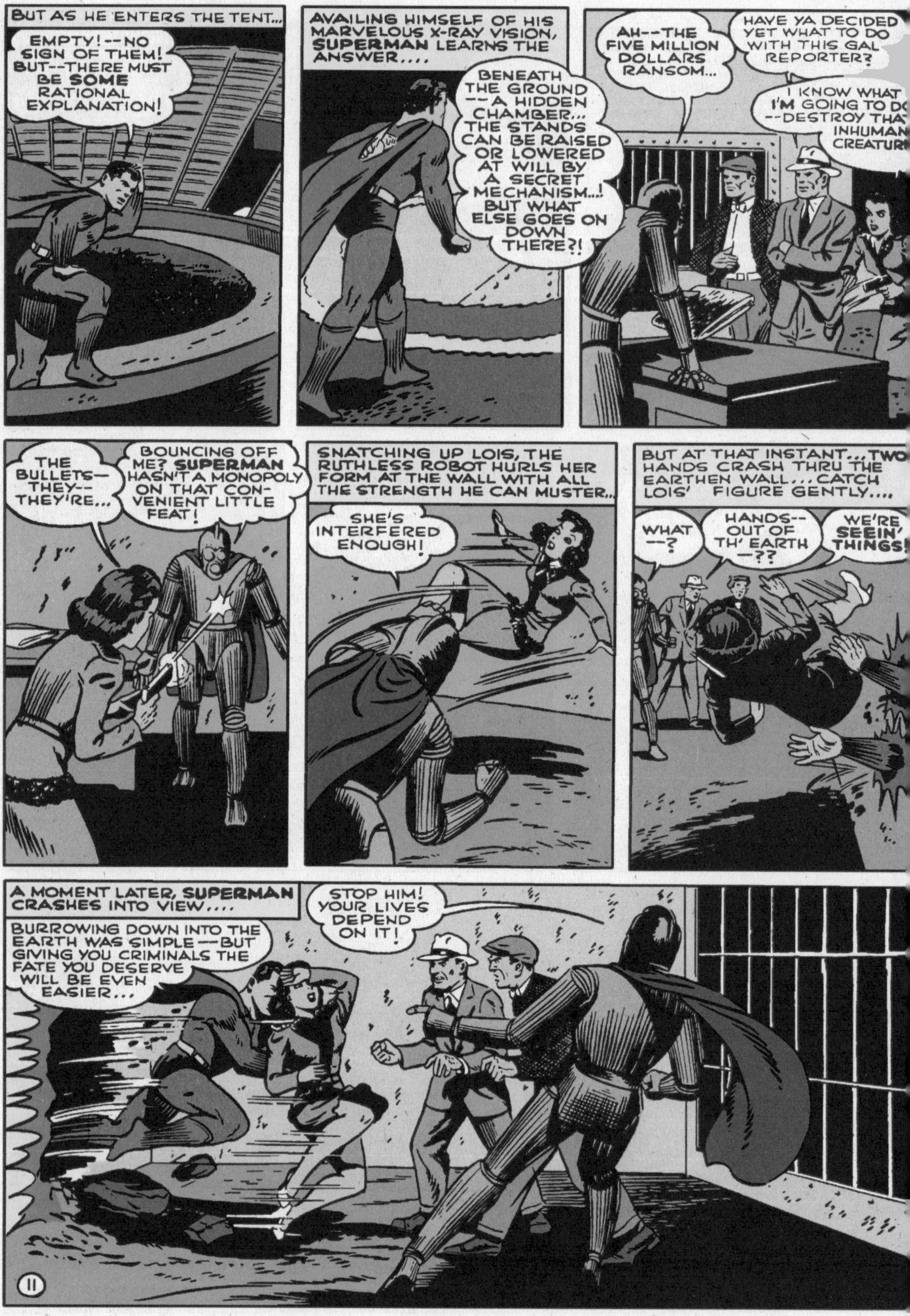
BUT AS HE ENTERS THE TENT...
EMPTY!--NO SIGN OF THEM! BUT--THERE MUST BE SOME RATIONAL EXPLANATION!
AVAILING HIMSELF OF HIS MARVELOUS X-RAY VISION, SUPERMAN LEARNS THE ANSWER....
BENEATH THE GROUND--A HIDDEN CHAMBER... THE STANDS CAN BE RAISED OR LOWERED AT WILL BY A SECRET MECHANISM...! BUT WHAT ELSE GOES ON DOWN THERE?!
AH--THE FIVE MILLION DOLLARS RANSOM...
HAVE YA DECIDED YET WHAT TO DO WITH THIS GAL REPORTER?
I KNOW WHAT I'M GOING TO DO --DESTROY THAT INHUMAN CREATURE
THE BULLETS--THEY--THEY'RE...
BOUNCING OFF ME? SUPERMAN HASN'T A MONOPOLY ON THAT CONVENIENT LITTLE FEAT!
SNATCHING UP LOIS, THE RUTHLESS ROBOT HURLS HER FORM AT THE WALL WITH ALL THE STRENGTH HE CAN MUSTER...
SHE'S INTERFERED ENOUGH!
BUT AT THAT INSTANT...TWO HANDS CRASH THRU THE EARTHEN WALL...CATCH LOIS' FIGURE GENTLY....
WHAT--?
HANDS--OUT OF TH' EARTH--??
WE'RE SEEIN' THINGS!
A MOMENT LATER, SUPERMAN CRASHES INTO VIEW....
BURROWING DOWN INTO THE EARTH WAS SIMPLE--BUT GIVING YOU CRIMINALS THE FATE YOU DESERVE WILL BE EVEN EASIER...
STOP HIM! YOUR LIVES DEPEND ON IT!
11

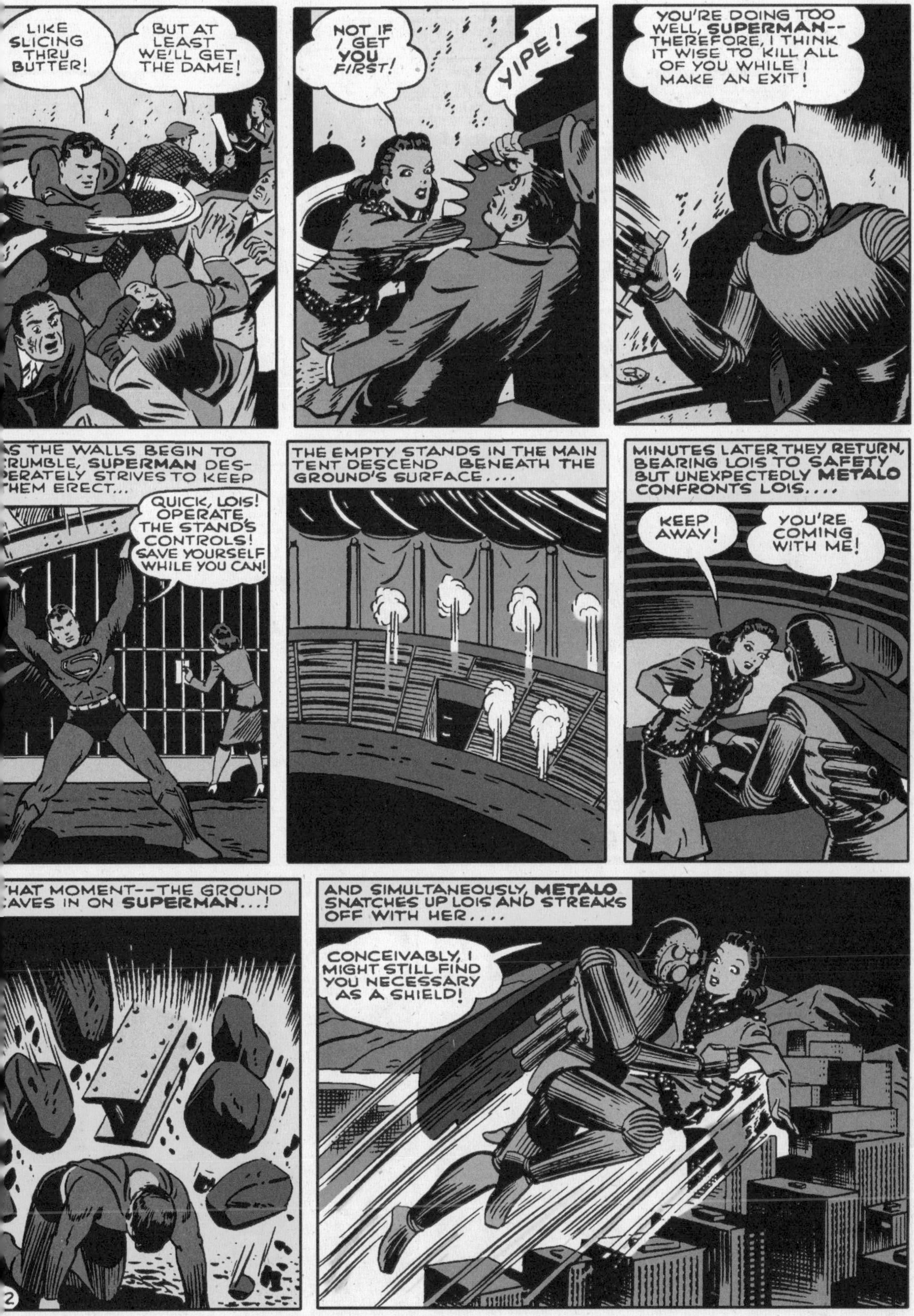
LIKE SLICING THRU BUTTER!
BUT AT LEAST WE'LL GET THE DAME!
NOT IF I GET YOU FIRST!
YIPE!
YOU'RE DOING TOO WELL, SUPERMAN-- THEREFORE, I THINK IT WISE TO KILL ALL OF YOU WHILE I MAKE AN EXIT!
S THE WALLS BEGIN TO RUMBLE, SUPERMAN DES-PERATELY STRIVES TO KEEP HEM ERECT...
QUICK, LOIS! OPERATE THE STAND'S CONTROLS! SAVE YOURSELF WHILE YOU CAN!
THE EMPTY STANDS IN THE MAIN TENT DESCEND BENEATH THE GROUND'S SURFACE....
MINUTES LATER THEY RETURN, BEARING LOIS TO SAFETY BUT UNEXPECTEDLY METALO CONFRONTS LOIS....
KEEP AWAY!
YOU'RE COMING WITH ME!
HAT MOMENT--THE GROUND AVES IN ON SUPERMAN...!
AND SIMULTANEOUSLY, METALO SNATCHES UP LOIS AND STREAKS OFF WITH HER....
CONCEIVABLY, I MIGHT STILL FIND YOU NECESSARY AS A SHIELD!
2

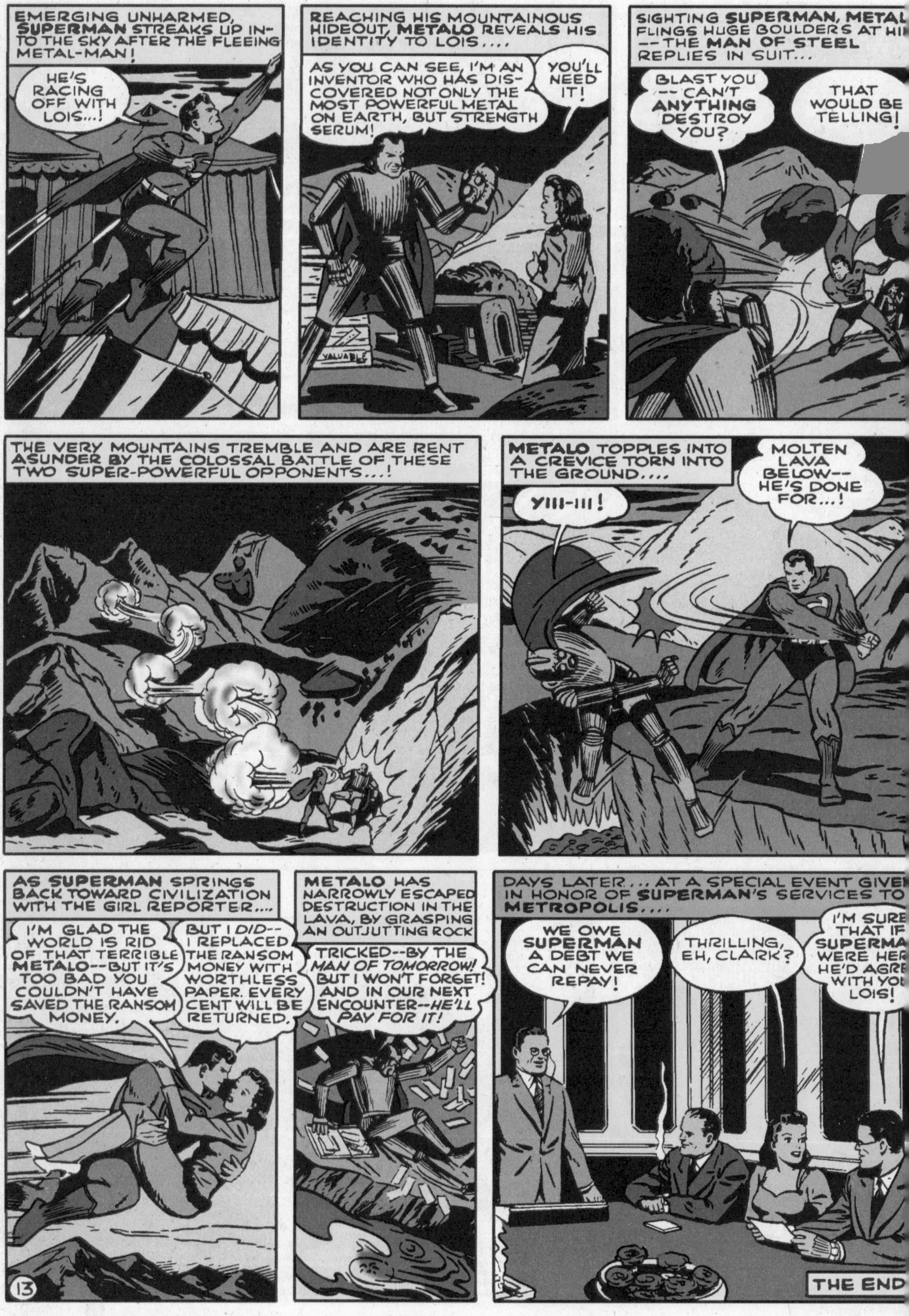
EMERGING UNHARMED, SUPERMAN STREAKS UP INTO THE SKY AFTER THE FLEEING METAL-MAN!
HE'S RACING OFF WITH LOIS...!
REACHING HIS MOUNTAINOUS HIDEOUT, METALO REVEALS HIS IDENTITY TO LOIS....
AS YOU CAN SEE, I'M AN INVENTOR WHO HAS DISCOVERED NOT ONLY THE MOST POWERFUL METAL ON EARTH, BUT STRENGTH SERUM!
YOU'LL NEED IT!
VALUABLE
SIGHTING SUPERMAN, METAL FLINGS HUGE BOULDERS AT HI --THE MAN OF STEEL REPLIES IN SUIT...
BLAST YOU --CAN'T ANYTHING DESTROY YOU?
THAT WOULD BE TELLING!
THE VERY MOUNTAINS TREMBLE AND ARE RENT ASUNDER BY THE COLOSSAL BATTLE OF THESE TWO SUPER-POWERFUL OPPONENTS...!
METALO TOPPLES INTO A CREVICE TORN INTO THE GROUND....
YIII-III!
MOLTEN LAVA BELOW--HE'S DONE FOR...!
AS SUPERMAN SPRINGS BACK TOWARD CIVILIZATION WITH THE GIRL REPORTER....
I'M GLAD THE WORLD IS RID OF THAT TERRIBLE METALO--BUT IT'S TOO BAD YOU COULDN'T HAVE SAVED THE RANSOM MONEY.
BUT I DID--I REPLACED THE RANSOM MONEY WITH WORTHLESS PAPER. EVERY CENT WILL BE RETURNED.
13
METALO HAS NARROWLY ESCAPED DESTRUCTION IN THE LAVA, BY GRASPING AN OUTJUTTING ROCK
TRICKED--BY THE MAN OF TOMORROW! BUT I WON'T FORGET! AND IN OUR NEXT ENCOUNTER--HE'LL PAY FOR IT!
DAYS LATER... AT A SPECIAL EVENT GIVE IN HONOR OF SUPERMAN'S SERVICES TO METROPOLIS....
WE OWE SUPERMAN A DEBT WE CAN NEVER REPAY!
THRILLING, EH, CLARK?
I'M SURE THAT IF SUPERMA WERE HER HE'D AGRE WITH YO LOIS!
THE END

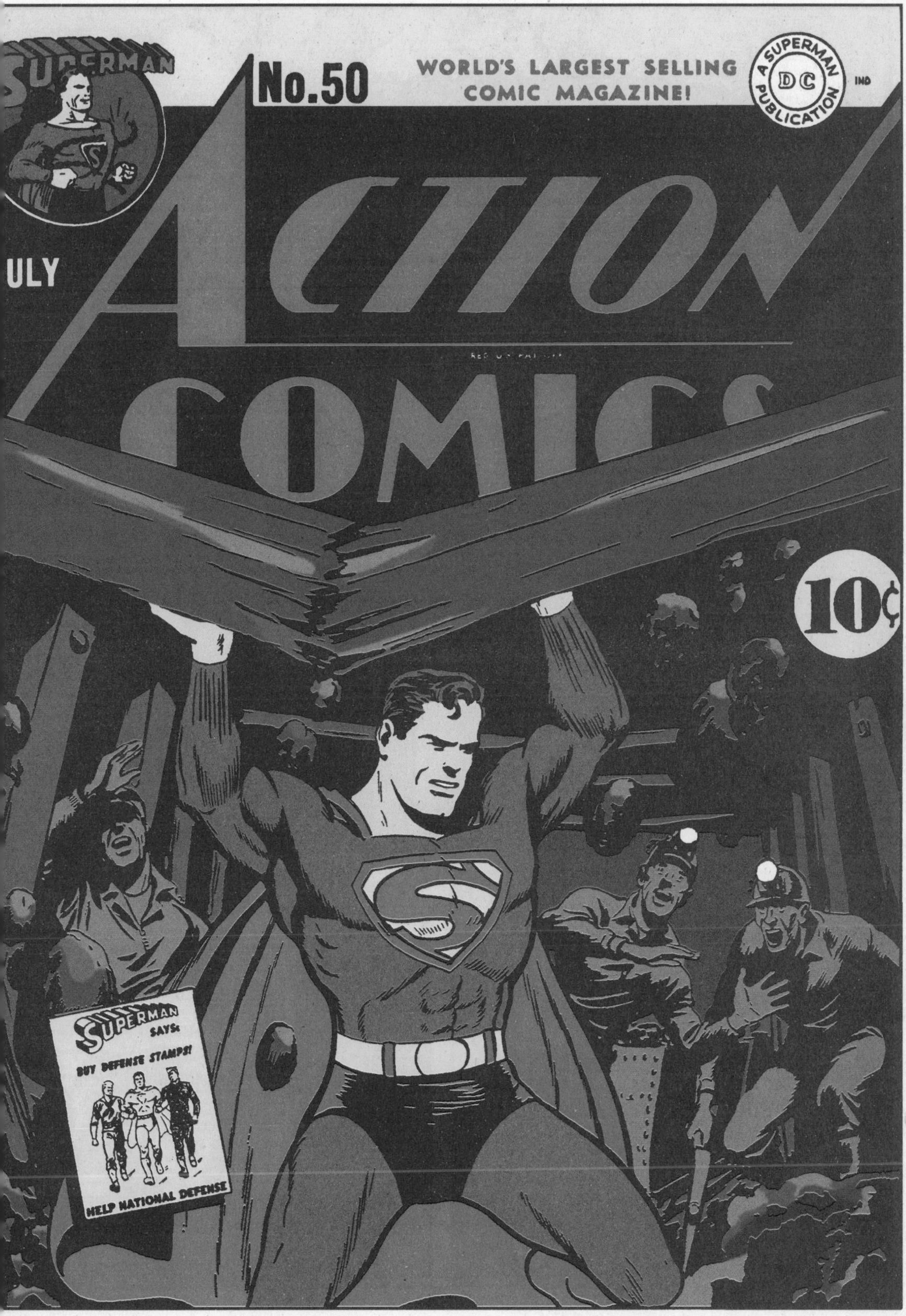
SUPERMAN
No.50
WORLD'S LARGEST SELLING
COMIC MAGAZINE!
A SUPERMAN
DC
PUBLICATION
IND
ULY
ACTION
COMICS
10¢
SUPERMAN
SAYS:
BUY DEFENSE STAMPS!
HELP NATIONAL DEFENSE

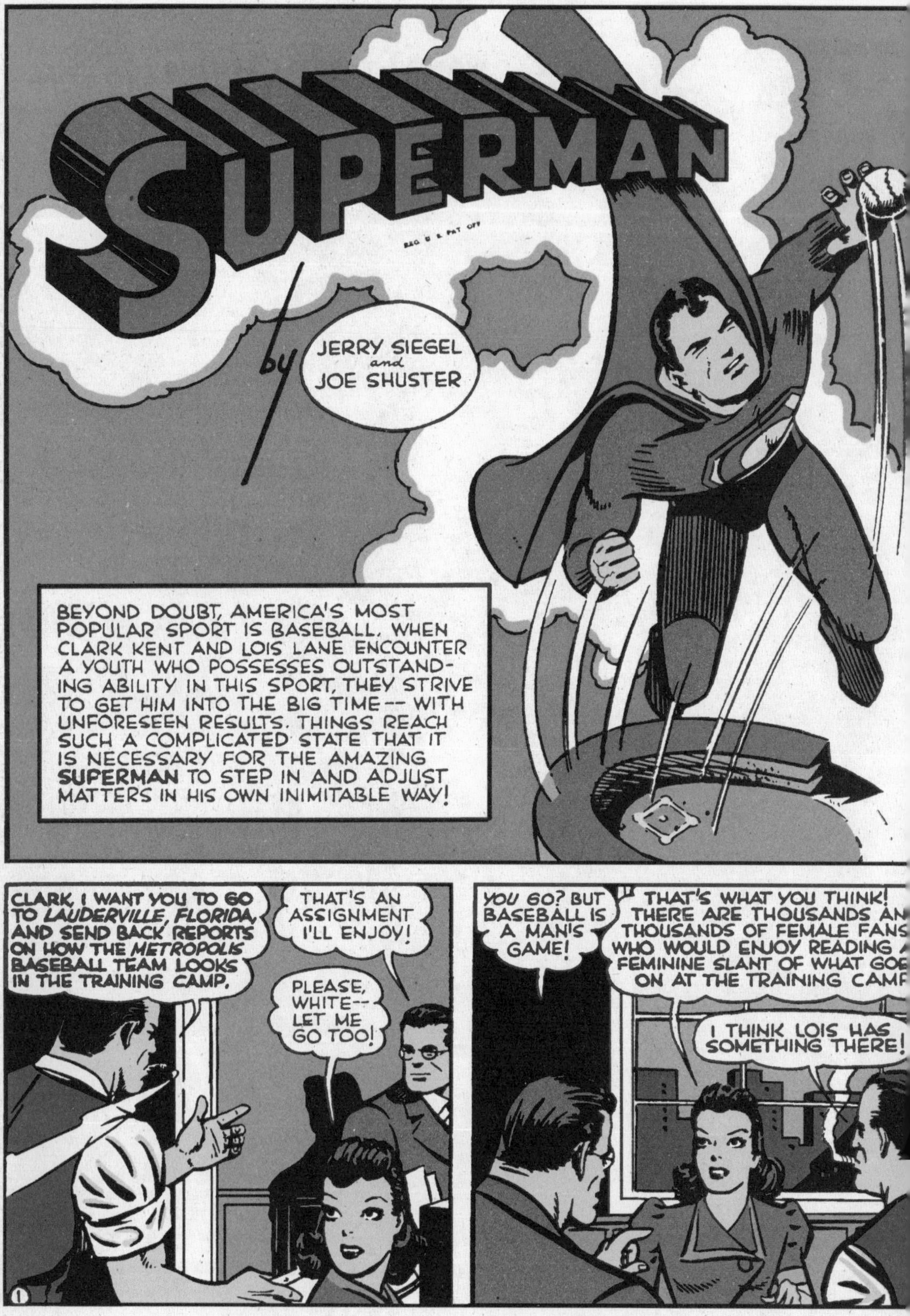
SUPERMAN
REG U.S. PAT OFF
by JERRY SIEGEL and JOE SHUSTER
BEYOND DOUBT, AMERICA'S MOST POPULAR SPORT IS BASEBALL. WHEN CLARK KENT AND LOIS LANE ENCOUNTER A YOUTH WHO POSSESSES OUTSTANDING ABILITY IN THIS SPORT, THEY STRIVE TO GET HIM INTO THE BIG TIME -- WITH UNFORESEEN RESULTS. THINGS REACH SUCH A COMPLICATED STATE THAT IT IS NECESSARY FOR THE AMAZING **SUPERMAN** TO STEP IN AND ADJUST MATTERS IN HIS OWN INIMITABLE WAY!
CLARK, I WANT YOU TO GO TO *LAUDERVILLE, FLORIDA*, AND SEND BACK REPORTS ON HOW THE *METROPOLIS* BASEBALL TEAM LOOKS IN THE TRAINING CAMP.
THAT'S AN ASSIGNMENT I'LL ENJOY!
PLEASE, WHITE-- LET ME GO TOO!
1
YOU GO? BUT BASEBALL IS A MAN'S GAME!
THAT'S WHAT YOU THINK! THERE ARE THOUSANDS AN THOUSANDS OF FEMALE FANS WHO WOULD ENJOY READING FEMININE SLANT OF WHAT GOE ON AT THE TRAINING CAMP
I THINK LOIS HAS SOMETHING THERE!

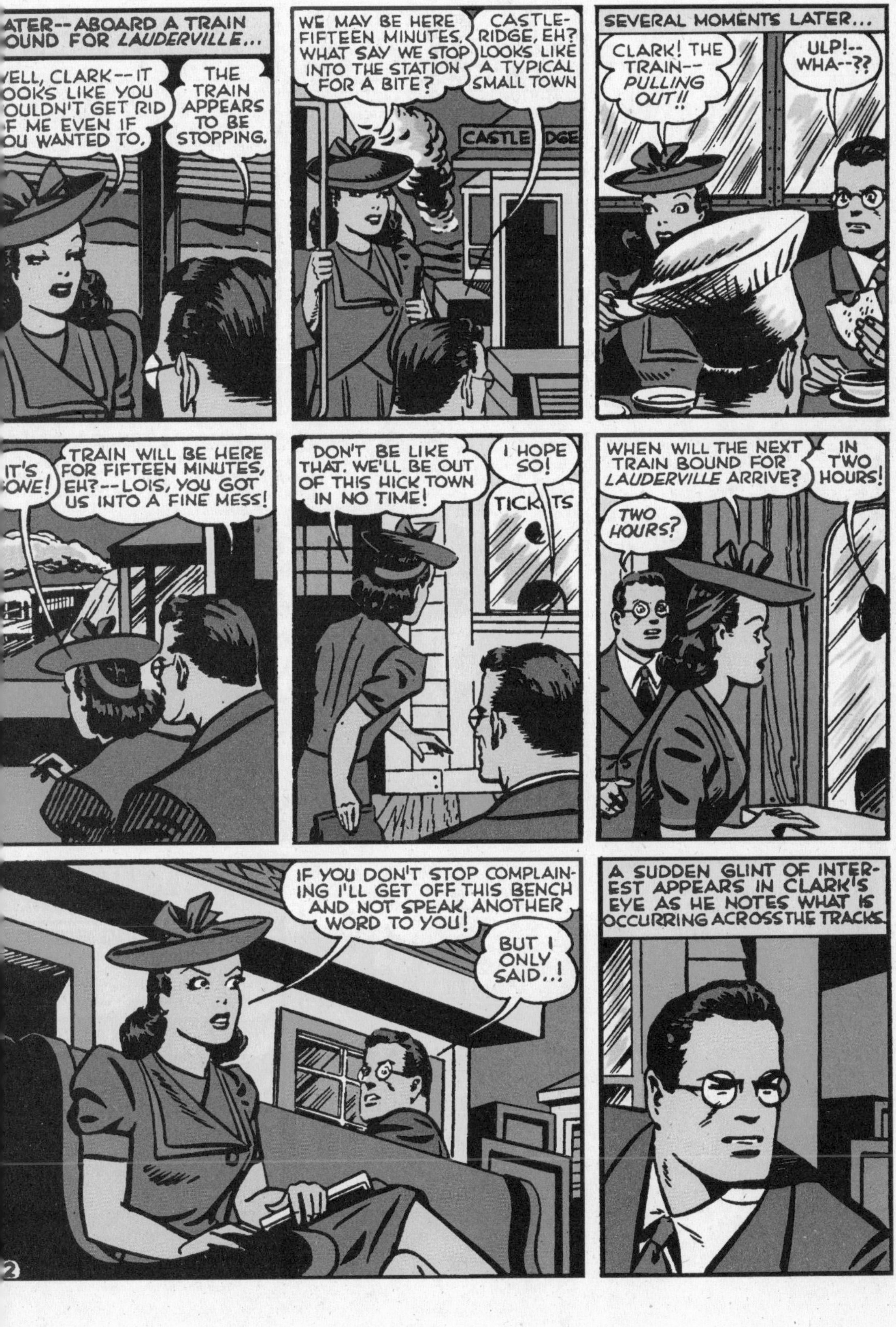
ATER--ABOARD A TRAIN
OUND FOR LAUDERVILLE...
VELL, CLARK--IT OOKS LIKE YOU OULDN'T GET RID F ME EVEN IF OU WANTED TO.
THE TRAIN APPEARS TO BE STOPPING.
WE MAY BE HERE FIFTEEN MINUTES. WHAT SAY WE STOP INTO THE STATION FOR A BITE?
CASTLE-RIDGE, EH? LOOKS LIKE A TYPICAL SMALL TOWN
CASTLE DGE
SEVERAL MOMENTS LATER...
CLARK! THE TRAIN-- PULLING OUT!!
ULP!-- WHA--??
IT'S ONE!
TRAIN WILL BE HERE FOR FIFTEEN MINUTES, EH?--LOIS, YOU GOT US INTO A FINE MESS!
DON'T BE LIKE THAT. WE'LL BE OUT OF THIS HICK TOWN IN NO TIME!
I HOPE SO!
TICK TS
WHEN WILL THE NEXT TRAIN BOUND FOR LAUDERVILLE ARRIVE?
IN TWO HOURS!
TWO HOURS?
IF YOU DON'T STOP COMPLAINING I'LL GET OFF THIS BENCH AND NOT SPEAK ANOTHER WORD TO YOU!
BUT I ONLY SAID..!
2
A SUDDEN GLINT OF INTEREST APPEARS IN CLARK'S EYE AS HE NOTES WHAT IS OCCURRING ACROSS THE TRACKS.

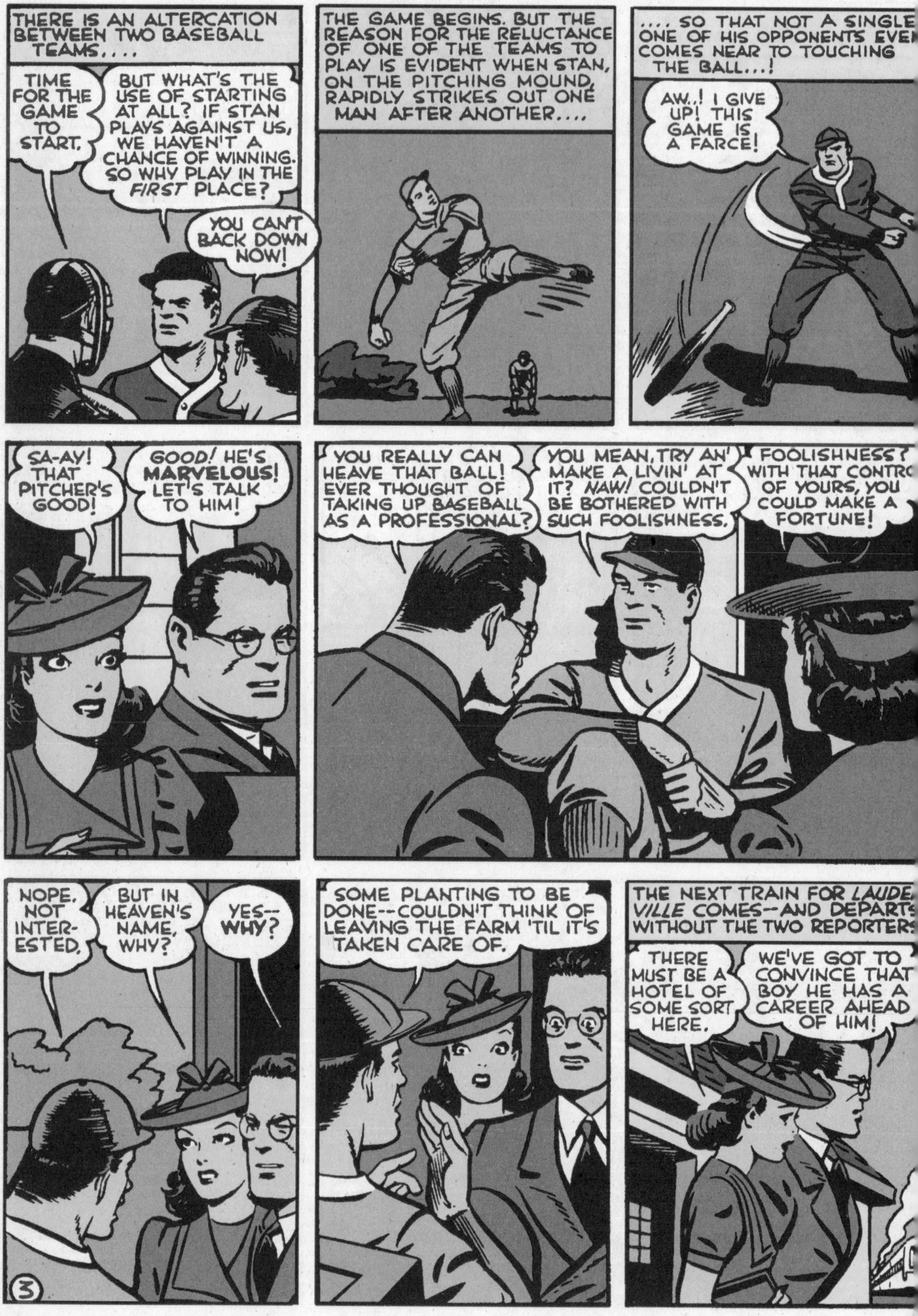

THERE IS AN ALTERCATION BETWEEN TWO BASEBALL TEAMS....
TIME FOR THE GAME TO START.
BUT WHAT'S THE USE OF STARTING AT ALL? IF STAN PLAYS AGAINST US, WE HAVEN'T A CHANCE OF WINNING. SO WHY PLAY IN THE FIRST PLACE?
YOU CAN'T BACK DOWN NOW!
THE GAME BEGINS. BUT THE REASON FOR THE RELUCTANCE OF ONE OF THE TEAMS TO PLAY IS EVIDENT WHEN STAN, ON THE PITCHING MOUND, RAPIDLY STRIKES OUT ONE MAN AFTER ANOTHER....
.... SO THAT NOT A SINGLE ONE OF HIS OPPONENTS EVEN COMES NEAR TO TOUCHING THE BALL...!
AW..! I GIVE UP! THIS GAME IS A FARCE!
SA-AY! THAT PITCHER'S GOOD!
GOOD! HE'S MARVELOUS! LET'S TALK TO HIM!
YOU REALLY CAN HEAVE THAT BALL! EVER THOUGHT OF TAKING UP BASEBALL AS A PROFESSIONAL?
YOU MEAN, TRY AN' MAKE A LIVIN' AT IT? NAW! COULDN'T BE BOTHERED WITH SUCH FOOLISHNESS.
FOOLISHNESS? WITH THAT CONTRO OF YOURS, YOU COULD MAKE A FORTUNE!
NOPE. NOT INTER-ESTED.
BUT IN HEAVEN'S NAME, WHY?
YES-- WHY?
3
SOME PLANTING TO BE DONE--COULDN'T THINK OF LEAVING THE FARM 'TIL IT'S TAKEN CARE OF.
THE NEXT TRAIN FOR LAUDE VILLE COMES--AND DEPARTS WITHOUT THE TWO REPORTERS
THERE MUST BE A HOTEL OF SOME SORT HERE.
WE'VE GOT TO CONVINCE THAT BOY HE HAS A CAREER AHEAD OF HIM!

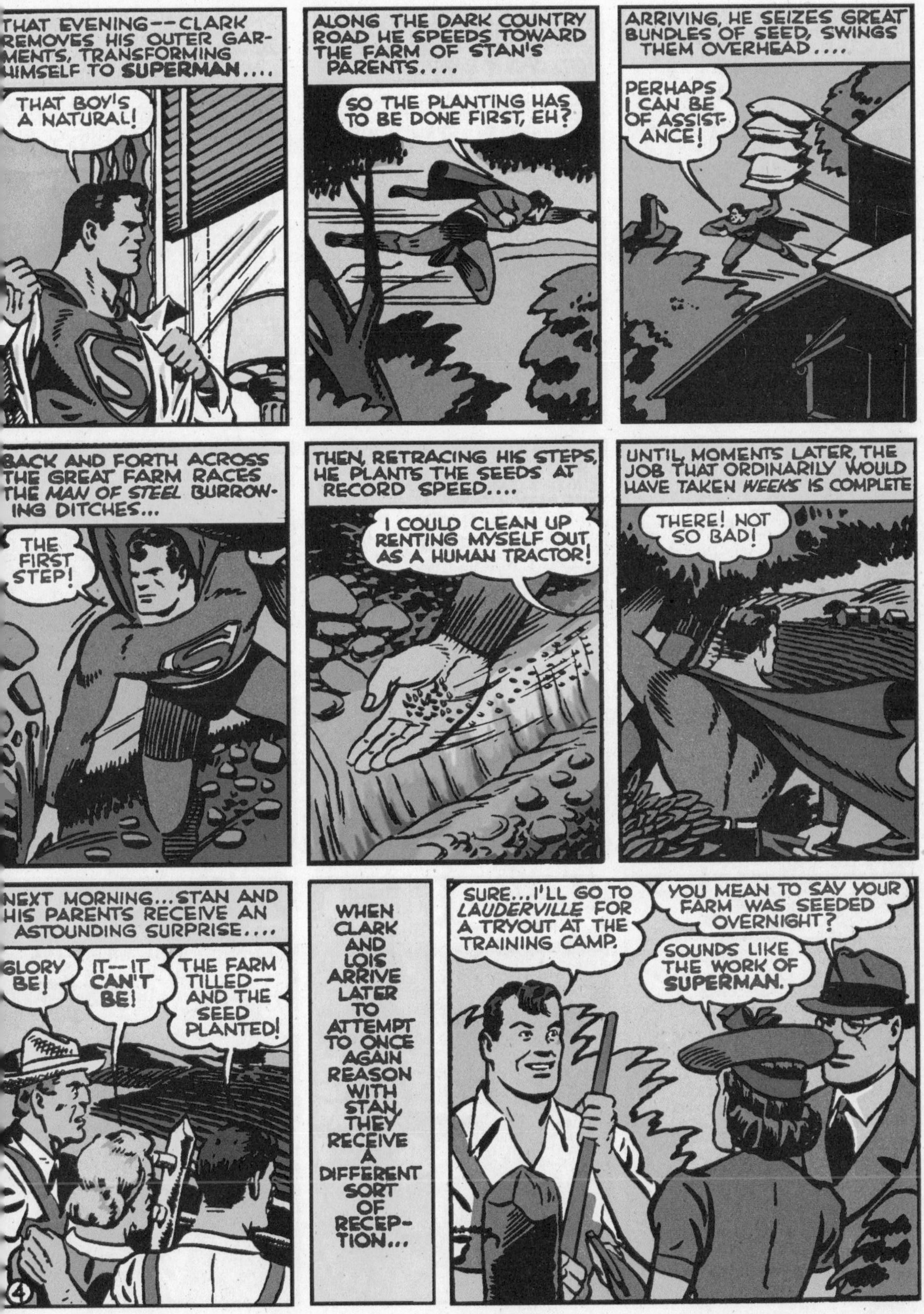
THAT EVENING--CLARK REMOVES HIS OUTER GARMENTS, TRANSFORMING HIMSELF TO SUPERMAN....
THAT BOY'S A NATURAL!
ALONG THE DARK COUNTRY ROAD HE SPEEDS TOWARD THE FARM OF STAN'S PARENTS....
SO THE PLANTING HAS TO BE DONE FIRST, EH?
ARRIVING, HE SEIZES GREAT BUNDLES OF SEED, SWINGS THEM OVERHEAD....
PERHAPS I CAN BE OF ASSISTANCE!
BACK AND FORTH ACROSS THE GREAT FARM RACES THE MAN OF STEEL BURROWING DITCHES...
THE FIRST STEP!
THEN, RETRACING HIS STEPS, HE PLANTS THE SEEDS AT RECORD SPEED....
I COULD CLEAN UP RENTING MYSELF OUT AS A HUMAN TRACTOR!
UNTIL, MOMENTS LATER, THE JOB THAT ORDINARILY WOULD HAVE TAKEN WEEKS IS COMPLETE
THERE! NOT SO BAD!
NEXT MORNING...STAN AND HIS PARENTS RECEIVE AN ASTOUNDING SURPRISE....
GLORY BE!
IT--IT CAN'T BE!
THE FARM TILLED--AND THE SEED PLANTED!
4
WHEN CLARK AND LOIS ARRIVE LATER TO ATTEMPT TO ONCE AGAIN REASON WITH STAN, THEY RECEIVE A DIFFERENT SORT OF RECEPTION...
SURE...I'LL GO TO LAUDERVILLE FOR A TRYOUT AT THE TRAINING CAMP.
YOU MEAN TO SAY YOUR FARM WAS SEEDED OVERNIGHT?
SOUNDS LIKE THE WORK OF SUPERMAN.

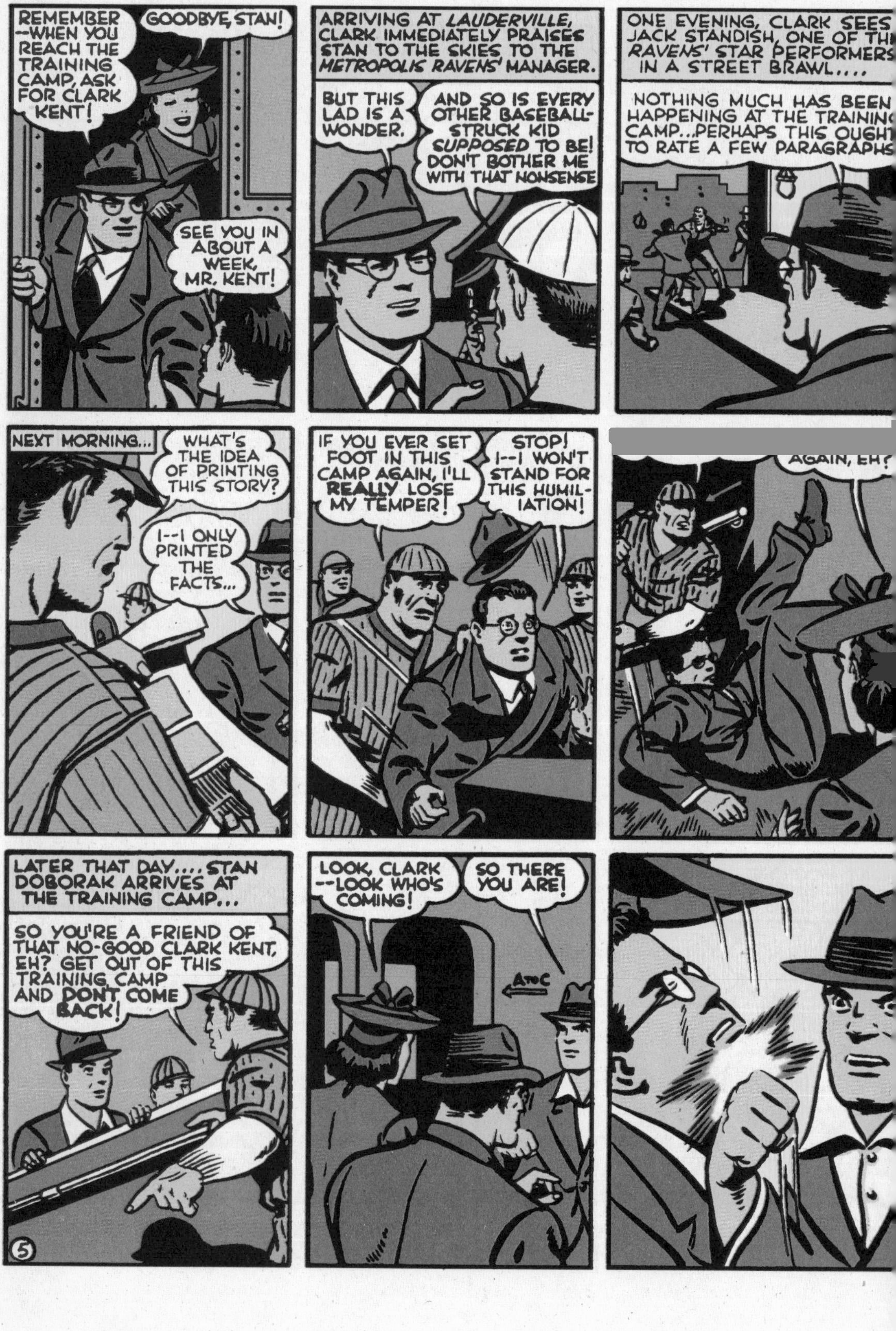
REMEMBER --WHEN YOU REACH THE TRAINING CAMP, ASK FOR CLARK KENT!
GOODBYE, STAN!
SEE YOU IN ABOUT A WEEK, MR. KENT!
ARRIVING AT *LAUDERVILLE,* CLARK IMMEDIATELY PRAISES STAN TO THE SKIES TO THE *METROPOLIS RAVENS'* MANAGER.
BUT THIS LAD IS A WONDER.
AND SO IS EVERY OTHER BASEBALL-STRUCK KID *SUPPOSED* TO BE! DON'T BOTHER ME WITH THAT NONSENSE
ONE EVENING, CLARK SEES JACK STANDISH, ONE OF TH *RAVENS'* STAR PERFORMERS IN A STREET BRAWL....
NOTHING MUCH HAS BEEN HAPPENING AT THE TRAININ CAMP...PERHAPS THIS OUGH TO RATE A FEW PARAGRAPHS
NEXT MORNING...
WHAT'S THE IDEA OF PRINTING THIS STORY?
I--I ONLY PRINTED THE FACTS...
IF YOU EVER SET FOOT IN THIS CAMP AGAIN, I'LL **REALLY** LOSE MY TEMPER!
STOP! I--I WON'T STAND FOR THIS HUMIL-IATION!
AGAIN, EH?
LATER THAT DAY.... STAN DOBORAK ARRIVES AT THE TRAINING CAMP...
SO YOU'RE A FRIEND OF THAT NO-GOOD CLARK KENT, EH? GET OUT OF THIS TRAINING CAMP AND **DON'T** COME BACK!
5
LOOK, CLARK --LOOK WHO'S COMING!
SO THERE YOU ARE!
A TO C

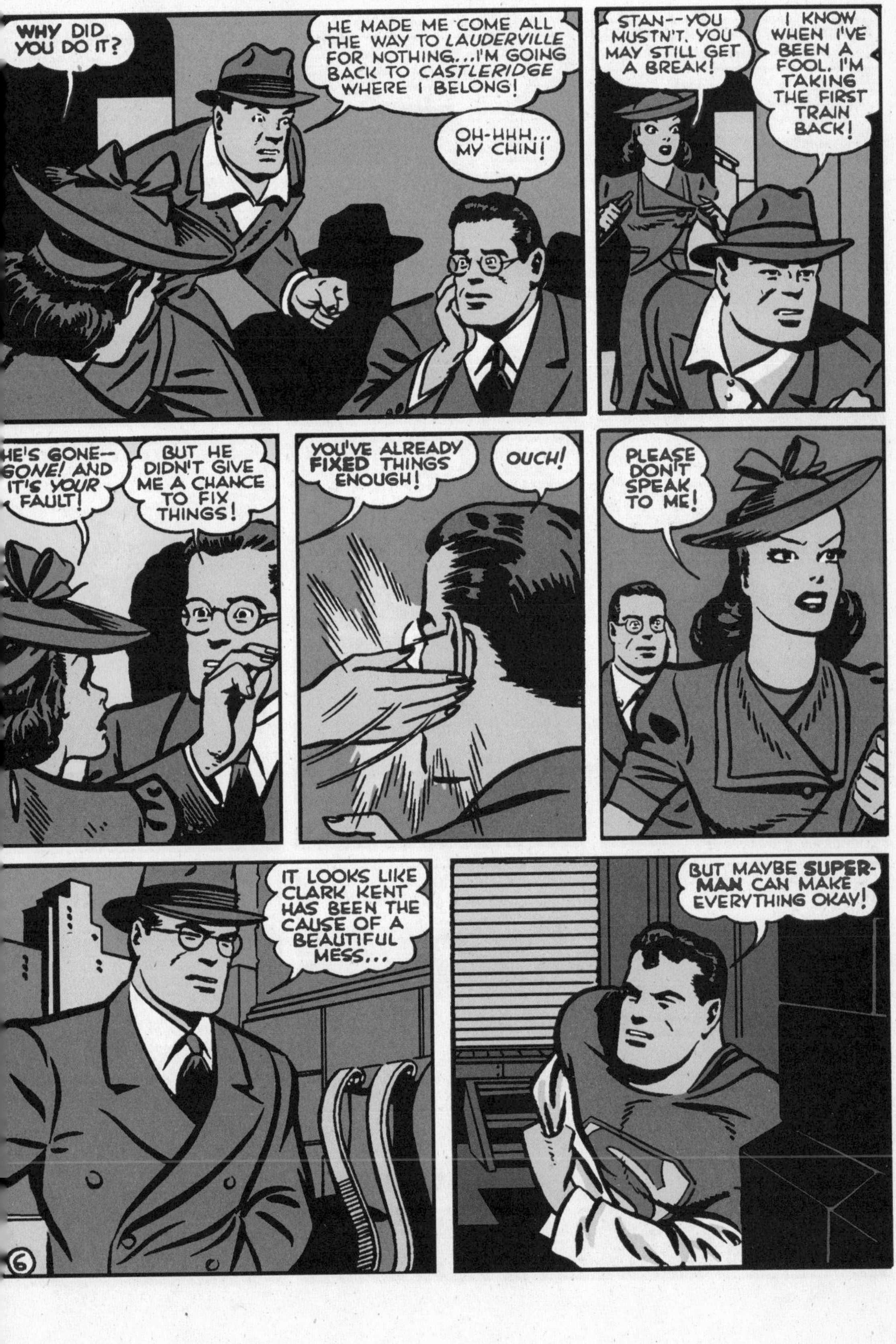
WHY DID YOU DO IT?
HE MADE ME COME ALL THE WAY TO LAUDERVILLE FOR NOTHING...I'M GOING BACK TO CASTLERIDGE WHERE I BELONG!
OH-HHH... MY CHIN!
STAN--YOU MUSTN'T. YOU MAY STILL GET A BREAK!
I KNOW WHEN I'VE BEEN A FOOL. I'M TAKING THE FIRST TRAIN BACK!
HE'S GONE--GONE! AND IT'S YOUR FAULT!
BUT HE DIDN'T GIVE ME A CHANCE TO FIX THINGS!
YOU'VE ALREADY FIXED THINGS ENOUGH!
OUCH!
PLEASE DON'T SPEAK TO ME!
6
IT LOOKS LIKE CLARK KENT HAS BEEN THE CAUSE OF A BEAUTIFUL MESS...
BUT MAYBE SUPERMAN CAN MAKE EVERYTHING OKAY!

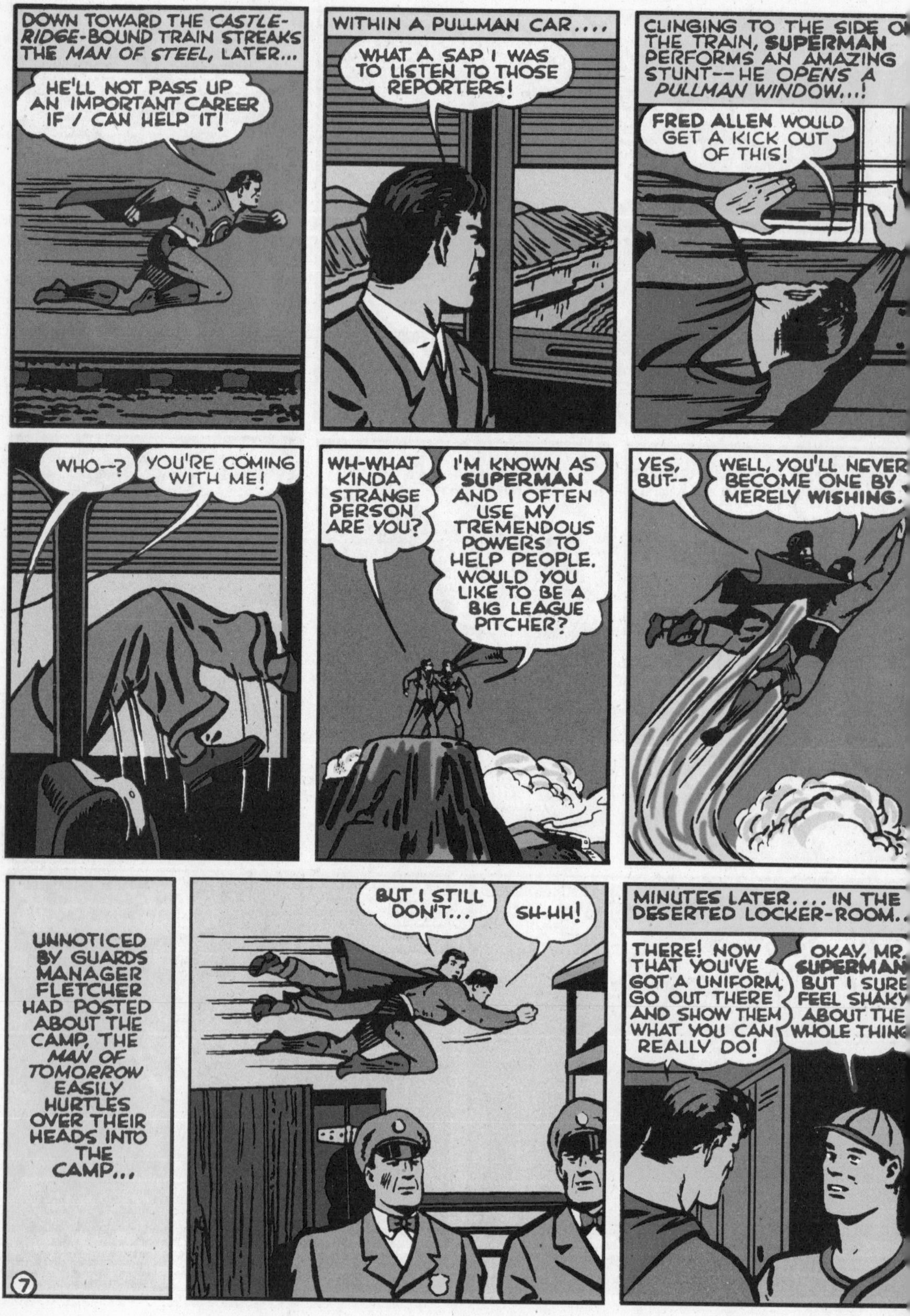

DOWN TOWARD THE CASTLE-RIDGE-BOUND TRAIN STREAKS THE MAN OF STEEL, LATER...
HE'LL NOT PASS UP AN IMPORTANT CAREER IF I CAN HELP IT!
WITHIN A PULLMAN CAR....
WHAT A SAP I WAS TO LISTEN TO THOSE REPORTERS!
CLINGING TO THE SIDE OF THE TRAIN, SUPERMAN PERFORMS AN AMAZING STUNT-- HE OPENS A PULLMAN WINDOW...!
FRED ALLEN WOULD GET A KICK OUT OF THIS!
WHO--?
YOU'RE COMING WITH ME!
WH-WHAT KINDA STRANGE PERSON ARE YOU?
I'M KNOWN AS SUPERMAN AND I OFTEN USE MY TREMENDOUS POWERS TO HELP PEOPLE. WOULD YOU LIKE TO BE A BIG LEAGUE PITCHER?
YES, BUT--
WELL, YOU'LL NEVER BECOME ONE BY MERELY WISHING.
UNNOTICED BY GUARDS MANAGER FLETCHER HAD POSTED ABOUT THE CAMP, THE MAN OF TOMORROW EASILY HURTLES OVER THEIR HEADS INTO THE CAMP...
7
BUT I STILL DON'T...
SH-HH!
MINUTES LATER.... IN THE DESERTED LOCKER-ROOM...
THERE! NOW THAT YOU'VE GOT A UNIFORM, GO OUT THERE AND SHOW THEM WHAT YOU CAN REALLY DO!
OKAY, MR. SUPERMAN BUT I SURE FEEL SHAKY ABOUT THE WHOLE THING

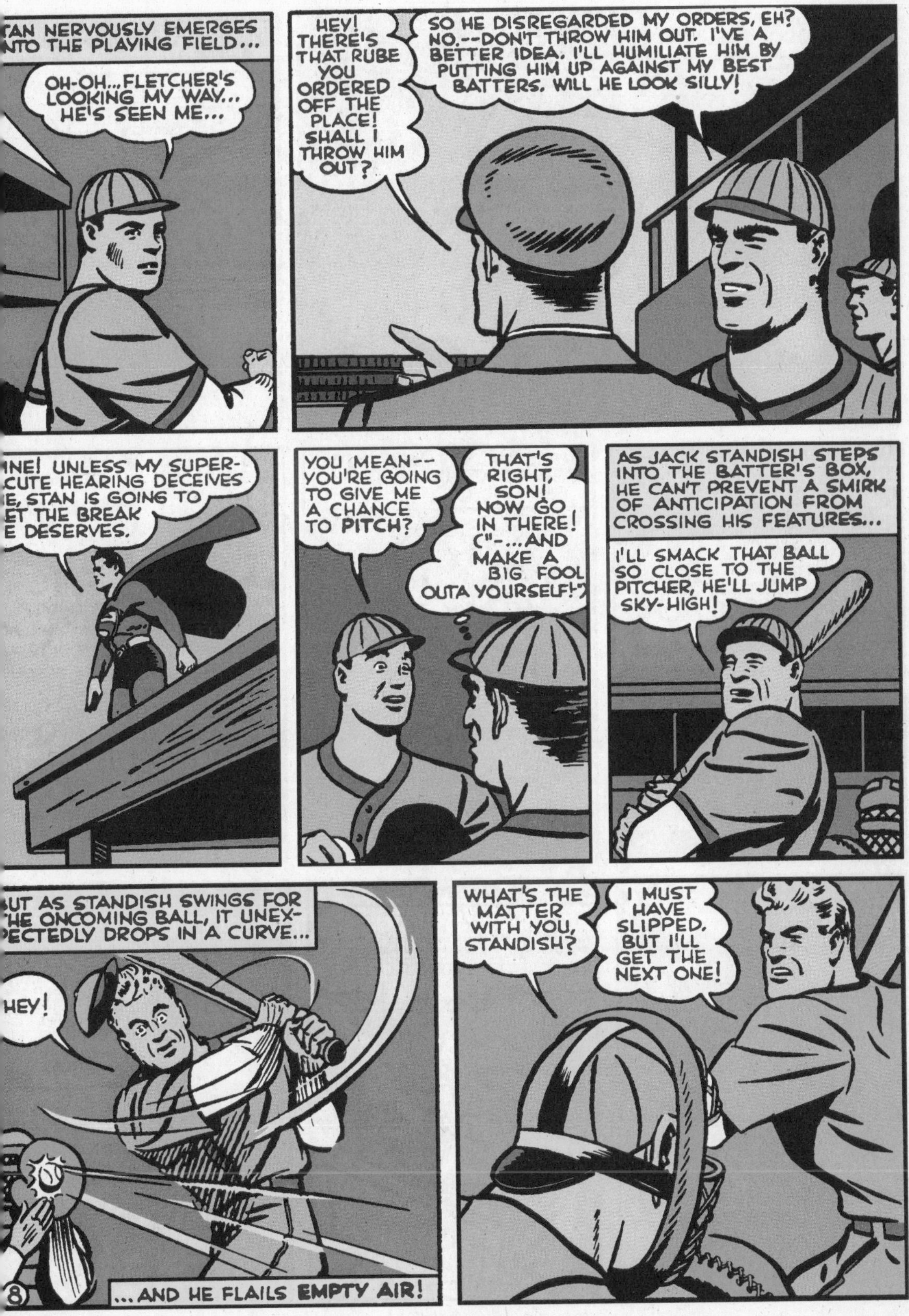
TAN NERVOUSLY EMERGES NTO THE PLAYING FIELD...
OH-OH...FLETCHER'S LOOKING MY WAY... HE'S SEEN ME...
HEY! THERE'S THAT RUBE YOU ORDERED OFF THE PLACE! SHALL I THROW HIM OUT?
SO HE DISREGARDED MY ORDERS, EH? NO.--DON'T THROW HIM OUT. I'VE A BETTER IDEA. I'LL HUMILIATE HIM BY PUTTING HIM UP AGAINST MY BEST BATTERS. WILL HE LOOK SILLY!
INE! UNLESS MY SUPER-CUTE HEARING DECEIVES E, STAN IS GOING TO ET THE BREAK E DESERVES.
YOU MEAN--YOU'RE GOING TO GIVE ME A CHANCE TO PITCH?
THAT'S RIGHT, SON! NOW GO IN THERE!
("-...AND MAKE A BIG FOOL OUTA YOURSELF!-")
AS JACK STANDISH STEPS INTO THE BATTER'S BOX, HE CAN'T PREVENT A SMIRK OF ANTICIPATION FROM CROSSING HIS FEATURES...
I'LL SMACK THAT BALL SO CLOSE TO THE PITCHER, HE'LL JUMP SKY-HIGH!
UT AS STANDISH SWINGS FOR HE ONCOMING BALL, IT UNEX-PECTEDLY DROPS IN A CURVE...
HEY!
8
...AND HE FLAILS EMPTY AIR!
WHAT'S THE MATTER WITH YOU, STANDISH?
I MUST HAVE SLIPPED. BUT I'LL GET THE NEXT ONE!

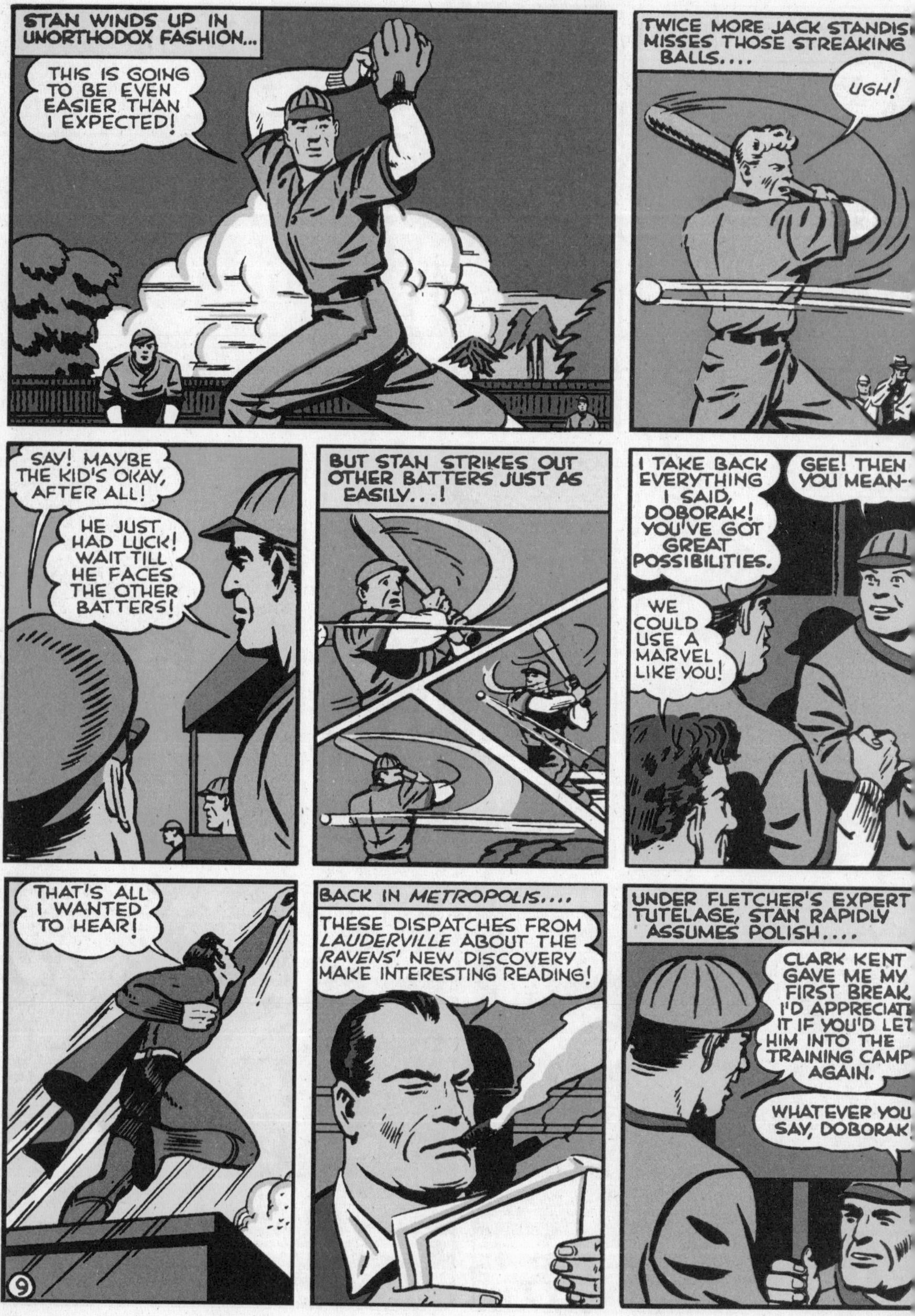
STAN WINDS UP IN UNORTHODOX FASHION...
THIS IS GOING TO BE EVEN EASIER THAN I EXPECTED!
TWICE MORE JACK STANDIS MISSES THOSE STREAKING BALLS....
UGH!
SAY! MAYBE THE KID'S OKAY, AFTER ALL!
HE JUST HAD LUCK! WAIT TILL HE FACES THE OTHER BATTERS!
BUT STAN STRIKES OUT OTHER BATTERS JUST AS EASILY...!
I TAKE BACK EVERYTHING I SAID, DOBORAK! YOU'VE GOT GREAT POSSIBILITIES.
GEE! THEN YOU MEAN--
WE COULD USE A MARVEL LIKE YOU!
THAT'S ALL I WANTED TO HEAR!
9
BACK IN METROPOLIS....
THESE DISPATCHES FROM LAUDERVILLE ABOUT THE RAVENS' NEW DISCOVERY MAKE INTERESTING READING!
UNDER FLETCHER'S EXPERT TUTELAGE, STAN RAPIDLY ASSUMES POLISH....
CLARK KENT GAVE ME MY FIRST BREAK. I'D APPRECIATE IT IF YOU'D LET HIM INTO THE TRAINING CAMP AGAIN.
WHATEVER YOU SAY, DOBORAK!

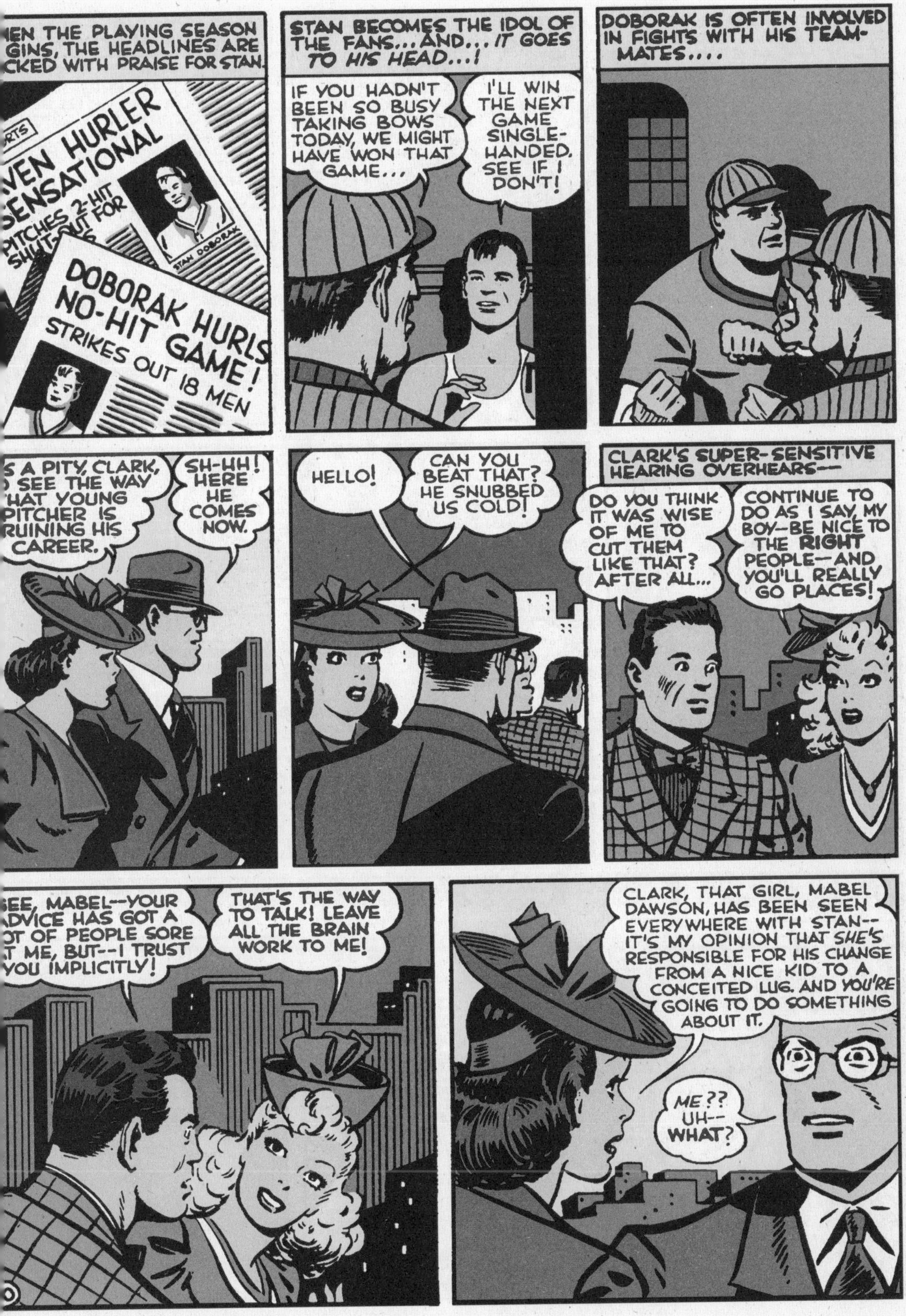
HEN THE PLAYING SEASON GINS, THE HEADLINES ARE CKED WITH PRAISE FOR STAN.
RTS
VEN HURLER SENSATIONAL
PITCHES 2-HIT SHUT-OUT FOR
STAN DOBORAK
DOBORAK HURLS NO-HIT GAME!
STRIKES OUT 18 MEN
STAN BECOMES THE IDOL OF THE FANS...AND...*IT GOES TO HIS HEAD...!*
IF YOU HADN'T BEEN SO BUSY TAKING BOWS TODAY, WE MIGHT HAVE WON THAT GAME...
I'LL WIN THE NEXT GAME SINGLE-HANDED. SEE IF I DON'T!
DOBORAK IS OFTEN INVOLVED IN FIGHTS WITH HIS TEAM-MATES....
S A PITY, CLARK, SEE THE WAY HAT YOUNG PITCHER IS RUINING HIS CAREER.
SH-HH! HERE HE COMES NOW.
HELLO!
CAN YOU BEAT THAT? HE SNUBBED US COLD!
CLARK'S SUPER-SENSITIVE HEARING OVERHEARS--
DO YOU THINK IT WAS WISE OF ME TO CUT THEM LIKE THAT? AFTER ALL...
CONTINUE TO DO AS I SAY, MY BOY--BE NICE TO THE **RIGHT** PEOPLE--AND YOU'LL REALLY GO PLACES!
SEE, MABEL--YOUR ADVICE HAS GOT A OT OF PEOPLE SORE T ME, BUT--I TRUST YOU IMPLICITLY!
THAT'S THE WAY TO TALK! LEAVE ALL THE BRAIN WORK TO ME!
CLARK, THAT GIRL, MABEL DAWSON, HAS BEEN SEEN EVERYWHERE WITH STAN--IT'S MY OPINION THAT *SHE'S* RESPONSIBLE FOR HIS CHANGE FROM A NICE KID TO A CONCEITED LUG. AND *YOU'RE* GOING TO DO SOMETHING ABOUT IT.
ME?? UH--**WHAT?**

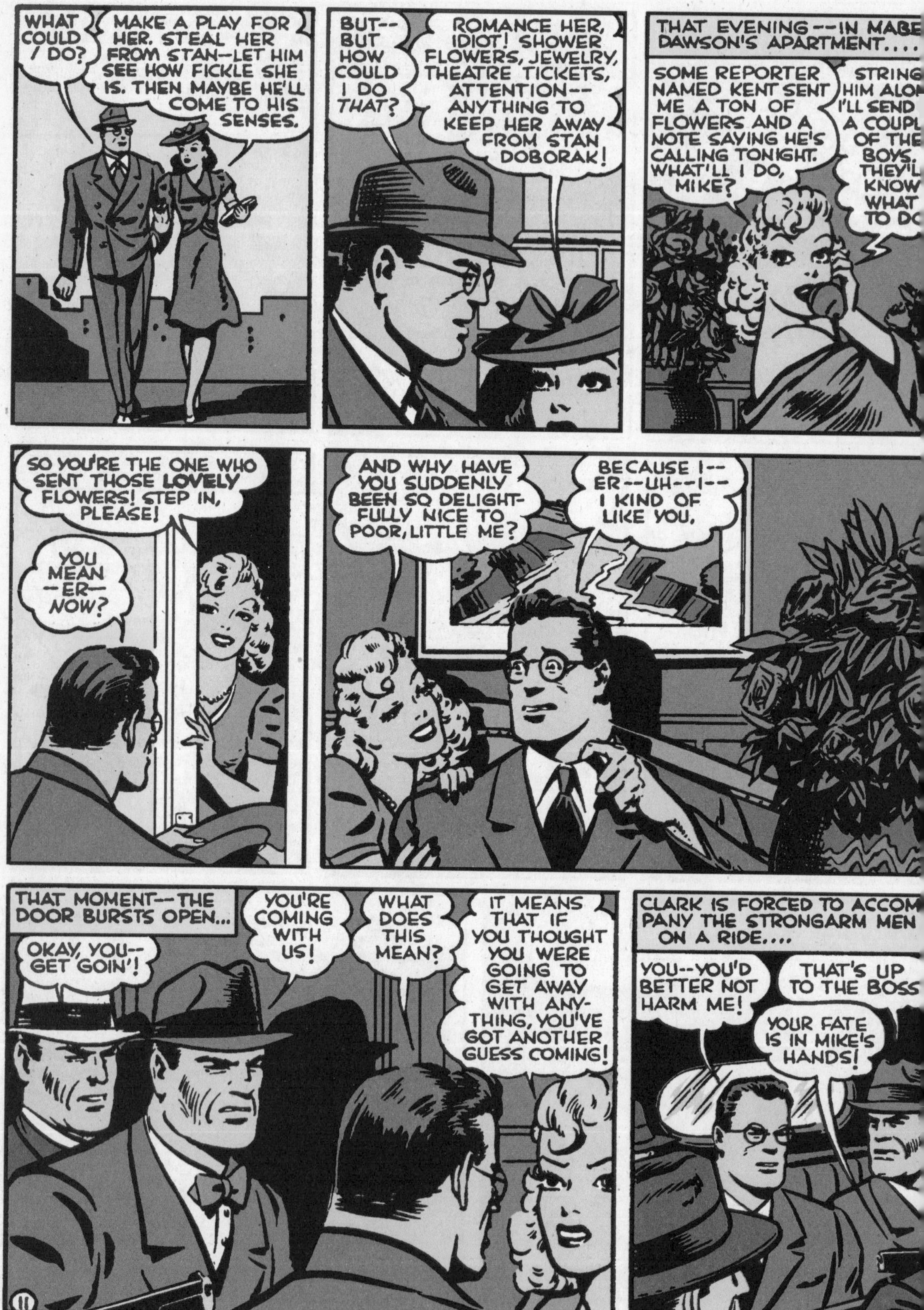
WHAT COULD *I* DO?
MAKE A PLAY FOR HER. STEAL HER FROM STAN--LET HIM SEE HOW FICKLE SHE IS. THEN MAYBE HE'LL COME TO HIS SENSES.
BUT--BUT HOW COULD I DO *THAT*?
ROMANCE HER, IDIOT! SHOWER FLOWERS, JEWELRY, THEATRE TICKETS, ATTENTION--ANYTHING TO KEEP HER AWAY FROM STAN DOBORAK!
THAT EVENING--IN MABE DAWSON'S APARTMENT....
SOME REPORTER NAMED KENT SENT ME A TON OF FLOWERS AND A NOTE SAYING HE'S CALLING TONIGHT. WHAT'LL I DO, MIKE?
STRING HIM ALO I'LL SEND A COUPL OF THE BOYS. THEY'L KNOW WHAT TO D
SO YOU'RE THE ONE WHO SENT THOSE **LOVELY** FLOWERS! STEP IN, PLEASE!
YOU MEAN -ER- *NOW*?
AND WHY HAVE YOU SUDDENLY BEEN SO DELIGHTFULLY NICE TO POOR, LITTLE ME?
BECAUSE I--ER--UH--I--I KIND OF LIKE YOU.
THAT MOMENT--THE DOOR BURSTS OPEN...
OKAY, YOU--GET GOIN'!
YOU'RE COMING WITH US!
WHAT DOES THIS MEAN?
IT MEANS THAT IF YOU THOUGHT YOU WERE GOING TO GET AWAY WITH ANYTHING, YOU'VE GOT ANOTHER GUESS COMING!
11
CLARK IS FORCED TO ACCOM PANY THE STRONGARM MEN ON A RIDE....
YOU--YOU'D BETTER NOT HARM ME!
THAT'S UP TO THE BOSS
YOUR FATE IS IN MIKE'S HANDS!

LATER-- CLARK IS LED INTO THE PRESENCE OF MIKE CAPUTO, BIG-TIME GAMBLER....

WHY HAVE YOU HAD OUR MEN BRING ME HERE?

I WANT TO KNOW YOUR ANGLE. WHY DID YOU *REALLY* MAKE A PLAY FOR MABEL?

I--I DON'T KNOW WHAT YOU'RE TALK-ING ABOUT...

I'VE NO TIME TO WASTE ON YOU!

CLARK IS LOCKED IN A ROOM....

WE'LL ATTEND TO HIM LATER! RIGHT NOW THERE'S SOME-THING ELSE I'VE GOT TO ATTEND TO. LET'S GET OUT OF HERE!

WITHIN THE ROOM, CLARK QUICKLY REMOVES HIS OUTER GARMENTS, TRANSFORMING HIMSELF TO-- *SUPERMAN*....

MIKE ISN'T THE ONLY ONE WHO WANTS INFORMATION. ONLY *I* AIM TO GET MINE *NOW!*

AS THE THUGS EMERGE FROM THE HOME, A COLOR-FULLY COSTUMED FIGURE CRASHES DOWN BEFORE THEM!

AWK!

SUPER-MAN!

GET HIM, MEN!

BUT AS THE THUGS CHARGE *SUPERMAN*, HE MOVES IRRESISTIBLY FORWARD, THEY CAREEN OFF HIM AS THO STRIKING A SOLID WALL...

LEGGO OF ME!

NOT-YET--!

UP INTO THE SKY HURTLES *SUPERMAN* WITH HIS SHRIEKING CAPTIVE,....

YEEEEE! I CAN'T STAND HEIGHTS!

THAT'S FINE! THEN MAYBE WE CAN SAVE A LOT OF TIME!

12

YOU KNOW WHAT I'M CAPABLE OF DOING, MIKE. DO I HAVE TO PUT YOU THRU THE WORKS OR--

OH-HHH-- MY HEAD --THE DIZZINESS... I'LL TELL YOU ANYTHING!

WHY ARE YOU AND MABEL INTERESTED IN STAN DOBORAK?

WE--WE PLANNED TO GET THE KID UNDER OUR THUMB-- GET HIM TO INVEST DOUGH IN AN APPAR-ENTLY "LEGITIMATE" INVESTMENT--THEN TELL HIM THAT UNLESS HE THREW GAMES WE'D BET ON, WE'D CLAIM HE REALLY GOT HIS "INVEST-MENT PROFITS" FOR THROWING GAMES.

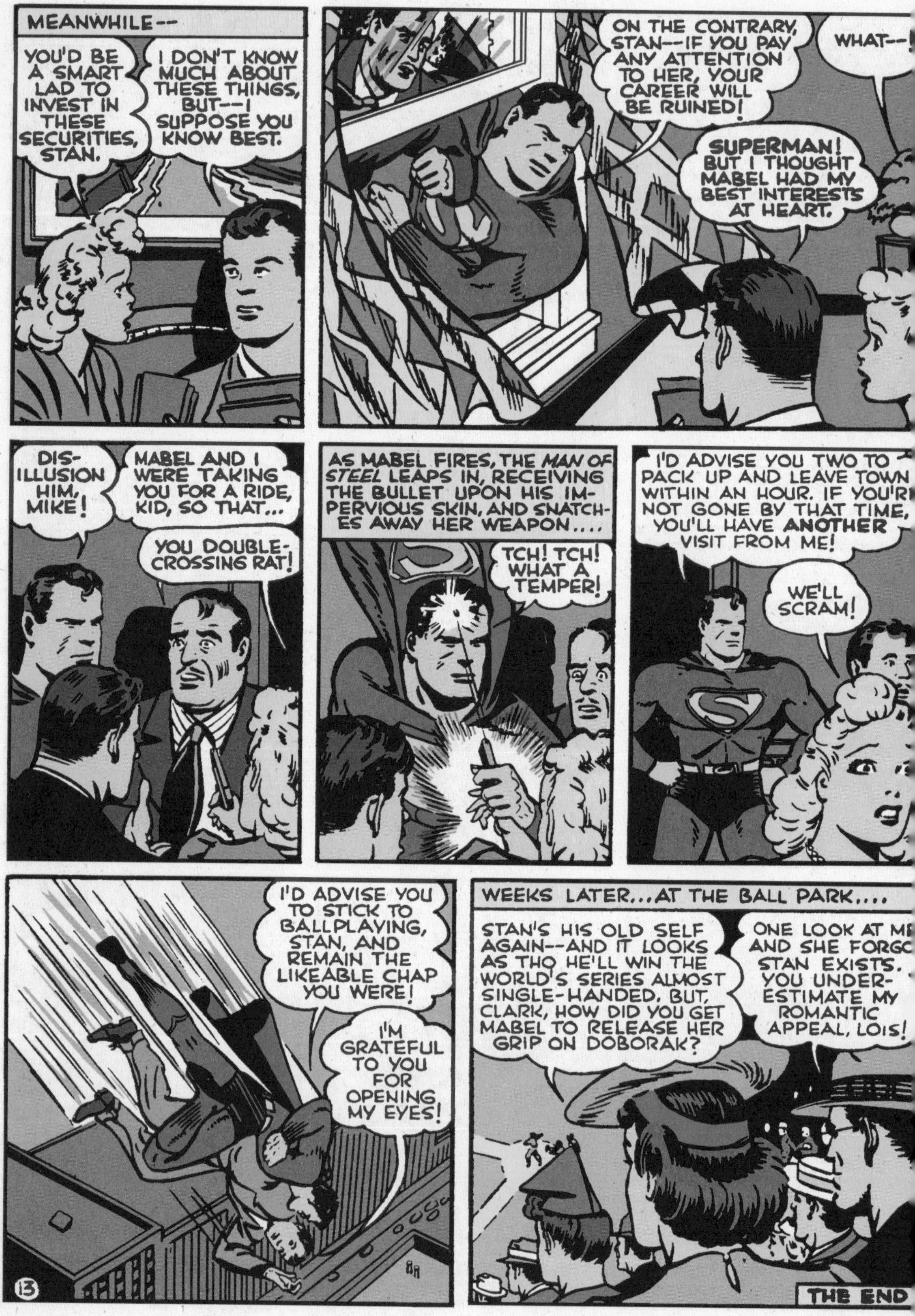
MEANWHILE--
YOU'D BE A SMART LAD TO INVEST IN THESE SECURITIES, STAN.
I DON'T KNOW MUCH ABOUT THESE THINGS, BUT--I SUPPOSE YOU KNOW BEST.
ON THE CONTRARY, STAN--IF YOU PAY ANY ATTENTION TO HER, YOUR CAREER WILL BE RUINED!
WHAT--!
SUPERMAN! BUT I THOUGHT MABEL HAD MY BEST INTERESTS AT HEART.
DIS-ILLUSION HIM, MIKE!
MABEL AND I WERE TAKING YOU FOR A RIDE, KID, SO THAT...
YOU DOUBLE-CROSSING RAT!
AS MABEL FIRES, THE MAN OF STEEL LEAPS IN, RECEIVING THE BULLET UPON HIS IMPERVIOUS SKIN, AND SNATCHES AWAY HER WEAPON....
TCH! TCH! WHAT A TEMPER!
I'D ADVISE YOU TWO TO PACK UP AND LEAVE TOWN WITHIN AN HOUR. IF YOU'R NOT GONE BY THAT TIME, YOU'LL HAVE ANOTHER VISIT FROM ME!
WE'LL SCRAM!
I'D ADVISE YOU TO STICK TO BALLPLAYING, STAN, AND REMAIN THE LIKEABLE CHAP YOU WERE!
I'M GRATEFUL TO YOU FOR OPENING MY EYES!
13
WEEKS LATER...AT THE BALL PARK....
STAN'S HIS OLD SELF AGAIN--AND IT LOOKS AS THO HE'LL WIN THE WORLD'S SERIES ALMOST SINGLE-HANDED. BUT, CLARK, HOW DID YOU GET MABEL TO RELEASE HER GRIP ON DOBORAK?
ONE LOOK AT M AND SHE FORGO STAN EXISTS. YOU UNDER-ESTIMATE MY ROMANTIC APPEAL, LOIS!
THE END

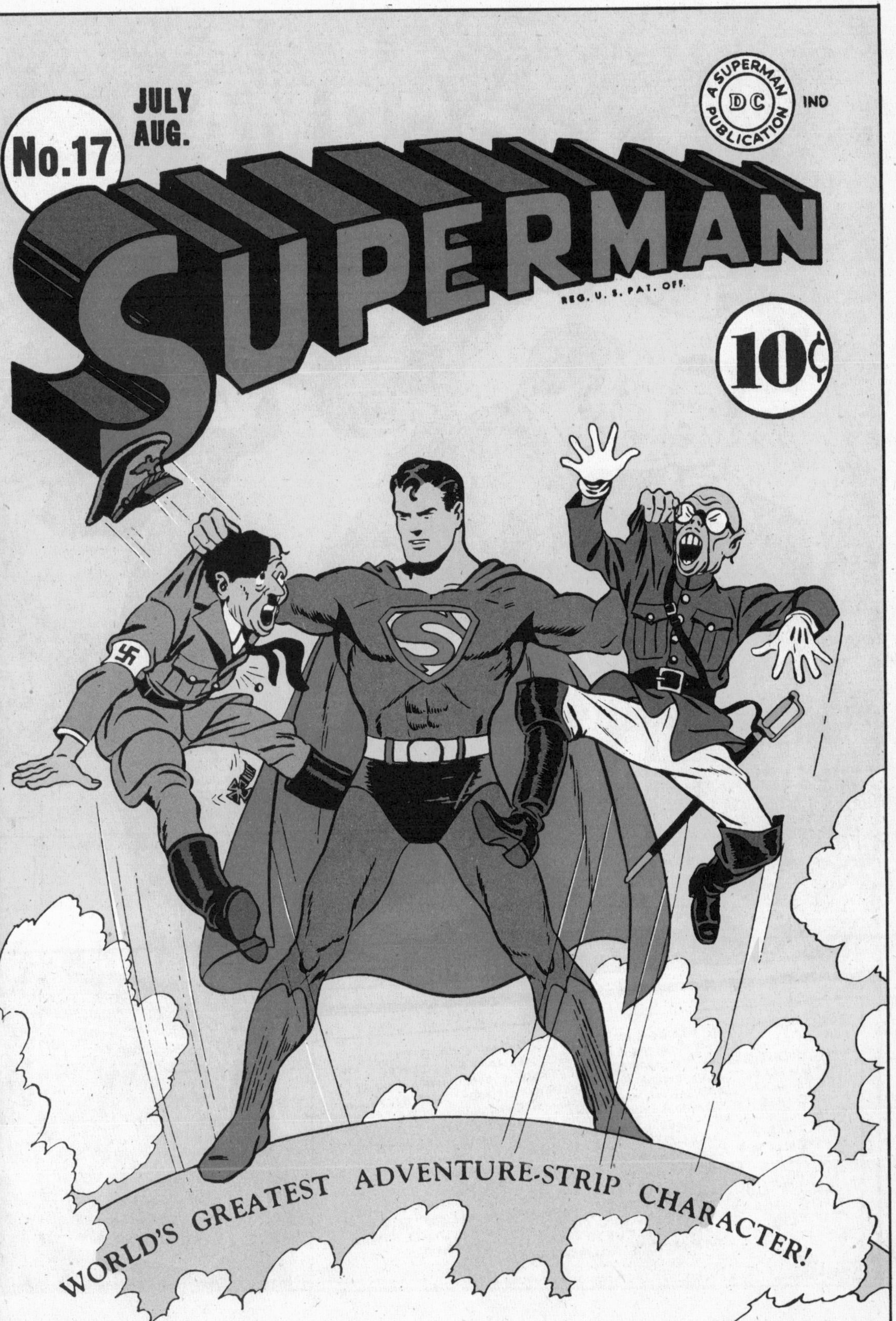

No.17
JULY
AUG.
A SUPERMAN DC PUBLICATION
IND
SUPERMAN
REG. U. S. PAT. OFF.
10¢
WORLD'S GREATEST ADVENTURE-STRIP CHARACTER!

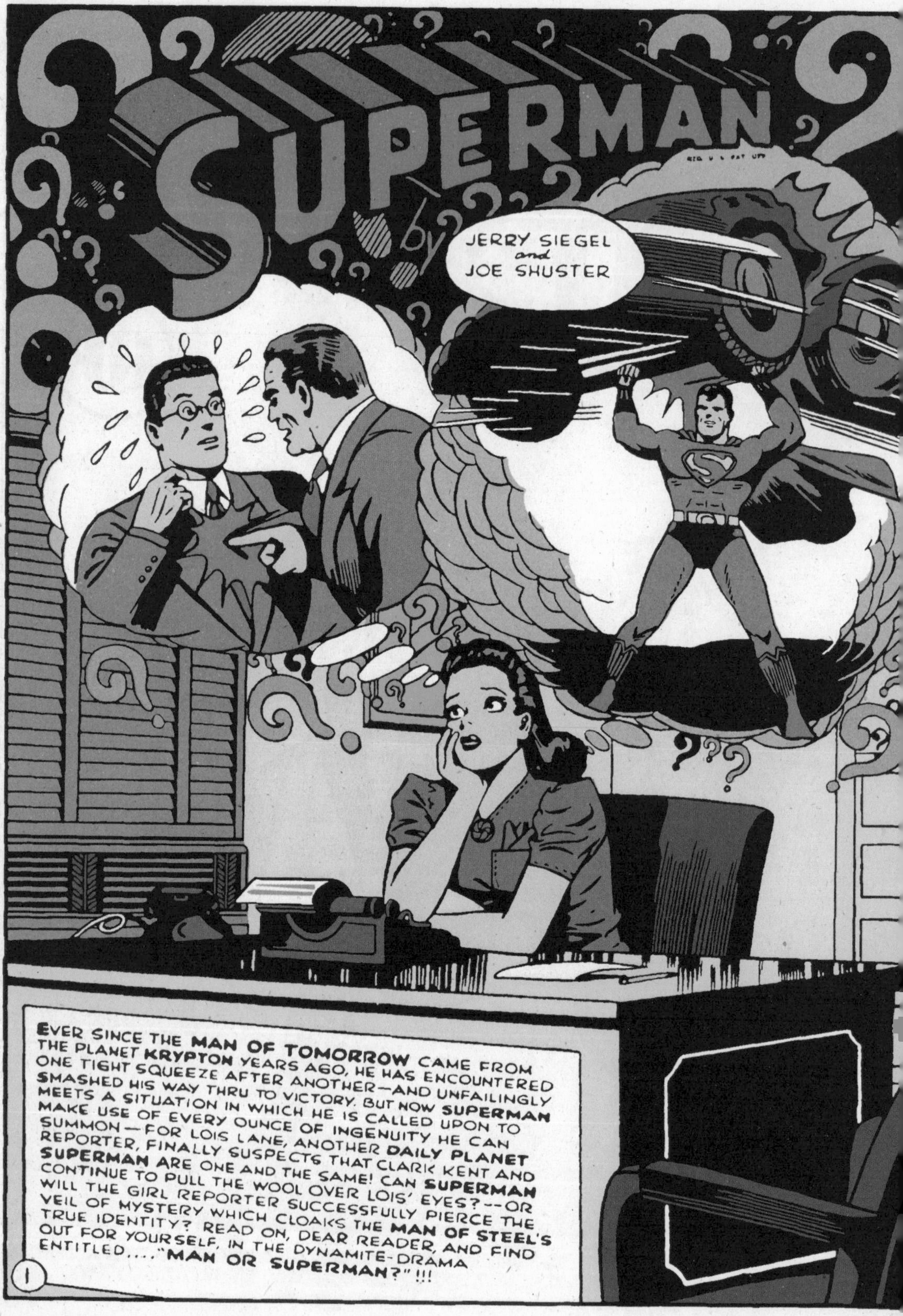
SUPERMAN
by
JERRY SIEGEL and JOE SHUSTER
EVER SINCE THE MAN OF TOMORROW CAME FROM THE PLANET KRYPTON YEARS AGO, HE HAS ENCOUNTERED ONE TIGHT SQUEEZE AFTER ANOTHER—AND UNFAILINGLY SMASHED HIS WAY THRU TO VICTORY. BUT NOW SUPERMAN MEETS A SITUATION IN WHICH HE IS CALLED UPON TO MAKE USE OF EVERY OUNCE OF INGENUITY HE CAN SUMMON—FOR LOIS LANE, ANOTHER DAILY PLANET REPORTER, FINALLY SUSPECTS THAT CLARK KENT AND SUPERMAN ARE ONE AND THE SAME! CAN SUPERMAN CONTINUE TO PULL THE WOOL OVER LOIS' EYES?--OR WILL THE GIRL REPORTER SUCCESSFULLY PIERCE THE VEIL OF MYSTERY WHICH CLOAKS THE MAN OF STEEL'S TRUE IDENTITY? READ ON, DEAR READER, AND FIND OUT FOR YOURSELF, IN THE DYNAMITE-DRAMA ENTITLED...."MAN OR SUPERMAN?"!!!
1

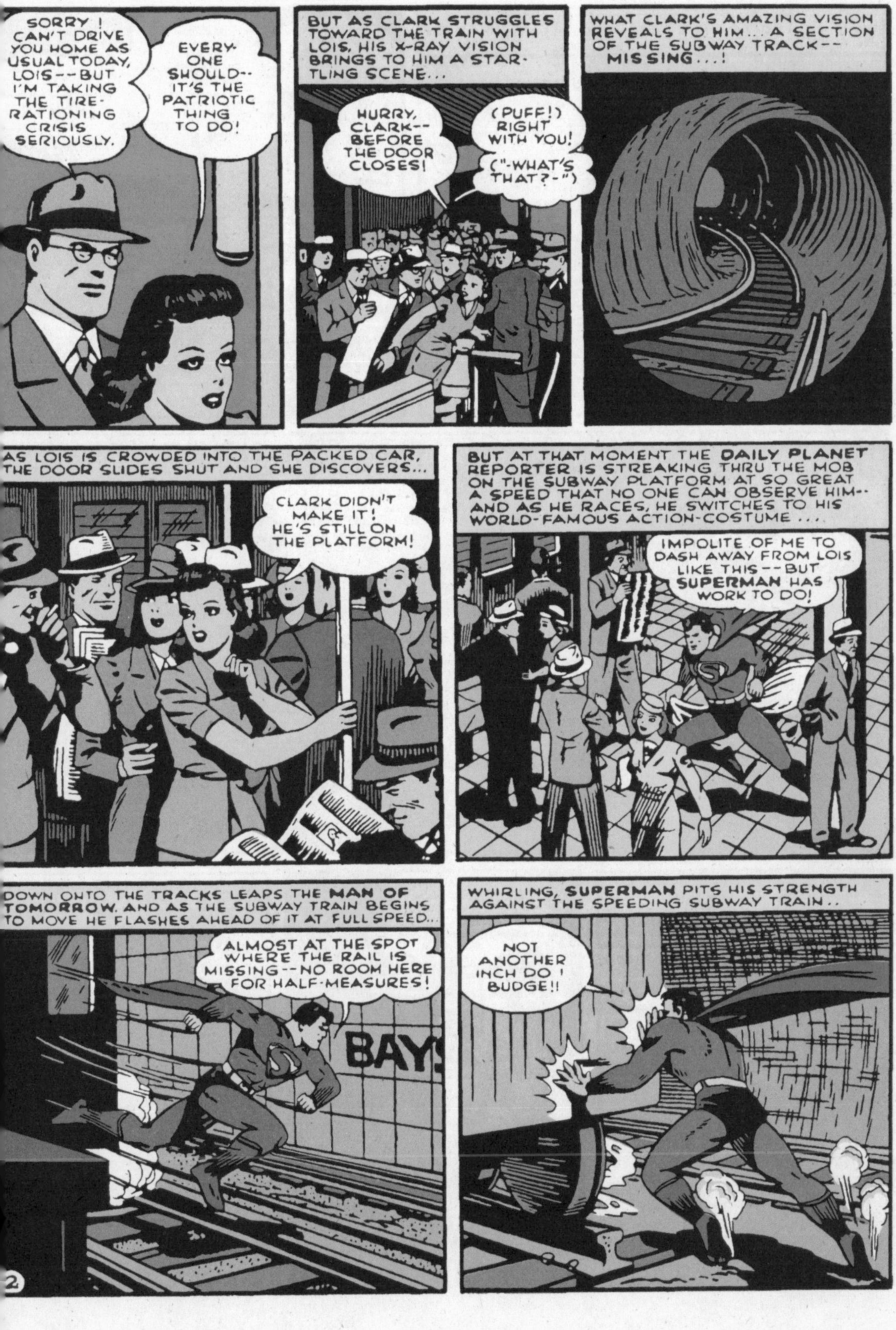
SORRY ! CAN'T DRIVE YOU HOME AS USUAL TODAY, LOIS--BUT I'M TAKING THE TIRE-RATIONING CRISIS SERIOUSLY.
EVERY-ONE SHOULD--IT'S THE PATRIOTIC THING TO DO!
BUT AS CLARK STRUGGLES TOWARD THE TRAIN WITH LOIS, HIS X-RAY VISION BRINGS TO HIM A STARTLING SCENE...
HURRY, CLARK--BEFORE THE DOOR CLOSES!
(PUFF!) RIGHT WITH YOU!
("-WHAT'S THAT?-")
WHAT CLARK'S AMAZING VISION REVEALS TO HIM... A SECTION OF THE SUBWAY TRACK--**MISSING**...!
AS LOIS IS CROWDED INTO THE PACKED CAR, THE DOOR SLIDES SHUT AND SHE DISCOVERS...
CLARK DIDN'T MAKE IT! HE'S STILL ON THE PLATFORM!
BUT AT THAT MOMENT THE **DAILY PLANET** REPORTER IS STREAKING THRU THE MOB ON THE SUBWAY PLATFORM AT SO GREAT A SPEED THAT NO ONE CAN OBSERVE HIM--AND AS HE RACES, HE SWITCHES TO HIS WORLD-FAMOUS ACTION-COSTUME ...
IMPOLITE OF ME TO DASH AWAY FROM LOIS LIKE THIS--BUT **SUPERMAN** HAS WORK TO DO!
DOWN ONTO THE TRACKS LEAPS THE **MAN OF TOMORROW**. AND AS THE SUBWAY TRAIN BEGINS TO MOVE HE FLASHES AHEAD OF IT AT FULL SPEED...
ALMOST AT THE SPOT WHERE THE RAIL IS MISSING--NO ROOM HERE FOR HALF-MEASURES!
BAYS
2
WHIRLING, **SUPERMAN** PITS HIS STRENGTH AGAINST THE SPEEDING SUBWAY TRAIN..
NOT ANOTHER INCH DO I BUDGE!!

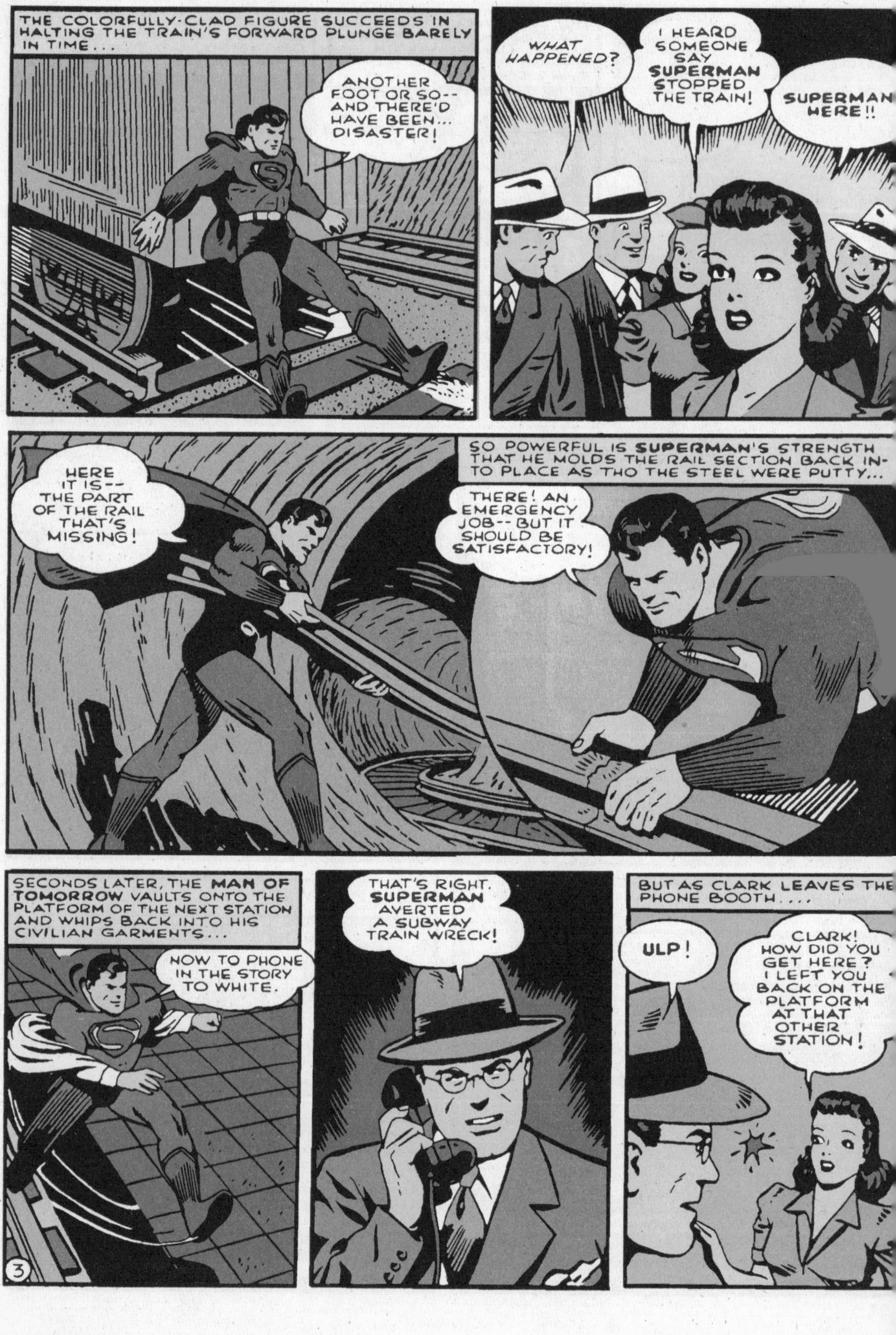
THE COLORFULLY-CLAD FIGURE SUCCEEDS IN HALTING THE TRAIN'S FORWARD PLUNGE BARELY IN TIME...
ANOTHER FOOT OR SO-- AND THERE'D HAVE BEEN... DISASTER!
WHAT HAPPENED?
I HEARD SOMEONE SAY SUPERMAN STOPPED THE TRAIN!
SUPERMAN HERE!!
HERE IT IS-- THE PART OF THE RAIL THAT'S MISSING!
SO POWERFUL IS SUPERMAN'S STRENGTH THAT HE MOLDS THE RAIL SECTION BACK INTO PLACE AS THO THE STEEL WERE PUTTY...
THERE! AN EMERGENCY JOB-- BUT IT SHOULD BE SATISFACTORY!
SECONDS LATER, THE MAN OF TOMORROW VAULTS ONTO THE PLATFORM OF THE NEXT STATION AND WHIPS BACK INTO HIS CIVILIAN GARMENTS...
NOW TO PHONE IN THE STORY TO WHITE.
3
THAT'S RIGHT. SUPERMAN AVERTED A SUBWAY TRAIN WRECK!
BUT AS CLARK LEAVES THE PHONE BOOTH....
ULP!
CLARK! HOW DID YOU GET HERE? I LEFT YOU BACK ON THE PLATFORM AT THAT OTHER STATION!

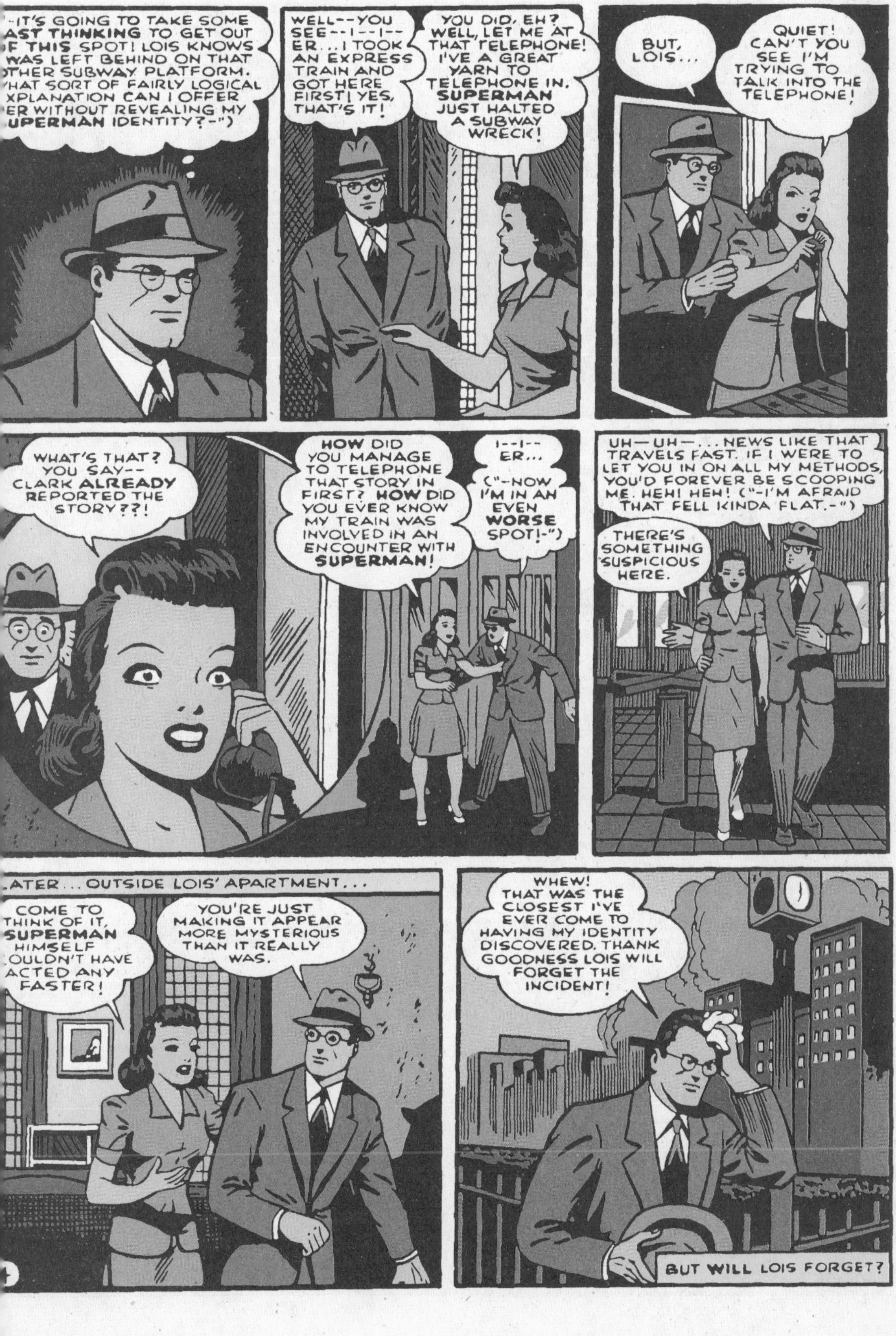

("-IT'S GOING TO TAKE SOME FAST THINKING TO GET OUT OF THIS SPOT! LOIS KNOWS I WAS LEFT BEHIND ON THAT OTHER SUBWAY PLATFORM. WHAT SORT OF FAIRLY LOGICAL EXPLANATION CAN I OFFER HER WITHOUT REVEALING MY SUPERMAN IDENTITY?-")
WELL--YOU SEE--I--I--ER...I TOOK AN EXPRESS TRAIN AND GOT HERE FIRST! YES, THAT'S IT!
YOU DID, EH? WELL, LET ME AT THAT TELEPHONE! I'VE A GREAT YARN TO TELEPHONE IN. SUPERMAN JUST HALTED A SUBWAY WRECK!
BUT, LOIS...
QUIET! CAN'T YOU SEE I'M TRYING TO TALK INTO THE TELEPHONE!
WHAT'S THAT? YOU SAY--CLARK ALREADY REPORTED THE STORY??!
HOW DID YOU MANAGE TO TELEPHONE THAT STORY IN FIRST? HOW DID YOU EVER KNOW MY TRAIN WAS INVOLVED IN AN ENCOUNTER WITH SUPERMAN!
I--I--ER...
("-NOW I'M IN AN EVEN WORSE SPOT!-")
UH—UH—...NEWS LIKE THAT TRAVELS FAST. IF I WERE TO LET YOU IN ON ALL MY METHODS, YOU'D FOREVER BE SCOOPING ME. HEH! HEH! ("-I'M AFRAID THAT FELL KINDA FLAT.-")
THERE'S SOMETHING SUSPICIOUS HERE.
LATER...OUTSIDE LOIS' APARTMENT...
COME TO THINK OF IT, SUPERMAN HIMSELF COULDN'T HAVE ACTED ANY FASTER!
YOU'RE JUST MAKING IT APPEAR MORE MYSTERIOUS THAN IT REALLY WAS.
WHEW! THAT WAS THE CLOSEST I'VE EVER COME TO HAVING MY IDENTITY DISCOVERED. THANK GOODNESS LOIS WILL FORGET THE INCIDENT!
BUT WILL LOIS FORGET?

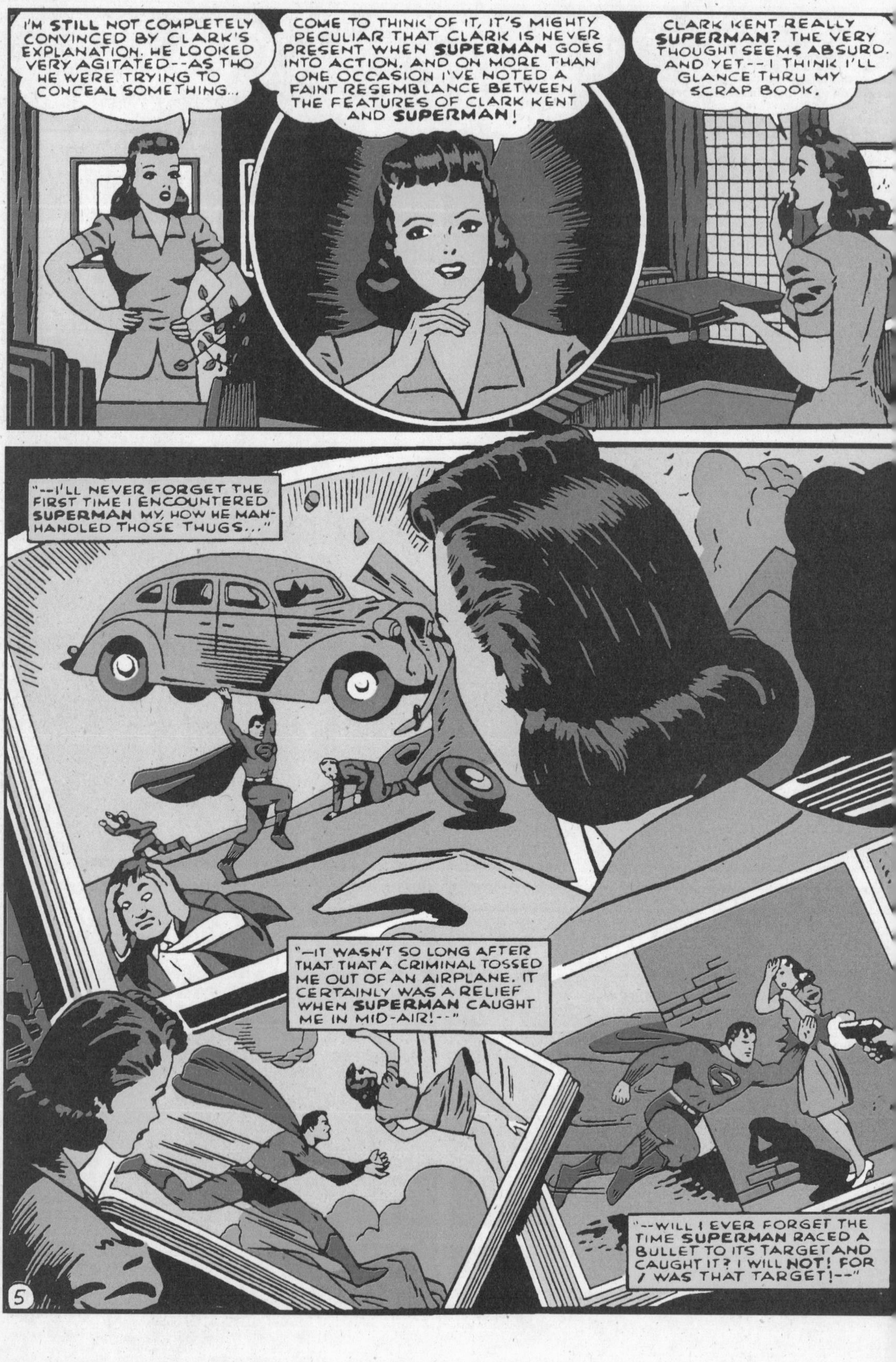
I'M STILL NOT COMPLETELY CONVINCED BY CLARK'S EXPLANATION. HE LOOKED VERY AGITATED--AS THO HE WERE TRYING TO CONCEAL SOMETHING...
COME TO THINK OF IT, IT'S MIGHTY PECULIAR THAT CLARK IS NEVER PRESENT WHEN SUPERMAN GOES INTO ACTION. AND ON MORE THAN ONE OCCASION I'VE NOTED A FAINT RESEMBLANCE BETWEEN THE FEATURES OF CLARK KENT AND SUPERMAN!
CLARK KENT REALLY SUPERMAN? THE VERY THOUGHT SEEMS ABSURD. AND YET-- I THINK I'LL GLANCE THRU MY SCRAP BOOK.
"--I'LL NEVER FORGET THE FIRST TIME I ENCOUNTERED SUPERMAN MY, HOW HE MAN-HANDLED THOSE THUGS..."
"--IT WASN'T SO LONG AFTER THAT THAT A CRIMINAL TOSSED ME OUT OF AN AIRPLANE. IT CERTAINLY WAS A RELIEF WHEN SUPERMAN CAUGHT ME IN MID-AIR!--"
"--WILL I EVER FORGET THE TIME SUPERMAN RACED A BULLET TO ITS TARGET AND CAUGHT IT? I WILL NOT! FOR I WAS THAT TARGET!--"
5

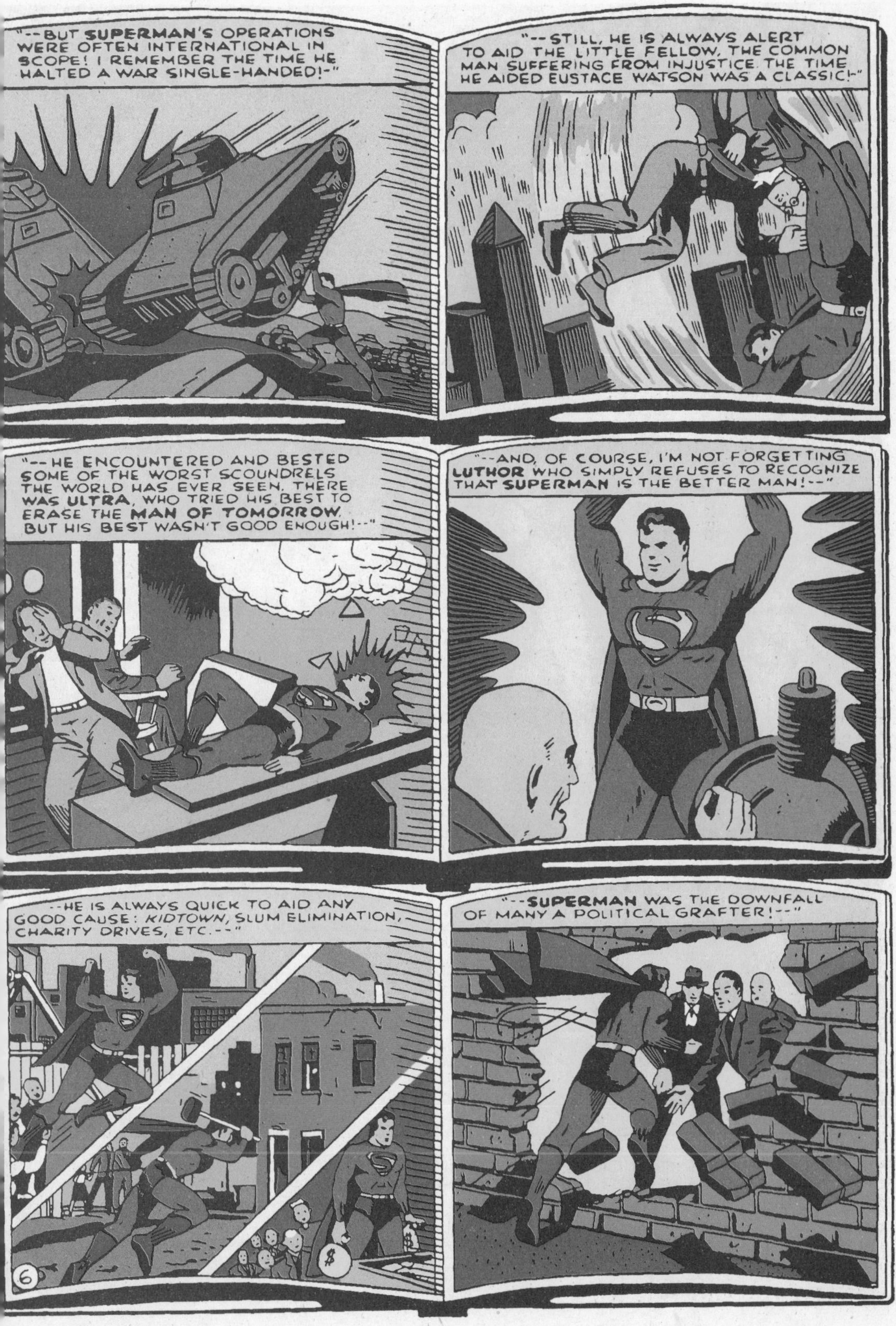
"--BUT SUPERMAN'S OPERATIONS WERE OFTEN INTERNATIONAL IN SCOPE! I REMEMBER THE TIME HE HALTED A WAR SINGLE-HANDED!-"
"--STILL, HE IS ALWAYS ALERT TO AID THE LITTLE FELLOW, THE COMMON MAN SUFFERING FROM INJUSTICE. THE TIME HE AIDED EUSTACE WATSON WAS A CLASSIC!-"
"--HE ENCOUNTERED AND BESTED SOME OF THE WORST SCOUNDRELS THE WORLD HAS EVER SEEN. THERE WAS ULTRA, WHO TRIED HIS BEST TO ERASE THE MAN OF TOMORROW. BUT HIS BEST WASN'T GOOD ENOUGH!--"
"--AND, OF COURSE, I'M NOT FORGETTING LUTHOR WHO SIMPLY REFUSES TO RECOGNIZE THAT SUPERMAN IS THE BETTER MAN!--"
--HE IS ALWAYS QUICK TO AID ANY GOOD CAUSE: KIDTOWN, SLUM ELIMINATION, CHARITY DRIVES, ETC.--"
$
$
6
"--SUPERMAN WAS THE DOWNFALL OF MANY A POLITICAL GRAFTER!--"

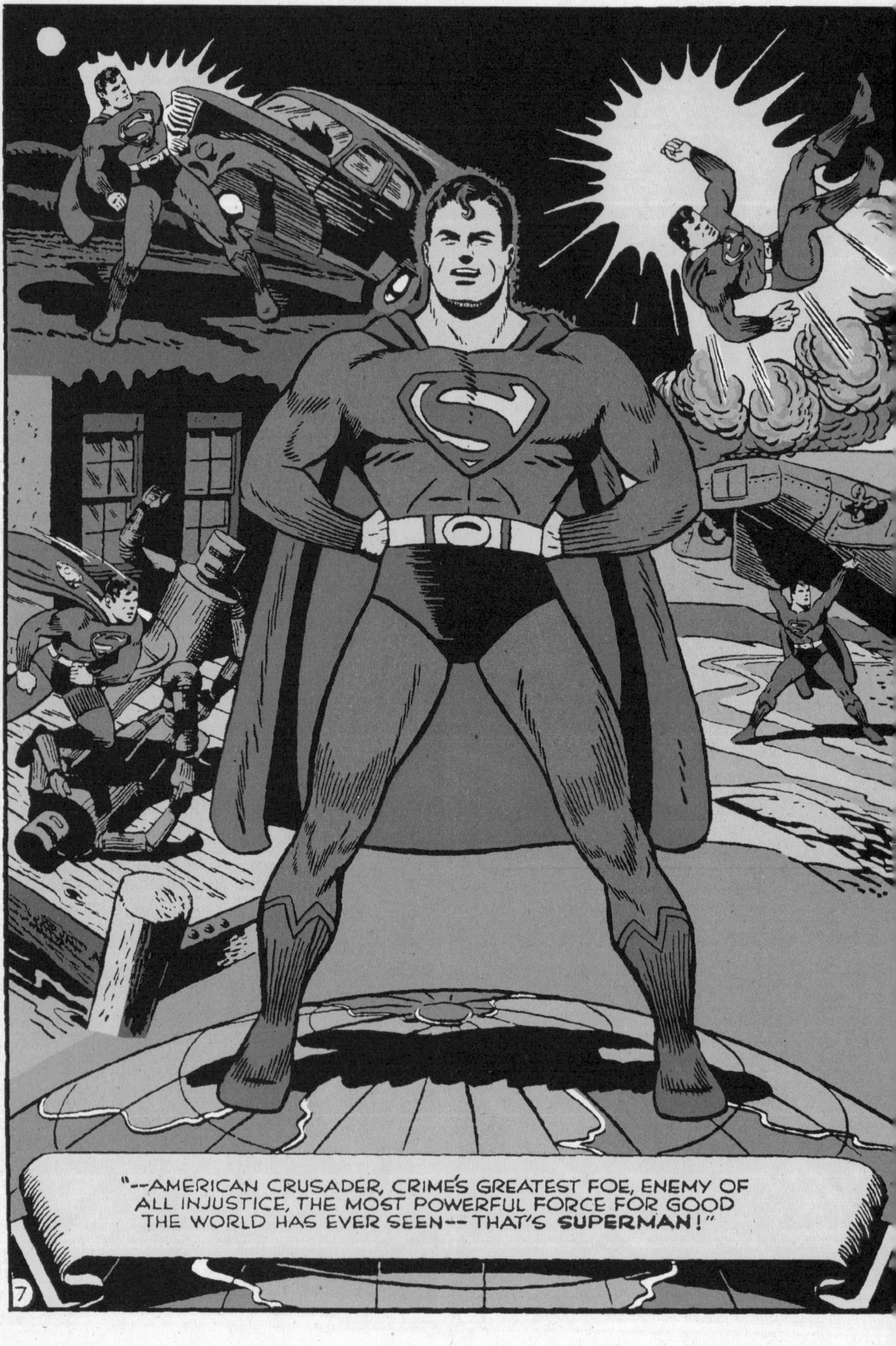

"--AMERICAN CRUSADER, CRIME'S GREATEST FOE, ENEMY OF ALL INJUSTICE, THE MOST POWERFUL FORCE FOR GOOD THE WORLD HAS EVER SEEN-- THAT'S **SUPERMAN!**"
7

HOW COULD I HAVE IMAGINED THAT MEEK, SHRINKING CLARK KENT COULD BE DYNAMIC SUPERMAN? A SILLY THOUGHT AND THE SOONER I FORGET IT, THE BETTER!

AFTER LOIS RETIRES THAT EVENING, CLARK FINDS THAT A PERSISTENT THOUGHT PREVENTS SLEEP. HE CHANGES TO SUPERMAN.

THAT SUBWAY RAIL WASN'T MISPLACED BY ACCIDENT! THERE'S SOMETHING WRONG GOING ON IN THE LABYRINTHS OF THE SUBWAY SYSTEM AND I'M GOING TO TRACK IT DOWN!

SHORTLY AFTERWARD, AS THE MAN OF TOMORROW RACES ALONG A SUBWAY TUNNEL, HIS SUPER-SENSITIVE HEARING DETECTS...

MASSIVE DYNAMOS-!

AVAILING HIMSELF OF HIS X-RAY VISION AND SUPER-HEARING, HE DETECTS A STARTLING SIGHT IN A NEARBY BUILDING....

THE WIRES HAVE BEEN CONNECTED TO THE SUBWAY TRACKS.... AFTER FLING THIS SWITCH, THE TREMENDOUS ELECTRICITY GENERATED BY THESE DYNAMOS WILL SURGE INTO THE TRACKS...THE PASSENGERS ABOARD TRAINS PASSING THIS SECTION, WILL BE ELECTROCUTED...!

WE KNOW ALL THAT! THROW THE SWITCH!

THE TALON DOESN'T LIKE DELAYS!

THRU THE EARTH BURROWS THE MAN OF TOMORROW AT DESPERATE SPEED...!

GOT TO PREVENT A MASS EXECUTION!

SUPERMAN!

AND NOT TOO LATE, I HOPE!

THROW THE SWITCH!

OUT OF MY WAY!

YOU'RE TOO LATE!!

THE SUBWAY TRACKS CRACKLE WITH ELECTRICAL ENERGY-- AND A SHORT DISTANCE OFF A TRAIN HURTLES TOWARD THE WAITING DOOM,....!

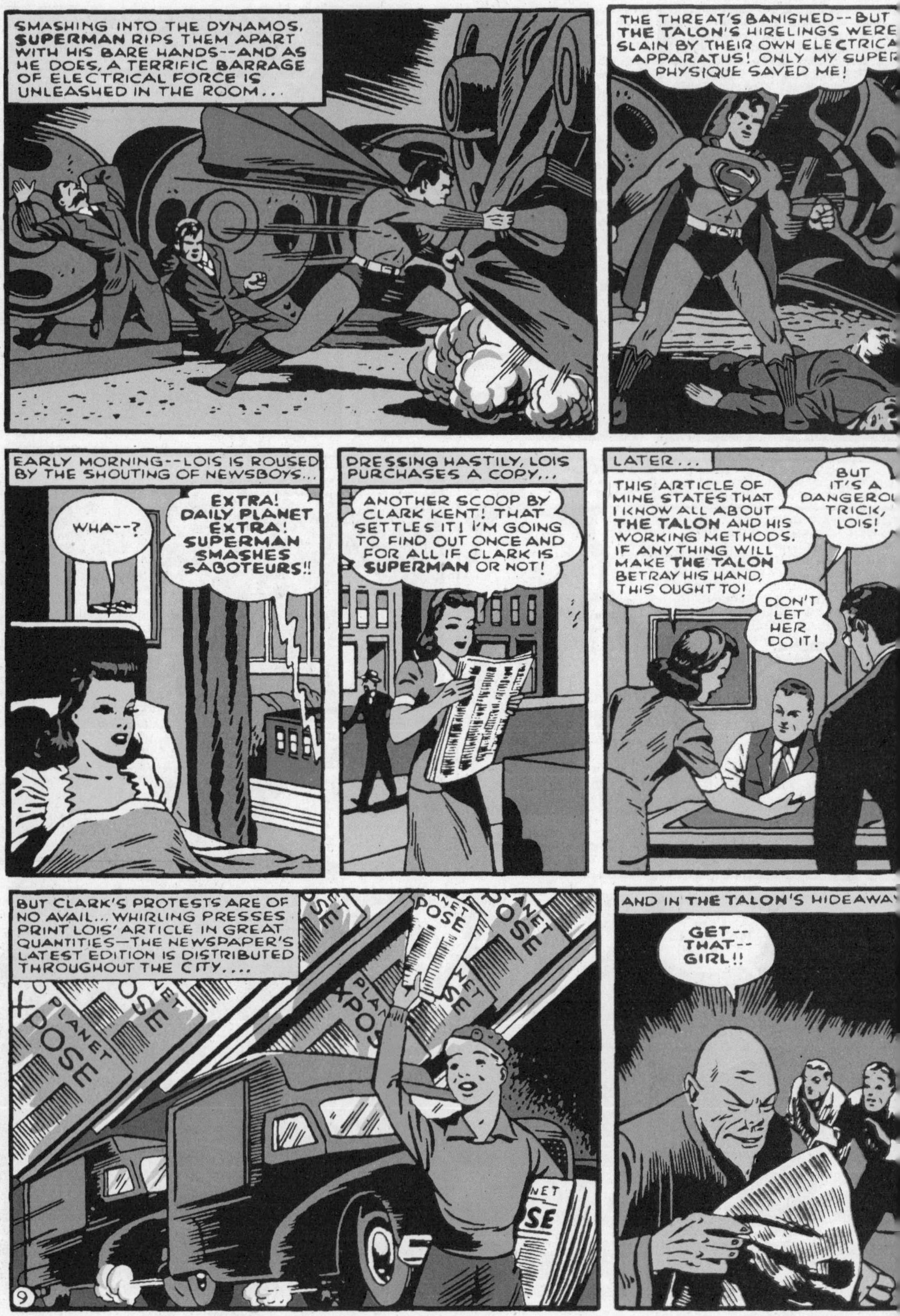

SMASHING INTO THE DYNAMOS, SUPERMAN RIPS THEM APART WITH HIS BARE HANDS--AND AS HE DOES, A TERRIFIC BARRAGE OF ELECTRICAL FORCE IS UNLEASHED IN THE ROOM...
THE THREAT'S BANISHED--BUT THE TALON'S HIRELINGS WERE SLAIN BY THEIR OWN ELECTRICA APPARATUS! ONLY MY SUPER PHYSIQUE SAVED ME!
EARLY MORNING--LOIS IS ROUSED BY THE SHOUTING OF NEWSBOYS...
WHA--?
EXTRA! DAILY PLANET EXTRA! SUPERMAN SMASHES SABOTEURS!!
DRESSING HASTILY, LOIS PURCHASES A COPY...
ANOTHER SCOOP BY CLARK KENT! THAT SETTLES IT! I'M GOING TO FIND OUT ONCE AND FOR ALL IF CLARK IS SUPERMAN OR NOT!
LATER...
THIS ARTICLE OF MINE STATES THAT I KNOW ALL ABOUT THE TALON AND HIS WORKING METHODS. IF ANYTHING WILL MAKE THE TALON BETRAY HIS HAND, THIS OUGHT TO!
BUT IT'S A DANGERO TRICK, LOIS!
DON'T LET HER DO IT!
BUT CLARK'S PROTESTS ARE OF NO AVAIL... WHIRLING PRESSES PRINT LOIS' ARTICLE IN GREAT QUANTITIES—THE NEWSPAPER'S LATEST EDITION IS DISTRIBUTED THROUGHOUT THE CITY....
PLANET XPOSE
9
AND IN THE TALON'S HIDEAWA
GET-- THAT-- GIRL!!

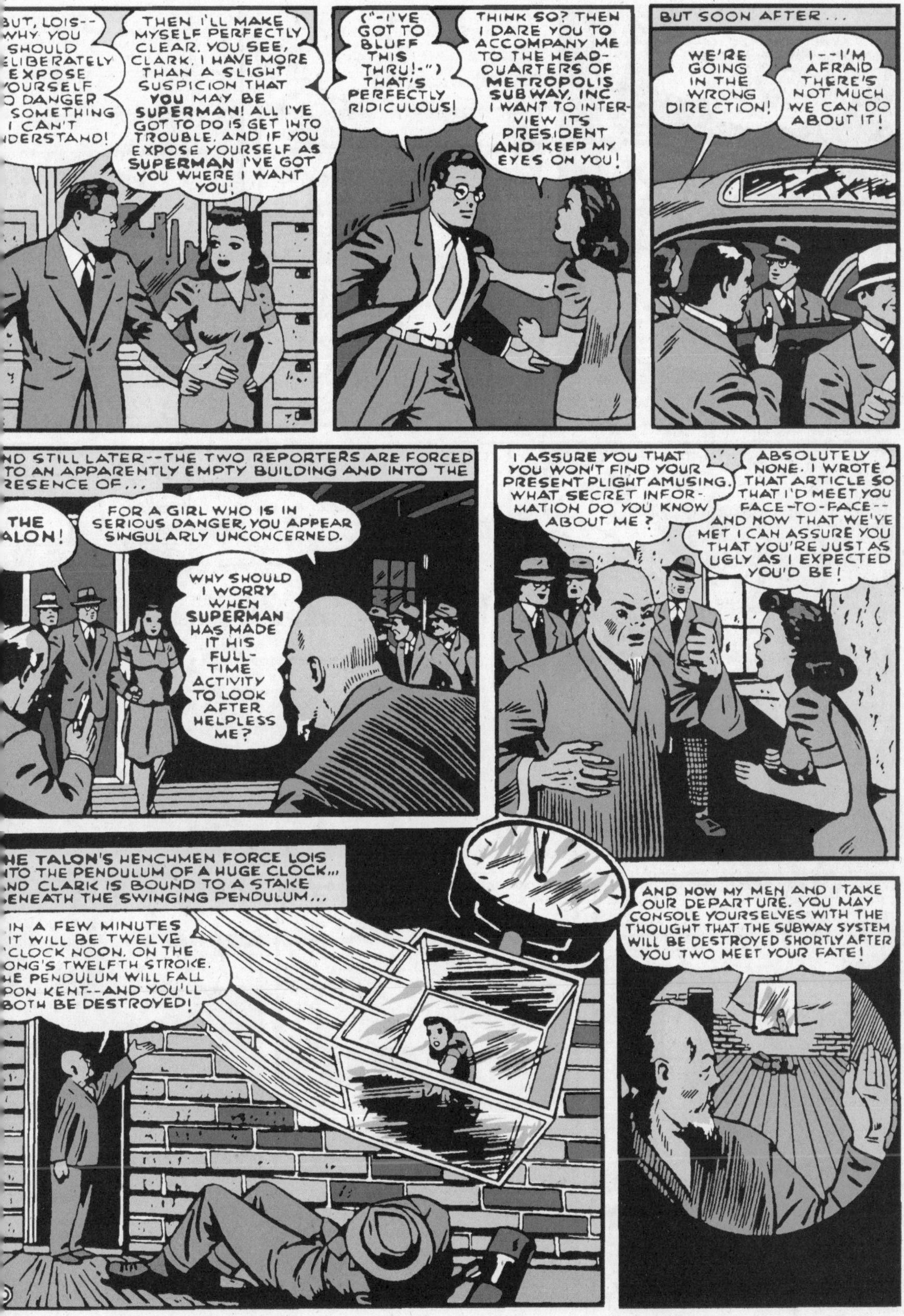
BUT, LOIS-- WHY YOU SHOULD ELIBERATELY EXPOSE OURSELF O DANGER SOMETHING I CAN'T NDERSTAND!
THEN I'LL MAKE MYSELF PERFECTLY CLEAR. YOU SEE, CLARK, I HAVE MORE THAN A SLIGHT SUSPICION THAT YOU MAY BE SUPERMAN! ALL I'VE GOT TO DO IS GET INTO TROUBLE, AND IF YOU EXPOSE YOURSELF AS SUPERMAN I'VE GOT YOU WHERE I WANT YOU!
("-I'VE GOT TO BLUFF THIS THRU!-") THAT'S PERFECTLY RIDICULOUS!
THINK SO? THEN I DARE YOU TO ACCOMPANY ME TO THE HEAD-QUARTERS OF METROPOLIS SUBWAY, INC. I WANT TO INTER-VIEW ITS PRESIDENT AND KEEP MY EYES ON YOU!
BUT SOON AFTER...
WE'RE GOING IN THE WRONG DIRECTION!
I--I'M AFRAID THERE'S NOT MUCH WE CAN DO ABOUT IT!
ND STILL LATER--THE TWO REPORTERS ARE FORCED TO AN APPARENTLY EMPTY BUILDING AND INTO THE RESENCE OF...
THE ALON!
FOR A GIRL WHO IS IN SERIOUS DANGER, YOU APPEAR SINGULARLY UNCONCERNED.
WHY SHOULD I WORRY WHEN SUPERMAN HAS MADE IT HIS FULL-TIME ACTIVITY TO LOOK AFTER HELPLESS ME?
I ASSURE YOU THAT YOU WON'T FIND YOUR PRESENT PLIGHT AMUSING. WHAT SECRET INFOR-MATION DO YOU KNOW ABOUT ME?
ABSOLUTELY NONE. I WROTE THAT ARTICLE SO THAT I'D MEET YOU FACE-TO-FACE--AND NOW THAT WE'VE MET I CAN ASSURE YOU THAT YOU'RE JUST AS UGLY AS I EXPECTED YOU'D BE!
HE TALON'S HENCHMEN FORCE LOIS INTO THE PENDULUM OF A HUGE CLOCK... ND CLARK IS BOUND TO A STAKE BENEATH THE SWINGING PENDULUM...
IN A FEW MINUTES IT WILL BE TWELVE 'CLOCK NOON. ON THE ONG'S TWELFTH STROKE, HE PENDULUM WILL FALL PON KENT--AND YOU'LL BOTH BE DESTROYED!
AND NOW MY MEN AND I TAKE OUR DEPARTURE. YOU MAY CONSOLE YOURSELVES WITH THE THOUGHT THAT THE SUBWAY SYSTEM WILL BE DESTROYED SHORTLY AFTER YOU TWO MEET YOUR FATE!

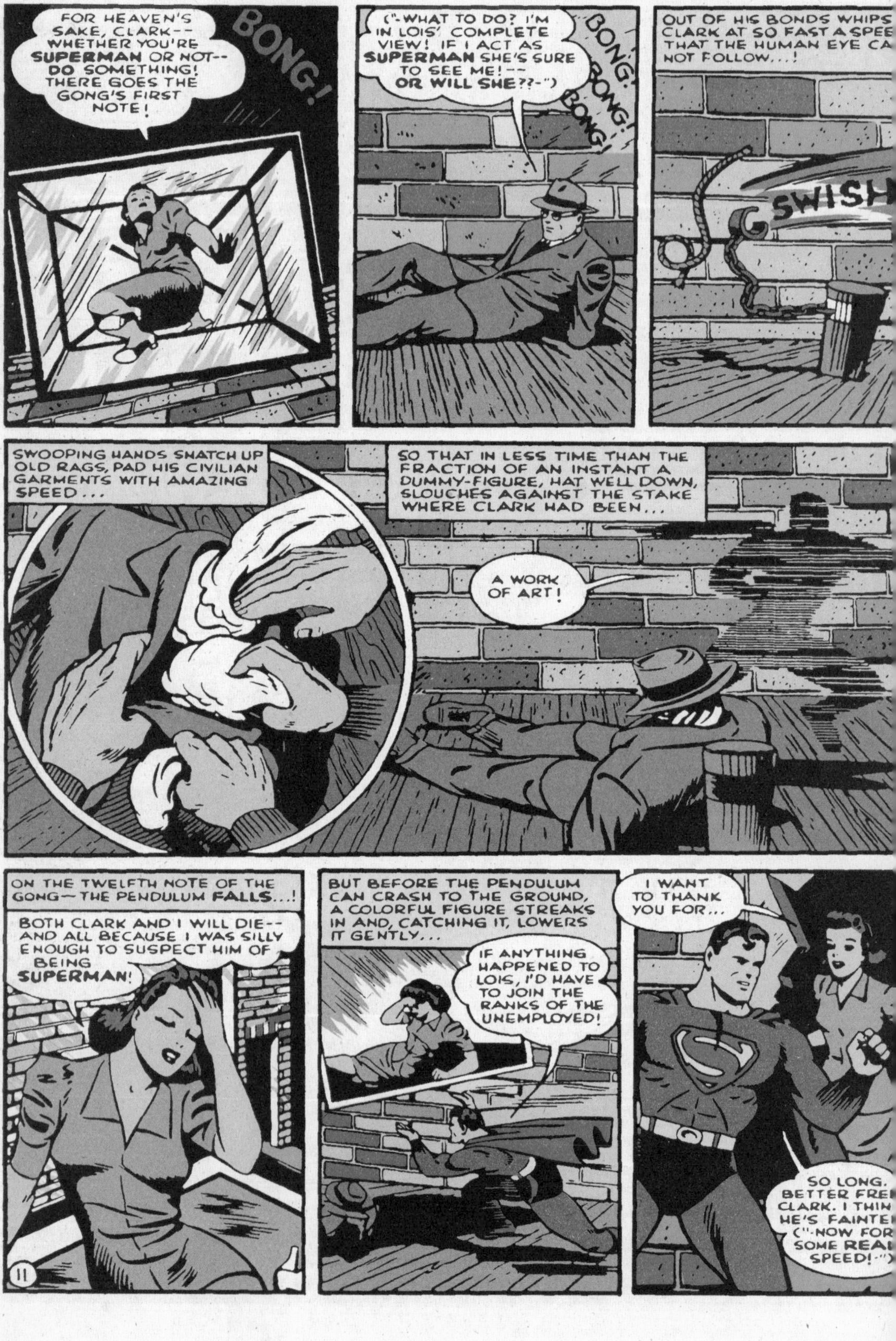
FOR HEAVEN'S SAKE, CLARK-- WHETHER YOU'RE SUPERMAN OR NOT-- DO SOMETHING! THERE GOES THE GONG'S FIRST NOTE!
BONG!
("-WHAT TO DO? I'M IN LOIS' COMPLETE VIEW! IF I ACT AS SUPERMAN SHE'S SURE TO SEE ME!-- OR WILL SHE??-")
BONG! BONG! BONG!
OUT OF HIS BONDS WHIPS CLARK AT SO FAST A SPEE THAT THE HUMAN EYE CA NOT FOLLOW...!
SWISH
SWOOPING HANDS SNATCH UP OLD RAGS, PAD HIS CIVILIAN GARMENTS WITH AMAZING SPEED...
SO THAT IN LESS TIME THAN THE FRACTION OF AN INSTANT A DUMMY-FIGURE, HAT WELL DOWN, SLOUCHES AGAINST THE STAKE WHERE CLARK HAD BEEN...
A WORK OF ART!
ON THE TWELFTH NOTE OF THE GONG—THE PENDULUM FALLS...!
BOTH CLARK AND I WILL DIE-- AND ALL BECAUSE I WAS SILLY ENOUGH TO SUSPECT HIM OF BEING SUPERMAN!
11
BUT BEFORE THE PENDULUM CAN CRASH TO THE GROUND, A COLORFUL FIGURE STREAKS IN AND, CATCHING IT, LOWERS IT GENTLY...
IF ANYTHING HAPPENED TO LOIS, I'D HAVE TO JOIN THE RANKS OF THE UNEMPLOYED!
I WANT TO THANK YOU FOR...
SO LONG. BETTER FREE CLARK. I THIN HE'S FAINTE ("-NOW FOR SOME REAL SPEED!-")

WHILE LOIS TURNS TOWARD THE STAKE, **SUPERMAN** WHIPS PAST HER AT SUPER-SPEED...

("-GOT TO MAKE IT BEFORE SHE COMPLETELY TURNS!-")

SWISH!

EMPTYING THE RAGS, HE DONS HIS OUTER GARMENTS AND ADJUSTS THE ROPES IN PLACE...

("-SHE'S ALMOST GOT HER EYES ON ME!-")

COME TO, CLARK! **SUPERMAN** SAVED US! WE'VE GOT TO GET TO THE SUBWAY SYSTEM HEADQUARTERS AND WARN THEM OF THE TALON'S THREAT!

I--I WANT TO KEEP AS FAR AWAY FROM THE TALON AS I CAN!

LATER...IN THE PRIVATE OFFICE OF ALBERT CALDWELL, PRESIDENT OF METROPOLIS SUBWAY, INC....

BUT I INSIST IT'S TRUE! THE TALON IS GOING TO DESTROY YOUR SUBWAY!

MELO-DRAMATIC NONSENSE!

("-MY X-RAY EYESIGHT...I SEE SOMETHING INTERESTING!-") NO SENSE WASTING TIME HERE, LOIS. I'M GOING BACK TO THE *PLANET* TO TURN IN WHAT WE'VE LEARNED!

BUT ONCE HE IS OUTSIDE THE OFFICE, CLARK CHANGES TO **SUPERMAN** AND RACES BACK IN....

SUPERMAN! STRANGE HOW YOU SHOWED UP SO SOON AFTER CLARK'S DEPARTURE!

WHAT DOES THIS INTERRUPTION MEAN?

I WAS WONDERING, CALDWELL, IF YOU DABBLE IN AMATEUR THEATRICALS?

OF COURSE NOT!

THEN THERE'S ONLY ONE OTHER EXPLANATION FOR THE TRACES OF YELLOW PIGMENT AND GREASE PAINT I CAN STILL DETECT ON YOUR SKIN, TALON!

MR. CALDWELL-- THE TALON!

HE'S MAD!

I'M BETTING HE'S THE BIRD WE'RE AFTER!

OBOY! IT'S OFF FOR THE DAILY PLANET FOR ME!

IF I'M FAST ENOUGH I MAY BE ABLE TO SCOOP CLARK!

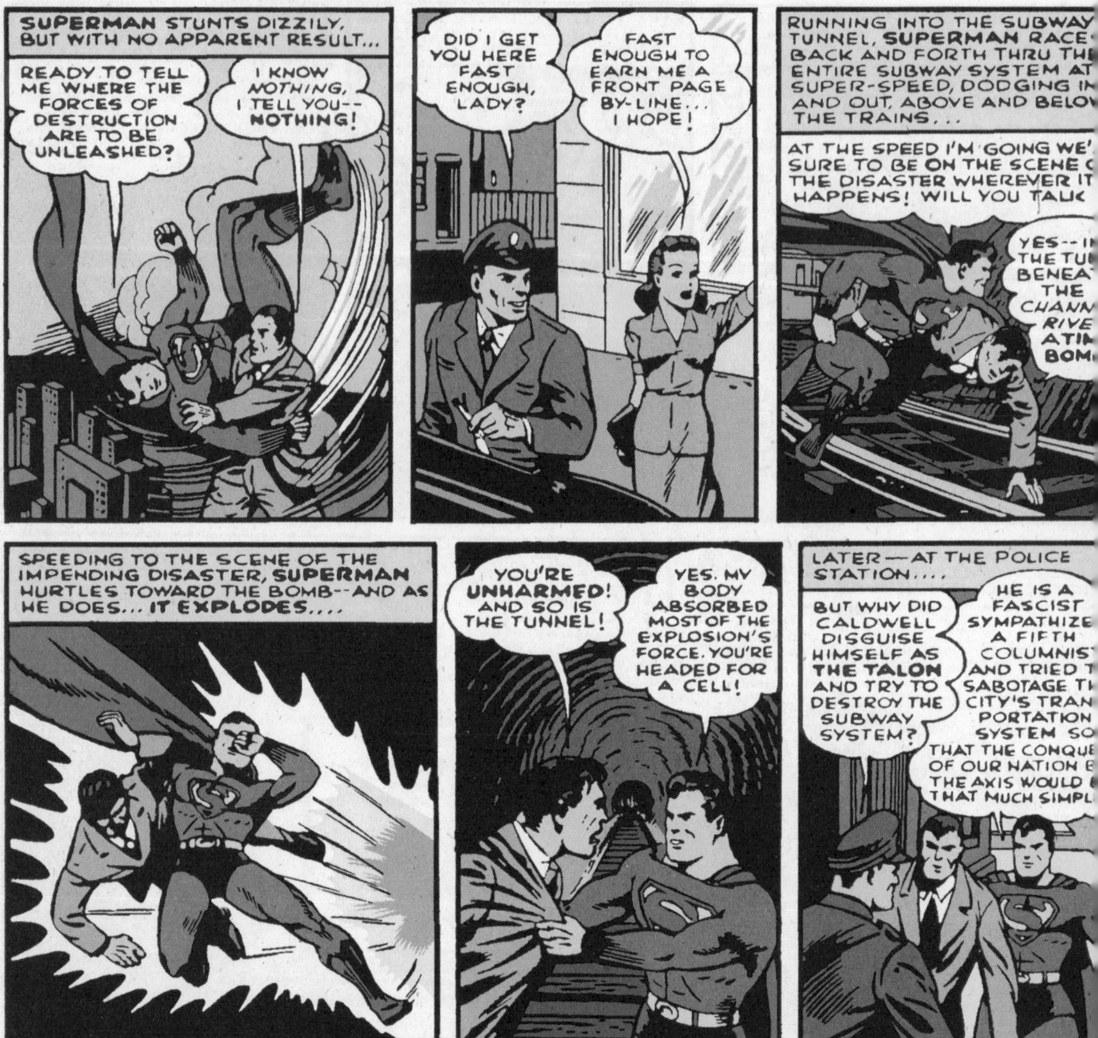
SUPERMAN STUNTS DIZZILY, BUT WITH NO APPARENT RESULT...
READY TO TELL ME WHERE THE FORCES OF DESTRUCTION ARE TO BE UNLEASHED?
I KNOW NOTHING, I TELL YOU-- NOTHING!
DID I GET YOU HERE FAST ENOUGH, LADY?
FAST ENOUGH TO EARN ME A FRONT PAGE BY-LINE... I HOPE!
RUNNING INTO THE SUBWAY TUNNEL, SUPERMAN RACE BACK AND FORTH THRU TH ENTIRE SUBWAY SYSTEM AT SUPER-SPEED, DODGING IN AND OUT, ABOVE AND BELO THE TRAINS...
AT THE SPEED I'M GOING WE' SURE TO BE ON THE SCENE THE DISASTER WHEREVER IT HAPPENS! WILL YOU TALK
YES--I THE TU BENEA THE CHANN RIVE ATI BOM
SPEEDING TO THE SCENE OF THE IMPENDING DISASTER, SUPERMAN HURTLES TOWARD THE BOMB--AND AS HE DOES... IT EXPLODES....
YOU'RE UNHARMED! AND SO IS THE TUNNEL!
YES. MY BODY ABSORBED MOST OF THE EXPLOSION'S FORCE. YOU'RE HEADED FOR A CELL!
LATER—AT THE POLICE STATION....
BUT WHY DID CALDWELL DISGUISE HIMSELF AS THE TALON AND TRY TO DESTROY THE SUBWAY SYSTEM?
HE IS A FASCIST SYMPATHIZE A FIFTH COLUMNIST AND TRIED T SABOTAGE TH CITY'S TRAN PORTATION SYSTEM SO THAT THE CONQUE OF OUR NATION B THE AXIS WOULD THAT MUCH SIMPL
SEVERAL MOMENTS LATER....
KENT AROUND? NO. I HAVEN'T SEEN HIM. WHY DO YOU ASK?
SWELL! THIS ONE TIME I SCOOPED HIM!
DID SOME-ONE MENTION MY NAME?
13
YOU HERE? ER--I--I GUESS I WAS MISTAKEN.
HERE'S A FULL EXPOSE OF THE TALON, WHITE.
THE END
BUT ARE LOIS' SUSPICIONS OF CLARK'S TRUE IDENTITY COMPLETELY ALLAYED? ONLY FUTURE RELEASES OF YOUR FAVORITE STRIP WILL TELL! DON'T MISS A SINGLE ADVENTURE OF-- SUPERMAN!

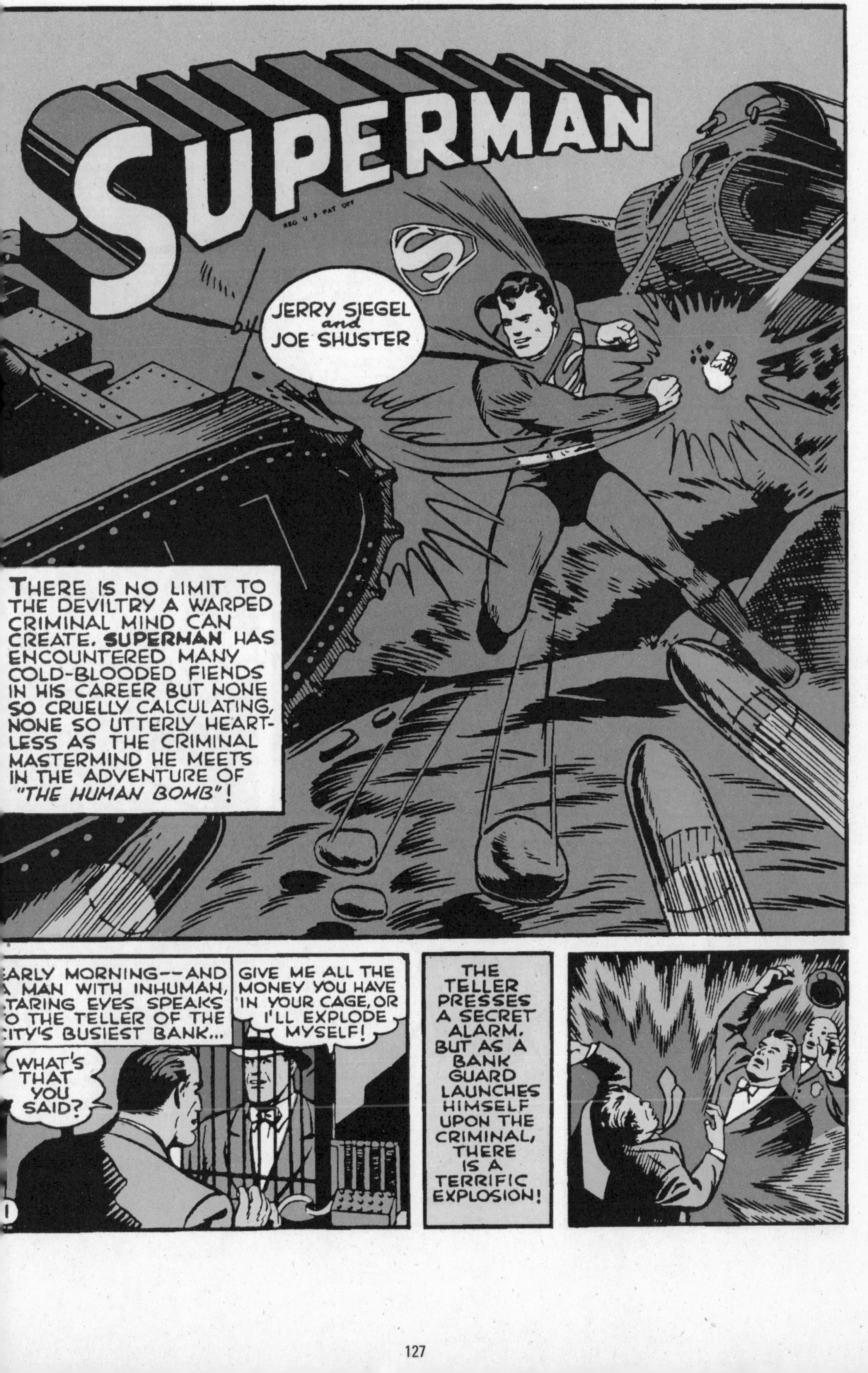
SUPERMAN
REG. U.S. PAT. OFF.
JERRY SIEGEL and JOE SHUSTER
THERE IS NO LIMIT TO THE DEVILTRY A WARPED CRIMINAL MIND CAN CREATE. **SUPERMAN** HAS ENCOUNTERED MANY COLD-BLOODED FIENDS IN HIS CAREER BUT NONE SO CRUELLY CALCULATING, NONE SO UTTERLY HEART-LESS AS THE CRIMINAL MASTERMIND HE MEETS IN THE ADVENTURE OF *"THE HUMAN BOMB"*!
ARLY MORNING--AND A MAN WITH INHUMAN, TARING EYES SPEAKS O THE TELLER OF THE ITY'S BUSIEST BANK...
GIVE ME ALL THE MONEY YOU HAVE IN YOUR CAGE, OR I'LL EXPLODE MYSELF!
WHAT'S THAT YOU SAID?
THE TELLER PRESSES A SECRET ALARM. BUT AS A BANK GUARD LAUNCHES HIMSELF UPON THE CRIMINAL, THERE IS A TERRIFIC EXPLOSION!

DAILY PLANET

BANDIT SLAYS HIMSELF IN BANK EXPLOSION

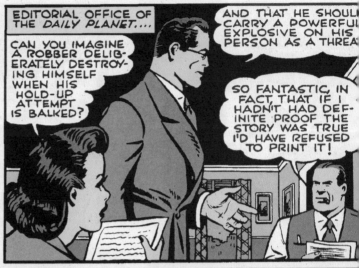

EDITORIAL OFFICE OF THE *DAILY PLANET*....

CAN YOU IMAGINE A ROBBER DELIBERATELY DESTROYING HIMSELF WHEN HIS HOLD-UP ATTEMPT IS BALKED?

AND THAT HE SHOUL[D] CARRY A POWERFUL EXPLOSIVE ON HIS PERSON AS A THREAT[?]

SO FANTASTIC, IN FACT, THAT IF I HADN'T HAD DEFINITE PROOF THE STORY WAS TRUE I'D HAVE REFUSED TO PRINT IT!

A MAN TO SEE YOU, SIR, BUT HE REFUSES TO GIVE HIS NAME.

SHOW HIM IN! I'M JUST IN THE RIGHT MOOD TO BAWL OUT A CRANK!

THE MOST OUTSTANDING FEATURE ABOUT PERRY WHITE'S CALLER ARE HIS STRANGE, STARING EYES...

YOU WANTED TO SEE ME?

YES. IT'S ABOUT THAT EXPLOSION AT THE BANK.

YOU GOT THE EXPLANATION ALL FIGURED OUT, EH? -- I'M NOT INTERESTED IN YOUR GUESSES.

BUT I'M *NOT* GUESSING -- BECAUS[E]

I, TOO, AM A *HUMAN BOMB!*

WHA--! (G-GULP!) W-WHY HAVE YOU COME HERE?

I WANT TO BE INTERVIEWED. AND YOU'D BETTER GRANT MY REQUEST OR I HAVE BUT TO PRESS THIS BUTTON... AND WE'LL BOTH DIE! THAT *WOULD* BE REGRETTABLE.

SA-AAY! THIS IS A BREAK! WHAT A STORY! YOU'D LIKE AN INTERVIEW, EH? I KNOW JUST THE REPORTER TO HANDLE THE ASSIGNMENT!

YES, MR. WHITE?

SEND IN CLARK KENT!

②

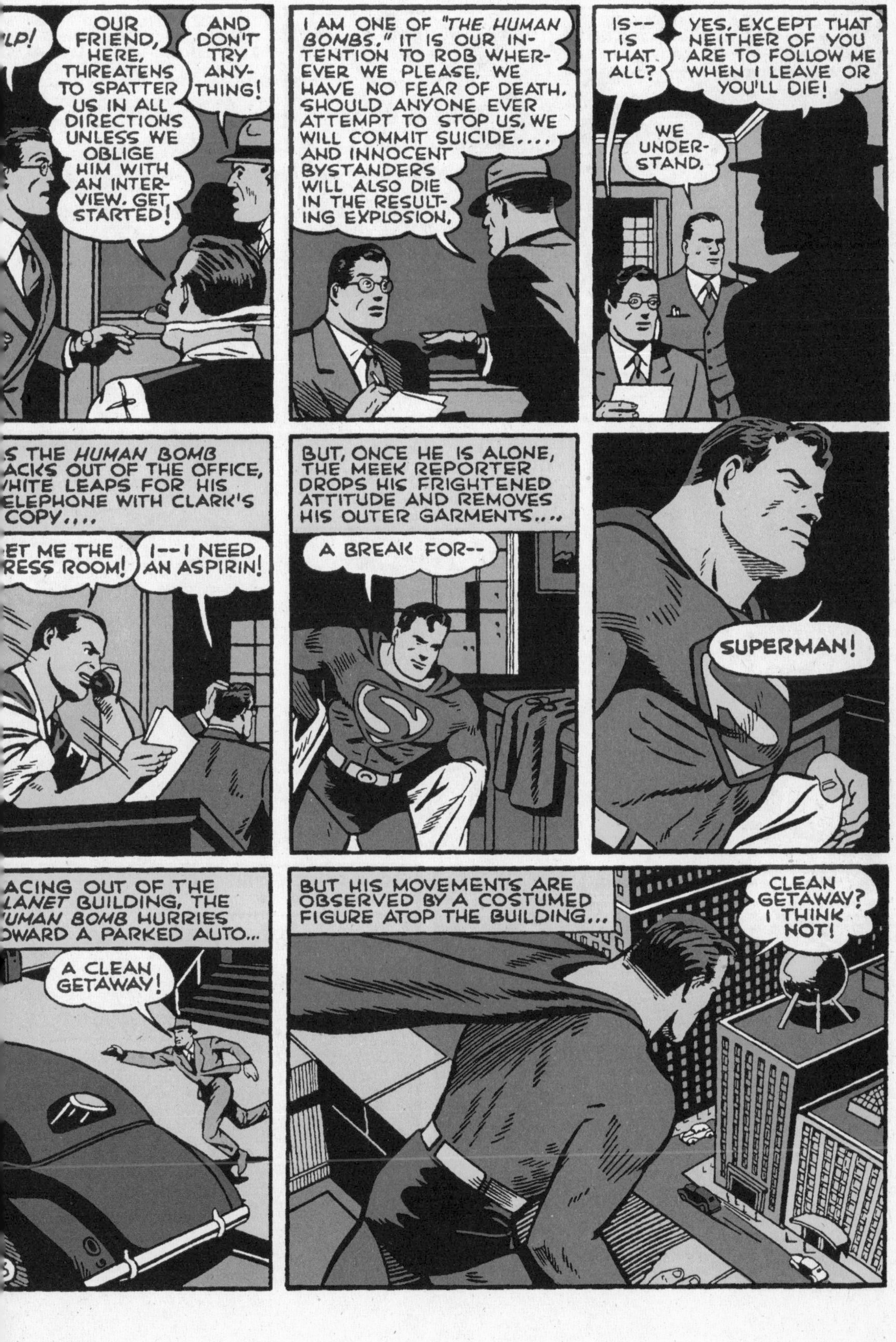

LP!
OUR FRIEND, HERE, THREATENS TO SPATTER US IN ALL DIRECTIONS UNLESS WE OBLIGE HIM WITH AN INTERVIEW. GET STARTED!
AND DON'T TRY ANYTHING!
I AM ONE OF "THE HUMAN BOMBS." IT IS OUR INTENTION TO ROB WHEREVER WE PLEASE. WE HAVE NO FEAR OF DEATH. SHOULD ANYONE EVER ATTEMPT TO STOP US, WE WILL COMMIT SUICIDE.... AND INNOCENT BYSTANDERS WILL ALSO DIE IN THE RESULTING EXPLOSION.
IS-- IS THAT ALL?
YES. EXCEPT THAT NEITHER OF YOU ARE TO FOLLOW ME WHEN I LEAVE OR YOU'LL DIE!
WE UNDERSTAND.
S THE HUMAN BOMB ACKS OUT OF THE OFFICE, HITE LEAPS FOR HIS ELEPHONE WITH CLARK'S COPY....
ET ME THE RESS ROOM!
I--I NEED AN ASPIRIN!
BUT, ONCE HE IS ALONE, THE MEEK REPORTER DROPS HIS FRIGHTENED ATTITUDE AND REMOVES HIS OUTER GARMENTS....
A BREAK FOR--
SUPERMAN!
ACING OUT OF THE LANET BUILDING, THE UMAN BOMB HURRIES OWARD A PARKED AUTO...
A CLEAN GETAWAY!
BUT HIS MOVEMENTS ARE OBSERVED BY A COSTUMED FIGURE ATOP THE BUILDING...
CLEAN GETAWAY? I THINK NOT!

A GREAT LEAP LAUNCHES THE *MAN OF STEEL* TOWARD THE DISTANT FIGURE....

HERE I GO!

HE CRASHES TO THE GROUND, UNINJURED BY THE GREAT FALL BECAUSE OF HIS TREMENDOUSLY POWERFUL MUSCLES....

SUPERMAN!

RIGHT!

OUT OF MY WAY, OR--

THREATS MERELY AMUSE ME!

STREAKING IN SO QUICKLY THE EYE CAN SCARCELY FOLLOW, **SUPERMAN** RIPS THE BOMB-APPARATUS OFF HIS FOE....

I'LL TAKE THAT!

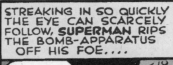

THE BOMB APPARATUS! --GONE!

AS THE MAN TRIES TO FLEE...

IT'S NOT POLITE TO RUN OUT IN THE MIDDLE OF A CONVERSATION!

AS A POLICE OFFICER DASHES UP....

WHAT'S THE DISTURBANCE?

YOU DON'T KNOW I OFFICER, BUT YOU'F ABOUT TO STUMBLE ON A PROMOTION YOU'VE JUST CAPTUR A MEMBER OF THE *HUMAN BOMB GAN*

RETURNING TO AN EMPTY OFFICE IN THE *DAILY PLANET* BUILDING, SUPERMAN DONS HIS CIVILIAN GARMENTS...ONCE AGAIN TRANSFORMING HIMSELF INTO THE DOCILE REPORTER...

NOT A BAD PIECE OF WORK!

BUT AS CLARK STEPS OUT OF THE ROOM, HE ENCOUNTERS—LOIS!

("—I'VE GOT TO THINK FAST!—")

CLARK! WHAT WERE YOU DOING IN THAT EMPTY ROOM?

ME? I—I HAPPENED TO WALK IN BY MISTAKE.

("—DOES SHE BELIEVE ME?—")

MISTAKE, EH?

("—I WONDER IF HE'S LYING? BUT WHY SHOULD HE?—")

SO HERE YOU ARE! GET DOWN TO POLICE HEADQUARTERS RIGHT AWAY. THEY'VE CAPTURED THE *HUMAN BOMB!*

COME ON, LOIS! ("—WHEW! IF WHITE HADN'T COME WHEN HE DID!—")

WHEN THE TWO REPORTERS REACH THE POLICE STATION...

ANY NEWS ABOUT THE *HUMAN BOMB*, CASEY?

HE REFUSES TO SAY ANYTHING. BUT...

WE'VE DISCOVERED WHO HE IS.— WELL-TO-DO, RESPECTABLE BUSINESS MAN WHO DISAPPEARED SOME TIME AGO. IT SEEMS STRANGE SUCH A MAN COULD TURN TO CRIME.

THERE'S A RATIONAL EXPLANATION FOR IT— IF WE COULD ONLY THINK OF IT!

AT THAT MOMENT....SIX MEN WITH STARING EYES WALK STIFFLY INTO POLICE HEADQUARTERS....

WE WANT THE *HUMAN BOMB!*

WHAT —?!

LOIS! THEY'RE NOT BLUFFING!

I'M AFRAID YOU'RE RIGHT!

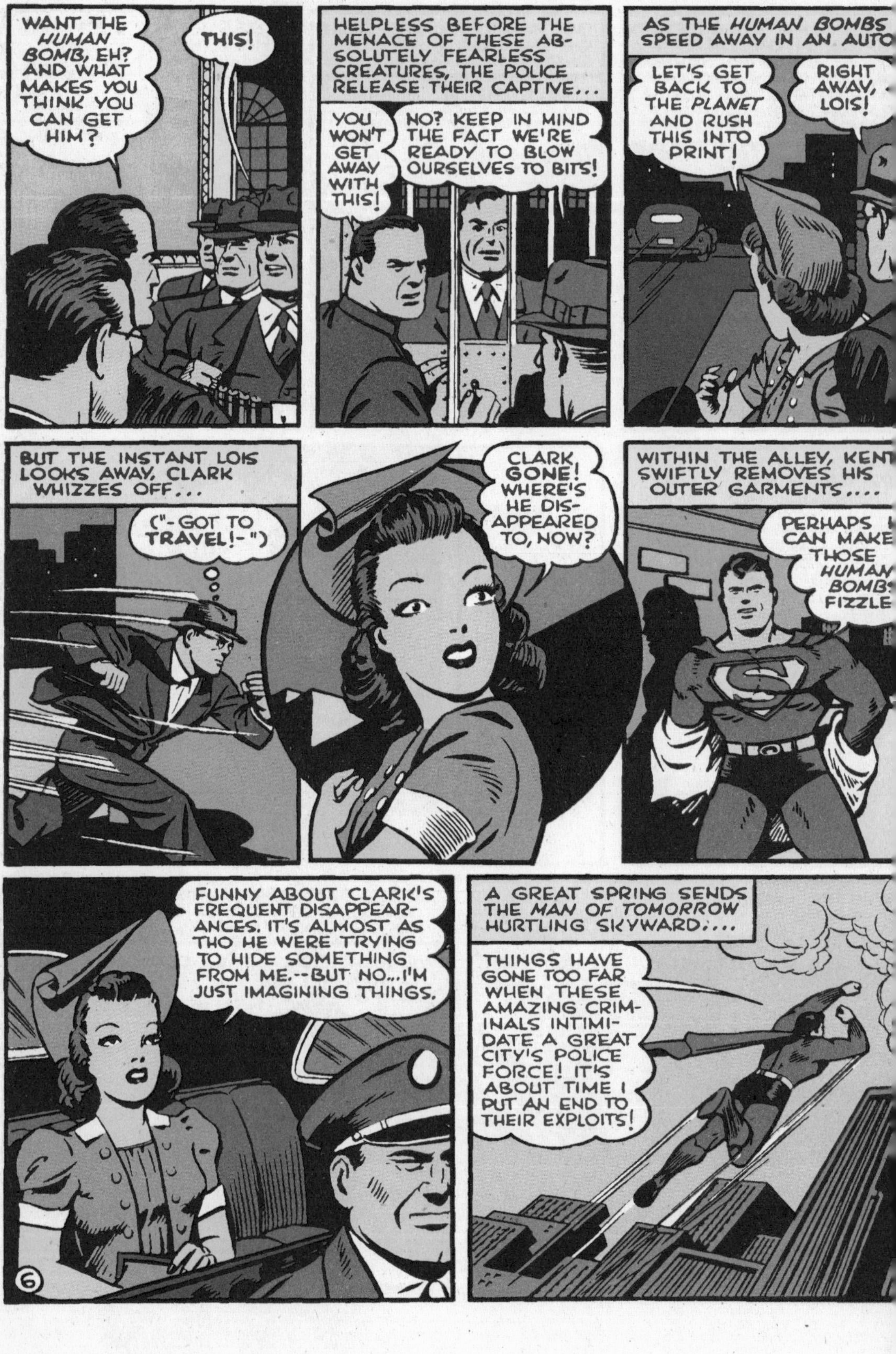

WANT THE HUMAN BOMB, EH? AND WHAT MAKES YOU THINK YOU CAN GET HIM?
THIS!
HELPLESS BEFORE THE MENACE OF THESE ABSOLUTELY FEARLESS CREATURES, THE POLICE RELEASE THEIR CAPTIVE...
YOU WON'T GET AWAY WITH THIS!
NO? KEEP IN MIND THE FACT WE'RE READY TO BLOW OURSELVES TO BITS!
AS THE HUMAN BOMBS SPEED AWAY IN AN AUTO
LET'S GET BACK TO THE PLANET AND RUSH THIS INTO PRINT!
RIGHT AWAY, LOIS!
BUT THE INSTANT LOIS LOOKS AWAY, CLARK WHIZZES OFF...
("-GOT TO TRAVEL!-")
CLARK GONE! WHERE'S HE DISAPPEARED TO, NOW?
WITHIN THE ALLEY, KENT SWIFTLY REMOVES HIS OUTER GARMENTS....
PERHAPS I CAN MAKE THOSE HUMAN BOMBS FIZZLE
FUNNY ABOUT CLARK'S FREQUENT DISAPPEARANCES. IT'S ALMOST AS THO HE WERE TRYING TO HIDE SOMETHING FROM ME.--BUT NO...I'M JUST IMAGINING THINGS.
6
A GREAT SPRING SENDS THE MAN OF TOMORROW HURTLING SKYWARD....
THINGS HAVE GONE TOO FAR WHEN THESE AMAZING CRIMINALS INTIMIDATE A GREAT CITY'S POLICE FORCE! IT'S ABOUT TIME I PUT AN END TO THEIR EXPLOITS!

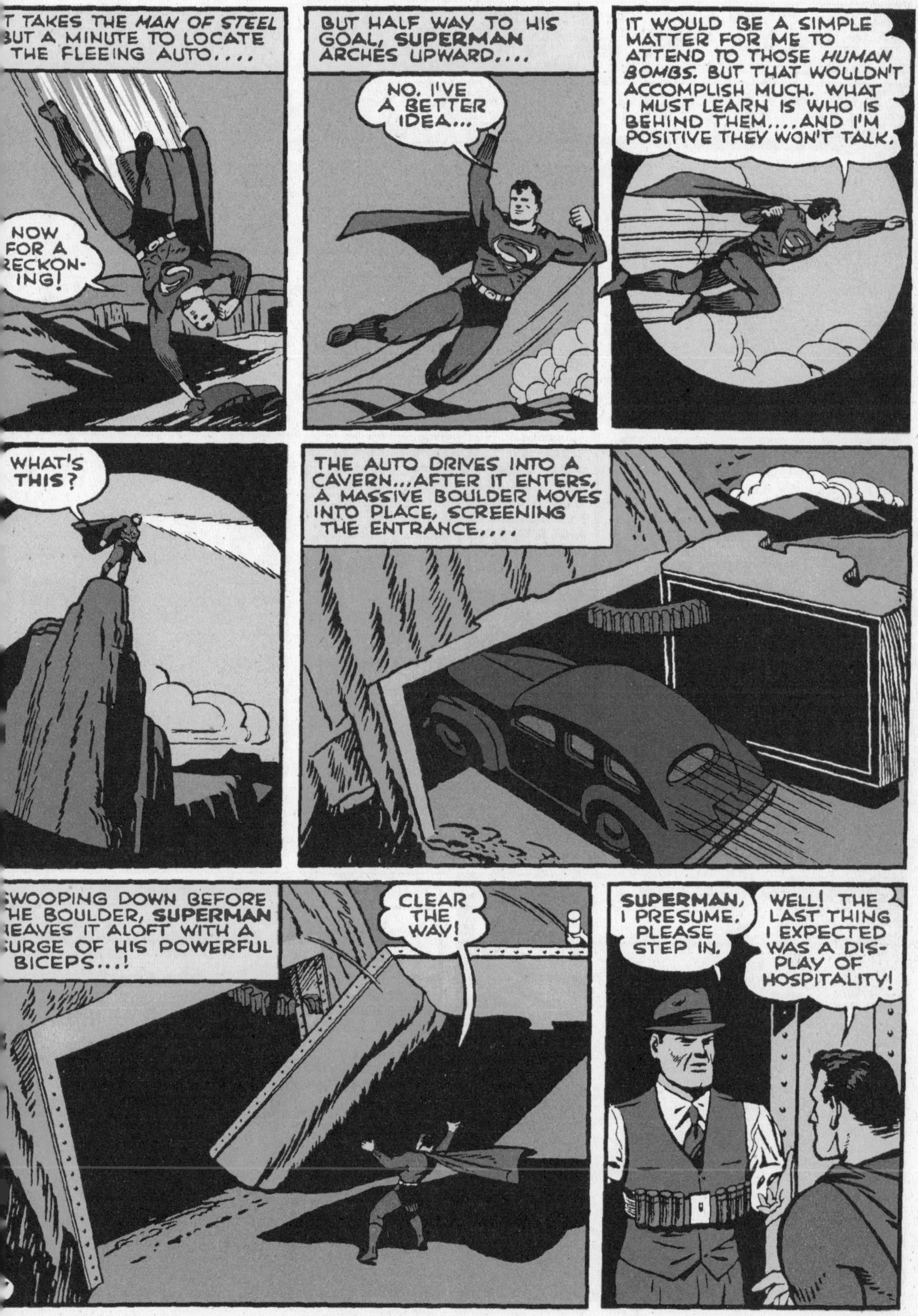

T TAKES THE *MAN OF STEEL* BUT A MINUTE TO LOCATE THE FLEEING AUTO....
NOW FOR A RECKON-ING!
BUT HALF WAY TO HIS GOAL, **SUPERMAN** ARCHES UPWARD....
NO, I'VE A BETTER IDEA...
IT WOULD BE A SIMPLE MATTER FOR ME TO ATTEND TO THOSE *HUMAN BOMBS*. BUT THAT WOULDN'T ACCOMPLISH MUCH. WHAT I MUST LEARN IS WHO IS BEHIND THEM....AND I'M POSITIVE THEY WON'T TALK.
WHAT'S **THIS**?
THE AUTO DRIVES INTO A CAVERN...AFTER IT ENTERS, A MASSIVE BOULDER MOVES INTO PLACE, SCREENING THE ENTRANCE....
SWOOPING DOWN BEFORE HE BOULDER, **SUPERMAN** HEAVES IT ALOFT WITH A SURGE OF HIS POWERFUL BICEPS...!
CLEAR THE WAY!
SUPERMAN, I PRESUME. PLEASE STEP IN.
WELL! THE LAST THING I EXPECTED WAS A DIS-PLAY OF HOSPITALITY!

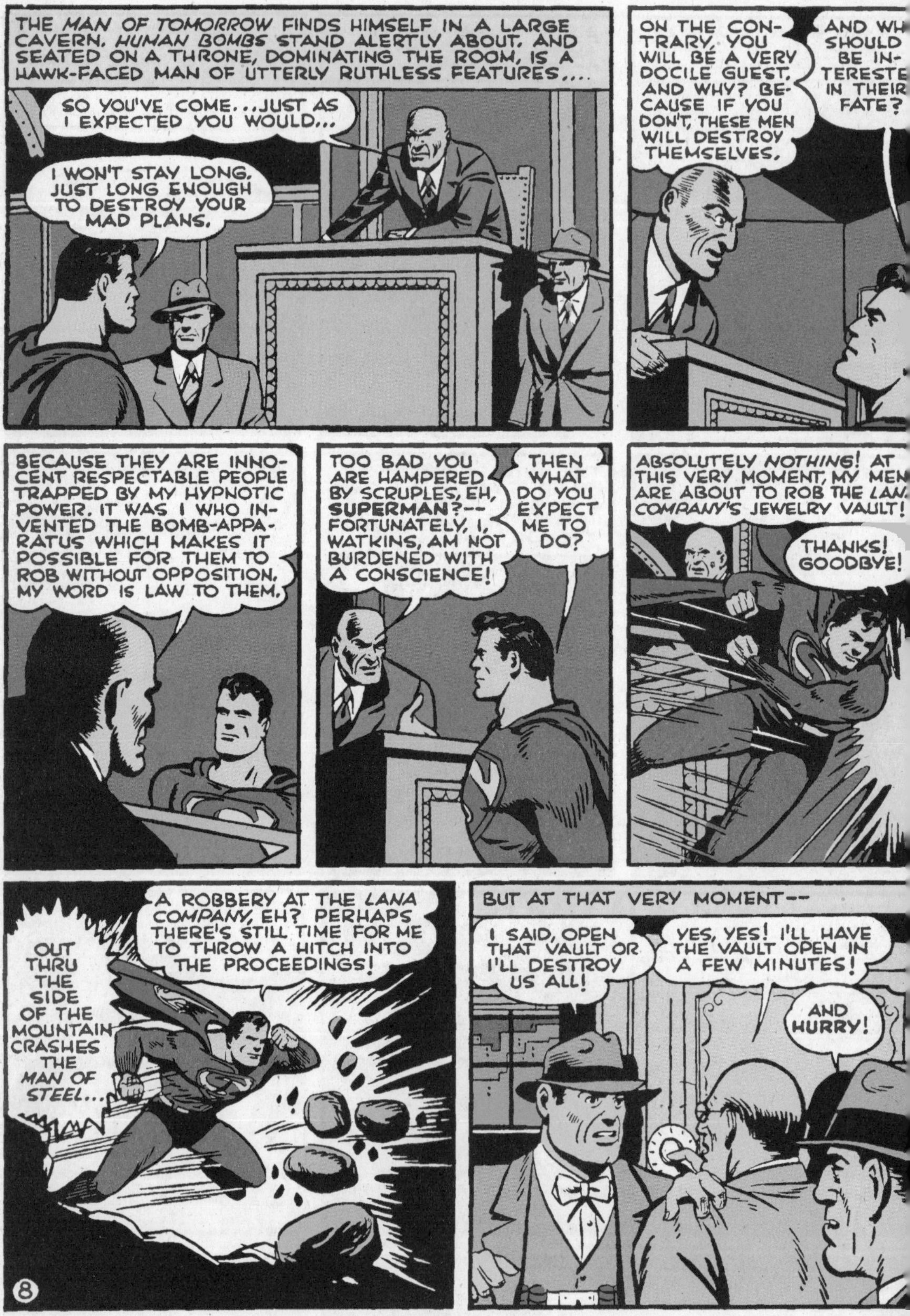
THE *MAN OF TOMORROW* FINDS HIMSELF IN A LARGE CAVERN. *HUMAN BOMBS* STAND ALERTLY ABOUT. AND SEATED ON A THRONE, DOMINATING THE ROOM, IS A HAWK-FACED MAN OF UTTERLY RUTHLESS FEATURES....
SO YOU'VE COME...JUST AS I EXPECTED YOU WOULD...
I WON'T STAY LONG. JUST LONG ENOUGH TO DESTROY YOUR MAD PLANS.
ON THE CONTRARY, YOU WILL BE A VERY DOCILE GUEST. AND WHY? BECAUSE IF YOU DON'T, THESE MEN WILL DESTROY THEMSELVES.
AND WH SHOULD BE INTERESTE IN THEIR FATE?
BECAUSE THEY ARE INNOCENT RESPECTABLE PEOPLE TRAPPED BY MY HYPNOTIC POWER. IT WAS I WHO INVENTED THE BOMB-APPARATUS WHICH MAKES IT POSSIBLE FOR THEM TO ROB WITHOUT OPPOSITION. MY WORD IS LAW TO THEM.
TOO BAD YOU ARE HAMPERED BY SCRUPLES, EH, **SUPERMAN**?-- FORTUNATELY, I, WATKINS, AM NOT BURDENED WITH A CONSCIENCE!
THEN WHAT DO YOU EXPECT ME TO DO?
ABSOLUTELY *NOTHING*! AT THIS VERY MOMENT, MY MEN ARE ABOUT TO ROB THE *LAN* *COMPANY*'S JEWELRY VAULT!
THANKS! GOODBYE!
OUT THRU THE SIDE OF THE MOUNTAIN CRASHES THE *MAN OF STEEL*...
A ROBBERY AT THE *LANA COMPANY*, EH? PERHAPS THERE'S STILL TIME FOR ME TO THROW A HITCH INTO THE PROCEEDINGS!
8
BUT AT THAT VERY MOMENT--
I SAID, OPEN THAT VAULT OR I'LL DESTROY US ALL!
YES, YES! I'LL HAVE THE VAULT OPEN IN A FEW MINUTES!
AND **HURRY**!

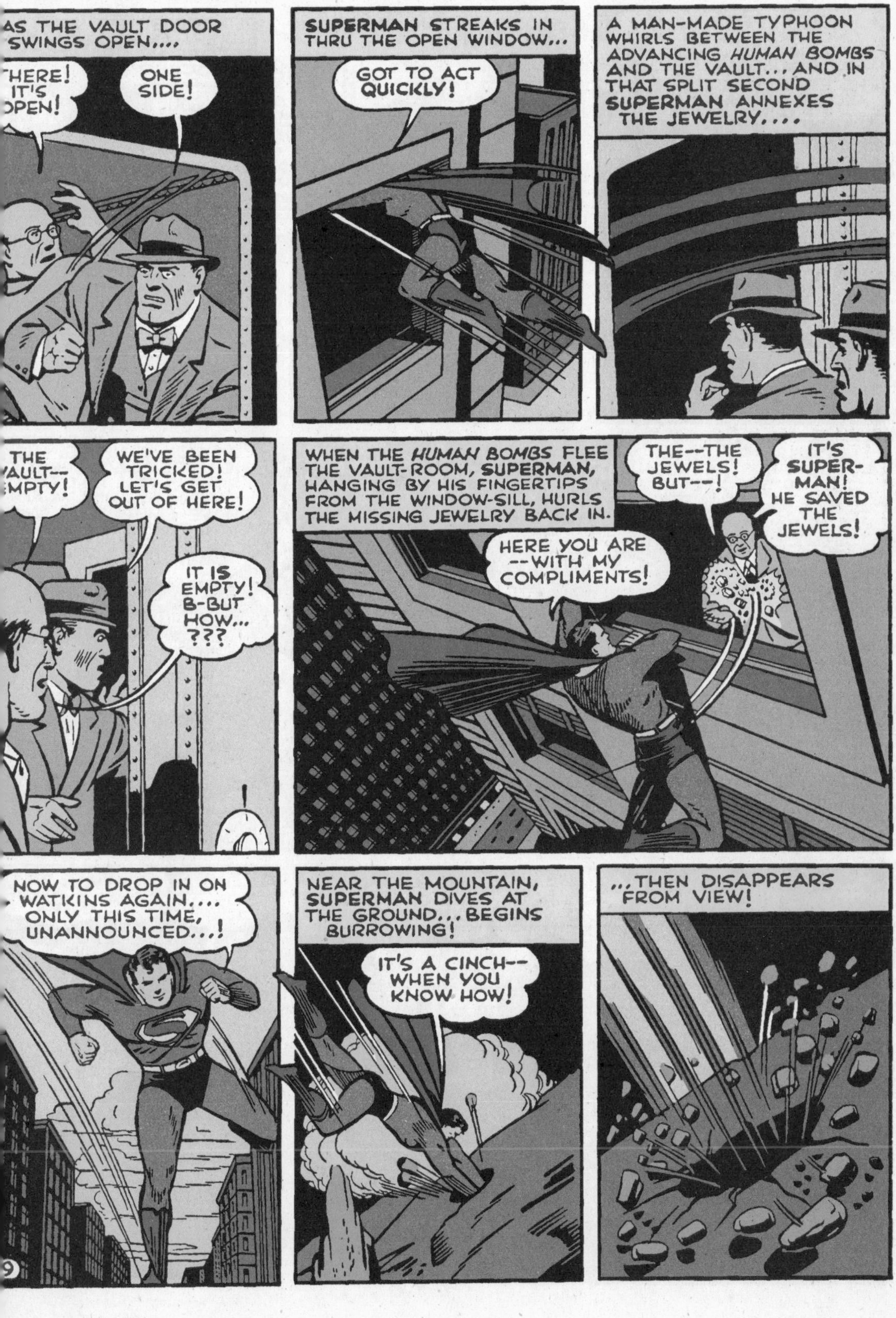
AS THE VAULT DOOR SWINGS OPEN....
HERE! IT'S OPEN!
ONE SIDE!
SUPERMAN STREAKS IN THRU THE OPEN WINDOW...
GOT TO ACT QUICKLY!
A MAN-MADE TYPHOON WHIRLS BETWEEN THE ADVANCING HUMAN BOMBS AND THE VAULT... AND IN THAT SPLIT SECOND SUPERMAN ANNEXES THE JEWELRY....
THE VAULT--EMPTY!
WE'VE BEEN TRICKED! LET'S GET OUT OF HERE!
IT IS EMPTY! B-BUT HOW... ???
WHEN THE HUMAN BOMBS FLEE THE VAULT-ROOM, SUPERMAN, HANGING BY HIS FINGERTIPS FROM THE WINDOW-SILL, HURLS THE MISSING JEWELRY BACK IN.
THE--THE JEWELS! BUT--!
IT'S SUPERMAN! HE SAVED THE JEWELS!
HERE YOU ARE --WITH MY COMPLIMENTS!
NOW TO DROP IN ON WATKINS AGAIN.... ONLY THIS TIME, UNANNOUNCED...!
9
NEAR THE MOUNTAIN, SUPERMAN DIVES AT THE GROUND... BEGINS BURROWING!
IT'S A CINCH--WHEN YOU KNOW HOW!
...THEN DISAPPEARS FROM VIEW!

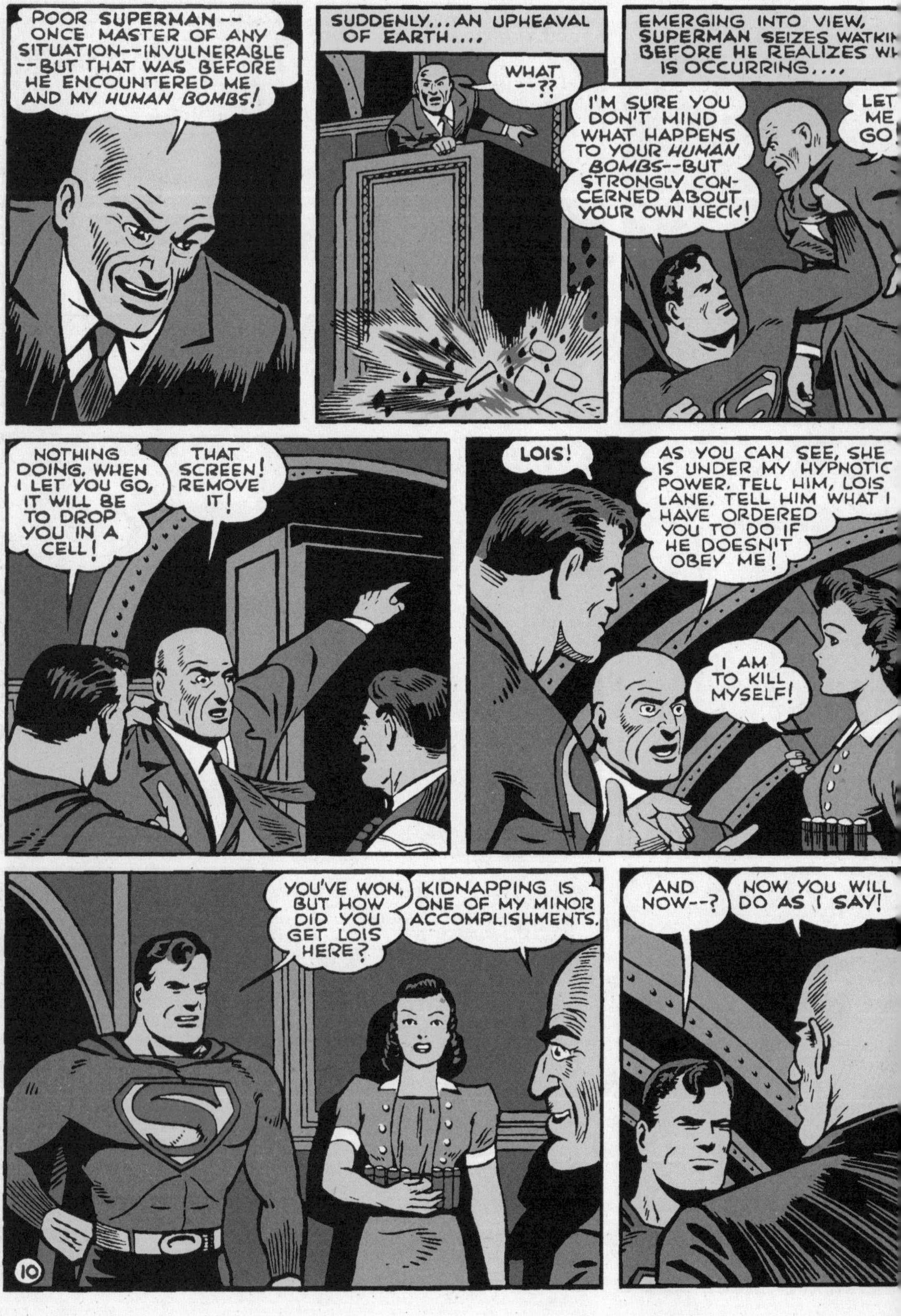
POOR SUPERMAN-- ONCE MASTER OF ANY SITUATION--INVULNERABLE --BUT THAT WAS BEFORE HE ENCOUNTERED ME AND MY *HUMAN BOMBS*!
SUDDENLY... AN UPHEAVAL OF EARTH....
WHAT --??
EMERGING INTO VIEW, SUPERMAN SEIZES WATKI BEFORE HE REALIZES W IS OCCURRING....
I'M SURE YOU DON'T MIND WHAT HAPPENS TO YOUR *HUMAN BOMBS*--BUT STRONGLY CONCERNED ABOUT YOUR OWN NECK!
LET ME GO!
NOTHING DOING. WHEN I LET YOU GO, IT WILL BE TO DROP YOU IN A CELL!
THAT SCREEN! REMOVE IT!
LOIS!
AS YOU CAN SEE, SHE IS UNDER MY HYPNOTIC POWER. TELL HIM, LOIS LANE. TELL HIM WHAT I HAVE ORDERED YOU TO DO IF HE DOESN'T OBEY ME!
I AM TO KILL MYSELF!
10
YOU'VE WON, BUT HOW DID YOU GET LOIS HERE?
KIDNAPPING IS ONE OF MY MINOR ACCOMPLISHMENTS.
AND NOW--?
NOW YOU WILL DO AS I SAY!

...ND
OUR
ORDERS?

ROBBERY, OF COURSE. I'LL LOOT THE TREASURIES OF THE WORLD! AND YOU WILL HELP MY *HUMAN BOMBS* ACCUMULATE THOSE RICHES!

A SPECIAL TRAIN--THE *CASCADE*--IS COMING INTO *METROPOLIS* IN AN HOUR, IT IS LADEN WITH A GREAT SUPPLY OF GOLD.

WHAT HAS THAT TO DO WITH ME?

MERELY THIS! YOU ARE GOING TO BRING THAT GOLD CARGO HERE TO ME!

AND SUPPOSE I TRICK YOU?

BUT YOU WON'T! FOR LOIS LANE WILL ACCOMPANY YOU! AND AT YOUR FIRST WRONG MOVE SHE WILL SLAY HERSELF! RIGHT, MISS LANE?

ABSOLUTELY RIGHT!

MOMENTS LATER... SUPERMAN STREAKS TOWARD THE RAILROAD YARD WITH LOIS....

YOU'D BETTER NOT TRY ANYTHING--OR I OBEY WATKINS' ORDER!

VERY WELL, I CAN DO NOTHING BUT OBEY. HERE COMES THE CASCADE NOW!

AS THE TRAIN IS ALMOST UPON HIM, SUPERMAN LIFTS THE ENGINE WITH ONE HAND...THEN RACES ALONG....

BUT YOU WERE SUPPOSED TO TAKE ALL THE GOLD!

I WILL. JUST WATCH!

SO SWIFT IS THE MOMENTUM OF SUPERMAN'S DASH THAT THE REMAINDER OF THE TRAIN RISES UP INTO THE AIR BEHIND THE ENGINE....

JUST LIKE A KITE!

11

LATER.... OUTSIDE THE MOUNTAIN HIDEAWAY....

ARE YOU PLEASED?

YOU HAVE DONE WELL!

BUT AS GOVERNMENT GUARDS SPRING FROM THE TRAIN, A PITCHED BATTLE ENSUES BETWEEN THEM AND THE HUMAN BOMBS!

BLAST THEM OUT OF EXISTENCE!

RACING BETWEEN THE TWO BATTLING PARTIES, SUPERMAN EXPERTLY CATCHES ALL THE BULLETS....

I DON'T WANT EITHER OF YOU TO GET HURT!

AND NOW FOR YOU!

HUMAN BOMBS! KILL YOURSELVES! I, WATKINS, COMMAND IT!

IN ANSWER TO THE MASTER HYPNOTIST'S COMMAND, THE HUMAN BOMBS PREPARE TO CARRY OUT THE ORDER...

HE WANTS US TO KILL OURSELVES...

...AND HIS WORD IS LAW!

THE END OF YOUR CROOKED SCHEMES!

THEIR LEADER KNOCKED UNCONSCIOUS BY SUPERMAN'S BLOW, THE HUMAN BOMBS ARE FREED FROM HIS HYPNOTIC INFLUENCE...

W-WAS I WEARING THIS?

WHERE HAVE I BEEN?

THESE MEN ARE GUILTLESS OF THE CRIMES THEY MAY HAVE COMMITTED, THEY WERE COMPLETELY DOMINATED BY WATKINS' WILL!

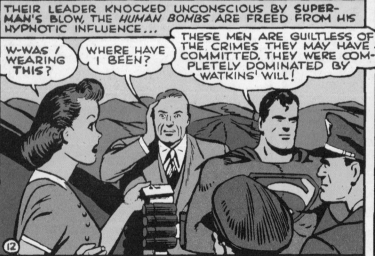

⑫

LATER...THE DAILY PLANET.

HOW DID YOU LIKE MY SCOOP?

EVEN SUPERMAN COULDN'T HAVE DONE BETTER!

THE END

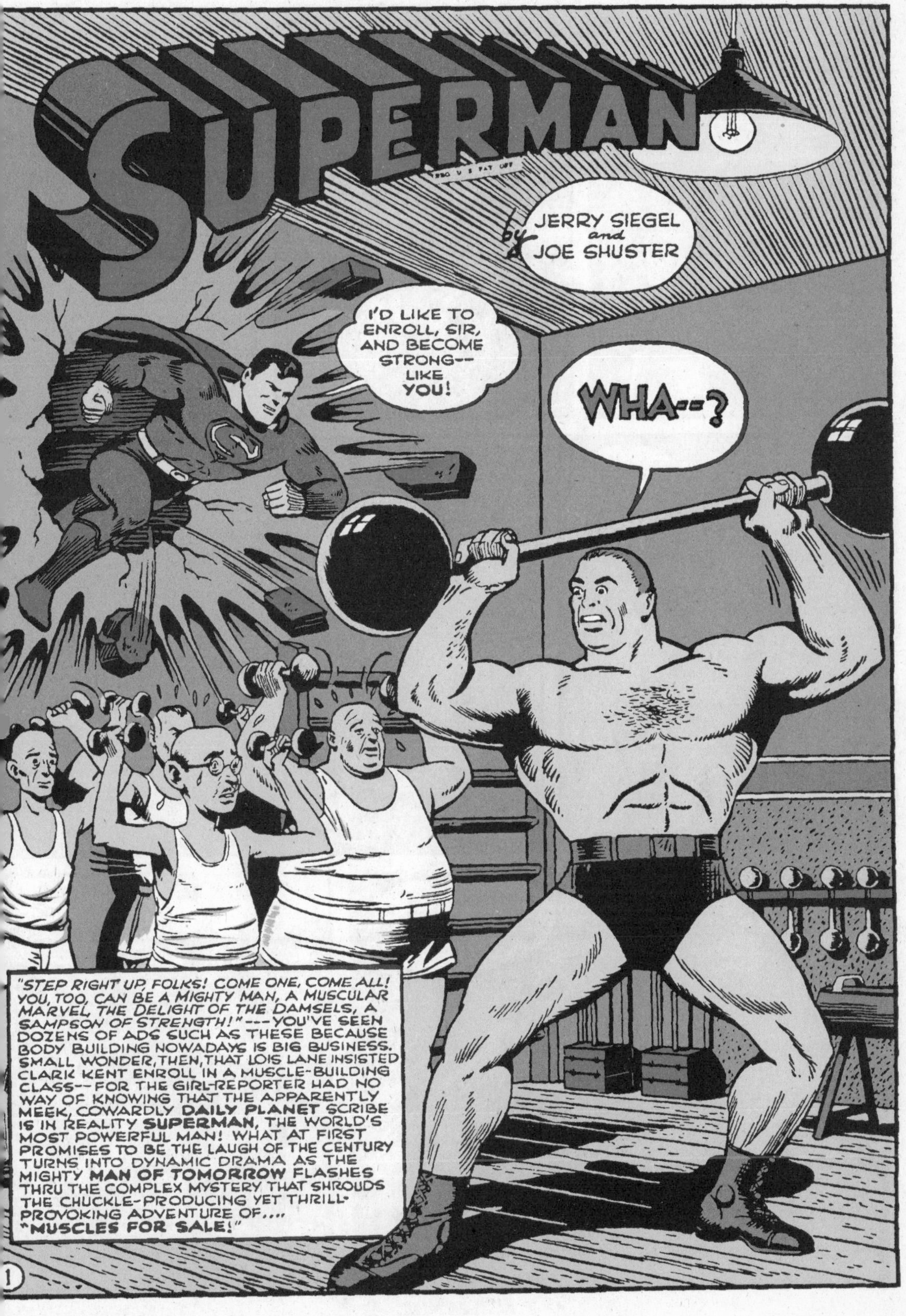
SUPERMAN
REG. U.S. PAT. OFF.
by JERRY SIEGEL and JOE SHUSTER
I'D LIKE TO ENROLL, SIR, AND BECOME STRONG-- LIKE YOU!
WHA--?
"STEP RIGHT UP, FOLKS! COME ONE, COME ALL! YOU, TOO, CAN BE A MIGHTY MAN, A MUSCULAR MARVEL, THE DELIGHT OF THE DAMSELS, A SAMPSON OF STRENGTH!" --- YOU'VE SEEN DOZENS OF ADS SUCH AS THESE BECAUSE BODY BUILDING NOWADAYS IS BIG BUSINESS. SMALL WONDER, THEN, THAT LOIS LANE INSISTED CLARK KENT ENROLL IN A MUSCLE-BUILDING CLASS-- FOR THE GIRL-REPORTER HAD NO WAY OF KNOWING THAT THE APPARENTLY MEEK, COWARDLY DAILY PLANET SCRIBE IS IN REALITY SUPERMAN, THE WORLD'S MOST POWERFUL MAN! WHAT AT FIRST PROMISES TO BE THE LAUGH OF THE CENTURY TURNS INTO DYNAMIC DRAMA AS THE MIGHTY MAN OF TOMORROW FLASHES THRU THE COMPLEX MYSTERY THAT SHROUDS THE CHUCKLE-PRODUCING YET THRILL-PROVOKING ADVENTURE OF.... "MUSCLES FOR SALE!"
1

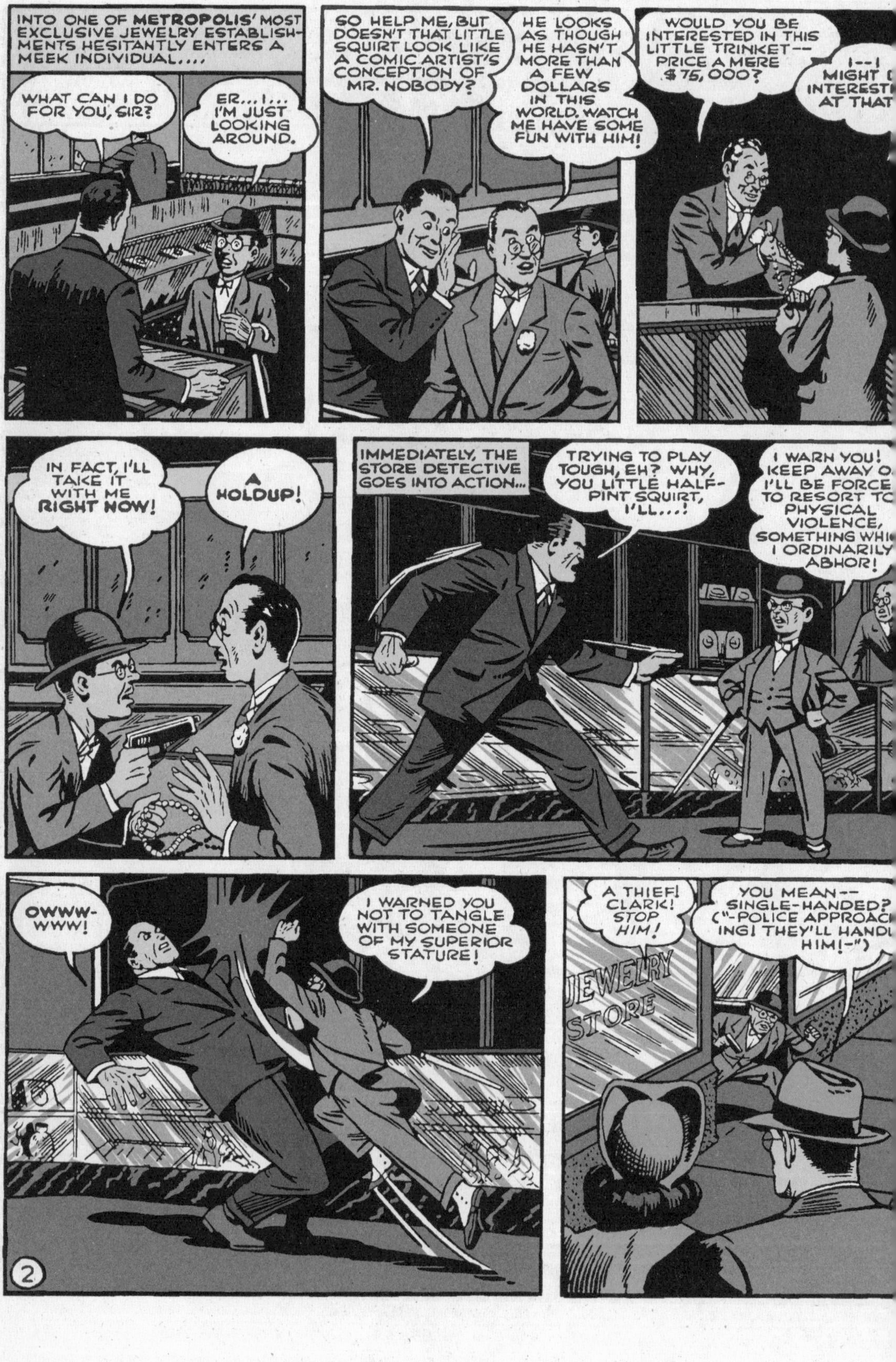
INTO ONE OF METROPOLIS' MOST EXCLUSIVE JEWELRY ESTABLISHMENTS HESITANTLY ENTERS A MEEK INDIVIDUAL....
WHAT CAN I DO FOR YOU, SIR?
ER...I... I'M JUST LOOKING AROUND.
SO HELP ME, BUT DOESN'T THAT LITTLE SQUIRT LOOK LIKE A COMIC ARTIST'S CONCEPTION OF MR. NOBODY?
HE LOOKS AS THOUGH HE HASN'T MORE THAN A FEW DOLLARS IN THIS WORLD. WATCH ME HAVE SOME FUN WITH HIM!
WOULD YOU BE INTERESTED IN THIS LITTLE TRINKET-- PRICE A MERE $75,000?
I--I MIGHT
INTEREST
AT THAT
IN FACT, I'LL TAKE IT WITH ME RIGHT NOW!
A HOLDUP!
IMMEDIATELY, THE STORE DETECTIVE GOES INTO ACTION...
TRYING TO PLAY TOUGH, EH? WHY, YOU LITTLE HALF-PINT SQUIRT, I'LL...!
I WARN YOU! KEEP AWAY O
I'LL BE FORCE
TO RESORT TO
PHYSICAL VIOLENCE, SOMETHING WH
I ORDINARILY ABHOR!
OWWW-WWW!
I WARNED YOU NOT TO TANGLE WITH SOMEONE OF MY SUPERIOR STATURE!
2
A THIEF! CLARK! STOP HIM!
YOU MEAN-- SINGLE-HANDED?
("-POLICE APPROAC
ING! THEY'LL HAND
HIM!-")
JEWELRY STORE

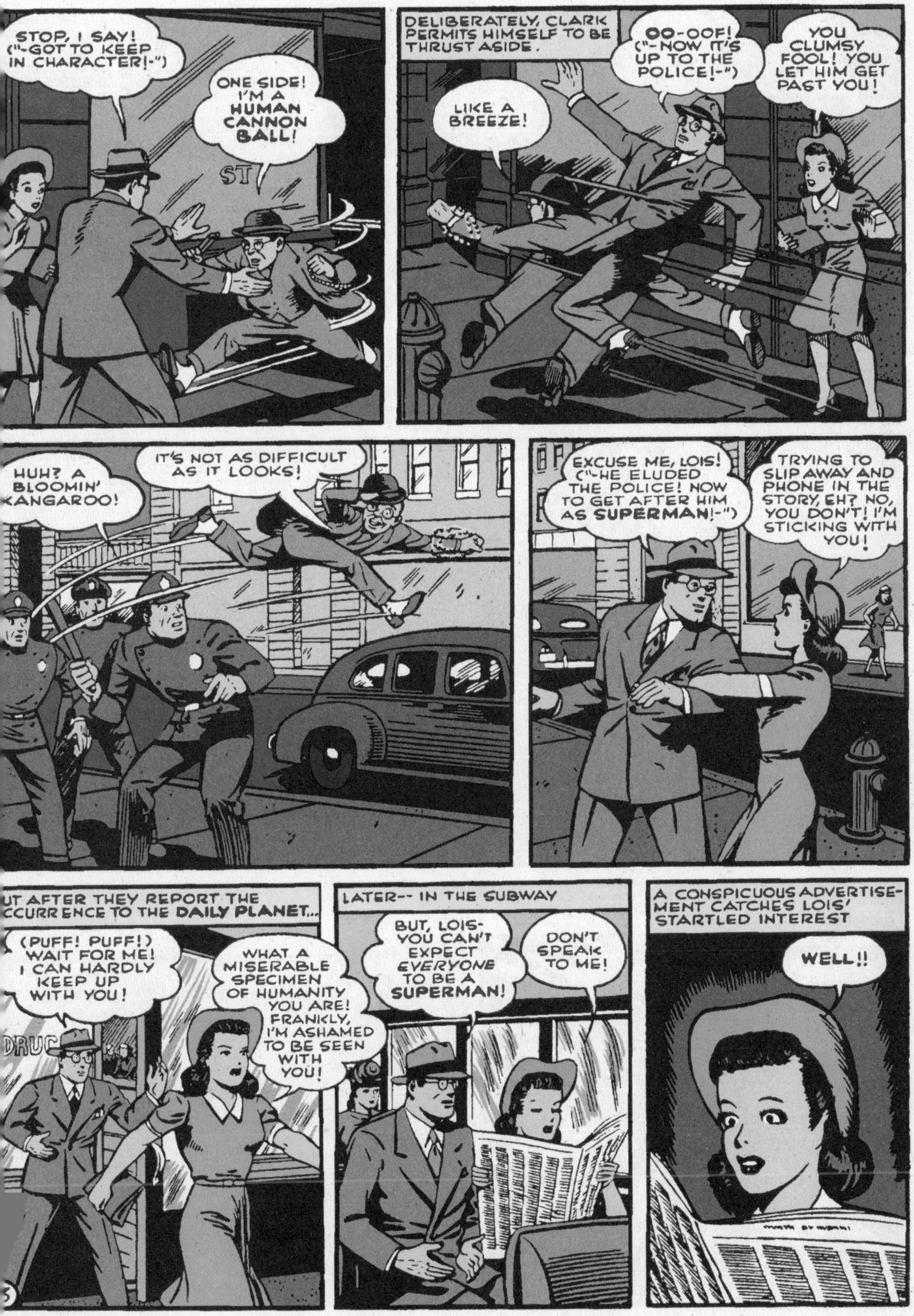
STOP, I SAY! ("-GOT TO KEEP IN CHARACTER!-")
ONE SIDE! I'M A HUMAN CANNON BALL!
DELIBERATELY, CLARK PERMITS HIMSELF TO BE THRUST ASIDE.
LIKE A BREEZE!
OO-OOF! ("-NOW IT'S UP TO THE POLICE!-")
YOU CLUMSY FOOL! YOU LET HIM GET PAST YOU!
HUH? A BLOOMIN' KANGAROO!
IT'S NOT AS DIFFICULT AS IT LOOKS!
EXCUSE ME, LOIS! ("-HE ELUDED THE POLICE! NOW TO GET AFTER HIM AS SUPERMAN!-")
TRYING TO SLIP AWAY AND PHONE IN THE STORY, EH? NO, YOU DON'T! I'M STICKING WITH YOU!
UT AFTER THEY REPORT THE CCURRENCE TO THE DAILY PLANET...
(PUFF! PUFF!) WAIT FOR ME! I CAN HARDLY KEEP UP WITH YOU!
WHAT A MISERABLE SPECIMEN OF HUMANITY YOU ARE! FRANKLY, I'M ASHAMED TO BE SEEN WITH YOU!
LATER-- IN THE SUBWAY
BUT, LOIS- YOU CAN'T EXPECT EVERYONE TO BE A SUPERMAN!
DON'T SPEAK TO ME!
A CONSPICUOUS ADVERTISEMENT CATCHES LOIS' STARTLED INTEREST
WELL!!

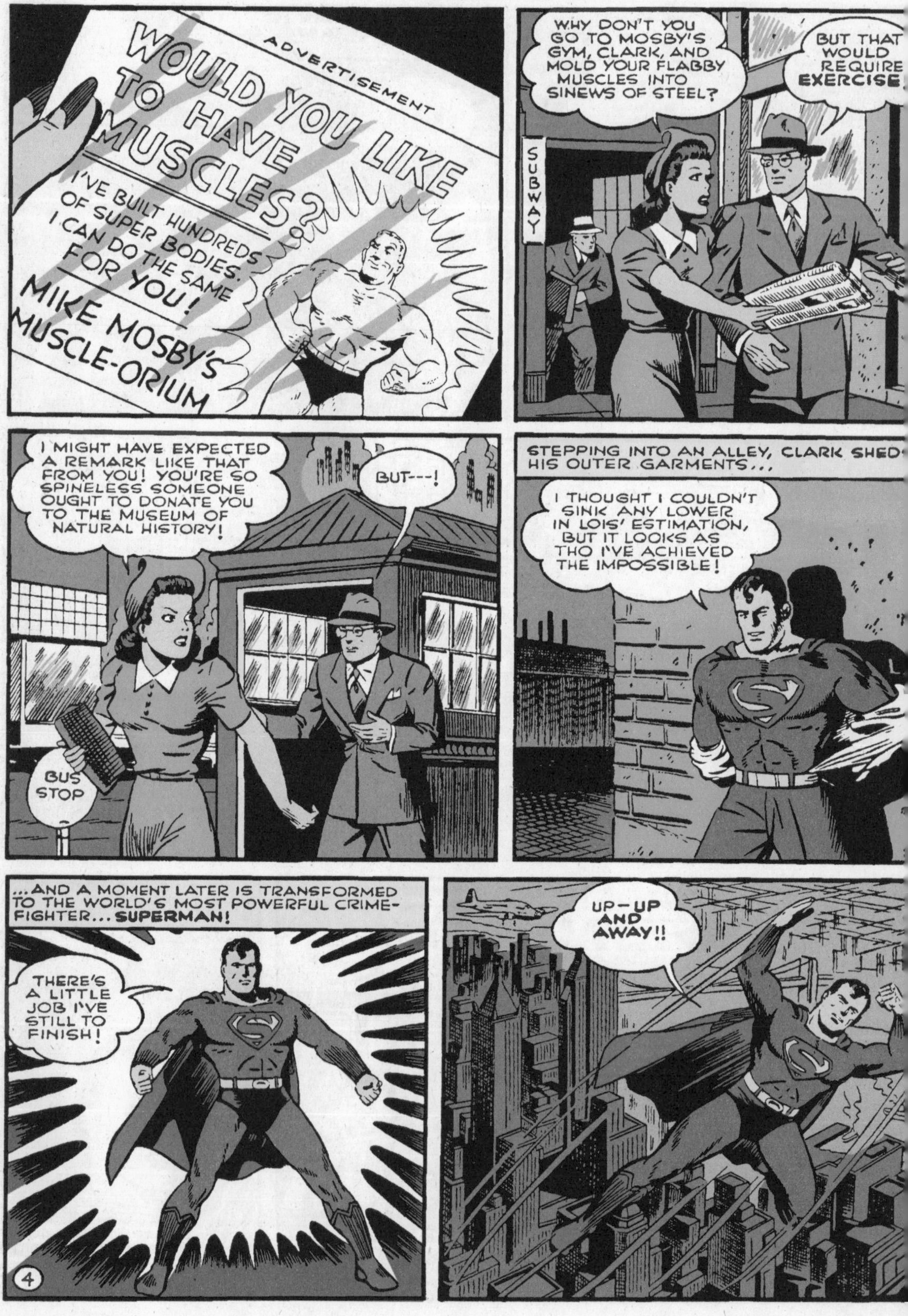
ADVERTISEMENT
WOULD YOU LIKE TO HAVE MUSCLES?
I'VE BUILT HUNDREDS OF SUPER BODIES. I CAN DO THE SAME FOR YOU!
MIKE MOSBY'S MUSCLE-ORIUM
WHY DON'T YOU GO TO MOSBY'S GYM, CLARK, AND MOLD YOUR FLABBY MUSCLES INTO SINEWS OF STEEL?
BUT THAT WOULD REQUIRE **EXERCISE**
SUBWAY
I MIGHT HAVE EXPECTED A REMARK LIKE THAT FROM YOU! YOU'RE SO SPINELESS SOMEONE OUGHT TO DONATE YOU TO THE MUSEUM OF NATURAL HISTORY!
BUT---!
BUS STOP
STEPPING INTO AN ALLEY, CLARK SHEDS HIS OUTER GARMENTS...
I THOUGHT I COULDN'T SINK ANY LOWER IN LOIS' ESTIMATION, BUT IT LOOKS AS THO I'VE ACHIEVED THE IMPOSSIBLE!
...AND A MOMENT LATER IS TRANSFORMED TO THE WORLD'S MOST POWERFUL CRIME-FIGHTER... **SUPERMAN!**
THERE'S A LITTLE JOB I'VE STILL TO FINISH!
4
UP-UP **AND AWAY!!**

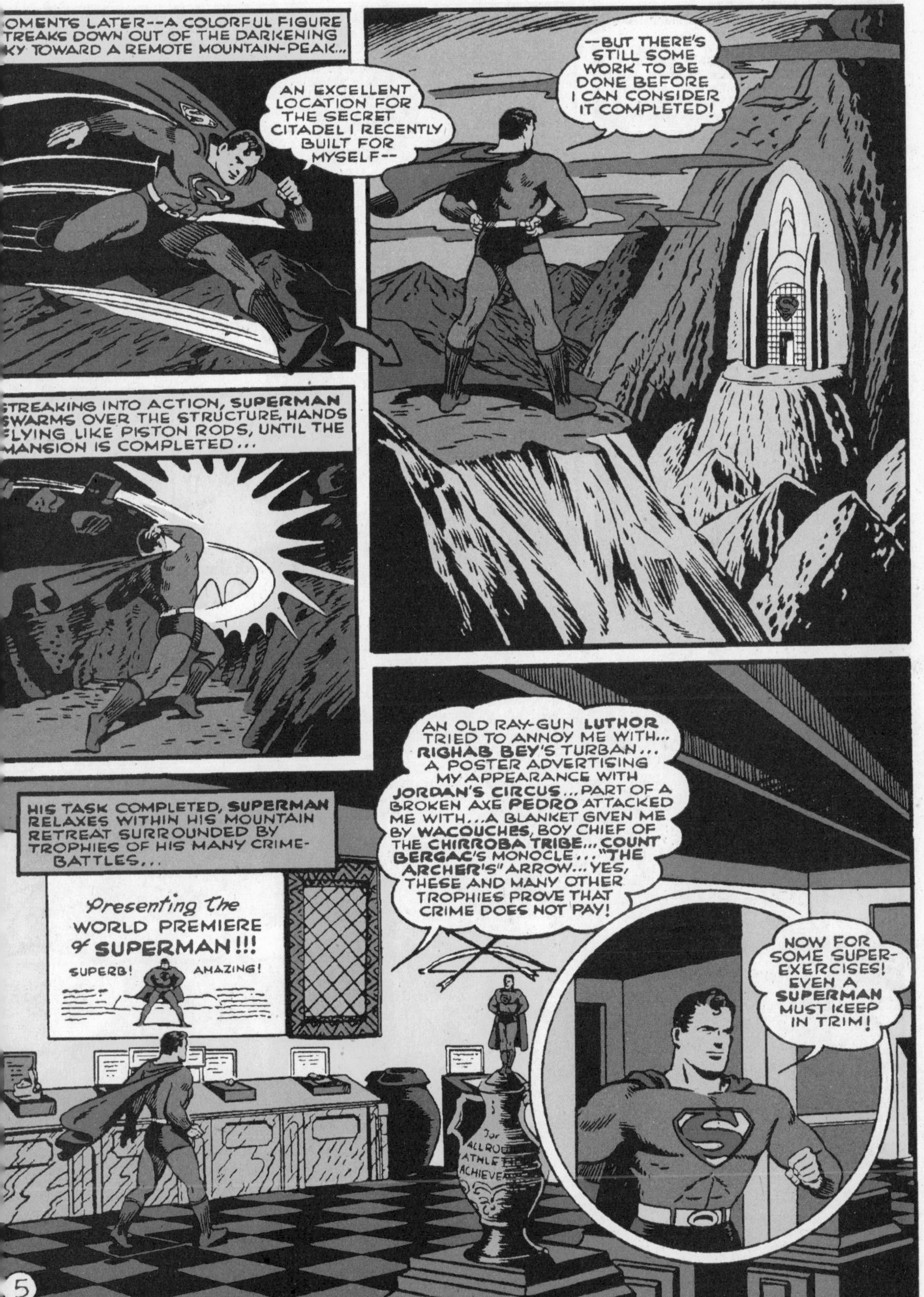

OMENTS LATER--A COLORFUL FIGURE TREAKS DOWN OUT OF THE DARKENING KY TOWARD A REMOTE MOUNTAIN-PEAK...
AN EXCELLENT LOCATION FOR THE SECRET CITADEL I RECENTLY BUILT FOR MYSELF--
--BUT THERE'S STILL SOME WORK TO BE DONE BEFORE I CAN CONSIDER IT COMPLETED!
STREAKING INTO ACTION, SUPERMAN SWARMS OVER THE STRUCTURE, HANDS FLYING LIKE PISTON RODS, UNTIL THE MANSION IS COMPLETED...
HIS TASK COMPLETED, SUPERMAN RELAXES WITHIN HIS MOUNTAIN RETREAT SURROUNDED BY TROPHIES OF HIS MANY CRIME-BATTLES...
Presenting The WORLD PREMIERE of SUPERMAN!!!
SUPERB!
AMAZING!
AN OLD RAY-GUN LUTHOR TRIED TO ANNOY ME WITH... RIGHAB BEY'S TURBAN... A POSTER ADVERTISING MY APPEARANCE WITH JORDAN'S CIRCUS... PART OF A BROKEN AXE PEDRO ATTACKED ME WITH... A BLANKET GIVEN ME BY WACOUCHES, BOY CHIEF OF THE CHIRROBA TRIBE... COUNT BERGAC'S MONOCLE... "THE ARCHER'S" ARROW... YES, THESE AND MANY OTHER TROPHIES PROVE THAT CRIME DOES NOT PAY!
NOW FOR SOME SUPER-EXERCISES! EVEN A SUPERMAN MUST KEEP IN TRIM!
5

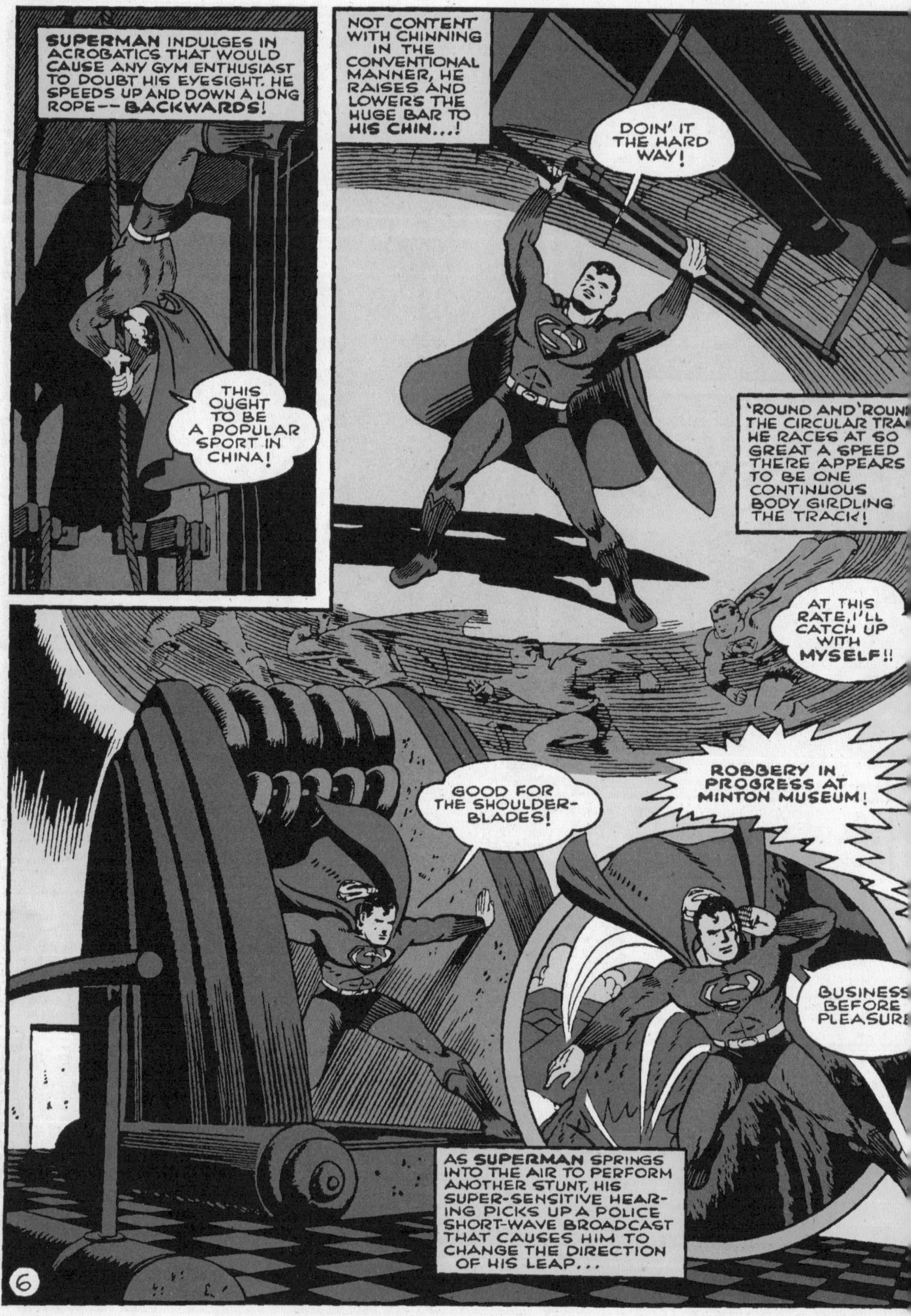
SUPERMAN INDULGES IN ACROBATICS THAT WOULD CAUSE ANY GYM ENTHUSIAST TO DOUBT HIS EYESIGHT. HE SPEEDS UP AND DOWN A LONG ROPE-- BACKWARDS!
THIS OUGHT TO BE A POPULAR SPORT IN CHINA!
NOT CONTENT WITH CHINNING IN THE CONVENTIONAL MANNER, HE RAISES AND LOWERS THE HUGE BAR TO HIS CHIN...!
DOIN' IT THE HARD WAY!
'ROUND AND 'ROUN THE CIRCULAR TRA HE RACES AT SO GREAT A SPEED THERE APPEARS TO BE ONE CONTINUOUS BODY GIRDLING THE TRACK!
AT THIS RATE, I'LL CATCH UP WITH MYSELF!!
GOOD FOR THE SHOULDER-BLADES!
ROBBERY IN PROGRESS AT MINTON MUSEUM!
BUSINESS BEFORE PLEASUR
AS SUPERMAN SPRINGS INTO THE AIR TO PERFORM ANOTHER STUNT, HIS SUPER-SENSITIVE HEARING PICKS UP A POLICE SHORT-WAVE BROADCAST THAT CAUSES HIM TO CHANGE THE DIRECTION OF HIS LEAP...
6

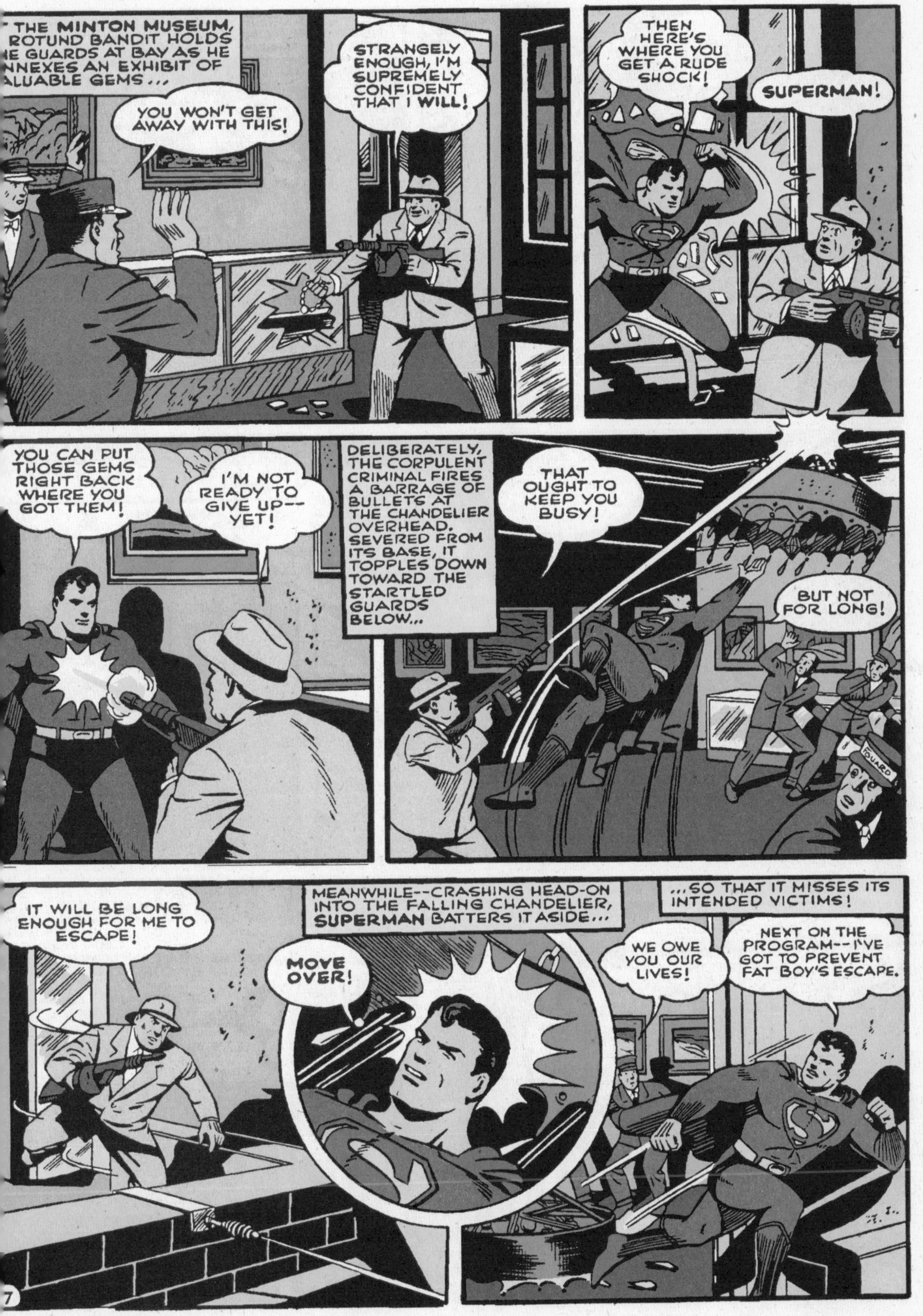
T THE MINTON MUSEUM, ROTUND BANDIT HOLDS E GUARDS AT BAY AS HE NNEXES AN EXHIBIT OF ALUABLE GEMS...
YOU WON'T GET AWAY WITH THIS!
STRANGELY ENOUGH, I'M SUPREMELY CONFIDENT THAT I WILL!
THEN HERE'S WHERE YOU GET A RUDE SHOCK!
SUPERMAN!
YOU CAN PUT THOSE GEMS RIGHT BACK WHERE YOU GOT THEM!
I'M NOT READY TO GIVE UP--YET!
DELIBERATELY, THE CORPULENT CRIMINAL FIRES A BARRAGE OF BULLETS AT THE CHANDELIER OVERHEAD. SEVERED FROM ITS BASE, IT TOPPLES DOWN TOWARD THE STARTLED GUARDS BELOW...
THAT OUGHT TO KEEP YOU BUSY!
BUT NOT FOR LONG!
GUARD
IT WILL BE LONG ENOUGH FOR ME TO ESCAPE!
MEANWHILE--CRASHING HEAD-ON INTO THE FALLING CHANDELIER, SUPERMAN BATTERS IT ASIDE...
MOVE OVER!
...SO THAT IT MISSES ITS INTENDED VICTIMS!
WE OWE YOU OUR LIVES!
NEXT ON THE PROGRAM--I'VE GOT TO PREVENT FAT BOY'S ESCAPE.
7

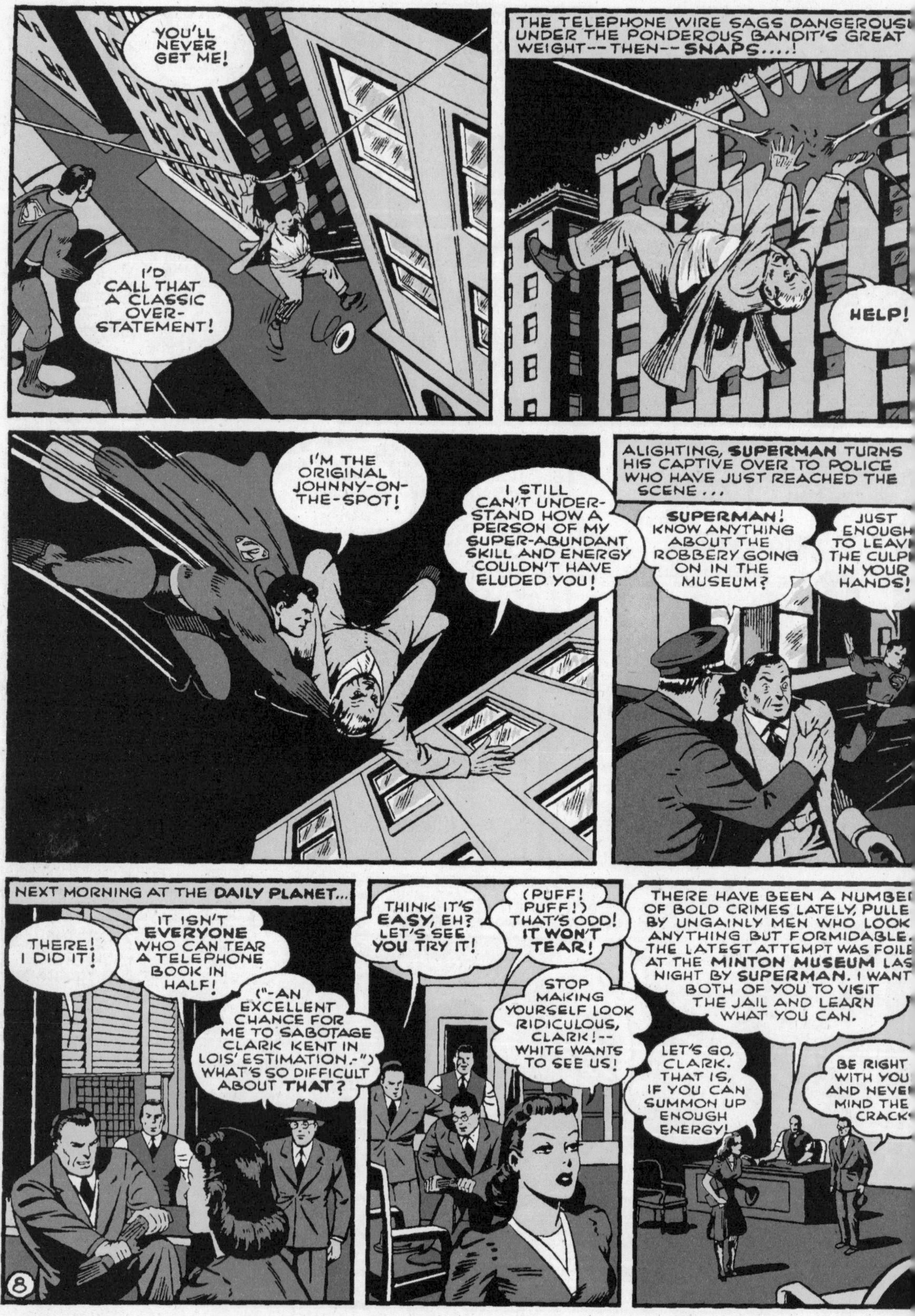

YOU'LL NEVER GET ME!
I'D CALL THAT A CLASSIC OVER-STATEMENT!
THE TELEPHONE WIRE SAGS DANGEROUS UNDER THE PONDEROUS BANDIT'S GREAT WEIGHT--THEN--SNAPS....!
HELP!
I'M THE ORIGINAL JOHNNY-ON-THE-SPOT!
I STILL CAN'T UNDER-STAND HOW A PERSON OF MY SUPER-ABUNDANT SKILL AND ENERGY COULDN'T HAVE ELUDED YOU!
ALIGHTING, SUPERMAN TURNS HIS CAPTIVE OVER TO POLICE WHO HAVE JUST REACHED THE SCENE...
SUPERMAN! KNOW ANYTHING ABOUT THE ROBBERY GOING ON IN THE MUSEUM?
JUST ENOUGH TO LEAV THE CULP IN YOUR HANDS!
NEXT MORNING AT THE DAILY PLANET...
THERE! I DID IT!
IT ISN'T EVERYONE WHO CAN TEAR A TELEPHONE BOOK IN HALF!
("-AN EXCELLENT CHANCE FOR ME TO SABOTAGE CLARK KENT IN LOIS' ESTIMATION.-") WHAT'S SO DIFFICULT ABOUT THAT?
8
THINK IT'S EASY, EH? LET'S SEE YOU TRY IT!
(PUFF! PUFF!) THAT'S ODD! IT WON'T TEAR!
STOP MAKING YOURSELF LOOK RIDICULOUS, CLARK!--WHITE WANTS TO SEE US!
THERE HAVE BEEN A NUMBE OF BOLD CRIMES LATELY, PULLE BY UNGAINLY MEN WHO LOOK ANYTHING BUT FORMIDABLE. THE LATEST ATTEMPT WAS FOIL AT THE MINTON MUSEUM LAS NIGHT BY SUPERMAN. I WANT BOTH OF YOU TO VISIT THE JAIL AND LEARN WHAT YOU CAN.
LET'S GO, CLARK. THAT IS, IF YOU CAN SUMMON UP ENOUGH ENERGY!
BE RIGHT WITH YOU AND NEVE MIND THE CRACK

LATER--
WHAT I CAN'T UNDERSTAND, MR. BRANT, IS WHY A QUIET, SANE, RESPECTABLE BUSINESS MAN OF YOUR FINE INTEGRITY SHOULD HAVE TURNED TO CRIME.

DON'T PREACH TO ME!

GEORGE-- GEORGE... THAT DOESN'T SOUND LIKE YOU AT ALL!

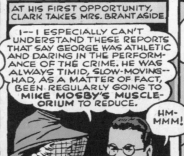

AT HIS FIRST OPPORTUNITY, CLARK TAKES MRS. BRANT ASIDE.
I--I ESPECIALLY CAN'T UNDERSTAND THESE REPORTS THAT SAY GEORGE WAS ATHLETIC AND DARING IN THE PERFORMANCE OF THE CRIME. HE WAS ALWAYS TIMID, SLOW-MOVING-- HAD, AS A MATTER OF FACT, BEEN REGULARLY GOING TO MIKE MOSBY'S MUSCLE-ORIUM TO REDUCE.

HM--MMM!

LOIS... I'VE BEEN GIVING YOUR SUGGESTION SOME SERIOUS THOUGHT. I THINK I'LL ENROLL AT MOSBY'S GYM AFTER ALL!

SOME SENSE AT LAST!

MR. MOSBY, CLARK IS PUNY AND WEAK-- EVERYONE ALWAYS PICKS ON HIM...

("-HERE'S WHERE I MAKE A BIG IMPRESSION ON THIS SWELL DISH BY BEATING UP HER BOY FRIEND!-") GET INTO A GYM SUIT, KENT. WE'LL GIVE MISS LANE A PREVIEW OF THE TOUGHENING PROCESS YOU'LL RECEIVE HERE!

ULP! ("-THAT LITTLE FELLOW STROLLING BY! HE'S THE CHAP WHO ROBBED THE JEWELRY STORE!")

NOT BAD! WHY, CLARK-- YOU HAVEN'T SUCH A POOR PHYSIQUE, AT THAT!

ER-- THINK SO?

HE'S GOT SOME GOOD BASIC MATERIAL THERE, BUT IT'S GOT TO BE WHIPPED INTO SHAPE. PUT ON THESE GLOVES!

OUCH! THAT HURT!!

PUT UP YOUR MITTS. WE'LL PUT ON A SPARRING EXHIBITION FOR TH' LITTLE LADY! ("-HO! HO! AFTER I BEAT HIS EARS OFF, SHE'LL BE DELIGHTED TO GO OUT TO LUNCH WITH ME!")

BUT CLARK SKILLFULLY DODGES MIKE'S POWER-HOUSE PUNCHES, AND THE INFURIATED PHYSICAL INSTRUCTOR CONTINUALLY FLAILS EMPTY SPACE...!

FIGHT LIKE A MAN, YA CRAZY JACK-IN-TH'-BOX!!

DISCRETION IS THE BETTER PART OF VALOR!

YOW-W!

TCH! TCH!

I'VE SEEN ENOUGH OF THIS FARCE! WHILE YOU TWO PLAY HIDE-AND-GO SEEK, I'VE IMPORTANT WORK TO DO!

I'M CLARK KENT. CAN YOU TELL ME WHO THAT FELLOW IS?

HE'S NAT FOLSOM, A BANKER, BUT THEY SAY HE MADE HIS FORTUNE OUT OF PROHIBITION. ME, I'M JAKE MASSEY, JUST AN ORDINARY GUY.

DOES ANYTHING-- ER--UNUSUAL--THAT IS, OTHER THAN GYM INSTRUCTION, GO ON AROUND HERE? ("--SO FOLSOM MAY HAVE BEEN A RACKETEER!--")

THE ONLY THING I'VE NOTICED IS THAT THEY EXERCISE YOU TO TH' POINT OF EXHAUSTION. IT'S TOO MUCH FOR ME. I'M THINKING OF QUITTING!

MEANWHILE--AS MIKE BANDAGES HIS BRUISED FIST IN HIS PRIVATE OFFICE....

BLAST THAT KENT! I'LL MAKE HIM PAY FOR MAKING ME LOOK LIKE A SAP BEFORE HIS GIRL!

YOU'LL DO NOTHING OF THE KIND, MIKE!

IT'S TH' SPOOK AGAIN!-- WH-WHAT ARE YOUR ORDERS JOHN L.?

OUR PARTNERSHIP HAS PROVEN EXCEEDINGLY LUCRATIVE THUS FAR. IF YOU WISH IT TO CONTINUE SO, MIKE, YOU MUST KEEP YOUR PERSONAL ANIMOSITIES UNDER CONTROL. GET OUT IN THE GYM--PUT THOSE CREAMPUFFS THRU THEIR PACES--AND LEAVE THE REST TO ME....!

MIKE PUTS HIS CLIENTS THRU A GRUELING SET OF EXERCISES.

PUSH-UPS...!

FASTER YOU DECREPIT DODOS!

MEDICINE-BALL BARRAGE!

HARDER! THIS AIN'T BEAN BAG!

WRESTLING...!

HELP! I'M STUCK!

SO THAT HALF AN HOUR LATER MIKE'S CUSTOMERS LAY WINDED AND PANTING ON THE MATS,, AND AS THEY RECLINE THERE HALF CONSCIOUS, COMPLETELY EXHAUSTED, A COMMANDING VOICE BOOMS FORTH....

STRONG! STRONG! ALL OF YOU ARE DARING, SUPERB ATHLETES--AND COMPLETELY SUBJECT TO MY WILL!

SUPERB ATHLETES-- SUBJECT TO YOUR WILL...

("--MASS HYPNOTISM! I'LL PRETEND TO BE HYPNOTIZED WITH THE OTHERS!--")

YOU WHO CALL YOURSELF CLARK KENT--YOU ARE NOW SUPERMAN! YOU POSSESS ALL HIS MIGHTY POWERS!

HERE. PUT ON THIS ESPECIALLY MADE SUPERMAN UNIFORM.

("--WHAT A LAUGH! THEY'RE TRYING TO HYPNOTIZE ME INTO THINKING I'M SUPERMAN AND THE JOKE OF IT IS--I AM!--")

AFTER CLARK DONS THE UNIFORM....

UNDERSTAND? YOU ARE NOW ALL-POWERFUL! YOUR STRENGTH IS TERRIFIC!

LIKE THIS?

HOLY COW! HE SOCKED CLEAR THRU TH' WALL!

AN' TH' MIRACLE OF IT IS, HE DIDN'T BREAK A BONE, OR GET A SCRATCH!

WHAT ELSE DO YOU EXPECT OF SUPERMAN

ATTENTION! YOUR INSTRUCTIONS ARE TO LOOT A BAZAAR BEING HELD AT THE HOTEL HANSOM PENTHOUSE BALLROOM THIS AFTERNOON. BRING THE LOOT HERE--THEN--FORGET EVERYTHING!!!

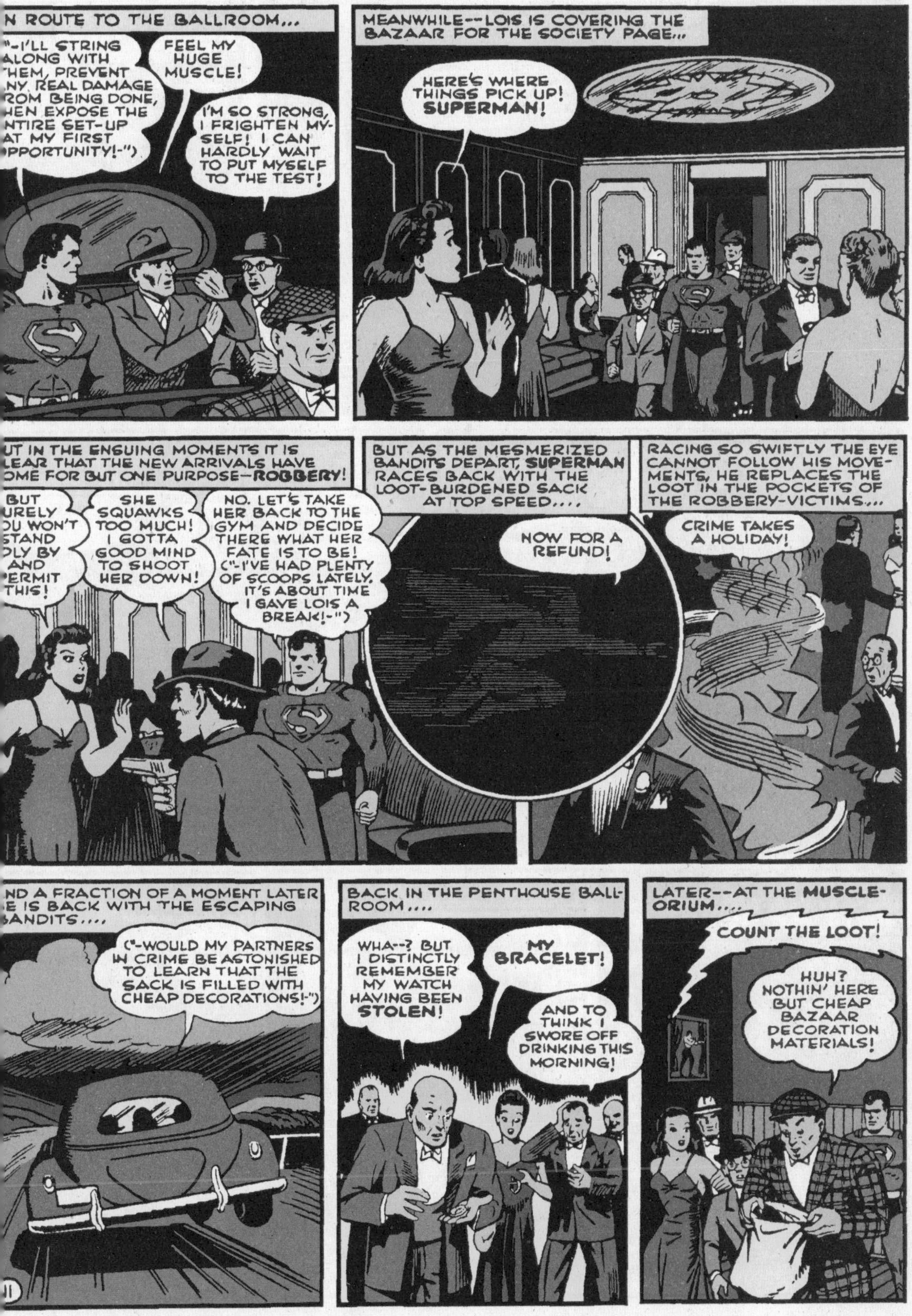
N ROUTE TO THE BALLROOM...
"-I'LL STRING ALONG WITH THEM, PREVENT NY REAL DAMAGE ROM BEING DONE, HEN EXPOSE THE NTIRE SET-UP AT MY FIRST PPORTUNITY!-")
FEEL MY HUGE MUSCLE!
I'M SO STRONG, I FRIGHTEN MYSELF! I CAN HARDLY WAIT TO PUT MYSELF TO THE TEST!
MEANWHILE--LOIS IS COVERING THE BAZAAR FOR THE SOCIETY PAGE...
HERE'S WHERE THINGS PICK UP! SUPERMAN!
UT IN THE ENSUING MOMENTS IT IS LEAR THAT THE NEW ARRIVALS HAVE OME FOR BUT ONE PURPOSE--ROBBERY!
BUT URELY OU WON'T STAND DLY BY AND ERMIT THIS!
SHE SQUAWKS TOO MUCH! I GOTTA GOOD MIND TO SHOOT HER DOWN!
NO. LET'S TAKE HER BACK TO THE GYM AND DECIDE THERE WHAT HER FATE IS TO BE! ("-I'VE HAD PLENTY OF SCOOPS LATELY. IT'S ABOUT TIME I GAVE LOIS A BREAK!-")
BUT AS THE MESMERIZED BANDITS DEPART, SUPERMAN RACES BACK WITH THE LOOT-BURDENED SACK AT TOP SPEED....
NOW FOR A REFUND!
RACING SO SWIFTLY THE EYE CANNOT FOLLOW HIS MOVEMENTS, HE REPLACES THE LOOT IN THE POCKETS OF THE ROBBERY-VICTIMS...
CRIME TAKES A HOLIDAY!
ND A FRACTION OF A MOMENT LATER E IS BACK WITH THE ESCAPING ANDITS....
("-WOULD MY PARTNERS IN CRIME BE ASTONISHED TO LEARN THAT THE SACK IS FILLED WITH CHEAP DECORATIONS!-")
11
BACK IN THE PENTHOUSE BALLROOM....
WHA--? BUT I DISTINCTLY REMEMBER MY WATCH HAVING BEEN STOLEN!
MY BRACELET!
AND TO THINK I SWORE OFF DRINKING THIS MORNING!
LATER--AT THE MUSCLE-ORIUM....
COUNT THE LOOT!
HUH? NOTHIN' HERE BUT CHEAP BAZAAR DECORATION MATERIALS!

WHAT SORT OF A DOUBLE-CROSSER'S TRICK IS THIS?

CUT IT OUT, MASSEY, OR THE SPOOK OF JOHN L. SULLIVAN WILL TAKE CARE OF YOU!

("-HERE'S WHERE THINGS START POPPING!-")

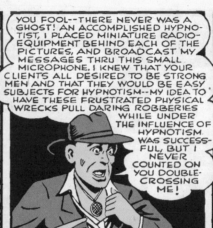

YOU FOOL--THERE NEVER WAS A GHOST! AN ACCOMPLISHED HYPNOTIST, I PLACED MINIATURE RADIO-EQUIPMENT BEHIND EACH OF THE PICTURES, AND BROADCAST MY MESSAGES THRU THIS SMALL MICROPHONE. I KNEW THAT YOUR CLIENTS ALL DESIRED TO BE STRONG MEN AND THAT THEY WOULD BE EASY SUBJECTS FOR HYPNOTISM--MY IDEA TO HAVE THESE FRUSTRATED PHYSICAL WRECKS PULL DARING ROBBERIES WHILE UNDER THE INFLUENCE OF HYPNOTISM WAS SUCCESS-FUL, BUT I NEVER COUNTED ON YOU DOUBLE-CROSSING ME!

BUT I DIDN'T DOUBLE-CROSS YA, CHIEF!

YOU'RE LYING!

ON THE CONTRAR THE CREDI IS ENTIREL MINE!

RUSH HIM! CRUSH HIM! I COMMAND YOU!

HOW TO OVERCOME THEM--WITH-OUT HARMING THEM--??

THEY SHOULD KNOW THEY HAVEN'T A CHANCE AGAINST SUPERMAN!

BUT THAT'S NOT SUPERMAN --THAT'S YOUR REPORTER FRIEND, CLARK KENT, MADE UP TO LOOK LIKE HIM!

AN INSPIRATION STRIKES THE MAN OF STEEL SNATCHING UP SEVERAL EXERCISE-CABLES, H LINKS THEM TOGETHER ABOUT THE CHARGING MEN, EFFECTIVELY IMPRISONING THEM....

THERE! THAT OUGHT TO HOLD YOU!

TAKE HIM, MIKE!

WITH PLEASURE!

THE PLEASURE IS ALL MINE!

OOOO-OOF!

NICE GOING!

AWK!

SCRAMBLING ERECT, MASSEY DRAWS A BEAD ON LOIS....

AT LEAST I'LL GET YOUR GIRL FRIEND!

NO YOU WON'T!

ABRUPTLY, MASSEY DUCKS OUT THE WINDOW TOPPLES SUPERMAN!

LOOK OUT!

THE END OF THAT FOOL!

⑫

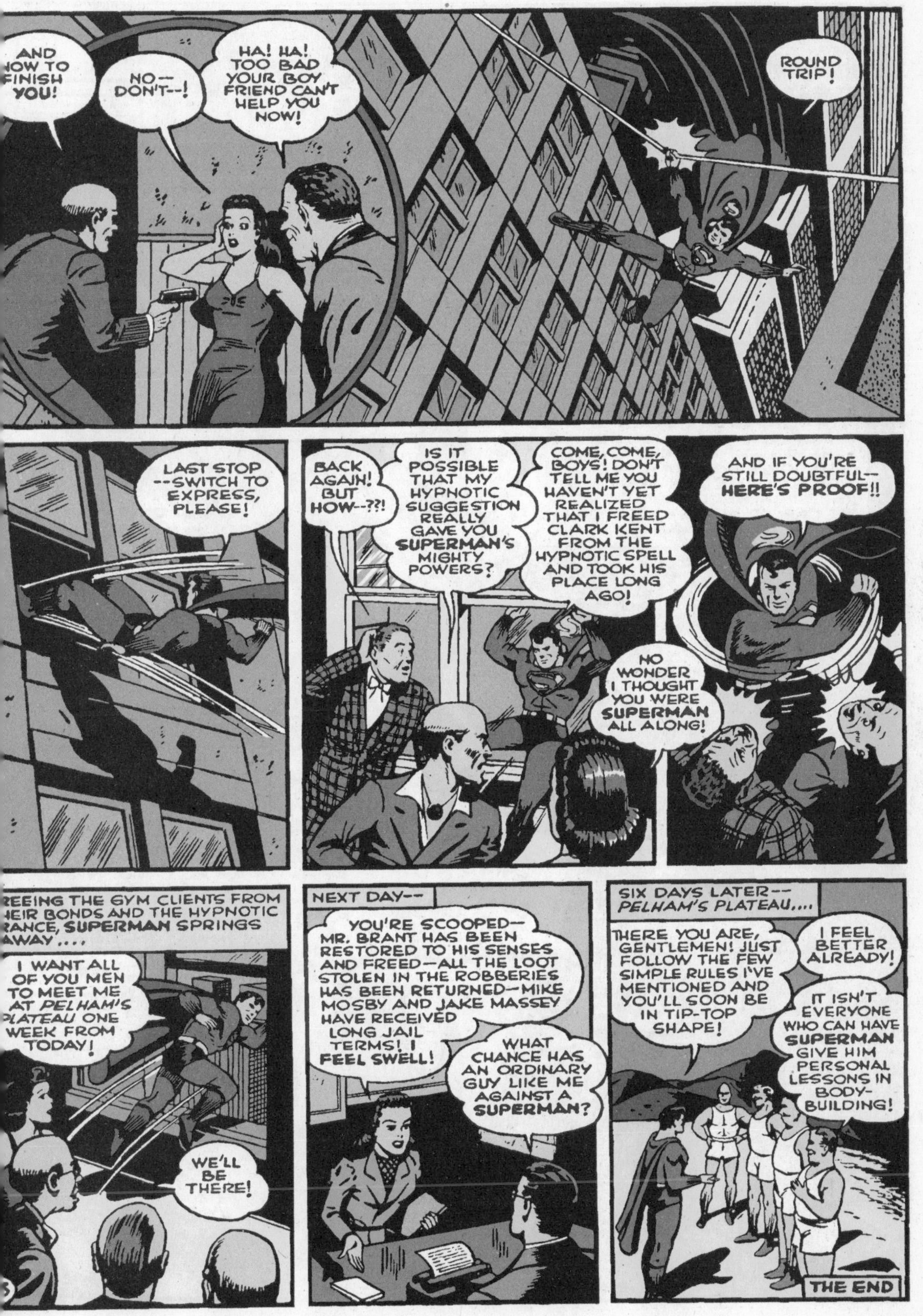
AND NOW TO FINISH YOU!
NO— DON'T--!
HA! HA! TOO BAD YOUR BOY FRIEND CAN'T HELP YOU NOW!
ROUND TRIP!
LAST STOP --SWITCH TO EXPRESS, PLEASE!
BACK AGAIN! BUT HOW--??!
IS IT POSSIBLE THAT MY HYPNOTIC SUGGESTION REALLY GAVE YOU SUPERMAN'S MIGHTY POWERS?
COME, COME, BOYS! DON'T TELL ME YOU HAVEN'T YET REALIZED THAT I FREED CLARK KENT FROM THE HYPNOTIC SPELL AND TOOK HIS PLACE LONG AGO!
AND IF YOU'RE STILL DOUBTFUL— HERE'S PROOF!!
NO WONDER I THOUGHT YOU WERE SUPERMAN ALL ALONG!
FREEING THE GYM CLIENTS FROM THEIR BONDS AND THE HYPNOTIC TRANCE, SUPERMAN SPRINGS AWAY....
I WANT ALL OF YOU MEN TO MEET ME AT PELHAM'S PLATEAU ONE WEEK FROM TODAY!
WE'LL BE THERE!
NEXT DAY--
YOU'RE SCOOPED— MR. BRANT HAS BEEN RESTORED TO HIS SENSES AND FREED—ALL THE LOOT STOLEN IN THE ROBBERIES HAS BEEN RETURNED—MIKE MOSBY AND JAKE MASSEY HAVE RECEIVED LONG JAIL TERMS! I FEEL SWELL!
WHAT CHANCE HAS AN ORDINARY GUY LIKE ME AGAINST A SUPERMAN?
SIX DAYS LATER-- PELHAM'S PLATEAU....
THERE YOU ARE, GENTLEMEN! JUST FOLLOW THE FEW SIMPLE RULES I'VE MENTIONED AND YOU'LL SOON BE IN TIP-TOP SHAPE!
I FEEL BETTER ALREADY!
IT ISN'T EVERYONE WHO CAN HAVE SUPERMAN GIVE HIM PERSONAL LESSONS IN BODY-BUILDING!
THE END

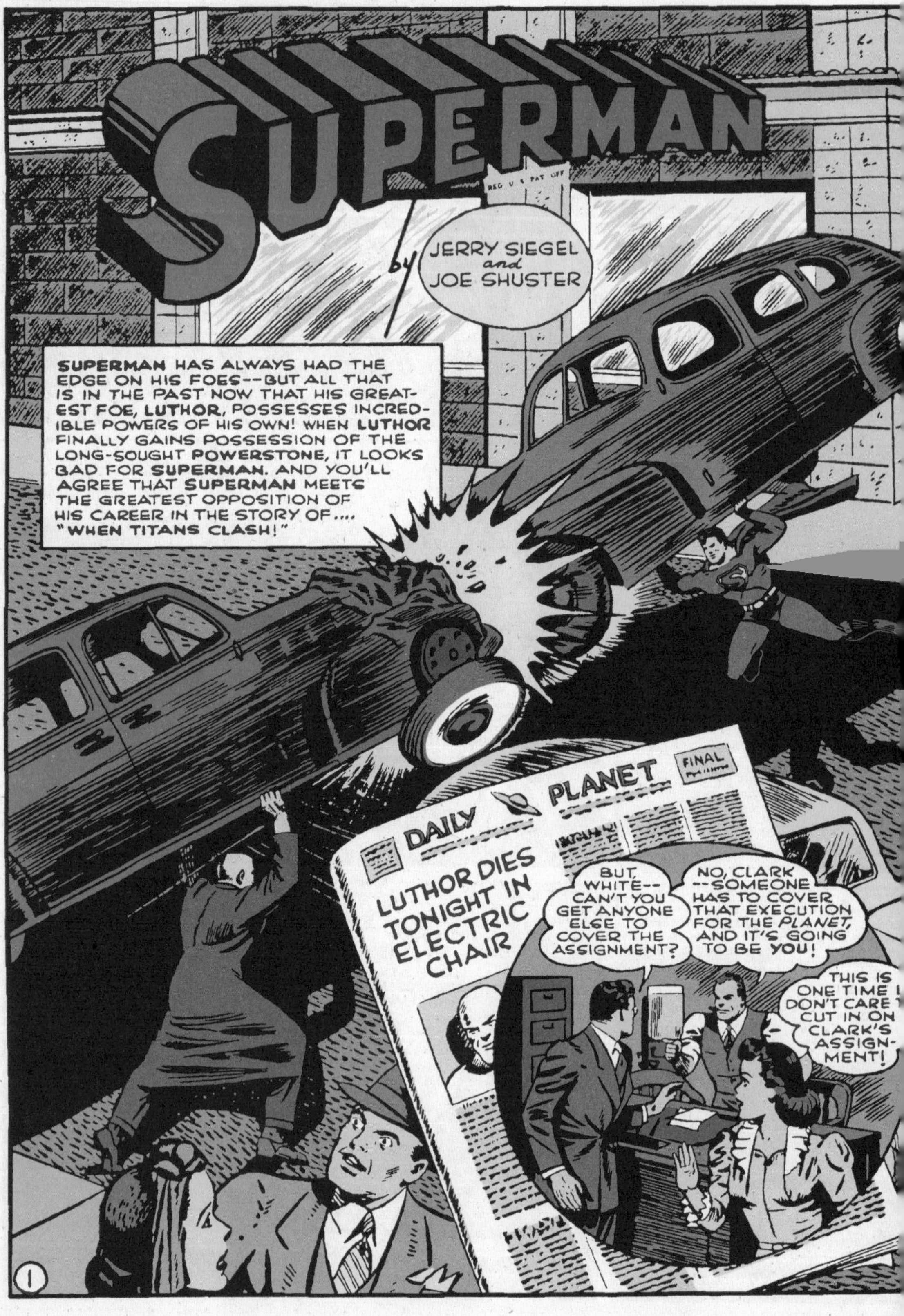
SUPERMAN
REG. U.S. PAT. OFF.
by JERRY SIEGEL and JOE SHUSTER
SUPERMAN HAS ALWAYS HAD THE EDGE ON HIS FOES--BUT ALL THAT IS IN THE PAST NOW THAT HIS GREATEST FOE, LUTHOR, POSSESSES INCREDIBLE POWERS OF HIS OWN! WHEN LUTHOR FINALLY GAINS POSSESSION OF THE LONG-SOUGHT POWERSTONE, IT LOOKS BAD FOR SUPERMAN. AND YOU'LL AGREE THAT SUPERMAN MEETS THE GREATEST OPPOSITION OF HIS CAREER IN THE STORY OF.... "WHEN TITANS CLASH!"
DAILY PLANET
FINAL
LUTHOR DIES TONIGHT IN ELECTRIC CHAIR
BUT, WHITE-- CAN'T YOU GET ANYONE ELSE TO COVER THE ASSIGNMENT?
NO, CLARK --SOMEONE HAS TO COVER THAT EXECUTION FOR THE PLANET, AND IT'S GOING TO BE YOU!
THIS IS ONE TIME I DON'T CARE TO CUT IN ON CLARK'S ASSIGNMENT!
1

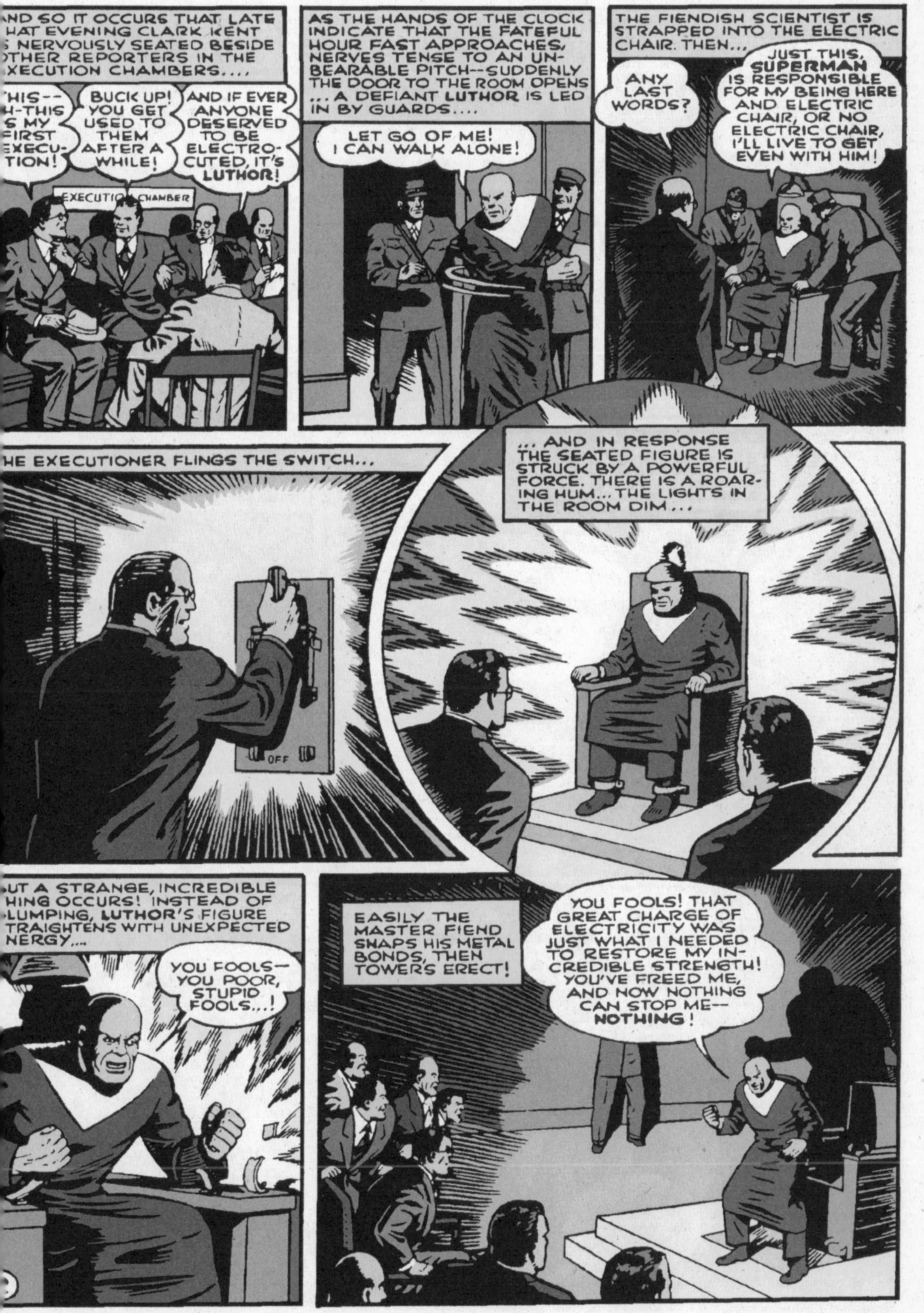

ND SO IT OCCURS THAT LATE HAT EVENING CLARK KENT S NERVOUSLY SEATED BESIDE OTHER REPORTERS IN THE EXECUTION CHAMBERS....
THIS-- H-THIS S MY FIRST EXECU- TION!
BUCK UP! YOU GET USED TO THEM AFTER A WHILE!
AND IF EVER ANYONE DESERVED TO BE ELECTRO- CUTED, IT'S LUTHOR!
EXECUTION CHAMBER
AS THE HANDS OF THE CLOCK INDICATE THAT THE FATEFUL HOUR FAST APPROACHES, NERVES TENSE TO AN UN- BEARABLE PITCH--SUDDENLY THE DOOR TO THE ROOM OPENS ... A DEFIANT LUTHOR IS LED IN BY GUARDS....
LET GO OF ME! I CAN WALK ALONE!
THE FIENDISH SCIENTIST IS STRAPPED INTO THE ELECTRIC CHAIR. THEN...
ANY LAST WORDS?
JUST THIS, SUPERMAN IS RESPONSIBLE FOR MY BEING HERE AND ELECTRIC CHAIR, OR NO ELECTRIC CHAIR, I'LL LIVE TO GET EVEN WITH HIM!
HE EXECUTIONER FLINGS THE SWITCH...
OFF
... AND IN RESPONSE THE SEATED FIGURE IS STRUCK BY A POWERFUL FORCE. THERE IS A ROAR- ING HUM... THE LIGHTS IN THE ROOM DIM...
UT A STRANGE, INCREDIBLE HING OCCURS! INSTEAD OF LUMPING, LUTHOR'S FIGURE TRAIGHTENS WITH UNEXPECTED NERGY....
YOU FOOLS— YOU POOR, STUPID FOOLS...!
EASILY THE MASTER FIEND SNAPS HIS METAL BONDS, THEN TOWERS ERECT!
YOU FOOLS! THAT GREAT CHARGE OF ELECTRICITY WAS JUST WHAT I NEEDED TO RESTORE MY IN- CREDIBLE STRENGTH! YOU'VE FREED ME, AND NOW NOTHING CAN STOP ME-- NOTHING!

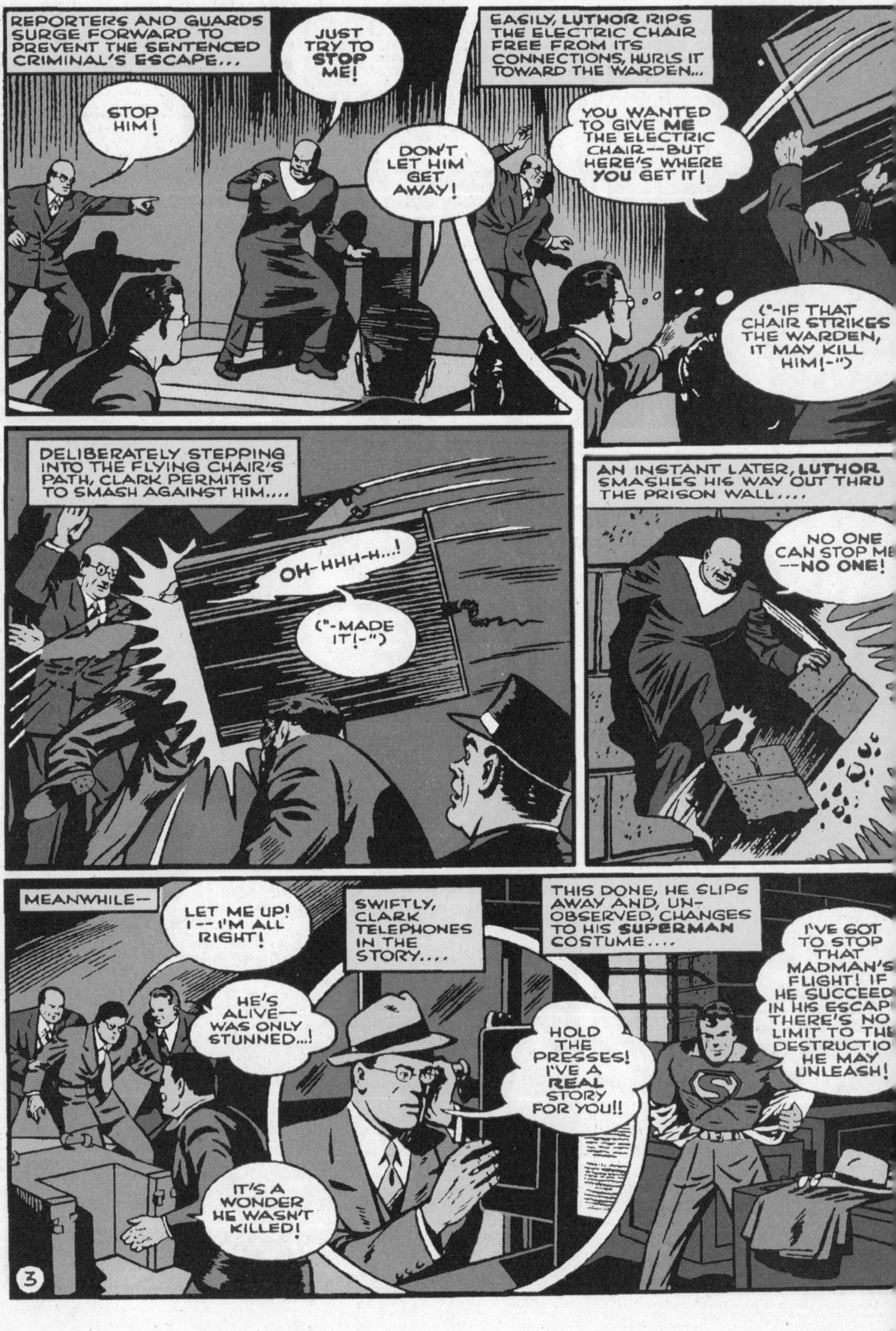

REPORTERS AND GUARDS SURGE FORWARD TO PREVENT THE SENTENCED CRIMINAL'S ESCAPE...
JUST TRY TO STOP ME!
STOP HIM!
DON'T LET HIM GET AWAY!
EASILY, LUTHOR RIPS THE ELECTRIC CHAIR FREE FROM ITS CONNECTIONS, HURLS IT TOWARD THE WARDEN...
YOU WANTED TO GIVE ME THE ELECTRIC CHAIR--BUT HERE'S WHERE YOU GET IT!
("-IF THAT CHAIR STRIKES THE WARDEN, IT MAY KILL HIM!-")
DELIBERATELY STEPPING INTO THE FLYING CHAIR'S PATH, CLARK PERMITS IT TO SMASH AGAINST HIM....
OH-HHH-H...!
("-MADE IT!-")
AN INSTANT LATER, LUTHOR SMASHES HIS WAY OUT THRU THE PRISON WALL....
NO ONE CAN STOP ME --NO ONE!
MEANWHILE—
LET ME UP! I--I'M ALL RIGHT!
HE'S ALIVE—WAS ONLY STUNNED...!
IT'S A WONDER HE WASN'T KILLED!
SWIFTLY, CLARK TELEPHONES IN THE STORY....
HOLD THE PRESSES! I'VE A REAL STORY FOR YOU!!
THIS DONE, HE SLIPS AWAY AND, UN-OBSERVED, CHANGES TO HIS SUPERMAN COSTUME....
I'VE GOT TO STOP THAT MADMAN'S FLIGHT! IF HE SUCCEED IN HIS ESCAP THERE'S NO LIMIT TO TH DESTRUCTIO HE MAY UNLEASH!
3

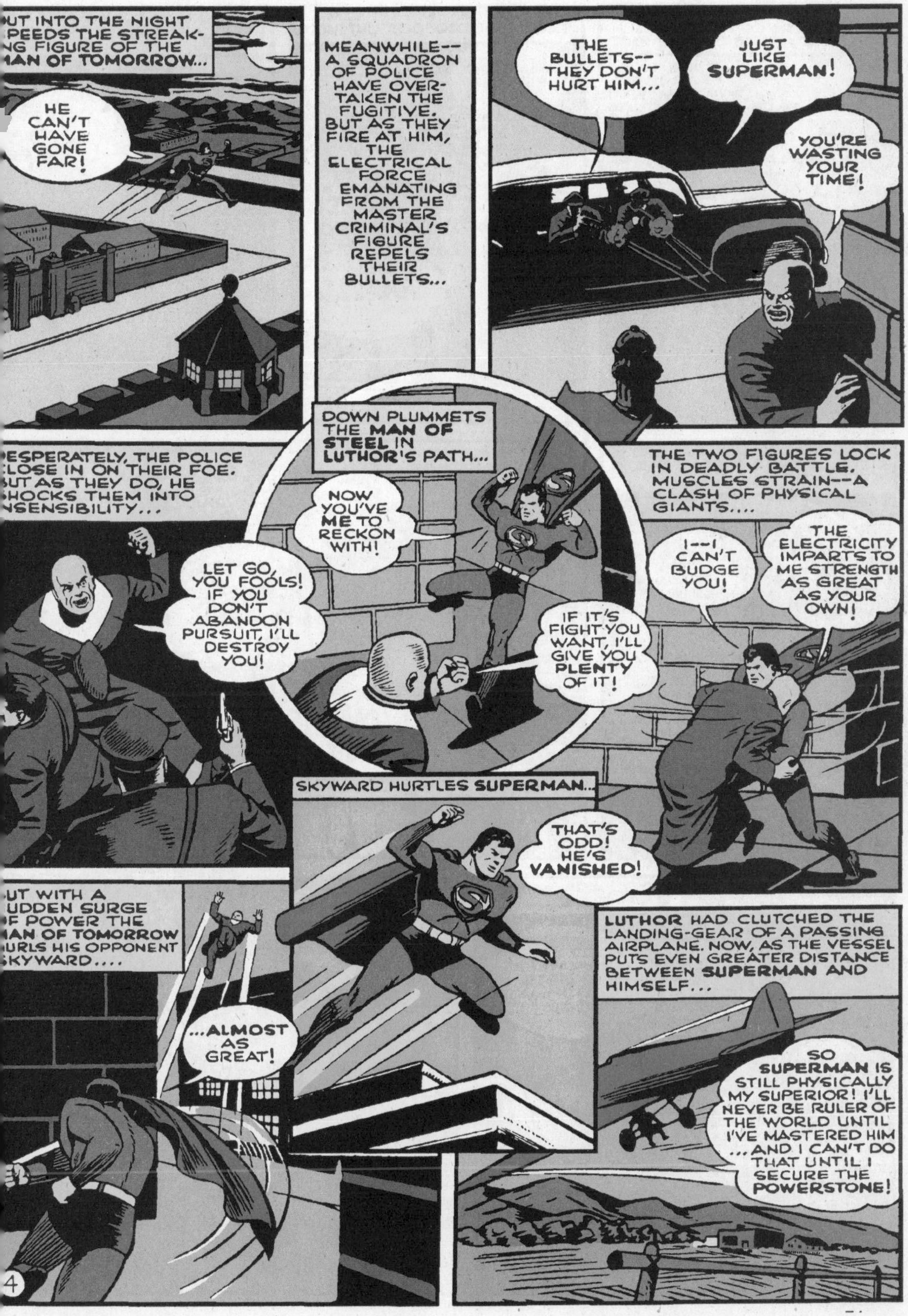

UT INTO THE NIGHT PEEDS THE STREAK-NG FIGURE OF THE MAN OF TOMORROW...
HE CAN'T HAVE GONE FAR!
MEANWHILE-- A SQUADRON OF POLICE HAVE OVER-TAKEN THE FUGITIVE. BUT AS THEY FIRE AT HIM, THE ELECTRICAL FORCE EMANATING FROM THE MASTER CRIMINAL'S FIGURE REPELS THEIR BULLETS...
THE BULLETS-- THEY DON'T HURT HIM...
JUST LIKE SUPERMAN!
YOU'RE WASTING YOUR TIME!
ESPERATELY, THE POLICE CLOSE IN ON THEIR FOE. BUT AS THEY DO, HE SHOCKS THEM INTO INSENSIBILITY...
LET GO, YOU FOOLS! IF YOU DON'T ABANDON PURSUIT, I'LL DESTROY YOU!
DOWN PLUMMETS THE MAN OF STEEL IN LUTHOR'S PATH...
NOW YOU'VE ME TO RECKON WITH!
IF IT'S FIGHT YOU WANT, I'LL GIVE YOU PLENTY OF IT!
THE TWO FIGURES LOCK IN DEADLY BATTLE. MUSCLES STRAIN--A CLASH OF PHYSICAL GIANTS....
I--I CAN'T BUDGE YOU!
THE ELECTRICITY IMPARTS TO ME STRENGTH AS GREAT AS YOUR OWN!
UT WITH A UDDEN SURGE F POWER THE MAN OF TOMORROW URLS HIS OPPONENT SKYWARD....
...ALMOST AS GREAT!
SKYWARD HURTLES SUPERMAN...
THAT'S ODD! HE'S VANISHED!
LUTHOR HAD CLUTCHED THE LANDING-GEAR OF A PASSING AIRPLANE. NOW, AS THE VESSEL PUTS EVEN GREATER DISTANCE BETWEEN SUPERMAN AND HIMSELF...
SO SUPERMAN IS STILL PHYSICALLY MY SUPERIOR! I'LL NEVER BE RULER OF THE WORLD UNTIL I'VE MASTERED HIM ...AND I CAN'T DO THAT UNTIL I SECURE THE POWERSTONE!
4

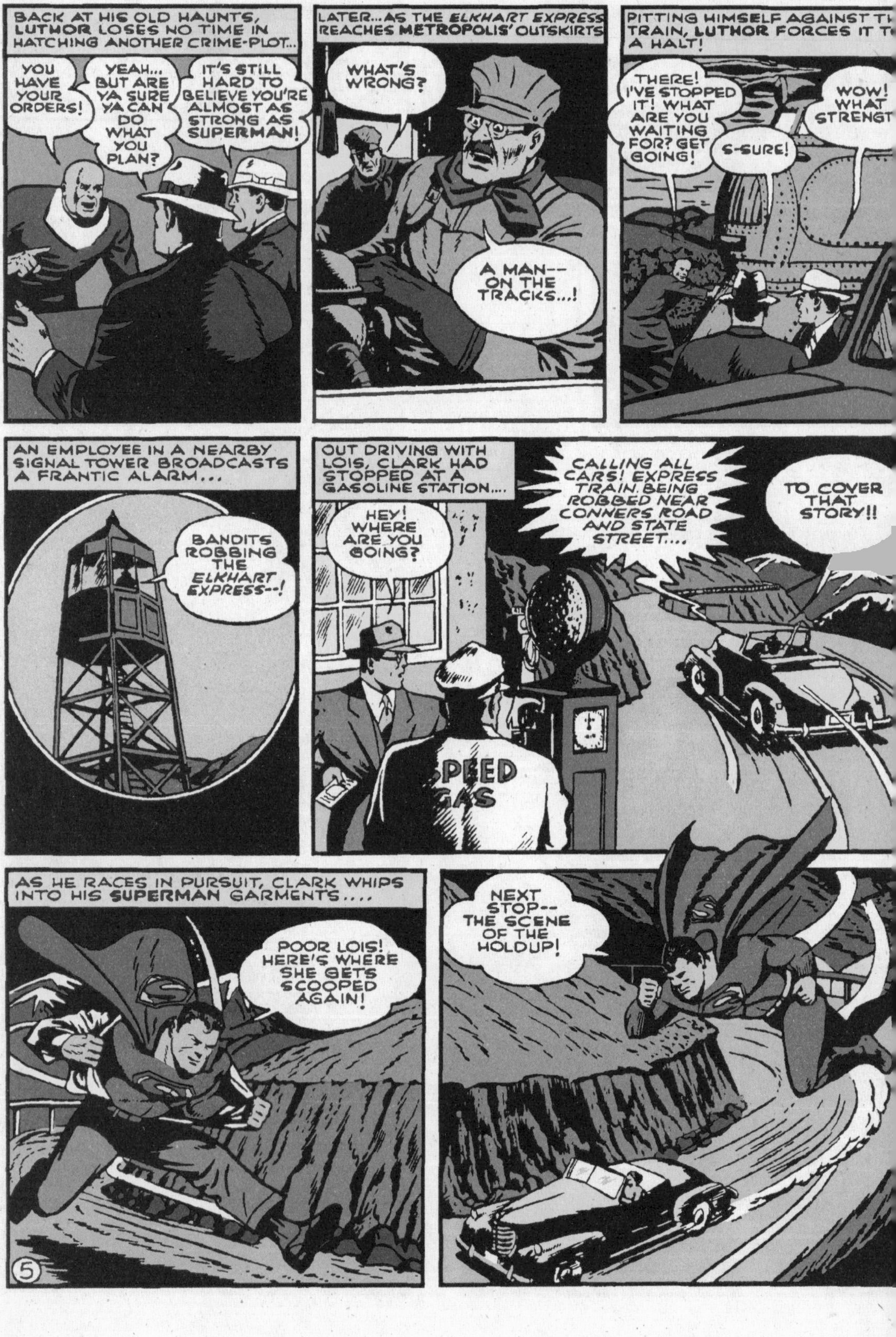

BACK AT HIS OLD HAUNTS, LUTHOR LOSES NO TIME IN HATCHING ANOTHER CRIME-PLOT...
YOU HAVE YOUR ORDERS!
YEAH... BUT ARE YA SURE YA CAN DO WHAT YOU PLAN?
IT'S STILL HARD TO BELIEVE YOU'RE ALMOST AS STRONG AS SUPERMAN!
LATER... AS THE ELKHART EXPRESS REACHES METROPOLIS' OUTSKIRTS
WHAT'S WRONG?
A MAN-- ON THE TRACKS...!
PITTING HIMSELF AGAINST TH TRAIN, LUTHOR FORCES IT TO A HALT!
THERE! I'VE STOPPED IT! WHAT ARE YOU WAITING FOR? GET GOING!
S-SURE!
WOW! WHAT STRENGT
AN EMPLOYEE IN A NEARBY SIGNAL TOWER BROADCASTS A FRANTIC ALARM...
BANDITS ROBBING THE ELKHART EXPRESS--!
OUT DRIVING WITH LOIS, CLARK HAD STOPPED AT A GASOLINE STATION....
HEY! WHERE ARE YOU GOING?
SPEED GAS
CALLING ALL CARS! EXPRESS TRAIN BEING ROBBED NEAR CONNERS ROAD AND STATE STREET....
TO COVER THAT STORY!!
AS HE RACES IN PURSUIT, CLARK WHIPS INTO HIS SUPERMAN GARMENTS....
POOR LOIS! HERE'S WHERE SHE GETS SCOOPED AGAIN!
5
NEXT STOP-- THE SCENE OF THE HOLDUP!

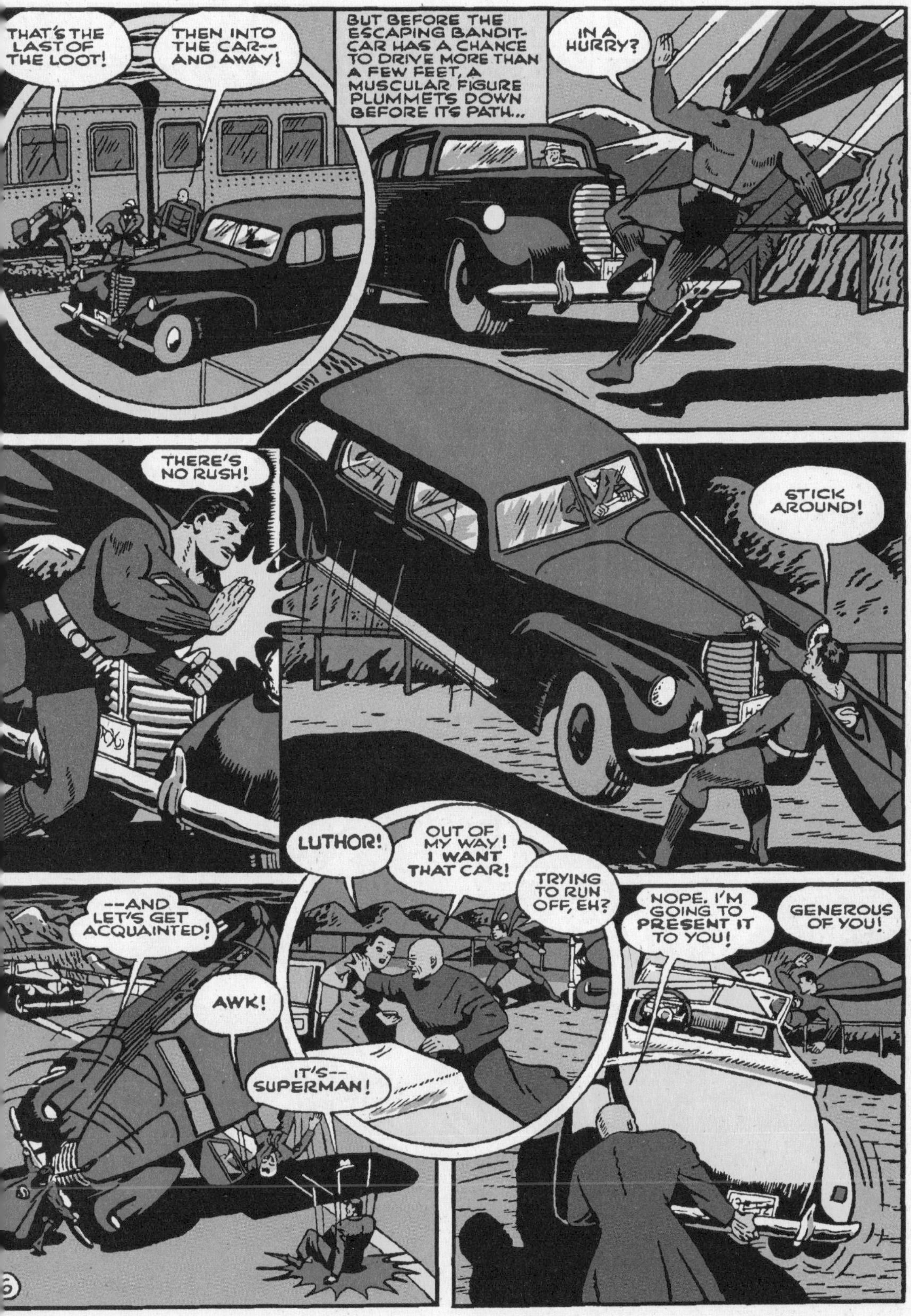
THAT'S THE LAST OF THE LOOT!
THEN INTO THE CAR--AND AWAY!
BUT BEFORE THE ESCAPING BANDIT-CAR HAS A CHANCE TO DRIVE MORE THAN A FEW FEET, A MUSCULAR FIGURE PLUMMETS DOWN BEFORE ITS PATH...
IN A HURRY?
THERE'S NO RUSH!
STICK AROUND!
--AND LET'S GET ACQUAINTED!
AWK!
LUTHOR!
OUT OF MY WAY! I WANT THAT CAR!
IT'S--SUPERMAN!
TRYING TO RUN OFF, EH?
NOPE. I'M GOING TO PRESENT IT TO YOU!
GENEROUS OF YOU!
6

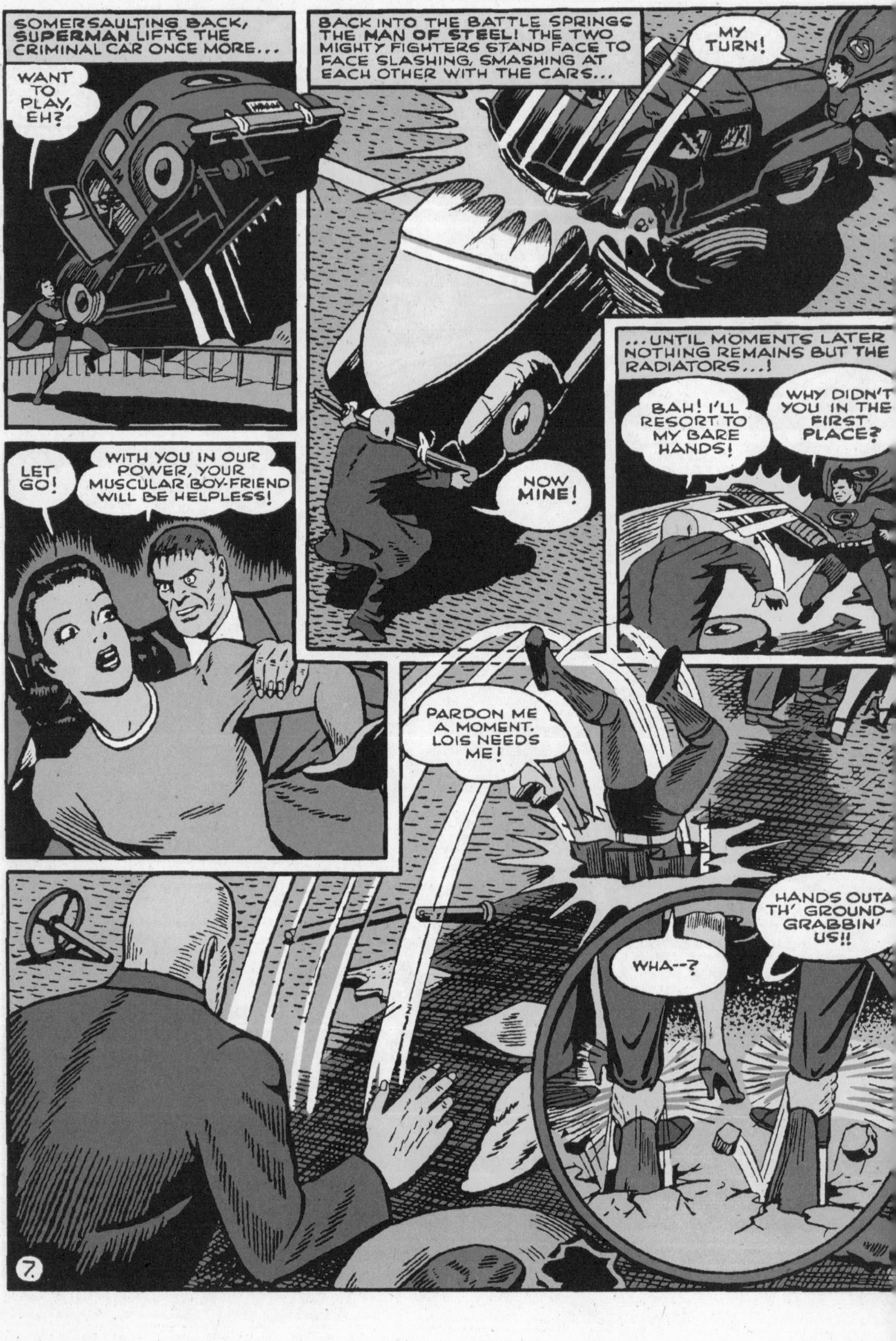
SOMERSAULTING BACK, SUPERMAN LIFTS THE CRIMINAL CAR ONCE MORE...
WANT TO PLAY, EH?
BACK INTO THE BATTLE SPRINGS THE MAN OF STEEL! THE TWO MIGHTY FIGHTERS STAND FACE TO FACE SLASHING, SMASHING AT EACH OTHER WITH THE CARS...
MY TURN!
NOW MINE!
...UNTIL MOMENTS LATER NOTHING REMAINS BUT THE RADIATORS...!
BAH! I'LL RESORT TO MY BARE HANDS!
WHY DIDN'T YOU IN THE FIRST PLACE?
LET GO!
WITH YOU IN OUR POWER, YOUR MUSCULAR BOY-FRIEND WILL BE HELPLESS!
PARDON ME A MOMENT. LOIS NEEDS ME!
HANDS OUTA TH' GROUND-GRABBIN' US!!
WHA--?
7.

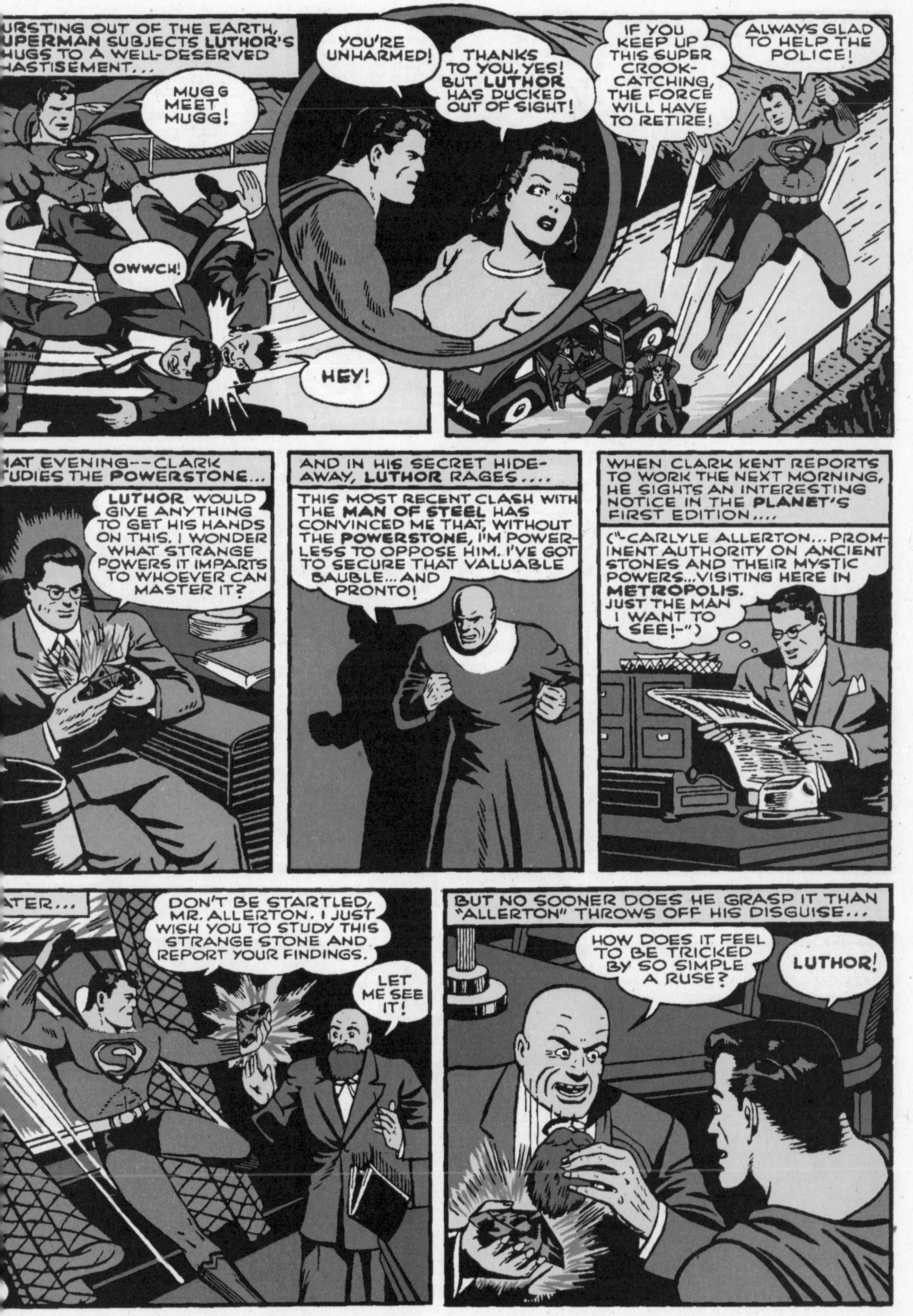
URSTING OUT OF THE EARTH, UPERMAN SUBJECTS LUTHOR'S HUGS TO A WELL-DESERVED HASTISEMENT...
MUGG MEET MUGG!
OWWCH!
HEY!
YOU'RE UNHARMED!
THANKS TO YOU, YES! BUT LUTHOR HAS DUCKED OUT OF SIGHT!
IF YOU KEEP UP THIS SUPER CROOK-CATCHING, THE FORCE WILL HAVE TO RETIRE!
ALWAYS GLAD TO HELP THE POLICE!
HAT EVENING--CLARK TUDIES THE POWERSTONE...
LUTHOR WOULD GIVE ANYTHING TO GET HIS HANDS ON THIS. I WONDER WHAT STRANGE POWERS IT IMPARTS TO WHOEVER CAN MASTER IT?
AND IN HIS SECRET HIDE-AWAY, LUTHOR RAGES....
THIS MOST RECENT CLASH WITH THE MAN OF STEEL HAS CONVINCED ME THAT, WITHOUT THE POWERSTONE, I'M POWERLESS TO OPPOSE HIM. I'VE GOT TO SECURE THAT VALUABLE BAUBLE... AND PRONTO!
WHEN CLARK KENT REPORTS TO WORK THE NEXT MORNING, HE SIGHTS AN INTERESTING NOTICE IN THE PLANET'S FIRST EDITION....
("-CARLYLE ALLERTON... PROMINENT AUTHORITY ON ANCIENT STONES AND THEIR MYSTIC POWERS... VISITING HERE IN METROPOLIS. JUST THE MAN I WANT TO SEE!-")
ATER...
DON'T BE STARTLED, MR. ALLERTON. I JUST WISH YOU TO STUDY THIS STRANGE STONE AND REPORT YOUR FINDINGS.
LET ME SEE IT!
BUT NO SOONER DOES HE GRASP IT THAN "ALLERTON" THROWS OFF HIS DISGUISE...
HOW DOES IT FEEL TO BE TRICKED BY SO SIMPLE A RUSE?
LUTHOR!

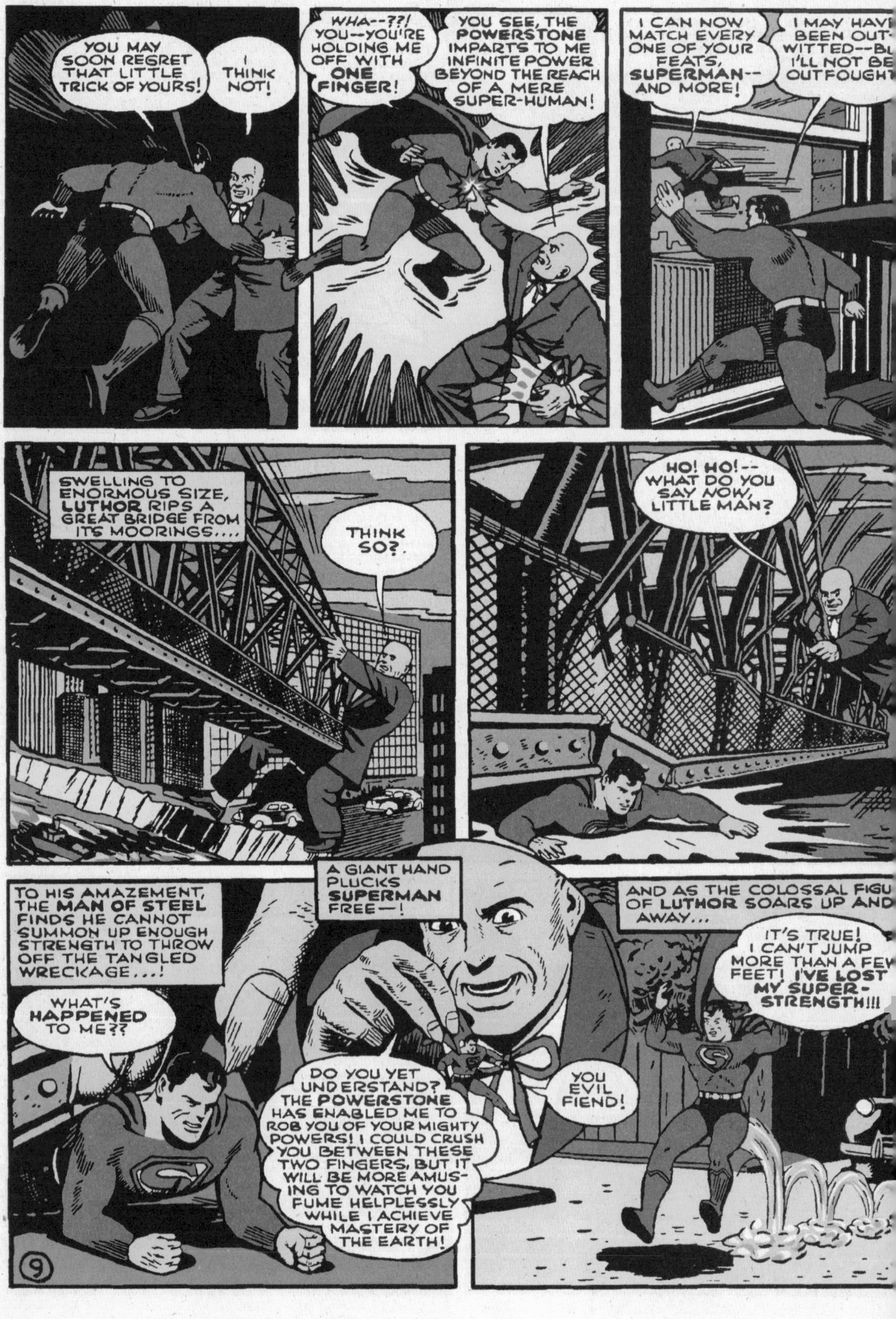
YOU MAY SOON REGRET THAT LITTLE TRICK OF YOURS!
I THINK NOT!
WHA--??! YOU--YOU'RE HOLDING ME OFF WITH ONE FINGER!
YOU SEE, THE POWERSTONE IMPARTS TO ME INFINITE POWER BEYOND THE REACH OF A MERE SUPER-HUMAN!
I CAN NOW MATCH EVERY ONE OF YOUR FEATS, SUPERMAN-- AND MORE!
I MAY HAV BEEN OUT- WITTED--B I'LL NOT BE OUTFOUGHT
SWELLING TO ENORMOUS SIZE, LUTHOR RIPS A GREAT BRIDGE FROM ITS MOORINGS....
THINK SO?.
HO! HO!-- WHAT DO YOU SAY NOW, LITTLE MAN?
TO HIS AMAZEMENT, THE MAN OF STEEL FINDS HE CANNOT SUMMON UP ENOUGH STRENGTH TO THROW OFF THE TANGLED WRECKAGE...!
WHAT'S HAPPENED TO ME??
9
A GIANT HAND PLUCKS SUPERMAN FREE—!
DO YOU YET UNDERSTAND? THE POWERSTONE HAS ENABLED ME TO ROB YOU OF YOUR MIGHTY POWERS! I COULD CRUSH YOU BETWEEN THESE TWO FINGERS, BUT IT WILL BE MORE AMUSING TO WATCH YOU FUME HELPLESSLY WHILE I ACHIEVE MASTERY OF THE EARTH!
YOU EVIL FIEND!
AND AS THE COLOSSAL FIGU OF LUTHOR SOARS UP AND AWAY...
IT'S TRUE! I CAN'T JUMP MORE THAN A FEV FEET! I'VE LOST MY SUPER-STRENGTH!!!

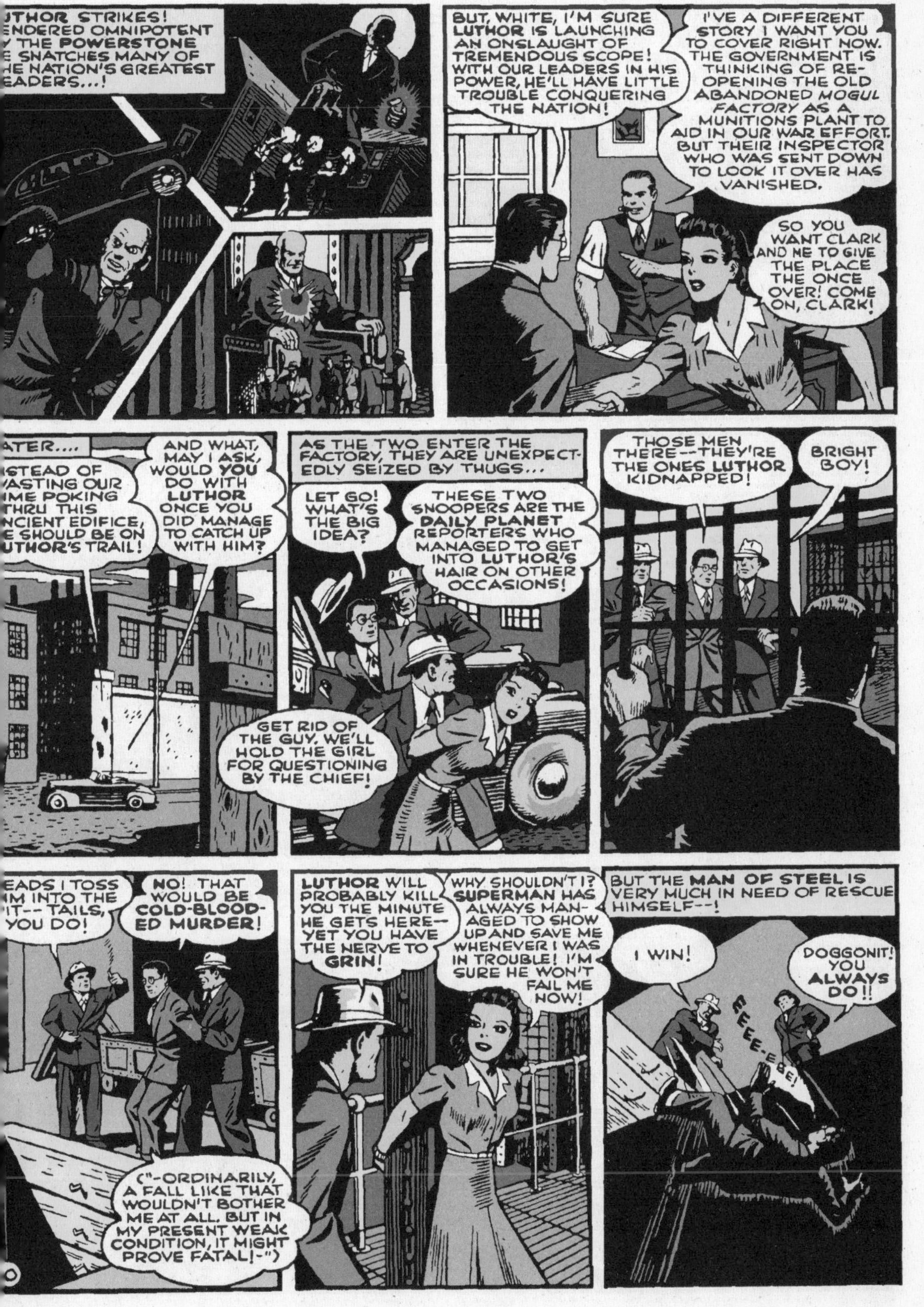
UTHOR STRIKES! ENDERED OMNIPOTENT Y THE POWERSTONE E SNATCHES MANY OF HE NATION'S GREATEST EADERS...!
BUT, WHITE, I'M SURE LUTHOR IS LAUNCHING AN ONSLAUGHT OF TREMENDOUS SCOPE! WITH OUR LEADERS IN HIS POWER, HE'LL HAVE LITTLE TROUBLE CONQUERING THE NATION!
I'VE A DIFFERENT STORY I WANT YOU TO COVER RIGHT NOW. THE GOVERNMENT IS THINKING OF RE-OPENING THE OLD ABANDONED MOGUL FACTORY AS A MUNITIONS PLANT TO AID IN OUR WAR EFFORT. BUT THEIR INSPECTOR WHO WAS SENT DOWN TO LOOK IT OVER HAS VANISHED.
SO YOU WANT CLARK AND ME TO GIVE THE PLACE THE ONCE OVER! COME ON, CLARK!
ATER....
NSTEAD OF VASTING OUR IME POKING THRU THIS NCIENT EDIFICE, E SHOULD BE ON UTHOR'S TRAIL!
AND WHAT, MAY I ASK, WOULD YOU DO WITH LUTHOR ONCE YOU DID MANAGE TO CATCH UP WITH HIM?
AS THE TWO ENTER THE FACTORY, THEY ARE UNEXPECT-EDLY SEIZED BY THUGS...
LET GO! WHAT'S THE BIG IDEA?
THESE TWO SNOOPERS ARE THE DAILY PLANET REPORTERS WHO MANAGED TO GET INTO LUTHOR'S HAIR ON OTHER OCCASIONS!
GET RID OF THE GUY. WE'LL HOLD THE GIRL FOR QUESTIONING BY THE CHIEF!
THOSE MEN THERE--THEY'RE THE ONES LUTHOR KIDNAPPED!
BRIGHT BOY!
EADS I TOSS IM INTO THE IT-- TAILS, YOU DO!
NO! THAT WOULD BE COLD-BLOOD-ED MURDER!
("-ORDINARILY, A FALL LIKE THAT WOULDN'T BOTHER ME AT ALL. BUT IN MY PRESENT WEAK CONDITION, IT MIGHT PROVE FATAL!-")
LUTHOR WILL PROBABLY KILL YOU THE MINUTE HE GETS HERE--YET YOU HAVE THE NERVE TO GRIN!
WHY SHOULDN'T I? SUPERMAN HAS ALWAYS MAN-AGED TO SHOW UP AND SAVE ME WHENEVER I WAS IN TROUBLE! I'M SURE HE WON'T FAIL ME NOW!
BUT THE MAN OF STEEL IS VERY MUCH IN NEED OF RESCUE HIMSELF--!
I WIN!
DOGGONIT! YOU ALWAYS DO!!
EEEE-EEE!

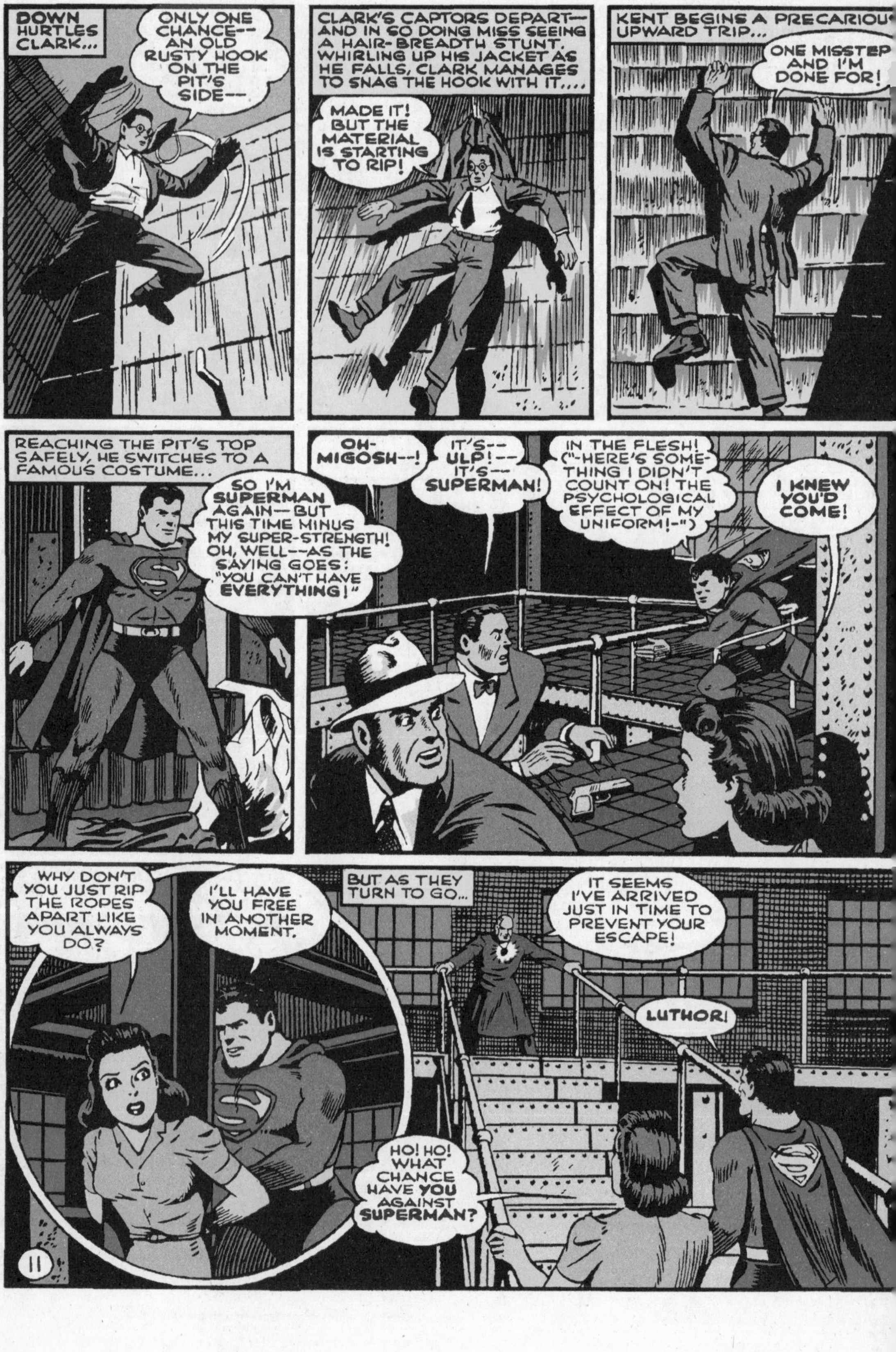
DOWN HURTLES CLARK...
ONLY ONE CHANCE-- AN OLD RUSTY HOOK ON THE PIT'S SIDE--
CLARK'S CAPTORS DEPART-- AND IN SO DOING MISS SEEING A HAIR-BREADTH STUNT. WHIRLING UP HIS JACKET AS HE FALLS, CLARK MANAGES TO SNAG THE HOOK WITH IT....
MADE IT! BUT THE MATERIAL IS STARTING TO RIP!
KENT BEGINS A PRECARIOU UPWARD TRIP...
ONE MISSTEP AND I'M DONE FOR!
REACHING THE PIT'S TOP SAFELY, HE SWITCHES TO A FAMOUS COSTUME...
SO I'M SUPERMAN AGAIN--BUT THIS TIME MINUS MY SUPER-STRENGTH! OH, WELL--AS THE SAYING GOES: "YOU CAN'T HAVE EVERYTHING!"
OH-MIGOSH--!
IT'S-- ULP!-- IT'S-- SUPERMAN!
IN THE FLESH! ("-HERE'S SOMETHING I DIDN'T COUNT ON! THE PSYCHOLOGICAL EFFECT OF MY UNIFORM!-")
I KNEW YOU'D COME!
WHY DON'T YOU JUST RIP THE ROPES APART LIKE YOU ALWAYS DO?
I'LL HAVE YOU FREE IN ANOTHER MOMENT.
11
BUT AS THEY TURN TO GO...
IT SEEMS I'VE ARRIVED JUST IN TIME TO PREVENT YOUR ESCAPE!
LUTHOR!
HO! HO! WHAT CHANCE HAVE YOU AGAINST SUPERMAN?

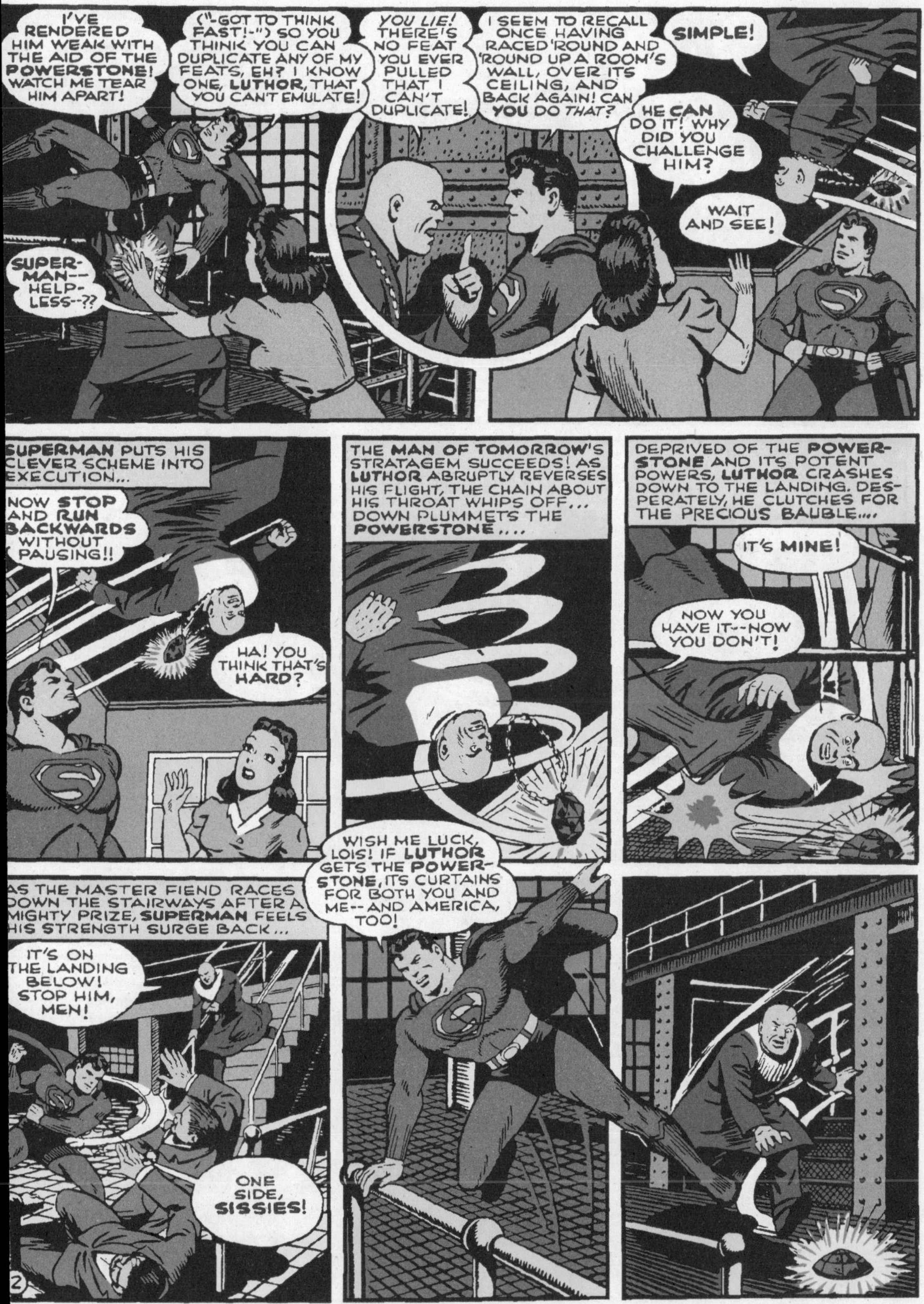
I'VE RENDERED HIM WEAK WITH THE AID OF THE POWERSTONE! WATCH ME TEAR HIM APART!
SUPER-MAN--HELP-LESS--??
("--GOT TO THINK FAST!--") SO YOU THINK YOU CAN DUPLICATE ANY OF MY FEATS, EH? I KNOW ONE, LUTHOR, THAT YOU CAN'T EMULATE!
YOU LIE! THERE'S NO FEAT YOU EVER PULLED THAT I CAN'T DUPLICATE!
I SEEM TO RECALL ONCE HAVING RACED 'ROUND AND 'ROUND UP A ROOM'S WALL, OVER ITS CEILING, AND BACK AGAIN! CAN YOU DO THAT?
SIMPLE!
HE CAN DO IT! WHY DID YOU CHALLENGE HIM?
WAIT AND SEE!
SUPERMAN PUTS HIS CLEVER SCHEME INTO EXECUTION...
NOW STOP AND RUN BACKWARDS WITHOUT PAUSING!!
HA! YOU THINK THAT'S HARD?
THE MAN OF TOMORROW'S STRATAGEM SUCCEEDS! AS LUTHOR ABRUPTLY REVERSES HIS FLIGHT, THE CHAIN ABOUT HIS THROAT WHIPS OFF... DOWN PLUMMETS THE POWERSTONE....
DEPRIVED OF THE POWER-STONE AND ITS POTENT POWERS, LUTHOR CRASHES DOWN TO THE LANDING. DES-PERATELY, HE CLUTCHES FOR THE PRECIOUS BAUBLE....
IT'S MINE!
NOW YOU HAVE IT--NOW YOU DON'T!
AS THE MASTER FIEND RACES DOWN THE STAIRWAYS AFTER A MIGHTY PRIZE, SUPERMAN FEELS HIS STRENGTH SURGE BACK...
IT'S ON THE LANDING BELOW! STOP HIM, MEN!
ONE SIDE, SISSIES!
2
WISH ME LUCK, LOIS! IF LUTHOR GETS THE POWER-STONE, ITS CURTAINS FOR BOTH YOU AND ME--AND AMERICA, TOO!

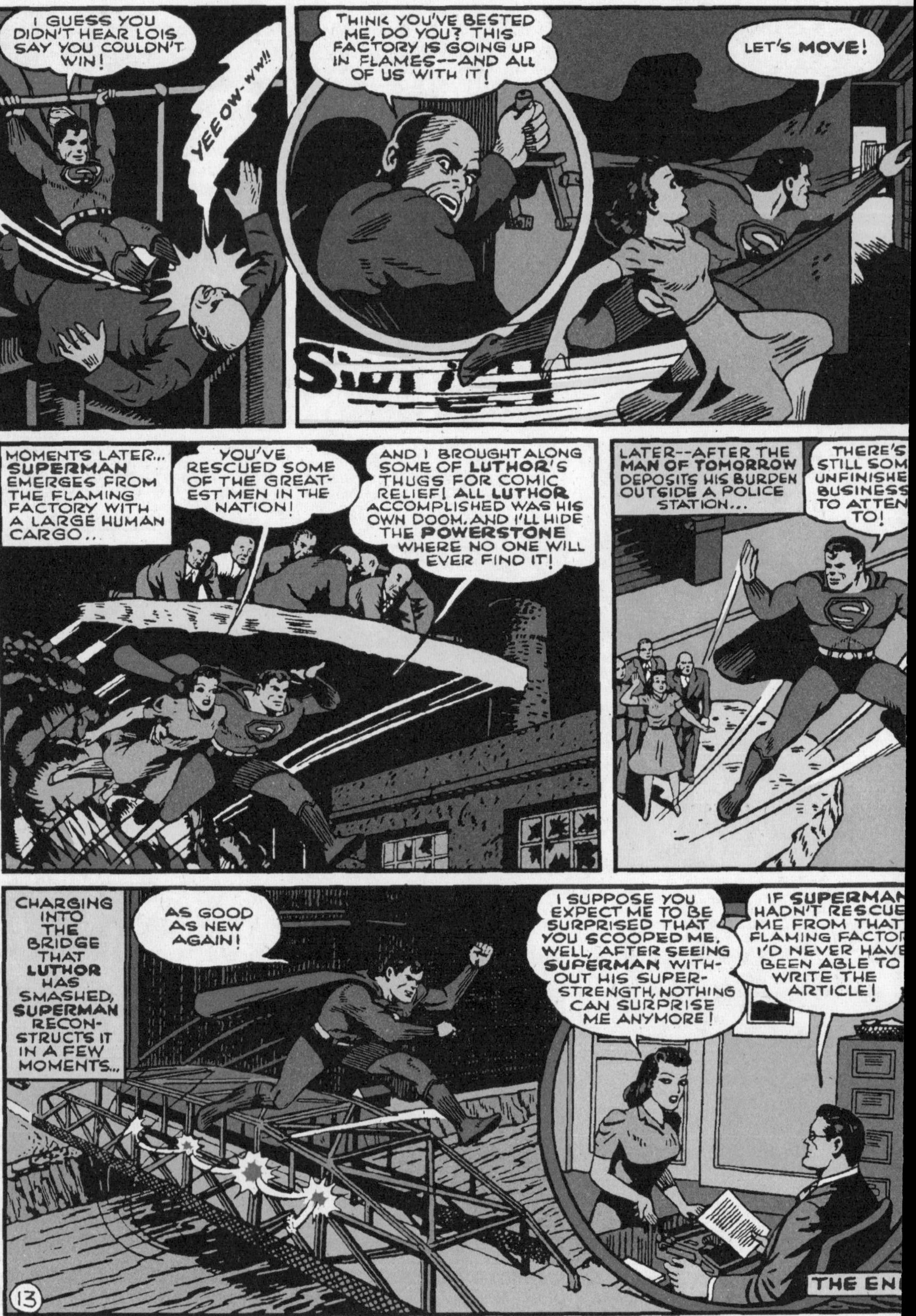

I GUESS YOU DIDN'T HEAR LOIS SAY YOU COULDN'T WIN!
YEEOW-WW!!
THINK YOU'VE BESTED ME, DO YOU? THIS FACTORY IS GOING UP IN FLAMES--AND ALL OF US WITH IT!
LET'S MOVE!
MOMENTS LATER... SUPERMAN EMERGES FROM THE FLAMING FACTORY WITH A LARGE HUMAN CARGO...
YOU'VE RESCUED SOME OF THE GREAT-EST MEN IN THE NATION!
AND I BROUGHT ALONG SOME OF LUTHOR'S THUGS FOR COMIC RELIEF! ALL LUTHOR ACCOMPLISHED WAS HIS OWN DOOM, AND I'LL HIDE THE POWERSTONE WHERE NO ONE WILL EVER FIND IT!
LATER--AFTER THE MAN OF TOMORROW DEPOSITS HIS BURDEN OUTSIDE A POLICE STATION...
THERE'S STILL SOM UNFINISHE BUSINESS TO ATTEN TO!
CHARGING INTO THE BRIDGE THAT LUTHOR HAS SMASHED, SUPERMAN RECON-STRUCTS IT IN A FEW MOMENTS...
AS GOOD AS NEW AGAIN!
I SUPPOSE YOU EXPECT ME TO BE SURPRISED THAT YOU SCOOPED ME. WELL, AFTER SEEING SUPERMAN WITH-OUT HIS SUPER-STRENGTH, NOTHING CAN SURPRISE ME ANYMORE!
IF SUPERMAN HADN'T RESCUE ME FROM THAT FLAMING FACTOR I'D NEVER HAVE BEEN ABLE TO WRITE THE ARTICLE!
13
THE EN

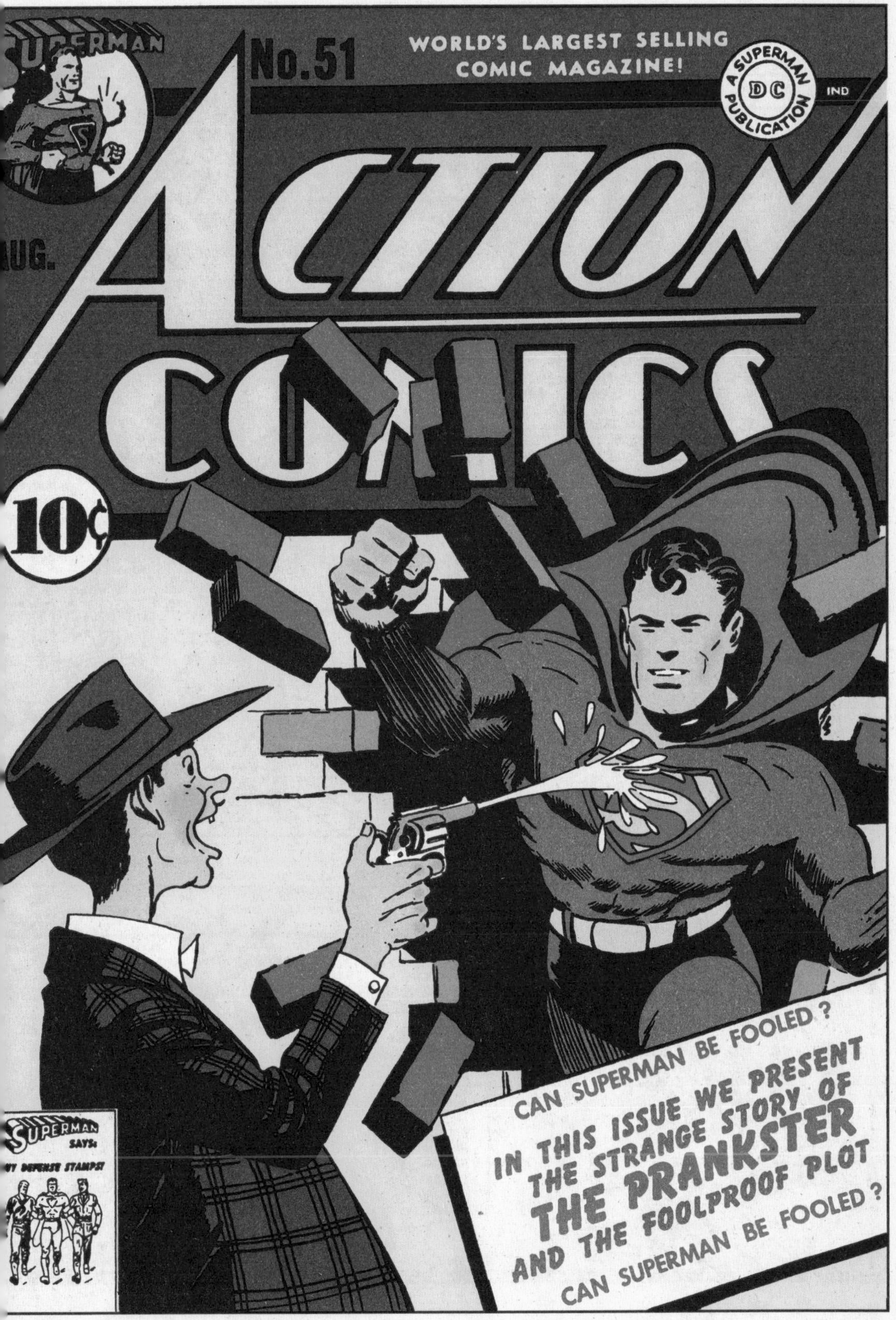

SUPERMAN
No. 51
WORLD'S LARGEST SELLING
COMIC MAGAZINE!
A SUPERMAN DC PUBLICATION
IND
AUG.
ACTION COMICS
10¢
CAN SUPERMAN BE FOOLED?
IN THIS ISSUE WE PRESENT
THE STRANGE STORY OF
THE PRANKSTER
AND THE FOOLPROOF PLOT
CAN SUPERMAN BE FOOLED?
SUPERMAN
SAYS:

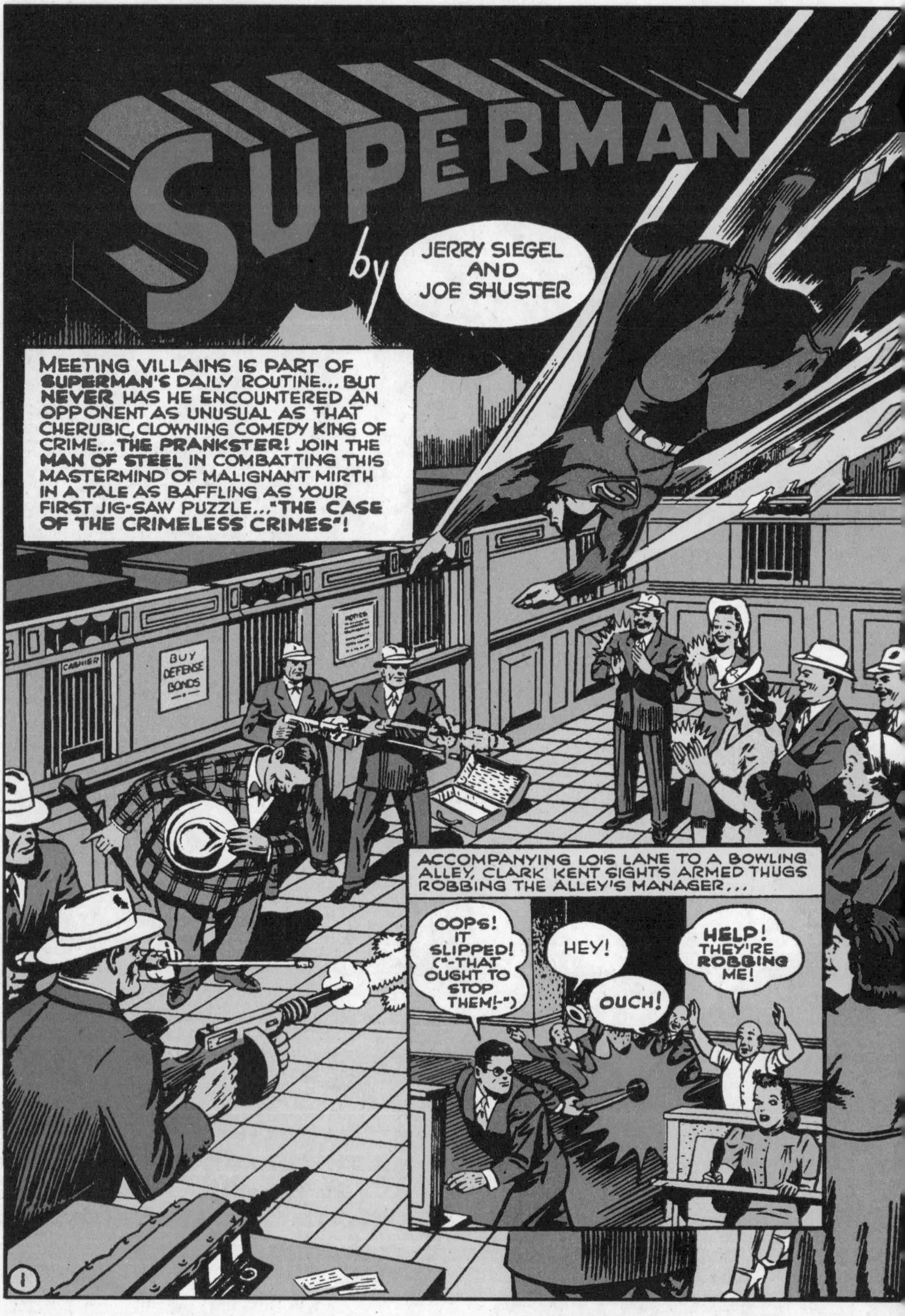
SUPERMAN
by JERRY SIEGEL AND JOE SHUSTER
MEETING VILLAINS IS PART OF SUPERMAN'S DAILY ROUTINE... BUT NEVER HAS HE ENCOUNTERED AN OPPONENT AS UNUSUAL AS THAT CHERUBIC, CLOWNING COMEDY KING OF CRIME... THE PRANKSTER! JOIN THE MAN OF STEEL IN COMBATTING THIS MASTERMIND OF MALIGNANT MIRTH IN A TALE AS BAFFLING AS YOUR FIRST JIG-SAW PUZZLE..."THE CASE OF THE CRIMELESS CRIMES"!
CASHIER
BUY DEFENSE BONDS
ACCOMPANYING LOIS LANE TO A BOWLING ALLEY, CLARK KENT SIGHTS ARMED THUGS ROBBING THE ALLEY'S MANAGER...
OOPS! IT SLIPPED! ("-THAT OUGHT TO STOP THEM!-")
HEY!
OUCH!
HELP! THEY'RE ROBBING ME!

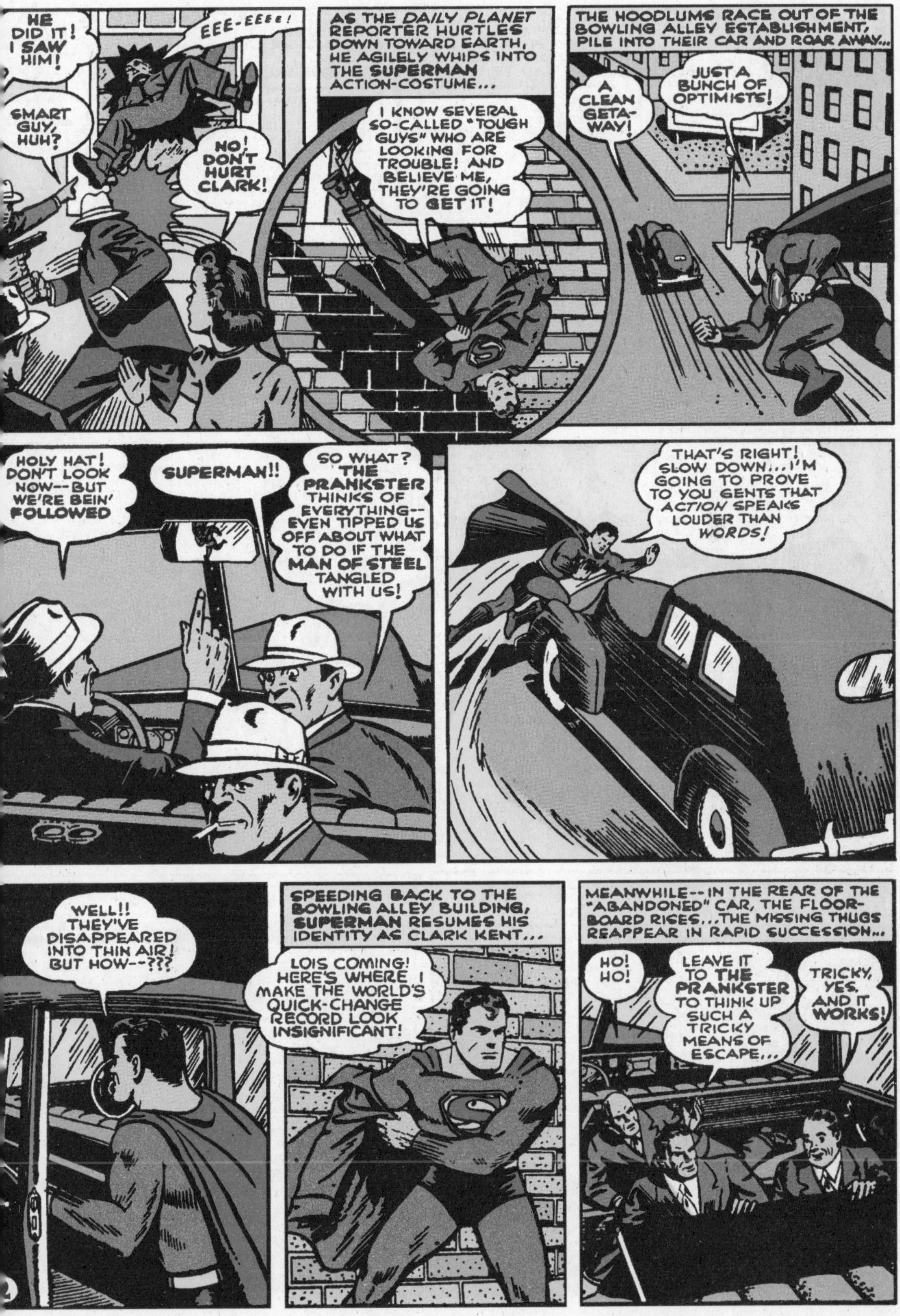

HE DID IT! I SAW HIM!
EEE-EEEE!
SMART GUY, HUH?
NO! DON'T HURT CLARK!
AS THE DAILY PLANET REPORTER HURTLES DOWN TOWARD EARTH, HE AGILELY WHIPS INTO THE SUPERMAN ACTION-COSTUME...
I KNOW SEVERAL SO-CALLED "TOUGH GUYS" WHO ARE LOOKING FOR TROUBLE! AND BELIEVE ME, THEY'RE GOING TO GET IT!
THE HOODLUMS RACE OUT OF THE BOWLING ALLEY ESTABLISHMENT, PILE INTO THEIR CAR AND ROAR AWAY...
A CLEAN GETA-WAY!
JUST A BUNCH OF OPTIMISTS!
HOLY HAT! DON'T LOOK NOW--BUT WE'RE BEIN' FOLLOWED
SUPERMAN!!
SO WHAT? THE PRANKSTER THINKS OF EVERYTHING--EVEN TIPPED US OFF ABOUT WHAT TO DO IF THE MAN OF STEEL TANGLED WITH US!
THAT'S RIGHT! SLOW DOWN...I'M GOING TO PROVE TO YOU GENTS THAT ACTION SPEAKS LOUDER THAN WORDS!
WELL!! THEY'VE DISAPPEARED INTO THIN AIR! BUT HOW--???
SPEEDING BACK TO THE BOWLING ALLEY BUILDING, SUPERMAN RESUMES HIS IDENTITY AS CLARK KENT...
LOIS COMING! HERE'S WHERE I MAKE THE WORLD'S QUICK-CHANGE RECORD LOOK INSIGNIFICANT!
MEANWHILE--IN THE REAR OF THE "ABANDONED" CAR, THE FLOOR-BOARD RISES...THE MISSING THUGS REAPPEAR IN RAPID SUCCESSION...
HO! HO!
LEAVE IT TO THE PRANKSTER TO THINK UP SUCH A TRICKY MEANS OF ESCAPE...
TRICKY, YES, AND IT WORKS!

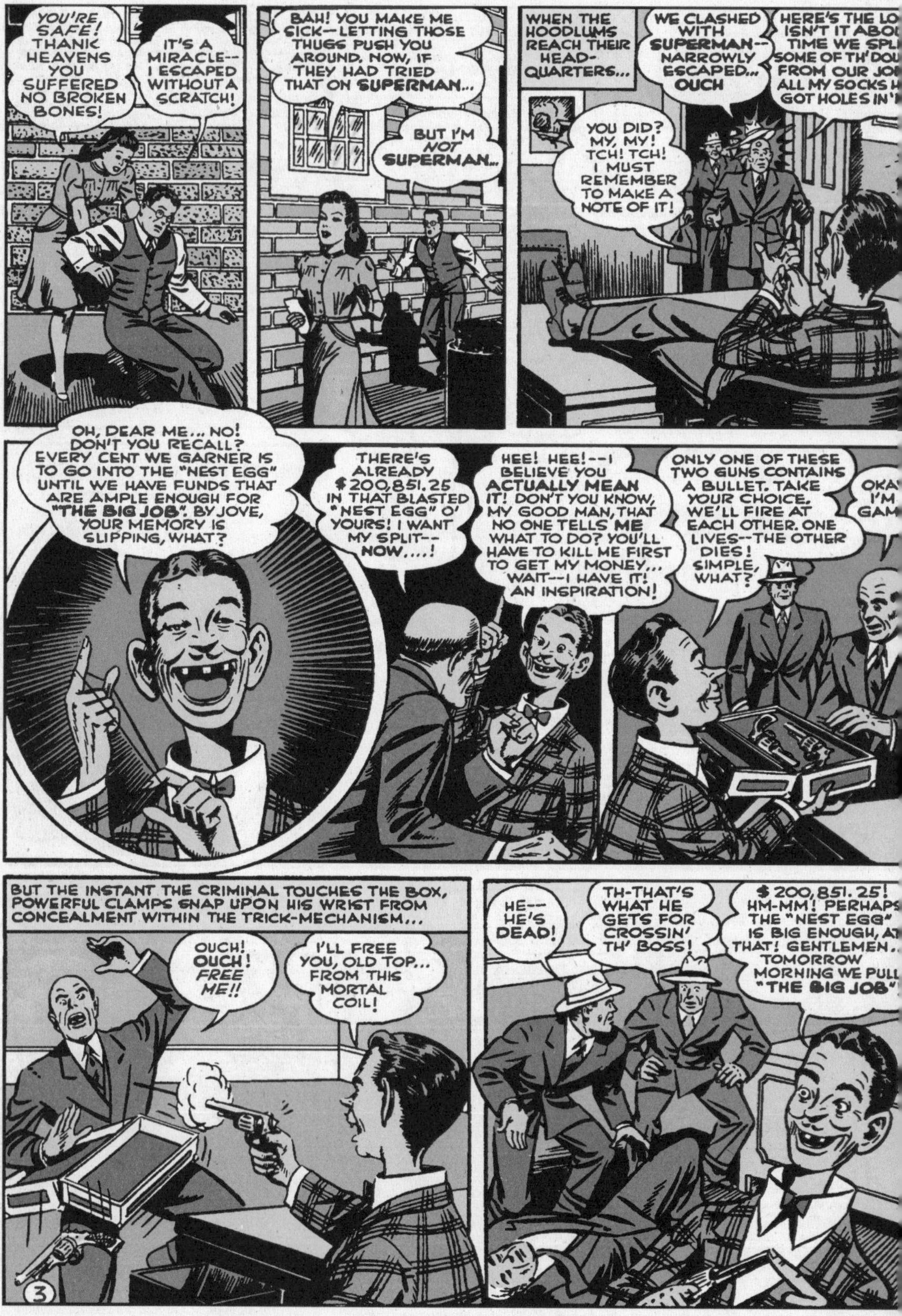
YOU'RE SAFE! THANK HEAVENS YOU SUFFERED NO BROKEN BONES!
IT'S A MIRACLE-- I ESCAPED WITHOUT A SCRATCH!
BAH! YOU MAKE ME SICK--LETTING THOSE THUGS PUSH YOU AROUND. NOW, IF THEY HAD TRIED THAT ON SUPERMAN...
BUT I'M NOT SUPERMAN...
WHEN THE HOODLUMS REACH THEIR HEAD-QUARTERS...
WE CLASHED WITH SUPERMAN-- NARROWLY ESCAPED... OUCH
HERE'S THE LO ISN'T IT ABOU TIME WE SPLI SOME OF TH' DOU FROM OUR JO ALL MY SOCKS H GOT HOLES IN'
YOU DID? MY, MY! TCH! TCH! I MUST REMEMBER TO MAKE A NOTE OF IT!
OH, DEAR ME... NO! DON'T YOU RECALL? EVERY CENT WE GARNER IS TO GO INTO THE "NEST EGG" UNTIL WE HAVE FUNDS THAT ARE AMPLE ENOUGH FOR "THE BIG JOB". BY JOVE, YOUR MEMORY IS SLIPPING, WHAT?
THERE'S ALREADY $200,851.25 IN THAT BLASTED "NEST EGG" O' YOURS! I WANT MY SPLIT-- NOW....!
HEE! HEE!--I BELIEVE YOU ACTUALLY MEAN IT! DON'T YOU KNOW, MY GOOD MAN, THAT NO ONE TELLS ME WHAT TO DO? YOU'LL HAVE TO KILL ME FIRST TO GET MY MONEY... WAIT--I HAVE IT! AN INSPIRATION!
ONLY ONE OF THESE TWO GUNS CONTAINS A BULLET. TAKE YOUR CHOICE. WE'LL FIRE AT EACH OTHER. ONE LIVES--THE OTHER DIES! SIMPLE, WHAT?
OKA I'M GAM
BUT THE INSTANT THE CRIMINAL TOUCHES THE BOX, POWERFUL CLAMPS SNAP UPON HIS WRIST FROM CONCEALMENT WITHIN THE TRICK-MECHANISM...
OUCH! OUCH! FREE ME!!
I'LL FREE YOU, OLD TOP... FROM THIS MORTAL COIL!
3
HE-- HE'S DEAD!
TH-THAT'S WHAT HE GETS FOR CROSSIN' TH' BOSS!
$200,851.25! HM-MM! PERHAPS THE "NEST EGG" IS BIG ENOUGH, A THAT! GENTLEMEN... TOMORROW MORNING WE PULL "THE BIG JOB"

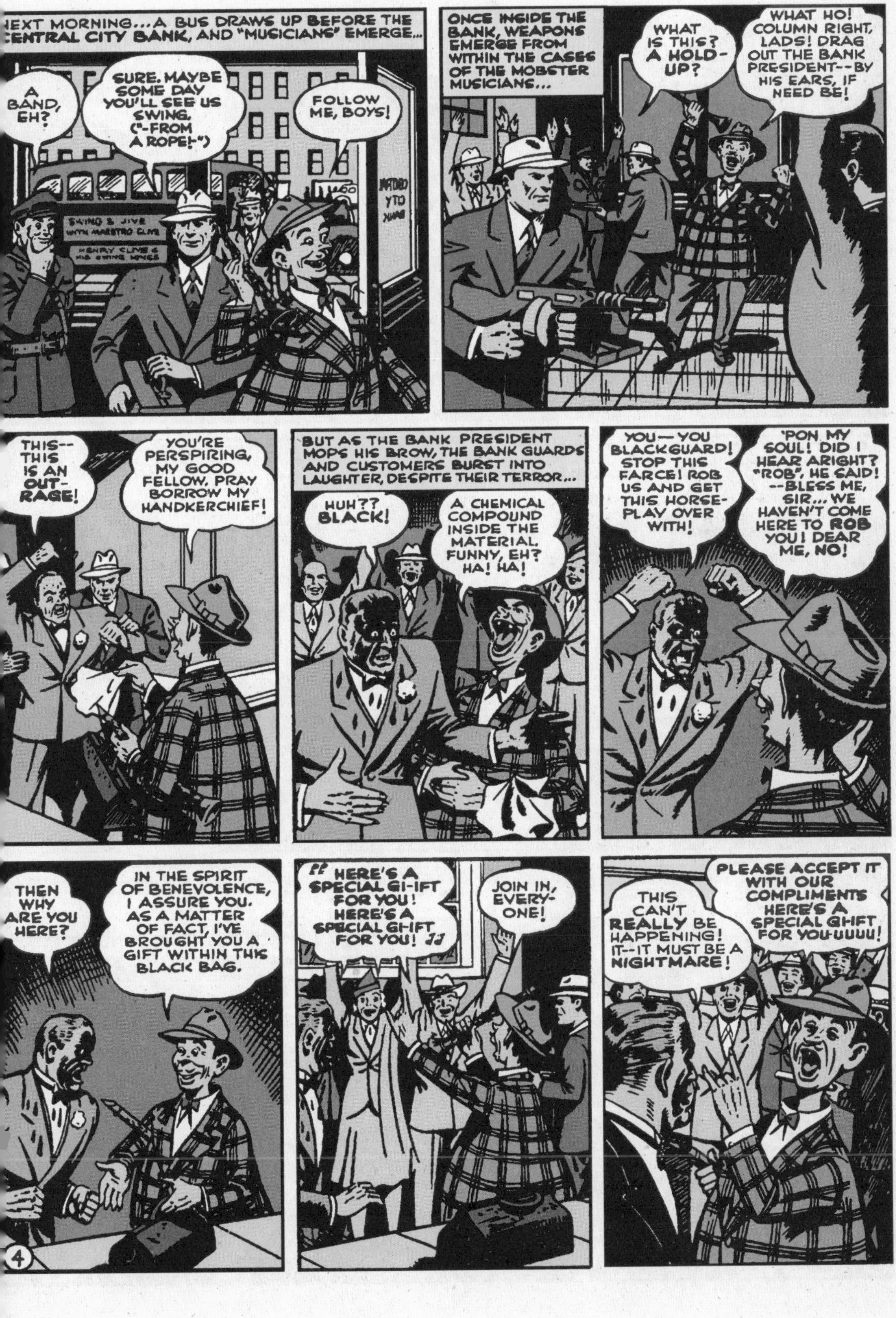
NEXT MORNING...A BUS DRAWS UP BEFORE THE CENTRAL CITY BANK, AND "MUSICIANS" EMERGE...
A BAND, EH?
SURE. MAYBE SOME DAY YOU'LL SEE US SWING. ("-FROM A ROPE!-")
FOLLOW ME, BOYS!
SWING & JIVE WITH MAESTRO CLIVE
HENRY CLIVE & HIS SWING KINGS
ONCE INSIDE THE BANK, WEAPONS EMERGE FROM WITHIN THE CASES OF THE MOBSTER MUSICIANS...
WHAT IS THIS? A HOLD-UP?
WHAT HO! COLUMN RIGHT, LADS! DRAG OUT THE BANK PRESIDENT--BY HIS EARS, IF NEED BE!
THIS--THIS IS AN OUT-RAGE!
YOU'RE PERSPIRING, MY GOOD FELLOW. PRAY BORROW MY HANDKERCHIEF!
BUT AS THE BANK PRESIDENT MOPS HIS BROW, THE BANK GUARDS AND CUSTOMERS BURST INTO LAUGHTER, DESPITE THEIR TERROR...
HUH?? BLACK!
A CHEMICAL COMPOUND INSIDE THE MATERIAL. FUNNY, EH? HA! HA!
YOU—YOU BLACKGUARD! STOP THIS FARCE! ROB US AND GET THIS HORSE-PLAY OVER WITH!
'PON MY SOUL! DID I HEAR ARIGHT? "ROB", HE SAID! --BLESS ME, SIR... WE HAVEN'T COME HERE TO ROB YOU! DEAR ME, NO!
THEN WHY ARE YOU HERE?
IN THE SPIRIT OF BENEVOLENCE, I ASSURE YOU. AS A MATTER OF FACT, I'VE BROUGHT YOU A GIFT WITHIN THIS BLACK BAG.
4
♪♪ HERE'S A SPECIAL GI-IFT FOR YOU! HERE'S A SPECIAL GI-IFT FOR YOU! ♪♪
JOIN IN, EVERY-ONE!
THIS CAN'T REALLY BE HAPPENING! IT--IT MUST BE A NIGHTMARE!
PLEASE ACCEPT IT WITH OUR COMPLIMENTS HERE'S A SPECIAL GI-IFT FOR YOU-UUUU!

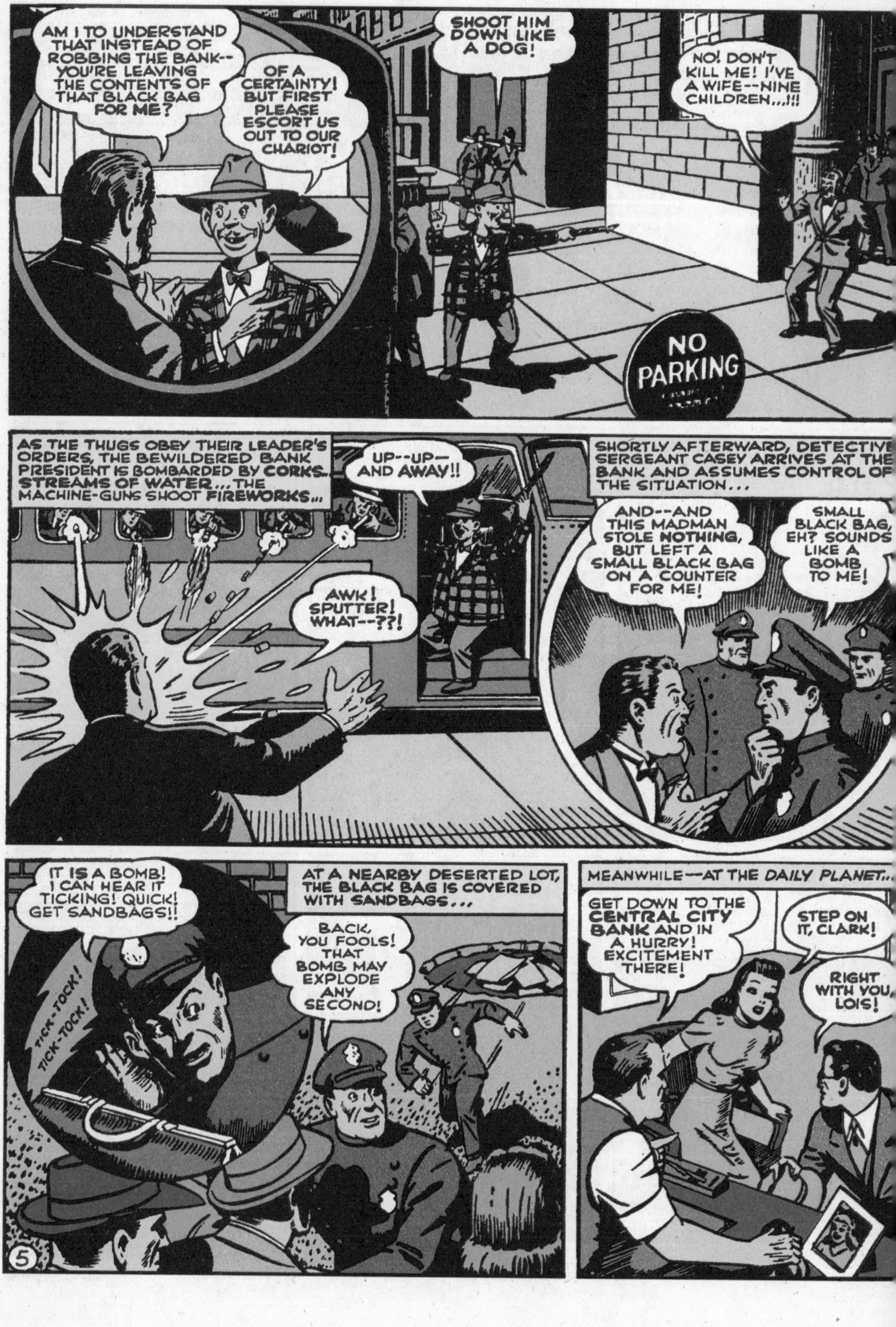
AM I TO UNDERSTAND THAT INSTEAD OF ROBBING THE BANK-- YOU'RE LEAVING THE CONTENTS OF THAT BLACK BAG FOR ME?
OF A CERTAINTY! BUT FIRST PLEASE ESCORT US OUT TO OUR CHARIOT!
SHOOT HIM DOWN LIKE A DOG!
NO! DON'T KILL ME! I'VE A WIFE--NINE CHILDREN...!!!
NO PARKING
AS THE THUGS OBEY THEIR LEADER'S ORDERS, THE BEWILDERED BANK PRESIDENT IS BOMBARDED BY CORKS... STREAMS OF WATER... THE MACHINE-GUNS SHOOT FIREWORKS...
UP--UP-- AND AWAY!!
AWK! SPUTTER! WHAT--??!
SHORTLY AFTERWARD, DETECTIVE SERGEANT CASEY ARRIVES AT THE BANK AND ASSUMES CONTROL OF THE SITUATION...
AND--AND THIS MADMAN STOLE NOTHING, BUT LEFT A SMALL BLACK BAG ON A COUNTER FOR ME!
SMALL BLACK BAG, EH? SOUNDS LIKE A BOMB TO ME!
IT IS A BOMB! I CAN HEAR IT TICKING! QUICK! GET SANDBAGS!!
TICK-TOCK! TICK-TOCK!
AT A NEARBY DESERTED LOT, THE BLACK BAG IS COVERED WITH SANDBAGS...
BACK, YOU FOOLS! THAT BOMB MAY EXPLODE ANY SECOND!
5
MEANWHILE--AT THE DAILY PLANET...
GET DOWN TO THE CENTRAL CITY BANK AND IN A HURRY! EXCITEMENT THERE!
STEP ON IT, CLARK!
RIGHT WITH YOU, LOIS!

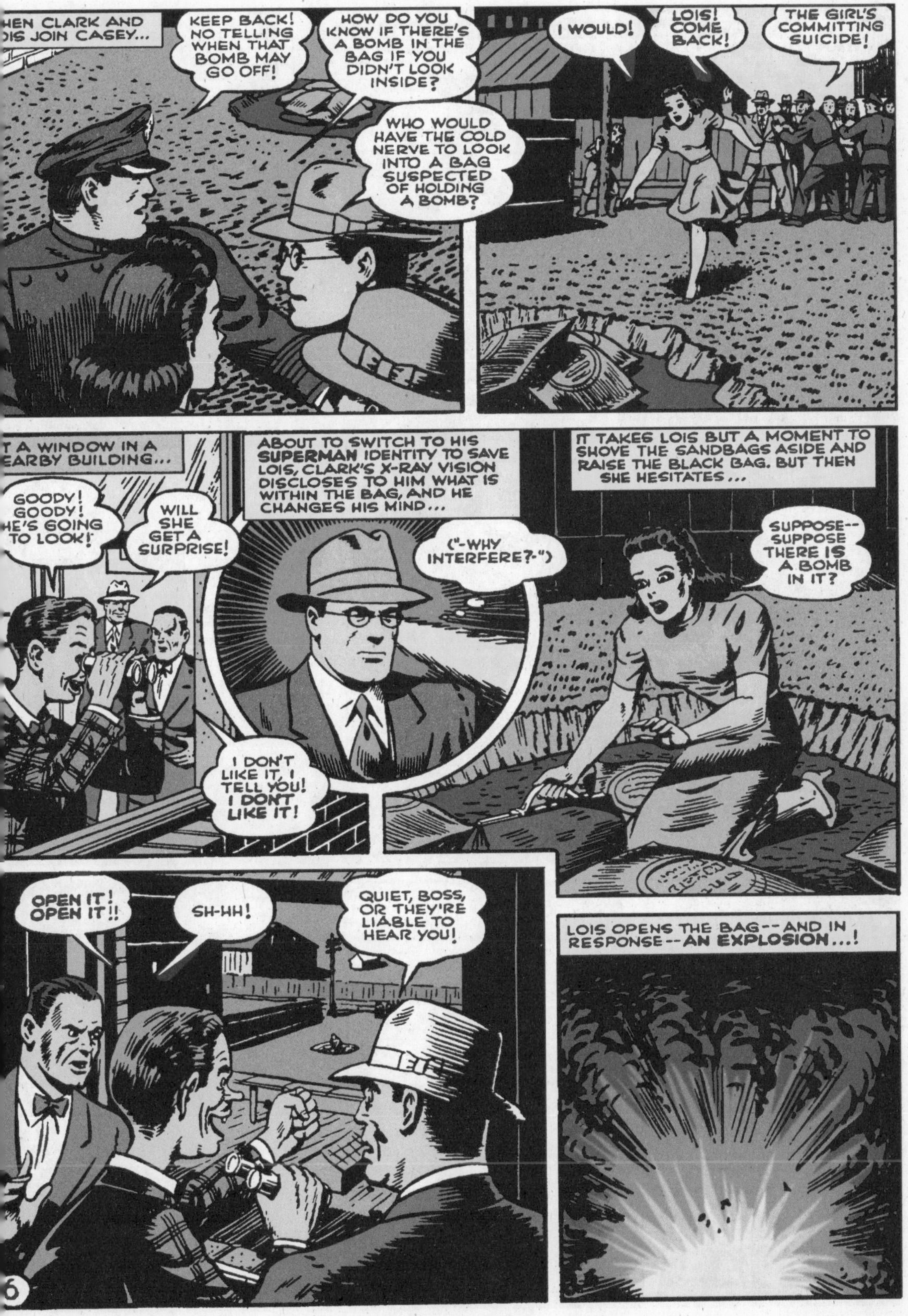

HEN CLARK AND
OIS JOIN CASEY...
KEEP BACK! NO TELLING WHEN THAT BOMB MAY GO OFF!
HOW DO YOU KNOW IF THERE'S A BOMB IN THE BAG IF YOU DIDN'T LOOK INSIDE?
WHO WOULD HAVE THE COLD NERVE TO LOOK INTO A BAG SUSPECTED OF HOLDING A BOMB?
I WOULD!
LOIS! COME BACK!
THE GIRL'S COMMITTING SUICIDE!
T A WINDOW IN A
EARBY BUILDING...
GOODY! GOODY! HE'S GOING TO LOOK!
WILL SHE GET A SURPRISE!
I DON'T LIKE IT, I TELL YOU! I DON'T LIKE IT!
ABOUT TO SWITCH TO HIS SUPERMAN IDENTITY TO SAVE LOIS, CLARK'S X-RAY VISION DISCLOSES TO HIM WHAT IS WITHIN THE BAG, AND HE CHANGES HIS MIND...
("-WHY INTERFERE?-")
IT TAKES LOIS BUT A MOMENT TO SHOVE THE SANDBAGS ASIDE AND RAISE THE BLACK BAG. BUT THEN SHE HESITATES...
SUPPOSE-- SUPPOSE THERE IS A BOMB IN IT?
OPEN IT! OPEN IT!!
SH-HH!
QUIET, BOSS, OR THEY'RE LIABLE TO HEAR YOU!
LOIS OPENS THE BAG--AND IN RESPONSE--AN EXPLOSION...!
6

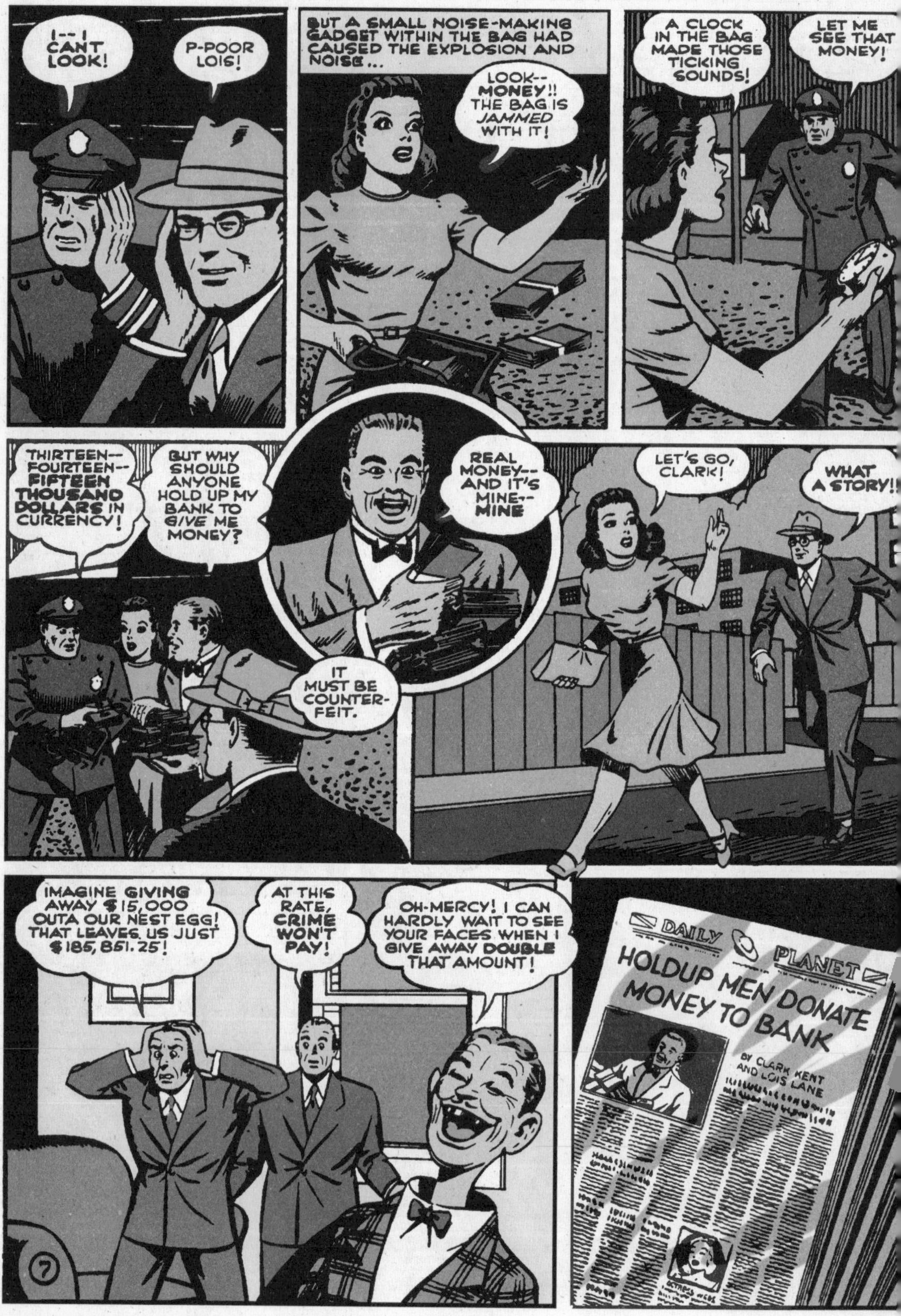

I-- I CANT LOOK!
P-POOR LOIS!
BUT A SMALL NOISE-MAKING GADGET WITHIN THE BAG HAD CAUSED THE EXPLOSION AND NOISE...
LOOK-- MONEY!! THE BAG IS JAMMED WITH IT!
A CLOCK IN THE BAG MADE THOSE TICKING SOUNDS!
LET ME SEE THAT MONEY!
THIRTEEN-- FOURTEEN-- FIFTEEN THOUSAND DOLLARS IN CURRENCY!
BUT WHY SHOULD ANYONE HOLD UP MY BANK TO GIVE ME MONEY?
IT MUST BE COUNTER-FEIT.
REAL MONEY-- AND IT'S MINE-- MINE
LET'S GO, CLARK!
WHAT A STORY!!
IMAGINE GIVING AWAY $15,000 OUTA OUR NEST EGG! THAT LEAVES US JUST $185,851.25!
AT THIS RATE, CRIME WON'T PAY!
OH-MERCY! I CAN HARDLY WAIT TO SEE YOUR FACES WHEN I GIVE AWAY DOUBLE THAT AMOUNT!
7
DAILY PLANET
HOLDUP MEN DONATE MONEY TO BANK
BY CLARK KENT AND LOIS LANE

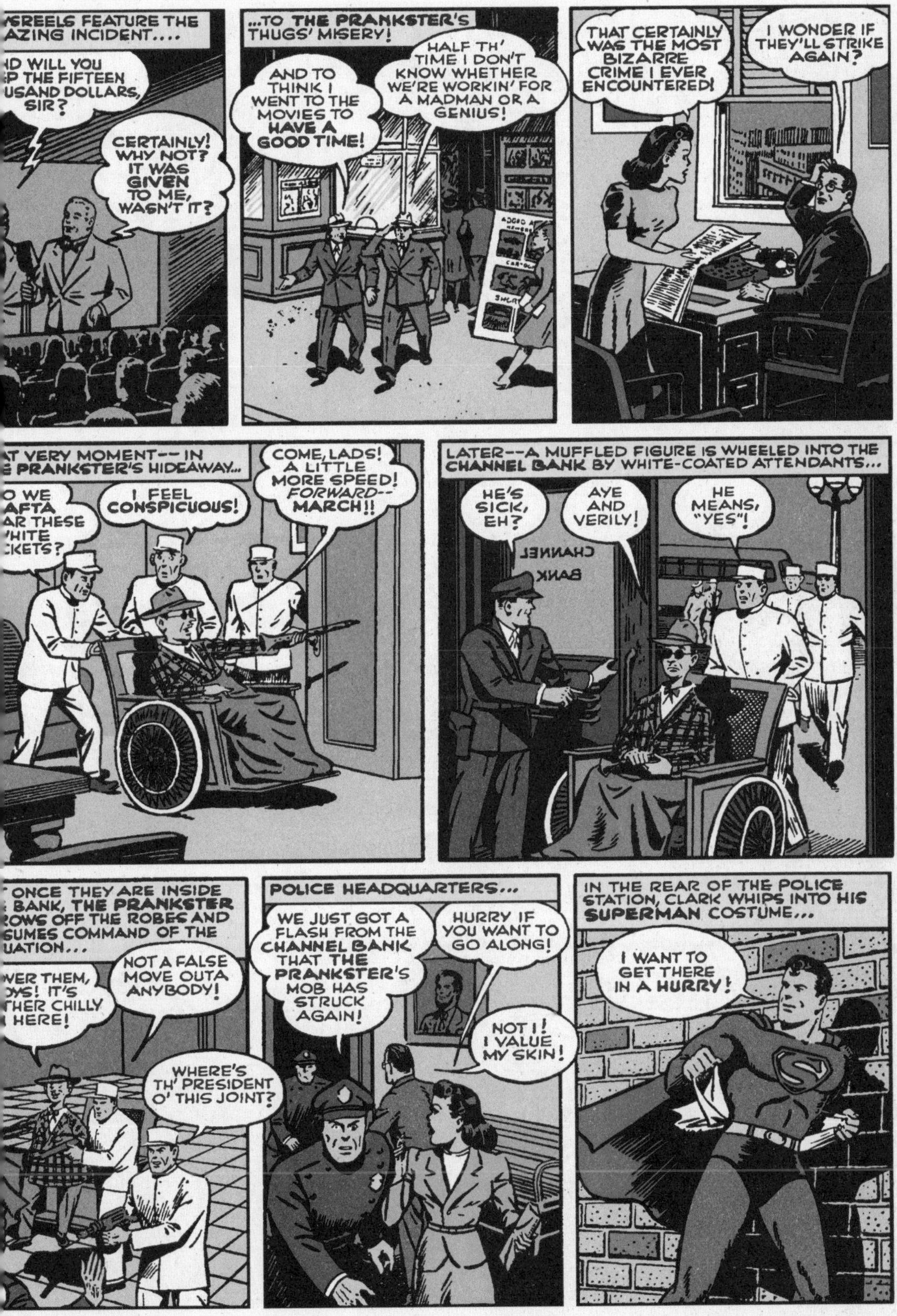
WSREELS FEATURE THE AZING INCIDENT....
ND WILL YOU EP THE FIFTEEN USAND DOLLARS, SIR?
CERTAINLY! WHY NOT? IT WAS GIVEN TO ME, WASN'T IT?
...TO THE PRANKSTER'S THUGS' MISERY!
AND TO THINK I WENT TO THE MOVIES TO HAVE A GOOD TIME!
HALF TH' TIME I DON'T KNOW WHETHER WE'RE WORKIN' FOR A MADMAN OR A GENIUS!
THAT CERTAINLY WAS THE MOST BIZARRE CRIME I EVER ENCOUNTERED!
I WONDER IF THEY'LL STRIKE AGAIN?
AT VERY MOMENT-- IN E PRANKSTER'S HIDEAWAY...
O WE AFTA AR THESE HITE CKETS?
I FEEL CONSPICUOUS!
COME, LADS! A LITTLE MORE SPEED! FORWARD-- MARCH!!
LATER--A MUFFLED FIGURE IS WHEELED INTO THE CHANNEL BANK BY WHITE-COATED ATTENDANTS...
HE'S SICK, EH?
AYE AND VERILY!
HE MEANS, "YES"!
ONCE THEY ARE INSIDE BANK, THE PRANKSTER ROWS OFF THE ROBES AND SUMES COMMAND OF THE UATION...
WER THEM, OYS! IT'S THER CHILLY HERE!
NOT A FALSE MOVE OUTA ANYBODY!
WHERE'S TH' PRESIDENT O' THIS JOINT?
POLICE HEADQUARTERS...
WE JUST GOT A FLASH FROM THE CHANNEL BANK THAT THE PRANKSTER'S MOB HAS STRUCK AGAIN!
HURRY IF YOU WANT TO GO ALONG!
NOT I! I VALUE MY SKIN!
IN THE REAR OF THE POLICE STATION, CLARK WHIPS INTO HIS SUPERMAN COSTUME...
I WANT TO GET THERE IN A HURRY!

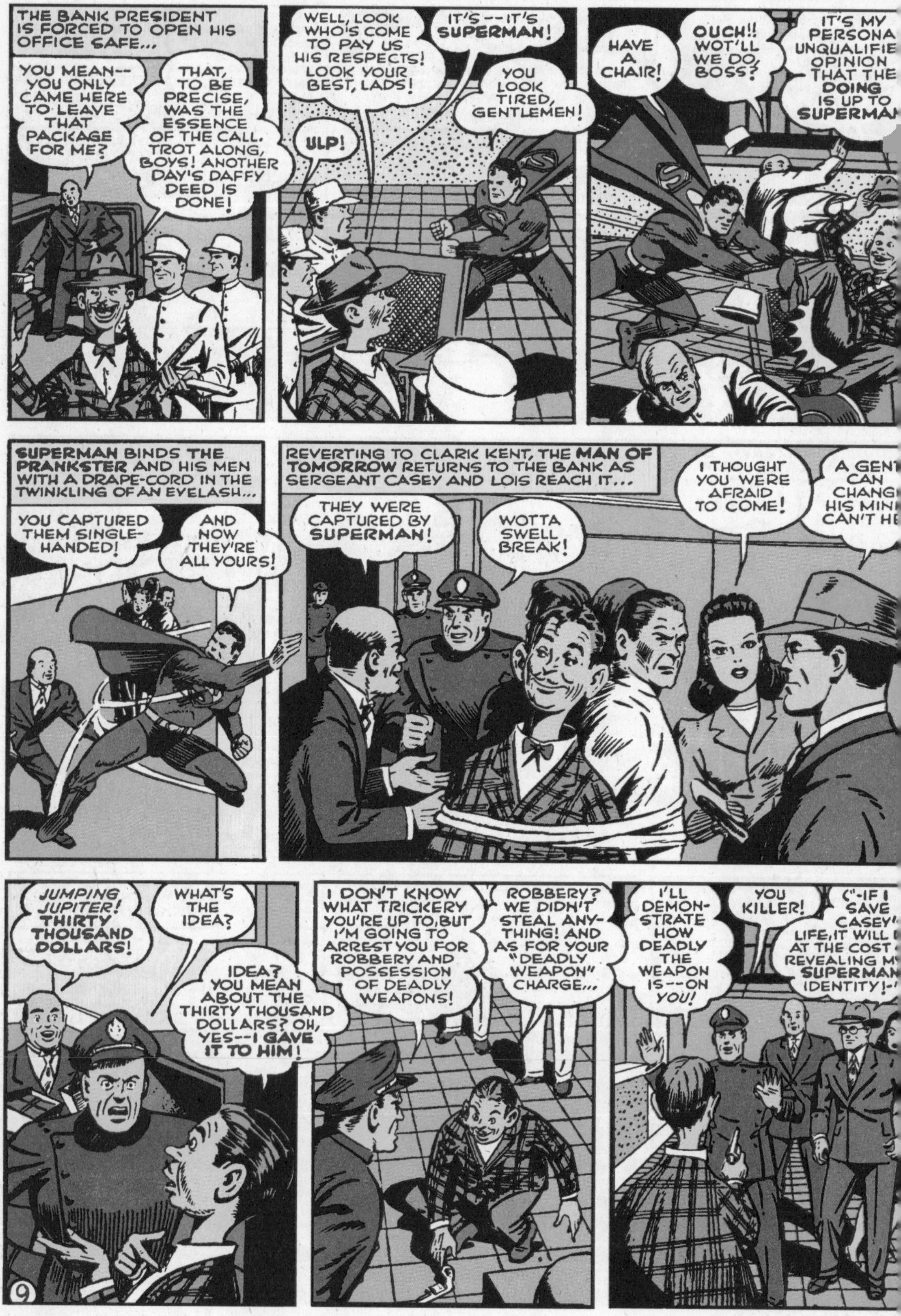
THE BANK PRESIDENT IS FORCED TO OPEN HIS OFFICE SAFE...
YOU MEAN--YOU ONLY CAME HERE TO LEAVE THAT PACKAGE FOR ME?
THAT, TO BE PRECISE, WAS THE ESSENCE OF THE CALL. TROT ALONG, BOYS! ANOTHER DAY'S DAFFY DEED IS DONE!
WELL, LOOK WHO'S COME TO PAY US HIS RESPECTS! LOOK YOUR BEST, LADS!
IT'S--IT'S SUPERMAN!
ULP!
YOU LOOK TIRED, GENTLEMEN!
HAVE A CHAIR!
OUCH!! WOT'LL WE DO, BOSS?
IT'S MY PERSONA UNQUALIFIE OPINION THAT THE DOING IS UP TO SUPERMAN
SUPERMAN BINDS THE PRANKSTER AND HIS MEN WITH A DRAPE-CORD IN THE TWINKLING OF AN EYELASH...
YOU CAPTURED THEM SINGLE-HANDED!
AND NOW THEY'RE ALL YOURS!
REVERTING TO CLARK KENT, THE MAN OF TOMORROW RETURNS TO THE BANK AS SERGEANT CASEY AND LOIS REACH IT...
THEY WERE CAPTURED BY SUPERMAN!
WOTTA SWELL BREAK!
I THOUGHT YOU WERE AFRAID TO COME!
A GENT CAN CHANG HIS MIN CAN'T HE
JUMPING JUPITER! THIRTY THOUSAND DOLLARS!
WHAT'S THE IDEA?
IDEA? YOU MEAN ABOUT THE THIRTY THOUSAND DOLLARS? OH, YES--I GAVE IT TO HIM!
I DON'T KNOW WHAT TRICKERY YOU'RE UP TO, BUT I'M GOING TO ARREST YOU FOR ROBBERY AND POSSESSION OF DEADLY WEAPONS!
ROBBERY? WE DIDN'T STEAL ANYTHING! AND AS FOR YOUR "DEADLY WEAPON" CHARGE...
I'LL DEMONSTRATE HOW DEADLY THE WEAPON IS--ON YOU!
YOU KILLER!
("-IF I SAVE CASEY' LIFE, IT WILL AT THE COST REVEALING M SUPERMAN IDENTITY!-"
9

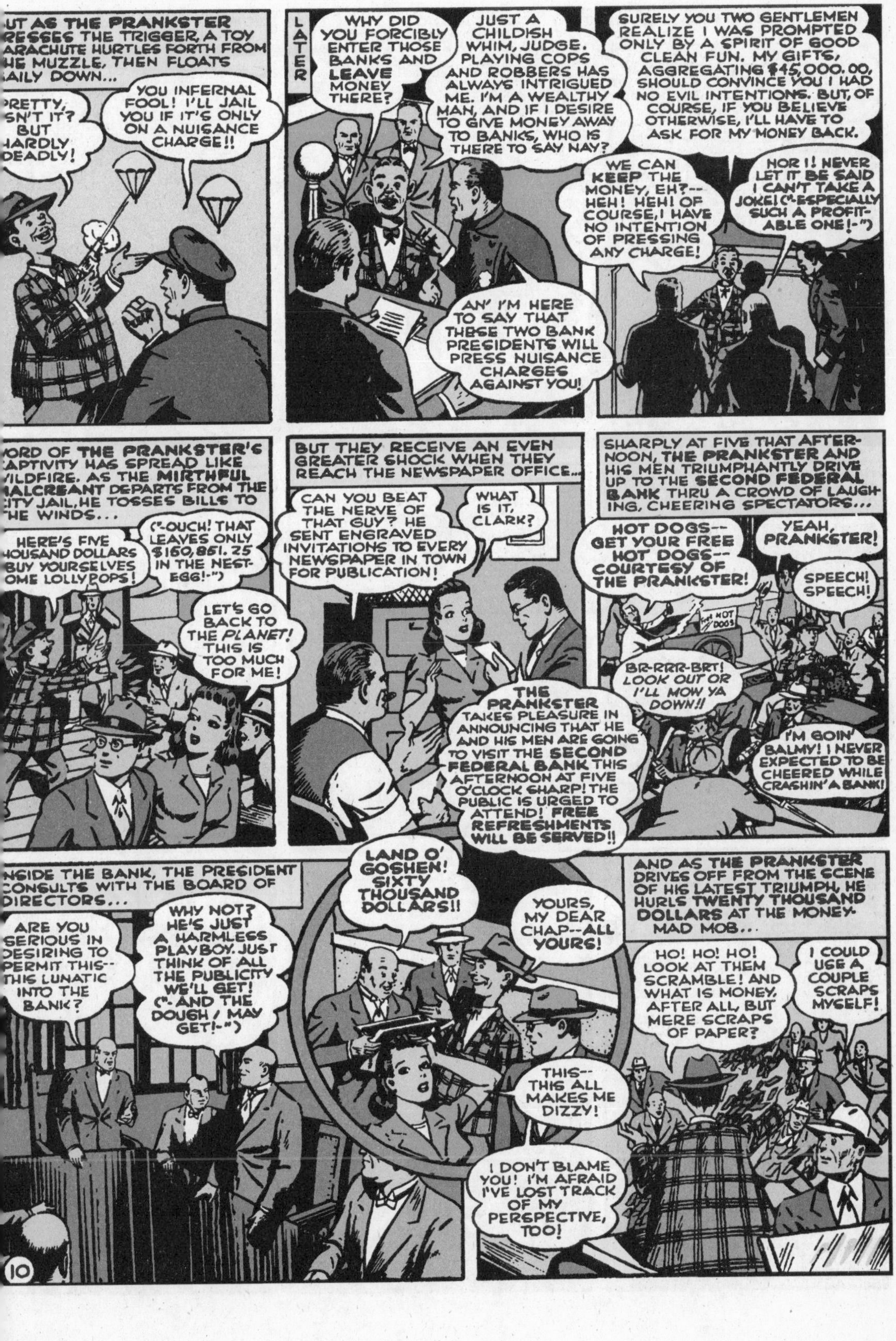
UT AS THE PRANKSTER RESSES THE TRIGGER, A TOY ARACHUTE HURTLES FORTH FROM HE MUZZLE, THEN FLOATS AILY DOWN...
PRETTY, SN'T IT? BUT HARDLY DEADLY!
YOU INFERNAL FOOL! I'LL JAIL YOU IF IT'S ONLY ON A NUISANCE CHARGE!!
LATER
WHY DID YOU FORCIBLY ENTER THOSE BANKS AND LEAVE MONEY THERE?
JUST A CHILDISH WHIM, JUDGE. PLAYING COPS AND ROBBERS HAS ALWAYS INTRIGUED ME. I'M A WEALTHY MAN, AND IF I DESIRE TO GIVE MONEY AWAY TO BANKS, WHO IS THERE TO SAY NAY?
AN' I'M HERE TO SAY THAT THESE TWO BANK PRESIDENTS WILL PRESS NUISANCE CHARGES AGAINST YOU!
SURELY YOU TWO GENTLEMEN REALIZE I WAS PROMPTED ONLY BY A SPIRIT OF GOOD CLEAN FUN. MY GIFTS, AGGREGATING $45,000.00, SHOULD CONVINCE YOU I HAD NO EVIL INTENTIONS. BUT, OF COURSE, IF YOU BELIEVE OTHERWISE, I'LL HAVE TO ASK FOR MY MONEY BACK.
WE CAN KEEP THE MONEY, EH?-- HEH! HEH! OF COURSE, I HAVE NO INTENTION OF PRESSING ANY CHARGE!
NOR I! NEVER LET IT BE SAID I CAN'T TAKE A JOKE! ("-ESPECIALLY SUCH A PROFITABLE ONE!-")
ORD OF THE PRANKSTER'S APTIVITY HAS SPREAD LIKE ILDFIRE. AS THE MIRTHFUL ALCREANT DEPARTS FROM THE ITY JAIL, HE TOSSES BILLS TO HE WINDS...
HERE'S FIVE HOUSAND DOLLARS BUY YOURSELVES OME LOLLYPOPS!
("-OUCH! THAT LEAVES ONLY $160,851.25 IN THE NEST-EGG!-")
LET'S GO BACK TO THE PLANET! THIS IS TOO MUCH FOR ME!
BUT THEY RECEIVE AN EVEN GREATER SHOCK WHEN THEY REACH THE NEWSPAPER OFFICE...
CAN YOU BEAT THE NERVE OF THAT GUY? HE SENT ENGRAVED INVITATIONS TO EVERY NEWSPAPER IN TOWN FOR PUBLICATION!
WHAT IS IT, CLARK?
THE PRANKSTER TAKES PLEASURE IN ANNOUNCING THAT HE AND HIS MEN ARE GOING TO VISIT THE SECOND FEDERAL BANK THIS AFTERNOON AT FIVE O'CLOCK SHARP! THE PUBLIC IS URGED TO ATTEND! FREE REFRESHMENTS WILL BE SERVED!!
SHARPLY AT FIVE THAT AFTERNOON, THE PRANKSTER AND HIS MEN TRIUMPHANTLY DRIVE UP TO THE SECOND FEDERAL BANK THRU A CROWD OF LAUGHING, CHEERING SPECTATORS...
HOT DOGS-- GET YOUR FREE HOT DOGS-- COURTESY OF THE PRANKSTER!
YEAH, PRANKSTER!
SPEECH! SPEECH!
HOT DOGS
BR-RRR-BRT! LOOK OUT OR I'LL MOW YA DOWN!!
I'M GOIN' BALMY! I NEVER EXPECTED TO BE CHEERED WHILE CRASHIN' A BANK!
NSIDE THE BANK, THE PRESIDENT CONSULTS WITH THE BOARD OF DIRECTORS...
ARE YOU SERIOUS IN DESIRING TO PERMIT THIS-- THIS LUNATIC INTO THE BANK?
WHY NOT? HE'S JUST A HARMLESS PLAYBOY. JUST THINK OF ALL THE PUBLICITY WE'LL GET! ("-AND THE DOUGH I MAY GET!-")
LAND O' GOSHEN! SIXTY THOUSAND DOLLARS!!
YOURS, MY DEAR CHAP--ALL YOURS!
THIS-- THIS ALL MAKES ME DIZZY!
I DON'T BLAME YOU! I'M AFRAID I'VE LOST TRACK OF MY PERSPECTIVE, TOO!
AND AS THE PRANKSTER DRIVES OFF FROM THE SCENE OF HIS LATEST TRIUMPH, HE HURLS TWENTY THOUSAND DOLLARS AT THE MONEY-MAD MOB...
HO! HO! HO! LOOK AT THEM SCRAMBLE! AND WHAT IS MONEY, AFTER ALL, BUT MERE SCRAPS OF PAPER?
I COULD USE A COUPLE SCRAPS MYSELF!
10

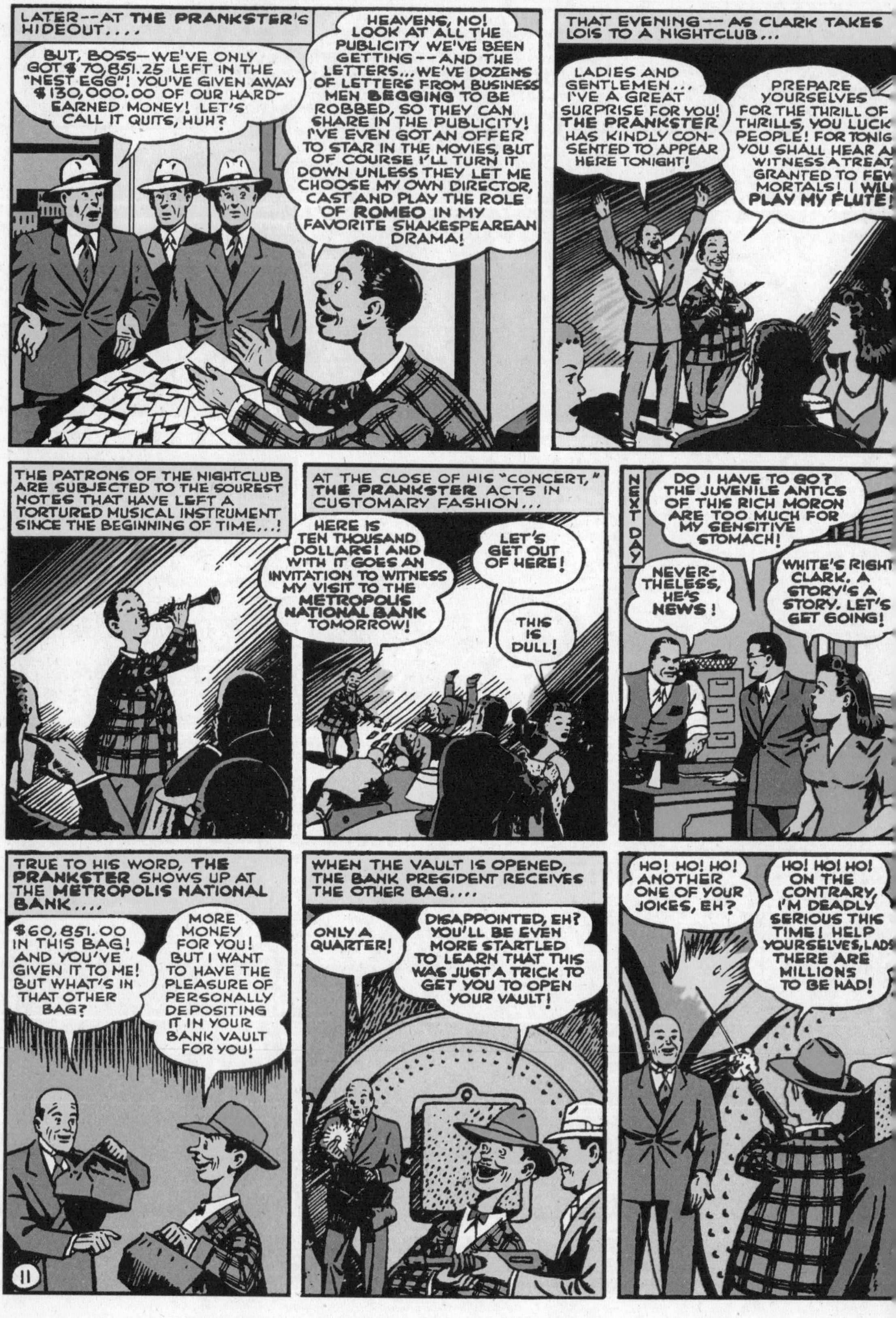

LATER--AT THE PRANKSTER'S HIDEOUT....
BUT, BOSS--WE'VE ONLY GOT $70,851.25 LEFT IN THE "NEST EGG"! YOU'VE GIVEN AWAY $130,000.00 OF OUR HARD-EARNED MONEY! LET'S CALL IT QUITS, HUH?
HEAVENS, NO! LOOK AT ALL THE PUBLICITY WE'VE BEEN GETTING--AND THE LETTERS... WE'VE DOZENS OF LETTERS FROM BUSINESS MEN BEGGING TO BE ROBBED, SO THEY CAN SHARE IN THE PUBLICITY! I'VE EVEN GOT AN OFFER TO STAR IN THE MOVIES, BUT OF COURSE I'LL TURN IT DOWN UNLESS THEY LET ME CHOOSE MY OWN DIRECTOR, CAST AND PLAY THE ROLE OF ROMEO IN MY FAVORITE SHAKESPEAREAN DRAMA!
THAT EVENING--AS CLARK TAKES LOIS TO A NIGHTCLUB...
LADIES AND GENTLEMEN... I'VE A GREAT SURPRISE FOR YOU! THE PRANKSTER HAS KINDLY CONSENTED TO APPEAR HERE TONIGHT!
PREPARE YOURSELVES FOR THE THRILL OF THRILLS, YOU LUCK PEOPLE! FOR TONIG YOU SHALL HEAR A WITNESS A TREAT GRANTED TO FEW MORTALS! I WIL PLAY MY FLUTE!
THE PATRONS OF THE NIGHTCLUB ARE SUBJECTED TO THE SOUREST NOTES THAT HAVE LEFT A TORTURED MUSICAL INSTRUMENT SINCE THE BEGINNING OF TIME...!
AT THE CLOSE OF HIS "CONCERT," THE PRANKSTER ACTS IN CUSTOMARY FASHION...
HERE IS TEN THOUSAND DOLLARS! AND WITH IT GOES AN INVITATION TO WITNESS MY VISIT TO THE METROPOLIS NATIONAL BANK TOMORROW!
LET'S GET OUT OF HERE!
THIS IS DULL!
NEXT DAY
DO I HAVE TO GO? THE JUVENILE ANTICS OF THIS RICH MORON ARE TOO MUCH FOR MY SENSITIVE STOMACH!
NEVERTHELESS, HE'S NEWS!
WHITE'S RIGHT CLARK. A STORY'S A STORY. LET'S GET GOING!
TRUE TO HIS WORD, THE PRANKSTER SHOWS UP AT THE METROPOLIS NATIONAL BANK....
$60,851.00 IN THIS BAG! AND YOU'VE GIVEN IT TO ME! BUT WHAT'S IN THAT OTHER BAG?
MORE MONEY FOR YOU! BUT I WANT TO HAVE THE PLEASURE OF PERSONALLY DEPOSITING IT IN YOUR BANK VAULT FOR YOU!
11
WHEN THE VAULT IS OPENED, THE BANK PRESIDENT RECEIVES THE OTHER BAG....
ONLY A QUARTER!
DISAPPOINTED, EH? YOU'LL BE EVEN MORE STARTLED TO LEARN THAT THIS WAS JUST A TRICK TO GET YOU TO OPEN YOUR VAULT!
HO! HO! HO! ANOTHER ONE OF YOUR JOKES, EH?
HO! HO! HO! ON THE CONTRARY, I'M DEADLY SERIOUS THIS TIME! HELP YOURSELVES, LADS THERE ARE MILLIONS TO BE HAD!

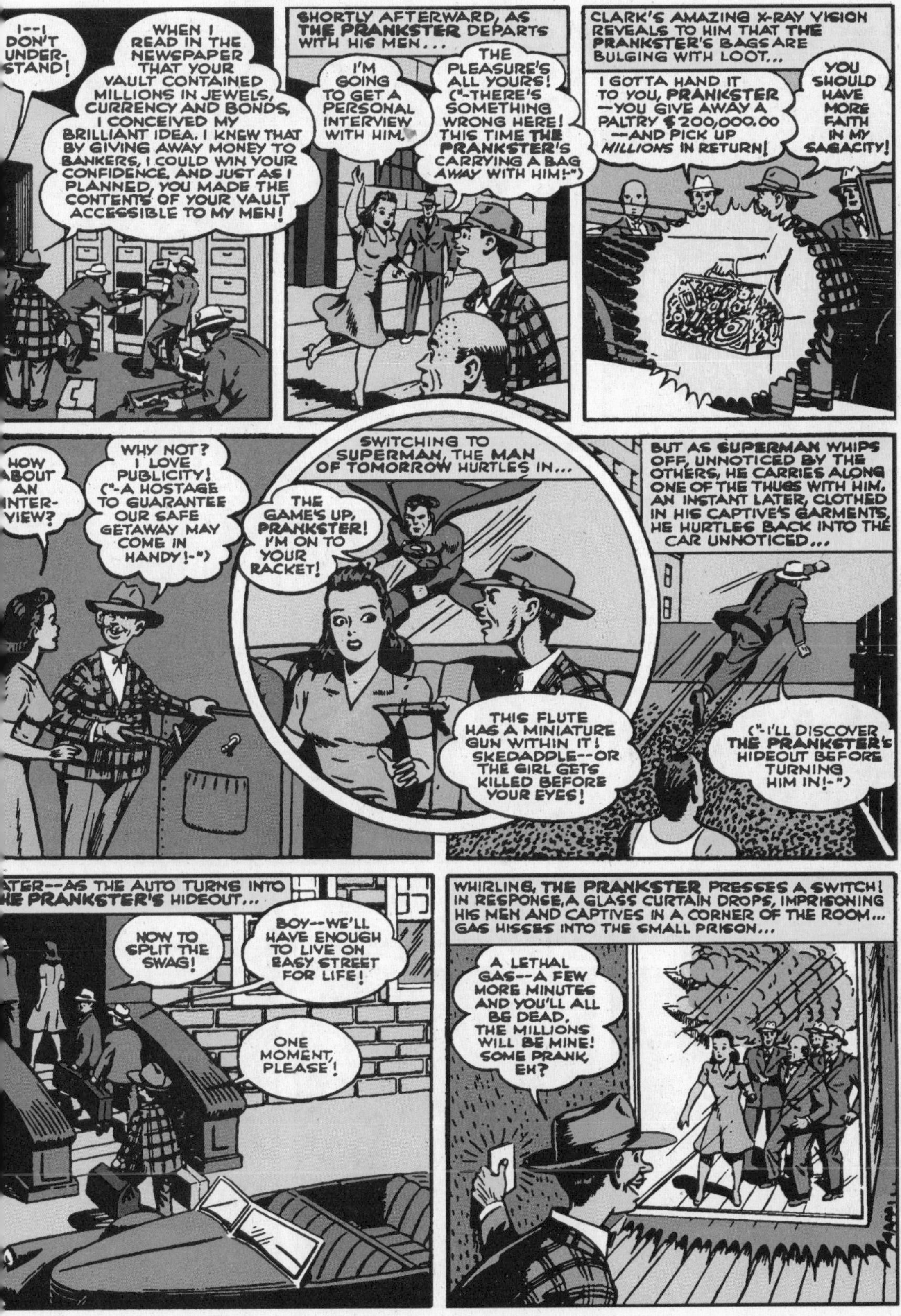

I--I DON'T UNDER-STAND!
WHEN I READ IN THE NEWSPAPER THAT YOUR VAULT CONTAINED MILLIONS IN JEWELS, CURRENCY AND BONDS, I CONCEIVED MY BRILLIANT IDEA. I KNEW THAT BY GIVING AWAY MONEY TO BANKERS, I COULD WIN YOUR CONFIDENCE, AND JUST AS I PLANNED, YOU MADE THE CONTENTS OF YOUR VAULT ACCESSIBLE TO MY MEN!
SHORTLY AFTERWARD, AS THE PRANKSTER DEPARTS WITH HIS MEN...
I'M GOING TO GET A PERSONAL INTERVIEW WITH HIM.
THE PLEASURE'S ALL YOURS! ("-THERE'S SOMETHING WRONG HERE! THIS TIME THE PRANKSTER'S CARRYING A BAG AWAY WITH HIM!-")
CLARK'S AMAZING X-RAY VISION REVEALS TO HIM THAT THE PRANKSTER'S BAGS ARE BULGING WITH LOOT...
I GOTTA HAND IT TO YOU, PRANKSTER --YOU GIVE AWAY A PALTRY $200,000.00 --AND PICK UP MILLIONS IN RETURN!
YOU SHOULD HAVE MORE FAITH IN MY SAGACITY!
HOW BOUT AN NTER-VIEW?
WHY NOT? I LOVE PUBLICITY! ("-A HOSTAGE TO GUARANTEE OUR SAFE GETAWAY MAY COME IN HANDY!-")
SWITCHING TO SUPERMAN, THE MAN OF TOMORROW HURTLES IN...
THE GAME'S UP, PRANKSTER! I'M ON TO YOUR RACKET!
THIS FLUTE HAS A MINIATURE GUN WITHIN IT! SKEDADDLE--OR THE GIRL GETS KILLED BEFORE YOUR EYES!
BUT AS SUPERMAN WHIPS OFF, UNNOTICED BY THE OTHERS, HE CARRIES ALONG ONE OF THE THUGS WITH HIM. AN INSTANT LATER, CLOTHED IN HIS CAPTIVE'S GARMENTS, HE HURTLES BACK INTO THE CAR UNNOTICED...
("-I'LL DISCOVER THE PRANKSTER'S HIDEOUT BEFORE TURNING HIM IN!-")
ATER--AS THE AUTO TURNS INTO HE PRANKSTER'S HIDEOUT...
NOW TO SPLIT THE SWAG!
BOY--WE'LL HAVE ENOUGH TO LIVE ON EASY STREET FOR LIFE!
ONE MOMENT, PLEASE!
WHIRLING, THE PRANKSTER PRESSES A SWITCH! IN RESPONSE, A GLASS CURTAIN DROPS, IMPRISONING HIS MEN AND CAPTIVES IN A CORNER OF THE ROOM... GAS HISSES INTO THE SMALL PRISON...
A LETHAL GAS--A FEW MORE MINUTES AND YOU'LL ALL BE DEAD. THE MILLIONS WILL BE MINE! SOME PRANK, EH?

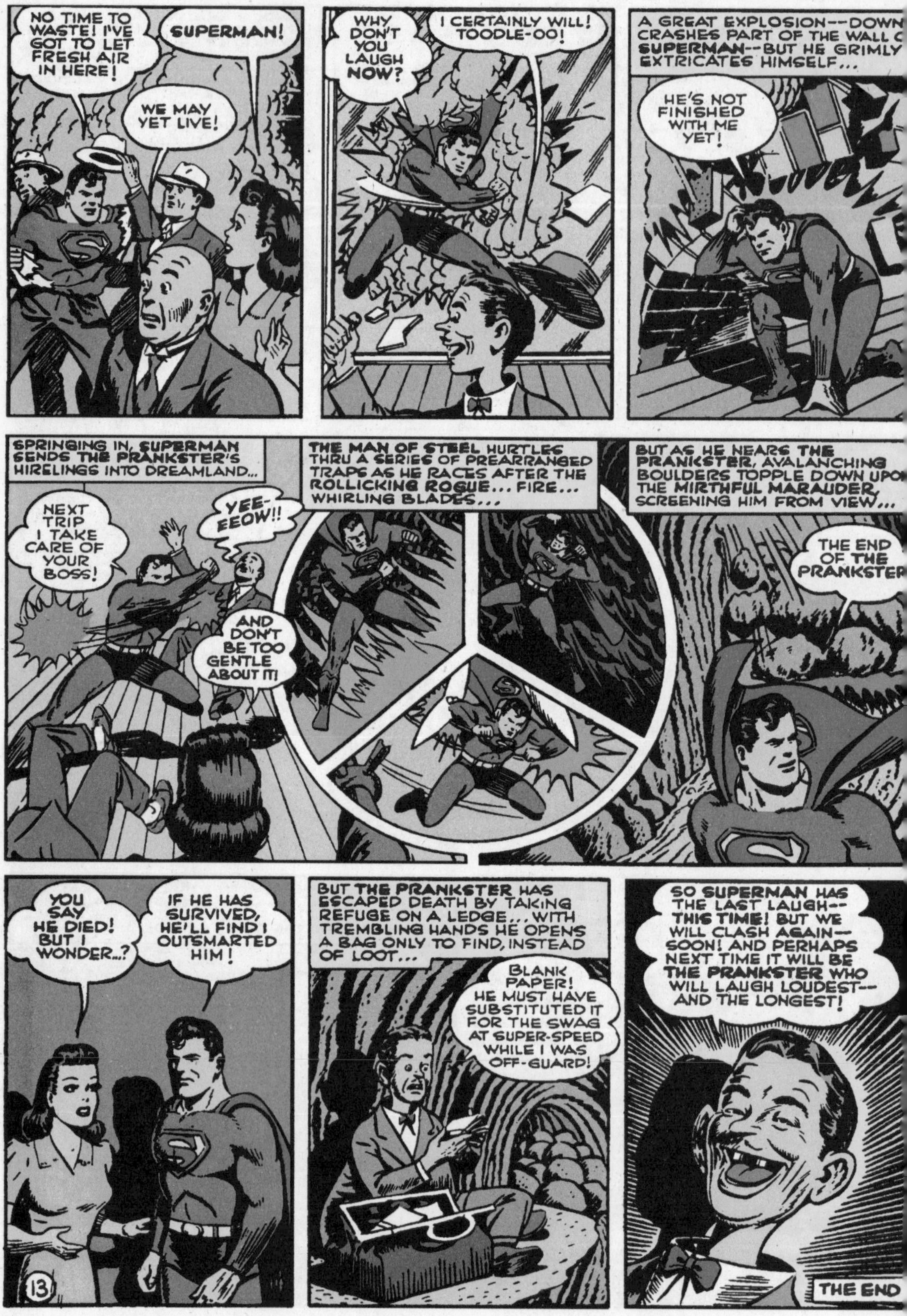

NO TIME TO WASTE! I'VE GOT TO LET FRESH AIR IN HERE!
SUPERMAN!
WE MAY YET LIVE!
WHY DON'T YOU LAUGH NOW?
I CERTAINLY WILL! TOODLE-OO!
A GREAT EXPLOSION--DOWN CRASHES PART OF THE WALL ON SUPERMAN--BUT HE GRIMLY EXTRICATES HIMSELF...
HE'S NOT FINISHED WITH ME YET!
SPRINGING IN, SUPERMAN SENDS THE PRANKSTER'S HIRELINGS INTO DREAMLAND...
NEXT TRIP I TAKE CARE OF YOUR BOSS!
YEE-EEOW!!
AND DON'T BE TOO GENTLE ABOUT IT!
THE MAN OF STEEL HURTLES THRU A SERIES OF PREARRANGED TRAPS AS HE RACES AFTER THE ROLLICKING ROGUE... FIRE... WHIRLING BLADES...
BUT AS HE NEARS THE PRANKSTER, AVALANCHING BOULDERS TOPPLE DOWN UPON THE MIRTHFUL MARAUDER, SCREENING HIM FROM VIEW...
THE END OF THE PRANKSTER
YOU SAY HE DIED! BUT I WONDER...?
IF HE HAS SURVIVED, HE'LL FIND I OUTSMARTED HIM!
13
BUT THE PRANKSTER HAS ESCAPED DEATH BY TAKING REFUGE ON A LEDGE... WITH TREMBLING HANDS HE OPENS A BAG ONLY TO FIND, INSTEAD OF LOOT...
BLANK PAPER! HE MUST HAVE SUBSTITUTED IT FOR THE SWAG AT SUPER-SPEED WHILE I WAS OFF-GUARD!
SO SUPERMAN HAS THE LAST LAUGH--THIS TIME! BUT WE WILL CLASH AGAIN--SOON! AND PERHAPS NEXT TIME IT WILL BE THE PRANKSTER WHO WILL LAUGH LOUDEST--AND THE LONGEST!
THE END

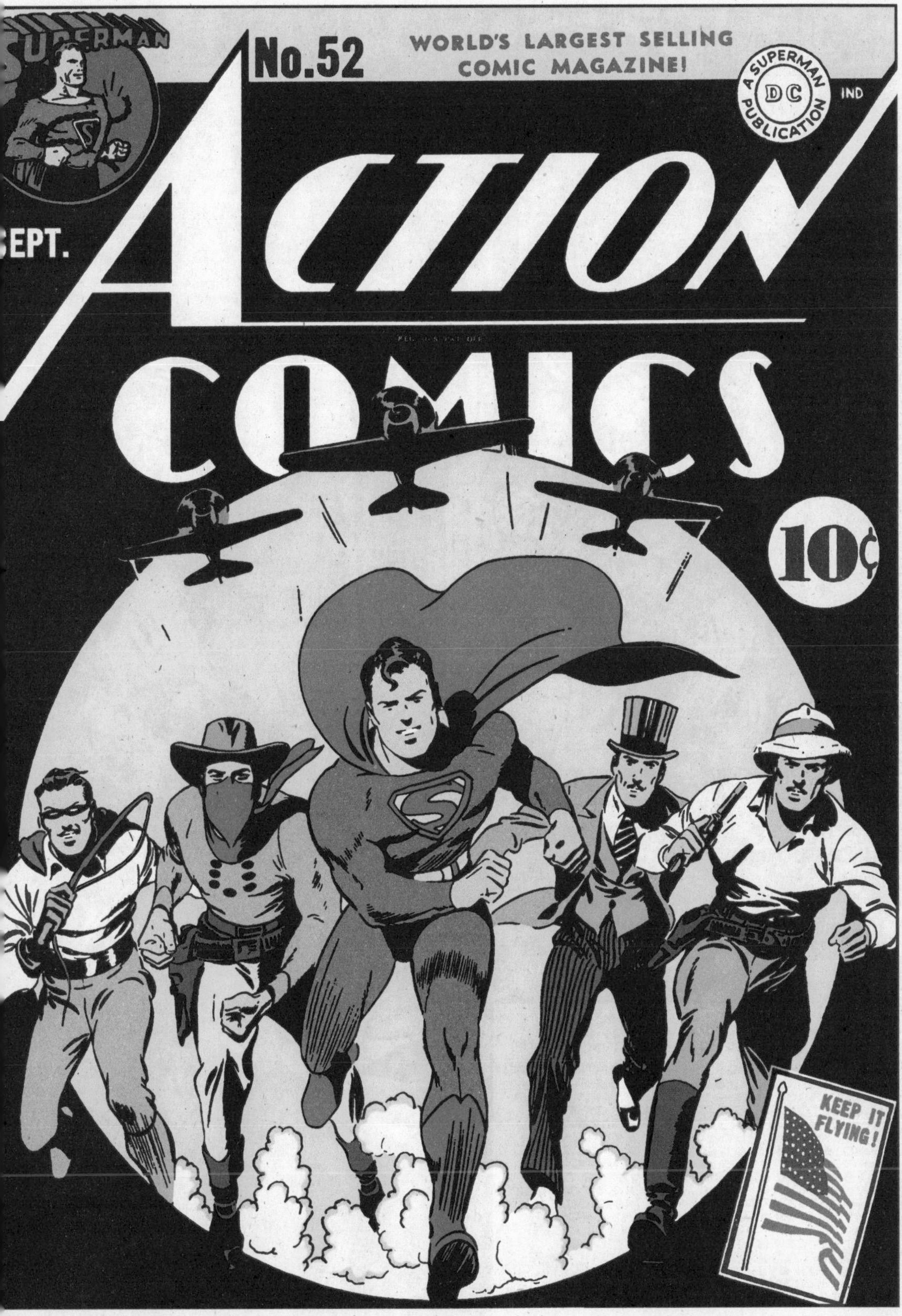
SUPERMAN
No.52
WORLD'S LARGEST SELLING
COMIC MAGAZINE!
A SUPERMAN
DC
PUBLICATION
IND
SEPT.
ACTION
COMICS
10¢
KEEP IT
FLYING!

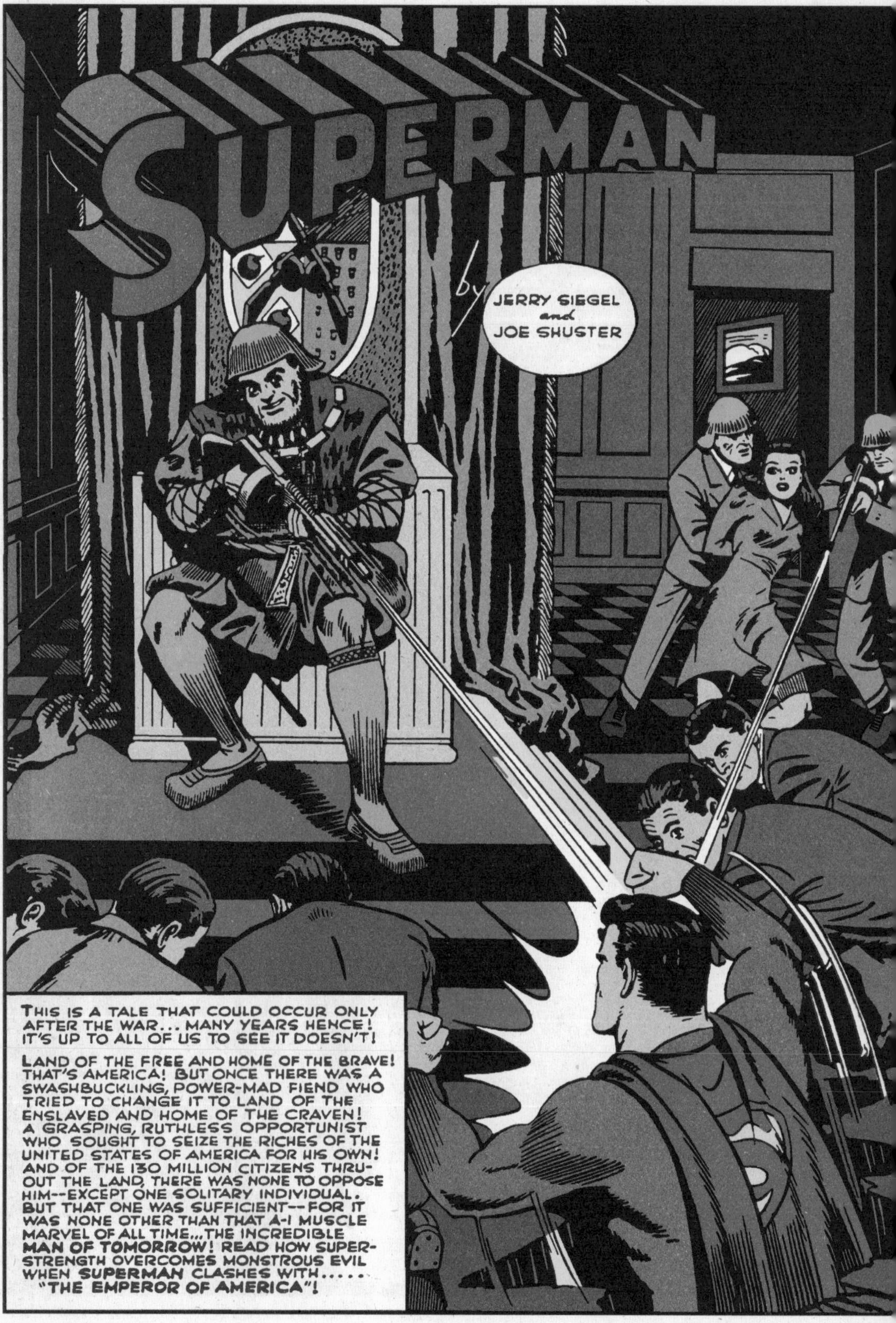
SUPERMAN
by JERRY SIEGEL and JOE SHUSTER
THIS IS A TALE THAT COULD OCCUR ONLY AFTER THE WAR... MANY YEARS HENCE! IT'S UP TO ALL OF US TO SEE IT DOESN'T!
LAND OF THE FREE AND HOME OF THE BRAVE! THAT'S AMERICA! BUT ONCE THERE WAS A SWASHBUCKLING, POWER-MAD FIEND WHO TRIED TO CHANGE IT TO LAND OF THE ENSLAVED AND HOME OF THE CRAVEN! A GRASPING, RUTHLESS OPPORTUNIST WHO SOUGHT TO SEIZE THE RICHES OF THE UNITED STATES OF AMERICA FOR HIS OWN! AND OF THE 130 MILLION CITIZENS THRU-OUT THE LAND, THERE WAS NONE TO OPPOSE HIM--EXCEPT ONE SOLITARY INDIVIDUAL. BUT THAT ONE WAS SUFFICIENT--FOR IT WAS NONE OTHER THAN THAT A-1 MUSCLE MARVEL OF ALL TIME...THE INCREDIBLE MAN OF TOMORROW! READ HOW SUPER-STRENGTH OVERCOMES MONSTROUS EVIL WHEN SUPERMAN CLASHES WITH..... "THE EMPEROR OF AMERICA"!

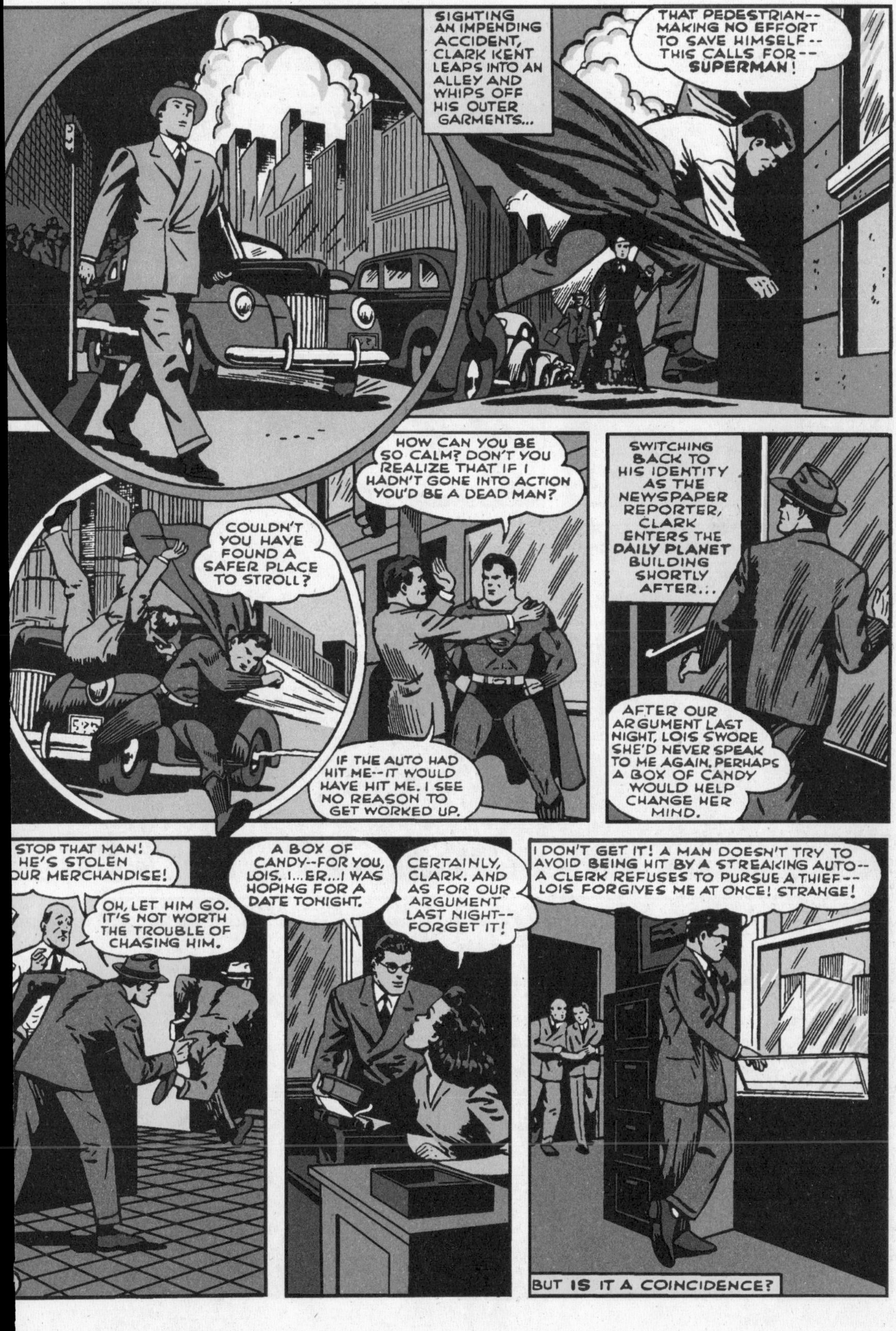
SIGHTING AN IMPENDING ACCIDENT, CLARK KENT LEAPS INTO AN ALLEY AND WHIPS OFF HIS OUTER GARMENTS...
THAT PEDESTRIAN--MAKING NO EFFORT TO SAVE HIMSELF--THIS CALLS FOR--SUPERMAN!
COULDN'T YOU HAVE FOUND A SAFER PLACE TO STROLL?
HOW CAN YOU BE SO CALM? DON'T YOU REALIZE THAT IF I HADN'T GONE INTO ACTION YOU'D BE A DEAD MAN?
IF THE AUTO HAD HIT ME--IT WOULD HAVE HIT ME. I SEE NO REASON TO GET WORKED UP.
SWITCHING BACK TO HIS IDENTITY AS THE NEWSPAPER REPORTER, CLARK ENTERS THE DAILY PLANET BUILDING SHORTLY AFTER...
AFTER OUR ARGUMENT LAST NIGHT, LOIS SWORE SHE'D NEVER SPEAK TO ME AGAIN. PERHAPS A BOX OF CANDY WOULD HELP CHANGE HER MIND.
STOP THAT MAN! HE'S STOLEN OUR MERCHANDISE!
OH, LET HIM GO. IT'S NOT WORTH THE TROUBLE OF CHASING HIM.
A BOX OF CANDY--FOR YOU, LOIS. I...ER...I WAS HOPING FOR A DATE TONIGHT.
CERTAINLY, CLARK. AND AS FOR OUR ARGUMENT LAST NIGHT--FORGET IT!
I DON'T GET IT! A MAN DOESN'T TRY TO AVOID BEING HIT BY A STREAKING AUTO--A CLERK REFUSES TO PURSUE A THIEF--LOIS FORGIVES ME AT ONCE! STRANGE!
BUT IS IT A COINCIDENCE?

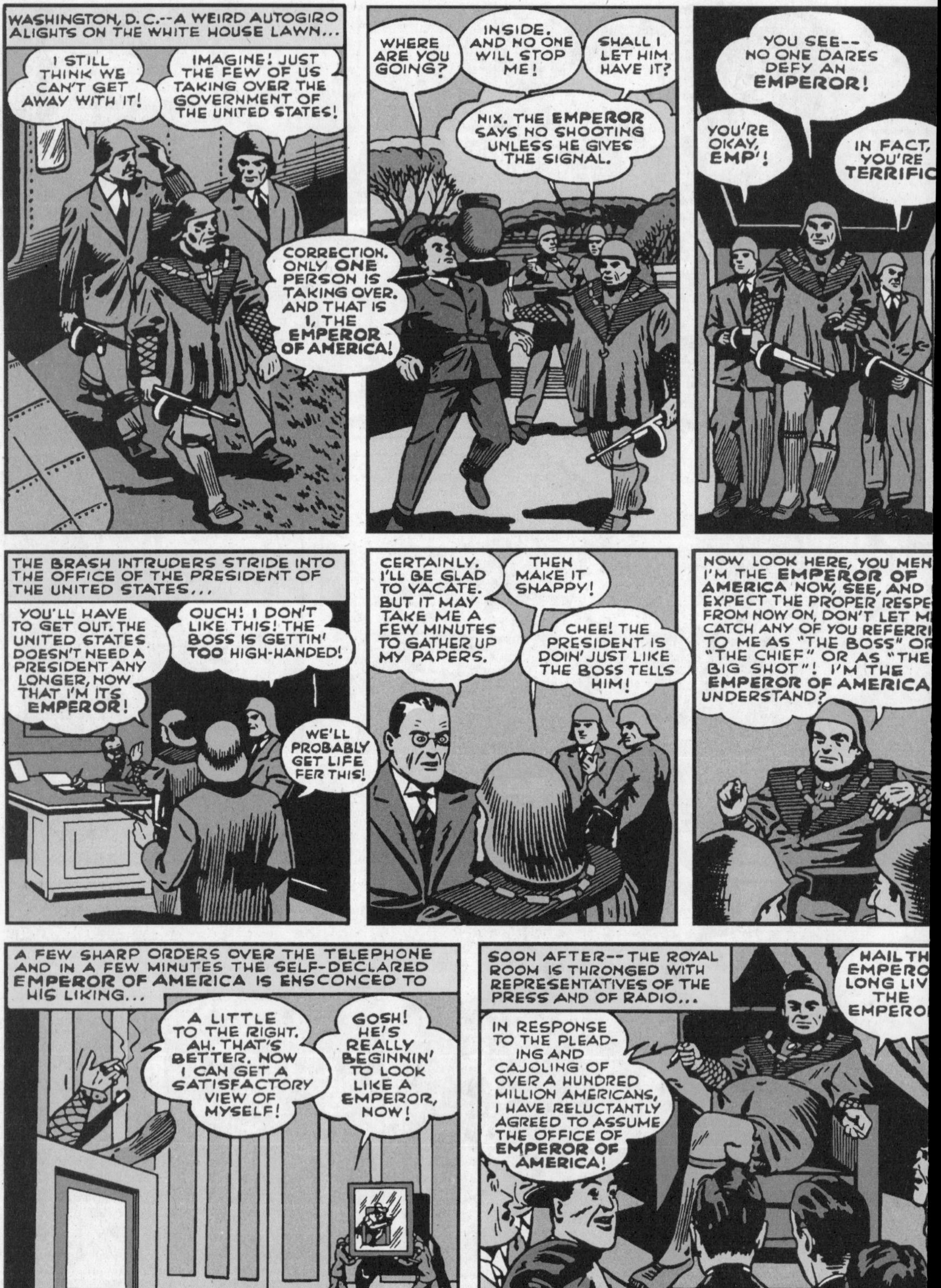
WASHINGTON, D. C.--A WEIRD AUTOGIRO ALIGHTS ON THE WHITE HOUSE LAWN...
I STILL THINK WE CAN'T GET AWAY WITH IT!
IMAGINE! JUST THE FEW OF US TAKING OVER THE GOVERNMENT OF THE UNITED STATES!
CORRECTION. ONLY ONE PERSON IS TAKING OVER. AND THAT IS I, THE EMPEROR OF AMERICA!
WHERE ARE YOU GOING?
INSIDE. AND NO ONE WILL STOP ME!
SHALL I LET HIM HAVE IT?
NIX. THE EMPEROR SAYS NO SHOOTING UNLESS HE GIVES THE SIGNAL.
YOU SEE-- NO ONE DARES DEFY AN EMPEROR!
YOU'RE OKAY, EMP'!
IN FACT, YOU'RE TERRIFIC
THE BRASH INTRUDERS STRIDE INTO THE OFFICE OF THE PRESIDENT OF THE UNITED STATES...
YOU'LL HAVE TO GET OUT. THE UNITED STATES DOESN'T NEED A PRESIDENT ANY LONGER, NOW THAT I'M ITS EMPEROR!
OUCH! I DON'T LIKE THIS! THE BOSS IS GETTIN' TOO HIGH-HANDED!
WE'LL PROBABLY GET LIFE FER THIS!
CERTAINLY. I'LL BE GLAD TO VACATE. BUT IT MAY TAKE ME A FEW MINUTES TO GATHER UP MY PAPERS.
THEN MAKE IT SNAPPY!
CHEE! THE PRESIDENT IS DOIN' JUST LIKE THE BOSS TELLS HIM!
NOW LOOK HERE, YOU MEN I'M THE EMPEROR OF AMERICA NOW, SEE, AND EXPECT THE PROPER RESPE FROM NOW ON. DON'T LET M CATCH ANY OF YOU REFERRI TO ME AS "THE BOSS" OR "THE CHIEF" OR AS "THE BIG SHOT"! I'M THE EMPEROR OF AMERICA UNDERSTAND?
A FEW SHARP ORDERS OVER THE TELEPHONE AND IN A FEW MINUTES THE SELF-DECLARED EMPEROR OF AMERICA IS ENSCONCED TO HIS LIKING...
A LITTLE TO THE RIGHT. AH. THAT'S BETTER. NOW I CAN GET A SATISFACTORY VIEW OF MYSELF!
GOSH! HE'S REALLY BEGINNIN' TO LOOK LIKE A EMPEROR, NOW!
3
SOON AFTER-- THE ROYAL ROOM IS THRONGED WITH REPRESENTATIVES OF THE PRESS AND OF RADIO...
HAIL TH EMPERO LONG LIV THE EMPERO
IN RESPONSE TO THE PLEAD-ING AND CAJOLING OF OVER A HUNDRED MILLION AMERICANS, I HAVE RELUCTANTLY AGREED TO ASSUME THE OFFICE OF EMPEROR OF AMERICA!

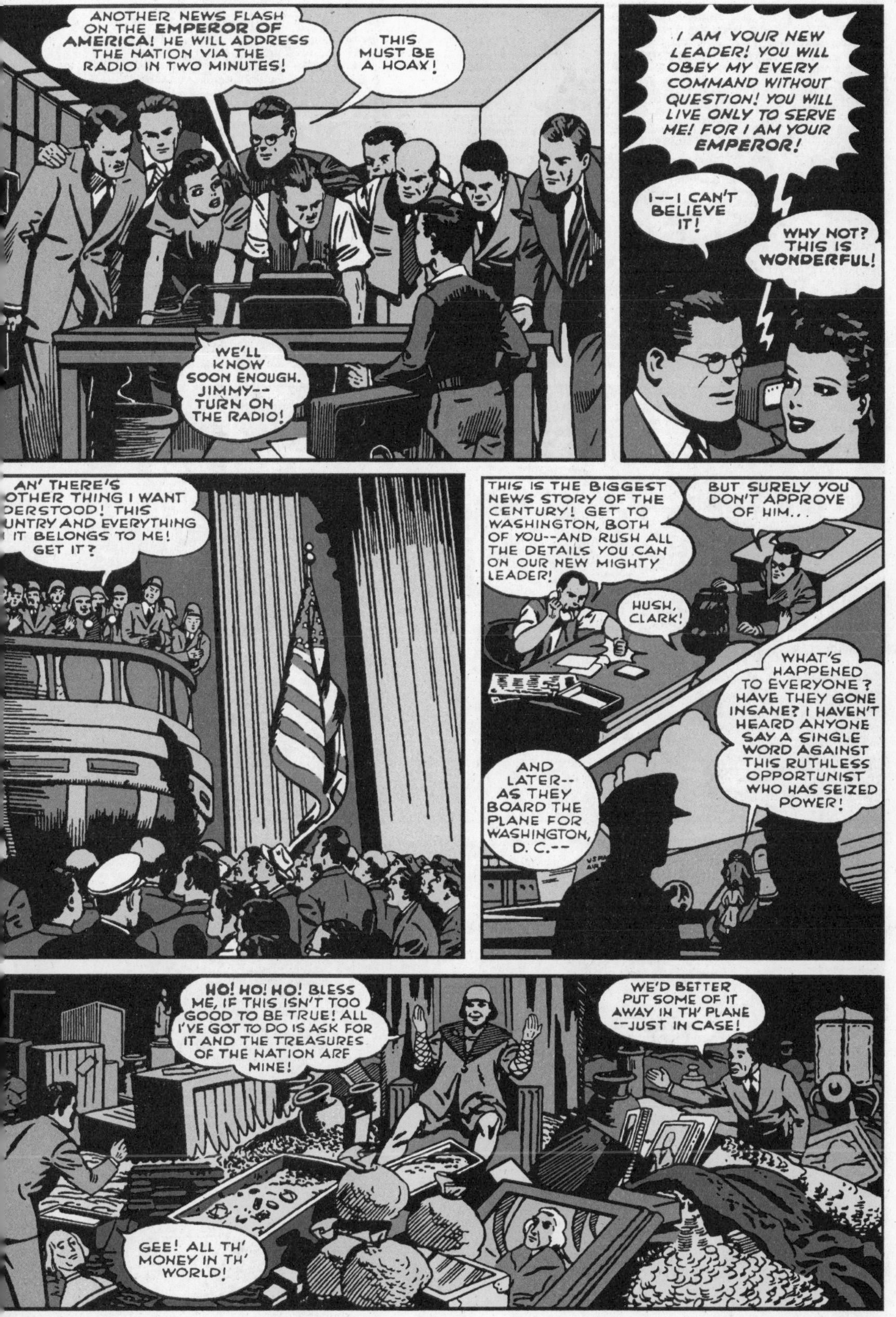

ANOTHER NEWS FLASH ON THE **EMPEROR OF AMERICA!** HE WILL ADDRESS THE NATION VIA THE RADIO IN TWO MINUTES!
THIS MUST BE A HOAX!
WE'LL KNOW SOON ENOUGH. JIMMY-- TURN ON THE RADIO!
I AM YOUR NEW LEADER! YOU WILL OBEY MY EVERY COMMAND WITHOUT QUESTION! YOU WILL LIVE ONLY TO SERVE ME! FOR I AM YOUR **EMPEROR!**
I--I CAN'T BELIEVE IT!
WHY NOT? THIS IS **WONDERFUL!**
AN' THERE'S OTHER THING I WANT DERSTOOD! THIS UNTRY AND EVERYTHING IT BELONGS TO ME! GET IT?
THIS IS THE BIGGEST NEWS STORY OF THE CENTURY! GET TO WASHINGTON, BOTH OF YOU--AND RUSH ALL THE DETAILS YOU CAN ON OUR NEW MIGHTY LEADER!
BUT SURELY YOU DON'T APPROVE OF HIM...
HUSH, CLARK!
AND LATER-- AS THEY BOARD THE PLANE FOR WASHINGTON, D. C.--
WHAT'S HAPPENED TO EVERYONE? HAVE THEY GONE INSANE? I HAVEN'T HEARD ANYONE SAY A SINGLE WORD AGAINST THIS RUTHLESS OPPORTUNIST WHO HAS SEIZED POWER!
HO! HO! HO! BLESS ME, IF THIS ISN'T TOO GOOD TO BE TRUE! ALL I'VE GOT TO DO IS ASK FOR IT AND THE TREASURES OF THE NATION ARE MINE!
WE'D BETTER PUT SOME OF IT AWAY IN TH' PLANE --JUST IN CASE!
GEE! ALL TH' MONEY IN TH' WORLD!

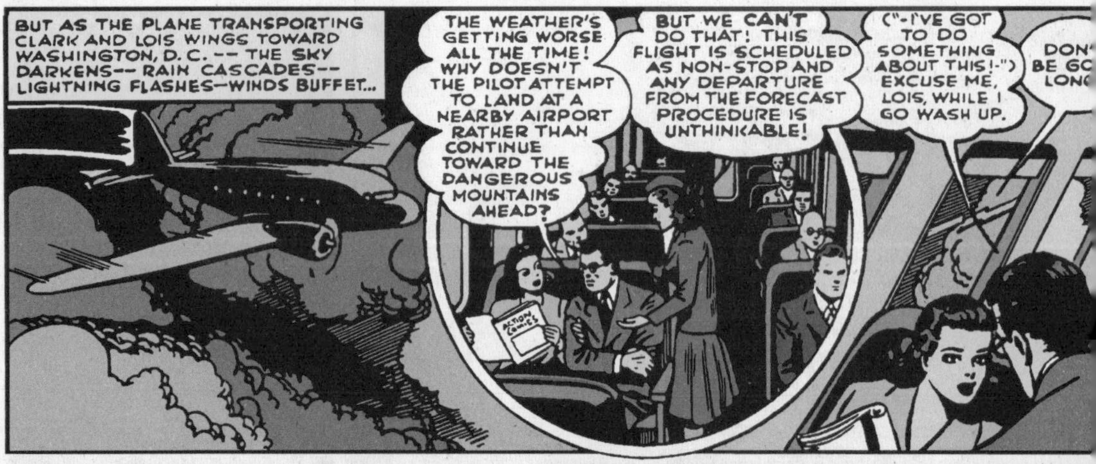
BUT AS THE PLANE TRANSPORTING CLARK AND LOIS WINGS TOWARD WASHINGTON, D. C. -- THE SKY DARKENS-- RAIN CASCADES-- LIGHTNING FLASHES--WINDS BUFFET...
THE WEATHER'S GETTING WORSE ALL THE TIME! WHY DOESN'T THE PILOT ATTEMPT TO LAND AT A NEARBY AIRPORT RATHER THAN CONTINUE TOWARD THE DANGEROUS MOUNTAINS AHEAD?
BUT WE CAN'T DO THAT! THIS FLIGHT IS SCHEDULED AS NON-STOP AND ANY DEPARTURE FROM THE FORECAST PROCEDURE IS UNTHINKABLE!
ACTION COMICS
("-I'VE GOT TO DO SOMETHING ABOUT THIS!-") EXCUSE ME, LOIS, WHILE I GO WASH UP.

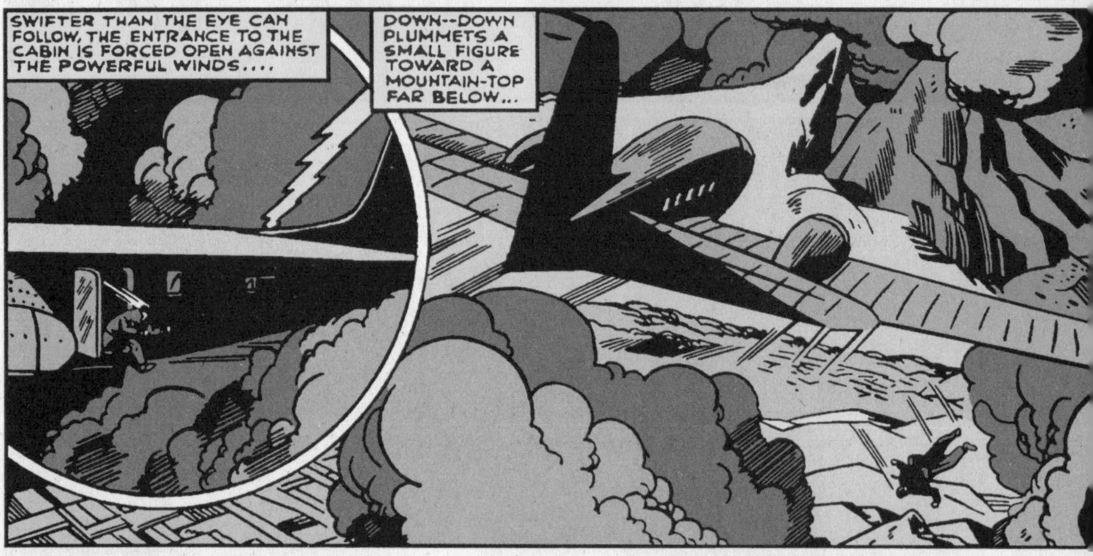
SWIFTER THAN THE EYE CAN FOLLOW, THE ENTRANCE TO THE CABIN IS FORCED OPEN AGAINST THE POWERFUL WINDS....
DOWN--DOWN PLUMMETS A SMALL FIGURE TOWARD A MOUNTAIN-TOP FAR BELOW...

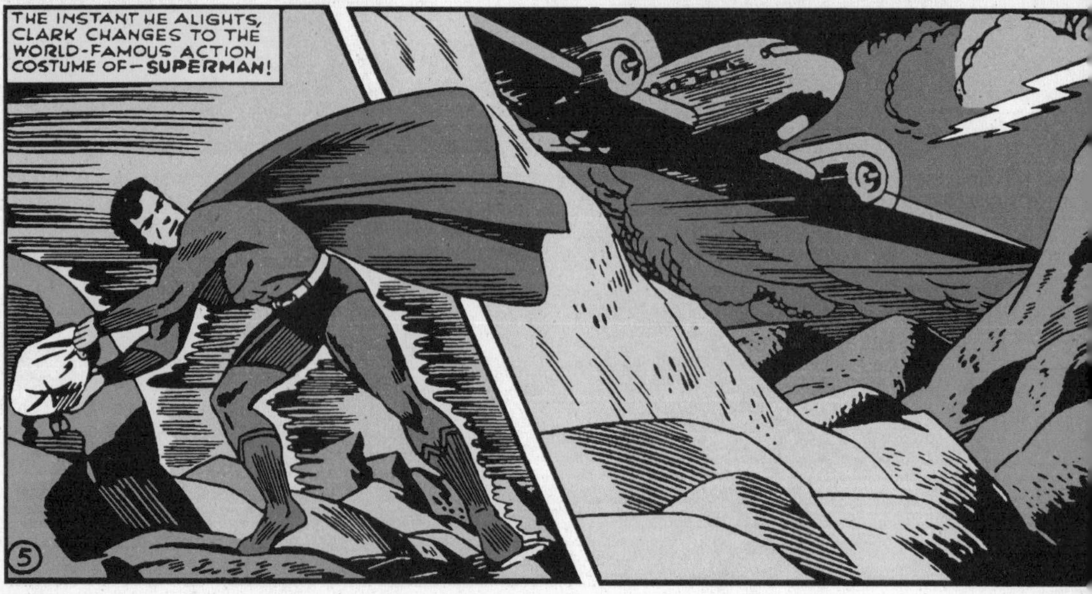
THE INSTANT HE ALIGHTS, CLARK CHANGES TO THE WORLD-FAMOUS ACTION COSTUME OF--SUPERMAN!
5

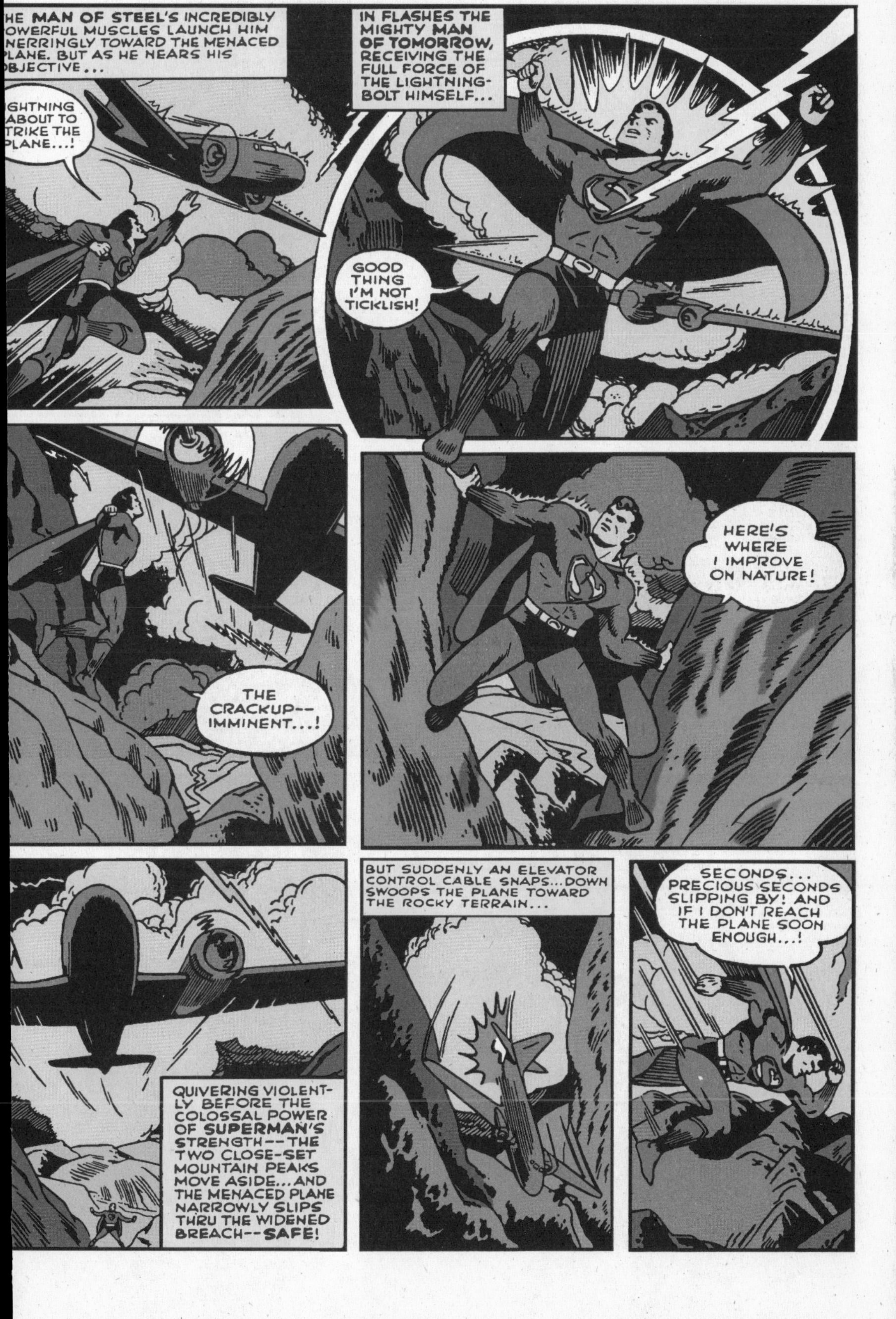
HE MAN OF STEEL'S INCREDIBLY OWERFUL MUSCLES LAUNCH HIM NERRINGLY TOWARD THE MENACED PLANE. BUT AS HE NEARS HIS OBJECTIVE...
IGHTNING ABOUT TO TRIKE THE PLANE...!
IN FLASHES THE MIGHTY MAN OF TOMORROW, RECEIVING THE FULL FORCE OF THE LIGHTNING-BOLT HIMSELF...
GOOD THING I'M NOT TICKLISH!
THE CRACKUP--IMMINENT...!
HERE'S WHERE I IMPROVE ON NATURE!
QUIVERING VIOLENTLY BEFORE THE COLOSSAL POWER OF SUPERMAN'S STRENGTH--THE TWO CLOSE-SET MOUNTAIN PEAKS MOVE ASIDE...AND THE MENACED PLANE NARROWLY SLIPS THRU THE WIDENED BREACH--SAFE!
BUT SUDDENLY AN ELEVATOR CONTROL CABLE SNAPS...DOWN SWOOPS THE PLANE TOWARD THE ROCKY TERRAIN...
SECONDS... PRECIOUS SECONDS SLIPPING BY! AND IF I DON'T REACH THE PLANE SOON ENOUGH...!

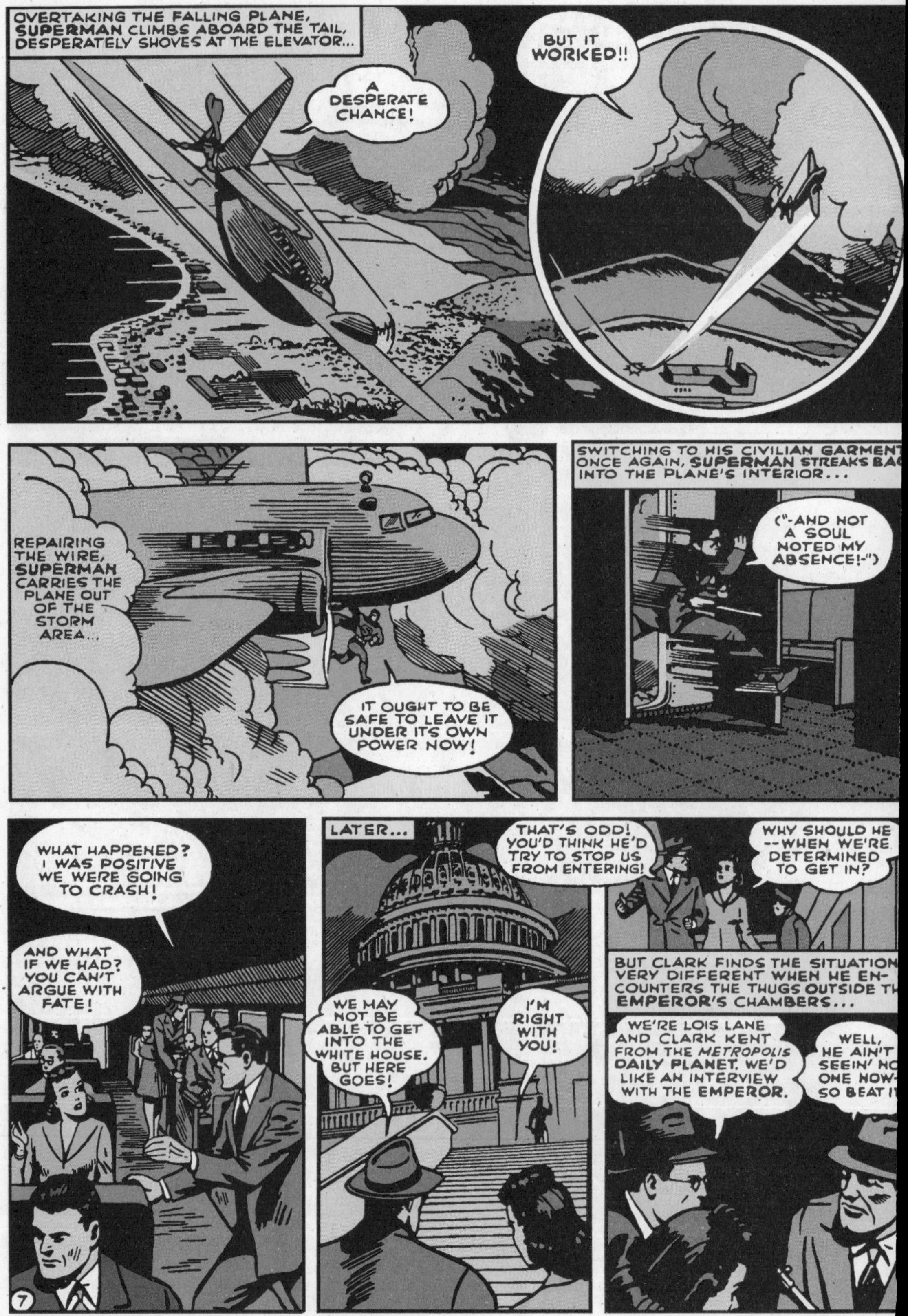
OVERTAKING THE FALLING PLANE, SUPERMAN CLIMBS ABOARD THE TAIL, DESPERATELY SHOVES AT THE ELEVATOR...
A DESPERATE CHANCE!
BUT IT WORKED!!
REPAIRING THE WIRE, SUPERMAN CARRIES THE PLANE OUT OF THE STORM AREA...
IT OUGHT TO BE SAFE TO LEAVE IT UNDER ITS OWN POWER NOW!
SWITCHING TO HIS CIVILIAN GARMENT ONCE AGAIN, SUPERMAN STREAKS BAC INTO THE PLANE'S INTERIOR...
("-AND NOT A SOUL NOTED MY ABSENCE!-")
WHAT HAPPENED? I WAS POSITIVE WE WERE GOING TO CRASH!
AND WHAT IF WE HAD? YOU CAN'T ARGUE WITH FATE!
7
LATER...
WE MAY NOT BE ABLE TO GET INTO THE WHITE HOUSE, BUT HERE GOES!
I'M RIGHT WITH YOU!
THAT'S ODD! YOU'D THINK HE'D TRY TO STOP US FROM ENTERING!
WHY SHOULD HE --WHEN WE'RE DETERMINED TO GET IN?
BUT CLARK FINDS THE SITUATION VERY DIFFERENT WHEN HE ENCOUNTERS THE THUGS OUTSIDE TH EMPEROR'S CHAMBERS...
WE'RE LOIS LANE AND CLARK KENT FROM THE METROPOLIS DAILY PLANET. WE'D LIKE AN INTERVIEW WITH THE EMPEROR.
WELL, HE AIN'T SEEIN' NO ONE NOW- SO BEAT IT

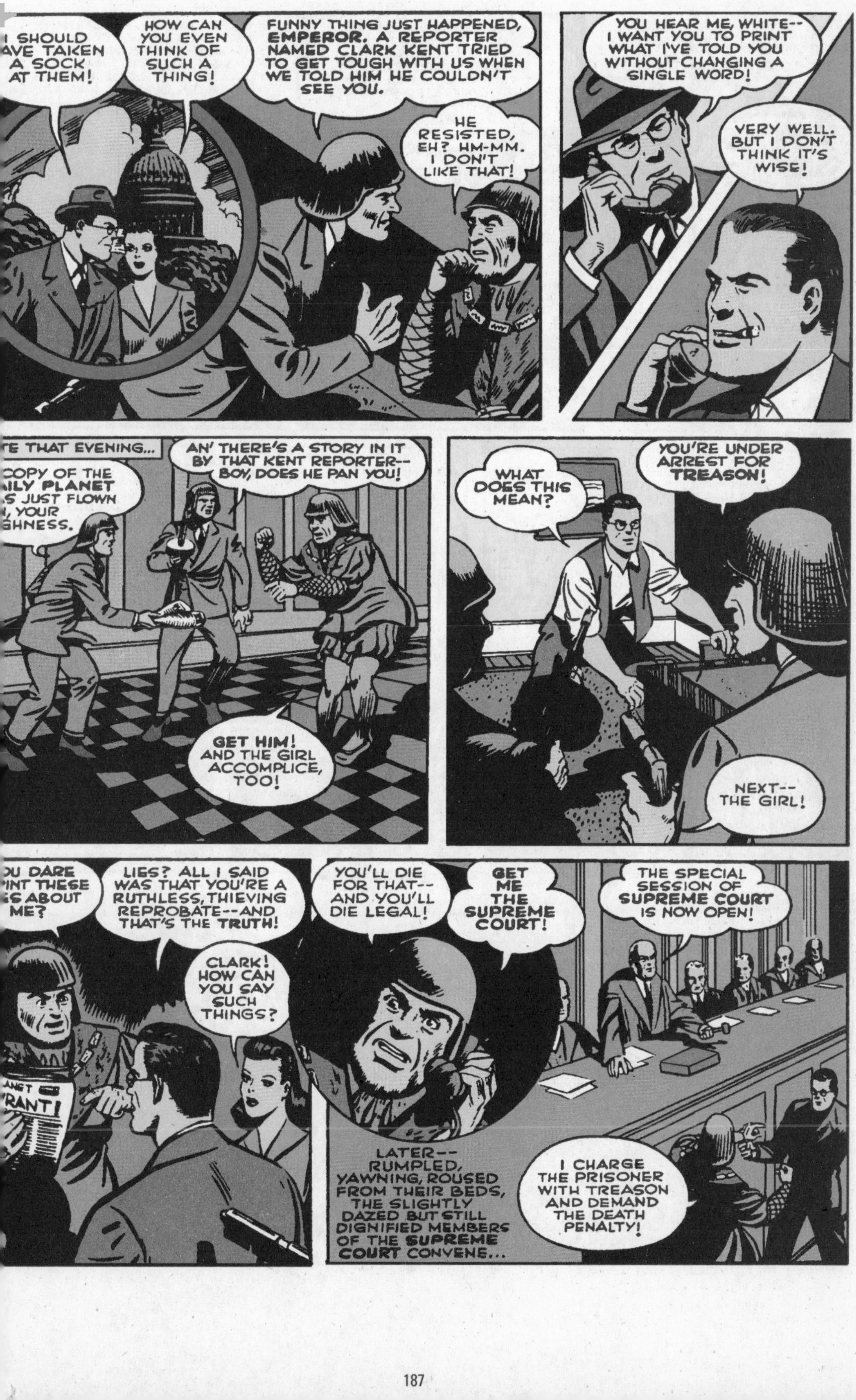

I SHOULD AVE TAKEN A SOCK AT THEM!
HOW CAN YOU EVEN THINK OF SUCH A THING!
FUNNY THING JUST HAPPENED, EMPEROR. A REPORTER NAMED CLARK KENT TRIED TO GET TOUGH WITH US WHEN WE TOLD HIM HE COULDN'T SEE YOU.
HE RESISTED, EH? HM-MM. I DON'T LIKE THAT!
YOU HEAR ME, WHITE-- I WANT YOU TO PRINT WHAT I'VE TOLD YOU WITHOUT CHANGING A SINGLE WORD!
VERY WELL. BUT I DON'T THINK IT'S WISE!
TE THAT EVENING...
COPY OF THE AILY PLANET S JUST FLOWN N, YOUR GHNESS.
AN' THERE'S A STORY IN IT BY THAT KENT REPORTER-- BOY, DOES HE PAN YOU!
GET HIM! AND THE GIRL ACCOMPLICE, TOO!
WHAT DOES THIS MEAN?
YOU'RE UNDER ARREST FOR TREASON!
NEXT-- THE GIRL!
OU DARE INT THESE S ABOUT ME?
LIES? ALL I SAID WAS THAT YOU'RE A RUTHLESS, THIEVING REPROBATE--AND THAT'S THE TRUTH!
CLARK! HOW CAN YOU SAY SUCH THINGS?
YOU'LL DIE FOR THAT-- AND YOU'LL DIE LEGAL!
GET ME THE SUPREME COURT!
THE SPECIAL SESSION OF SUPREME COURT IS NOW OPEN!
LATER-- RUMPLED, YAWNING, ROUSED FROM THEIR BEDS, THE SLIGHTLY DAZED BUT STILL DIGNIFIED MEMBERS OF THE SUPREME COURT CONVENE...
I CHARGE THE PRISONER WITH TREASON AND DEMAND THE DEATH PENALTY!

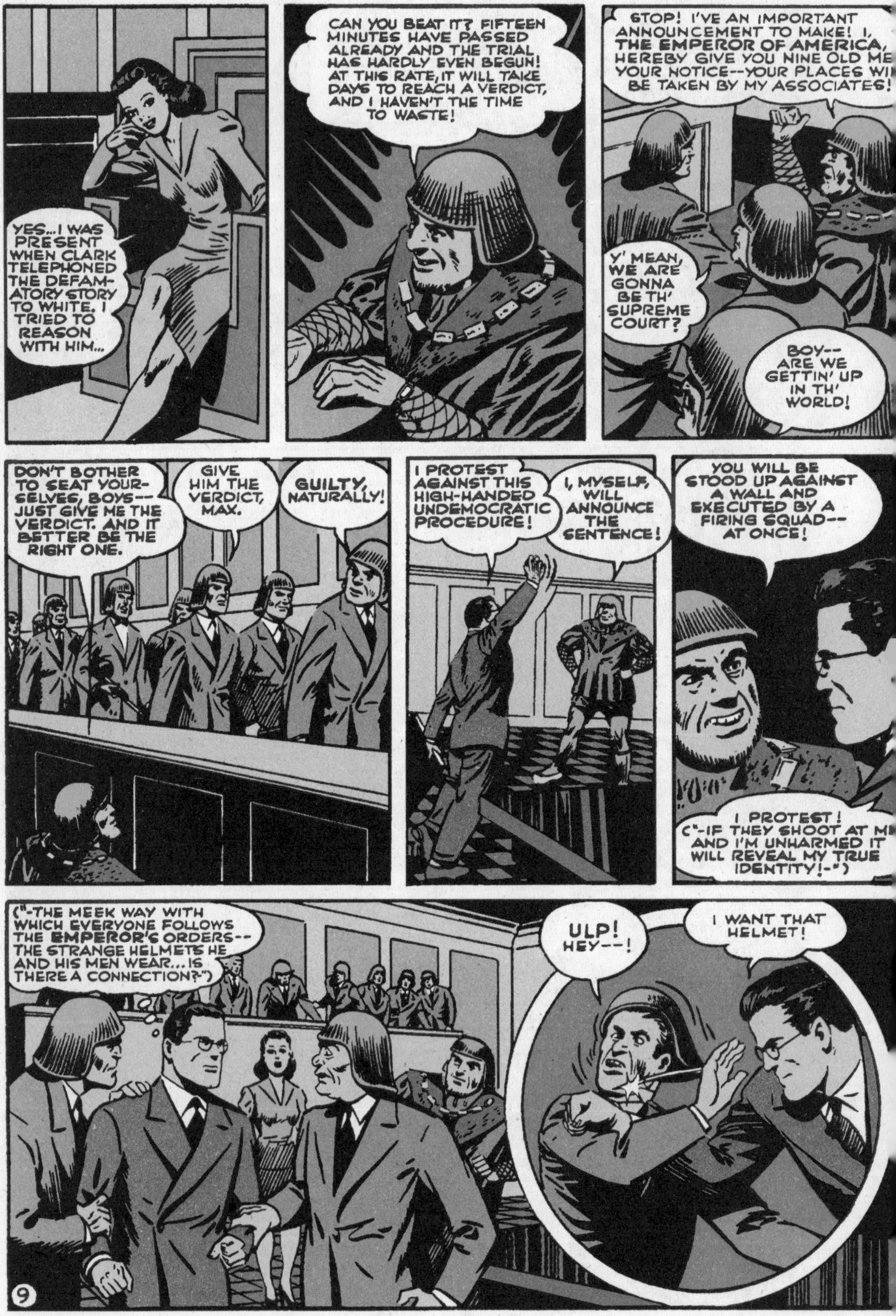
YES...I WAS PRESENT WHEN CLARK TELEPHONED THE DEFAMATORY STORY TO WHITE. I TRIED TO REASON WITH HIM...
CAN YOU BEAT IT? FIFTEEN MINUTES HAVE PASSED ALREADY AND THE TRIAL HAS HARDLY EVEN BEGUN! AT THIS RATE, IT WILL TAKE DAYS TO REACH A VERDICT, AND I HAVEN'T THE TIME TO WASTE!
STOP! I'VE AN IMPORTANT ANNOUNCEMENT TO MAKE! I, THE EMPEROR OF AMERICA, HEREBY GIVE YOU NINE OLD ME YOUR NOTICE--YOUR PLACES WI BE TAKEN BY MY ASSOCIATES!
Y' MEAN, WE ARE GONNA BE TH' SUPREME COURT?
BOY-- ARE WE GETTIN' UP IN TH' WORLD!
DON'T BOTHER TO SEAT YOURSELVES, BOYS-- JUST GIVE ME THE VERDICT. AND IT BETTER BE THE RIGHT ONE.
GIVE HIM THE VERDICT, MAX.
GUILTY, NATURALLY!
I PROTEST AGAINST THIS HIGH-HANDED UNDEMOCRATIC PROCEDURE!
I, MYSELF, WILL ANNOUNCE THE SENTENCE!
YOU WILL BE STOOD UP AGAINST A WALL AND EXECUTED BY A FIRING SQUAD-- AT ONCE!
I PROTEST! ("-IF THEY SHOOT AT M AND I'M UNHARMED IT WILL REVEAL MY TRUE IDENTITY!-")
("-THE MEEK WAY WITH WHICH EVERYONE FOLLOWS THE EMPEROR'S ORDERS-- THE STRANGE HELMETS HE AND HIS MEN WEAR... IS THERE A CONNECTION?-")
ULP! HEY--!
I WANT THAT HELMET!
9

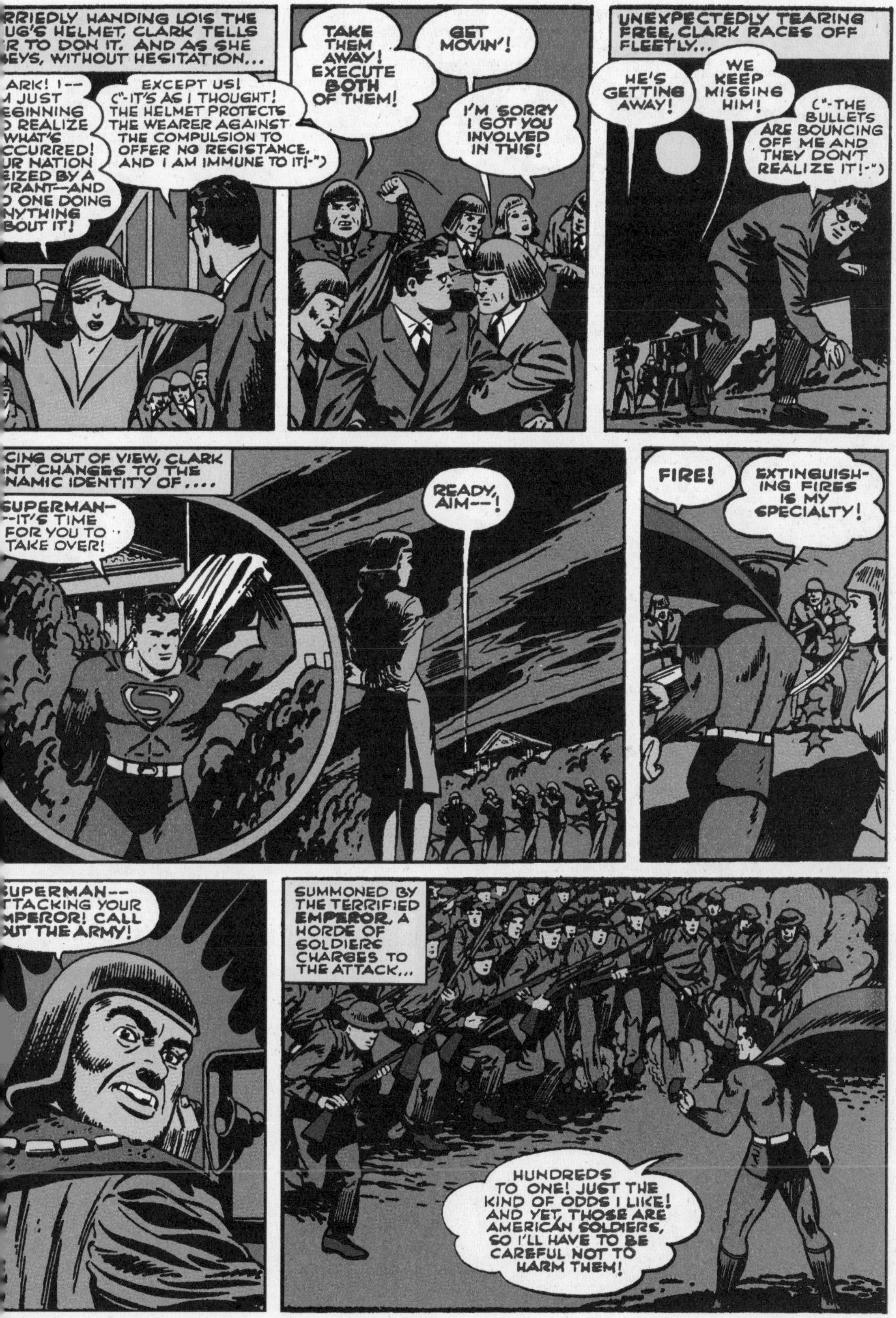
RRIEDLY HANDING LOIS THE UG'S HELMET, CLARK TELLS R TO DON IT. AND AS SHE BEYS, WITHOUT HESITATION...
ARK! I-- M JUST EGINNING O REALIZE WHAT'S CCURRED! UR NATION EIZED BY A YRANT--AND O ONE DOING NYTHING BOUT IT!
EXCEPT US! ("-IT'S AS I THOUGHT! THE HELMET PROTECTS THE WEARER AGAINST THE COMPULSION TO OFFER NO RESISTANCE. AND I AM IMMUNE TO IT!-")
TAKE THEM AWAY! EXECUTE BOTH OF THEM!
GET MOVIN'!
I'M SORRY I GOT YOU INVOLVED IN THIS!
UNEXPECTEDLY TEARING FREE, CLARK RACES OFF FLEETLY...
HE'S GETTING AWAY!
WE KEEP MISSING HIM!
("-THE BULLETS ARE BOUNCING OFF ME AND THEY DON'T REALIZE IT!-")
CING OUT OF VIEW, CLARK NT CHANGES TO THE NAMIC IDENTITY OF....
SUPERMAN--IT'S TIME FOR YOU TO TAKE OVER!
READY, AIM--!
FIRE!
EXTINGUISHING FIRES IS MY SPECIALTY!
SUPERMAN--TTACKING YOUR MPEROR! CALL OUT THE ARMY!
SUMMONED BY THE TERRIFIED EMPEROR, A HORDE OF SOLDIERS CHARGES TO THE ATTACK...
HUNDREDS TO ONE! JUST THE KIND OF ODDS I LIKE! AND YET, THOSE ARE AMERICAN SOLDIERS, SO I'LL HAVE TO BE CAREFUL NOT TO HARM THEM!

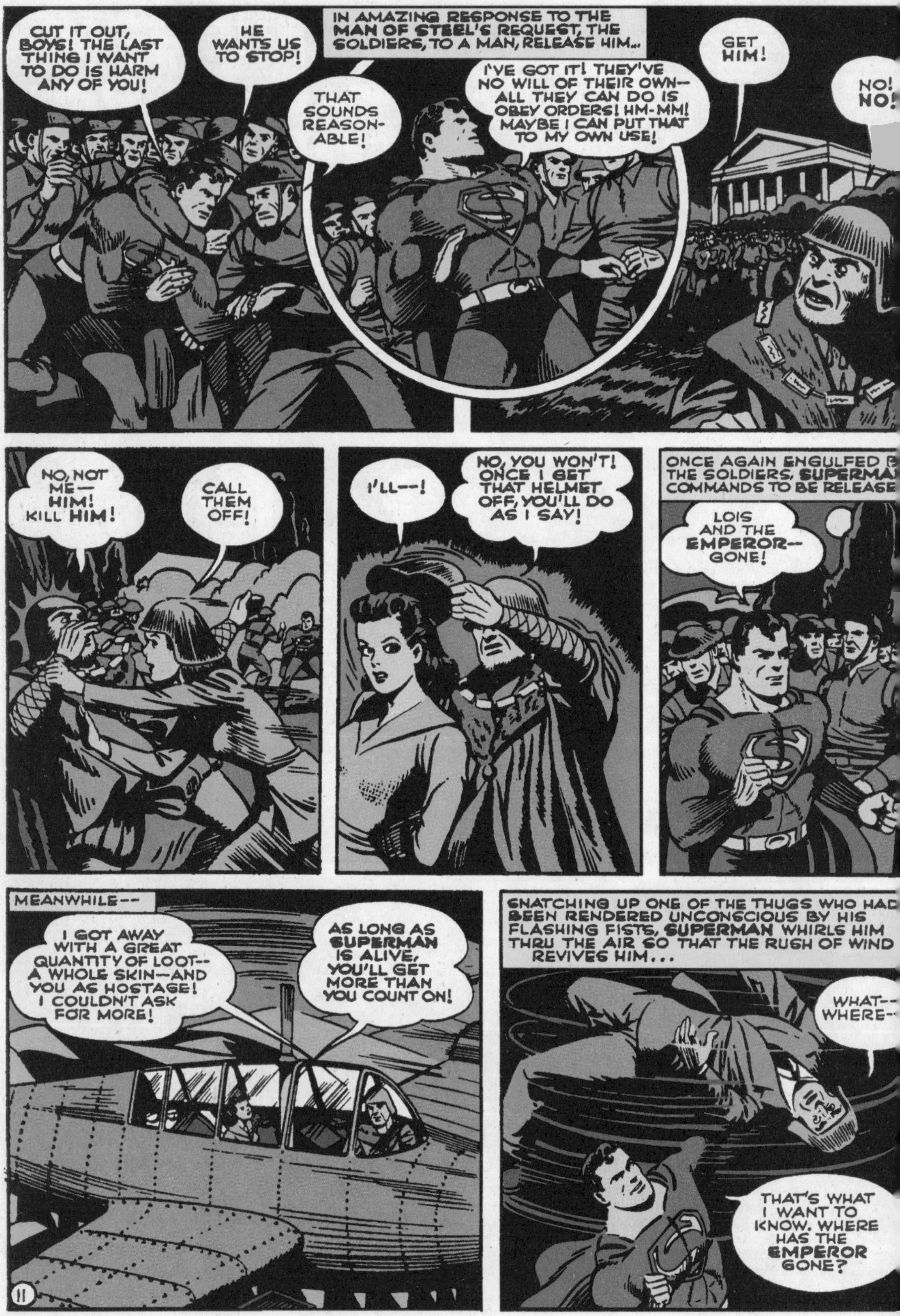

CUT IT OUT, BOYS! THE LAST THING I WANT TO DO IS HARM ANY OF YOU!
HE WANTS US TO STOP!
IN AMAZING RESPONSE TO THE MAN OF STEEL'S REQUEST, THE SOLDIERS, TO A MAN, RELEASE HIM...
THAT SOUNDS REASON-ABLE!
I'VE GOT IT! THEY'VE NO WILL OF THEIR OWN-- ALL THEY CAN DO IS OBEY ORDERS! HM-MM! MAYBE I CAN PUT THAT TO MY OWN USE!
GET HIM!
NO! NO!
NO, NOT ME-- HIM! KILL HIM!
CALL THEM OFF!
I'LL--!
NO, YOU WON'T! ONCE I GET THAT HELMET OFF, YOU'LL DO AS I SAY!
ONCE AGAIN ENGULFED B THE SOLDIERS, SUPERMA COMMANDS TO BE RELEASE
LOIS AND THE EMPEROR-- GONE!
MEANWHILE--
I GOT AWAY WITH A GREAT QUANTITY OF LOOT-- A WHOLE SKIN--AND YOU AS HOSTAGE! I COULDN'T ASK FOR MORE!
AS LONG AS SUPERMAN IS ALIVE, YOU'LL GET MORE THAN YOU COUNT ON!
11
SNATCHING UP ONE OF THE THUGS WHO HAD BEEN RENDERED UNCONSCIOUS BY HIS FLASHING FISTS, SUPERMAN WHIRLS HIM THRU THE AIR SO THAT THE RUSH OF WIND REVIVES HIM...
WHAT-- WHERE--
THAT'S WHAT I WANT TO KNOW. WHERE HAS THE EMPEROR GONE?

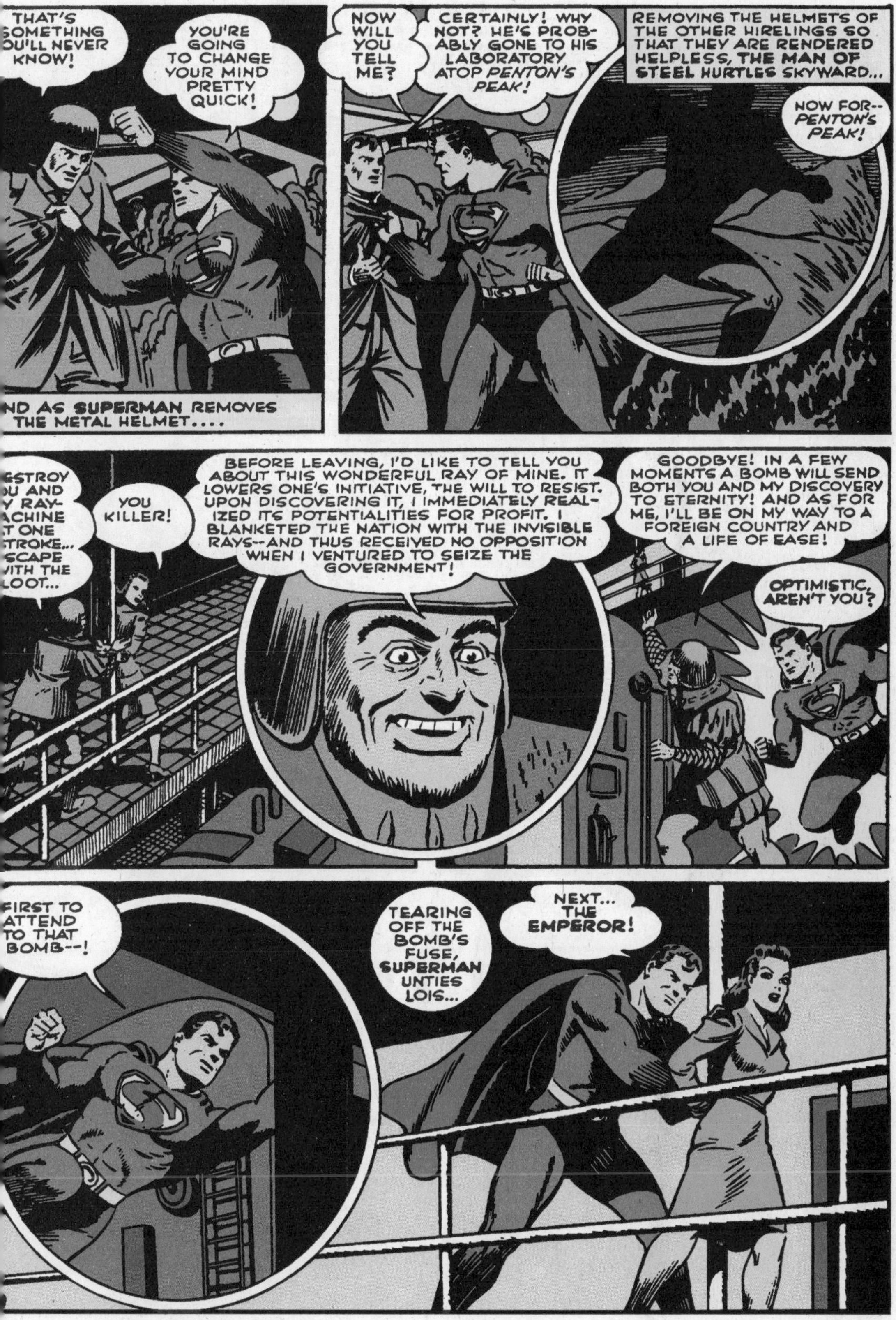

THAT'S SOMETHING OU'LL NEVER KNOW!
YOU'RE GOING TO CHANGE YOUR MIND PRETTY QUICK!
ND AS SUPERMAN REMOVES THE METAL HELMET....
NOW WILL YOU TELL ME?
CERTAINLY! WHY NOT? HE'S PROBABLY GONE TO HIS LABORATORY ATOP PENTON'S PEAK!
REMOVING THE HELMETS OF THE OTHER HIRELINGS SO THAT THEY ARE RENDERED HELPLESS, THE MAN OF STEEL HURTLES SKYWARD...
NOW FOR-- PENTON'S PEAK!
ESTROY OU AND Y RAY- ACHINE T ONE STROKE... SCAPE WITH THE LOOT...
YOU KILLER!
BEFORE LEAVING, I'D LIKE TO TELL YOU ABOUT THIS WONDERFUL RAY OF MINE. IT LOWERS ONE'S INITIATIVE, THE WILL TO RESIST. UPON DISCOVERING IT, I IMMEDIATELY REALIZED ITS POTENTIALITIES FOR PROFIT. I BLANKETED THE NATION WITH THE INVISIBLE RAYS--AND THUS RECEIVED NO OPPOSITION WHEN I VENTURED TO SEIZE THE GOVERNMENT!
GOODBYE! IN A FEW MOMENTS A BOMB WILL SEND BOTH YOU AND MY DISCOVERY TO ETERNITY! AND AS FOR ME, I'LL BE ON MY WAY TO A FOREIGN COUNTRY AND A LIFE OF EASE!
OPTIMISTIC, AREN'T YOU?
FIRST TO ATTEND TO THAT BOMB--!
TEARING OFF THE BOMB'S FUSE, SUPERMAN UNTIES LOIS...
NEXT... THE EMPEROR!

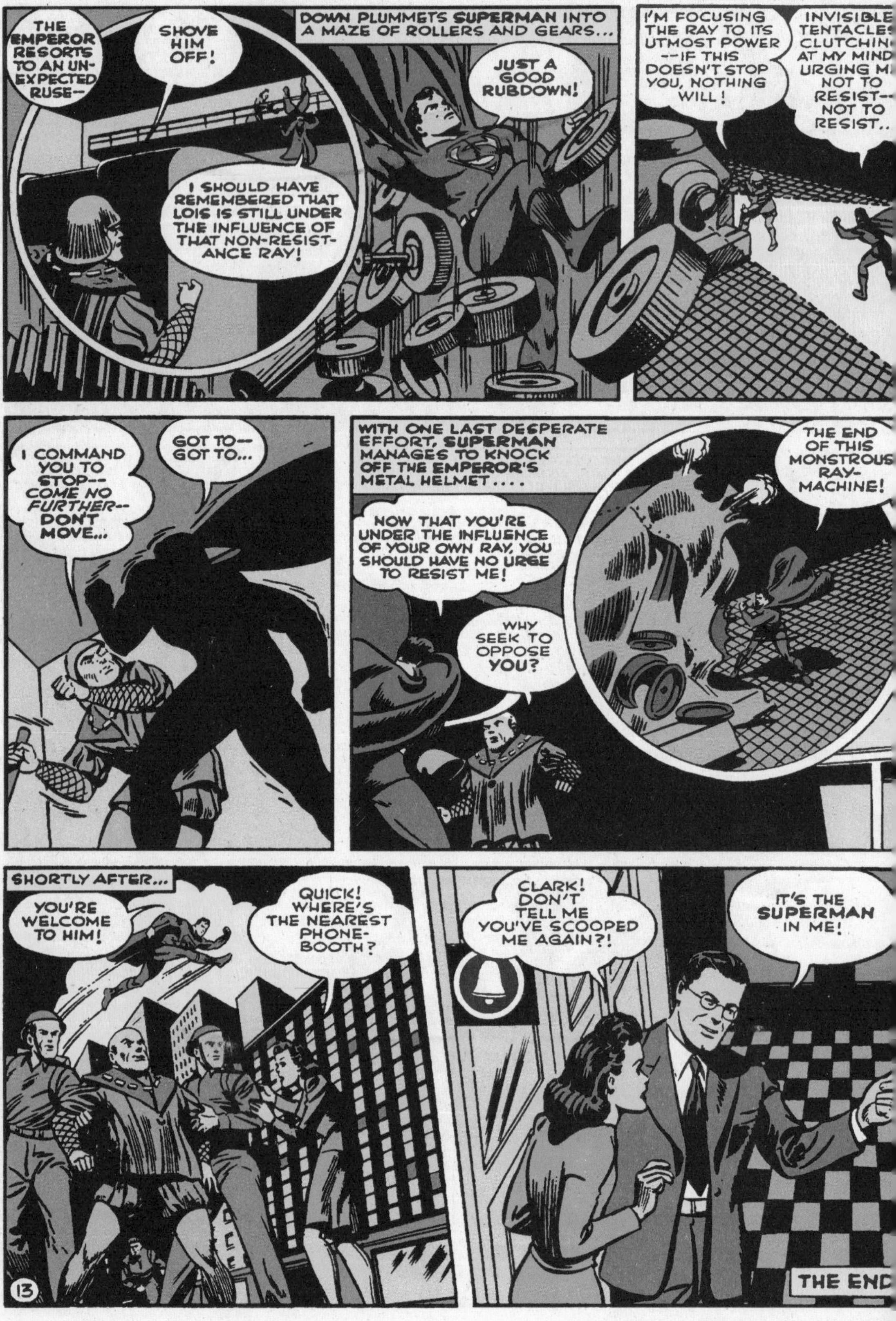
THE EMPEROR RESORTS TO AN UN-EXPECTED RUSE--
SHOVE HIM OFF!
I SHOULD HAVE REMEMBERED THAT LOIS IS STILL UNDER THE INFLUENCE OF THAT NON-RESIST-ANCE RAY!
DOWN PLUMMETS SUPERMAN INTO A MAZE OF ROLLERS AND GEARS...
JUST A GOOD RUBDOWN!
I'M FOCUSING THE RAY TO ITS UTMOST POWER --IF THIS DOESN'T STOP YOU, NOTHING WILL!
INVISIBLE TENTACLES CLUTCHING AT MY MIND URGING ME NOT TO RESIST-- NOT TO RESIST..
I COMMAND YOU TO STOP-- COME NO FURTHER-- DON'T MOVE...
GOT TO-- GOT TO...
WITH ONE LAST DESPERATE EFFORT, SUPERMAN MANAGES TO KNOCK OFF THE EMPEROR'S METAL HELMET....
NOW THAT YOU'RE UNDER THE INFLUENCE OF YOUR OWN RAY, YOU SHOULD HAVE NO URGE TO RESIST ME!
WHY SEEK TO OPPOSE YOU?
THE END OF THIS MONSTROUS RAY-MACHINE!
SHORTLY AFTER...
YOU'RE WELCOME TO HIM!
QUICK! WHERE'S THE NEAREST PHONE-BOOTH?
13
CLARK! DON'T TELL ME YOU'VE SCOOPED ME AGAIN?!
IT'S THE SUPERMAN IN ME!
THE END